FIELDING'S
SCANDINAVIA

Fielding Titles

Fielding's Amazon
Fielding's Australia
Fielding's Bahamas
Fielding's Belgium
Fielding's Bermuda
Fielding's Borneo
Fielding's Brazil
Fielding's Britain
Fielding's Budget Europe
Fielding's Caribbean
Fielding's Europe
Fielding's Far East
Fielding's France
Fielding's Guide to the World's Most Dangerous Places
Fielding's Guide to the World's Great Voyages
Fielding's Guide to Kenya's Best Hotels, Lodges & Homestays
Fielding's Guide to the World's Most Romantic Places
Fielding's Hawaii
Fielding's Holland
Fielding's Italy
Fielding's London Agenda
Fielding's Los Angeles Agenda
Fielding's Malaysia and Singapore
Fielding's Mexico
Fielding's New York Agenda
Fielding's New Zealand
Fielding's Paris Agenda
Fielding's Portugal
Fielding's Scandinavia
Fielding's Seychelles
Fielding's Southeast Asia
Fielding's Spain
Fielding's Vacation Places Rated
Fielding's Vietnam
Fielding's Worldwide Cruises

FIELDING'S SCANDINAVIA

The Most In-Depth and Entertaining Guide to Denmark, Sweden, Norway, Finland and Iceland

Martha Berman

Fielding Worldwide, Inc.
308 South Catalina Avenue
Redondo Beach, California 90277 U.S.A.

Fielding's Scandinavia

Published by Fielding Worldwide, Inc.

Text Copyright ©1995 Martha Berman

Icons, Illustrations Copyright ©1995 FWI

FIELDING WORLDWIDE INC.

PUBLISHER AND CEO	**Robert Young Pelton**
PUBLISHING DIRECTOR	**Paul T. Snapp**
ELECTRONIC PUBLISHING DIRECTOR	**Larry E. Hart**
PROJECT DIRECTOR	**Tony E. Hulette**
ADMINISTRATIVE COORDINATOR	**Beverly Riess**
ACCOUNT SERVICES MANAGER	**Christy Harp**

EDITORS

Linda Charlton   **Kathy Knoles**

PRODUCTION

Gini Martin   **Chris Snyder**

Craig South

COVER DESIGNED BY	**Digital Artists, Inc.**
COVER PHOTOGRAPHERS — Front Cover	**Robert Young Pelton/Westlight**
Background Photo, Front Cover	**Chad Ehlers/Allstock**
Back Cover	**Chad Ehlers/Tony Stone Images**
INSIDE PHOTOS	**Danish Tourist Board, Finnish Tourist Board, Norwegian Tourist Board, Swedish Tourist Board**

Inquiries should be addressed to: Fielding Worldwide, Inc., 308 South Catalina Ave., Redondo Beach, California 90277 U.S.A., Telephone (310) 372-4474, Facsimile (310) 376-8064, 8:30 a.m.–5:30 p.m. Pacific Standard Time.

ISBN 1-56952-049-6

Library of Congress Catalog Card Number

94-068325

Printed in the United States of America

Dedication

To my father, Marven Lasky,
   who taught me to look for adventure in uncommon places.

Letter from the Publisher

In 1946, Temple Fielding began the first of what would be a re-markable new series of well-written, highly personalized guidebooks for independent travelers. Temple's opinionated, witty and oft-imitated books have now guided travelers for almost a half-century. More important to some was Fielding's humorous and direct method of steering travelers away from the dull and the insipid. Today, Fielding Travel Guides are still written by experienced travelers for experienced travelers. Our authors carry on Fielding's reputation for creating travel experiences that deliver insight with a sense of discovery and style.

Martha Berman offers the Fielding reader an unprecedented knowledge of Scandinavia, gleaned through seven years of observing the region via every possible means—from in the sky aboard a mail plane to on the ground as part of a reindeer safari. She leads the reader into remote and little-discovered fjords, as well as fairy-tale castles and other attractions that will make Scandinavia the warmest place on earth.

Today, the concept of independent travel has never been bigger. Our policy of *brutal honesty* and a highly personal point of view has never changed; it just seems the travel world has caught up with us.

Enjoy your Scandinavian adventure with Martha Berman and Fielding.

Robert Young Pelton

Publisher and C.E.O.

Fielding Worldwide, Inc.

ABOUT THE AUTHOR

Martha Berman

Martha Berman, a writer of fiction and travel and the former owner of a travel agency in Indianapolis, has spent the last seven years exploring the Scandinavian countries by all modes of available transportation, including mail planes, snowmobiles and reindeer. Martha, who has taught English Literature and Composition at Butler University in Indianapolis, earned her B.A. from the University of Michigan and her M.A. from Butler University. She also studied at Wellesley College and the University of Florence, Italy. Her collection of short stories, *Dancing on Sand*, was awarded the Indiana Short Fiction Award in 1986.

ACKNOWLEDGMENTS

For their friendliness, helpfulness, and wonderful sense of humor, I thank all my Scandinavian friends who have made the work of this book into pleasure. In particular, I wish to thank the tourist boards of Denmark, Finland, Iceland, Norway and Sweden and to acknowledge the help and hospitality of the Silja, Birka and Viking lines, as well as Icelandair and Finnair Airlines.

I must also thank my children, Joseph, Anne and Thomas Berman, who assisted me on many of my trips and were unsparing in their assessments of hotels, restaurants and sights, indeed of entire cities. They kept my eye jaundiced, a healthy condition for a guidebook writer.

Fielding Rating Icons

The Fielding Rating Icons are highly personal and awarded to help the besieged traveler choose from among the dizzying array of activities, attractions, hotels, restaurants and sights. The awarding of an icon denotes unusual or exceptional qualities in the relevant category.

RATINGS: Fielding Award, Author Selection, Money Saver, Expensive, Quality, Warning, Danger, Inexpensive, Mild Disapproval, Spacious, Cramped

CULTURAL: Museum/Art, Interesting Architecture, History, Book Reference, Artistically Important, Musically Interesting, Cultural Archeology, Crafts, Theatre

SIGHTS: Picturesque, Great Scenery, Market, Beaches/Resorts, Cultural, Fortress, Castle, Church

WHERE TO STAY: Simple, Luxurious, Cottage, Bed & Breakfast, Scenic, Business, Honeymoon, Chateau

TRAVEL TIPS: Arrival/Departure, By Air, By Water, By Train, By Car, Bus/Local Transit, Barge, River Boat, Calendar, Itinerary, Compass, Kids

ACTIVITIES: Downhill Skiing, X–country Skiing, General Sports, Water-Sports, Sailing, Scuba Diving, Snorkeling/Diving, Deep-sea Fishing, Freshwater Fishing, Swimming, Hiking, Walking, Relaxing, Golf, Tennis, Horseback Riding, Cycling, Workout

SPECIAL INTEREST: Mystery, Singles, Romantic, Nude Beaches, Lecture, Spectacular Cuisine, Wine Tasting, Shopping, Nightlife, Cafe Stops, Gardening, Pro Sports

TABLE OF CONTENTS

LIST OF MAPS

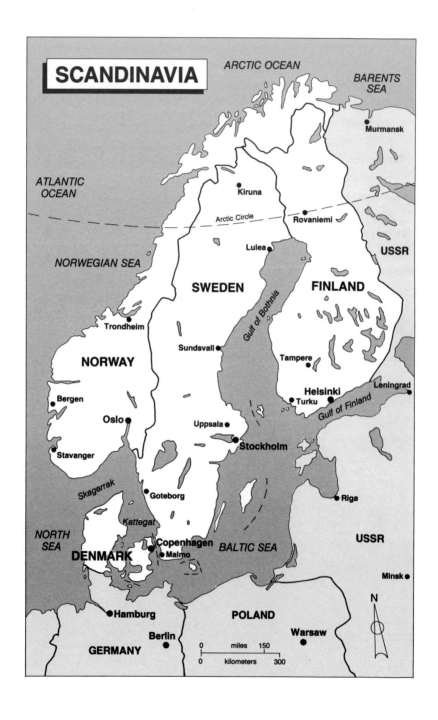

HOW TO USE
THIS BOOK

The introduction to each country provides an overview of the geography and character of the area, something about the people and the culture and, where pertinent, a bit of history, just enough to familiarize readers with the names and events they will hear of in their sightseeing. In the introduction, a section is also included on the basic information travelers will need concerning currency, discounts on accommodations and travel, national holidays, language, weather and food and drink.

The countries are organized similarly, with chapters devoted to regions that generally can be covered in a minimum of three to five days, depending on the mode of travel and the pace the traveler sets. Destinations listed under "Excursions from…" are half- to full-day trips from that city. At the end of some chapters, a section called "On the Way" suggests stops between cities or regions, or ways to get from one place to another. Special trips, such as canal boat cruises, are listed in the cities from which they depart. In the major cities, a Directory with a listing of services and important phone numbers is included. In large cities, hotels are categorized by price; restaurants and sightseeing are organized by location.

THE STAR SYSTEM

I have tried to give as much detail about hotels as possible so that travelers will be able to judge which spot might most appeal to them. The star system is a shortcut guide and highly subjective, but I hope not unfair. The judgment is based on the overall quality of the hotel: the comfort and attractiveness of the rooms; amenities offered (hair-dryers, shampoo, plenty of big towels); pool and sauna; service, with serious consideration given to efficiency, friendliness and ambience. A big, comfortable, commercial hotel might not rate as high as a smaller, quieter one with special charm or friendliness. And some expensive hotels might not have a star at all if they have nothing to recommend them. In the smaller cities, where there are few choices, I often do not use a star rating at all and simply try to tell readers enough about the hotel to let them judge for themselves.

★★★★★ Exceptional quality of accommodations and service (very few get this rating). Hotels so rated must have impeccable service, very luxurious rooms and something extra, a special ambience.

★★★★ Generally excellent accommodations and service.

★★★ Very good quality.

★★ Pleasant and comfortable though not luxurious.

★ Worth looking into because of price.

+Top choice in category. This rating is based simply on my personal opinion, and I reserve the right to have more than one + in each category because sometimes I just can't make up my mind, or perhaps there are qualifications such as location, which make it practical to tag more than one hotel. On the other hand, if most of the hotels are of equal quality, I do not use this symbol at all.

No star. This does not mean the hotel is unacceptable. It just suggests that the hotel has nothing special to recommend it, but you might find it perfectly fine.

PRICES

The exchange rate at the time of publication will be found in the introduction to each country. Prices, where given, are only an approximation, and categories for hotel prices are given in the currency of the country rather than in dollars in an effort to maintain some stability. But prices are, of course, subject to change. Categories are, by nature, subjective. Some might find a $100-a-night hotel exorbitant, while others will think it a great bargain. In the introduction to each country, the price range for the hotels is listed.

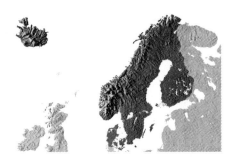

SCANDINAVIA:
AN INTRODUCTION

Geiranger is the most spectacular of all the fjords.

Scandinavia is a sweeping term, pulling into its arc the vast northern reaches of Europe and eons of geological and cultural history. Within its compass, Scandinavia embraces some of the most beautiful land in the world, from the dramatic fjords and mountains of Norway to the tranquil, pine-fringed lakes of eastern Finland. Much of Europe's most colorful and violent history was played out in these lands, from the glorious era of the Viking forays to the tragic devastation wrought during the second world war. And within those historical parentheses lived characters like Harald Fairhair, who unified Norway; Gustavus Vasa, who saved Sweden from the oppression of Denmark; Harald Blue-Tooth (Danish, of course, with a fairy-tale name like that) and some extraordinary women: Queen Margaret, who orchestrated the Kalmar Union and proved herself a stateswoman on a par with Catherine the Great and Elizabeth I; and young Queen Christina of Sweden, who gathered to her court in Uppsala the greatest minds of Europe and then, in a dramatically staged scene at Uppsala Castle, renounced her throne in order to spend her life in Rome in the shadow of the Vatican.

Until recently, the Scandinavian countries were largely ignored by tourists, who contented themselves with remaining within the confines of central Europe, writing off the Nordic countries as cold, austere landscapes with people to match. In the United States, we spoke of "little Finland," not stopping to think that Finland is the fifth largest country in Europe and that this so-called tiny place has managed to survive occupation by Sweden, Russia and Germany, and to bob up to the surface with one of the healthiest economies of western Europe, the only country in Europe to have paid off its war debt. We thought of Norway as a remote but pretty spot where those crazy polar explorers did their stuff, and of Sweden as a life-long Ingmar Bergman film, or a Strindberg play with angst-ridden farmers and landed gentry loosening their tightly laced lives once a year, with disastrous results, on Midsummer Eve. Only Denmark was blessed with our grace. That country wasn't so strange; after all, it had Victor Borge and Hans Christian Andersen and all those cute little thatched cottages.

But times have changed and North Americans are discovering Scandinavia, a region of rare beauty, civilized towns and gracious people. Because most Scandinavians speak English and are fond of Americans, these countries make easy trips. Even going into the remote wilderness of Lapland is almost disappointingly simple, with air and train service available and, for the most part, excellent roads. But the ease of travel does not remove the adventure. These are exotic lands, sparsely populated and wildly beautiful. In Finnish Lapland, the reindeer outnumber the people; in the town of Honnigsvag, Norway, at the gateway to the North Cape, no trees grow. In Spitzbergen, Norway, a tourist board advisory warns visitors to watch out for polar bears.

At the other end of the spectrum from these wilderness outposts are the cities of Scandinavia: sophisticated, civilized and fun, with what I call a three-E rating: Excellent, Elegant, and Expensive. Yes, expensive. Scandinavia is costly. It has always had that reputation and nothing has changed, except that many other European cities have now come to match the Scandinavian prices, and a few, like London and Paris, have outstripped Scandinavia by a sackful of pounds or francs.

A BRIEF HISTORY

Though the history of these countries stretches back to 10,000 B.C., the cities and towns bear little testimony to any life before the 19th century. You will find rune stones, Viking graves and plenty of excavated relics, but, for the most part, the towns themselves look relatively new. Because most of the buildings in Scandinavia were constructed of wood, a dangerous material in a cold country where houses were heated by roaring fires, fires devastated the towns many times, so only the castles and churches, which were built of stone, remain. In some cases, this destruction has proven to be an architectural blessing, especially in Finland, where the center of Helsinki was virtually designed by one man, Carl Ludwig Engels, who created a perfectly balanced, neoclassical composition.

More than fire destroyed these countries, however. From the times of the Vikings onward, the history of the Nordic lands has been tempestuous, riddled with border skirmishes and all-out wars. Over the centuries, the scepter passed back and forth between Denmark and Sweden, with Norway and Finland simple tag-alongs who fell under the sweep of grander powers. It has only been in this century, since 1917, when Finland threw off the yoke of Russian rule and Norway gained her freedom from Sweden, that all four countries have been independent. And even then, one cannot say they lived together peacefully, for during World War II, Finland, in a move to save herself from being caught once again in Russia's smothering bear hug, allied with Germany.

The history of the Nordic regions begins long before the birth of Christ, when nomadic tribes, probably the predecessors of the Sames or Lapps of today, crossed into Finland by way of the Ural Mountains. Evidence of Stone Age hunters in Denmark points to life in that area as long ago as 10,000 B.C. And excavations throughout Scandinavia have yielded relics of well-developed agricultural settlements and pagan cultures. By A.D. 100, business on the high seas was beginning to develop, and by the eighth century A.D., the Vikings had launched what were to be two centuries of seafaring trade, piracy and plunder, which made Europe a smaller place and traded influences both ways. The Danish and Norwegian Vikings carried their navigational skills and business acumen west to the Shetland

and Orkney Islands and into England and France, while the Swedes sailed eastward as far as Russia, arriving at what is now Leningrad and moving on up to Lake Ladoga. In all these journeys, the purpose was not only conquest but commercial and even spiritual gain. The Vikings carried goods to the countries they visited and brought back new treasures, among them Christianity. In fact, it was the conversion of the Viking chieftains that brought the end of the Viking era around the year 1030. Christianity had made a quiet entrance into Sweden in the ninth century, when St. Ansgar began spreading the gospel, but it was really King Eric of Sweden, along with Bishop Henry, in the 12th century, who established the religion more solidly in Sweden and then embarked on a missionary attack on Finland. In Denmark, King Harald Blue-Tooth had easily converted his subjects in the 10th century, and the Norwegian King Olav brought religion to his subjects with little resistance.

The Reformation, in the 16th century, obliterated all traces of Catholicism in the Scandinavian countries. The churches were gutted of their embellishments, the frescoes whitewashed, and the treasures sold. Though many of the churches have now been restored to their original beauty, all four Scandinavian countries remain Lutheran.

Since Viking times, the political history of these nations has been one of swapping power. Finland remained under the grip of Sweden for more than 600 years until it was ceded to Russia. Sweden was dominated by Denmark until Gustavus Vasa liberated his country, and Norway was traded off between Sweden and Denmark from time to time. The only moment of unity was the brief Kalmar Union, in 1397, when the three countries, with Finland as part of Sweden, were united under one ruler, King Eric (the nephew of Queen Margaret, who actually held the power). Once Margaret died, Eric's poor judgment led to the breakup of the union and allowed Denmark to grasp power over Sweden, a power that was relinquished only through the efforts of the above-mentioned Gustavus Vasa.

It is understandable that these nations would want to remain neutral in the world wars, but they only partially succeeded. By the onset of World War II, only Sweden found itself able to maintain neutrality. Finland, as its only protection against Russia, allied with Germany and ended up destroyed by both nations. Norway was forced into the war and, along with Denmark, undertook an elaborate resistance movement. Denmark, with the cooperation of Sweden, managed to smuggle almost all its Jewish population safely out of the country and into neutral Sweden. Norway was not so successful. Most of the

Norwegian Jews died in concentration camps, but Norway's resistance effort was remarkable in all other ways.

THE SCANDINAVIAN NATIONS TODAY

All four nations have highly socialized states with health care and education provided for all citizens. The standard of living in these countries is very high, but so are the taxes. However, the visitor to any of these countries will see almost no poverty and no homelessness. The state provides a home for every citizen who needs it. Mothers are given at least one year's maternity leave, and fathers often can take paternity leave. The laws governing alcohol in all the countries are stringent, with stiff penalties imposed on anyone found driving with even a low level of blood alcohol. Consequently, the Scandinavians are very careful. Usually a designated driver is appointed and that individual does not drink.

THE SCANDINAVIANS

Foreigners tend to generalize about the residents of these northernmost countries, assuming they are all brooding and silent variations of the melancholy Dane who, we should remember, was conceived by an Englishman. But each of these nations has a distinctive personality and, while it is just as dangerous to generalize about one nation as about all four, even the least observant visitor will find that the people of each country can be characterized in some way. The Danes are the most outgoing, with a zany sense of fun and a real desire to extend themselves to a stranger. The Norwegians have an earthier sense of humor beneath a cordial dignity; the Finns are rather shy, but once they feel comfortable, they will reveal their wonderful dry and ironic wit. The Swedes are the quietest and the most serious of the lot, but those in the southern regions, where the Danish influence lasted longest, are much more outgoing and open and will be quick to treat a visitor as a dear friend. What all Scandinavians have in common is innate courtesy and graciousness.

THE LAPPS

The Sames, or Lapps, were among the first settlers of the Nordic regions, probably arriving in Finland and in Finnmark, in Norway, during the Stone Age. The Sames are a race generally characterized by dark hair, high cheekbones and wide-set eyes. They came as hunters and fishermen, and to this day maintain their way of life as fishermen, farmers and reindeer herders. Their culture is distinctive, and in recent years the Lapps have worked hard at the dual challenge of maintaining their unique heritage while becoming part of contemporary Scandinavian life.

Lapland stretches across the uppermost areas of Finland, Sweden and Norway, and in most ways, the Lapps are more closely united as a race than they are with the people of their own countries. A Nordic Lapp Council crosses territorial boundaries to handle the problems and concerns of this minority race. But the Lapps are no longer a primitive people. Though some live in simple huts or even tents in summertime, many of the successful reindeer herders and fishermen have comfortable houses with central heating, VCRs and computers. They are in step with today and are beginning to develop their own tourism business, offering reindeer safaris and snowmobile expeditions to interested visitors.

THE LANGUAGES OF SCANDINAVIA

Swedish, Norwegian and Danish are all closely related, Germanic-based languages. The people of these countries can usually understand one another with little trouble, but the most universally spoken of the languages is Swedish, so if you are planning to learn one language, that would be the most practical choice. Icelandic is the purest of the Nordic tongues, almost unchanged since Iceland was first settled almost 1100 years ago. It is very close to the Old Norse of the Vikings. Finnish is another matter altogether. Even the Finns admit that their language is impossible. It is related only to an obscure Uralic tongue that bears a distant resemblance, I am told, to Hungarian. It is courteous, in visiting any country, to try to learn a few words of the language, but no one will fault you in Finland if you do not succeed. In all the Scandinavian countries, English is widely and well spoken. As you travel into the more remote areas, it will be somewhat more difficult, but not impossible, to find English-speaking people.

PRACTICAL MATTERS

TAX-FREE SHOPPING

All the Scandinavian countries have a value-added tax, often called MOMS, which is added to every purchase, from restaurant food to fur coats. For nonresidents of Scandinavia who will be taking goods out of the country before using them, a refund of the tax, up to 25 percent in some cases, can be collected upon leaving the country. To qualify for the refund, shoppers must fill out a certificate given to them by the shop and hand in that certificate at the tax-free counter at the point of departure. In some cases, the tourist may be asked to show the goods, so you do have to carry these with you rather than send them through in your luggage. Refunds are given on the spot, in the currency of the country. If you are traveling from one country to another within Scandinavia, you can wait until leaving for the last time to collect your tax refund regardless of where your purchases were made. When shopping, be sure to carry your passport with you in order to obtain the tax-free certificate. There is a minimum purchase required in each country in order to qualify for the refund.

ACCOMMODATIONS IN SCANDINAVIA

The central railway stations in most of the big towns and cities have a hotel booking center where travelers can make reservations and obtain information on budget accommodations. The tourist offices in all the cities and towns can give visitors information on alternatives to hotels, such as holiday villages, self-catering cottages and farmhouse holidays.

CUTTING THE HIGH COSTS OF SCANDINAVIA

Each country has particular discount plans on travel, accommodations and meals. Readers will find details on these in the introductory sections for each country. Below are a few that are valid throughout Scandinavia.

SCANDINAVIAN BONUS PASSES

Scandinavian Bonus Passes are hotel discount passes valid in certain hotels in each country. In Denmark, it is the Danway hotels; in Finland the Arctia chain; the Sara Hotels in Sweden; and the Inter Nor Hotels in Norway. Consult the sections on individual countries for details. Available through travel agents and the following North American companies: **Scantours**, ☎ *(800) 223-SCAN*; **Scanworld**, ☎ *(818) 506-4114*; **Royal World Holidays**, ☎ *(206) 789-6144*; **Nortour**, ☎ *(612) 822-1688*; **Scandinavian American World Tours**, ☎ *(800) 223-0599*.

BEST WESTERN HOTEL CHEQUES SCANDINAVIA

Best Western Hotel Cheques Scandinavia offer flat rates for double rooms, all with private bath and breakfast included. Each cheque costs $30 and is valid from June 1 to Sept. 1. These are available through travel agents in the U.S. Some restrictions and variations apply, depending on the country and the particular hotel.

SCANDIC HOTELS

Scandic Hotels also offers prepaid vouchers which cut the cost of a room dramatically. Breakfast and tax are included. The vouchers are sold by **Scantours**, ☎ *(800) 223-7226*; **Holiday Tours of America**, ☎ *(800) 223-0567*; and **Crownline Tours**, ☎ *(800) 255-9509*.

DAILY MENU

In almost every city or town, restaurants offer a daily menu, usually for lunch, of two courses and a drink for a very low price. Many Scandinavians take advantage of the daily menu, eating their big meal at noon and saving money by eating more lightly at dinner.

VISIT SCANDINAVIA PACKAGES

SAS offers a variety of packages to ease the burden on your billfold. Enticements range from a $395 round-trip fare for long weekends including hotel, breakfast and city card, to ski packages and Norwegian coastal voyages.There is also an all-inclusive package through SAS for a five-day cruise from Stockholm to St. Petersburg on the Swedish-managed M/S *Ann Karenina*. Cost is $999 to $1245 per person double occupancy. Details are available from your travel agent or from SAS, ☎ *1-800-221-2350.*

SCANDINAVIAN RAIL PASSES

Offered by the state railways of all the Scandinavian countries, they provide unlimited travel over a period of 21 days throughout Norway, Denmark, Finland and Sweden. Passes are also good for many of the ferries crossing between countries. These can be bought in Scandinavia at any railway station and through **Scantours**, *1535 Sixth St., Suite 205, Santa Monica, CA 90401,* ☎ *(800) 223-7226.* For further information, contact the Scandinavian Tourist Board.

Eurail Passes are valid for travel in Scandinavia and on several of the boats running between the countries. Your travel agent can obtain information for you.

French Rail will offer a Scanrail Pass for unlimited travel on trains and on certain ferries and buses in the four countries. *Contact French Rail, 226 Westchester Ave., White Plains, NY 10604,* ☎ *(800) 844-7245.*

BOAT SERVICE IN SCANDINAVIA

One of the most pleasant ways to travel in Scandinavia is by boat. Ferries ply the waters between the countries and their islands, while steamers chug through the lakes and canals within the countries. The big liners that sail between Stockholm and Finland are spiffily decorated luxury ships, with gourmet restaurants, nightclubs and discos, and, of course, saunas. These boats have comfortable overnight accommodations and are popular with Finns and Swedes for weekend getaways or family vacations. The cruises have duty-free shops on board where passengers can buy perfume, liquor and gift items. The Scandinavians use these trips as a chance to buy liquor and wine, which are otherwise heavily taxed. One word of warning: There has been a great deal of negative press about the rowdiness of passengers on board these boats. These cruises provide an opportunity for the Scandinavians to drink with impunity since no one need worry about who is going to drive home. You may see some pretty raucous behavior from time to time, but unless you are planning to stay up very late in one of the bars or lounges, your chances of being bothered by any of this activity are slim. Most of the passengers are well-behaved, certainly lively and out for a good time, but rarely offensive, so do not let the bad press put you off. The cruises are fun and provide a good chance to meet Scandinavians in pleasant surroundings. More detailed information on such trips is given in conjunction with the boat routes. For scheduling and booking information, contact the Silja, Viking, or Birka lines. Look in the Goteborg section of Sweden and the Saimaa Lake section of Finland in this book for information on steamers in those areas.

WHEN TO TRAVEL

Several centuries ago, a French king was reported to say that Denmark had eight months of winter, and the rest of the year the weather is awful. Weather is certainly a factor in Scandinavian travel, but it need not be an impediment. While it does rain quite a bit in Denmark and Norway, the temperatures in all the Scandinavian countries are not so frigid as you might expect. Average temperatures are about 30°F. in winter and in the 60s and 70s in the summer, though an occasional heat wave will carry the thermometer into the 80s. Warmed by the Gulf Stream, Western Norway has mild winters, with snow in the high country above Bergen but not much in the cities along the coast. In the central mountains and on the east coast of Norway, where Lillehammer, the site of the 1994 Winter Olympics is located, you will find plenty of the white stuff, however. And if you are longing for expanses of frozen tundra, you can find that in the northern reaches of Norway, Sweden and Finland. Stockholm and Helsinki are usually snow covered in winter, while Copenhagen contends more with wind and rain. Residents of Oslo cross-country ski along lighted paths after work in wintertime.

Always be prepared for rain. The weather is capricious and a sunny day does not always fulfill its promise. The best months for travel are June and July, but May can be sunny and pleasant, and it is an especially beautiful time to be in the fjord region of Norway, as the fruit trees are in bloom. Do check with the tourist offices, however, if you plan to travel off season, as many of the fjord steamers do not operate regularly at that time.

Winter, while on-season for winter sports, is definitely off-season for sightseeing. Many of the attractions are closed or open on limited schedules, and it is all but impossible to get into the fjord areas of Norway at that time. But Finland promotes winter travel to Lapland, and it is an extraordinary experience to cross the great stretches of snow-covered fields and pine forests. Reindeer safaris and cross-country skiing are the attractions in the frozen north, and access to these areas is more convenient than you might expect. If you wish to see the Midnight Sun, you can travel to the far north any time between May 23 and July 31. And, conversely, if you want to experience the dark period, go north in the months of December and January.

FOR MORE INFORMATION

Scandinavian Tourist Board: *655 Third Avenue, New York, NY 10017,☎ (212) 949-2333. All the tourist boards of the Scandinavian countries are located at the above address.*

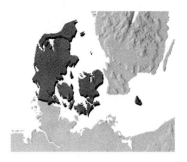

DENMARK

Kronborg Castle supposedly inspired Shakespeare's "Hamlet."

AN INTRODUCTION

Any country that numbers among its patron saints Hans Christian Andersen, Victor Borge and an ancient king named Harald Bluetooth, must have a sense of whimsy, wonder and humor. Though the sea-wrapped landscape is lush and lovely, the thatched cottages and half-timbered houses charming and cozy, and the capital one of the most welcoming and pleasant cities of Europe, Denmark's greatest asset is its people. The Danes, with their wacky sense of humor and their all-out friendliness, are the most attractive of the many treasures this country offers the tourist, though the food may run a close second, and the beer a strong third. So pack your sense of fun when you take off for Denmark, a land where good food, good beer and a good laugh are plentiful.

With its small cottages and tiny hamlets, Denmark appears idyllic, almost a toy nation. Its emphasis on fantasy and fun (it has two of the best amusement parks in the world) makes it ideal for children. But it is a place for adults as well. Tivoli Gardens is not aimed only at children; in fact, much of its beauty and elegance is lost on the younger crowd; and Hans Christian Andersen had much to say to adults as well as children. Adults will enjoy the sophisticated restaurants and the lively night scene. And there is more to buy in Denmark than Lego. Browse through the porcelain wares of Royal Copenhagen and Bing and Grondahl or the silver treasures of Georg Jensen. Or treat yourself to a fur coat to ward off the cold that never really gets to Denmark, where even in winter, the temperature rarely falls below 30°F.

The term the Danes use to describe the style that is so much a part of their life is *hyggelig*, an almost untranslatable word that suggests a combination of friendliness, coziness and cheer. The houses, the restaurants and the people themselves all exude this ever-so-Danish quality. Even Copenhagen has a warmth and a whimsical charm, surprising in a sophisticated European capital.

A LAND OF ISLANDS

Because Denmark consists of islands and is connected to Europe only at the peninsula of Jutland, travelers will find themselves hopping on and off boats and ferries at every step of the way. Denmark is not dramatic, but its charm lies in its rolling green landscape, its sea-washed coasts and its sandy beaches. Add to these the thatched-roofed, half-timbered cottages, and you have an illustration for a fairy tale—by Hans Christian Andersen, of course. This complex of islands makes travel somewhat like an amusement-park ride, with combinations of trains, buses and boats coming into play any time a traveler wants to move from one island to the next. Since Denmark is relatively flat, bicycling is a good way to get around. The highest hill, **Himmelbjergetin** in Jutland, is only 490 feet. The Danes refer to this as their mountain. On Funen, northeast of Faborg, are the **Svanninge Bakker** low hills that are, nonetheless, high enough to offer a panorama of the islands south of Funen.

Jutland is the largest area of Denmark. Its landscape is varied, from the dunes and flat meadows of the east coast to the more dramatic

cliffs of the west coast. In Jutland more than in other sections of Denmark, one is aware of the blend of old and new. Close to one another are **Ribe**, Denmark's oldest city, and **Esbjerg**, her youngest. **Arhus**, the second largest city in the country, is located in the northeast amid the woods and beaches of that coast. **Aalborg**, one of the most successful mixes of old and new, is a delightful town, full of old, important buildings beside more modern ones. The city, with its more than 300 restaurants and night spots, has earned the nickname "Little Paris of the North." North of Aalborg is **Skagen**, a windblown resort town at the northernmost point of Denmark where the two seas, the Kattegat and the Skaggerak, meet. **Funen** is the fairy-tale island, not just because its main city, **Odense**, is the birthplace of Hans Christian Andersen, but because it looks like a fairy-tale landscape. It may seem that only Funen could have spawned that famous teller of tales. The island of **Zealand** has **Copenhagen** as its claim to fame, but there is also the fascinating town of **Roskilde**, where the great ancient cathedral holds the tombs of Denmark's kings, and **North Zealand**, with its castles (among them Kronborg, which is the castle said to have been the model for Elsinore of Shakespeare's *Hamlet*). The islands of **Lolland**, **Falster** and **Mon**, with its chalk cliffs, lie south of Zealand; farther east is **Bornholm**, closer to Sweden than to Denmark. **Greenland** and the **Faroe Islands** are also Danish, but they are so far away that they are often forgotten, certainly by tourists traveling to Copenhagen.

Denmark is an agricultural country with three-quarters of the land area devoted to farming. Travelers driving across Denmark will notice the unique farm buildings called *gaards*. All the buildings of the farm, including the main house as well as the barns, are connected in a U-shape around a central court. The thatched roofs that visitors see on so many of the half-timbered cottages are uniquely Danish. These roofs are expensive both to construct and to insure, but many Danes persevere, not wanting to relinquish this pretty tradition. The roofs are made from rush, which grows in fresh water lakes. The rush is bundled and then put on the frame of the roof, working from below toward the peak. Wooden boards, made of oak and heavy enough to secure the rush against the wind, are put on top. A roof lasts about 30 years, barring disasters, of which fire is the most threatening.

THE CULTURAL SIDE

Of course, the first name in literature to spring to mind is that of Hans Christian Andersen, who made of the fairy tale something adults as well as children can enjoy. By now, enough is known of Andersen's humble beginnings that it suffices here to say that he grew up in the poorest of surroundings in Odense. What is not known so well, perhaps, is that Andersen had aspirations beyond the simple fairy tales that developed almost accidentally as he was pursuing a career in drama. He went to Copenhagen to try his luck in the theater, both as an actor and playwright, and met with little success in either department. In fact, his story tells us that after his rival, Denmark's most esteemed playwright and director, Johan Heiberg, had turned down one of his plays, Mr. Andersen submitted another one, *The Lying-in Room*, anonymously. It was promptly accepted and ran for a year to full houses. Sometime later, Andersen asked the famous director if he would reconsider the first play he had submitted. Absolutely not, the director told Andersen. "But if you could write something as good as *The Lying-in Room*, that would be another matter." Andersen waited several years even then before admitting that he was the author of that successful play. Many of the manuscripts of Andersen's writings for adults are displayed in the Hans Christian Andersen Museum in Odense. A visit there will also give you an idea of the writer's loneliness and of his unrequited loves. But as a teller of tales, none surpassed him. He began by telling stories to children and, seeing the reception these were accorded, began writing them down, remembering, as he himself said, that parents, who would be reading these to their children, needed to be entertained as well. Frequently Andersen read or told his stories on stage, and he usually opened by describing the role of the poet as that of discovering and revealing the connection of man with God through stories and poems that prick at the heart and truth of mankind. It sounds like pretty lofty stuff, but what distinguishes the fairy tales of H.C. Andersen is his ability to hone in on the nature of human beings, to reveal what people have felt but could never quite express themselves.

Denmark's other most famous literary light is Karen Blixen, who wrote under the pen name of Isak Dinesen. In Mrs. Blixen's work there is also the strain of the fantastical, a preoccupation with the strangeness of human experience. In prose that is elegant and almost poetic, Dinesen's stories weave elaborate and imaginative tapestries of mystery, romance and violence. Her biographical work, *Out of Africa*, was the source for the very successful American film of the same name. But Karen Blixen was, like H.C. Andersen, a storyteller above all else. And, interestingly, she wrote much of the time in English and then translated the work into Danish. This was done at first because American publishers seemed more interested in publishing her books than did the Danish.

Ludvig Holberg, the 18th-century dramatist, is claimed by both Norway and Denmark. Born in Bergen, he left his home at an early age, and after wandering the continent for several years settled in Denmark. His plays are acid comedies, satiric in nature, and have earned him the title of the "Molière of the North."

The Danes are also renowned for their contemporary design and for the beauty of their applied art. As long ago as 1775, Denmark was exhibiting its love for beautiful things in the products of the Royal Porcelain factory, which was opened that year. A set of Flora Danica dinnerware was made for King Frederick VI in 1790, and is on display at Rosenborg Castle when it is not in use by the queen for special occasions. Royal Porcelain's signature pattern, Royal Copenhagen, won the Grand Prix at the world exhibition in Paris in 1889, and, in 1900, the Bing and Grondahl Porcelain works was awarded a grand prize for its entry. Georg Jensen, silversmith extraordinaire, brought a new eye for design to a traditional field. His remarkable silver patterns reflected to some extent the art nouveau movement. And Denmark's design prowess is nowhere so well known as in the furniture style called Danish Modern, which aims for a purity of style and the blending of form and functionalism. Arne Jacobsen, an architect and designer, is perhaps the foremost name in this field.

In a more traditional vein, Bertel Thorvaldsen's monumental sculptures are classical in conception and style. Born to a poor family near Odense (and a lifelong friend of Hans Christian Andersen), Thorvaldsen realized enormous success in his own lifetime. He was given commissions by royalty and even the pope, and was frequently called on to make busts of well-known people. In 1838, the king of Denmark sent a warship to accompany Thorvaldsen on his triumphal return from Rome. The sculptor arrived with all his works and most were given to the city of Copenhagen, where they are housed in the monumental Thorvaldsen Museum.

Kai Nielsen (1882–1924) is another sculptor of international prominence. His works can be found throughout Denmark, but perhaps the most famous, or at least the most talked about, is the controversial figure, *Ymer Well*, in the main square of **Faaborg** on Funen.

Danish painting reached its apotheosis in the so-called "Golden Age" of the late 19th century, and it was the Skagen group in particular that best expressed the new realism of this movement. Because they painted outdoors, many artists came to Skagen, at the northern tip of Denmark, for the rare quality of the light. P. S. Kroyer was one of the leaders of this group, painting peasants and fishermen as they worked at Skagen. Michael Ancher and his wife Anna were also well-known exponents of the Skagen school. Their house in Skagen is open to the public.

The Funen painters created works that were more impressionistic than those of the Skagen group. The two most famous artists of Funen are Johannes Larsen, many of whose works are exhibited at the museum of his name in Kerteminde, and Poul Christiansen, whose works, along with those of other representatives of this group, can be seen at the Faaborg Museum.

The most acclaimed contemporary Danish painter is Asger Jorn, who died in 1972. The entire collection of his work was bequeathed to the Silkeborg Art Museum in Jorn's hometown. Mention should be made here also of the COBRA group. The name is an acronym for Copenhagen, Brussels and Amsterdam, and is given to a group of abstract painters founded by Asger Jorn and others.

In music, the name of composer Carl Nielsen (1865-1931) stands out above all others. Nielsen is considered the father of modern Danish music. He is the third artistic son of Odense and, like Hans Christian Andersen and Bertel Thorvaldsen, was born into a poor family. His works include several symphonies as well as a chorale and chamber music.

It is difficult to classify Victor Borge, the humorist/pianist who is a truly gifted and classically educated musician as well as Denmark's most popular comic export. Mr. Borge is the premier ambassador of Danish charm, whimsy and wackiness.

KING CHRISTIAN IV

Though there is not space here to give readers an elaborate account of Denmark's history and her succession of kings, it is worth taking a moment to mention King Christian IV, the "builder king," because travelers will come upon his name frequently as they move through the country, visiting palaces and state buildings that were built by this extraordinary monarch. King Christian IV ruled Denmark for 60 years during the 16th and 17th centuries, first under a regent, as he was only 11 years old when his father, Frederik II, died. But the young king took off running, beginning by building a bigger military and developing trading companies that extended Denmark's commerce. His greatest legacy came through his interest in the arts and architecture. He laid out new towns, both in Denmark and Norway, which he also ruled, and rebuilt the city of Oslo after a disastrous fire. He named the rebuilt city Christiana, a name that stuck until 1924. His two greatest gifts to Copenhagen were the Rosenborg Palace and the Borsen, where it is said that he himself worked on the dragon's tail spire. King Christian IV also built the main palace of Frederiksborg and commissioned the elaborate fountain, which stands in the central courtyard. And, with his interest in and concern for the navy (he was called the "sailor king"), he built rows of small houses for sailors near the harbor in Copenhagen. To this day, the houses are used for sailors. They are the dwelling places of retired seamen of the Royal Danish Navy.

THE DANISH RESISTANCE IN WORLD WAR II

There are many tales about Denmark's courage during World War II, but Danes most often relate with great pride the story of their king, Christian X, who rode out from the palace every day during the Nazi occupation to rally his people. There is a tale which is probably apocryphal but widespread nonetheless, which tells us that when the Nazis declared that all Jews had to wear a yellow star, the King rode out from the Palace wearing a yellow star of his own. The more accepted version of the story says that King Christian X simply said that if the Jews were made to wear yellow stars, he would wear one as well.

With all the varying tales, however, Denmark's courageous resistance in World War II, when this tiny country was able to smuggle more than 7000 Danish Jews to safety in Sweden, is undisputed. Word had come that the Germans were searching for Danish Jews and planned to round them all up on October 1. Two German troopships were already in Copenhagen harbor. An anti-Nazi staff member at the German embassy leaked word of the plan, and the resistance movement sprang into action. Resistance groups called lists of names and spread the word. Some Danish citizens used the telephone directory to find Jewish names, then went to the houses to warn the Jews and help them hide. Throughout Denmark, incidents of Danes aiding the Jews abounded; by nighttime on October 1, most Jews in Denmark were in hiding. On the following Sunday, the Bishop of Copenhagen and Lutheran ministers throughout Denmark read a statement protesting the persecution of the Jews and vowing their own responsibility as Christians to stop it. Groups of citizens worked together to smuggle hundreds of Jews across the Kattegat into Sweden, and by early November, over 7000 of the nearly 8000 Danish Jews had reached safety. A fine exhibition of the

Danish resistance in World War II is offered at the Resistance Museum in Copenhagen. For a list of points of Jewish interest, pick up a copy of the pamphlet, *Denmark: Jewish Points of Interest*, at the tourist information center in Copenhagen or request it from the Danish Tourist Office in New York City.

TRAVEL ESSENTIALS

Danish Tourist Board: *655 Third Ave., New York, NY 10017,* ☎ *(212) 949-2333. You will find local tourist information centers in almost every town. Most of these are centrally located in or on the main square or near the railway station. To write ahead to these offices, consult the New York office of the Danish Tourist Board for addresses and telephone numbers.*

GETTING THERE

SAS, which would be the first choice for service and efficiency, offers daily non-stop service from Newark as well non-stop several times a week from Chicago and Seattle. If you choose SAS, look into their Weekend Money Saver packages leaving on Thursdays from Newark and returning on Sundays. The package includes hotel, breakfast and the Copenhagen Card, but it is available for limited dates only. Delta also flies non-stop from Kennedy.

GETTING AROUND

Denmark is a small country, but because of its geography, travelers will find themselves on various combinations of ferries and trains in order to get anywhere. If you are driving, you must book car space on the ferries well ahead of time in the summer. If you are not driving, you will probably start out from Copenhagen by train, which will not just connect with, but will actually chug onto a ferry.

DSB is the state-owned railway service. There are several different types of trains in Denmark. The Lyntog are express trains; the Inter-city trains run between major cities on different islands. If you are crossing the "Great Belt" between Zealand and Funen, you will take an Inter-city train and you must have a reservation. Buy your tickets at the railway stations for buses, trains and ferries. If you are traveling from Copenhagen to a nearby city like Roskilde, you can take a local train for much less money and you won't need a reservation.

PRACTICAL TIPS

Once in a while, a slip-up could occur if the local and the Inter-city are departing from the same track within minutes of each other; show your ticket to the conductor before you get on the train to make sure you are on the correct one. Otherwise, you may have to pay a rather steep additional fare. Discount passes and senior citizen fares are available. Inquire at the tourist offices or the train station. A Eurail Pass is also valid for Denmark.

Car Rental: Hertz and Avis have offices in most Danish cities, and Budget is located in a few towns. Travelers can arrange ahead from the U.S. for a rental car. Car rentals are expensive in Europe, especially if you require an automatic shift. In that case, you should book ahead, as cars with automatic transmission are not as easily available as those with stick shift.

Driving Regulations: Speed limits are 50 kilometers in town, 80 outside town, and 100 kilometers on motorways. Roads are generally excellent, though the major highways are often only two lanes and there can be truck traffic, which slows the going. Seatbelts are compulsory for drivers and front-seat passengers. **Parking disks** are required in many towns, unless you park at a meter. Pick up a disk at banks, gas stations or tourist offices, and place it in the right front window of your car with the dial pointed at the time of your arrival.

Bicycling: Cyclists think of Denmark as an ideal spot for bicycling, though it is not so flat as one might think and the wind and rain can make it rough going at times. However, the countryside is excellent for bicycling, and most of the major roads and the towns have bicycle paths. The Danes are accustomed to cyclists since they themselves use this mode of transportation. Some tourist offices in the smaller towns rent bicycles, and all can give you a list of where to rent bikes. Copenhagen has begun an experiment by making 5000 bicycles available to anyone wishing to ride through the city. There is no charge, just a 20Dkr. (about $4) deposit which will be refunded upon return of the bicycle to any of the 800 bike racks located all over town.

Air travel: Danair, in cooperation with some subsidiary companies, provides the domestic service between Copenhagen and all the major cities of Denmark. Flights are frequent and quick, no flight taking more than an hour. A **Visit Scandinavia Fare** on SAS is a seven-coupon ticket for a low fare, which allows for travel anywhere SAS flies in Scandinavia between April 1 and September 30. These coupons are sold by SAS and by travel agents in North America only; check with them for the current price.

MONEY MATTERS

The Danish krone, written Dkr., is the currency of Denmark. At the time of publication, the exchange rate was 6.10Dkr. to the U.S. dollar. Like all Scandinavian countries, Denmark is expensive, but much less so once you get out of Copenhagen. Also, as in the other Scandinavian countries, value-added tax, called MOMS, is incorporated in the price of everything, including hotels and meals. In Denmark, the tax is over 18 percent. Service is included on restaurant bills and in taxi fares, so there is no need to tip. Danes will also warn you not to tip, as they claim the Americans are spoiling the service industry, but that is a matter left up to the individual. A few extra coins to round out the cab fare or to the person who carries your luggage will not be turned down.

TAX-FREE SHOPPING

This system is the same as in the other Scandinavian countries. After purchasing a minimum amount (the current requirement is 300Dkr, or about $46, a reduction of 50 percent from the previous minimum), request a form from the shop and hand this in at the airport when you leave the country. You may be asked to show the goods, so plan to carry them with you. You will receive your refund, ranging from 15–19 percent in Danish kroner. You can also claim your refund at the Stockholm, Oslo and Helsinki airports as you leave Scandinavia. The Copenhagen Airport has the best airport shopping in Europe and it is tax-free, so you may want to wait to purchase certain items until you are at the airport. A pamphlet listing goods and prices at the airport is available at SAS offices in Copenhagen, so you can make sure what you want is available. The prices are regulated and shops at the airport are not allowed to charge more than the ones in town.

HOLIDAYS

Everything closes down on December 25 and 26; January 1; several days over the Easter holiday; Day of Common Prayer in April; Ascension Day in May; and June 5, Constitution Day, when the shops close at noon.

SPECIAL EVENTS IN 1995

Copenhagen Jazz Festival: a 10-day event featuring local and international performers appearing in parks, squares and along the canals of Copenhagen. The event starts the first Friday in July.

Copenhagen Water Festival Musical: events from ballet to rock concerts will enliven the city from the harbor esplanades near Amalienborg Palace and at other sites along the water during this third annual festival which occurs Aug. 11–20. A Water Pass provides half-price entry.

Louisiana Museum of Art: a retrospective, entitled "Toulouse-Lautrec and Paris," will be on view through Feb. 5, 1995. Asger Jorn, the Danish painter who died in 1973, will be the focus of a retrospective March 3– Sept. 7.

Roskilde Festival: One of Denmark's major summer events, the festival attracts more than 100 singers and bands. In the past, guest performers have included Paul Simon, Neil Young, Bob Dylan, Sting, Eric Clapton, Phil Collins.

ACCOMMODATIONS

Kiosk P in the Central Railway Station in Copenhagen can help you with booking hotels or private accommodations. If you are looking for very inexpensive places to stay, your best bet for help is usually at the train station in the town you are visiting. For youth hostels, contact the **Danish Tourist Board** in New York or Denmark's **Vandrehjem**, *Vesterbrogade 39, DK 1620, Copenhagen V.* Kro means inn in Danish. You will find many places to eat and/or stay with the word kro after the name. Though the word seems to conjure up a picture of a half-timbered, thatched cottage, many kros are modern, and not all kros have rooms to rent. Some are simply eating places. Nor are they all uniformly casual. Another misconception is that kros are always inexpensive. Though many are, several of the most expensive and nicest places to stay and to eat in Denmark are kros.

Danish Inn Holidays is an association of 66 recommended inns throughout the country. A system called "Inn Cheques" provides discounts at these inns. Each cheque covers a one-night stay in a double room with private bath and breakfast included. In some of the inns an additional minimal charge may be applicable. Travelers can purchase "Inn Cheques" through travel agencies or through the local tourist offices in Denmark.

Self-catering holidays are very popular in Denmark. Travelers wishing to rent a cottage for a week or more should contact the Danish Tourist Board for a list of available rentals.

Farm Holidays are a special way to see the rural life in Denmark. Again, the list of Danish families who wish to share their homes and their way of life with foreign travelers is available through the local tourist boards, who will make the arrangements for you. Prices include room and three meals a day, and are reasonable. Opportunities for these farm holidays abound throughout the countryside. You should understand that often there will be more than one family staying at the farm, and while accommodations are comfortable, these are not hotels and do not offer comparable service. But they are a wonderful way to meet the Danes and glean an understanding of the Danish rural life.

Danish Country Holidays offer another unique way of experiencing Denmark. These are self-catering houses or flats in Jutland that are often connected with a farm. They have all the essentials except bed linen, table linen and tea towels. The accommodations are heated and usually have a garden. This is the closest tourists can come to feeling as if they are living in their own home in the Danish countryside. The tourist offices have a brochure with listings of available rentals. Prices are reasonable.

CASTLES AND MANOR HOUSES

The organization for castles and manor houses offers a new program for tourists wishing to spend a night in one of the castles or manor houses of Denmark. For a price of 650Dkr. per person, the traveler is entitled to one night in a double room with a three-course dinner, a welcoming drink, coffee and cake and breakfast. In a few of the hotels, a surcharge is added and the prices could be subject to change in 1995. You can book these hotels through your travel agent. The Danish Tourist Board in New York has a well-illustrated and detailed brochure on the castles and manors that are part of the program.

HOTEL RATES

I have classified the hotels according to price as follows:

Very Expensive: ----------------------More than 1000Dkr.

Expensive: --------------------------------- 801-1000Dkr.

Moderate: ------------------------------------600-800Dkr.

Inexpensive: ----------------------------Less than 600Dkr.

The rates are subject to change; a hotel in the expensive category could have slid up into the very expensive category by the time readers are ready to travel. Where possible I have indicated the approximate price in Danish kroner.

Several discount passes for hotels are available. Travelers purchasing the **Scandinavian Bonus Pass** before coming to Denmark are entitled to a 15–40 percent discount at all Danway Hotels. The pass is valid for an unlimited number of nights, but travelers can stay only a maximum of three nights at one hotel. Buy the Bonus Pass through your travel agent.

Best Western Hotel Cheques Scandinavia offer discounts for double rooms, all with private bath and breakfast included. A voucher costs $25 and will entitle you to discounted rates from June 1 to September 1. Buy them through travel agents in the U.S.

LANGUAGE

In Copenhagen, Zealand and Funen, almost everyone speaks English. In Jutland, travelers may occasionally find that English is not spoken, as the second language there is German, understandably, because Germany is so close. This is rarely a problem, however, and usually there is someone around who can help out. As far as the Danish language is concerned, it is almost futile to try to learn even a few phrases without a tape to go along with the phrase book. While Danish looks fairly similar to Swedish and Norwegian, it is pronounced entirely differently. Victor Borge says that Danish is not so much a language as "a disease of the throat." And another description claims that Danes "swallow the first half of the word, jump over the second and end up with a rumble in the throat."

WEATHER

All that green grass and bright flowers have to cost something, and the price is rain. Because Denmark is made up of islands, it also gets its share of wind, so come prepared to weather the weather. That means a rain garment that will not billow out in the wind and carry you off like a hot-air balloon, and a hat that will stay on your head midst the gustiest breezes. Temperatures are generally cool, but rarely frigid even in winter, though the best months for travel are generally from April to October.

FOOD AND DRINK

The Danes enjoy the pleasures of the table and are imaginative cooks. One need not confine oneself only to fish here, though that is always excellent, especially the herring, and especially the herring from Bornholm. Game and beef are also popular and generally beautifully prepared. And then there are the other specialties that have become almost a part of our own language, and which we and others have failed so miserably at reproducing. The first that comes to mind is Danish pastry, called *wienbrot*. In Denmark, these bear no resemblance to the limp, cheese-filled American version. In fact, wienbrot rivals, and some, I among them, would say, surpasses the croissant as the breakfast of choice at any time of the day. I try to choose my hotels on the basis of their wienbrot, which is why I will suffer a sleepless night lying above the train tracks at the Astoria Hotel in Copenhagen, counting only the minutes until I get to that establishment's superb breakfast buffet. *Smorrebrod* is the other Danish specialty that has been corrupted abroad. I am not speaking here of smorgasbord, the word Americans use for the Scandinavian buffet, but rather of the openfaced sandwiches that are a Danish delight. In Danish, smorrebrod means bread and butter, but in Denmark that might go down as the culinary understatement of the century. The Danes have raised smorrebrod to unimagined pinnacles, and you can hardly avoid them if you spend one lunchtime in Denmark. There are, of course, smorrebrod and smorrebrod, so try at least once to go out of your way and out of pocket to find the extraordinary ones like those at **Ida Davidsen** in Copenhagen. The Danes cook and serve exquisitely and are imaginative with their use of sauces and vegetables.

The cold table, or *koldt bord*, is another adventure in Denmark, and is usually served only at lunch. Budget watchers can stoke up at one of these at lunchtime and eat lightly and inexpensively at dinner.

As for drink, the beer flows freely, as you might expect, even at 11:00 in the morning, and no wonder. There is no topping Danish beers. The best known are Carlsberg and Tuborg, but there are many other labels as well, and almost every medium-sized town or area has its local beer, which is usually excellent. In Odense, try Albani; in Svendborg, drink Bock. Schnapps is also a popular drink, served in tiny glasses at any time of the day. If you are eating herring, accompany it with a thimbleful (that's all anyone can handle) of *Aquavit* and follow that with beer. *Gammel Dansk*, Bitter Dram, is just what it sounds like, but the Danes swear by it as a cure for whatever ails you, especially headaches and stomach upsets. *Cherry Heering* (note two e's and one r; even the ever-imaginative Danes have not yet resorted to cherry-flavored herring) is Denmark's sweet liqueur. The best use I have seen it put to is inside a chocolate bonbon.

Travelers will find that Denmark has some extraordinarily fine restaurants, but the Danish food is so good that you need not look for a five-star restaurant to ensure a good meal. Once out of Copenhagen, especially, you will find excellent food at reasonable prices.

Casinos in Denmark. The Danes started off the year of 1991 with a roll of the dice in six new casinos. As of December 31, 1990, the Danish Parliament approved gambling for those 18 years and older in six institutions throughout Denmark. These first casinos are in the SAS Hotel Scandinavia in Copenhagen, the Hotel Marienlyst in Helsingor, the Hotel Hans Christian Andersen in Odense, the Hotel Munkebjerg in Vejle, the Hotel Royal in Aarhus and the Hotel Limfjorden in Aalborg.

COPENHAGEN

Nyhavn is the heart of Copenhagen.

COPENHAGEN: THE TOP TEN

There is far more to Copenhagen than the sights listed below, but these are the spots most tourists head to first and then hope to have plenty of time for more exploring through the narrow streets and along the canals that are the true heart of the city. All the sights listed below are described in detail in the appropriate sections of "What to See and Do."

- Amalienborg Palace
- Brewery Tours
- The Carlsberg Glyptotek Museum
- City Hall
- Langelinie and The Little Mermaid
- North Zealand trip along the "Danish Riviera" with stops at the Louisiana Art Museum, Frederiksborg Castle and Kronborg Castle
- Nyhavn, Rosenborg Castle and the King's Gardens
- The Museum of Denmark's Fight for Freedom: 1940–45
- Stroget: the Walking Street
- Tivoli Gardens

Tourist Information Office: *1, Bernstorffogade by the entrance to Tivoli.* Open June 1–September 15, daily from 9:00 a.m. to 6:00 p.m; May 1–May 31,

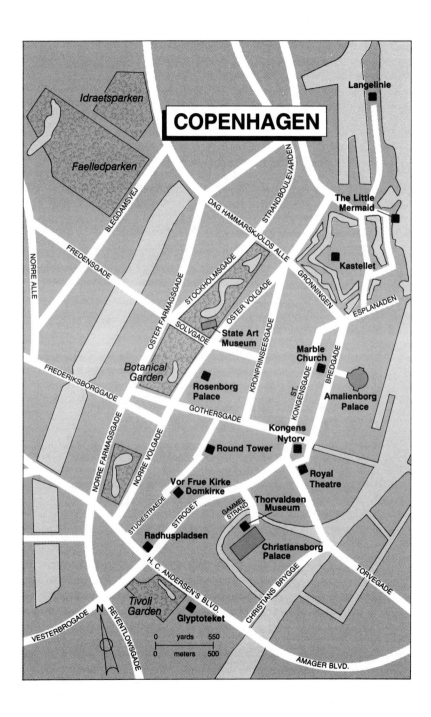

COPENHAGEN

Idraetsparken

Langelinie

Faelledparken

BLEGDAMSVEJ

DAG HAMMARSKJOLDS ALLE

STRANDBOULEVARDEN

The Little Mermaid

NORRE ALLE

FREDENSGADE

OSTER FARMAGSGADE

STOCKHOLMSGADE

OSTER VOLGADE

GRONNINGEN

Kastellet

ESPLANADEN

SOLVGADE

State Art Museum

KRONPRINSESSGADE

Marble Church

BREDGADE

FREDERIKSBORGGADE

Botanical Garden

Rosenborg Palace

ST. KONGENSGADE

Amalienborg Palace

NORRE FARMAGSGADE

NORRE VOLGADE

GOTHERSGADE

Kongens Nytorv

Round Tower

Royal Theatre

STUDIESTRAEDE

STROGET

Vor Frue Kirke Domkirke

GAMMEL STRAND

Thorvaldsen Museum

Radhuspladsen

Christiansborg Palace

H. C. ANDERSEN'S BLVD

CHRISTIANS BRYGGE

TORVEGADE

VESTERBROGADE

REVENTLOWSGADE

N

Tivoli Garden

Glyptoteket

0   yards   550

0   meters   500

AMAGER BLVD.

Monday–Friday, 9:00 a.m–5:00 p.m. and Saturday, 9:00 a.m.–2:00 p.m.;
Sunday and holidays, 9:00 a.m.–1:00 p.m. Open September 16–April 30,
Monday–Friday, 9:00 a.m.–5:00 p.m.; Saturday 9:00 a.m.–noon; closed
Sundays and holidays.

COPENHAGEN CARD

The card entitles the holder to free admission to museums and sights; to discounts on crossings to Sweden; and to free travel on buses and trains throughout
Copenhagen and the surrounding area, which includes Roskilde, Koge and
North Zealand. A word of warning on using the card for trains out of Copenhagen: For travel within the island of Zealand, avoid if possible the Inter-city
trains that go from island to island. They require reserved seats and are more expensive. Travel on the SAS airport bus is not included in the card. An adult can
include two children under five on his card, and children from ages five to 11 pay
half price for their own cards. The card must be dated with the first date of use
and signed. It can be validated at the Tourist Information Office, at the SAS Passenger Service Desk at Copenhagen Airport, at the Central Railway Station, and
at all DSB stations in Copenhagen. A one-day card costs 140Dkr.; two days
230Dkr.; and three days 295Dkr.

DIRECTORY

American Embassy • *24 Dag Hammerskjolds Alle, 2100 Copenhagen 0,*
☎ *31 42 31 44.*

Banks • Hours 9:30 a.m.–4:00 p.m.; Thursday until 6:00 p.m. Closed Saturday
and Sunday.

Bicycle Rental • Bicycle rental runs about 35Dkr. per day, with a deposit of
100–200Dkr. You can rent bicycles at the train stations in Elsinore, Holle-
rod, Klampenborg and Lyngby from April to October.

Chemist • For day and night service in the city: *Steno Apotek, 6C, Vesterbrogade,* ☎ *33 14 82 66.*

Church Services • Roman Catholic services in English, *Sanki Anna Kirke,* Saturday and Sunday, 5:00 p.m.; *First Baptist Church,* Sunday at 9:00 a.m.;
First Church of Christian Scientist, Sunday at 11:15 a.m. There is also a
synagogue at *12 Krystalgade.* Services weekdays at 7:00 a.m. and at sunset;
Saturday at 8:30 and 11:30 a.m., and at sunset. *The Church of England St.
Alban's Church* in Churchillparken at Langelinie holds services on Sunday
at 8:30 and 10:30 a.m.

Emergency • ☎ *113* For fire, police or ambulance. State the nature of the
emergency. Emergency calls from public phones are free.

Exchanges outside banking hours • Main Railway Station: October to mid-
April from 7:00 a.m. to 9:00 p.m. daily; mid-April to September from 6:45
a.m. to 10:00 p.m. The lines here can be long, so allow plenty of time.
Money can also be exchanged at the American Express office, which is open
April–October weekdays from 9:00 a.m. to 5:00 p.m. and Saturday until
noon. The rest of the year, the office is closed on Saturday. Den Danske

Bank at Copenhagen Airport is open in the departure hall from 6:30 a.m. to 8:30 p.m., and in the arrival and transit areas from 6:30 a.m. to 10:00 p.m.

Medical Service • ☎ *112* in Copenhagen. Available 24 hours.For non-emergencies, weekdays from 9:00 a.m.–4:00 p.m, call ☎ *33 93 63 00.*

Dentists • Emergencies only: *Tandlaegevagten 14, Oslo Plads.* All year daily from 8:00 a.m. to 9:30 p.m.; Saturday, Sunday, and holidays from 10:00 a.m. to noon. Dentists' fees are also paid in cash.

Missing Credit Cards • For most cards other than American Express, ☎ *42 65 88 66* from 7:00 a.m. to midnight.

Porters • Copenhagen's Central Railway Station has a convenient service. Travelers can reserve a porter ahead of their arrival by calling ☎ *33 15 74 00, ext. 11281.*

Room Reservations • Kiosk P Central Station will find hotels and private accommodations for you. The booking fee is about 10Dkr. per bed. Open from May to mid-September daily from 9:00 a.m. to midnight. Open September 15–September 30 from 9:00 a.m. to 10:00 p.m. In October, Monday–Saturday, 9:00 a.m. to 5:00 p.m. In November and December, Monday–Friday, 9:00 a.m. to 5:00 p.m.; Saturday, 9:00 a.m. to noon. In April, Monday-Saturday, 9:00 a.m. to 5:00 p.m.

Telephone • For calls to the U.S., ☎ *04300010.* This toll-free number will reach an operator in the U.S. Public phones take two 25-ore coins for local calls, or one-krone pieces for long distance. For operator assistance on public phones, go to the post office in the Central Railway Station or the main Telegraph Office at *37, Kobmagergade.*

Tipping • Hotels, restaurants and taxis include the tip in the charge. It is up to the traveler's discretion to give tips for other services such as porters. In public restrooms, there is usually a charge of 1 or 2Dkr.

She's not pretty, she's even a little dowdy with her stolid red brick buildings, but everyone loves this old sea queen. Copenhagen is the largest city in Scandinavia and probably the one most visited by tourists; under her rather frumpy exterior and eccentric skyline beats a very sophisticated and generous heart.

There have been settlements on the site of Copenhagen for more than 6000 years, but the first mention of the city was in 1043 when there was a small fishing village on the site. The harbor and the abundance of herring in the sea brought prosperity to any who settled here. So in 1157, when King Valdemar the Great gave the town to Bishop Absalon, it was a most generous gift. Absalon built a castle on the island by the harbor, and the developing town became known as *Kobmandens Havn,* or the Merchants' Harbor. In the 17th century, King Christian IV, the builder king, extended the city eastward at

Christianshavn and northeast to Amalienborg and Rosenborg. In the first years of the 18th century, the bubonic plague laid waste to the city, killing one-third of the residents. And in 1728 the first of two major fires destroyed much of the city. In 1795, another fire destroyed Christiansborg Palace. The last major destruction of the city occurred in 1807 when the English, in retaliation for Denmark's support of Napoleon, demanded surrender of the Danish ships. The assaulting forces bombarded Copenhagen, decimating much of the civilian population and large sections of the city. But much of Copenhagen's eccentric charm can be attributed to the gabled, high-windowed buildings that were constructed after that great fire.

Copenhagen welcomes the walker. The center of town is small enough to cover on foot, and the narrow streets that wind off the main ones offer enchanting discoveries to the adventurous explorer. For the visitor, it is a city with fascinations as complex as its wonderful winding streets. The quirky, twisting spires are always there, watching over the tourist and giving him an instant landmark. All you need do is look up and you will get your bearings. So pick up a map and set off. You cannot get really lost, but wandering a little off the beaten path, even at the risk of a small loss of bearings, is well worth the effort.

GETTING THERE

SAS offers service from New York, Chicago, Los Angeles and Seattle. Delta Airlines flies nonstop from Atlanta.

GETTING AROUND AND OUT OF TOWN

From Copenhagen's Kastrup Airport, the SAS bus will take passengers to the Central Railway Station.

Most of the museums and sights in the Copenhagen area are accessible by bus or train or a combination of the two. A joint fare system allows travelers to use the same ticket on both bus and train routes. A basic ticket is good for one hour's travel and unlimited transfers within adjacent zones. Travelers with a discount card or ticket must stamp the ticket face up in the automatic machines at the front door of the buses or in the yellow machines on railway platforms. Most buses leave from Radhuspladsen. **Taxis** indicate availability by a sign FRI. Be sure that the taxi has a meter. Basic fare is 12Dkr., with an additional 7Dkr. per kilometer. Rates are higher from 6:00 p.m. to 6:00 a.m. and on Saturdays and Sundays. Most taxi drivers understand English. To call a taxi, ☎ *31 35 35 35.*

CAR RENTAL

Avis, *1, Kampmannsagade,* ☎ *33 15 22 99; airport office,* ☎ *31 51 22 99.* **Budget,** *6, Nyropsgade,* ☎ *33 13 39 00; airport,* ☎ *32 52 39 00;* **Hertz,** *3 Ved Vesterport,* ☎ *33 12 77 00; airport,* ☎ *31 50 93 00.*

BUS SERVICE TO SWEDEN

Bus 999 leaves from Bernstorffsgade for Malmo and Lund; ☎ *44 68 09 99.*

BOAT SERVICE TO SWEDEN

The Hydrofoil to Malmo takes 40 minutes from Havnegade; ☎ *33 12 80 88.*
To Helsingborg, ☎ *33 32 14 31*; to Gothenborg, ☎ *33 32 14 31.*

SERVICE TO BORNHOLM

Boats from Copenhagen to Ronne depart nightly at 11:30 p.m.; ☎ *33 13 18 66.*

CAR FERRIES

The ride to Funen from Halskov takes one hour; to Jutland (Arhus) from Kalundborg is a three-hour trip. Call Danish State Railways, Central Station, ☎ *33 14 88 80.*

TRAIN SERVICE

There is frequent railway service to towns on Funen and in Jutland. The trains roll right onto the ferries, and passengers can either remain on the train or walk around the boat during the trip.

Information on all the above is available at the Transit Information Office or at any travel agent in Copenhagen.

WHAT TO SEE AND DO

The center of Copenhagen runs from the harbor to **Radhuspladsen** (town hall) square. The walking street, called **Stroget,** links the two major squares, **Kongens Nytorv** and Radhuspladsen. Between the two lie the University, several cathedrals, excellent shopping and some fine restaurants. Northeast of Kongens Nytorv you will find nautical Copenhagen, with Nyhavn, the canal street; and Langelinie, with its promenade along the harbor to Copenhagen's most famous lady, The Little Mermaid.

SIGHTSEEING TOURS

Most of these tours can be booked through your hotel or at the Tourist Information Office, and most leave from Radhuspladsen. They are popular, so be sure to book ahead in high season. As with all tours, the success depends on the guide. It is a good idea to take a city tour upon arrival, just to get an idea of the layout of Copenhagen and the major sites. As for more outlying areas, tours are also available, but if you have several in your party, it may be almost as economical, and probably more fun, to rent a car and explore the environs of Copenhagen yourself. **The Grand Tour of Copenhagen** departs every day, throughout the year, from City Hall Square next to the Lur Blower Column. This tour will take visitors past the major sights of the city. Though it does not include visits inside the sights, it is a good way of getting your bearings and deciding what you want to come back to see. The tour takes about 2-1/2 hours.

The City Tour runs daily from May 10 to September 15 at 10:00 a.m. and 4:00 p.m. In July and August, there is an additional departure at noon. The trip lasts 1-1/2 hours. **City and Harbor Tours** leave daily from April 30 to September 10 at 9:30 a.m., 1:00 p.m., and 3:00 p.m. The early and late tours also pick up at some hotels. Inquire at the Tourist Information Office. **Royal Tours** will take you inside the Royal Reception Rooms at Christiansborg Palace and Rosenborg Castle where you will see the crown jewels Tuesday, Thursday and Saturday at 10:00 a.m. from June 1 to September 10. The trip lasts 2-3/4 hours. The **Castle Tour of North Zealand** takes you along the coast to **Helsingor,** site of Kronborg Castle, the Elsinore Castle of *Hamlet* fame. Passengers will also stop for a tour of Frederiksborg Castle and a walk through the gardens of the Queen's summer residence, Fredensborg Palace. **Harbor and Canal Tours** offer you an easy, quick way to get out onto the water. Tours leave from Gamle Strand and Kongens Nytorv every half hour from May 1 to September 15. Some tours are unguided, so be sure to inquire. The trip lasts about 45 minutes and takes passengers out into the harbor and through the main canals of Copenhagen. **Guided Walking Tours** conducted by an English-speaking guide are available in July and August. The tours are listed in *Copenhagen This Week*. They last about 2 hours. Inquire at the Tourist Information office. There are all-day tours to **Legoland**, to **Roskilde** for a Vikingland tour and to **Odense** for a Hans Christian Andersen tour. Inquire at your hotel or at the Tourist Information Office.

KONGENS NYTORV, AMALIENBORG PALACE AND THE LITTLE MERMAID

Most tourists head straight for The Little Mermaid statue at Langelinie, and that is not a bad way to make your first acquaintance with Copenhagen. But allow yourself some time, because there is much to see on the way. Since Copenhagen is such a walkable city, we'll assume you have on your most comfortable shoes and we will start at Kongens Nytorv, the square (though it is actually round) where you will find the grand old Hotel D'Angleterre, the mammoth department store Magasin du Nord and the Royal Theater. Walk around the square to Nyhavn, the canal that runs right up to the square. You can walk all the way down Nyhavn, and you will probably be here often, as it is a pleasant place to stroll and has many attractive restaurants to lure you back. But for now, the more direct route for our purposes is to take Bredgade off Kongens Nytorv to **Sankt Annae Plads**. If you want to just step into Nyhavn, you can also take the first street off Nyhavn to your left as you walk toward the harbor and reach Sankt Annae Plads that way. From Sankt Annae Plads, Amaliegade will lead you straight to Amalienborg Palace.

Amalienborg Palace

The palace is actually four separate limestone mansions, curving around a central square with the equestrian figure of King Frederik V in the center. The domed building in line with the statue is the Marble Church. The mansions were originally built by order of the king in 1749 for four of Copenhagen's most influential and wealthy businessmen. The buildings were designed by the architect Nicolai Eigtved, and the first recipient of a mansion was Count Adam Gottlob Moltke, a personal friend of Frederik V. Though all four buildings are identical on the exterior, Moltke's is the most lavish on the interior. It is the one on the left as you enter through the colonnade. Now this building is used only for the most important state occasions. Queen Margrethe II and her husband Prince Henrik live in the mansion to the right of the colonnade. The building across from the Queen's residence eventually came into the hands of Admiral Peter Frederik Wulff, who befriended the young Hans Christian Andersen and invited him to the mansion frequently. Today, it is the residence of the Queen Mother, Ingrid, who, according to the constitution, holds regency rights she can exercise if Queen Margrethe is incapacitated.

When the **Royal Family** is in residence, the Royal Guard marches from Rosenborg Castle to Amalienborg every day. Should you wish to follow the route or catch them midway, the Guard leaves Rosenborg Castle at 11:30 a.m. and marches to Kongens Nytorv, along Bredgade to Sankt Annae Plads and then along Amaliegade to the palace, where the changing of the guard occurs at noon.

The Gefion Fountain, Langelinie and The Little Mermaid

From the palace, turn toward Amalienhavn, the park with the fountain in the center. You have a choice here. You can continue along the quay, where you will see the old warehouses, many of them renovated now, until you come to Langelinie, where The Little Mermaid holds court. Or you can go the back way, along Toldbodgade, the next street up from the harbor, and into Amaliegade again. This was Copenhagen's most fashionable residential area and is still a beautiful spot. At the northern end of Amaliegade, you will see the **Gefion Fountain**, a huge, wonderfully energetic piece, illustrating the legend of the origins of Copenhagen. The story tells us that the goddess Gefion turned her four sons into oxen so that they could pull the plough with which she dug Denmark out of the soil of Sweden.

From the fountain, you can go left to St. Alban's Church and the Resistance Museum. You are now in Churchill Park.

The Museum of Denmark's Fight for Freedom: 1940–45

The museum traces the Danish resistance movement during World War II. Though the story about King Christian X wearing a yellow star when the Germans ordered all Danish Jews to do so may be apocryphal, the courage and commitment of the Danes during the war is well documented. In one night, with only a few hours' warning, the Danish people managed to smuggle most of their Jewish compatriots across the water to Sweden. That and other acts of valor are documented here. The exhibit is well displayed, with an audio tour available. Among the exhibits are those on underground communications, on importing of arms and munitions from England and on sabotage efforts. *Open May to mid-September, Tuesday–Saturday from 10:00 a.m. to 4:00 p.m.; Sunday, 10:00 a.m. to 5:00 p.m; closed Monday. From mid-September to April, the museum is open Tuesday–Saturday from 11:00 a.m. to 3:00 p.m. and Sunday from 11:00 a.m. to 4:00 p.m. Closed Monday.*

From the Resistance Museum, you have two choices. Continue through the park to the **Kastellet** fortifications, built in the 17th century when Copenhagen was a fortified city, entirely surrounded by walls. This fortress has been left much as it was. Or go uphill behind the Gefion fountain and you will come to **Lange-linie**, the site of Copenhagen's landmark, the statue of The Little Mermaid.

The first lady of Copenhagen, **The Little Mermaid**, is actually quite small. She sits just a few feet out in the water, and the temptation to wade out and touch her is almost irresistible. She was a gift to the city from the brewer Carl Jacobsen in 1913. In 1964, a truly misanthropic vandal decapitated her, and a new head was made from the original cast. The Little Mermaid is the official tourism trademark of the city and almost every tourist picks up at least one souvenir statue to take home. The Royal Copenhagen Porcelain Factory has the monopoly on this lady, however, and is the only company allowed to reproduce the statue.

NYHAVN

To many, Nyhavn seems to be the heart of Copenhagen. For years, this canal street was an unsavory spot, with drunken sailors, rough bars, tattoo parlors—all the sordid elements of harbor life. But several years ago renovation began, and now it is a delightful area with plenty of good restaurants and cafes, and still enough of the nautical flavor to satisfy an old salt. The exteriors of the mostly 18th-century houses are virtually unchanged, except for tasteful painting and careful restoration; solid, heavy-masted wooden boats still bob in the canal, tangling the air with their halyards and stays. Hans Christian Andersen lived at three different addresses here. First, in 1835, he lived at No. 20, where he wrote his earliest fairy tales; from 1848 to 1865, he rented rooms at number 67; and late in his life, from 1873 to 1875, he moved into number 18. No. 9 is one of the earliest houses in the area, bearing the inscription 1681 under the front window. No. 71, at the harbor end of the canal, was an old warehouse that has now become a first-class hotel, named for its address: **71 Nyhavn**. At the Kongens Nytorv end of the canal, on the southwest side, is Charlottenborg Palace, a Dutch baroque building from the year 1670. It is the home of the Royal Academy of Arts. A small cafe in the Exhibition Hall is open from 10:00 a.m. to 5:00 p.m. all year. In summer, meals are served in the courtyard.

ALONG STROGET FROM KONGENS NYTORV TO RADHUSPLADSEN AND TIVOLI

Stroget is the chain of streets running roughly east to west that make up the pedestrian mall of central Copenhagen. It provides an easy way to get back and forth between Kongens Nytorv and Radhuspladsen, the two anchor squares of the city. But tourists must allow themselves to stray from Stroget, for there are many little streets and inlets that wind off the main drag here that are more interesting. Much of the good shopping in Copenhagen is found here, not just on Stroget but in the streets around it. Stroget begins at its more fashionable end just by the D'Angleterre Hotel. And right away, you can make a little detour by going off to the right and winding around the charming street called **Ny Adelgade**. You can also get to this street by turning left out of the D'Angleterre Hotel—in Copenhagen, with its higglety-pigglety layout, you always seem to end up where you began. On this street and just off it, are elegant galleries and shops. Stop in at #12, the shop of **Tage Andersen**, a most unusual and elegant florist. It's worth going inside to see the elegant clutter of exotic plants, stone, marble, iron and caged birds. Mr. Andersen has also designed furniture for many public buildings and restaurants.

For a healthful bite: As you wind back to the Stroget, you will pass **Crank's Gronne Buffet**, a vegetarian restaurant where you might want to stop for lunch. It's reasonable and good. Farther along the Stroget, you will see a sign for **Pistolstraede.** This alleyway winds back to several fine shops and a restaurant. **Torvehallen**, the market, is fun to explore. **Lunch Break:** If you are hungry after looking at those sumptuous wares, the **Bee Cee Cafe** (open from 11:00 a.m. to 4:00 p.m.) or the bakery, **Kransekehusets Konditorei**, are both good spots. You will see the name Bee Cee here several times. It derives from the initials of Birger Christiansen, the furrier and entrepreneur, who has embellished much of this part of Copenhagen with his Midas touch. When you come out of Pistolstraede, you will still be on **Ostergade**, the first section of Stroget.

Ostergade runs into **Amagertorv**, a large square with the famous **Stork Fountain**. Number 6 Amagertorv is one of the oldest buildings in Copenhagen, built in 1606. It houses the **Royal Copenhagen** store. **The Church of the Holy Spirit** is located just down the street and is open for visitors. The font is the work of the sculptor Thorvaldsen. At times, a bake sale is set up in the courtyard of the church and passersby can stop for a cup of coffee and a snack. From the east side of the church, you can take the street called Niels Hemmensgade, which will lead you to **Grabrodre Torv**, site of a Franciscan monastery in the Middle Ages and now one of the most pleasant squares in the city. Two of Copenhagen's very popular restaurants are located here: **Peder Oxe** with its lively wine cellar and, next door, **Bof and Ost**, another popular and reasonable eating spot.

A Detour to the Round Tower and the Latin Quarter

If you want to wander a little more, go through the square to Skindergade, where you will find some very old houses. Take Skindergade to the right and you will end up on **Kobmagergade**, another pedestrian mall. To the left is the Round Tower, built by Christian IV as an observatory and a library. Visitors can climb the winding walk which twists around the outside of the tower. The library at the top is now an exhibition hall. As you come from the tower, you will see **Arnold Busck**, a bookstore with a good selection of books in English. You are now in the University area. Continue on **Store Kannikestraedet** to arrive at the **Cathedral of Copenhagen** and the **University**. Inside the cathedral is Bertel Thorvaldsen's most famous work, his statue of Christ. Thorvaldsen also created the marble statues of the twelve apostles, which are here as well. Not far past the Cathedral, on your left, will be Jorcks Passage, which leads back to Stroget.

Back on Stroget

The next square is a double one, with Gammeltorv, the oldest square in Copenhagen, on the right, and Nytorv on the left. The original town hall of Copenhagen, destroyed in a fire in 1795, was located at a point just between these two squares. The building on the corner of Nytorv was built in 1880 as the new Town Hall, and then it became the city courthouse when the present Town Hall at Radhuspladsen was constructed. The **Caritas Fountain** in Gammeltorv is fed by a well, in existence since Renaissance times. The figures of the fountain date from the early 17th century.

From the double square, Stroget leads into Frederiksberggade. A bank now occupies the site of the house where the philosopher Soren Kierkegaard grew up. From here it is a straight shot into Radhuspladsen.

Radhuspladsen

This huge square is often considered the center of Copenhagen, and certainly every tourist will walk through it at least once as all roads seem to lead here. The square is always a busy place. Many buses leave from here, as do most of the city sightseeing tours. At night, with the crowds spilling out of Tivoli, the scene is bustling. The square is punctuated by three sculptures; the *Dragon Fountain* in front of the Town Hall and, at the other end, the *Soldier and the Little Horn Blower*, created in memory of the soldiers who died in the wars against Germany in the late 19th century. At the corner of the hall, by H.C. Andersen Boulevard, is the statue of *H.C. Andersen* himself, looking toward Tivoli Gardens.

The Town Hall

The impressive landmark sits stolidly in red brick dignity in the middle of the square. Visitors can go into the Hall, where Jens Olsen's World Clock is located, and can also climb the tower.

TIVOLI GARDENS

Tivoli is a world unto itself, but visitors do not really need a guide to Tivoli, as it reveals its own charms effortlessly. However, a few words on procedure are in order. Tivoli can become expensive. At last check, admission was 38Dkr. with children half price.But each time you enter the park, you must buy a new ticket, so plan to stay several hours and make just one visit if you are budgeting. But it is not the cost of admission so much as the cost of amusements and the food in Tivoli that will boost your bill.

There are ways to beat the high prices a bit. Admission to the gardens is free with a Copenhagen Card, and you can also buy a Tivoli Tour Pass, which costs about $24. It is valid for unlimited use on all amusements for the day and evening of the purchase. You can also buy 10-tour tickets at a savings of about 10Dkr. And to further cut the cost, you can eat before or after you have been to Tivoli. Don't let the high cost of Tivoli Gardens deter you, however. Tivoli is unique and enchanting, and at its most magical at night when the lights are twinkling in the trees and illuminating the gardens. On Saturday and Sunday at 6:30 p.m. and 8:30 p.m., the Tivoli Guards, selected boys of ages 9–16, march through the park. For the first time in its 151 year history, Tivoli opened for Christmas in 1994. This was an experiment, but plans are in the works to continue this new tradition which opens the Gardens from mid-November until New Year's Eve when the festivities explode in a burst of spectacular fireworks.

Restaurants in Tivoli: Eating in Tivoli can be a problem. It is not that there is no place to eat inside the gardens; in fact, the opposite is true. You will find many places to eat, all expensive and some exorbitantly so. You can pick up snacks at the many kiosks, but if you are planning to sit down to a meal, you will have to plan to spend at least $30 per person for the most simple fare, and, all too frequently, the food is mediocre and the service lackadaisical. Among the best spots are **Divan II** and **Belle Terrasse**. These two restaurants are as beautiful and the cuisine as fine as any you will find in Denmark, but they are very, very expensive. **At Divan I**, another pretty spot, you may save a few kroner. The food here is generally high caliber, but it is not quite so consistent as at the above-mentioned places. Stay away in particular from **Pafuglen**, where the rude service is matched by the mediocre food. You would do better, especially if you are not in the market for Divan II or Belle Terrasse, to eat before you come into Tivoli or to satisfy yourself with snacks from the kiosks. *The gardens open every day at 10:00 a.m. and the children's amusements start up at 11:30 a.m. At 1:30 p.m., all the amusements are in full swing. From 3:00 p.m. to midnight there are promenade concerts, and throughout the day, various band concerts and shows take place on the different stages and are free. Fireworks on Wednesday, Friday, and Saturday at 11:45 p.m. and Sunday at 11:30 p.m. The gardens close at midnight every night.Tivoli opens on April 27 in 1995 and closes on Sept. 10.*

The new Tivoli Museum, opened in 1993 in honor of Tivoli's 150th birthday, houses exhibits of paintings and drawings of the gardens throughout its history, and costumes and models of some of the old rides. *Open 10 am–10pm daily.*

SLOTTSHOLMEN, THE CASTLE ISLAND

Slottsholmen is the island, wedged between the harbor and the mainland, where Bishop Absalon built his castle in 1167. The ruins of that castle are still visible in the museum, which is located under Christiansborg. On Slottsholmen is the Borsen, or Stock Exchange, a Renaissance building topped by a tower with a design of four intertwined dragons' tails. Also, the newest edition of Christiansborg Palace is here. This is the home of the Parliament, the Supreme Court and many state offices. The Thorvaldsen Museum, dedicated to the work of Danish sculptor Bertel Thorvaldsen, is also located on Slottsholmen.

Just across the bridge on Gammel Strand is a good place for lunch, **Gammel Strand 46**. Choose from an assortment of herring, smorrebrod and hot dishes. This is a tiny homey spot, popular with Copenhagen businessmen.

CHRISTIANSHAVN

Christianshavn is the section of Copenhagen to the east, developed by Christian IV in his effort to expand the city in the early part of the 17th century. The twisting spire of the Church of Our Saviour dominates the skyline of the island and offers a spectacular view of the city. Back down to earth, the visitor will find Christianshavn a pleasant, green island, bisected by the picturesque Christianshavn Canal. The canal tours, which leave from Kongens Nytorv, offer an effortless way to see this part of Copenhagen. The island is also the site of **Christiana**, the experimental community that reached the height of its notoriety in the 1960s when those mostly young people, who were unhappy with the establishment, chose to flock to this green and welcoming enclave and live according to their own plan. In the best Danish tradition, the city has always allowed this area to govern itself. There are not so many people living here now, but they are left alone. Visitors can walk here, but one might feel a little strange as it is not really to be considered a tourist attraction and you might have the feeling that you are intruding.

If you wish to spend some time walking through the other parts of Christianshavn, try peeking into some of the courtyards and gardens along the canal. No. 30 has an especially pretty garden. Remember, though, that most of these are private homes.

The Restaurant Kanellen, at the end of the canal, is a very pleasant spot with good food. A three-course lunch will run about 125Dkr., dinner about 195Dkr. It is housed in a small, pink building right on the water.

MUSEUMS AND OTHER SIGHTS

There are so many museums that only the top attractions can be listed here, but if you buy a Copenhagen Card, the accompanying booklet will list them all for you.

NOTE: *Most museums are closed on Mondays.*

Rosenborg Castle

Built by Christian IV in 1633, Rosenborg is largely unchanged on the exterior, since it is one of the few buildings to have escaped the fires of the 18th century. But the purposes of the castle have changed over the centuries, and, consequently, the interior has undergone some transformations. This was Christian IV's favorite castle and the place he chose to die. Visitors can go through many of the rooms, gleaning a good idea of what life here must have been like. The castle was last used as a royal residence by King Frederik IV, who renovated many of the rooms and slowly shifted the style of decoration from Renaissance to baroque. From 1740 until the present, Rosenborg has been a repository for the royal collections. It has been open to the public since 1833. Be sure to see the silver collection in the banquet hall on the top floor. There is also some very fine porcelain there. And don't miss the ceilings of the banquet hall. Downstairs, accessible by a separate entrance, are the crown jewels. These are charming rather than splendid, but of special interest is Christian IV's exquisite crown. New this year is the permanent exhibit, in the Green Room, located in the vaults next to the Treasury. The display in the Green Room includes 16th- and 17th- century heirlooms of the Danish Royal Family. In addition, be sure to visit **the grounds of the castle, which are called Kongens Have or the King's Garden.** This is a lovely place to spend an hour or so. There is a pleasant restaurant of the same name here as well. Opening hours of the castle vary with the seasons because there is no electricity in the castle itself. *Generally, the museum is open every day May–September 25 from 10:00 a.m. to 4:00 p.m., and from the end of September through most of October, 11:00 a.m. to 3:00 p.m. The rest of the year, the castle is open only Tuesday, Friday and Sunday from 11:00 a.m. to 1:00 p.m.; but the Treasury housing the Crown Jewels is open Tuesday–Sunday from 11:00 a.m. to 3:00 p.m.*

The State Museum of Art

Located across from the gardens of Rosenborg Castle, this is the largest art museum in Denmark with both Danish and international paintings. Most of the Danish collection dates from the late 18th century through the 20th. The foreign exhibit contains an impressive display of Dutch and Flemish art as well as a significant collection of the work of Matisse. *Open Tuesday–Sunday from 10:00 a.m. to 5:00 p.m. all year. Closed Monday.*

Ny Carlsberg Glyptotek

Located across the street from Tivoli Gardens, this museum, the gift of brewer Carl Jacobsen, houses the largest collection of ancient art in northern Europe. In addition to an extraordinary collection of artifacts from ancient Egypt, the museum has exhibits of Greek, Italian and 19th- and 20th-century French art with a particularly fine selection of Gauguin's work. You will find Danish art exhibited as well. Open May–August, Tuesday–Sunday 10:00 a.m.–4:00 p.m.; September–April, noon–3:00 p.m. Sunday 10:00 a.m.–4:00 p.m. Closed Monday.

The Thorvaldsen Museum

Every time you drive by Slottsholmen on your way from Radhuspladsen to Kongens Nytorv, you cannot help but notice this building with its mustard-colored facade embellished with green and blue frescoes. It was built for the express purpose of housing the monumental sculptures of Bertel Thorvaldsen, the 19th-century Danish sculptor. The interior design is as interesting as the outside, with vaulted, painted ceilings and beautiful wall colors. In addition to an extensive exhibit of Thorvaldsen's own sculptures, including small models for some of the pieces, the museum also contains Thorvaldsen's own collection of ancient art. Closed Monday. Open all year Tuesday–Sunday, from 10:00 a.m. to 5:00 p.m.

Christiansborg Palace

The Royal Reception rooms are open to the public. A guided tour in English will take you through the Throne Room, the library and the banqueting hall. (Visitors may also go into the Danish Parliament, where tours in English are given every day but Saturday; check on hours.) The ruins of Bishop Absalon's Castle were carefully excavated and preserved during the building of the present castle. They are in the museum beneath the castle. The tour is offered May–September, Tuesday–Sunday at 11:00 a.m., 1:00 p.m. and 3:00 p.m. At other times of the year, the English tour is given every day at 2:00 p.m., except Monday and Saturday. Open May–September daily from 9:30 a.m. to 4:00 p.m. The rest of the year, the museum is closed on Saturday. Also on the grounds are the Royal Stables, the Theater Museum and the Royal Arsenal Museum.

Grundtvigskirken

The architecture of this extraordinary yellow brick church, built between 1921 and 1940, is described as a combination of a Danish village church and a Gothic cathedral, with touches of Danish National Romanticism. The church is a stop on the Grand Tour of Copenhagen. *Open May–September, Tuesday–Saturday from 9:00 a.m. to 4:45 p.m.; Sunday, noon to 4:00 p.m. From October to April, the church is open Monday–Saturday from 9:00 a.m. to 4:00 p.m.; Sunday, noon to 1:00 p.m.* These hours are subject to change if there is a church function in progress.

Brewery Tours

Both Carlsberg and Tuborg offer tours of the brewery and free samples. The Carlsberg Brewery has a museum on the premises. **Carlsberg's** guided tours of the brewery begin at *9:00 a.m., 11:00 a.m. and 2:30 p.m., Monday–Friday.* **Tuborg's** tours are scheduled at *10:00 a.m., 12:30 p.m. and 2:30 p.m., Monday–Friday.*

The Eksperimentarium

A new concept in science museums. Located in the old mineral bottling hall of the Tuborg Brewery, it houses hands-on exhibits in science and technology. *Open Monday, Wednesday, Friday from 9:00 a.m. to 6:00 p.m.; Tuesday and Thursday, 9:00 a.m.–9:00 p.m.; weekends, 11:00 a.m.–6:00 p.m.* There is a cafe where you can eat your "brown bag" lunch.

The Erotic Museum

This latest addition to the museum scene features exhibits of erotica through the ages as well as the sex lives of well-known people, like Freud.

The National Museum

There are exhibits on the cultural development of Denmark from the Stone Age to the present day, in addition to collections of western and eastern antiquities. The museum has recently undergone a major renovation and hosts several important exhibitions throughout the year. *Open mid-June to mid-September, Tuesday–Sunday from 10:00 a.m. to 4:00 p.m. The rest of the year, it is open Tuesday–Friday from 11:00 a.m. to 3:00 p.m., and Saturday and Sunday, noon to 4:00 p.m. Closed Monday.*

The Hans Christian Andersen Center

Located at Nyhavn 69 in a restored townhouse, the center features exhibits, readings and theatrical performances depicting the fairy tales and the life of this most famous of Denmark's citizens. *Open every day but Tuesday from 10:00 a.m. to 5:00 p.m.*

The Copenhagen City Museum

The history of Copenhagen, with a model of the city as it was in 1530, is displayed in front of the museum during summer. The museum also houses a Soren Kierkegaard exhibit. *Open May–September, Tuesday–Sunday from 10:00 a.m. to 4:00 p.m.; rest of the year, Tuesday–Sunday from 1:00 p.m. to 4:00 p.m. Closed Monday.*

Kunstindustrimuseet (Museum of Decorative Art)

European decorative art from the Middle Ages to the present. Also, collection of art from China and Japan. *Open all year, Tuesday–Sunday from 1:00 p.m. to 4:00 p.m. Closed Monday.*

The Hirschsprungske Collection

Danish painters of the 19th and 20th centuries with emphasis on the Golden Age and Skagen painters. *Open May–September, Wednesday–Sunday from 1:00 p.m. to 4:00 p.m. From October to April, additional hours are Wednesday evenings, 7:00 p.m. to 10:00 p.m. Closed Monday and Tuesday.*

The Ordrupgaard Collection
Collection of paintings of the French impressionists and works by painters of Denmark's "Golden Age." Frequent visiting exhibits as well. The collection is located in a lovely old home. *Open all year, Tuesday–Sunday from 1:00 p.m. to 5:00 p.m. Closed Monday.*

The Storm P. Museum
Storm P. was the pen name of Robert Storm Petersen, a cartoonist who lived from 1882 until 1949. For a glimpse of Danish humor and insight into the social and political issues of those years in Denmark, visit this museum. *Open May–August, Tuesday–Sunday from 10:00 a.m. to 4:00 p.m. The rest of the year, open Wednesday, Saturday and Sunday from 10:00 a.m. to 4:00 p.m. Closed Monday.*

The Bakkehusmuseet Museum of Literary and Cultural History from 1780-1830
The museum is located in the home of Kamma and Knud Lyne Rahbek, which was a meeting spot for Danish intellectuals of the time. The house is furnished as it was in those years. *Open Wednesday, Thursday, Saturday and Sunday from 11:00 a.m. to 3:00 p.m.*

The Georg Jensen Museum
Handmade silver objects from 1904–1940; also Georg Jensen memorabilia. *Open Monday–Friday from 10:00 a.m. to 5:30 p.m.; Saturday, 10:00 a.m. to 2:00 p.m. Closed Sunday.*

Louis Tussaud's Wax Museum
Children will probably beg to go to this museum, which is highly noticeable, right next to Tivoli with both a Tivoli and a street entrance. It is a pale copy of Mme. Tussaud's in London and as such is, in my opinion, overpriced. The best exhibits are of the H.C. Andersen fairy tales. *Open May to mid-September daily from 10:00 a.m. to 11:00 p.m. The remainder of the year, the closing hours vary, so check ahead.*

The Copenhagen Zoo
Among the sections are an Ape Jungle, an African Savannah and a Children's Zoo. *Open every day June–August from 9:00 a.m. to 6:00 p.m.; September and October, 9:00 a.m. to 5:00 p.m.; April and May, 9:00 a.m. to 5:00 p.m., with 9:00 a.m. to 6:00 p.m. hours on weekends. January–March, the Zoo is open every day from 9:00 a.m. to 4:00 p.m.*

The Royal Copenhagen Porcelain Factory
Smallegade 45. Tours of this factory, which makes all the beautiful Royal Copenhagen porcelain as well as many other objects, are on Tuesday and Thursday at 9:30 a.m. *Closed from July 15 to August 5.*

Holmegaard Glassworks
Holmegaard is Denmark's only major glass manufacturer. It was started by a woman in the 19th century. The glassworks at Fensmark near Naestved, about 80 kilometers southwest of Copenhagen, are *open weekdays from 9:00 a.m. to noon and from 12:30 p.m. to 1:30 p.m.*

The Tycho Brahe Planetarium

A striking new planetarium set beside Sankt Jorgens Lake on Gl. Kongevej. The building designed by the architect Knud Munk contains, in addition to the space theater and Omnimax performances, a library, shop and the restaurant Cassiopeia. *Open daily from 10:30 a.m. to 9:00 p.m. Performances occur on the hour, every hour between 1:00 p.m. and 9:00 p.m.; noon and 10:00 p.m. showings on Friday and Saturday.*

West India Warehouse

The Royal Cast Collection. Display of approximately 2000 plaster casts of famous works of art covering more than 4000 years of the history of sculpture.

The Royal Opera House

For those who are looking for evening entertainment aside from the nightclub and bar scene, the Royal Opera House is the home of both the Royal Opera and the Royal Ballet. Highlights of the 1995 season include *Les Sylphides* on May 11; *Romeo and Juliet* on Jan. 10, 11, 14, 17, 18; *Giselle* on Mar. 5, 6, 11, 13, 17, 22, 30, April 1 and May 18. *The Abduction from the Seraglio* will be performed on Jan. 16, 20, 22, 25, Feb. 8, 13, 16, 24 and March 4, 8 and 21. *Tannhauser* will be presented on Feb.23 and 26 and March 1, 10, 28 and 31 as well as April 29 and May 4, 8 and 21, with *Turandot* the attraction on March 20, 23, 25, April 3, 6, 8 and 11.

SHOPPING

Antiques, silver, porcelain, glass, furs and fashions—Copenhagen has them all, and all are easily accessible. Most of the men's and women's fine fashions are at the Kongens Nytorv end of Stroget. Antiques are pocketed on several streets running east off the Stroget.

Shopping hours • Monday–Thursday from 9:00 a.m. to 5:00 p.m.; Friday, 9:00 a.m. to 7:00 or 8:00 p.m.; and Saturday, 9:00 a.m. to 1:00 or 2:00 p.m. On Monday, some shops do not open until 10:00 a.m. On Sunday and holidays, some bakeries, service stations and kiosks open for a few hours. The supermarket and kiosks at the Central Station are open daily until midnight. Most gift shops in hotels remain open later than other shops. In summertime, the Royal Copenhagen Gift Shop, next to the main store on Stroget, is open later on Saturday and for a few hours on Sunday. But check ahead.

Tax-free shopping • See introduction for details. Just remember to ask for the form in the shop.

PORCELAIN

Royal Copenhagen Porcelain, *Amagertorv*, is the largest porcelain store in Denmark. Royal Copenhagen also owns Bing and Grondahl Porcelain, so you will find those products here as well. Be sure to climb the stairs to the tiny museum with beautiful old pieces. In season, a small gift shop near the Royal Porcelain store stays open on Saturdays and Sundays and has gifts from Holmegaard and Georg Jensen, as well as Royal Porcelain, since all these companies, along with Illums Bolighus, are now under the same ownership. Sometimes there are small exhibits in the courtyard annex. Check the hours. Royal Porcelain also operates a cafe on its premises. In many of the **antique shops** *on Kompagnistraede*, you can find old Royal Porcelain in the traditional Blue Fluted design, which was created in 1775 with the backing of the Royal Family. These pieces may not be certified antiques, but they are very pretty, sometimes prettier than the newer ones, though all are the same pattern. They are generally a bit less expensive than the items you will buy in the regular retail shops. Of course, the selection is limited. The three wavy lines on the bottom of the pieces are the trademark of Royal Porcelain. The lines stand for the Great Belt, the Little Belt and the Sound, which connect the main areas of Denmark.

H. Danielsens Eftf., *in Laederstraede, off Stroget*, sells secondhand silver, glass and porcelain, and offers Christmas plates from every year. A vast inventory.

GLASS

Holmegaard, *on Stroget*, sells the only glass made in Denmark. Many enchanting pieces are here, and the prices seem a little lower than for Swedish glass. See section on "Museums and Other Sights" for details on visiting the glassworks.

SILVER

Georg Jensen has the monopoly here. Again, you will find this shop on Stroget. **Hans Hansen Silver**, also on Stroget, is one of Copenhagen's most well-known silversmiths, with contemporary jewelry designs. If you are looking for vintage silver, **Georg Jensen has moved its antiques to the Georg Jensen shop. Bredgade**, the street behind Amalienborg Palace, contains several choices for antique silver as well.

Peter Krog, *Bredgade 4*, is a good source for large pieces of antique silver as well as jewelry. **Straedet** is a walking street which houses several secondhand silver shops, among them **H. Danielsen's Successors** which is in a building that once served as headquarters for the Danish Resistance. For less expensive offerings, try **Soelvkaelderen** *at Kompagnistraede 1*, a cornucopia of old silver and new and old silver plate. You can also trek to **Noerrebro**, which is a working-class area filled with secondhand shops that occasionally will yield a treasure at a more reasonable price than those in the more up-market areas. **ABC Antik**, *at Ravnsborggade 15*, and **Kim Antons and Company**, *at Ravnsborggade 20B*, are worth rummaging through. There is also a flea market of sorts on Saturdays in summertime from 8:00 a.m. to 2:00 p.m. *in Israels Plads, behind the Norreport Station.*

ANTIQUES

Rather than mention specific names here, I think it is best for shoppers simply to meander through the two major areas for antiques, **Bredgade** and the Stroget area. Take **Laederstrade**, *which runs off Hojbro Plads by the Nicolai Church.* This street has a few antique shops, and it will lead you into **Kompagnistraede**, with even more shops. This is the place for silver, antique and modern. You can pick up pieces of secondhand Georg Jensen silver and Royal Copenhagen porcelain in these shops. For lunch, you can either stop at the Nicolai Cafe in the church before you start on your expedition—a good place if you are saving up kroner for your antique spree—or turn left at **Nabolos**, which crosses Laeder-straede, and follow it to Gamle Strand.

GALLERIES

Galeri Asbaek at 20 Bredgade is one of Copenhagen's major art galleries. Open Mon–Fri. 11:00 a.m.–6:00 p.m., Sat. 11:00 a.m.–4:00 p.m. There is a pleasant little cafe in the garden.

Tage Andersen, *on Ny Adelgade*, is an anomaly, a florist with a few exquisite accessories and some pieces of furniture designed by Mr. Andersen. The tiny shop itself is museum-like in more ways than one, for it does charge an admission fee of approximately $6.

NEEDLEWORK

Eva Rosenstand, *on Stroget*, is justifiably famous. **Galerie Norby** *at Vestergade 8* is a new and exciting gallery for Danish and international art.

FURS

Birger Christensen, *in Stroget*, dominates the fur business here, and will offer you the best designs and the finest furs. You may pay top kroner in Copenhagen terms, but you will get the best quality and design. If you know what you want and it is not top of the line, you may be able to do well at **Otto Madsen**, evidently designed for tourists. The prices are the best you will find, but you have to sift through a lot of things you would not want in hope of finding a hidden treasure.

MEN'S AND WOMEN'S FASHIONS

Pistolstraede, *off Stroget*, has the most exclusive women's shops, with many specialty and design shops. **Brodrene Andersen,** *at Ostergaade 7–9 in Stroget*, offers classic men's and women's wear. For knitwear, **The Sweater Market** seems almost too obvious to be true with its English name and its prominent location *on Stroget*, but it has an endless supply of all the things you are probably looking for—sweaters, knit caps, gloves and scarves made in Denmark and Iceland.

BOOKS

Arnold Busck, *near the University*, has books in English. **Antikvariat**, in the newspaper *Politiken building in Radhuspladsen*, has old books and also a good selection of books in English. **Magasin du Nord** has a good supply of paperbacks in English on the fourth floor. **Danisk Boghandel,** *on Stroget*, has a fairly large selection of English books, mostly paperbacks and best sellers. **Branner's** *at Bredgade 10* has a good selection of old books.

DANISH DESIGN

Artium, *on Vesterbrogade*, is a small gallery-like shop for contemporary Danish artifacts and household objects. **Illums Bolighus,** not to be confused with Illums department store just next to it on Stroget, is the center for contemporary Scandinavian and international design. Many splendid temptations here. *Illums Bolighus is open Saturday until 5:30 p.m. and Sunday from noon to 5:30 p.m., but check these hours as they are subject to change.* A relatively new and quirky trend has sprung up in Copenhagen for shoppers who are nostalgic for Danish modern furniture. At Klassic, each item carries two price tags, the current one and the price of the piece if new. in most cases the savings are at least 50 percent. Other shops offering secondhand Danish modern are Dansk Mobelkunst, Permanent Design (not to be confused with the old Den Permanent) and Design Kompagniet.

PAUSTIAN FURNITURE HOUSE

Located at the harbor, at *Kalkbraenderilobskaj 2*, Paustian House has long been a respected name in contemporary furniture design. Its new headquarters offer museum-like displays of new designs. ☎ *31 18 45 11* for information on hours.

EIDERDOWN QUILTS

Messen, *on Kobmagergade, near the Round Tower,* has a good selection. Several department stores sell quilts, and at Kastrup Airport you can pick up eiderdown.

DEPARTMENT STORES

Magasin du Nord—You cannot miss this massive, gray stone building that dominates the *Kongens Nytorv.* This is the largest department store in Denmark, and you will find just about everything you need here. On Saturday mornings, it is so crowded with shoppers trying to complete their business before the 2:00 p.m. closing, you will hardly be able to move through the aisles. Try to come here on another day. In the basement is a small service center with a shoe repair and benches for resting weary bones. **Illums,** *on Stroget,* is the other major department store. **Scala** is a brand new, unique complex of shops, theaters and restaurants *on Axeltorv, in the thick of the Radhus and Tivoli area.* One attraction here is the assemblage of Charlie Chaplin's hat, walking stick and shoes, which the developers of Scala bought at auction for one million krone.

SHOPPING AT KASTRUP AIRPORT

You will not even mind waiting for your plane when you depart from Copenhagen, as the shopping in the duty-free section is so much fun. A little bit of everything is here, from smoked salmon, packaged to survive a long flight home, to Royal Porcelain and Georg Jensen. The prices here are not really any better than those in Copenhagen if you have been careful to retrieve all your tax-free benefits. But it is just fun to browse and pick up last-minute items. *The airport shops are open from 7:00 a.m. to 10:00 p.m. every day.*

WHERE TO STAY

VERY EXPENSIVE

The Hotel D'Angleterre   +★★★★★

Kongens Nytorv 34. If you can afford it, and maybe even if you can't, you should stay here. Scrimp a little someplace else and treat yourself to this grand old hotel in the best European and Danish traditions. Since 1775, the D'Angleterre has sat like a wedding cake, in white, frothy splendor on the Kongens Nytorv, and the city has grown up around it. It is two steps from the Stroget and around the corner from Ny Adelgade with its upscale galleries and restaurants. It is also a three-minute walk from Nyhavn, so the location could not be better. The D'Angleterre is a large hotel, but it offers the personal service and intimacy of a small one. The interiors here have all been renovated within the last five years; the old dark rooms and corridors have been redone in soft, light colors and opulent fabrics. They retain an old-world elegance, but offer every modern comfort including beautiful, up-to-date bathrooms; big, fluffy towels and bathrobes; hairdryers, minibar and TV. At night, guests will find their beds turned down and fresh towels along with a bottle of Perrier water by the bed. This is one of the few hotels in Scandinavia that provide "turn-down" service in the evenings. The lobby is more like a living room in a Danish manor house and is a very pleasant place to have tea in the afternoon. The English-style bar with its leather chairs and wood-panelled walls is a cozy retreat. Le Restaurant, the gourmet dining room that used to be the Reine Pedauque, is an elegant and quiet retreat with excellent food. Be sure to avail yourself of the concierge service. Prices at the D'Angleterre are high and generally do not include breakfast. The best rooms are on the inside, away from the traffic. Rooms numbered 33 and 35 on all floors should be quiet. It is best to avoid the first-floor rooms, which can be noisy. The hotel is under new ownership and some changes are planned, including an exercise room and swimming pool.

The SAS Royal   ★★★★

1 Hammerichsgade. A modern hotel, originally designed by Arne Jacobsen. It has been redone several times and the feeling here is cold and somewhat commercial, but the rooms are luxurious, and the location is handy to the Tivoli side of town, just across from that park and near the railway station. This is the choice of many businessmen and groups. For the same price, the D'Angleterre offers more charm. But the Royal is an SAS hotel, which means it comes with all the conveniences that affiliation offers travelers. It is also air-conditioned, not too important in Copenhagen, except that it is often nice not to have to open a window onto the noisy street, especially in this area. TV/VCR, minibar, health club, restaurant and cafe.

The Plaza   ★★★★

4 Bernstorffsgade. Old-world charm, here, with comfortable rooms and the well-known and beautiful Library Bar. Conveniently located near Tivoli and the Central Station. Rooms are large, and most have been redecorated recently.

71 Nyhavn   ★★★★

71 Nyhavn. Though the rooms here tend to be small, this is a very appealing spot. It has just 82 rooms, so the feeling is intimate. Its location is excellent, as its name suggests. It is right on Nyhavn, and on the water, opposite the Malmo hydrofoil station. The hotel occupies a 19th-century warehouse which has, of course, been totally renovated. Exposed beams, contemporary furniture of wood, leather and warmly colored fabrics make this an attractive and welcoming spot. 71 Nyhavn is one of the Romantik Hotels, the designation given only to hotels with an extra degree of charm and individuality. All rooms have TV and minibar.

The SAS Scandinavia

70 Amager Blvd. Tall and sleek, and with 543 rooms, much larger than its sister, the SAS Royal, this is a busy place, frequented mainly by groups and business travelers. It is a stop on the SAS airport shuttle route, so it is convenient if you do not need to be right in the middle of town. Indoor pool, jogging track and fitness center. The Casino Copenhagen in the hotel offers roulette, baccarat and slot machines.

The Sheraton

6 Vestersogade. It's certainly more than adequate as far as comfort is concerned, but why not get a little charm for your money? Though the Sheraton is in a pretty setting, it is not quite as convenient to the center of activity as the hotels listed above. However, it is a comfortable, efficient place.

EXPENSIVE

The Hotel Phoenix

This brand-new hotel promises to be one of Copenhagen's premier hostelries. Occupying a renovated 17th-century building, it has 211 rococo-style rooms, three restaurants, a swimming pool and sauna. It is located near the Amalienborg Palace.

The Hotel Opera

15 Tordenskjoldsgade. A pleasant, small hotel with old-world charm and a very pretty bar and restaurant. The rooms are tiny, but attractive. It is a bit overpriced for the comforts it provides, but it is long on friendliness and appeal. Well located, not far from the Royal Theater and Nyhavn.

The Kong Frederik

25 Vester Volgade. Owned by Remmen Hotels which also owns the D'Angleterre. This one is a bit less expensive, but comfortable nonetheless. Well located and welcoming, with several appealing restaurants.

The Astoria

4 Banegaardspladsen. This hotel serves the best breakfast in town in one of the most attractive art deco dining rooms around. The rooms are adequate, if a little dark, and the bathrooms small, but the major problem here is the noise. The hotel bills itself as being located near the Central Railway Station, but it is actually almost on top of part of the station—the noisy part. Some guests do not appear to be bothered by this and enjoy the hotel for the friendliness of the staff and the really extraordinary art deco renovation of the public rooms.

MODERATE

The Admiral

24 Toldbodsgade. One of the best buys in Copenhagen. This hotel, in a restored 18th-century warehouse right on the water, is so popular you must book months in advance. The rooms vary in size and shape, and some might be a bit awkward or small because an effort was made to retain the feeling of the old building with exposed beams and thick walls and all the quirky angles. Some might find the hotel a bit too busy, as many groups come here. But for those who like a lively place, this is the spot. Its location, right on the harbor, is convenient and fun. The Pinafore restaurant is excellent, and the Nautilus Bar is always crowded.

Sophie Amalie

*21 Skt. Annae Plads.*Owned by Remmen Hotels, along with the D'Angleterre and the Kong Frederik, this hotel is located next door to the Admiral and is a fine choice if you cannot get into the Admiral, a not unusual occurrence. The Sophie Amalie is small, with airy, modern rooms and an excellent location. Some might prefer this to the Admiral, since it is much quieter.

Hotel Ascot

Studiestraede 61. Designed and constructed in 1901 by the architect Martin Nyrop as a bath house for the bourgeoisie of Copenhagen, the building has been transformed into a thoroughly modern, small hotel with clean, comfortable rooms.

Hotel Neptun

18 Skt. Annae Plads. Just 54 rooms in this very pleasant, family hotel with an inner courtyard where guests can enjoy a drink in good weather. The rooms are modern and bright, all with TV and minibar. The rooms on the courtyard can be noisy if there is a crowd on a summer evening, but the hotel takes no groups, so it is generally a quiet place. There are also small apartments that can be rented by the day or week. These sleep three and have rather ingenious cooking facilities in the living room. The hotel's restaurant Agnete is most attractive, with murals depicting the legend of Agnete and the Man from the Sea.

Hotel City

24 Peder Skramsgade. Although it falls into the moderately priced category, with rooms running just under $125 a night at last check, it still seems a little overpriced, considering the small size and plainness of the rooms. The bathrooms are tiny and the breakfast room was downright dreary at last visit. But this is a friendly place with a most helpful manager/concierge, and it is well located in the area behind Kongens Nytorv and on the way to the water. TV, hairdryers. No minibar, but soft drinks available from reception.

The Savoy Hotel ★★

34 Vesterbrogade. A comfortable hotel in a quiet courtyard in the area of the central station. The rooms are dowdy but clean and cozy, and the hotel is not without charm. Centrally located near Central Station, just on the fringe of the more unsavory area around the station.

THE HOTELS OF HOTELGADEN

Hotelgaden is the name given to Helgolandsgade, the street behind the Central Railway Station, which contains several pleasant, moderately priced hotels. There has been a serious effort on the part of the city and the tourist industry to revitalize this area, as it had become a problem in recent years. After the gentrification of Nyhavn, the rougher crowds, who were accustomed to hanging out in that area, moved to this part of town. Travelers should be aware that they may not be quite at ease here. But all that having been established, these hotels are comfortable and offer good value, friendly atmosphere and helpful staff. The hotels are on the fringe of the undesirable area—not actually in it—and you will be focusing on the attractions in the other direction, toward Vesterbrogade and H.C. Andersen Blvd. Additional note: These hotels were originally mission hotels and retain some of the vestiges of those days. None of the four hotels allows you to bring a guest to your room.

The Absalon Hotel ★

The biggest of the four hotels, this is the only one with a restaurant, open from May 1 to September. The rooms are comfortable and modern, and most have private baths, TV and hairdryers.

The Triton ★★★

This is the most modern of the group, with pleasantly decorated rooms in light woods and bright colors. All have private baths, TV/VCR and some refrigerators (not minibars) and hairdryers. Most rooms have wonderfully modern, big bathrooms.

The Hebron Hotel

This hotel has retained its older style and is a bit drearier than the above two, but the rooms are in the process of being redecorated in brighter colors. *Inexpensive.*

The Selandia

A good bet for young people or families, as some rooms are fitted out with four beds in dormitory-style. Some rooms do not have private baths. *Inexpensive.*

The Mayfair

Though on the same street, The Mayfair is not actually part of the above group, which shares a management and booking office. It is in the process of building itself into a first-class hotel and is well on the way. All the rooms have been newly renovated most attractively. The bathrooms are modern, though some are small. TV, minibar, hairdryers. Good value here.

AIRPORT HOTEL

Sara Hotel Dan ★★★

This hotel, at Kastrup Airport, has all the comforts, but it is a noisy, chaotic place, as an airport hotel can be. It is convenient, but the service is slipshod and the staff frequently uncooperative and unfriendly, an unusual occurrence in this friendliest of nations. The shuttle to the airport runs only until 9:30 a.m. and after 5:00 p.m. At other times, you will have to call a cab, which is sometimes difficult. Unfortunately, it is about the only choice if you must stay at the airport. (For the price, I would recommend staying at the SAS Scandinavian and picking up the airport shuttle bus which stops there. The Scandinavian is a busy place too, but a little better organized.

You will just have to leave some extra time the morning of your flight.)

Expensive.

WHERE TO EAT

Copenhagen offers a cornucopia of wonderful restaurants, serving excellent food in attractive surroundings. It is not inexpensive to eat in this city, but the quality of the food, service and ambience make a meal in Copenhagen kroner well spent.

RESTAURANTS IN THE AREA OF NYHAVN AND KONGENS NYTORV

As you walk along Nyhavn, you can choose for yourself which restaurant appeals to you. There are many, and most are good and not too expensive. Among the choices are:

Restaurant Els, Store Strandstaede

This intimate restaurant, with its wonderful murals depicting the seasons and the muses of dance and music, has a warm, informal elegance, and is one of the most pleasant dining spots in town, with friendly, unpretentious service and excellent food. The restaurant has been on this spot since 1853, first as a coffeehouse and gathering place for actors from the Royal Theater around the corner. The ubiquitous H.C. Andersen made his way here frequently, and wrote a poem on the occasion of the opening. There is an unpublished cover charge of about 55Dkr., perhaps to cover, among other things, the Perrier water served at every table. The set-price fish menu runs about 270Dkr. without wine.

Kommandanten

Ny Adelgade 7, Across from the D'Angleterre. This is possibly the loveliest and best restaurant in Copenhagen. There are several small rooms, each with no more than five or six tables, set as if in a Danish home with silver candelabra and Royal Copenhagen dinnerware. The furniture was designed by Tage Andersen, whose shop is just across the street. If you are seated in one of the upstairs rooms, my favorites, you can get a glimpse of the chefs at work on their exquisite presentations. The three-course set menu with one glass of wine will be about 325Dkr.

Mary Rose

Nyhavn. A freshly and simply decorated restaurant. Quiet, pleasant service and food. A two-course dinner with a glass of wine will run about 225Dkr.

Leonore Christine

Nyhavn 9. Another gracious, quiet dining spot, slightly more formal and somewhat more expensive than Mary Rose. It is quite popular with Danes, as well as tourists, and is usually crowded. Try the grilled smoked salmon.

Gilleleje

Nyhavn 10. This cluttered, nautically flavored restaurant is a pleasant hodgepodge of style and cuisine. The menu includes a rice table, fish entrees, game and beef. A few too many Americans for those who are looking to meet the Danes instead of their own neighbors, but there are enough

Danish customers to make you feel this is not just for tourists. A meal with entree, dessert and a glass of wine will run about 250Dkr.

Skipperkroen

Nyhavn. I have not tried this one, but it is very lively and always crowded. Owned by the brothers who also have the Streckers restaurants, which are a small chain of informal, snack-type places.

Bronnum

Kongens Nytorv (By the Royal Theater). This is a good place for after-theater and late dining, since food is served until 3:00 a.m. and the popular bar remains open until 5:00 a.m. A friendly bartender handles late night overindulgers with ease and diplomacy. The back room is more suited for quiet dining. Light snacks to full dinners. Reasonable. This is one of the few restaurants open on Sunday.

In Lille Kongensdade, a street running west off Kongens Nytorv, you will find two restaurants popular with Copenhagen residents:

Parnas

Lille Kongensgade 16. A busy, lively spot that serves late. Hearty fare at moderate to somewhat higher prices. This is a cozy, typically old Copenhagen hangout. Live music.

Skindbuksen

Lille Kongensgade 4. Here is another lively place with a jolly crowd and good, robust food. It gets crowded, so come early.

IN THE NEIGHBORHOOD OF AMALIENBORG PALACE

Ida Davidsen

70 Kongensgade, the street which runs off Kongens Nytorv behind the Marble Church. This landmark restaurant was called Oscar Davidsen until Oscar's daughter Ida took over. Danes and tourists alike flock to this extraordinary spot, where Ms. Davidsen presides over a succulent display of culinary skill. The smorrebrod are exquisite and different from any you will find elsewhere. There are other tempters besides. The best part is that guests come up to the display case to choose their own sin. More often than not, Ms. Davidsen will guide you through the repertoire, describing each selection in detail. The restaurant is open only for lunch, and is closed on Saturdays and Sundays. Lunch, if you choose more than one item—and how can you avoid it—will cost about 175Dkr.

Svend Larsen's

Down the street from Ida Davidsen. Here you can carry out smorrebrod, so it is a good place to know about if you are planning to take a picnic to Lygnby. (See section on "Trips Out of Copenhagen.")

Sankt Annae

Sankt Annae Plads 12. This tiny basement cafe serves lunch only. Mainly smorrebrod with some hot dishes. Reasonable and popular. Closed Sunday and Monday.

ON AND OFF STROGET

Alsace
Pistolstraede 11. Serves primarily French cuisine, in a beautiful old court-yard. Though I have not eaten here, it is highly recommended by Copen-hagen natives, and since it has been busy every time I passed by, it seems safe to say that the food is good. Prices are fairly reasonable by Copenhagen standards.

Kransekagehuset *in Ny Ostergade,* and **Kransekagehusets Konditori,** *Pistol-straede,* are good places for quick, sweet bites of Danish confections.

Pasta Basta
Valkendorfsgade 22. Farther down the Stroget and around the corner from the Church of the Holy Spirit, this is one of the best buys in town. For about 59Dkr., diners can help themselves from the cold pasta table. Or you can order from the menu at equally reasonable prices. Order wine by the glass or bottle, or pour your own from the open, marked bottles on your table and pay only for what you drink. This is a popular place with the Dan-ish people on a Sunday afternoon. *Open every day from 11:00 a.m. to 5:00 a.m.*

J. Christian Andersen
32 Kobmagergade. Take-out sandwiches and cheese.

Peder Oxe
Grabrodretorv 2. An informal, attractive restaurant in one of the old build-ings on this lovely square. The salad bar is the main attraction, along with good beef and fish offerings. A two-course meal with a glass of wine will be about 250Dkr., but you can eat less expensively here if you are careful.

Bof and Ost
Next door to Peder Oxe. This restaurant is a little less expensive than its neighbor, though you can dine well here on a variety of interesting menu items.

Cafe Nikolai
Nikolai Church. The place for lunch if you are counting your krone. The cafe serves simple sandwiches, soups and desserts as well as hot meals. *Open Monday–Friday from noon to 6:00 p.m.*

GAMLE STRAND AND VED STRANDEN

If you wind southeast from the Nikolai Church, you will come to the canal where the old fish market used to be. There are three good spots here:

Gamle Strand 46
Gamle Strand 46. One of the old cellar restaurants of Copenhagen, this is a place where Danes love to lunch. Choose from a selection of smorrebrod, hot dishes and herring. The latter should be accompanied by aquavit fol-lowed by beer. Come on, you can do it. *Lunch only.*

Krog's Fiskerestaurant
Gamle Strand 38. The granddaddy of Danish fish restaurants, Krog's has

enjoyed a deservedly fine reputation for years. In an 18th-century building, with paintings by the Danish folk artist Valdemar Andersen on the walls, the service and food of this excellent, unpretentious restaurant can always be counted on. For that reason, you will find plenty of tourists here. Expensive. *Open 11:00 a.m.-11:00 p.m.*

Fiskehuset

Next door to Krog's. Another Copenhagen landmark, a little more casual than Krog's and very good as well.

St. Gertrud's Kloster

32 Hauser Plads. This is probably the best-known restaurant in Copenhagen, and one of the most expensive. It is an experience to eat here. The food is certainly more than adequate, and the decor authentic, but you can eat better for less elsewhere in the city. Because the dining rooms are in the catacombs of an ancient building, electrical wiring, which would have required drilling into the fragile, old, brick walls, was prohibited. Consequently, 1200 candles illuminate the brick-walled restaurant. Somehow, however, in spite of the restriction against wiring through the walls, an engineer did manage to pipe in Muzak. If you tend towards claustrophobia, this is probably not the place for you, though the underground labyrinth of small, candlelit rooms is most attractive. Many people love this restaurant and celebrate special occasions here. I find it somewhat gimmicky and the hasty but most cordial service, smacking just a bit of the assembly-line approach. Guests are almost forced to order a drink before dinner, as when they arrive for their reservation (and you must have one), they are first ushered into the library bar, a very attractive place, where they place their order and wait for their table.

HOTEL DINING

Pinafore

In the Admiral. A lively, most attractive restaurant, rustic in style, with excellent food at reasonable prices. A cold buffet is one of the main attractions, along with the steaks, which are cooked on an open grill.

Queen's Garden

In the Kong Frederik Hotel. Outdoor dining in good weather, with an indoor English-style pub and grill. Good food and a little less expensive than some of the other hotel dining spots.

LUNCH RESTAURANTS

Lunch can often be a problem in a foreign city. You don't want a lavish meal—although a good budget tactic is to eat your main meal at lunch—and it's hard to find good restaurants with light fare. Copenhagen offers the visitor several choices. Because of the signature Danish smorrebord or open-face sandwich, you will find many small cafes and shops serving those beautiful delicacies. Among the most well-known is Ida Davidsen, mentioned above in the Amalienborg area. Also recommended by those who are in the know are Hos Gitte Kid at *4 Fortunstraede* and Kanal Cafeen *at 18 Frederiksholms Kanal.* Prices for sandwiches range from about $5 to $11.

NIGHTLIFE

Tordenskjold Discoteque, *near the Royal Theater, is open from 10:00 p.m. to 5:00 a.m.* May require membership, so call ahead. ☎ *33 12 03 04.*

Annabel's, *Lille Kongensgade 16 (off Kongens Nytorv) is open from 10:00 p.m. to 5:00 a.m.*

Daddy's Dance Hall *is open until 8:00 a.m. in July and August, rest of the year until 4:00 a.m., and offers different types of music on different nights.* It is located in the cellar of the Palads Cinema.

De Tre Musketerer, *near the Nikolai Cathedral, has jazz every night from 10:00 p.m. to 2:00 a.m. Closed Sunday.*

On the Rocks *in Pilestraede is a cafe and discotheque open until 5:00 a.m. Food is served until 3:00 a.m. Closed Sunday.*

The Nautilus Bar *in the Admiral Hotel has dancing and stays open till 2:00 a.m.*

Hvids Winstue is a wine bar *near the Royal Theater in Lille Kongensgade.*

Cafe Victor, *in Ny Ostergade,* is open late for food and drink.

The Duke, a wine bar *in Gothersgade, is open 4:00 p.m.–5:00 a.m.*

Den Rode Pimpernel (The Scarlet Pimpernel), a dance restaurant *on H.C. Andersen Boulevard,* is popular with the middle-aged clientele.

Cafe Sommersko, *in Kronprinsensgade near Stroget,* serves meals at moderate prices *until 10:00 p.m.* and stays crowded late with young people, especially students from the nearby University.

The Palace Theater, newly spruced up, has 14 movie theaters.

Scala, *the new shopping center next to the Palace,* also has several cinemas and restaurants as well as shops. Here you will find the city's newest disco,**Axel Dansebar.** *Open Thursday from 10:00 p.m. to 4:00 a.m.; Friday, Saturday and Sunday, 10:00 p.m. to 5:00 a.m. Admission is 40Dkr.*

There is a casino in the **SAS Scandinavia**.

QUICK TRIPS OUT OF TOWN

DRAGOR

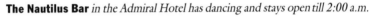

Take Bus 30 or 33. Ask the bus driver where to get off. The first thing you have to learn is to pronounce the name of this town so you can ask your way. It is pronounced, like everything else in Denmark, totally differently from the way it looks. So, with mouth barely open and tongue locked in place, simply say "druh-yr," choke a bit, and you might make yourself understood. This charming old seaside town just three kilometers from Kastrup Airport is an easy bus ride from Radhuspladsen. The town was originally settled by the Dutch with the idea of developing a herring industry here. Now it is a desirable residential area with modern houses as well as the 18th-century cottages. The thatched roofs have proven to be a problem for Dragor, and there have been frequent fires.

Dragor Museum

The museum houses an exhibit showing how the Dutch, who were the principal residents here for centuries, lived. *Open May–September, Tuesday–Friday from 2:00 p.m. to 5:00 p.m.; weekends and holidays from noon to 6:00 p.m.*

Take a walk: In addition to visiting the museum, you should simply walk the streets and look at the half-timbered, thatched or tile roofed cottages. Peek over walls and behind hedgerows to see the exquisitely kept gardens. Wind through the streets, eventually heading toward the water, and then take the small well-trodden path that runs between hedgerows on one side and the beach grass on the other. You will not see throngs of tourists, but instead, residents of Dragor who come to walk along the water and to stop in at the **Strandhotel** or **Dragor Kro** for a drink. **The Dragor Kro**, established in 1721 at *23 Kongevejen* just up from the harbor, is a charmer, with deep rose and yellow walls and a beautiful flower-filled courtyard where food is served in summer. There is a very cozy bar as well. Danish meals at reasonable prices, a set menu from 109Dkr. to 139Dkr. The **Strandhotel**, located by the water, is a restaurant, not a hotel. Sit on the terrace and watch the action in the lively marina.

LYGNBY AND KLAMPENBORG

A 20-minute train ride north of Copenhagen will bring you to these two recreational areas with the Open Air Museum, a shopping complex and acres of park and lakes for hiking and boating. The S train from Copenhagen stops at Klampenborg, site of **Jaegersborg Deer Park** and **Bakken Amusement Park**, and at Lyngby station. The tourist information office at Lyngby Torv 5 will give you information on boat service and tourist attractions. The river **Molleaaen** links the three lakes of Lyngby and runs past several old mills. Visitors can rent canoes and rowboats along the river, or can take a ferry from Lake Lyngby into either of the other two lakes. The boat service on the lakes runs in summer only, every day but Mondays. Check with the tourist information office in Copenhagen for exact opening and closing dates. Also check on the prices. At last count, the rates for the ferry were rather high.

The Frilandsmuseet *(Open Air Museum)*

With about 100 reconstructed old houses from various regions of Denmark, this is one of the main attractions of Lygnby. If you stay on the S train, it will let you off at Sorgenfri nearby. Or take Bus 84 from Lyngby. Another possibility, and this is my choice, is to take the small **Jaegersborg** train from the Lyngby station. *The museum is open April 15–September every day from 10:00 a.m. to 5:00 p.m. and October 1–14 every day from 10:00 a.m. to 3:00 p.m. The rest of the year, it is open Sunday and all public holidays, except December 24 and 25, from 10:00 a.m. to 3:00 p.m.*

Bakken

The world's oldest amusement park is *situated in the Deer Park*, just a 10-minute walk from Klampenborg station. Young children may even prefer Bakken to Tivoli because there are more rides for them and it is a more manageable size. It is very pretty, set among the trees of the Deer Park in a more rural landscape than the sophisticated Tivoli. The restaurants here are small and unpretentious. There is no admission fee. *Open March 30 every day from noon to midnight. Many of the rides do not open until 2:00 p.m., however.*

Lyngby Church
A medieval structure with 500-year-old frescoes.

Damhuset
Shoppers will find a fine handicraft shop in this 17th century building. It is *located at the spot where Molleaen crosses Lyngby Hovedgade at the water mill.*

Sorgenfri Palace
Located just outside Lyngby, opens its gardens to the public.

Jaegersborg Deer Park
The former royal hunting grounds stretch between Klampenborg and Lyngby. Take the S train from Copenhagen and get off at Klampenborg.

Ordrupgaard Museum
Located near the Deer Park. You can take bus 160 from Lyngby for the most efficient route. See the "Museum" section of Copenhagen for details.

WHERE TO EAT

You might want to pack a lunch, since this is the ideal spot for a picnic. This is your chance to buy some of those delectable smorrebrod and pastries that seem to call out from Copenhagen bakeries and to enjoy them in a setting worthy of their quality. If you prefer to eat in a restaurant, you will find several in the area. The restaurant **Lottenborg**, *near Sorgenfri Palace,* is located in a 17th-century building. There is a bistro that is open only in summer and more formal service all year round. Also, the **Regatta Pavillonen**, *situated right on Lake Bagsvaerd,* serves a cold buffet. *Closed on Mondays.* I have not tried either of these restaurants, but both are attractive, the latter decorated by Bjorn Winblads. As with most restaurants in and around Copenhagen, a full meal will be fairly expensive.

A QUICK TRIP TO SWEDEN

For a pleasant family outing on a pretty day, take the ferry to a little Swedish island called Hven, just a 45-minute ride from Copenhagen. There you can rent bicycles and, in about one hour, ride all around the island. There is also a beach at the marina where the boat arrives. Tourists can purchase tickets, which include bike rental and a picnic lunch. The concierge at your hotel in Copenhagen will have information on this excursion or you can write ahead to *Flyvebadene, Havnegade 49, Postbox 1509, 1020 Copenhagen.*

ROSKILDE

Viking Ship Museum houses five Viking ships raised off Roskilde.

Roskilde Tourist Office: *Located by the cathedral,* ☎ *02 35 27 00. Open daily in summer from 9:00 a.m. to 6:00 p.m. All other months open Monday–Thursday, 9:00 a.m.–5:00 p.m.; Friday, 9:00 a.m.–4:00 p.m.; and Saturday, 10:00 a.m.–1:00 p.m.*

GETTING THERE

A train from Copenhagen will get you to Roskilde in about 35 minutes. Be sure to take the local train, not the Inter-City.

A pleasant day trip from Copenhagen, Roskilde has much to recommend it. Travelers watching their budgets could consider staying here instead of in Copenhagen, as the hotels are less expensive. Roskilde is one of Denmark's oldest towns and was an important commercial center as well as a stopping point for the traveling kings and queens of Denmark. Since its cathedral has always been the burial place for Danish royalty, the town has enjoyed prominence throughout the centuries. Now it is a pleasant place with parks, a pedestrian shopping mall and a market on Wednesdays and Saturday. You can walk from the center of town to the Roskilde fjord through attractive parks and gardens.

WHAT TO SEE AND DO

Roskilde Cathedral

This is the burial place of the kings and queens of Denmark and serves as an excellent textbook on the history of the country. Built by Bishop Absalon, this cathedral is on the site of two earlier ones. The first, a wooden structure, was built by Harald Blue-tooth, who Christianized Denmark. The second was built of limestone, and this last one was constructed of brick, a material new to Denmark at the time. Workers had to be imported from Italy to make the bricks, and this need, along with the lack of sufficient kilns, slowed construction drastically. The early builders worked out the plan as they went along, and near the door you can see one row of bricks at eye level that was obviously inserted to account for an error in measurement. The church is over 800 years old and, since it was more than 100 years in construction, Bishop Absalon did not live to see his dream accomplished.

The chapel of Christian I was built in 1460, that of Christian IV 1614–1642, the chapel of Frederik V in 1774, and the newest, the Gludcksobrgian Chapel, from 1917–1924. The current royal family will be buried in a small, walled, burial ground open to the sky just outside the cathedral. The cathedral was begun when Denmark was a Catholic country, but during the Reformation much of the decorative painting was whitewashed and then later uncovered. Of special interest are the royal chapels where the kings and queens are buried. The first on your right, as you face the altar, shelters the tombs of the early kings, from Christian I. The royal column in the middle of the chapel bears prominent red lines marking the heights of Danish and visiting royalty who have come to Roskilde. You can see the height of the present queen, Margrethe, who is quite tall, and who insisted on being measured barefoot in order to have an accurate record. The highest line, marked with a red "P," is Peter the Great of Russia.

The next chapel, that of Frederik V, is a splendidly austere, neoclassical design. From that chapel, look through the side aisle toward the apse to see the earliest part of the church, begun around 1175. Queen Margrethe I lies in a black marble sarcophagus behind the altarpiece, which was given to the cathedral by King Christian IV. On the north side of the cathedral is King Christian IV's chapel with its elaborate iron gate. The statue of Christian IV is the work of Bertel Thorvaldsen. As you move from chapel to chapel, you will be struck by the differences in architecture and design, reflecting the changing styles of the times. Also, look at the clock with a 16th-century mechanism that causes St. George's horse to attack the dragon.

Walk outside the church toward the yellow building, called the Palace, which is not really a palace but the place where the kings and queens rested when they came from Copenhagen for a funeral. Look up and you will see an arch of gray limestone between the yellow brick walls of the palace and the red brick of the cathedral. That is a remnant of the earlier cathedral, and it was through the passageway above this arch that the French soldiers of Napoleon, who had come to aid Denmark in its fight against the Swedes, escaped when word of Napoleon's defeat arrived.

The Viking Museum

A pleasant walk from the cathedral on a fair day, this attractive concrete and glass building houses the five Viking ships that were raised in the waters off Roskilde. There are two merchant ships, two warships and a fishing boat. A film, shown in several languages including English, describes the excavation methods. The cafeteria serves light food, reasonably priced, and it is a fine place to sit and look over the harbor. A copy of a Viking ship, seaworthy enough to take occasional short voyages, floats serenely in view. *Open April–October daily from 9:00 a.m. to 5:00 p.m.; remainder of year, 10:00 a.m. to 4:00 p.m.*

The Roskilde Museum

Contains costumes and toys in addition to anthropological finds. There is also an old grocer's shop where visitors can make purchases of items available in the 19th century. *The museum is open June–August daily from 11:00 a.m. to 5:00 p.m.; remainder of year, Monday–Saturday, 2:00 p.m. to 4:00 p.m.*

The M/S *Sagafjord*

An old wooden steamer sails out from Roskilde around the lake every day at noon, 2:30 and 7:00 p.m. in summer. On the noon sailings, lunch is served. The hours are different in winter. For a Sunday excursion, consider coming to Roskilde in the morning to look at the cathedral, then boarding the lake steamer for a lunchtime sail, and ending with a visit to the Viking Ship Museum. Check on the opening hours for all the above, as they are subject to change, and the church might be closed for a wedding or funeral.

Roskilde Festival

From June 29 through July 2, this major pop/rock festival has featured the top names in music. The 1995 festival promises to be a gala since it is the celebration of the festival's 25th anniversary. More than 75,000 fans are expected, so plan your visit to Roskilde according to your priorities.If the concerts are the focus of your interest, this is the time to be in Roskilde. On the other hand, there are probably better dates for seeing the town and visiting its museums.

Ledreborg

*Just a few kilometers from Roskilde at Lejre*you will find the country estate of Ledreborg, built in the 18th century for Count Johan Ludvig Hostein, a councillor of Christian IV and at one time prime minister. It is a fine example of the Danish baroque style and boasts a vast collection of Dutch and Danish paintings, as well as an impressive array of tapestries, porcelain and silver. *Open every day from June through August 11:00 a.m. to 4:30 p.m.; the rest of the year Sunday only.*

The Historical-Archeological Research Center

An experiment in living at a reconstructed Iron-Age village. Visitors can spend time living the life of the Iron Age, 2000 years ago, sailing in a dugout canoe, baking bread over an open fire, cutting firewood with an Iron-Age axe or grinding grain on a primitive grinder. But if you are not inclined toward taking on the hardships of the Iron Age, you can just come to look and learn. There are workshops, slide shows, nature walks and 17th-century farmhouses, in addition to the Iron-Age village. *Open May–September*

daily from 10:00 a.m. to 5:00 p.m. From Copenhagen, take the Holbaek/ Kalundborg train to Lejre Station, where in season an HT bus runs from Lejre station, departing every hour during the open hours of the center. Outside the entrance to the center is a restaurant/cafeteria. **Schweizerhuset** is a new country inn, located not far from the center and the Iron-Age village. It serves à la carte lunch and dinner every day from 11:30 a.m. to 10:00 p.m.

Selso Castle

At Skibby. The castle was built in the 16th century but renovated in the baroque style 200 years later. It is a rather simple castle, as castles go, but the caring renovations begun in 1972 by two journalists, Grete and Bernhard Linder, have given to the manor house an aura of past life, richly lived.Of special interest is the baroque banqueting hall.

WHERE TO STAY

The Scandic Roskilde is so new that I have not yet seen it, but it promises to be comfortable and modern. The **Prinsen** is the other option, an old standby right in the center of town. The Roskilde Tourist Office has a list of accommodations in private homes, most with private bath, at exceptionally reasonable rates. The **Horgarden Youth Hostel** is one of Denmark's best.

Sorup Herregaard

Outside Roskilde, this structure was converted into a hotel in 1986, but it still retains the ambience of a country house, with all the activities of a working farm. There are 32 rooms and one suite, all well decorated and very comfortable. Tennis, a pool and sauna are on the grounds, and there is golf nearby. The restaurant offers a range of selections, all prepared from locally grown produce, game and meat.

The Hotel Sofryd

At Jyllinge, 12 kilometers from Roskilde, is a modern hotel overlooking the Roskilde Fjord. The simply decorated restaurant commands a lovely view of the fjord, and the rooms are comfortable and modern, all with private bath.

NORTH ZEALAND

Frederiksborg Castle houses the Museum of Danish National History.

A drive north from Copenhagen along the "Danish Riviera" is a pleasant day trip. You can combine a visit to Helsingor with Frederiksborg Castle and Fredensborg Palace; in fact, that is what the "Castle Tour of North Zealand" does, but it is really more fun to do it on your own and to allow time for wandering in Hillerod or Helsingor and for lunch at the **Store Kro** beside Fredensborg Palace. On your way back, you might want to stop at the **Sollerod Kro**, a deservedly popular restaurant that is a member of the prestigious Relais & Chateaux organization. Dinner will be expensive but excellent, and served in picturesque surroundings.

HUMLEBAEK

The Louisiana Museum of Modern Art

The Louisiana Museum is remarkable not only for its fine collection of post-World War II painting and sculpture, but also for the dynamics of the art, the landscape and the architecture. These three elements work together to make a visit to the museum, on the shore of Humlebaek Lake, a "happening." Walk through the glass-windowed galleries where the scene outside the windows complements the paintings on the walls. Sculpture of Alexander Calder, Henry Moore, Arp and Dubuffet, among others, is displayed in the park, as well as inside. The Giacometti collection is extensive, and now a new east wing, housing primarily graphic arts, as well as special exhibitions, has been completed. Concerts, films and theater performances occur frequently. The museum is so named because the gentleman who built the main house on the property in the 1860s had three wives all named Louisa. *Open all year round, daily from 10:00 a.m. to 5:00 p.m.*

Your Copenhagen card is good here. Take the train from Copenhagen to Humlebaek and or Bus No. 188 from Klampenborg. There is a cafeteria with indoor and outdoor service, and a bookstore with a wide selection of books and posters.Special Exhibits in 1995 include a retrospective of the paintings and graphic works of the renowned Danish artist Asger Jorn. The exhibit runs from March 3 through Sept. 7.

HILLEROD

Take the S train from Copenhagen; bus 701 or 703. Hillerod is the site of Frederiksborg Castle, and it is also a pleasant town to stroll through, so tourists should try to allow enough time to explore a bit beyond the castle. There is a pedestrian street, and behind many of the modern shops on the main street are old houses.

Frederiksborg Castle

The castle has always been an important place for the Danish people, and its destruction by fire in the 19th century was a tragedy for Denmark. Now the castle is the Museum of Danish National History, one of Denmark's most important museums. The castle is built on three islands in the castle lake. Enter through the Town Gate on the southern island, and walk through Straedet to the castle. The first buildings you pass are all that remain of Frederik II's castle. The two towers at the end of this section were built in 1562. The bridge goes to the middle island where the castle of Christian IV, built in the first 20 years of the 17th century as a hunting castle, is situated. The large Barbicap Tower heralds the entrance to the King's Castle. The tower was the last structure Christian IV built at the castle, and was completed in 1623. Standing in the courtyard, at the Neptun fountain, you look ahead to the main castle with its central King's Wing. The Neptun fountain is not the original one designed with its 16 bronze figures by Christian IV. This newer one was completed in 1886. As you cross to the castle yard, notice the portal inscribed with the date 1609. Enter the castle through the King's Wing, where the museum is located.

Much of the interior of the castle was destroyed in the fire in 1859, but restoration, with the help of a donation from J. C. Jacobsen of the Carlsberg Breweries, proceeded quickly after the fire. It was at this time that Mr. Jacobsen suggested the castle be made into a museum. There was an effort made to restore the Knight's Room and the King's Oratory to their original style, but the rest of the interior was changed to accommodate the Museum of Danish National History. In the museum, you will find decorative art, paintings and art objects of historical significance. Among the treasures is the first Bible printed in Danish. It was this Bible that established the standard for written Danish.

The museum is set up chronologically, beginning with the late baroque period and moving forward 10 years with each room. Be sure to see the chapel, one of the few parts of the King's Castle not destroyed by the fire. The organ at the south end of the chapel is the Compenius organ, which was installed in this spot in 1617 and later moved. Notice the exquisite vaulting and the ornate pillars of the chapel. The other section of the castle that was left intact after the fire is the Privy Passage, or the Council Hall Corridor. Many of the paintings here were acquired by Lambert van Haven, Christian IV's architect. The paintings throughout the King's Wing depict moments in the history of Denmark. The bed in room 41 was Christian IV's "official bed," and was a gift from Louis XIV of France, who knew something about official and unofficial beds. Evidently, Christian IV did also, as he fathered so many children that the Danish say it was "a joke in Europe and an environmental problem in Denmark." As you move through the rooms, you will notice that the furniture becomes more elegant and lighter in line. In the Knights' Hall are portraits of the royal families who occupied the castle. Among others, you will find Christian IX, whose son Wilhelm was chosen King of Greece. King Christian IX also had two other sons and three daughters. One, Alexandra, married King Edward VII of Great Britain. Another, Dagmar, became the empress of Russia and was the mother of Czar Nicholas II.

For students of the decorative arts, Frederiksborg is an important stop. The porcelain collection is particularly beautiful. Here is the set of white porcelain, Blonde Chine, which was a gift to the Danish king from Russia. The Danes, in their turn, made a set of 2600 pieces of Flora Danica in 1800 as a gift for Catherine of Russia, but Catherine died, so the Danes kept the porcelain. For more detail on the rooms and their objects, buy the illustrated guidebook on sale at the museum. It will take you room by room through the castle.

If you're hungry: **Slotsherrens Kro,** near the castle, serves meals at varying prices *from 10:00 a.m. to 9:00 p.m., from April to October.* **Slotskroen**, another restaurant beside the castle, is one of the oldest houses in Hillerod. It was converted into an inn in 1794. *Closed Monday.*

Bauneholm Manor House

The newest manor house in New Zealand is located about 5 kilometers from Hillerod. Situated near the forest of Gribskov, it contains 18 double rooms, all with private bath. The Restaurant Laroche specializes in Danish country cuisine as well as French haute cuisine and boasts an impressive wine cellar. A golf course nearby, as well as biking and horseback, are available for guests.

HELSINGOR

Get here by train from Copenhagen, or drive along the beautiful section of coast nicknamed the "Danish Riviera."

Best known as the home of Kronborg (Hamlet's Elsinore) Castle, Helsingor is a busy, pleasant port town. For years, it was Denmark's largest city and enjoyed a position of importance because of its strategic location on the sea and just across from Sweden. For over 400 years, the ruler of the sound in Helsingor collected tolls from every ship of every nation passing through the sound. In addition, the number of foreigners who lived here made Helsingor an international city, and that is evident even today in the varied character of the old, preserved buildings and neighborhoods.

Helsingor is the site of many restored old houses. You will find the stately merchants' houses near the harbor. Farther from the center are the artisans' and ferrymen's homes. Near St. Olai Church are several restored medieval houses. Fairs are held in the center of town, in Axel Square every Wednesday and Saturday from 7:00 a.m. to noon. It is between Helsingor in Denmark and Helsingborg in Sweden that the two countries are at their closest points. Ferry service to Sweden runs three times an hour. Travelers can buy duty-free goods on board.

Kronborg Castle

The purported inspiration for Shakespeare's Elsinore Castle of Hamlet renown. Whether old Will ever came to Denmark or saw this castle is beside the point. No one seems to care, and even if it is only an apocryphal tale, it does not deter the tourists at all. In the year 1200, a monk wrote down a story of a Danish prince who, unlike hesitating Hamlet, actually went ahead and killed his uncle and took power. It is probable that the prince of the monk's tale lived in the 8th century and was the son of a minor king in Jutland. In 1589, a group of English actors came to Kronborg, and it is highly likely that they told Shakespeare the story. The original building on the site was a fortress built in 1425, largely for the purpose of defending this Danish coast against any assault from the Swedish side, which was also fortified. It was King Frederik II who, in 1574, began renovating and enlarging the medieval fort of Krogen. His work was not to last, however, as fire destroyed most of its interior in 1629, and in 1658 Sweden took it over and ruined a great deal of it. King Christian IV rebuilt the ruined sections, leaving the exterior walls intact, but renovating the facades which were originally similar to the exterior of Frederiksborg Castle. During the 18th century, the castle served as a Danish garrison because of its strategic position. In 1920, the castle was made a national monument and underwent extensive restoration.

Most of the castle, including the Royal Apartments in the north wing, is open to the public. The Knights' Hall is one of the largest and oldest of its kind in northern Europe. Go into the church, which has been restored to its appearance during the time of Frederik II. Continue through the royal rooms of the west wing, and then through the catacombs, where Holger Danske, the national hero, is said to sleep. The legend has it that as long as he sleeps, Denmark will be safe.

While in Helsingor, take the time to look at the **St. Olai Church,** a medieval church with a fine altarpiece and beautiful baptistery. The **Carmelite Monastery** and **St. Mariae Church** are considered to be among the best preserved Gothic structures in the world. In the church, notice the organ which was used by the well-known baroque organist and composer Dietrich Buxtehude in the 1660s. The monastery is the place where King Christian II's mistress, Dyveke, was buried. The old Carmelite House, which was a hospital run by the nuns for foreign seamen, is now the **Helsingor Town Museum. Marienlyst Palace,** at Lappen, north of old Elsinore, is a particularly beautiful small palace. Built in the 1580s by King Frederik II, it was enlarged and modernized by the French architect N. H. Jardin. The Hamlet Memorial is in the park. In the Palace are exhibitions of painting, while the top floor contains the original Louis XVI interiors. The **Hotel Marienlyst** has a casino.

SCANTICON BORUPGAARD

This modern hotel is built around an historic manor house, circa A.D. 1000, which has numbered King Christian III and Hans Paaske, master builder of Kronborg Castle, among its illustrious residents. The hotel has 149 rooms with private bath, minibar and TV. A fitness center with swimming pool, sauna and work-out area plus nearby tennis courts and golf course are available. The interiors are furnished with objects on loan from the museums of Elsinore, and the restaurant offers both Danish and French cuisine.

FREDENSBORG

The attraction here is the **Fredensborg Palace**, the summer residence of Queen Margrethe and Prince Henrik. Begun by King Frederik IV in 1722, it was embellished by some of Denmark's greatest architects until its completion in 1766. The French landscape architect, N. H. Jardin, designed the gardens in the French style. Since no fires have touched it, Fredensborg remains one of the best examples of 18th-century Danish architecture. Though it fell into some disuse at the beginning of the 19th century, King Christian IX revitalized it and brought his large family here. His son-in-law, Czar Alexander III, enjoyed the beautiful park and frequently bicycled through the grounds and into the surroundings. Though the interior of the palace is open only in July from 1:00 p.m. to 5:00 p.m., the public is always welcome to wander the grounds. Enter through the main gate and you will be facing the palace, with smaller buildings running along the promenade leading to the palace. The Chapel Wing lies to the east of the palace, and attached to it is a stable that includes the gentlemen's residence. But the main interest for visitors is the park which leads to Denmark's second largest lake, Lake Esrum. Several avenues lead to the lake, and you can also wander off these main roads on the paths that run between them. Be sure to walk to the lake and see the two pavilions, designed by Jardin in 1765 as summer houses.

If you wish to spend the night, the **Hotel Store Kro**, built in 1723 by King Frederik IV, is one of the treats of Denmark. It has traditionally been the choice of visiting European royalty and statesmen, but it is just as available to you. There are 49 rooms, each decorated a bit differently and all with private bath. Double rooms will be about 1000Dkr. If you do not plan to stay overnight, just stop for a meal.

SOUTHERN ZEALAND

KOGE

The Koge Tourist Office: *Vestergade 1 in the main square.* The S train from Copenhagen will take you to this town, known for its many old half-timbered houses. Just 25 miles from Copenhagen, it is an easy day trip. Your Copenhagen card will be valid here.

Kirekstraede is the street with many half-timbered houses. At **No. 20** is Denmark's oldest half-timbered house. Also be sure to look at **No. 16 Vestergade.** But actually, look at them all.

The Koge Museum, a series of 17th-century buildings, contains exhibitions of Koge in the Middle Ages and the Renaissance. *Open every day all year round, but hours vary with the seasons, so check before you go.* The **Koge Art Museum** exhibits contemporary paintings, graphics and sculpture. *Open all year, Tuesday–Friday from 2:00 p.m. to 5:00 p.m.; Saturday and Sunday, 11:00 a.m. to 5:00 p.m.* **Koge Skitsesamling** is a museum dedicated to the process of creating a work of art. In addition, there is a permanent collection of 20th-century art, visiting exhibitions, and films. *Open early July–April every day, but Monday, from 11:00 a.m. to 5:00 p.m.*

Vallo Castle and Park used to be the place where the unmarried daughters of the Danish aristocracy could live in apartments suitable to the style to which they had grown accustomed. Now it is an old-age home, so it is not open to the public, but you can enjoy the elegant gardens. *April–October from 10:00 a.m. to dark.*

JUST FOR FUN

Fishing: *In the Tryggevaelde river near Vallo Castle.* Permit required.

Swimming: *At the beaches between Koge and Stroby.*

Horse Racing: *At Skovbo Travbane (trotting course).* Races Thursday and Sunday during school holidays. Take the bus from Koge Station.

Every Wednesday and Saturday throughout the year, a **market** is set up in town. During the summer, there is often **folk dancing** in the streets and courtyards of Koge. Saturday is a traditionally lively evening with jazz and folk music out of doors as well as inside.

THE ISLAND OF MON

Tourist Office: *Storegade 5. Open all year round.*

It is worth driving the 80-odd miles southeast of Copenhagen just for the sake of emerging from some of Denmark's steepest roads to the startling vision of the ancient chalk cliffs against the sea. Here on Mon, the visitor will find plenty to catch his eye. The cliffs, of course, are breathtaking, but beyond that the casual stroller walking along the foot of the cliffs might pick up a few fossils or find orchids in the forest behind the cliff. The ornithologist will also be rewarded, as there are many rare birds to be found in the area. This is an excellent spot for bicycling as well, and the beaches at Ulsvhale, which is a nature preserve, are beautiful. Contact the tourist office for bicycle rental. The staff can suggest bicycle tours and give you information on camping, of which there is plenty. Ancient barrows and chambered tombs are found all over the island. And the churches of Mon, with their exuberantly painted frescoes, are an important attraction. At Stege, Keldby, Fanefjord and Elmelunde, are churches decorated with narrative painting. **Borre** is the site of an impressive brick church. And at **Damsholte**, the architect Philip de Lange designed the outstanding 18th-century church. **Stege**, just about 10 miles from the bridge that links Mon to Zealand, is an old town that has retained its medieval ramparts and moat. Walk along the main street with the old merchants' houses. Sonderstien is a pleasant street running behind the gardens. Molleporten is the impressive town gate, next to the Mons Museum. In the Stege Church, you will find frescoes in a typically exuberant and naive Danish mode. At the Centrum Galleriet is an exhibition and sales gallery with ten artists displaying their work in glass, tile, and other media. At **Liselund**, a folly inspired by traditional English gardens and by Marie Antoinette's Le Hameau, you will find a miniature thatched palace with a Norwegian exterior and a Pompeiian interior. The "Swiss Cottage" is the spot where Hans Christian Andersen wrote "The Tinder Box." There were more buildings here, but they were destroyed by the erosion of part of the cliff.

THE ISLANDS OF LOLLAND AND FALSTER

Falster Tourist Information: *Ostegade 2, DK 4800 Nykobing F. Open all year.*

Nysted Tourist Information: *Adelgade 65, DK4880 Nysted. Open June 1– August 31. Sakskobing Tourist Information: Torvegade 4, DK 4990 Sakskobing. Open June 1–September 15. Off-season, Parkvej 30, DK 4990, Sakskobin. Naskov Tourist Office (on Lolland): Axeltorv 6. Open all year, but the hours vary. From June 22–August 8, the office is open Monday– Friday from 9:00 a.m. to 5:00 p.m., and Saturday from 9:00 a.m. to noon.*

The two islands south of Copenhagen are pleasant recreation spots: Falster with its moors, and Lolland, a rich farming area. These are good places for family vacations, for sailors, fishermen and nature lovers. However, if you are pressed for time and want to explore a Danish island, my choice would be Funen rather than Lolland and Falster. If you choose Lolland/Falster, you will need a car or a bicycle in order to explore the countryside. Inquire at the tourist offices for bicycle rental.

Falster calls itself the "south sea island," since it boasts over 20 kilometers of sandy beaches and pleasant swimming. **Nykobing F**, a market town, is the so-called capital of Falster. The main attraction is the Czarens Hus, built in 1700 and named after the visit of Peter the Great in 1716. Visit the Abbey Church with the monks' herb garden; stop at No. 18 Langgade to see a half-timbered building constructed in 1580; Ritmestergarden on the corner of Frisegade and St. Kirkestraede was built around 1620. Take in the view from the water tower, the zoo and the regional museum. An excellent golf course is just 10 kilometers from town.

Gedser, a ferry port, is the southernmost point of Denmark. Ferries to East and West Germany leave from here. You can climb to the top of Gedser Lighthouse for a fine view. A holiday center with a covered, "subtropical swimming pool" is in the middle of town. One of Denmark's best beaches stretches from the southern tip of Gedser north along the Boto Wood with its nude beach, to **Marielyst**, a seaside resort with stretches of lovely beach, clear water and an amusement park, *Familieland Falster*. **Stubbekoning** is the oldest town on Falster. Ravaged by fires and floods, it is now a picturesque spot with low merchant houses and a fishing and yachting harbor. And for a true meeting of old and new, there is an 800-year-old church and the largest motorcycle and radio museum in northern Europe.

For **cottage rental**, contact the **Falster Ferie Service Center** at ☎ *0045-3-895442*.

The main town of Lolland is **Sakskobing**, a busy, commercial center with many old buildings. **Nakskov** is the principal town of West Lolland. *The Mail Boat Tour* departs daily at 9:15 a.m. to the islands and to Albuen, where you can catch a bus back to Nakskov. During the Danish summer school holidays, a boat also leaves at 3:30 every day for **Vejlo**, and a sunset tour of the fjord departs at 6:00 p.m. on Wednesday and Thursday. The trip lasts about 2-1/2 hours. It does not go in bad weather. Book at the tourist office.

Aalholm Castle at Nysted was built in 1250, and contains unusual collections of furniture, weapons, birds and butterflies. Open June 1–September 4 from 11:00 a.m. to 6:00 p.m. daily.

THE FUNEN ARCHIPELAGO

Aero/Marstal offers pleasant beaches and fishing.

For tourist office listings see the section on the appropriate town.

GETTING THERE

Flights from Copenhagen serve Odense regularly. The "L" trains will also take you from Copenhagen to Odense. Inter-City train ferries go between Zealand and Nyborg. At Middlefart, the bridges of the Little Belt link Funen and Jutland.

The search for the Denmark of the fairy tales brings tourists to Hans Christian Andersen's birthplace in Odense, but the beauty and charm of Denmark is much more evident once you have gone beyond the rather contrived area that has grown up around the Hans Christian Andersen House in Odense; you will be missing the most beautiful part of the country if you do not further explore Funen and its archipelago. Funen, with its gently rolling farmland, washed by rain and unfortunately often whipped by the wind, and the islands trailing off to the south, Aero, Langeland and Tasinge, are picture-perfect. Aside from Copenhagen, these central islands are the heart of Denmark's spirit and charm. Here, the tourist will find dignified manor houses, cozy inns and richly painted half-timbered cottages edging crooked, sea-drenched, cobbled streets.

If you prefer to stay in private accommodations on Funen, you can book these through the tourist offices in Odense, Aero and Svendborg. It will cost about 100Dkr. per bed with an additional 25Dkr. for breakfast. The tourist offices in Aero and Svendborg can also help visitors with holiday cottages and pensions. Inquire at the tourist office about **Inn Checks**, travelers vouchers that can be purchased for either one night or several. An association of inns located on Funen offers these checks, and you can book from inn to inn as you travel across the island. It will cost about 195Dkr. per bed and half price for children in the same room. The price includes breakfast. **Funen Combi Pension** is an arrangement by which travelers stay in one place, but lunch and dine at different spots on Funen, Langeland and Aero. Upon arrival at the pension where you will spend the night, you are given vouchers that may be redeemed at participating establishments. Pick up a brochure on the program at any Funen tourist office.

NOTE

Travelers should be aware that many smaller hotels and pensions in the countryside do not accept credit cards. Also, many hotels close for the winter months, so be sure to check ahead.

ODENSE

Odense Tourist Office: *Radhuset, KD 5000, Odense. Open mid-June to August 31, Monday–Saturday from 9:00 a.m. to 7:00 p.m.; Sunday, 11:00 a.m. to 7:00 p.m. Off-season, Monday–Friday from 9:00 a.m. to 5:00 p.m.; Saturday, 9:00 a.m. to noon. Closed Sunday.*

DIRECTORY

Banks • Open 9:30 a.m.–4:00 p.m.; Thursday until 6:00 p.m. Closed Saturday and Sunday.

Emergency • ☎ *000* or *09 111 22 22*; Doctor on night duty, ☎ *09 14 14 33* from 4:00 p.m. to 7:00 a.m.

Pharmacy • ☎ *09 12 07 19.*

Police • ☎ *09 14 14 48.*

Shopping • 9:00 a.m.–5:30 p.m.; Friday, 9:00 a.m.–8:00 p.m.; Saturday, 9:00 a.m.–noon.

Insider Tip

Meet the Danes: *A program designed to bring together foreigners and Danes matches visitors with families who share similar interests. The visitors are invited to spend a few hours with their Danish family, for coffee and cake or wine and sandwiches. To participate, go to the tourist office in Odense and fill out a questionnaire. You should make arrangements as early as possible during your stay on Funen in order to allow time for arrangements to be completed.*

Odense was first mentioned in a letter from the German Emperor Otto III dated March 18, 988. The letter exempts the Odense Church from taxes and establishes the city as the seat of the bishop. Because of its monasteries and churches, the city attracted many visitors. In 1086, King Knud the Holy was assassinated by rebellious subjects in front of the altar of St. Alban's Church. Shortly afterwards, the king was canonized. His tomb is now in the cathedral that bears his name. In 1482, the first two books ever printed in Danish were produced in Odense by the German printer, Johan Snell, who had come here at the request of the church. In the early 12th century, the English monk, Aelnoth came to Odense to write a book about Knud the Holy and his ancestors. This book is the first known work written in Danish, and the earliest attempt at describing Denmark's history. Claus Berg, a woodcarver, also found his way here and produced work for Queen Christine, who resided in Odense from 1504–1521. Berg's masterpiece is the altarpiece, which, now restored, is in the cathedral.

SIGHTSEEING TOURS

A two-hour tour is conducted every day but Sunday at 3:00 p.m. during July and August. The tour begins at St. Knud's Cathedral and then goes by bus to the modern sections of Odense, passing the hospital, the university, new housing area, and the harbor. It concludes at the Hans Christian Andersen Museum. Departure from the Odense Tourist Office by the town hall.

WHAT TO SEE AND DO

The Hans Christian Andersen Museum

The central part of the museum occupies an 18th-century, half-timbered house that may or may not have been the birthplace of the writer. Andersen did not know exactly where he was born, as his parents, at the time of his birth, had not found a home of their own. Later, this building was considered his birthplace because his grandmother had at one time lived there. Do not be put off by the contrived surroundings of the museum. In the 19th century, the area was occupied by poor families, but now it has been restored far beyond what it might have looked like in Andersen's day. It is so clean and shiny that it looks like a Disney World village. However, Hans Christian Andersen had a side far darker than anything Disney ever conceived. This museum offers a serious and thoughtful portrait of Denmark's most famous son. The sorrow and frequent loneliness of Andersen's life are addressed in the museum through the carefully documented and ordered exhibits. Andersen's serious side, his deeper literary aspirations and the complexity of some of the tales are all illustrated here.

This is not particularly a museum for children, unless parents are prepared to read and explain the exhibits. But it is well worth the time to examine carefully if you are interested in learning about Hans Christian Andersen.

The exhibit consists of several rooms of memorabilia, snapshots, early books, manuscripts and the writer's own sketches. These are accompanied by text that explains the course of Andersen's life, his friendships, his failed romances and his travels. A slide show offers a series of old photographs that bring the fabled man to life. Be sure also to visit the library and exhibit of illustrations for the fairy tales. Here, children can push a button and listen to one of four tales read in English by Michael Redgrave or Laurence Olivier, and there is a video of an animated story as well.

St. Knud's Cathedral

A 13th-century church built on the site of the assassination of King Knud. The tomb of the martyred king is here as well as the tombs of King Hans and King Christian II. Of particular interest is Claus Berg's elaborate triptych.

Funen Village

A collection of old farm buildings from different parts of Funen have been arranged to approximate the layout of a typical Funen town of the last century. Farming in the old way is still carried on here, and in summer, visitors can observe various trades and crafts. In December, one day is given over to the demonstration of a 19th-century farm family's Christmas preparations. *Open April and May from 9:00 a.m. to 4:00 p.m.; June–August, 9:00 a.m.– 6:30 p.m.; September and October, 9:00 a.m.–4:00 p.m.; and November– March, Sunday and holidays only, 10:00 a.m.–4:00 p.m.* Just outside the entrance is the **Sortebro Kro**, a 19th-century inn serving a fine cold buffet for about $20, as well as an à la carte menu.

The Carl Nielsen Museum

Open only two years, the museum is dedicated to the life and work of the Danish composer and his wife, sculptress Anna Marie Carl-Nielsen. Visitors will be treated to excerpts of Nielsen's music as they go through the exhibits. The museum adjoins the Odense Concert Hall.

Monterstraede

A complex of four houses from the mid-16th to mid-17th centuries. The DSB Jernbanemuseum, a railway museum, is located here, as well as the Prehistory Museum mentioned below.

The Funen Prehistoric Museum

Exhibits of Stone, Bronze and Iron Age settlements on Funen. *Open all year from 10:00 a.m. to 4:00 p.m daily.; Wednesday from 7:00 a.m. to 10:00 p.m. Closed December 24 and 25 and January 1.*

Funen Prehistoric Museum at Hollufgard

A new complex that opened its first stage in 1988. A reconstruction of a Funen Viking farm is underway, and should be completed by the time of this printing. A Bronze-Age house has also been reconstructed.

Montergarden

(Museum of Urban and Cultural History.) Old buildings from Odense and Nyborg, among them several from the Renaissance, from the beginning of the 18th century and from the industrial period of 1850–1900. In addition, there are exhibitions of the history of Odense and an extensive collection of coins and medals. The texts are in Danish, but there is a guidebook with a summary in English available. *Open daily from 10:00 a.m. to 4:00 p.m. Closed December 24, 25, and January 1.*

H.C. Andersen's Childhood Home

From 1807–1819, Hans Christian Andersen and his parents occupied one of three tiny apartments in the house. This is the house which Andersen described in detail in *The Fairy Tale of My Life.* A few items from his childhood are on display. *Open April–September daily from 10:00 a.m. to 5:00 p.m.; October–March, noon to 3:00 p.m daily.*

Carl Nielsen's Childhood Home

The composer lived here from 1874–1879. Two rooms with exhibits of memorabilia from Nielsen's childhood. *Open April–September daily from 10:00 a.m. to 5:00 p.m. Closed the remainder of the year.*

Funen Art Museum

Danish art from 1750 to the present. *Open daily from 10:00 a.m. to 4:00 p.m.; Wednesday from 7:00 a.m. to 10:00 p.m. Closed December 24, 25 and Jan 1.*

Brandts Glass Factory/Cultural Center

This complex of galleries, shops and restaurants was awarded the 1988 European Museum Prize. It is located just off the pedestrian street.

WHERE TO STAY

The H.C. Andersen Hotel

The newest and sleekest. It is very attractive and conveniently situated. There is a Hans Christian Restaurant and a Fairy Tale Bar. Also a nightclub with live music and a gambling casino. About 1000Dkr. for a double room.

The Grand

Some visitors may prefer this place, which has a bit more old-world charm than the H.C. Andersen. Most rooms are large, comfortable and quiet, though perhaps a bit dowdy, decorated in that insipid green that sometimes seems to be the official color of Danish hotel rooms. At last visit, the bathrooms were sadly in need of updating. All rooms have minibar and TV. The lobby is attractive, and the dining room rather formal with piano music every evening. There is also a cozy little bar. A cafe serving light meals is open only in season and never on Mondays. Double rooms run between 800Dkr. and 1000Dkr.

The Plaza

Just across from the railway station. This hotel has been recently renovated with lovely, modern bathrooms. There is a quiet restaurant serving simple, reasonably priced meals. Double rooms run between 700 and 1000Dkr., but these rates are negotiable depending on availability. Do not let the location by the railway station deter you. This is a pretty part of town with a pleasant park just across the way.

The Windsor Hotel ★ ★

In the center of town. This is a lower-priced choice. It has a popular restaurant and bar and the rooms are more than adequate. A double room will be about 660Dkr.

Hotel Knudsens Gaard

About 1-1/2 kilometers from town. The motel was an old farm, rebuilt as a motel in the 1950s. It has recently added a new wing.

WHERE TO EAT

Den Gamle Kro

A cozy old inn dating from 1683. There are several half-timbered rooms attractively cluttered with old pottery and copper, Viking ship models and other odds and ends hanging from the heavy wood beams. The food is excellent and moderately expensive. A two-course meal will cost between 150Dkr. and 200Dkr. without wine. The Hans Christian Andersen crêpe looks ordinary, just ice cream in a crêpe, but a few drops of a mysterious elixir, discouragingly called Caloric Punch, turn this dessert into an extraordinary experience. A children's menu is available, and if you eat here at lunch rather than dinner, the price is quite reasonable. The service is friendly if a bit frantic, but once you have been served you are left to enjoy your meal in peace and linger as long as you wish.

Marie Louise

Here is a truly pleasant spot, located in Lottrups Gard, a small passage off Vestergade, the walking street. Danish nouvelle cuisine, simple, contemporary decor in an old building. The kitchen is partially visible from the dining room. There are only a few tables, so book ahead. The food is exquisite and the prices moderate to expensive. An entree will run about 150Dkr. A salad is included in the price if you ask for it. The house wine is good.

Unter Linetraeet

Across from the H.C. Andersen museum. Beautiful, elegant and popular, it is moderate to expensive. A one-course meal will run about $20.

Rode 7

Danish haute cuisine in elegant surroundings. Diners will do best with the three-course set menu for about $25. Beef and lamb are specialties.

Franck A

For inexpensive, simple fare, this is a popular spot. For a quick lunch, drop into the bar side of the restaurant and order one or more smorrebrod.

Prior Cafe

Another quick lunch or snack place at the end of Vestergade. Not much charm, but efficient. Self-service sandwiches, quiche and pastries.

Sortebro Kro

This is the restaurant at Funen Village. It's worth going out there just for this spot.

In addition, many so-called "Day Restaurants" serve inexpensive meals from around 11:00 a.m. to 8:00 p.m. You can have a good meal for about 40Dkr.

EXCURSIONS FROM ODENSE

KERTEMINDE

Twenty-two kilometers from Odense, this is a beach town and a good place from which to have a glimpse of north Funen. Kerteminde is a pretty spot with a picturesque old town and a pleasant harbor. If you are a cyclist, this makes a nice ride along the coast, but you can also get here by bus. Buses leave frequently from behind the Odense train station. The ride by bike is lovely, as there are paths running most of the way, with the water on one side and the serene Danish countryside stretching on the other.

The Johannes Larsen Museum

Larsen was one of the last of the great Funen painters, and this museum is devoted to his paintings and sketches. *Open April 15–October 31 from 10:00 a.m. to 4:00 p.m. every day but Monday.*

The Kerteminde Museum

A museum of local history. *Open daily from 10:00 a.m. to 4:00 p.m.*

Ladbyskibet

A 1000-year-old Viking chieftain's burial ship. *Open May–September from 10:00 a.m. to 6:00 p.m.; October–April, 10:00 a.m. to 3:00 p.m. Closed Monday.*

If you're hungry, you can eat by the water at **Rudolf Mathis Fiske Restaurant**, which has a three-course set menu for about 250Dkr. At lunch, the three-course meal is 175Dkr. *Open every day except Monday, noon–2:00 p.m. and 6:00 p.m.–9:30 p.m.*

If you want to stay overnight, **Munkebro Kro**, on the road to Kerteminde, is an old, thatched-roof inn with a view of the water. Licensed in 1816, it was rebuilt in 1977 after a fire. Twenty comfortable modern rooms all with private bath. TV in parlor. Private tennis court.

EGESKOV CASTLE

Buses from Faborg and Nyborg stop right outside the castle gates. The train from Odense pulls in at the train station, 2 kilometers from the castle.

Egeskov and Valdemar Slot are the only castles on Funen that are open to the public. Unlike Valdemar, Egeskov is still lived in. Though the present count and countess live in apartments that are not open to visitors, the rooms available to sightseers still seem livable, as the elder count and countess occupied them until their deaths in an auto accident several years ago.

The rooms are full of the personalities of the family members. Count Gregers Ahlefeldt-Laurvig-Bille, father of the present count, was a hunter of worldwide renown, and his wife, the Countess Nonni, was a needleworker of great accomplishment. The Countess' needlework hangs throughout the castle, and hunters will be especially interested in the collection of the count's hunting weapons and trophies. On one wall of the hunting room, visitors will see an impala with horns that are listed in the Guiness Book of Records because of their length. In the same room, the large octagonal iron stoves in the corners are very rare. There is also a harpoon the count used for whale-hunting in Greenland. Drawings and cartoons of the count portray him as a jolly man. He was extremely popular and often went around to the schools to speak to the children of his adventures. He wrote three books, one on hunting, the other two on his travels.

Egeskov was originally a farm and part of a large estate. In the 16th century, a man named Frands Brockenhuus inherited the farm as part of the dowry of his wife. Brockenhuus began to buy up the surrounding land, and finally built the castle which was completed in 1554. The name Egeskov, which means oak forest, refers to the legend that an entire oak forest was used to build the foundation of the castle.

In the Yellow Room, so named because the Louis XVI furniture has been gilded, notice the Louis XVI clock with the organ base and the 16th-century Dutch bureau. Even the staircases here are interesting. The one in the tower is unique because it turns to the left instead of the right, as was the usual case in order to give the defender a free right sword arm. On the walls and in the niches are family portraits and beautiful objects—some as simple as a copper bowl, but striking just the right note against the thick white plaster walls. The stairs lead up to the attics of the castle, where you can see evidence of the extensive restoration that was done in 1987. There are also drawings of the old castle. Beneath one of the spires lies the figure of the *Traemanden*, the wooden man. Legend says that if the figure is ever removed from this spot, the castle will tumble into the moat.

The main hall has been restored to look as it did in 1554. Of interest here are the paintings of King Christian IV and Niels Juel, the naval hero who was married to the daughter of a former owner of Egeskov.

Collectors of romance will be fascinated by the Rigborg Room where Rigborg Brockenhuus, the daughter of the 16th-century owner of the castle, was locked up for years by her father after she fell in love with a young man named Frederik Rosenkrantz, and, as the story goes, "got so close that she accidentally gave birth to a son."

From the Rigborg Room, visitors can enter the Tower Room, with a spectacular view of the Renaissance Gardens. Hanging in the room is a patchwork quilt made by the Countess Nonni.

The Victorian Room was restored in 1977 with furniture and possessions of the Ahlefeldt-Laurvig and Bille Brahe families. It offers an interesting insight into the daily lives of the residents of Egeskov. The Music Room is notable for its Hepplewhite furniture and an old square piano. Also, visitors will see a portrait of Countess Nonni. The Butler's Room has patchwork quilts which are the work of Countess Nonni's mother. And in the Admiral's Room is a collection of photographs of the family and guests of Egeskov.

The extensive gardens are of special interest. They were laid out in 1730 by Niels Krag the Younger in the French manner. In the 1960s, a Renaissance Garden with fountains, box hedges and topiaries was created. The Fuchsia Garden contains the largest collection of fuchsias in Europe. In winter, they are kept in greenhouses. There is also a kitchen garden, which was laid out in the time of

Christian IV. It contains all the herbs, vegetables and flowers that would have been necessary for a large household in the 17th century. In the park-like English Garden, the tree-shaded lawn slopes toward the lake. Farther west and south along the lake is the Cottage Garden and beyond that, the Water Garden and the Herbaceous Garden. Rose beds border the lawns that lead to the cafeteria. The Egeskov Rose is cultivated here, and visitors can buy Egeskov Rose Jelly. Don't miss the maze, which is renowned. Visit also the museum of vintage cars and carriages. In summer, concerts are given in the Baronial Hall. *Egeskov is open in May and September from 10:00 a.m. to 5:00 p.m. In June, July and August, the castle is open from 10:00 a.m. to 5:00 p.m., and the grounds until 6:00 p.m.*

FAABORG

Of interest here are the remains of the old ramparts, the belfry of the old St. Nicolai Church, and several carefully preserved old houses. This is also something of a center for exhibitions of the Funen artists. The **Old Merchant's House** is a museum of cultural history. Open May 15–September 15 every day from 10:30 a.m. to 4:30 p.m. The **Faaborg Museum of Funen Art** contains an excellent collection of the Funen painters and sculptors, particularly of the work of Kai Nielsen. Be sure to take a look at Nielsen's controversial sculpture, *Ymer Well*, in the main square. **Kaleko Molle** is a 600-year-old mill, now a museum. *Open May 15–September 15 from 10:00 a.m. to 5:00 p.m daily.*

WHERE TO STAY AND EAT

Two of the most enchanting inns in Denmark are located near Faaborg.

The Falsled Kro
> *Near Millinge north of Faaborg.* This 15th-century inn has been exquisitely updated into an elegant and comfortable country hotel with some of the most beautiful rooms I have seen, and a first-rate restaurant. It is a member of the prestigious Relais & Chateaux organization. If you don't stay here, at least stop for a meal. Expensive and worth every krone.

Steensgaard Herregardspension
> Another excellent country hotel at Millinge. The main building was built in 1310, and the renovations have been carefully attentive to the tradition of this elegant, half-timbered, red-brick country house, complete with a moat. Just 14 rooms, each with its own unique character. The dining room here is renowned, and occasionally there is space for diners who are not staying at the inn. Book ahead.

NYBORG

There is Inter-city train service from Zealand. This is an old port town, the site of the granting of Denmark's first constitution.

WHAT TO SEE AND DO

Nyborg Castle

Built in 1171, the castle served as a royal residence and was the place where the constitution of Denmark was signed in 1282. Christian IV turned his hand to the renovation and refurbishing of the castle, and his work is evident today. *Open June to August every day from 10:00 a.m. to 5:00 p.m. During the off-season, hours are 10:00 a.m. to 3:00 p.m. every day but Monday. Closed December–February.*

Hindemae Manor House

Built in 1787, this is one of Denmark's outstanding manor houses. Original furnishings in the rooms, and permanent exhibition and sale of art objects. There is a lunch restaurant and cafe. *Open June–August from 11:00 a.m. to 5:00 p.m. Off-season, it is open only on Saturday, Sunday and public holidays from 11:00 a.m. to 5:00 p.m.*

WHERE TO STAY

The Hotel Hesselet

The top choice, with the style and elegance that earns it a place in the coveted Relais & Chateaux. It is Oriental rather than Danish in flavor. A double room will run about $140.

SVENDBORG

Tourist Office: *Mollergade 20, Torvet, on the main square.*

A 700-year-old city, Svendborg is a lively town, successfully mixing the old and the new. It is a good center for exploring south Funen, as ferries leave frequently from its harbor for Troense, Thuro and Aero, and there are bridges to Langeland and Tasinge.

WHAT TO SEE AND DO

Vor Frue Kirke (Our Lady Church)

Built between 1253 and 1279.

Anne Hvides Gard

3 Furestraede • The oldest half-timbered house in Svendborg houses the museum. You can walk here from the church. The house was built around 1560, and its interiors are from the 18th and 19th centuries. There is a museum shop here.

The Svendborg Theater

Not impressive on the outside, but the interior is a miniature replica of the Royal Theater in Copenhagen. Performances are in Danish only, however. The main square is the scene of a market held every Wednesday and Saturday morning.

WHERE TO STAY

The Hotel Svendborg
In the center of town. All rooms with private bath, TV and minibar. Double room will run about 650Dkr., including breakfast. Restaurant.

The Hotel Royal
Located near the railway station with a view of the harbor. The hotel attracts a young crowd. I have not seen the rooms.

The Hotel Aero
The hotel has an excellent restaurant, but its rooms are not up to par, and the hotel service falls short.

Tre Rosor Holiday Center
Really a motel with family rooms that have kitchens, as well as a few double rooms. All with private bath. TV in all rooms and apartments. Though it's not very pretty, this could be a good spot for families, and its restaurant is well recommended.

Christiansminde Hotel and Holiday Center
Close to the beach but still in town. This is a new hotel with indoor pool. Ninety apartments with kitchens and private baths. The hotel is popular, so book ahead. A double room will be about 600Dkr. Apartments by the week will run around 3940Dkr. and accommodate eight people.

The Villa Pension Strandbo
A boarding house in a beautiful private home on the water. There are no private baths. About 200Dkr. per person with breakfast. Three miles from town.

The Stenstrup Kro and Hotel
A very reasonably priced inn. All rooms with private bath. Seven miles from Svendborg. Double rooms about 350Dkr.

Youth Hostel: The Vandrerhjemmet Soro
A pleasant place in an excellent location by the water, just out of Svendborg center.

WHERE TO EAT

The Hotel Aero
The restaurant here serves fine meals with fish the specialty.

The Restaurant Sandig
Excellent new Danish cuisine with a "surprise" four-course dinner at about 170Dkr.

The Vester Skerninge Kro
Just six miles from Svendborg, this is a picturesque, historic inn, built in 1772 and known as a stopping-off point for important travelers on their way through Funen. Good Danish fare in homey surroundings. Menu in English as well as Danish. Reasonable. *Closed Tuesday.*

Strandkroen

Six miles from Svendborg on the water, highly recommended.

Expensive.

NIGHTLIFE

Las Vegas and **Bios** are nightclubs. **Chess** and **Humlebien** are discos.

Kloster Moster, a music pub with different live music each night, attracts a young crowd.

THE ISLAND OF TASINGE

Tasinge is the third largest island of the Funen archipelago. Until 1911, the entire island belonged to Valdemars Slot, which served as the manor house of the land.

TROENSE

The main town of Tasinge is the stuff of fairy tales. Its narrow streets and brightly painted thatched cottages are Denmark at its most delightful. Troense was the spot many sea captains chose as their home port, and the houses are somewhat larger and more substantial than one finds in the fishing and farming villages. Take the time to walk along the best known street, **Gronnegade**.

The Tasinge Skippers' Home and Folklore Museum

The complex has four buildings: three old houses and a modern exhibition hall with exhibits on Stone-Age findings, clothing and the story of Elvira Madigan. The "Skippers' Home" is furnished as it would have been for a 19th-century Troense sea captain. *The museum is open June 20–August 15 daily from 10:00 a.m. to 6:00 p.m. From May 1 to June 19 and from August 16 to mid-September, it is open weekdays 10:00 a.m. to 3:30 p.m.; Saturday and Sunday, 10:00 a.m. to 5:00 p.m.*

Near the museum is a National Trust area where visitors can climb the 72-meter Bregninge hill for a view of the sea and the islands. A good picnic spot.

Landet Church

Interesting in its own right, the church is best known as the burial place of the ill-fated lovers, Elvira Madigan and Sixten Sparre. Elvira, whose real name was Hedvig Jensen, was a tightrope walker whose beauty had gained her some fame and notoriety. Sixten Sparre, the son of an aristocratic family, was married at the time he met Hedvig. According to the tale, he deserted the army to run off with the enchanting performer. With no money between them, they lived hand-to-mouth, but managed to find a sympathetic widow living near Troense who took them in for a brief time. On what was to be the last day of their lives in July of 1889, the widow fixed the fated pair a picnic lunch, which they took into the forest where they were later found, victims of a double suicide. Their grave lies just southeast of the large oak tree in the Landet churchyard.

The Danish Mechanical Doll Museum

Located at an old farm formerly owned by Tasinge's most famous citizen, Soren Lolk, who championed the cause of the farmers of Funen, the farm has been used as a setting for lectures and festivals. The museum is quite an adventure for children and adults. Owners Jytte and Kjeld Hansen are constantly adding to the collection. Visitors can make the toys go through their paces with a push of a button.

Valdemars Slot (Funen Manor House Museum)

Though privately owned, this castle on the island of Tasinge is open to the public and accessible by ferry from Svendborg. Visitors are free to wander the grounds and to visit most of the rooms of the palace. Of note are the tapestries, the book collection, the Knight's Hall and the chapel. The elegant interiors and art treasures, the setting by the sea and the fine restaurant make Valdemars Slot a rewarding outing from Svendborg. Construction on the castle began in 1639 when King Christian IV won the land from his mother-in-law in a card game. Though he started building the castle, he did not live to see it completed. It was given in 1677 to naval hero Niels Juel as payment for the Swedish fleet, which he defeated and brought back to Denmark. Juel enlarged the main building to its present size. In the 18th century, the gatehouses, stables and carriage houses that stand beside the pond were added, as well as the beach pavilion.

Lunch Break: There are two restaurants on the grounds. **Den gra dame** is a gourmet restaurant located beneath the church. Its vaulted ceilings and elegantly simple furnishings are as tasteful as the excellent food. A garden pavilion and a bistro, **Aeblehaven** (The Apple Orchard), offers lighter fare in summer. Visitors are also welcome to bring picnic lunches. *The museum is open May–September every day from 10:00 a.m. to 5:00 p.m. In October, and from Easter to April 30, it is open Saturday, Sunday and holidays from 10:00 a.m. to 5:00 p.m. The restaurants are open all year, every day except Monday, noon to 3:00 p.m. and from 6:00 p.m. to 10:00 p.m.*

WHERE TO STAY AND EAT

Hotel Troense

A pleasant and reasonably priced hotel on the water. The comfortable and modern rooms will run about 600Dkr. with breakfast. Choose between the new section, in which all the rooms are updated and have private baths but no view, or the old building, which will guarantee you a view, but not necessarily a private bath.

The Troense Motel

This half-timbered, rose-colored cottage is more like a pension than a hotel, and it is inexpensive.

Valdemars Slot

The castle has cottages for rent in the area as well. Contact the Svendborg tourist office.

For fine fare, a good choice and an expensive one is the excellent and beautiful restaurant at **Valdemars Slot** mentioned above. **The Hotel Troense** also has an excellent restaurant.

THURO ISLAND

Thuro, reached by bridge from Tasinge, is the tiniest island of the archipelago. The narrow sound nestled between the two crescents of this horseshoe-shaped island was a perfect hideout for pirates. The island is hilly and wooded, with fine beaches at Smormosen and Thuro Rev. Of interest is the church, with an especially beautiful terraced graveyard. Legends and mystery surround the island, which is said to have been the birthplace of Rolf Krake, a king whose story is one of violence, revenge and incest. There is a monument to Rolf Krake on the island.

WHERE TO STAY AND EAT

The Hotel Pension Rogeriet

A family-owned hotel with comfortable rooms, a wonderfully homey atmosphere and a beautiful setting by the water. The hotel is on the site of an old smokehouse, now used by the family as their home. The smokehouse has been in the family for five generations, and the hotel is now run by brother and sister Niels Hansen and Dorta Petersen. There are 30 beds and only two rooms without bath. The new wing was built in 1962. Dinner is served in a family dining room or on an enclosed veranda, and coffee is taken in the book-lined living room or, in good weather, outside. There is a small beach and a boat for guests to use. The paintings in the living room are the work of the grandfather of the present owners, who was an artist and sailor of some fame. He smuggled weapons in the Spanish Civil War, and sailed to South Africa and to northern Russia in the course of his naval career. A double room with half-board ran, at last check, 600Dkr., and with breakfast only, 380Dkr. Singles range from 325Dkr. to 360Dkr. half-board and 250Dkr. with breakfast only. These rates are for several nights. One night will be more expensive. A cold buffet lunch is available for hotel guests only, but you must inform the management if you plan on lunch. The pension accepts no credit cards.

THE ISLAND OF LANGELAND

A causeway links Tasinge to Langeland (so-called because it is a long, narrow island). Dotted by whitewashed churches and old mills, Langeland's gentle hills, woods and pretty coast make it a pleasant place for nature lovers who, in winter, can also enjoy the flocks of birds who make this a stopping point in their migrations south.

RUDKOBING

The main town of the island has an old apothecary shop with a chemist's laboratory and items like Dragon's blood and pulverized mummy on display. *Open May 15–August 31, Monday–Friday from 1:00 p.m. to 4:00 p.m.* The **Langeland Museum** in Rudkobing is a museum of regional history. *Open June, July and August, Monday–Friday from 10:00 a.m. to 4:00 p.m. Off-season, open Sunday and public holidays from 2:00 p.m. to 4:00 p.m.*

TRANEKAER

This small town on Langeland has a castle at one end of its winding main lane and a church at the other. Between them nestle fairy-tale cottages with tiny farmyards and flowers sprouting everywhere. The bus from Rudkobing stops here, just down from the Tranekaer Gaestgivergard, an historic inn.

Tranekaer Slotsmolle

A restored windmill in the town of Tranekaer. There is an exhibition of mill history. *Open May 15–August 31, Monday–Friday from 10:00 a.m. to 5:00 p.m.; Sunday and public holidays from 1:00 p.m. to 5:00 p.m. Closed Saturday.*

Carriage Exhibition

At Skovsgard manor. Horse-drawn carriages from around 1900. *Open May 15–September 30, Monday–Friday from 10:00 a.m. to 5:00 p.m.; Sunday and public holidays from 1:00 p.m. to 5:00 p.m. Closed Saturday.*

Sailors, swimmers and fishermen take note: Langeland has six marinas and makes an excellent center for sailors wishing to cruise the Funen archipelago. Spring and autumn are the best times for fishing off the shore or from a boat. The beaches at Ristinge Strand, Spodsbjerg Strand and at the northern point of Lohals and Hous are excellent bathing and windsurfing spots. **Bicycle and Dinghy Rental** *Ole Dehn, at Lohals, Sondergade 22,* ☎ *09 55 17 00.*

WHERE TO STAY AND EAT

The Tranekaer Gaestgivergard   ★★★

The best choice here. It is an old inn of rich tradition. In fact, Queen Margrethe visited it some years ago to commemorate its anniversary. The rooms in the main, older building are a bit dark, but very comfortable. In the new wing, the rooms are brighter and more contemporary. Restaurant.

THE ISLAND OF AERO

Tourist Information: *Torvet, DK 5970 Aeroskobing. Open in summer Monday–Friday from 9:00 a.m. to 5:00 p.m.; Saturday, 9:00 a.m. to 1:00 p.m.; Sunday, 10:00 a.m. to noon.*

The ferry from Svendborg takes a little over an hour to Aeroskobing. From Faaborg, a ferry will take you to Soby, and from Rudkobing, you can take a ferry to Marstal.

AEROSKOBING

The principal town of this salty little island is protected as a historical entity, the only town so designated in Denmark. Consequently, it looks much as it did in the 1680s. But during the last two weeks of July, the 20th century comes to Aeroskobing, and its narrow streets swell with jazz lovers flocking to the jazz festival that attracts international visitors.

The nicest thing to do in Aeroskobing is wander along the narrow, cobbled streets and enjoy the colorful houses, many with the extraordinary doors unique to Aero. Aeroskobing was named the community of the year because of its alternative energy program using hay as fuel.

Aero lends itself to biking or driving, as it is interesting to get out into the countryside. There are many dolmens and passage graves. The churches of the island are also worth visiting.

Start at the **Aeroskobing Church**, which was built in 1756 and is the third one to be built on the site. (Inside are votive ship models, found in many churches of coastal towns.) The font dates from 1250 and was part of the original church. The pulpit is 17th century, and the altarpiece from 1821. Across the square from the church is the Old Merchant's House, a warehouse built in 1848. If you walk down **Brogade,** you will see on your left an old bakery that has been owned by the same family for five generations. At the corner of Brogade and Gyden are three attached half-timbered houses, known as **Hammerichs Hus**. This is a museum with a collection of old furniture, faience, handicrafts, and artwork from the area, all collected by Gunnar Hammerich, a sculptor. *Open daily from 10:00 a.m. to noon and from 2:00 p.m. to 4:00 p.m.*

On the corner of Norregade is the **Aeroskobing Museum**, located in the former bailiff's house. Farther along Norregade are the old sea captains' houses, and if you walk through the alley by the church, you will come to Sondergade, where the two oldest houses in town are located. The **Prior's House** was built in 1690. Notice the oak door that was stained with ox blood and has remained intact to this day. Farther along the street is **Kjobinghus**, the oldest house in Aeroskobing.

Also visit **Museumsgarden**, where the unique **Peter's Bottle Ship Museum** is located. This museum is filled with the work of an old ship's cook, Peter Jacobsen, who made almost all the bottle ships and ship models in the museum himself. No bottle was deemed unworthy for Peter's art, and you will find ships built in everything from milk to brandy bottles. Some claim that Peter personally emptied all the bottles himself. *The museum is open June–August from 9:00 a.m. to 5:00 p.m. daily; May and September from 10:00 a.m. to noon and 2:00 p.m. to 4:00 p.m daily. Also in Museumsgarden is a small house displaying the wood carvings of Hans the Sculptor.*

ON THE ROAD AROUND AERO

Northeast of Aeroskobing, you will find **Bregninge Church**, a 12th-century church with an extraordinary altarpiece. The spire, thatched with wooden shingles, is of particular interest. Inside, the extraordinary triptych is justifiably famous. It was carved before the Reformation by the woodcarver Claus Berg, who also carved the triptych in St. Knud's Cathedral in Odense.

The other two main towns on Aero are **Soby**, a fishing village of roughly the same size as Aeroskobing, and **Marstal**, a sailing town, from where travelers can catch the ferry to **Rudkobing** on Langeland. If you are driving or biking, the island is small enough to get around easily, and you should try to cover most of it, as the sea-wrapped landscape is beautiful, and there are worthy sights and pleasant beaches along the way. Pick up a map and guide pamphlet at the tourist office in Aeroskobing, and then start your exploration. Drive to **Tranderup**, where you will find hilly terrain and high cliffs. If you walk down to the beach and to the left, you will come to the point where the valley opens to the sea. Tranderup village has a newly restored 19th-century church with an altarpiece from before the Reformation. **Voderup Klint** is a naturally terraced landscape that is now a nature reserve. Walk along the path to the beach. **Sobygard Voldanlaeg** is the site of medieval fortifications and a farm. From here, visitors can walk up a path to **Vestner Molle**, one of the oldest Dutch windmills to be found in Denmark. The present mill was built in 1834 to replace the old one. Fine view, but visitors cannot go into the mill.

WHERE TO STAY AND EAT

The Hotel Aerohus
An old family hotel with modern comforts, though not all rooms have private baths. Pleasant restaurant. This is a good choice. Reasonable.

Det Lille Hotel
Just six rooms in what was an old sea captain's house. Simple meals are served in cozy surroundings.

The Vindeballe Kro

At Tranderup. The inn has some cottages in the garden, as well as hotel rooms.

The Dunkaer Kro

On the road to Marstal. Picturesque and cozy. Not all rooms have private bath. Also inquire at the tourist office for cottages to rent.

Insider Tip

On Aero, it is possible to rent one of the charming half-timbered houses that are so much a part of Aero's appeal. Contact the Aero tourist office.

JUTLAND

Legoland is a miniature world built of Lego Blocks.

GETTING THERE

Frequent flights from Copenhagen service Billund, Aalborg, Arhus (Tistrup airport is 50 kilometers from the city) and Esbjerg; and ferry connections are convenient from Kalundborg on Zealand and from Funen. Airfares are reasonable, especially if you plan to spend at least three days in Jutland.

Unlike the rest of Denmark, Jutland's beauty and fascination lie in the bleak landscape, the windswept moors and the pale beaches. This is the only part of Denmark attached to the European continent. As a result, it attracts visitors to and from Germany. The major attractions for tourists are the town of **Ribe** in the southwest, the oldest town in Denmark and one of the best preserved in Europe; **Legoland** at Billund, not far from Ribe; **Arhus** and **Aalborg**, two large towns in the north; and **Skagen**, at the northern tip of Denmark, a typically Danish resort town with its blown and scarred beaches and its charming yellow cottages.

BILLUND: THE HOME OF LEGOLAND

Many visitors to Jutland will fly from Copenhagen to Billund in the southeast, and then drive north. The first stop, just across the parking lot at the Billund airport, should be **Legoland**. This is a miniature world built entirely of Lego blocks. It is an amusement park of sorts, and a museum of the ingenuity and whimsy that is the soul of Denmark. Certainly if you have children, and probably even if you don't, you should try to make the excursion here. Legoland itself will require only a few hours of your time, but you could then go on to Ribe, well worth a detour. No one needs a guidebook to Legoland, but my one word of advice is not to eat in the McDonald's-like fast-food restaurants just inside the gates. Wait until you get to **Wild West Land** and choose one of the restaurants in that area, where you will find Denmark's version of "food on the range." There are a few rides for children, but most of the fascination is just in seeing the marvels created with Lego blocks. One ride that children really love is the driving school, where they are allowed to drive battery-powered toy cars, but are given instruction in the rules of the road and must obey the traffic signals and signs. The indoor exhibits include Titania's Palace, with 3000 miniature pieces of furniture and art objects, a collection of old mechanical toys and dolls and doll houses, and a playroom for children with thousands of Lego bricks. *Open May 1–September from 10:00 a.m. to 8:00 p.m daily. In peak season, the park remains open until 9:00 p.m. There is a tourist office at the entrance to the park.*

OTHER ATTRACTIONS IN THE BILLUND AREA

The Sand Dunes of Grene Sande in an area protected by the National Trust are a good place for walking and sunbathing and for skiing in winter. The **Billund Trotting Course** holds races *every Thursday at 6:45 p.m. all year round and on Sunday evenings in July.*

WHERE TO STAY

If you are planning to go on to explore *Jutland*, or at least to see *Ribe*, it is advisable and certainly more fun to spend the night in Ribe. (See below.) If you are planning to leave Legoland late in the evening and do not want to drive all the way to Ribe, you could stop at the **Hovberg Kro,** at *Holmeavej 2* in *Hovberg*, about 20 kilometers from Billund. The Kro is situated in a lovely park area with good fishing and pleasant walks. The original Kro was built in 1790, but it has been expanded and renovated into a modern building with up-to-date comforts. Moderate. If you wish to stay in *Billund*, the **Hotel Legoland** is convenient and comfortable.

RIBE

Tourist Office: *Torvet, 6760 Ribe*

Ribe is one of the "must-sees" on the peninsula of Jutland. With its ancient cathedral and beautifully preserved half-timbered houses, it is a living museum and a very pleasant place to spend a few hours or a day walking the cobbled streets and relaxing in the picturesque square. At one time an important port, Ribe is now surrounded by marshland and its major claim to fame is the beauty of its preserved old buildings and the storks that perch upon the medieval rooftops.

There was a community at Ribe as long ago as A.D. 700, and in the latter half of the eighth century a trading center developed. Excavations have yielded evidence of foreign trade and such skills as blacksmithing, shoemaking and the production of glass beads. In the ninth and 10th centuries, Ribe became the episcopal seat with the erection of a church by Bishop Ansgar, no evidence of which is left today. Writings at the end of the 11th century mention the town of Ribe, "surrounded by water flowing in from the ocean." Construction of the present cathedral was begun at the end of the 12th century.

Writings and excavations have established that a second or twin town developed on the south side of the river. It was at this time that Ribe began to flourish as a trading center, connecting routes between the Baltic and the North Sea. Ribe's golden era lasted from the early 13th century to 1536, the year of the Reformation in Denmark. In those years, the town claimed the dubious distinction of paying more taxes than any other community in Denmark and was the most important town in Denmark. Merchants, pilgrims and students all traveled through Ribe on their way to and from Europe and the Holy Land, but the Reformation brought dramatic changes to Ribe with the selling of the monasteries and the stripping of the ecclesiastical riches. At the same time, easier sailing routes around North Jutland shifted much of the trade to Copenhagen. In the 17th century, wars with Sweden brought further decline.

Throughout its history, Ribe also contended with devastating fires and, as early as 1581, established a ban on thatched roofs. The building designs began to change around this time as well, with the narrow, gabled ends of the houses facing the street. In many Danish towns, the wealthy families built their houses of brick and others were half-timbered, which means that the framework of the structure was timber and the walls were of brick or wattle and daub. In Ribe, because of the marshy ground, half-timber was the preferred mode of building as it adapts more easily to the shifting soil; and so even the prosperous merchants built their gabled houses in the half-timbered style. Many of these are still standing, and the center of the old town has been preserved under the National Trust.

SIGHTSEEING TOURS

Every day in summertime, a tour with an English-speaking guide departs at 11:30 a.m. Check with the tourist office in the square.

The Night Watchman's Tour

For a touch of atmosphere, join the night watchman as he makes his rounds every night at 10:00 p.m. The watchman, Aga Grann, appears in his watchman's garb and cap, carrying the "Morning Star" staff and lantern, and sings the 10:00 p.m. refrain of the watchman's song. At this hour, the song advises everyone to go to sleep. He will take you through many of the streets and corners mentioned below, swinging his lantern, calling out the hour, and telling you, in Danish and English, something of the history of Ribe as he goes. This walk through the darkened town with the marvelous Mr. Grann really piques the imagination and carries the traveler back to the medieval times of Ribe's heyday. Moreover, this is a fine opportunity to snatch a peek inside some of the houses where the lamps are lit and the shades happen to be up.

WHAT TO SEE AND DO

The center of the old town is small, and the greatest attractions are the old, half-timbered houses, many with beautiful doors. The square, fronted by the Dagmar Hotel and Wies' Stue, one of the oldest inns in Denmark, is a good starting point and a pleasant place to have a drink or coffee in good weather.

Ribe Cathedral

Located on the square, the late Romanesque basilica that forms the heart of the church was built from the mid-12th to the mid-13th centuries. The south door of the transept, the "Cat's Head Door," bears witness to the skill of the early stonemasons. The north tower collapsed in 1283 and was replaced with a larger, brick tower, completed about 1333. It was in this tower that the alarm bell was installed. Also at this time, several Gothic chapels were added to the building.

After the Reformation of 1536, the cathedral became the parish church, but the central portion fell gradually into disrepair and attempts at repair resulted in the demolition of several of the chapels and the cloisters, as well as the south tower. In the late 19th century, a more careful renovation began. The latest change occurred in 1987 when the painter Carl-Henning Pedersen decorated the apse with frescoes and stained glass. The view from the top of the tower is worth the climb. Notice as you exit the cathedral that the structure stands slightly below street level. This is due to the soft, marshy ground on which the cathedral was built. Today, because of the rubble of the past, the foundations of Ribe's buildings stand more solidly.

Torvet and the old streets

The best way to see Ribe is to walk down the streets running off the square. On Skolegade, you will come to **The Grammar School**, which is the oldest in Denmark. It was used from the early 16th century until 1856 and turned out some of Denmark's most well-known personages. **Hans Tausen's House**, also on Skolegade, is now an archeological museum exhibiting materials relating to the early history of Ribe. The house itself was the residence of the bishop and is the oldest in existence.

Puggaardsgade and **Sonderportsgade** are streets that run off Skolegade. At the corner of these two streets are several well-preserved half-timbered houses, which are still occupied. **Tarnborg**, in Puggaardsgade, is a 16th-century house that served as the residence for noblemen, the bishop and the canon. It now houses city offices.

The Town Hall

On the square. The building was constructed in 1496 and at first was filed with shops, then became residential quarters. In 1709, it became the Town Hall. A small museum occupies the portion of the structure that was the debtors' prison.

St. Catharine's Church and Abbey

Along with the cathedral, these are all that are left of the former churches and abbeys which proliferated at one time in Ribe. This church was built in the 15th century, though an earlier church did occupy the site. At present, the abbey is a home for the elderly. Walk here through a lovely park with a small pond, a picturesque bridge and a fountain.

Quedens Gaard

A half-timbered merchant's house, on the way to the harbor; several wings were built around 1580 and the central portion in the 18th century. It is a museum, furnished as it was in its prime during the 16th and 17th centuries. Also in this direction, **Fiskergade** is an ancient street, developed in 1400 but later destroyed by a fire. There are several half-timbered merchants' houses here, lining the streets that run to the harbor.

The Ribe Art Museum

Exhibits of Danish 19th-century artists, in addition to collections of later artists. The museum occupies a stately mid-19th-century mansion in a beautiful garden by the river.

WHERE TO STAY AND EAT

The Dagmar Hotel

The first choice of everyone here, so book ahead—way ahead. Right on the square, it is old, dating from 1581, but beautifully renovated and charming. The restaurant, which consists of four dining rooms, is sumptuously hospitable and expensive. You can dine more modestly in the cellar restaurant. All rooms with private baths, TV/VCR. *Moderate.*

The Weis Stue

The rooms are not as comfortable as in the Dagmar and do not have private baths, but this is a historic spot and its restaurant is cozy and less formal than the Dagmar. *Inexpensive.*

The Restaurant Saelhunden

At Skibbroen. A good choice for simple fare and a chance to see the local residents. The atmosphere here is unaffected and friendly and the food is good. It is situated right on the water. The menu is in English and German as well as Danish. Inexpensive. No credit cards.

Some travelers choose to stay at Gram, not far from Ribe, where there are two inns. **Den Gamle Kro** is more of a motel with small apartments. **Schloss Kroen** is connected to the old castle.

ESBJERG

Tourist Office: *Skolegade 33, DK 6700 Esbjerg.*

In contrast to **Ribe**, the oldest town in Denmark, **Esbjerg** is the youngest, just 120 years old. It is also the fifth largest Danish city, an offshore oil center, and the largest fishing port in Denmark. Ferries leave from here for England, and there is train service up the west coast of **Jutland** and across to **Copenhagen**. While the city is not a prime tourist attraction in itself, the city leaders have done their best to provide enough of interest to the traveler who finds himself here on the way to somewhere else. The museums of Esbjerg, in particular, are well worth visiting, and the "chessboard" town plan, designed in the 1870s, should be of interest to town planners.

WHAT TO SEE AND DO

The Fishery Museum

This large, attractive, modern museum has excellent exhibits on the history of fishing, an aquarium with every kind of saltwater fish found in Denmark, as well as a seal tank. This is the only place in Denmark where seals are bred in captivity. An open-air exhibit of old boats is still in the development stage, but there is a miniharbor here and old summer fishing huts, as well as a workshop where demonstrations of net-making are given. There is also a German bunker here that you can walk into. Cafeteria and picnic tables. Bus service from the center of town. *Open daily from 10:00 a.m. to 4:00 p.m. The museum remains open later in season.*

The Esbjerg Museum

Exhibits on the history of the city. A replica of a street and town square with houses containing apartments, workshops and shops, including an actual grocery store and a "harbor." There is also an exhibit on the period from the Stone Age to the Viking Age. *Open all year from 10:00 a.m. to 4:00 p.m. Closed Monday.*

The Printing Museum

A printing office, bookbinders shop and an exhibit on the development of printing. *Open May 1–September 30 weekdays, from 2:00 p.m. to 5:00 p.m.*

Collection of the Esbjerg Art Association

Museum of modern Danish art from 1920 until today. There are also graphic works by Danish and foreign artists. In addition, there is a small collection of handicrafts. *Open daily from 10:00 a.m. to 5:00 p.m.*

The Main Library

Located in Norregade • This is a cultural center as well as a library. Of particular interest is the children's division, decorated with paintings by the Danish humorist Storm P. In the Cafe Biografen, a cafe and cinema located in the library complex, the Esbjerg Ensemble performs classical music.

The Marbaek Area Nature Preserve

About 12 kilometers north of Esbjerg, you will find large lakes, heather-covered moors and the remains of two Iron-Age settlements. There are marked footpaths for hikers, bicycle trails and bridle paths. An 18-hole golf course with a clubhouse, shop and restaurant is located in the northeast part of Marbaek. Marbaekgard center offers information, a farming exhibit, minigolf course and restaurant. In season, get here by taking Bus 21 from Esbjerg to Hjerting and changing to interurban Bus No. 43 to Sjelborg Camping. From there, Marbaek is a 2.5-kilometer walk.

The Cemetery

Graves of Allied airmen who were shot down over the west coast of Jutland during World War II. Across the road is a small cemetery with the graves of refugees and over 1000 German soldiers.

Music in Esbjerg

During the last week of June and the first week of July, there is a municipal summer entertainment program. Most performances are given in the open-air theater in the town park.

WHERE TO STAY

The Hotel Brittania

In the center of town, this is a modern, rather commercial, but comfortable hotel, the first choice of most business travelers. All rooms with private bath and TV/VCR. Two restaurants, bar and pub.   *Moderate.*

The Scandic Hotel Olympic

Another comfortable, modern and commercial hotel. All rooms with private bath, TV. Private parking facilities. Restaurant.   *Moderate.*

The Hermitage Hotel West

Outside town is this pleasant and new hotel. Actually more of a motel, it is nonetheless a first-class establishment, attractive and comfortable.

Moderate.

Hotel Hjerting

Seven kilometers northwest of the center of Esbjerg and on the water, this is a good choice if you are looking for a less urban environment, particularly if you wish to be closer to the Marbaek area. Modern rooms and an excellent restaurant.

The Youth Hostel

Worth mentioning. It is housed in the old Maritime School.

WHERE TO EAT

Pakehuset
The first choice here. Danish specialties in a pleasant setting near the ferry pier for Fano.   *Moderate.*

The two restaurants in the **Hotel Hjerting** outside town are also very good.

FANO

Fano Tourist Office: *Havnen, Nordby, 6720 Fano. Open Monday–Friday from 9:00 a.m. to 4:00 p.m.; Saturday, 9:00 a.m. to noon. In July and August, open weekdays until 5:30 p.m.; Saturday, 8:00 a.m. to 9:00 p.m.; and Sunday, 10:00 a.m. to noon.*

A 20-minute ferry ride from Esbjerg will bring you to this seafaring island and a round-the-island bus service in Fano connects with the ferry. One warning to those who do not like waiting in line: Try to travel here on a weekday as the weekend ferries are jammed in summertime. This congestion is partly because the ferries are small and are thus a way of regulating the flow of visitors to the island. While you might have to wait in line for a boat, you will not feel crowded once you are on the island. Fano has 18 kilometers of white sand beaches and limitless stretches of clear water. Marked paths lead through the nature preserve with sand dunes, forest and heath. This is the place for surfers (lessons for beginners available), kite flyers and cyclists, and there is an 18-hole golf course in the Dunes. Fano is a very popular camping spot as well. The two towns on the island are Nordby, where the ferry lands, and Sonderhor, on the southern end. Both are filled with the thatched cottages and winding streets that are so much a part of Denmark, past and present.

Fano has always been a marine island, owned until 1741 by the king and then sold to the residents when the Royal Treasury was a bit slim. The new owners obtained the rights to shipbuilding, and at one time four shipyards were thriving here. From 1741 to 1900, 1000 ships were built on Fano.

WHAT TO SEE AND DO

The Fano Museum in Nordby
Collections of furniture and implements showing how people lived 150-200 years ago on Fano. Exhibits also of the treasures the sailors brought home from their travels.

The Fano Seafaring and National Costume Museum
Exhibits on the history and daily life of the island. (*In Nordby.*)

Hannes Hus at Sonderhor
The house of an ordinary family of 100 years ago, left much as it was.

The Fano Fair

Throughout the first weekend in July, folk dancing and fiddle music fill the streets, and participants appear in their traditional costumes. The "Seaman's Return" and a wedding feast are also part of the celebrations.

The Sonderhor Fair

Has its day on the third Sunday in July. Festivities include dancing and a bridal procession by the famed old mill in Sonderhor.

WHERE TO STAY

The tourist office has listings of private guest houses as well as summer houses.

Sonderhor Kro

This is everyone's first choice, so book ahead. A member of the Relais & Chateaux group, the inn dates from the 1770s and is full of Danish thatched-roof charm. There are only seven rooms, but even if you do not stay here, you should take one meal in its excellent and inviting restaurant.

Krogarden

Located at Nordby, it is an old inn with comfortable rooms and a pleasant restaurant. The rooms here will be somewhat less expensive than at the Sonderhor Kro.

SILKEBORG AND THE LAKE DISTRICT

Tourist Office: *Torvet 9/ P.O. Box 950, 8600 Silkeborg.*

Surrounded by forests and lakes, Silkeborg is the largest town of the Danish Lake District in the middle of Jutland. The lake district is made up of several small, connected lakes and is hillier and prettier than much of southern Jutland. Americans looking for the Danish equivalent of Michigan or New England lakes might be disappointed, however. The towns of mid-Jutland are more livable than visitable, with lovely houses in the wooded hills and town centers that are pleasant and tranquil but not especially charming. Silkeborg has a large, open square with several pedestrian streets running off it. As in many of the cities in Denmark, these walking streets are pedestrian in every sense of the word, displaying only very ordinary merchandise in rather uninteresting shops. However, the food shops here are attractive. Silkeborg Harbor is small and pretty, situated on a narrow river.

WHAT TO SEE AND DO

The Silkeborg Museum

Situated in a pretty old manor house, this is a fine museum with a most extraordinary possession, the **Tollund Man**. If you come to Silkeborg only to see this ancient human, it will be worth the trip. The Tollund Man, the most famous of the three bog-bodies found in Bjaeldskovdal, lies curled on his side as if he were asleep and in such perfect condition, because of the preservative qualities of the bog in which he was found, that he seems almost alive. He was discovered in 1950 by two brothers who were cutting peat. When they found the body, it was so perfectly preserved that they called the police, imagining not-so-distant foul play. Archaeologists studying the Tollund Man and the Elling Woman, who was found in a nearby bog twelve years before the Tollund Man, have concluded that both were from the same period of the Iron Age and had been hanged, probably as a sacrifice to the gods. There also are other interesting exhibits in the museum, so allow time.

The Silkeborg Art Museum
The major exhibit is the collection of Asger Jorn, a Silkeborg native and the leader of the COBRA art movement. There are works by other contemporary artists also.

The Lake Steamers
It is possible to take short cruises on the lake in summertime. Hjejlen is the oldest operating paddle steamer in the world. In season, it sails at 10:00 a.m. and 1:45 p.m. on Sundays. At other times, you can take newer boats through the lakes.

Himmelbjerget
The name means "Sky Mountain," but this is a mountain only by Danish flatland standards. It is located at **Ry**, a small town that grew up in the 1870s when the railway connection between Silkeborg and Skanderborg was constructed. This is a good starting point for hiking through the area. Excursion boats make the trip from Ry to the Sky Mountain.

WHERE TO STAY

The Impala Hotel ★★★★
A good choice, two kilometers out of town. Facing the lake, a first-class resort hotel. A double room with bath will run about 800Dkr.

Hotel Dania ★★
Right in town on the square, this is an older hotel with a comfortably shabby lobby. The rooms are modern and not especially charming, but homey. A double with bath will run about 650 Dkr.

The Svostrup Kro
Located outside town, this is an old inn situated beside the river.
Inexpensive.

The Hotel Himmelbjerget
In Himmelbjerget, this is a venerable family hotel in the midst of the wooded lake area. Just 18 rooms, none with private bath. Open only from April to October.

The Silkeborg Tourist Office has a list of private accommodations at very low rates.

WHERE TO EAT

The restaurant at the **Hotel Himmelbjerget** at Himmelbjerg is highly recommended. The **Hotel Ny Hattenaes** has a restaurant which is reachable by boat. The **Impala Hotel** and the **Hotel Dania** also have agreeable restaurants. And **Spisehuset** in Silkeborg serves good, simple Danish food; **Godt Gemt** and **Hjorten** are also reliable spots in town.

ARHUS

Arhus Tourist Bureau, *Radhuset DK-8000 Arhus C. (at the foot of the City Hall tower). Open June 19–August 6 every day from 9:00 a.m. to 9:00 p.m.; August 7–September 10, every day, 9:00 a.m.–7:00 p.m. Open May 1–June 18, Monday-Friday, 9:00 a.m.–5:00 p.m.; Saturday, 9:00 a.m.– noon. The rest of the year the office is open Monday–Friday from 9:00 a.m. to 4:30 p.m.; Saturday, 9:00 a.m.–noon.*

DIRECTORY

Banks • Banks are open Monday, Tuesday, Wednesday, and Friday from 9:30 a.m. to 4:00 p.m.; Thursday, 9:30 a.m. to 6:00 p.m.

Car Rental • InterRent, *Sonder Alle 35,* ☎ *06 12 35 00.*

Doctors • ☎ *06 19 21 22* from 4:00 p.m. to 7:30 a.m. ☎ *06 12 72 11* from 7:30 a.m. to 4:00 p.m.

Emergency • ☎ *000* or *06 12 12 22.*

Hotel Booking • Information on hotels and private accommodations is available through the tourist office.

Market • Every Wednesday and Saturday morning at Bispetorov near the cathedral.

Police • ☎ *06 13 30 00.*

Taxis • Taxis with English speaking drivers can be ordered through the tourist board. ☎ *06 12 16 00* or direct ☎ *06 15 11 00.*

Insider Tip

Apply at the tourist office on your arrival if you would like to be invited into a Danish home for an evening of conversation, coffee and cake. The tourist office can arrange home exchanges between Danish and foreign families.

Arhus grew because of the railway and harbor, which expanded industrial and agricultural shipping from this center on the east coast of Jutland. Merchants, seeing the potential, began investing in the city, and it has grown to be the second largest town in Denmark. It is a somber, even unattractive town with heavy brick buildings and dark streets, brought to life mainly by the university and its students, and redeemed by its surroundings—the sea and the lush forests of eastern Jutland. While there is enough of interest to keep the traveler occupied, Arhus itself is more of a commercial than a tourist center; the real beauty of Arhus can be found in its surroundings, with its thick beech woods and its miles of beach. So my advice to travelers is to stay outside the center of town, perhaps venturing into the beautiful, wooded Marselisborg section. Arhus makes an excellent base for exploration of this area of Jutland as it is well situated for trips to Randers, Viborg, Ebeltoft and Silkeborg. The very helpful tourist office can help you plan trips to the many manor houses in the area.

GETTING THERE

Tirstrup Airport is 50 kilometers east of Arhus and has frequent daily service to and from Copenhagen. Train/ferry service runs from Kalundborg on Zealand to Arhus. Express bus service goes between Copenhagen (Valby Station) and Arhus via Ebeltoft and Odden.

GETTING AROUND

Arhus has a well-developed public transport system, which is important because much of the interest of Arhus lies outside the center. The yellow buses run within the city, to the suburbs and the surrounding areas, and travelers can buy a money-saving **Multi-Ride** ticket at various newsstands, the tourist office in the Town Hall or from the city office of Arhus Public Transport (Arhus Sporveje). Timetables with maps are also available at those points for a nominal fee. The tourist office has worked with the bus company to arrange city and outer ring tours by bus. Some of these are listed below. You can also buy a **Holiday 7-day Bus Pass** valid for all bus routes within the municipal boundaries of Arhus, with free entrance to several museums and activities of Arhus, including **The Old Town Museum** and the **Prehistory Museum**. *Issued from late June to early August; 120Dkr. for adults, 65Dkr. for people under 18 years of age.*

SIGHTSEEING TOURS

Round about the City Tour
A 2-1/2-hour bus tour to all the city's attractions with time allowed to walk around the Old Town and to visit the cathedral and the lobby of the Concert Hall and out to Marselisborg Castle. A multilingual guide accompanies the tour. *Departures daily at 10:00 a.m. from the tourist office from June 19 to September 22.* The 3-1/2 hour tour includes the above plus the beech forests to the south and the Moesgaard Prehistory Museum with the 2000-year-old Grauballe Man and the reconstructions of Viking houses.

Guided City Walking Tour of Old Arhus
Conducted by a multilingual guide who will take you to the Viking

Museum, the Church of Our Lady and the old streets of Arhus. *From June 22 to August, Thursday from 2:00 p.m. to 4:00 p.m.* Departure from the tourist office.

Excursions by public transport from Arhus

Available to Mols, Ebeltoft, and the Lake District. The tourist office sells 24-hour tourist tickets valid for all routes in the county. There is also a brochure available at the tourist office with suggestions for sightseeing and bus schedules. The tourist office will be happy to assist you in planning a driving tour should you have a car.

Castle Tour

Offered from June 21 until the beginning of August. Bus tours depart from the tourist office at 1:30 every Wednesday to the baroque castle of Clausholm and to the Renaissance castle of Rosenholm.

WHAT TO SEE AND DO

Den Gamle By

This is one of the outstanding open-air museums of Scandinavia and is reason in itself to come to Arhus. The museum consists of 65 old buildings from all over Denmark and constitutes a living picture of life and period design from the late 16th until the 20th century. *Open all year but the hours vary. In June, July and August, every day from 9:00 a.m. to 5:00 p.m. In September, every day from 10:00 a.m. to 5:00 p.m. The rest of the year it is open weekdays, Sunday and holidays, but the hours change so check with the tourist office. Bus No. 3 to the Old Town.*

City Hall

The surprising lightness and airiness of this contemporary building strikes a contrast with the more somber side of Arhus. Some love it; others hate it. You decide. *Tours of the Council Chamber and the Wedding Room are available from mid-June to early September, Monday–Friday, at 4:00 p.m. Visitors can also go up into the tower in the summer months at noon and 2:00 p.m.*

Arhus Cathedral

Built in the mid-15th century, this is the longest church in Denmark, with a nave of almost 85 feet. The altarpiece was carved by Bernt Notke in 1479 and the frescoes date from the early 16th century. *Open May–September every day, except Sunday and holidays, from 9:30 a.m. to 4:00 p.m. The rest of the year from 10:00 a.m. to 3:00 p.m.*

The Church of Our Lady

A Gothic church with an altarpiece by the well-known woodcarver, Claus Berg. The real interest here is the crypt church, which was discovered in 1955 beneath the choir of the larger church and has been found to be the first stone church in Arhus, built around the year 1060. There is a cloister church here as well. *All the churches are open May–August, weekdays from 10:00 a.m. to 4:00 p.m., and Saturday, 10:00 a.m. to 2:00 p.m. The* remainder of the year, it is open weekdays from 10:00 a.m. to 2:00 p.m.; Saturday, 10:00 a.m. to noon.

The Viking Museum

The remains of a 1000-year-old Viking rampart were discovered during the construction of the Andelsbanken building on Clemstorv. In the basement of the bank, you will see a reconstruction of the ramparts with a typical Viking house. *Open Monday, Tuesday, Wednesday and Friday from 8:00 a.m. to 4:00 p.m.; Thursday, 8:00 a.m. to 6:00 p.m.*

Arhus Art Museum

Fine collection of Danish art from 18th century to contemporary, in addition to works of German and American artists. *Open every day but Monday from 10:00 a.m. to 5:00 p.m. Take Bus No. 1, 2, 3, 6 or 9 to Norreport.*

The Women's Museum

Changing exhibits on women's life and work in rural and urban environments with emphasis on the 20th century. There are also exhibits of works by women artists. This is one of the few such museums in the world. It is located next to the cathedral in the old police station. *Open daily from noon to 5:00 p.m. Closed Monday.*

Moesgaard Prehistory Museum

In the forest south of Arhus. Here you will find the 2000-year-old Grauballe Man, a well-preserved bog man from the Iron Age. In addition to archeological exhibitions from the Stone Age, the Bronze Age, the Iron Ages and the Viking Era, there is also a "Prehistoric Trail" running through the forest and park that leads past layouts from the Stone and Bronze Ages, and several reconstructed houses from the Iron and Viking Ages. *Open* *from the end of March through the first week in September, daily from 10:00 a.m. to 5:00 p.m. The rest of the year, it is open on Sunday, Tuesday and Friday from 10:00 a.m. to 5:00 p.m. Bus No. 6 from main railway station to Moesgaard Museum.*

Marselisborg Palace and Park

A summer residence of the Danish Royal Family. The park, but not the palace, is always open to visitors from sunrise to sunset. When the queen is in residence the Royal Guards are present, and the changing of the guard takes place every day at noon. Behind the palace is an arboretum.

Tivoli Friheden

An amusement park at the edge of the Marselisborg woods. Rides, concerts, revues, in a pretty garden setting. *Open April 15 to mid-August. Take Bus No. 4 to Skovbrynet.*

The Arhus Festival

This festival is held every year during the first week in September, and includes concerts, ballet and opera, as well as street festivals, puppet shows and an old-fashioned market in Old Town. Also jazz and reggae and sporting events, including the Marselis Cross Country Run, which has as many as 10,000 participants each year.

WHERE TO STAY

The hotel situation in Arhus is not especially good. Aside from the Royal, which is expensive, there is not really a good choice in town other than rather impersonal, commercial hotels.

The Royal Hotel

A traditional hotel with a small, lovely lobby crowned by a beautiful stained-glass window. The rooms are well furnished, light and airy, though a bit small. The Queen's Garden restaurant is bright and attractive, but I have not eaten there. There is gambling in the casino of the hotel.

Expensive.

The Atlantic

The location of this modern hotel at the harbor is not particularly attractive, but the rooms are nicely decorated and comfortable. Restaurant, pub and night club.   *Moderate to expensive.*

Hotel Marselis

Strandvejen 25. Located a few minutes out of town on the beach, this is a stunning modern hotel with luxurious rooms and a fine restaurant.

Very expensive.

The Mission Hotel

The budget choice that the tourist office often seems to recommend, so I include it here with a warning: It is clean and adequate, but very dreary. Located by the railway station, which is a convenient but not pretty area.

WHERE TO EAT

Restaurant Mahler

Vestergade 39 • Another of Arhus' top spots. Excellent French cuisine in a 19th-century building in town. A three-course meal will run about 300Dkr. *The restaurant is not open Sunday or Monday, and it closes in July.*

De Fire Arstider (The Four Seasons)

Aboulevarden 47 • A charmingly decorated restaurant in the middle of town. Jonna Hald, one of Denmark's best-known women chefs and a partner in the restaurant, holds court here with the emphasis on fish and shellfish dishes. *Closed Sunday.*   *Expensive.*

Hotel Marselis

Strandvejen 25, outside town • Cool and sleek, and right on the water. The food is generally very good, though the service can be a bit harried if there are large parties in the dining room.   *Expensive.*

Queen's Garden

In the Royal Hotel • A pretty, winter garden setting with good food. *Closed Sunday.*   *Expensive.*

Munkestuen

Klostertorv 5 • Proprietress Lise Poulsen fills the diminutive kitchen with her hospitable presence and casually serves up some of the best down-to-earth Danish fare around. This is a simple, friendly restaurant where you cannot help talking to the other diners, especially if you come for lunch in the outdoor courtyard. Inside, you can watch Lise Poulsen perform her magic with all fresh ingredients grown locally. Diners and visitors to the bar seem to wander in and out of the kitchen, and Mrs. Poulsen just keeps on cooking. On the bar, in beautiful decanters, are varieties of schnapps made from berries friends have brought. At lunch, Mrs. Poulsen might glance in the refrigerator and ask her guests what they feel like eating. The day we ate here, it was a variety of herring from Bornholm. Dinner is a set menu, which changes each night. There are only 40 seats, so it is a good idea to book ahead for dinner. *Moderate.*

Musikshusets Restaurant
Located in the concert hall, there is a cafe and restaurant here.

Moderate.

SHOPPING

Most of the shopping is on the complex of walking streets in the center of town.

Handicraft City Walk
The Arhus Tourist Office has joined with several artists to map out a walking tour of studios and handicraft shops. *Be sure to check on opening hours as they vary, but most are open weekdays from 10:00 a.m. until at least 4:00 p.m., and Saturdays until noon or 1:00 p.m.*

Bogform Helle Stisen
Jaegergardsgade 48, where handmade bookcovers and stationery are sold.

Keramikvaerkstedet Boutique and Workshop
Also on Jaegergardsgade, offers porcelain, stoneware and pottery.

Kokon
Ostboulevarden 1, a textile workshop, and shop with glass and wooden toys in addition to fabrics.

Lertoj
A cooperative ceramics boutique at *Badstuegade 4.*

Ase Rise
Boutique and workshop, at *Mejlgade 5,* sells pottery and glass.

Keramiker Kirsten Sloth
Amaliegade 19, a boutique and workshop with household items, teapots, jars, candlesticks, etc.

Johan Torp
Skt. Clemens Torv 17, a jeweler with original designs in silver and gold.

Volden 4
This shop sells stoneware, silver jewelry and wearable art.

EXCURSION FROM ARHUS
EBELTOFT

Ebeltoft Tourist Office: *in the square.*

This tiny town, one of Denmark's oldest, is a charmer, with an oak-beamed town hall, half-timbered houses and inviting gardens. Ebeltoft also makes a good base for enjoying the countryside and outdoor activities of Jutland. There is a golf course outside of town, and hiking and cycling trails across the countryside with its beech woods, open fields and sandy beaches. You can also take the time to explore some of the attractions of the town.

Old Town Hal
Rebuilt in 1789 and now houses a museum with an archeological exhibit and a collection from Thailand. *Open all year from 10:00 a.m. to 4:00 p.m.*

Missers Doll Museum
Houses an extensive collection of 19th- and 20th-century dolls, doll clothes and toys. *Open 10:00 a.m.–5:00 p.m. during the high season.*

Thorsager Round Church
Built in the 12th century.

Old Dyers Farm
Visit an old dye works dating from the 17th century, with living quarters furnished as they were in the 18th century. *Open all year from 10:00 a.m. to 4:00 p.m.*

Old Frigate Jutland
A 19th-century boat. *Open April–September from 10:00 a.m. to 8:00 p.m. Off-season, it is open on weekdays from 10:00 a.m. to 8:00 p.m.*

Night Watchman
Sings the hour every night at 8:00, 9:00 and 10:00 p.m. in front of the Old Town Hall.

WHERE TO STAY

The Hotel Hvide Hus
A lovely modern hotel on the beach with a golf course nearby, a swimming pool and sauna. All rooms with private baths, TV and minibars. Most with terraces. Doubles run about 880Dkr.

The Hotel Ebeltoft Strand
Also on the beach, with an indoor pool. All rooms have private baths, mini-bar and TV. The restaurant serves French cuisine. There is also a bar and a sitting room with an open fireplace. Prices will run about the same as the Hvide Hus.

ON THE WAY NORTH

The area north of Arhus, known as North Jutland, seems almost an entity unto itself with its sweep of dunes and grasses against the sea and its beautiful manor houses, which seem to appear from nowhere on the broad, sweeping landscape. At any tourist office in North Jutland you can pick up a tourist ticket that entitles you to an unlimited number of rides on all NT bus lines and private trains throughout the county of North Jutland. 60Dkr. for adults, 30Dkr. for children and senior citizens. These tickets are only available during June, July and August.

RANDERS AND MARIAGER

On your way north from Arhus to Aalborg, you will pass **Randers**, a large, industrial city with some redeeming streets of old half-timbered houses. But if you prefer to skip the big city and its hassles, you could veer off the E3 toward **Mariager**, a much more appealing town of half-timbered houses and cobbled streets. One of the reasons for heading this way, however, is to stop off at the **Hvidsten Kro**, a fabled old inn with just 12 rooms and a well-known kitchen. This is an old farmhouse, its dining room furnished with primitive antiques and plenty of old copper. The restaurant is known for its five-course meal, which should keep you going for the next few days.

AALBORG

Tourist Office: *Ostera 8. Open Monday–Friday from 9:00 a.m. to 4:30 p.m.; Saturday, 9:00 a.m.–noon. Open June 19–August 18, Monday–Friday, 9:00 a.m.–8:00 p.m.; Saturday 9:00 a.m.–2:00 p.m.; Sunday 10:00 a.m.–1:00 p.m. The tourist office will be happy to help you with car and bicycle tours of the surrounding area.*

DIRECTORY

Banks • Open Monday–Friday from 9:30 to 4:00 p.m.; Thursday until 6:00 p.m. At other times, the tourist office will exchange foreign currency.

Doctor • ☎ *98 13 62 11.* Monday, Tuesday, Thursday and Friday from 4:00 p.m. to 7:00 a.m.; Wednesday, 7:00 p.m. to 7:00 a.m. Weekends and public holidays, day and night.

Emergency • ☎ *000* or *98 12 22 22.*

Pharmacy • 24-hour pharmacy: *Budolfi Apotek at the corner of Vesterbro and Algade,* ☎ *98 12 06 77.*

Shopping • Monday–Thursday from 9:30 a.m. to 5:30 p.m; Friday until 7:00 p.m. or 8:00 p.m.; Saturday, from 9:00 a.m. to noon or 1:00 p.m.

As might be expected of the foremost producer of schnapps in the world, Aalborg, the home of Akvavit, is a jolly place, a fjord-side city with a sophisticated flavor. It successfully blends modern with old, and seems dedicated to the Danish philosophy that everyone should have a good time. There are more than 300 restaurants, and enough night spots to keep you going long past Cinderella's bedtime. The center of town is easily walked in a few minutes. An ingenious arrangement of pedestrian streets and a street devoted to restaurants and night spots makes this, Denmark's fourth largest city, a most manageable and pleasant place. In addition, most of the sightseeing past the beautiful old buildings and to the churches can be done on foot. Just outside the center is a large park area where the North Jutland Art Museum and Zoo are located. The Vikings were the first settlers at this site at the narrowest point of the Lim Fjord. The city always flourished as a busy trading center and the wealth of the town over the years is evident in some of the lovely old buildings that have survived to this day.

GETTING THERE

There are frequent air connections between Aalborg and Copenhagen. The airport is located just across the fjord at Norresundby. A bus leaves the Coach Station (Rutebilstationen) 40 minutes prior to flight departures.

SIGHTSEEING TOURS

Castle Tour: From around July 6 to mid-August, a bus tour to Voergard Manor, the town of Saeby and Dronninglund Castle departs every Thursday at 1:00 p.m. from Adlegade. Multilingual guide. The trip lasts approximately five hours. Buy tickets in advance at Aalborg tourist office.

A **bus tour** of the city departs Adlegade at 11:00 a.m., Monday–Friday from mid-June to mid-August; English-speaking guide available Tuesday and Thursday only. On other days, the tour is given in Danish and German only.

From mid-June until the beginning of September the **Old Steam Railway** runs on Sunday between Aalborg and the Greenland Harbor, which is the center for import and export with Greenland. The trip leaves at 2:00 p.m. and lasts about two hours.

At the tourist office you can pick up an excellent pamphlet, "Good Old Aalborg", which describes several **walking tours** of the old parts of town. The pamphlet was compiled by local historian Svend B. Olesen and the sketches were done by architect Christian Lomborg. The pamphlet will guide you on several easily walked tours and fill you in on the history and anecdotes that surround the landmarks of Aalborg.

WHAT TO SEE AND DO

The Nordjyllands Kunstmuseum

(North Jutland Art Museum) • This stunning, contemporary building, designed by Finnish architects Alvar and Elissa Aalto in collaboration with Jean Jacques Baruel, houses the foremost collection of international contemporary art in Jutland.

Jens Bang's House

Considered the finest domestic Renaissance building in northern Europe, this five-story, ornately decorated house was built in 1624 by a prominent merchant, Jens Bang. It is said that Mr. Bang retaliated against his enemies by having their caricatures carved into the facade of the house. He was evidently miffed at never being asked to sit on the town council, so on the south facade of his house, facing the Town Hall, he commissioned a carving of his face with the tongue sticking out.

Aalborg Town Hall

The beautiful, yellow rococo building is the second town hall built on the site. The first was the building at which Jens Bang directed his venomous tongue. On the north side, the date 1759 is inscribed and, on the front, the year 1762. The square in front of the building is the oldest square in Aalborg. This was where the courthouse stood and where executions took place. The stone post in the square is the zero kilometer mark from which distances in Aalborg are measured.

The Budolfi Cathedral

The oldest portions of this church date from around 1100, but most of it was built in the early 15th century. Its baroque spire added in the 18th century is a trademark of Aalborg.

The Monastery of the Holy Ghost

Built in 1431, this is Denmark's oldest social institution. There was a section for monks and one for nuns, whose duty it was to care for the elderly and ill. Today the monastery houses senior citizens.

The Aalborg Historical Museum

Exhibits on Aalborg history, including a fine collection of silver made in Aalborg, and a glass exhibit. The Aalborg Room from 1602 is an outstanding example of a Renaissance interior.

The Church of Our Lady

The tower, Lunge's Chapel and the murals in the west gable are the only remains from the original church, which was built around 1100. The present church was built in 1878. The granite portal on Peder Barkes Gade is evidence of the early origins and Norman influence of the church and is the oldest work of art in Aalborg. Inside the church near the north entrance is the tomb of Mayor Jorgen Olufsen. Notice the epitaphs on the side of the original chapel. Of interest are the epitaphs of Severinus Oali and Johannes Joannis, and next to those, one for Dorte Jensdatter who had been married to both men and who was burned as a witch in 1620.

The Danes Worldwide Archives

Located next to the Church of Our Lady, the archives contain the principal collection in Denmark on emigration history. Letters, books and photos from Danish emigrants around the world. *Open May–August, Monday–Thursday from 9:00 a.m. to 4:00 p.m.; Friday, 9:00 a.m. to 2:00 p.m. The rest of the year, Monday only, from 9:00 a.m. to 8:00 p.m.*

Jorgen Olufsen's House

No. 6 Maren Turis Gade • Considered the best-preserved Renaissance merchant's house in Denmark, this three-story structure was built in 1616. You can still see the hook from which the scales hung at the entrance so that customers could watch their purchases being weighed. Notice the ornamentation on the stone gable front where the initials of Jorgen Olufsen, who built this house, have been carved. Olufsen was the brother of Jens Bang, and the tale is told that when Jens Bang saw this house, he was goaded into outdoing his brother by building his more spectacular five-story house. The figure in the niche above is known as the Aalborg Girl.

Aalborghus Castle

Located at the harbor, the castle was built between 1539 and 1585 by King Christian III. It is now the residence and office of the Lord Lieutenant and the county administration. *The courtyard is open from 8:00 a.m. until sunset. The dungeon beneath the coach house, the underground passages and the ramparts are open Monday–Friday from 8:00 a.m. to 4:00 p.m.*

Lindholm Hoje

Across the fjord just beyond Norresundby is a large cemetery from the Viking Era and the Iron Age. Most of the graves are cremation graves in which the ashes of the deceased were buried along with his possessions in a tomb surrounded by stones in either triangular or oval shapes. During the Viking era, the stones were set in the shape of a ship, with large stones at the bow and stern. North of the cemetery are excavations of the settlement, with wood-paved roads and the post-holes of the houses evident. A coin dated from around 1050 was found in the course of these excavations. Many of the artifacts found here are now in the Aalborg Historical Museum. There is a shop at Lindholm Hoje where you can pick up a more detailed pamphlet on the cemetery and settlement. Bus No. 1 and then a short walk.

PARKS AND RECREATION

A large green area consisting of Kildeparken and Molleparken trims the city with a lush recreational area. It is here that you will find the zoo, the Aalborg Tower and the North Jutland Art Museum.

Aalborg Zoo

In Molleparkvej. The second largest zoo in Scandinavia houses animals from the world over. *Open all year round. Restaurant.*

Kildeparken

Developed in 1802, and has many sculptures by Danish artists including works of Thorvaldsen and Anne Marie Carl Nielsen.

Aalborg Tower

Offers the best vantage point for an eagle's-eye view of Aalborg. *Open last week in April to mid-June, and mid-August to mid-September from 10:00 a.m. to 5:00 p.m. From mid-June to mid-August, 10:00 a.m. to 7:00 p.m.*

Tivoliland. An amusement park with rides, shooting galleries, restaurants and gardens, in addition to **China Town**, with a China Fun House, gift shop and restaurant.

Fourth of July Celebration, Danish Style takes place every July 4th at Rebild National Park, about 20 miles south of Aalborg. Here you will also find a museum of Danish emigration.

WHERE TO STAY

Hvide Hus Hotel (The White House Hotel)   ★★★★
Set in Kilden Park, about a 10-minute walk from the center of town, this 20-year-old hotel has just been renovated and looks brand new. The rooms

are large and well furnished, and the large doubles have two bathrooms so they can serve as family rooms. With a pull-out sofa, they often accommodate four people. Ask for a parkside room, as such are quieter and the view is beautiful. The Kilden Restaurant on the 15th floor has a lovely view, but the restaurant was empty when I saw it and I did not eat there. Outdoor pool. Doubles are between 900Dkr. and 1000Dkr.

Limfjordshotellet

Located near the harbor, this is a bright, contemporary hotel with attractive but small rooms. The hotel is 10 years old, with a new section that was built four years ago. All the rooms are pleasant. The ones in the older wing tend to be larger, though they can be noisy on weekends as the hotel is located in a busy section of Aalborg, and the town is very lively on Friday and Saturday nights. To avoid noise, request a room on the top floor. All rooms with private bath, TV and minibar. The piano bar in the lobby is open until 1:00 a.m. And there is now a casino offering roulette, baccarat and black jack. The restaurant serves a set menu only. A double room will run about 850Dkr. *Expensive.*

Hotel Phoenix ★★★★

Well-located in the center of town on Vesterbro near Jens Bang's House, this is a venerable, elegant old hostelry. The hotel was the home of Brigadier Villiam von Halling, notorious for the cruelty with which he treated his servants and wife, and for the fact that he bought himself a title and the rank of Brigadier. It was from the money von Halling paid for his titles that the King of Denmark was able to pave Kongens Nytorv in Copenhagen. One story claims the Brigadier chose the brides for all the peasants on his farm and reserved the right to spend the wedding night with the bride. The rooms in the Brigadier's house, which is now the core of the hotel, are comfortable in a simple, old-fashioned way, with modern, good-sized bathrooms. The lobby is cozy and there are three popular restaurants here. Double rooms about 900Dkr. *Expensive.*

The Slottshotellet

Located on the harbor, this is a modern airy place with simple and comfortable, though small, rooms and a bright lobby containing a small bar and cafe. All rooms with private bath and TV. Double rooms run from 780Dkr. to 995Dkr.

The Hotel Scheelsminde ★★★

Just outside of town, this is a very delightful spot, and if you do not stay here, at least try to visit for a meal in the large, beautiful dining room, which sits amidst the trees and overlooks the gardens of the hotel. The hotel itself was built as a manor house in 1808 by Christian Paul Scheel. It was eventually given to a regimental surgeon by the king of Denmark. In 1920, the estate was bought by Akvavit as an experimental farm for growing potatoes. In 1959, a group of Aalborg businessmen bought it, and in 1961 opened it as the Motel Scheelsminde, run by the Jensen family. In 1977, the Jensens bought the hotel; their son Peter now manages it. Mrs. Jensen is Swiss and brings her country's hotel expertise to Scheelsminde. The 60 rooms are small, simple and comfortable, but not luxurious. It is the setting and the amenities of the hotel itself that make this a special place to stay. An indoor pool and tennis court are under construction. In the garden, a family of pets, including two African mountain goats, linger and occasionally find their way into the elegant, English-style lobby. Moderate. The double rooms are about 750Dkr. and 1000Dkr. for a family of four. All include breakfast, and all but one room have private baths. There is bus service here from the center of town at least every half hour.

WHERE TO EAT

Jomfru Ane Gade is the street devoted to fun. Here you will find a variety of restaurants for every taste. Aalborg is a lively city and this is the center of much of the celebrating. It is a pleasant, safe street and you can feel comfortable in any of the restaurants and night spots. Among my choices along this street are:

Faklen

Understated elegance with an English flavor in one of the oldest buildings on the street. The panelled dining room is cozy and inviting, with excellent food and pleasant service. The daily menu of two courses will run about 150Dkr., with three courses about 170Dkr. À la carte entrees range from 148Dkr. to 200Dkr.

Cafeen

This casual restaurant has the look of a Parisian brasserie. The menu is varied with interesting and well-prepared seafood dishes a specialty. A three-course set meal will run about 140Dkr.

Dufy

Located above Cafeen, Dufy has a somewhat more formal ambience than its downstairs sister. The same kitchen serves both restaurants.

Regensen

A family restaurant with casual service and a lively atmosphere. Steaks and beer are the order of the day, though there are plenty of other choices as well. On Saturday nights, there is music and dancing.   *Moderate.*

Fyrtojet

A small, vaulted, candlelit restaurant in an old building. It is a cozy and popular place. A two-course meal will run about 125Dkr. There is also a glass-roofed winter garden, which is pleasant all year round.

The Restaurant Halling

In the Hotel Phoenix. This is the hotel's premier restaurant. The excellence of the food here has been certified by the award of the Cordon Bleu de Saint Esprit Star.   *Expensive.*

Pista Pasta

An informal Italian restaurant in the Phoenix Hotel. Casual service with a pasta buffet and bottles of wine on the table.

Scheelsminde

A gracious, elegant dining room in the country manor hotel overlooking the hotel's garden. There is also a tiny, English club-style bar just off the lobby. The restaurant is a member of the Chaine des Rotisseurs Gastronomic Society.   *Expensive.*

Duus Vinjaelder

A wine cellar rather than a restaurant, but you can order light snacks, and you should come here just to see it, as the wine cellar is located in the cellars of the Jens Bang's House.

NIGHTLIFE

Once again, Jomfru Ane Gade is the place. You can simply wander up and down this street and pick your spot. **Cafe Rendez Vous**, **American Bar** and the **Music Cafe** are all located at 5 Jomfru Ane Gade. Lunch is also served here. **Ambassadeur** is the largest nightclub in Denmark, with four different choices, from disco to more sedate dancing.

EXCURSIONS FROM AALBORG

THE MANOR HOUSES OF NORTH JUTLAND

If you are interested in visiting old manor houses, you will find several in North Jutland, and you might want to meander on your way to and back from Skagen in order to take in a few of these. Not all of them are open to public, but visitors are welcome to walk through the grounds at most of them.

At Viborg, in the middle of North Jutland, is **Tjele Home Farm**, set near the lake of Tjele Langso, east of Viborg. This is a 16th-century farm, and is known as the inspiration for many of Denmark's writers. The house is not open, but you can stroll through the grounds all year round. Northeast of Viborg near Skive is **Spottrup Castle**, one of the oldest manor houses in Denmark, built around 1500. The castle and garden are open during summer months. **Krabbesholm** in Skive is now a folk high school. The oldest part of the manor house was built in 1560, and the two wings were added in 1755. The banquet hall is decorated in the unique Jutland rococo style.

East of Skive and Viborg, in the vicinity of Randers, **Stovringgard Convent**, a Renaissance-style building surrounded by a moat, was built in 1622 and became a home for the unmarried daughters of the aristocracy in the 18th century. **Gammel Estrup** was built in 1960 and now contains the Jutland Manor House Museum and the Danish Museum of Agriculture.

At Aalborg, you will find **Aalborghus Castle**, which was built in 1539 by King Christian III. The courtyard and dungeon are open to the public. **Dronninglund Castle**, northwest of Aalborg near the forest of Dronninglund, was built 800 years ago as a Benedictine convent. It is a seminar center and, in summertime, is used as a hotel. The rooms are well-furnished and the public rooms are filled with lovely antiques. A double room with bath runs about 600Dkr. with breakfast. But you must check ahead, as it is not always available as a hotel if seminars are in progress.

Voergard, on the way north from Aalborg, is considered one of the most beautiful Renaissance buildings in Denmark. It contains an impressive collection of European paintings and objets d'art. Open to the public during the summer months. A bus tour of Voergard is available from Aalborg.

Saebygaard, west of Saeby, on the way north from Aalborg, is a well-furnished Renaissance manor house. Open to the public during the month of July.

Bratskov Manor House in Brovst, east of Aalborg, was a farm until 1948. It now is a cultural center with a museum in the medieval cellar and is open to the public.

Drivers can choose to go north from Aalborg by either the west or east coast. Going east, you can take the E3 to Hjallerup, then 559 to Dronninglund to take a look at that manor house. If you want to stop there for lunch, you must call ahead; otherwise, lunch is not served, and even if you do call, you might be informed that they are not serving that day. From Dronninglund, pick up 541 to Saeby, where you can stop at another manor house, and then get back on the E3 to Frederikshavn.

FREDERIKSHAVN

Tourists may find themselves in this east coast town on their way to and from Norway and Sweden, for there are ferry connections to Gothenborg and Oslo here. Frederikshavn is also one of the largest fishing harbors in Denmark. Most tourists are here simply to make connections on their way to somewhere else, but if you have some time, visit the **Bangsbo Museum**, which occupies an ancient estate. It belonged to the church, but in 1573, a private citizen took it over. When he died, his widow built the main building. The present structure is built upon the foundations of the original building. At the turn of the century, it was a popular gathering spot for artists and writers. The collections include an exhibit of the history of Frederikshavn; a display of jewelry made from human hair; a reconstruction of a Victorian living room and a more rustic room from the area of Frederikshavn. There is also a Viking-style ship built in the 12th century; a carriage collection; a maritime exhibit; and an exhibition on World War II, depicting the German occupation and the Resistance movement. *Open every day from 10:00 a.m. to 5:00 p.m. Closed Monday, November–March.*

WHERE TO STAY

The Hotel Frederikshavn

The newest name in town. A modern hotel in an old building, it boasts a spectacular indoor swimming pool with a wave machine, whirlpool and sauna. All rooms with private baths, TV, minibars and hairdryers. *In the center of town.* **Expensive.**

The Jutlandia

Overlooking the harbor. This is a modern hotel with 105 rooms, all with private bath, TV/VCR and a restaurant with a fine harbor view. There is bus service from the hotel to the Aalborg Airport. *Expensive.*

The Motel Lisboa

On the south edge of town. This is a modern and comfortable motel with attractive, bright, contemporary rooms all with private baths, TV/VCR. A double room will run about 600Dkr. *Moderate.*

From Frederikshavn you can pick up road No. 40, which will take you up to Skagen through **Albaek**, a cute, tiny town on the east coast. You might want to stop at the **Albaek Kro**, which has a cozy restaurant, white walls, dark woodwork and red velvet furnishings against deep-set windows overlooking a garden. From Albaek, it is an easy drive along the coast to Skagen. You will see few trees, perhaps an evergreen here and there and silver, feathery grasses along the dunes.

SKAGEN

Skagen Tourist Office: *Sct. Laurentiivej 18 in the middle of town. At the tourist office, pick up a brochure with a map indicating the interesting old areas of town suitable for walking tours.*

Skagen (pronounced Skane), at the tip of Denmark, is the spot where the Skagerrak and the Kattegat meet. Americans will find this town a Danish Cape Cod, with windswept beaches and flower-decked frame cottages, mostly yellow rather than the New England white or gray. The center of Skagen, with its walking street, is very much a resort town, with boutiques and art galleries. And Skagen has always attracted artists, as there is something special about the light, or so they say. Since Skagen's weather is no different from that of the rest of Denmark, sunlight here is capricious, giving way more often than not to mist, gray skies and rain. But the bright orange roofs and cozy clusters of cottages are welcoming, and the Danes, who are not especially given to sunbathing and country-club sports, flock here for walks on the rain-drenched beaches or bicycle rides along the flat, windswept roads along the sea. And when the sun shines, it throws a glorious, luminescent light that seems reserved only for places at the ends of the earth.

The first person reputed to build a house at Skagen was a herdsman of wild horses, named Tronder. The town received a charter in 1413 and thrived during the Middle Ages. But by the beginning of the 19th century, the fortunes of Skagen had declined because of the drifting sands, which smothered the fields and even buried the houses. The few people who remained here lived from hand to mouth by fishing and salvaging whatever washed ashore from shipwrecks. It was the war with England in 1807 that briefly revived Skagen's fortunes when the privateers landed here for the 19th-century version of "R and R." Finally, just before the turn of the century, with the coming of the railway from Frederikshavn and the development of the harbor, Skagen came into its own. New Skagen is on the Kattegat side of the peninsula, and the old town (Gammel Skagen) is on the Skagerrak side.

WHAT TO SEE AND DO

Grenen

The main attraction for tourists is this point, where the Skagerrak and the Kattegat meet. Tourists come here to stand with a foot in two seas and you can do this, but be careful not to wade out more than a few feet. There are strict warnings against swimming here, as the currents are formidable. Jeep-pulled buses called Sandormen will take you out to the north tip of Skaw if you prefer not to walk. The ride out and back takes about 30 minutes including a 10-minute stay at the point. You should walk along the beaches of each coast to get a good look at the landscape, which is a tapestry of textures and colors, mostly varieties of green, from sea green to celadon, brightened here and there with heather and rose hips. There is a German bunker rising from the sand like a beached whale. **Drachmanns Grav** is out here as well. Holger Drachmann was a poet and artist who wrote one song for which he is known all over Denmark. You can walk out to his grave and then go on to the north point past the bunker.

The Skagen Museum

The museum is the other tourist drawing card, with a fine exhibition of the Skagen painters who worked in Skagen between the years of 1830 and 1928. *Open June, July and August from 10:00 a.m. to 6:00 p.m daily; April and October from 11:00 a.m. to 3:00 p.m.; May and September, 10:00 a.m. to 5:00 p.m.*

Drachmann's House

The painter/poet lived here during the last years of his life. *It is open to the public June to mid-September from 10:00 a.m. to 5:00 p.m daily.*

Michael and Anna Anchers House

The Anchers and their daughter Helga were all painters and worked in this house, built in 1884 and enlarged in 1914. The house has been restored to mirror the way it looked when it was occupied by this artistic family. *Open June 21–August 15 from 10:00 a.m. to 6:00 p.m. daily; April, 11:00 a.m. to 3:00 p.m.; May–June 20, 10:00 a.m. to 5:00 p.m., and October, 11:00 a.m. to 3:00 p.m.*

Skagen Fortidsminder (Open-air museum)

The house of a wealthy fisherman built in 1830 is open, as is the house once occupied by a much poorer fisherman and his family of 10. There is a 19th-century windmill here, a museum of fishing and a lifeboat station.

The Sand Buried Church

Only the tower of this 14th-century church, dedicated to St. Lawrence, is visible. Beneath the sands, the church remains a mystery and an invisible reminder of the drifting sands that have always threatened Skagen. It was after a brutal storm in 1775 that the congregation had to shovel its way into the church for every service. Finally, in desperation, the church fathers closed the church in 1795. Some of the stones were taken from the church and used in building houses in Skagen. The furnishings were sold at an auction in 1810, and the church's model ship is now hanging in the Arhus Cathedral.

The Fish Auction

This goes on at the docks every morning from 6:00 a.m. until about 9:00 a.m. For a look at more herring than you might ever have dreamed of seeing, drop by.

WHERE TO STAY

Your best bet is to inquire at the tourist office as there are many small hotels and private accommodations. **Brondums** is an old hotel with lots of atmosphere but small rooms without private baths. **The Strandhotellet** with nine pleasantly decorated rooms is recently renovated. You could also stay at the **Albaek Kro**, which is just a few minutes south of Skagen and is a pleasant, comfortable inn.

WHERE TO EAT

The **Skagen Fiske Restaurant**, an informal tavern, has a sand floor and also serves at outdoor tables. The thing to order here, especially at lunch, is a plate piled high with shrimp. The more formal dining room upstairs offers a variety of sophisticated fish dishes. The dining room of the **Hjorths Hotel**, a 100-year-old institution, is newly decorated with bare floors and white brick walls. The emphasis is on hearty presentations of fish and soups. Right in town, the **Bodilles Kro** is a pub-style restaurant with light snacks or full meals. Simple Danish fare. Inexpensive.

ON THE WAY SOUTH

Drive back along route 40 toward Albaek and pick up 597 just before Albaek for Hirtshals. Hirtshals is another ferry point for service to and from Norway and Sweden. At Hirtshals take Route 55 south to Lokken. This trip will take you through lovely farmland, a patchwork landscape of biscuit-colored grasses and dark green fields, and whitewashed churches with red roofs and square bell towers. A 10-kilometer side trip will bring you to the Rubjergknude, a 244-foot clay cliff where there is an old lighthouse and sand-drift museum. As you drive along the coast, you will see a landscape quite different from that of the east coast, with high cliffs and much rougher surf. The views from the dunes are spectacular and you should take time to walk up them. **Lokken** is a very Danish beach resort. The **Lokken Badehotel** looks like the best bet, but I was unable to see a room. Tourists are probably better off just coming here for a day at the beach and then returning to Aalborg, which is only 43 kilometers away. There are campgrounds here.

THE ISLAND OF BORNHOLM

Nordbornholms Turistbureau: *Kirkegade 6, DK 3770 Allinge.*

Though it floats in the Baltic, closer to southern Sweden than to the rest of Denmark, Bornholm, with its brightly painted, tile-roofed houses, narrow streets, and cozy fishing villages, is thoroughly Danish. However, there are some features that make Bornholm "Danish with a difference." The island boasts more hours of sunshine than any other spot in Denmark; pine woods fringe the purest white sand beaches in the country; and here you will also find the only rocky Danish coast. Plan to spend some time walking through the thick forests—Almindingen is Denmark's third largest forest. Rent a bicycle and tour the island, which is small enough to manage easily. It is said that Bornholm represents all faces of the Danish landscape, plus a little more.

The history buff will also find much of interest here. Bornholm's trademark is its round churches, which are unique to the island. These four cylindrical, white, stone structures, with their conical roofs, were important links in the island's medieval defenses, and have survived almost perfectly intact since the 10th and 11th centuries. The main defense, however, was the fortress **Hammershus**, built in 1255 by the archbishop of Lund, Sweden. Its magnificent ruins sit in splendor as the largest fortress ruins in northern Europe. The island is also laced with ancient grave mounds and monoliths.

Throughout history, Bornholm has found itself caught in the middle of conflict. For centuries during the Middle Ages, the island was the victim of pirate raids, and its round churches served as effective fortresses. In the year 1255, it became a protectorate of the bishop of Lund and was a pawn in the conflicts between Denmark and the see of Lund. The bishopric of Lund needed Bornholm, in particular Hammershus Fortress, and it was not until a violent conflict erupted in which 1000 Swedish inhabitants of the island were killed, that Denmark could claim Bornholm as its own.

During World War II, Bornholm suffered more than any other part of Denmark. The Nazis arrived on the island in April of 1940, and calmly took possession of all the hotels, casting the helpless islanders into despair and anger. The occupation lasted five years, yet through it all, a Bornholm branch of the Danish underground worked quietly to ensure that the island remained a port for Danish refugees going from Denmark to Sweden. No sabotage could occur; nothing could happen to arouse the suspicion or attention of the Nazis. The aim of the Bornholmers was to keep things as they were so that hundreds of Jews and other Danes threatened by the Gestapo would be able to leave safely for Sweden. The Bornholm residents suffered silently and deeply, and their ordeal continued even after the German occupation ended. On May 7 and 8, 1945, just as the island was celebrating the surrender of the German forces in Denmark, the Russians, believing the Germans on Bornholm would not be so quick to surrender to them, bombed the island. The Russians were correct in their assumption. The Germans had in fact refused to surrender to them, and had instead surrendered to the British, whom they were awaiting even as the Russian assault began. During these raids, 300 houses in Ronne were destroyed, and in Nexo almost all the houses were either destroyed or heavily damaged. The Russians occupied Bornholm for a year, a period that even Bornholmers too young to actually remember, resent bitterly.

GETTING THERE

The most efficient way is to fly. **Danair** has several daily departures every day to Ronne. Flying time is 35 minutes. Overnight ferry service is available from Copenhagen with some day service in peak periods. The boat trip takes seven hours.

GETTING AROUND

If you have the time and energy, biking is a fine way to see the island. Bicycles can be rented in all the major towns and at the Fredensborg Hotel near the Ronne airport. Otherwise, bus service crisscrosses the terrain. BAT bus has hourly connections between the major towns and also connects to all ferry arrivals and departures. Special one- or seven-day tickets are available at reduced prices. BAT has a tour guide called *Through Thick and Thin* with suggestions for walks, and also offers a Handicrafts and Arts bus that stops at the working exhibitions on the island. *For information: BAT "Det rode Parkhus," Snellemark 30/3700 Ronne.* Travelers wishing to visit the island of **Christianso** can get there by ferry from Allinge and Gudhjem from May 15 to September 15 and from Svaneke all year-round.

The towns and sights are listed in the order that tourists will come to them when traveling northwest from Ronne and then southeast around the island.

RONNE

This 650-year-old market town is the "capital" of Bornholm. It is a port town with a natural harbor situated between two barrier reefs. The old part of town is near the harbor, and the old streets are still there, much as they were in medieval times. The church, not an old one, is located in the old part of town, and Vimmelskaftet, a winding street running south from the church, is the site of many well-preserved 19th-century houses. A very pretty tour would be to explore Lakesegade, at the north end of town, and then go down to the fishing and yacht harbor Norrekas. The main square was built in 1834 and is neoclassical in design.

As you walk through town, notice some of the houses. **No. 11 Sondergade** is a fine example of an old sea captain's house, with its three-bayed attic and baroque-style segmented gable. There is an observation tower on the roof. **No. 12 Sondergade** is the old guardhouse, built in 1744 from stone taken from Hammershus. **No. 7 Lakesegade**, which used to be the Erichsenskegaard, an old residence, is now a museum with interiors as they were during the time of the Erichsen family. *Open May–September daily from 1:00 p.m. to 4:00 p.m.* At **No. 27 Landemarkeet,** in the garden, is a monolith thought to be 3000 years old. Strollers can see it from the street. **No. 7 Ostergade** is the Ronne Theater, Denmark's oldest private theater still in use. Built in 1823, it provided a stage for visiting actors as well as for local groups who performed in the Bornholm dialect. **No. 4 Gronnegade** has one wing that is thought to be the oldest building in Bornholm. **Kastellet** and remains of the old bastions are located just south of town. Kastellet itself is a round tower built in 1689, with a second story added in 1841. *There is a Defense Museum open here in June and September, Tuesday, Thursday and Saturday from 1:00 a.m. to 4:00 p.m.; July and August, Monday–Saturday, 1:00 a.m. to 4:00 p.m.*

HASLE

Hasle is an old market town with many half-timbered houses. In the old church, high above the town in a grove of trees, is a rare triple altarpiece from 1600. Along the road north, you will pass the fishing villages of Helligpeder and Teglkas, and then will reach a path leading to Jons Kapel, the spot where the monk, Brother Jon, gave his sermons. He lived in a nearby cave.

Continue on to the **Hammershus Fortress** ruins, which sit atop a knoll in the northwest corner of Bornholm. Construction of the fortress began around A.D. 1250, under the supervision of the archbishop of Lund. The central parts of the Mantel Tower, made of boulders, are the oldest portions of the fort. The tower housed two well-known political prisoners: Leonora Christina, the daughter of Christian IV, and her husband Corfitz Ulfedt were imprisoned here from 1660–1661 on charges of treason with Sweden. Against the walls of the fort, buildings were added as the need arose. The church stood against the north wall. There is also an inner wall enclosing another fort area. A rampart at the northeast gate is thought to have been built in the 17th century under the reign of Christian IV. It is interesting because it shows the use of earthworks rather than walls as protection against cannon fire.

At the northwest gate, remains of a drawbridge and an oriel window can be seen. On the cliff side, the outer wall of the fort is connected to the inner wall by a bridge, the only medieval bridge still intact in Denmark. The fort fell into disuse in 1743 when the island of Christianso was fortified with stones from the already partially ruined Hammershus. In that year, the commandant of Hammershus moved to Ronne, and the fort was left for people to ransack for the stones they needed. Since 1814, however, it has been forbidden to take stone from the fort, and in 1822 Hammershus was declared an ancient monument. The most significant archeological find occurred in 1967, when 22 gold coins and four gold rings were dug up. The coins, German guilders, were dated between 1420 and 1519, and were probably hidden when the fort was captured by ransackers from Lubeck in 1522. Hammershus has nurtured many legends, the most popular of which holds that the Bornholm trolls occupy it now.

SANDVIG AND ALLINGE

These twin towns, part of one municipality, are located next to one another with many well-kept, half-timbered farmhouses, and narrow streets with hollyhocks climbing the brightly painted walls of the houses. This is a sailing center, and also the spot where the smoked Bornholmers (smoked herring) is made. Of interest here are: **Allinge Church,** a late Gothic structure that has been extended and restored as recently as 1892; **Madsebakke,** Denmark's largest collection of rock carving, located between the two towns near the holiday resort of Madselokke. **Sandkas**, a sheltered white-sand beach lying between two cliffs; **Tejn,** nearby, one of Bornholm's main fishing harbors. South of Tejn at Stammershalle, you will find three monoliths from the Viking era.

GUDHJEM

The houses here creep up the rocky hills with just enough room between them for a tiny garden. In summer, a boat leaves every day for Christianso. Small boats also run to the *Hilligdoms Kipper* (cliffs) at Ro. Boats will take tourists into the cave called The *Wet Oven*. South of Gudhjem is a path running along the sea to *Melsted Beach*. And farther south the coast becomes rocky, ending in a huge granite gorge. The **Gudhjem Museum** contains exhibits of Bornholm textiles. The **Agricultural Museum** at Melstedgard in Gudhjem is a typical Bornholm farm with an exhibit of old farming tools.

SVANEKE

In 1975, Svaneke won the *European Gold Medal for Town Preservation*. With its narrow, winding streets and well-preserved, whitewashed, half-timbered houses, it is undoubtedly a winner. Here, on the southeast coast, you will find mulberry and fig trees hanging over the walled gardens. A walk north or south from town will bring you to small fishing villages.

NEXO

Here is Bornholm's second-largest harbor, and it is a busy place. Nexo is distinguished by the pale sandstone that surrounds the Nexo Church and fronts many of the half-timbered houses. Balka, to the south of town, is a fine beach sheltered by dunes. Going inland from Nexo, you will come to Akirkeby, the oldest merchant town on Bornholm. It is known for its beautiful church containing an extraordinary font which is as old as the church, around 1600. The font was made in Gotland and signed by the master craftsman, Sigraf. Akirkeby fell on hard times with the development of the coastal cities.

THE ROUND CHURCHES

The four round churches mentioned previously are located at Olsker, Nyker, Nylars and Osterlars. In medieval times, they were just as important as fortifications as they were as churches. The largest and perhaps most interesting is Osterlarskirke. Wall paintings from 1230 were rediscovered 600 years later under coats of whitewash. Check with the tourist offices for directions to all the churches and for opening hours.

CHRISTIANSO: THE FORTRESS ISLAND

Christianso is the largest of the Ertholmene Islands, about an hour's boat trip from Bornholm. In 1864, a naval base was established at the fortress. Now about 130 people live on the island, an idyllic spot with no automobiles permitted. Daily ferry service from Allinge, Svaneke and Gudhjem in summertime; all year-round from Svaneke.

RECREATION

Eighteen-hole **golf courses** can be found at Norbornholms, Golfbane and Bornholms, Golfbane. There is a nine-hole course at Dueodde. **Trotting races** are held at Almindingen. Check with tourist office for days and times. **Fishing** is available at Bornholm, at the beach south of the airport and at several points on the other coasts. A license, available through Bornholm's Sportsfiskertorening, is required for fishing in the lakes and rivers.

SHOPPING

For **ceramics** visit Michael Andersen Workshop and Boutique at Lille Torv/ Ronne. For **glass**: Baltic Sea Glass, a small glass studio and shop at Ostermaire between Nexo and Gudhjem. Hvide Hus at Ostermarie sells **handicrafts**, **housewares** and **furniture** in a charming, half-timbered, thatched-roof building. Bente Hammer's workshop and boutique eight kilometers north of Ronne is the place for **textiles**.

WHERE TO STAY

Hotels are listed below. There are also some very fine holiday homes available for rent with some near the beautiful, white sandy beaches. You will also find several youth hostels on the island. Contact the Danish Youth Hostel Association. (See "Introduction" for address of the Danish Youth Hostel Organization.)

For holiday home and hotel booking: *Bornholm Booking Center: Nordbornholms Turistbureau, DK 3770 Allinge; Gudhjem Turistbureau, DK 3760 Gudhjem; Nexo-Dueodde Turistbureau, DK 3730 Nexo.*

RONNE

The Hotel Fredensborg

Near the airport. A lovely modern hotel that manages to project a comfortable, almost homey atmosphere in spite of its sleek glass-and-tile interior. Much of this feeling is imparted by its energetic owner, Birte Jensen, who has designed much of the interior herself and is always on the premises overseeing all details of this first-class establishment. All rooms have views of the sea and either a balcony or terrace. The restaurant, Di 5 Stauerna, is first rate and as attractive as the rest of this contemporary, seaside hotel. The hotel is located near the airport, but since air traffic is minimal, noise is not a problem. Open all year.

The Hotel Hoffman

Located in the center of Ronne. 80 rooms, all with private bath. A pleasant choice if you do not care about being on the beach. Open all year.

SANDKAS

The Hotel Friheden

All rooms have private baths. There are also apartments with kitchen facilities. Open from May until beginning of November. Indoor pool.

Moderate.

The Hotel Abilgard

A modern hotel sitting high above the sea. There are 77 rooms, each with its own entrance from the park. Outdoor pool and tennis court.

Moderate to inexpensive.

NEXO

The Hotel Balka Sobad

On the beach with tennis court and outdoor pool. Modern rooms all with private bath.   *Moderate.*

The Hotel Balka Strand

A pleasant hotel near the beach.   *Moderate.*

SVANEKE

The Hotel Siemsensko

Located on the harbor in a group of older buildings that have been completely modernized. There are 44 rooms, most with private bath.

Moderate.

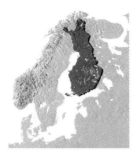

FINLAND

Helsinki's Pohjoisesplanadi Street is a parade of neoclassical buildings.

AN INTRODUCTION

If the generalization that the Finns are a silent people contains any truth, the alleged silence could be attributed to the difficulty of the Finnish language, which is enough to render anyone speechless. Many Finns, on first meeting, appear somewhat reticent and shy. But once they have crossed the barrier of introductions and the usual polite exchanges, the Finnish are not in the least tongue-tied. These feisty residents of the fifth-largest country in Europe, sandwiched between the two powers that occupied them for over 700 years, have had to speak up loudly and clearly to retain their own identity and gain their independence. They have clawed their way out of the grip of both Sweden and the czars, have seen their country devastated by fires, bombed by Russia and scorched by Germany. They have fought to establish their own culture and language in the face of the smugness of the Swedish occupiers; they have weathered the criticism of those who felt, until recently, that they were on terms just a bit too intimate with Russia. Now, in the late 20th century, Finland has proven itself the equal of any nation, savvy in business, skillful in politics and creative in design. No longer do people speak of "little Finland." No longer do foreigners scorn this remote country, which was for so many centuries considered a primitive outpost. The only country to pay off its war debt, Finland has emerged from its centuries of struggle with pride in its own accomplishments and a sense of its own identity.

Perhaps more than anything, that identity is one forged of antitheses. Finland is a land of wilderness and urbanity, primitiveness and sophistication, melancholy and joy. Though they have created some of the most beautiful and elegant home designs, no one loves nature and the wilderness more than the Finns. They will drop the trappings of civilization and all that tasteful comfort to run for the hills; they will leave the warmth of the sauna to plunge into the icy sea. They will spend the day skiing across rugged terrain in the coldest and darkest of weather and come into town at night to dance the tango at the local nightclub.

The duality is evident in more serious matters as well, particularly in Finland's relationship with the countries that lie on either side of her, and that have been part of her history since its beginnings. Lying in the shadow of an awesome next-door neighbor, and occupied for more than 600 years by her other neighbor, Finland has, over the years, developed a love-hate relationship with these two powers and learned to tolerate their presences, if not embrace them. For years, Finnish was the language of the peasants, scorned by the Swedes and Swedish-speaking Finns. Now, the languages co-exist, with street signs in both—Finnish is on top—and towns are often called by both their Finnish and Swedish names.

In the matter of food, as well, Finland offers two distinct cuisines. There is, so to speak, a fork in the road to the kitchen, with attention given to Russian as well as Finnish cuisine. In matters of religion, too, Finland is a bit of a split personality. The state religion is Lutheran, and a portion of every citizen's taxes goes to the church. But the Finns, for the most part, worship only nature. They show off

FINLAND

their beautiful old wooden churches, but they rarely attend them. The most religious Finns seem to be the Greek Orthodox, worshipping in churches that were built by the Russian soldiers during the time when Finland was a Grand Duchy of Russia.

In spite of these foreign influences, however, Finland and the Finns have their own distinctive character. The sparse population, 4,926,000 sprinkled over 130,500 square miles of land, which is in large part wilderness, is made up of rugged and fiercely individualistic people. As do all the Scandinavians, Finns must contend with almost six months of darkness and cold. Perhaps more than any other Nordic people, the Finns have come to terms with the extremes of climate, devising psychic insulation against the bleakness of the long, dark winters, and almost savoring the challenge. One of the insulators against dreariness is the Finnish sense of humor, as dry and warm as a sauna. The Finns are not given to the zaniness of the Danes or the hilarity of the Norwegians, but their quietly ironic view of life and their deadpan humor have stood them well against the vicissitudes of history and climate.

INTO THE WOODS

In a way, the things foreigners think of as most characteristically Finnish are born of the successful endeavor to manage life in a nature that is at once beautiful and hostile. Rather than rail against nature and the difficulties she brings, the Finns embrace the challenge, heading out to their summer cottages at the gleam of a sunny ray, or into the snow to ski or skate, or into the icy sea for a swim after a sauna. Perhaps it is that uniquely Finnish combination of feistiness and heartiness that sends the Finns grinning out into the cold and dark, to prove that neither the Swedes, nor the Russians, nor Mother Nature herself can ever get the best of them.

No matter how beautiful and comfortable a Finnish house may be, no self-respecting Finn is without an escape hatch—a cabin or a hut in the wilderness—the more remote the better. The Finns race to these cottages every summer weekend, gleefully shedding the creature comforts of their homes for a chance to carry their own water and lug their own wood; to, as one Finnish friend put it, "take all day to do the things that during the week they can do in a few minutes." They hike, fish, canoe and stay away from town so that they need not dress up or socialize. Foreigners seeking a bit of this Finnish experience usually head for the holiday villages where there are a few people around. But the Finns opt for solitude and an escape from organized activities.

A LAND OF WATER AND TREES

The bulbous southern half of Finland sparkles with a good percentage of those 187,000 lakes and acres of untouched woodland. One of the first things a traveler will notice in Finland is the profusion of trees. You will see it as you fly into Helsinki and even as you ride from the airport into town, passing office buildings and factories screened by birch and pine trees. Because of the abundance of trees, especially evergreens, the Finnish landscape, even in the depths of snow-buried winter, is never totally bleak. Fluffy pines fringe the snowy meadows and delicate birches veil the houses. The beauty of the Finnish landscape lies in its remoteness and tranquillity, the uncluttered stretches of meadow and woods, the still, dark lakes and the silent pines.

It is practical for itinerary planning to divide Finland into three parts: the coastal areas of western and southern Finland and the archipelago; the eastern lake district; and Lapland. The waters of the coastal areas, which are the Gulf of Bothnia, between Finland and Sweden, and the Gulf of Finland, lapping the shores of Russia, are generally calm. Here, travelers can take ferries and cruise ships to Sweden and St. Petersburg. The eastern lake district is one of Finland's most beautiful areas, with pleasant towns bordering the clear lakes and historic steamers chugging from island to island. Lapland, with its gentle fells, deep lakes and seething rapids, is the most exotic of the areas, with miles of untamed wilderness punctuated here and there by very civilized small towns. In the most remote corners of these northern wilds, the visitor should not be surprised to come upon a comfortable, modern hotel complete with a nightclub and live dance band.

FINNISH DESIGN

The Finnish flair for design is, in a way, an offspring of the Finns' affinity with nature. Finnish design is distinguished by the use of natural materials, the eye for balance and proportion and the subtle use of color, all properties of love and respect for nature and for man's place within the natural environment. It also springs from a tradition of national identity, of that same tenacity and determination to hold on to an identity in the face of the occupying countries. In the late 19th-century, the National Romantic (Jugend) movement was an effort to proclaim Finland's individualism and reject the Russian influence. In the face of those earlier 19th-century, Empire-style buildings that made Helsinki into a mini-Leningrad, the National Romantic style celebrated Finland's distinctiveness. Early in the

1900s, Eliel Saarinen and his partners Armas Lindgren and Herman
Geselius pulled the fundamentals of the movement into the 20th
Century and then took off from there. Saarinen's Railway Station in
Helsinki became the landmark of Finnish contemporary design. Eliel
Saarinen eventually moved to the United States where he designed,
in addition to many other structures, the buildings of Cranbrook
Academy in Michigan. The other well-known name in Finnish design is Alvar Aalto, who once said that architecture is the highest ex-
pression of Finnish culture because the language is too difficult.
Aalto's designs dot the landscape of Finland from Helsinki and the
University at Jyvaskyla to Rovaniemi in Lapland. Aalto was innovative in his efforts to design total environments with furniture and accessories. In his home designs, his emphasis was on suiting the
structure to the clients' needs and on creating a tranquil, welcoming
ambience.

Today, Finnish design is carrying on that tradition of style and
practicality in its private homes as well as in its public buildings.
From the simplest kitchen implement to the most sophisticated and
expensive home, the Finnish style is elegant, tasteful and original.
Ride the cruise ships that ply the waters between Finland and Sweden for a glimpse of Finnish design at its brightest and most glamorous, or visit the extraordinary library in Tampere to see the perfect
blend of ambience and usefulness. At Artek in Helsinki, you can ad-
mire and purchase Aalto-designed furniture and housewares; at Marimekko, you can buy splashy fabrics that almost sing with
exuberance; and the list goes on. Wherever you go in Finland, you
will find little corners, oases of man-made beauty, in addition to the
natural loveliness of the landscape.

MUSIC, LITERATURE AND ART

Finnish art is most often characterized by a reverence for nature. In
music, painting and sculpture, the celebration of the landscape is
central. From the works of Jean Sibelius, whose music sings of the
natural beauty of Finland, to Eila Hiutunen's sculpture monument
to the composer, it is Finland that is the substance of the work. Sibelius's tone poem *Finlandia* evokes the splendor of the forests and
lakes, while many of his other works are based on the Finnish epic
poem, the *Kalevala*. It might be harder to find the Finnish countryside in the contemporary music of Joonas Kokkonen, but this esteemed composer has also helped to maintain Finland's place on the
musical map. His works have been performed around the world to

great acclaim, and in 1968 he was awarded the Nordic Prize in music.

Perhaps we know little of Finnish literature because the language is so difficult, but among the Finnish literary lights, the name of Frans Eemil Sillanpaa shines; in 1939, he was the first Finn to win the Nobel Prize for literature. The two novels that have been translated into English are *Fallen Asleep While Young* and *Meek Heritage*. The writer Vaino Linna was awarded the 1963 Nordic Literary Prize for his novel, *The Unknown Soldier.*

One of the most distinctively Finnish painters is Akseli Gallen-Kallela, who often worked with Eliel Saarinen on interiors of buildings. Gallen-Kallela's *Flame Rug* has become a classic of Finnish design. His paintings illustrating the *Kalevala* are remarkable for their power and energy. His work can be seen, among other places, at his studio home outside Helsinki and in the Gosta Serlachius Museum of Fine Arts at Mantta, north of Tampere. Albert Edelfelt is another important name in Finnish painting. His portrait of Louis Pasteur is in the Louvre. The most popular of the Lapp painters is Reidar Sarestoniemi, whose house and studio museum, not far from Kittila in Lapland, is open to the public. Sarestoniemi's paintings, which most often treat Lapp themes—folk tales, landscape and wildlife—are remarkable for the energy of the brushwork and the vibrancy of the colors. Another name in Lapp painting is that of Andreas Alariesto, whose paintings are also centered on the Lapp culture and land.

In sculpture, the name of Waino Aaltonen stands above all others. His figure of Paavo Nurmi, the great Olympic runner, is world-renowned. The Waino Aaltonen Museum in Turku has many of the sculptor's other, equally impressive works. Eila Hiltunen created the *Sibelius Monument* in Helsinki, a national landmark that evoked a great deal of controversy when it was unveiled, since it was the first abstract monument to a human being. Bowing to public pressure, Ms. Hiltunen added a model of the face of the composer to the monument.

THE SAUNA

It might not be an art form, but it took a certain kind of creative genius to come up with this most extraordinary sybaritic pastime. For centuries the sauna, that uniquely Finnish invention, has been a central part of Finnish life. It has been used for everything from delivering babies to concluding business deals—though those deals are completed after the sauna, in the sauna lounge. Business is never actually discussed in the sauna, even though saunas are an important part of business entertaining and many corporations have their own.

The first saunas were holes in the ground, with stones piled at one edge. The sauna was used only once a week, for cleaning out all the impurities of both mind and body. Now there are all varieties of sauna, from the most primitive wooden huts built in the woods by a lake to the glitziest of tiled spas with Olympic pools and wave machines. But the basics of the sauna are simple: a wood-lined room, a bench, heated coals and a bucket of water. You can add whatever variations you wish, from birch branches that stir up the blood to a scrubwoman who will cleanse you squeaky-clean, even lounges serving beer and sandwiches. The important thing is the alternating of heat and cold, and the most vital step is the cool down after the sauna. This is when deals are completed and treaties are made. This is the social time, and it is not to be rushed or ignored. Most hotels in Finland have a sauna, or several. In some, you will be charged a nominal fee; in others, a morning sauna and swim, if there is a pool, are included in the room rate. Saunas are taken in the nude, and public saunas in Finland are not mixed, though in private homes, the entire family takes a sauna together.

For a real sauna experience, complete with smoke sauna and an ice hole, try the **Finnish Sauna Society in Helsinki**. (See the "Helsinki" section for details.)

A NUTSHELL HISTORY

Finland's history is long and complex, a tale of struggles against Russia and Sweden. At the risk of being simplistic, suffice it to say here that the Finns arrived in what is now Finland at about the time of the beginning of the Christian era. From 1154 until 1809, Finland was ruled by Sweden. It was King Eric of Sweden who, with the help of Henry, the bishop of Uppsala, Christianized Finland in the 12th century. The Finns were what one might call a hard sell, and poor Henry (later Saint Henry) was killed by a peasant named Lalli. It has never been established whether Lalli was resisting conversion or killing what he thought was a thief. The struggle against Sweden and Christianity continued for years, with Finland finally yielding religiously and politically to Sweden.

Within those nearly 700 years of Swedish domination, Russia managed to occupy Finland between the years of 1713 and 1721, and again between 1741 and 1743. Finally, in 1809, Finland became an autonomous Grand Duchy of Russia and continued as such until it declared itself independent in 1917 under the leadership of General

Carl Gustav Mannerheim. In November of 1939, the Russians, demanding that Finland close the Gulf of Finland and cede land in the eastern section of Karelia, attacked Finland. The rest of the world was appalled as Russia dropped bombs on Finland's defenseless cities, claiming that they were not bombs, but baskets of food. The Finns held their own for several months in this Winter War, and managed to push back the Russians, only to be knocked down again as World War II escalated. In what appeared to be the only way to save themselves against Russian aggression, Finland allied with Germany. At the end of the war, the country was caught between the two powers, burned by the retreating Germans and further devastated by the Russians. Finland was a heap of rubble with a vastly shrunken eastern border, and the problems of rebuilding almost all of its northern area and of absorbing more than 400,000 Finns back into the now diminished area of eastern Finland.

FINLAND'S MEDIEVAL TOWNS

Because Finland was built primarily of wood and suffered disastrous fires, the visitor will see little that was constructed before the 18th century. With few exceptions, the four medieval towns of Finland represent all that is left of this country's early history. At the time of the Reformation, only six coastal towns had charters. Two of these were Ulvila in the north, which was replaced by Pori at the more suitable site of the Kokemaenjoki River, and Viipuri in the east, which is now part of the USSR. What remains are Turku, Rauma and Naantali, on the east coast, and Porvoo, an easy day trip northeast of Helsinki. (See the sections on Helsinki and on the west coast for details of these medieval towns.)

TRAVEL ESSENTIALS

Finnish Tourist Board: *655 Third Ave., New York, NY 10017. ☎ (212) 949-2333. Almost every town has a local tourist information office with excellent material and willing help. Most of their addresses are indicated in this book.*

GETTING THERE

Finnair Has daily flights nonstop from JFK to Helsinki. Delta flies three times a week non-stop from JFK, with an additional flight both ways in summer. And **S.A.S.** connects through Copenhagen. SAS also flies from Stockholm to Tampere, Turku, Pori and Vaasa. **From Germany and Sweden by boat**: The **Silja Line** travels between Travemunde in Germany and Helsinki. Silja and Viking lines travel regularly between Stockholm and Helsinki or Turku. There is also service to Mariehamn on these lines as well as on the **Birka** and **Anedin** lines. The ferry tragedy in the autumn of 1994, which was not on a trip between Finland and Sweden, nor on any of the above-mentioned lines, might have dampened some enthusiasm for these cruises, but such disasters are extremely rare and it is fun to travel this way between Sweden and Finland. The boats are big and quite luxurious, with elegant dining rooms, nightclubs, discos and ingenious playrooms for the children. There are saunas and pools as well, and it is a good chance to meet the Scandinavians. On board, you can buy duty-free goods. Travelers can choose to spend the night on board or to take a day cruise.

GETTING AROUND

Train service is clean and efficient with sleeping berths and room for cars on many trains. Tourist tickets valid for one month entitle the bearer to a 20 percent reduction on rail tickets. If part of the trip is made by train, reductions are also allowed on the plane or bus portion of the trip as well. **Finnrail Passes** permit unlimited travel on the Finnish State Railways for the period indicated on the ticket. The holder must also show the ticket collector on the train a passport or identity card. Visitors over age 65 may buy a Senior Citizen Card entitling the holder to 50 percent discounts on rail travel. A $300 Finnair Holiday ticket gives the bearer unlimited air travel throughout Finland for 15 days. A Youth Holiday Ticket is available for 12–23 year olds at the reduced price of $250. Bus service is extensive and efficient and, in Lapland, is the primary mode of transportation. A Coach Holiday Ticket allows you up to 625 miles of travel during a two-week period for a cost of about $75 and there is a discount of 20 percent for families or groups of three or more traveling together for a minimum of 46 miles. They are available at any bus station or travel agency in Finland.

CAR RENTAL

A valid driver's license from the driver's country is required. The minimum age of the renter varies from 19 to 23 years. One year's driving experience is required.

TRAVELING TO THE FORMER USSR

Travelers planning to cross the border to Russia must have a **Russian visa**. It is advisable to obtain it in the traveler's home country, as it takes a minimum of eight working days to get one in Helsinki. If you are driving to Russia, you must have, in addition to your passport and visa, an **international driver's license**; an **international certificate of car registration** in the country of origin, or in cases where the car is rented or borrowed, a **certificate** indicating that the owner has given permission for the driver to take the car abroad. You also must show an **itinerary card**, issued on entering Russia, indicating your name, citizenship, registration and itinerary, including route, time and date of stops, and In-tourist service vouchers for accommodations. It is also advisable to take out car insurance from **Ingosstrakh**, the Russian Insurance Company, as no other insurance company covers damage within Russia. You can obtain this insurance in Helsinki from *Ingosstrakh, Salomonkatu 5, 00100 Helsinki*. Be sure to take spare parts for your car.

Cruises: For information on cruises, contact *Kristina Cruises, Tehtaankatu 25, Helsinki* or the Sally. The Finnish Tourist Board in New York will have information on these.

Trains: Trains leave Helsinki twice a day for St. Petersburg. The train to Moscow takes about six-and-a-half hours; to St. Petersburg about 12 hours. Reservations and visas are required.

MONEY MATTERS

The Finnish Mark or Markka, written FIM, is the currency of Finland. At the time of publication, the exchange rate was 4.7FIM to the US dollar. Taxes are included in everything from clothing to hotels and restaurants, but as in the other Scandinavian countries, visitors can obtain refunds on purchases of over 100FIM if they fill out the proper forms and turn those in as they leave the country.

HOLIDAYS

December 6 is Finnish Independence Day. In addition to Christmas, Boxing Day and New Year's Day, the following national holidays are observed: Epiphany, Good Friday, Easter, May Day Eve and Day, Ascension Day (in 1994 and in 1995), Whitsun on of 1994 and in 1995. Midsummer Eve and Day and All Saint's Day are also observed.

SPECIAL EVENTS IN 1995

March 8–12, Tampere: 24th International Film festival

June 9–12, Naantali: Naantali Music Festival

June 14–18, Sodankyla: Midnight Sun Film Festival

June 17–24, Joensuu: Joensuu Song Festival

July, Utsjoki to Helsinki: Finland Runs—Six-day relay, one of longest in the world

July 8–August 5, Savonlinna: Opera Festival

August Hameenlinna Series of chamber music concerts at Sibelius' birthplace

August 21–Sept. 3, Helsinki: Helsinki Festival

October, Helsinki: Baltic Herring Market. Specific dates were not available at printing.

ACCOMMODATIONS

Finland is an extremely clean country. All the accommodations listed here are immaculately clean and all are comfortable, with private baths unless otherwise noted. For booking Holiday Cottages and Farmhouse Holidays, contact the tourist information offices in the areas where you would like to stay, or the Finnish Tourist Board in New York. In some cases, booking agents are listed in this guidebook. Hotels here may be a little more expensive than those of the other Nordic nations, but not by much. In some instances, summer and weekend rates are available, so check with the hotels.

Farmhouse Holidays: There are approximately 150 farmhouses that accept guests on full board, half board or bed and breakfast. These are always in the country and often near water. The rooms are clean, but rarely have private baths. There is usually a bathroom in the house and guests are welcome to use the sauna at appointed times. Some farms have separate guest houses, though many accommodate visitors in the main house. Guests should expect to be treated as part of the family and are usually welcome to participate in the work of the farm.

Holiday Cottages seem to crop up in all the rural areas, and range from a simple fishing hut on the coast to a luxury log cottage in the lake area. All are furnished and include cooking utensils and tableware. Guests must supply bed linens and towels and their own food. The season for these cottages is from mid-June to mid-August and from the first of January to the end of April in Lapland ski areas.

HOTEL RATES

Very Expensive	More than 800FIM
Expensive	450–800FIM
Moderate	300–450FIM
Inexpensive	Less than 300FIM

There are several ways to beat the high prices of hotels in Finland. **Finncheques** cost approximately $41 per person for one night's accommodations. They are valid from June 1 through the end of August, and there is no limit to the number a traveler can buy. Hotels are divided into three price categories according to what is provided for one Finncheque. In some cases, a nominal charge is added for a second person in the room. Only the first night can be booked in advance, but bookings for successive nights at other hotels honoring Finncheques can be made at any Finncheque hotel. In the United States, the following agencies sell Finncheques: **Holiday Tours of America**, *425 Madison Ave., New York, NY, 10017;* ☎ *(800) 677-6454.* **Scantours, Inc.** *1535 6th St. (209), Santa Monica, CA 90401;* ☎ *(800) 223-SCAN.*

Holders of **Scandinavian bonus passes** may receive from 15 to 50 percent off room rates at more than 80 hotels, ☎ *(800) 677-6454* and *(800) 688-EURO.* **Travel Pass Finland** is valid for discounts at Sokos Hotels and on rental cars from Hertz. ☎ *(800) 545-2204.* **Best Western Hotelcheques** are available for double rooms at 11 Best Western Hotels. **Scandic Summer Cheques**, at $44 per person per night, are valid at more than 120 hotels in Finland and throughout Scandinavia, ☎ *(800) 677-6454* or *(800) 223-SCAN.* The **Pro Scandinavia Voucher** allows the traveler to stay at any of more than 400 hotels in Scandinavia for a price of about $100 per night. ☎ **Haman Scandinavia US Inc.**, *(800) 426-2687.* Most of these discount programs are valid only in summertime or on weekends in wintertime. Also be sure to ask for weekend rates at most hotels. The Helsinki Card entitles the holder to discounts at many hotels in Helsinki.

LANGUAGE

Finnish is inscrutable, but if you take your time and pronounce each letter, you will probably get it right, though your trip might be over before you get through the word. Most Finns in the major cities and towns speak English, though the taxi drivers do not, so it is a good idea to write down the name of your destination. As in any country, it is a courtesy to learn the simple words like please and thank you, or good morning. Your effort will be appreciated.

Please = *Olkaa hyva* (oalka hewvah); Thank you = *Kiitos* (keetos); Good morning = *Hyvaa huomenta* (hewvah hooahmentah); Yes = *Kylla* (kewluh); No = *Ej* (ayee). The Finns will be impressed. Swedish is the second language of Finland and about 6 percent of the population speak Swedish.

SPORTS AND RECREATION

Bicycling

Many hotels, campgrounds and tourist information offices will rent bicycles by the day or week. The Aland Islands and the lake region are a particularly good place to bicycle. The **Finnish Youth Hostel Association** and some tourist information offices have information on planned trails and tours.

Canoeing and white-water rafting

The local tourist information offices in the lake area and northern Finland will provide you with information on renting canoes and kayaks.

Fishing

With thousands of lakes and clear streams, Finland is mecca for the fisherman, but be sure to check on restrictions before casting into the waters. Fishing gear and licenses can be arranged through the local tourist information offices or you can purchase a fishing tour package.

Golf

Golf is the latest craze in Finland and there are now 78 golf courses in the country, most of them 18-holes. To play, bring your handicap certificate and a copy of your U.S. club membership with you. A special Green Zone Golf Package allows you to play golf at the Green Zone Golf Course with nine holes in Finland and nine in Sweden. The course is located just below the Arctic Circle and the package includes round-trip fare from Helsinki to Kemi and two nights at the Tornio City Hotel with breakfast included. Green fees and taxis are additional. Call **Holiday Tours of America**, ☎ *(800) 677-6454.*

FOOD AND DRINK

Finnish food is rather exotic and at the same time earthy, with hearty breads and plenty of potatoes. It has become more difficult to find typically Finnish dishes in the large cities, since the cuisine is now mostly Continental, but you should try some of the following if you can find them:

Vorschmak—a dish supposedly invented by General, later President, Mannerheim. It contains ground herring, lamb and potatoes, and is much better than it sounds.

Poronliha *(reindeer meat)*—The best way to eat this, in my opinion, is in the dried or smoked variety, often served with fruit as a kind of Finnish answer to prosciutto. You can get reindeer, like beef, in any form, however.

Sillisalaatti—herring salad.

Muikku—small whitefish, usually served fried.

Lakka *(cloudberries)*—These tart Arctic berries, which look something like an orange raspberry, ripen in the land of the Midnight Sun. They are used for a variety of concoctions, from a cream sauce for reindeer meat to sorbet and Lakka, a cloudberry liqueur.

In Finland, especially in Helsinki, you will find many Russian restaurants that serve excellent Russian specialties and Georgian wines. In Karelia, the eastern district of Finland, the Karelian cuisine is quite unique. Among the specialties are *sara*, a mutton and potatoes dish baked in a wooden trough, and *Rantakala* (shore fish), a fish stew that should be made at the lakeside with freshly-caught fish. *Rieska* bread and *Kalakukko*, a bread baked with fish and pork, are also Karelian delicacies.

TELEPHONE

The country code for Finland is *358*. To call from abroad to Finland, first dial the international prefix of the country you are calling from; second, the country code of Finland; third, the trunk code, without the prefix 9; and fourth, the number you want. In Finland, the trunk code is used with the prefix 9. For information in the Helsinki area, ☎ *012*; for other areas ☎ *020*.

TIME

Finland is two hours ahead of Greenwich Mean Time. The difference between Eastern Standard U.S. time and Finnish standard time is seven hours. Finland goes on Daylight Saving Time from late March until late September, at which time it is three hours ahead of Greenwich Mean Time.

HELSINKI

Senate Square is the last purely neoclassical square built in Europe.

HELSINKI: THE TOP TEN

Helsinki is a place to soak up atmosphere, and wander in the sunlit Market Square or along the broad avenues of Mannerheimintie and Esplanadi. Among the major sights you will want to take in are the following. All are described in detail in the appropriate sections under "What to see and do."

- Finlandia Hall
- Hvittrask: The Former Studio and Home of Eliel Saarinen at Kirkkonummi
- Market Square
- The National Museum
- Parliament House
- Railway Square and the Railway Station
- Senate Square
- The Sibelius Monument
- The Temppeliakio Church (Rock Church)
- The Uspenski Cathedral

Tourist Information Office: *Pohjoiseplanadi 19, by Market Square.* ☎ *169 3757 or 174 088.* Open May 16–Sept. 16, Monday–Friday from 8:30 a.m. until 6:00 p.m. and on Saturday from 8:30 a.m. until 1:00 p.m. The rest of the year, Monday from 8:30 a.m. until 4:30 p.m. and Tuesday–Friday from 8:30 a.m. until 4:00 p.m. Closed Saturday.

HELSINKI CARD

Visitors can buy a Helsinki Card for one, two or three days. The card gives tourists free travel on city buses, trams, the metro and the Suomenlinna ferry. In addition, the card offers a free sightseeing bus tour, free admission to many museums and sights, free boat trips in summertime and reduced rates for various other activities. Several hotels offer special rates for holders of the Helsinki Card. You can pick up a card at the Helsinki Tourist Office, at the central Hotel Booking Center (*3 Asemaaukio, next to Railway Station*), at most travel agencies, Stockmann's department store and many hotels. Or, if you wish to purchase it before you leave the U.S., you can contact Rahim Tours, ☎ *(800) 554-5305.* Cards are good for one to three days, and the cost ranges from 60 FIM to 95 FIM, with children's prices available.

DIRECTORY

American Embassy • *Itainen Puistotie 14.* ☎ *171-931.* **American Express** • *Located in Area Travel, Pohjoisesplanadi 2.* Open Monday–Friday from 9:00 a.m. to 5:00 p.m. ☎ *185-51.*

Banks • Usually open Monday–Friday, 9:15 a.m. to 4:15 p.m.

Currency exchange • You can exchange money in your hotel, but sometimes that is more expensive than at regular exchanges and banks. Exchanges are available at: Airport, 6:30 a.m.–11:00 p.m. daily; Olympic Harbor, 9:00 a.m.–noon and 3:00 p.m.–6:00 p.m. daily; Railway Station, 11:30 a.m.–6:00 p.m.

Bicycle rental • Bicycles are available for rental from the youth hostel at the Olympic Stadium. 25FIM per day. Half-price with Helsinki Card.

Church Services in English • Services in English every Sunday at the Temppeliaukio church, *Lutherinkatu 3* and at the FELM (Finnish Evangelical Lutheran Mission) *Tahtitorninkatu 18.*

Emergency numbers • General emergency is ☎ *112 or 181-000* for police, fire or medical emergency. You can also dial 002 for police and 006 for an ambulance. For private, nonemergency medical care, call the Alekski Medical clinic, *Manerheimintie 8;* ☎ *601-911.* Open Monday through Friday from 8:00 a.m. until 6:00 p.m. For an English speaking dentist, ☎ *736-166.* Available 24 hours.

Helsinki Today • ☎ *058* for a recording on what's happening each day in Helsinki.

Holidays • Museums and many other places of interest are often closed on Mondays, as well as on the following holidays: New Year's Day, Good Friday, Easter Sunday, May Day, Midsummer's Day, Independence Day, Christmas Eve and Christmas Day. Shops are closed on the above holidays and also on Epiphany, Easter Monday, Ascension Day, the day before Whitsunday, All Saints' Day and Boxing Day. Also check on possible early closings on Easter Saturday, Midsummer's Eve, the day before All Saints' Day, Christmas Eve and New Year's Eve.

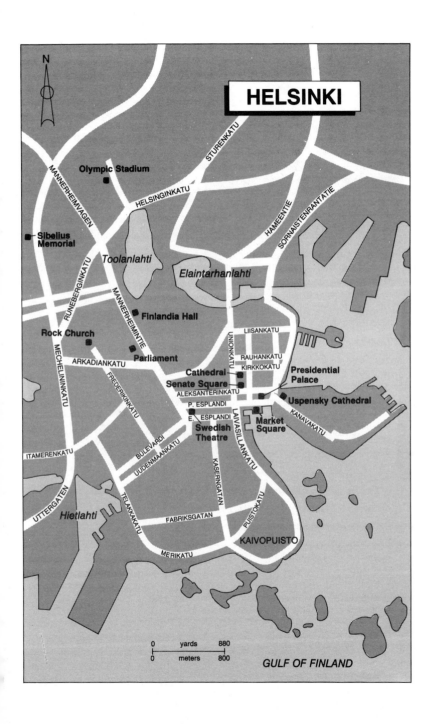

Hotel Booking Center • Central Railway Station. It is open daily in summer, but closed on Saturday and Sunday in winter. Check for hours.

Left Luggage • You can leave and pick up luggage at the bus station Monday–Thursday from 9:00 a.m. to 5:00 p.m. and Friday, 8:00 a.m. to 6:00 p.m. The Railway Station left luggage department is open every day from 6:15 a.m. to 11:00 p.m.

Pharmacy • 24-hour Yliopiston *apteekki. Mannerheimintie 96,* ☎ *415 778.*

Post Office • *Mannerheimintie 11.* Open Monday, 9:00 a.m.–5:00 p.m.; Tuesday–Friday, 9:00 a.m.–5:00 p.m. Teleservices—*Mannerheimintie 11 B,* open every day from 7:00 a.m. to 11:00 p.m.

Tax-free shopping • Most shops participate in the Finland Tax-free Shopping program. A foreign tourist who will be taking the purchases out of the country may receive a voucher for a cash refund of the value-added tax, which is approximately 11 percent. The tourist presents this voucher at his point of departure from the country and receives the cash on the spot. Goods must be taken out of the country and cannot be used before the visitor leaves Finland.

Telephone • The area code for Helsinki is *90.* You do not need to dial this prefix when calling within Helsinki. Phone boxes take 1 and 5 mark coins.

Tipping • Finland is one place you will not find a hand reaching out at every turn. 15 percent service is included on hotel and restaurant bills. You can add a small tip, a few marks, if you like, but it is not necessary. Taxi drivers will often refuse a tip as service is figured into the meter price. The one place a tip is mandatory is in the cloakrooms of restaurants. You are expected to check your coat and the fee is between three and fiveFIM. Cloakroom attendants tend to be rather burly, silent fellows and they will stand there glaring if you do not come up with the specified number of marks.

DAUGHTER OF THE BALTIC

They call her "Daughter of the Baltic," and indeed, this city does seem to be born of the sea. However, Helsinki is not exactly Venus rising from the half-shell. She is, with her gracious, pale, neoclassical buildings, more like an attractive, conservatively clad matron, extending a charming, warm, but reserved welcome to those who come to her sea-bordered boulevards and parks. Yet there is something exotic and even surprising about this city that stands so close to Russia. Helsinki bears testimony to Finland's history of occupation by foreign powers. The street signs are written in both Finnish and Swedish; the harbor is dominated by the eccentric, onion-domed Uspenski Cathedral; and Senate Square, especially under its winter blanket of snow, is almost Russian in character, with its yellow, Empire-style buildings and a statue of Czar Alexander II, the only czar the Finns liked well enough to immortalize in bronze.

Here is a city that builds a monument to manual labor at one of its busiest corners, that constructs a Parliament building in red granite, with a facade designed to suggest solidity and stability. And yet against the neoclassical restraint and the solid bourgeois mien, the city planners found space to erect Alvar Aalto's innovative Finlandia Hall, and to commission the astonishing monument to Jean Sibelius, a steel structure that suggests the pipes of an organ and bears, if one looks closely, a rather spectral cast of the composer's face. Helsinki is both elegant and earthy, conservative and inventive. The city bears testimony to Finland's trend-setting and creative gift for design, and to the Finnish character, which is tenacious, feisty and quietly fun-loving.

Founded in 1550 by the Swedish King Gustav Vasa, Helsinki did not become the capital of Finland until 1812, after Finland was made a Grand Duchy of Russia following the Swedish-Russian War of 1806–1809. At that time, the czar moved the capital from Turku to Helsinki, which was closer to Russia. A new city plan was drawn up to rebuild the fire- and war-damaged city, and the German architect Carl Ludwig Engels, who had designed buildings in St. Petersburg, was commissioned to design the center of the city. Further doom for Turku and a blessing for Helsinki was the great fire that destroyed most of Turku, including the university. Within a few years, the university was centered in Helsinki, and that city was thus the cultural and political capital of Finland. In those years, when Finland was a Grand Duchy of Russia, Helsinki was a stylish place, drawing aristocratic Russians because of its excellent water. At Kaivopuisto Park in the center of the city, a fashionable health spa was built and attracted visitors from all over Europe.

Helsinki is located on a peninsula, and most of the major buildings and sights are within an easy walk or tram ride. The heart of the city is the **Market Square** on the harbor, and that spot makes a fine starting point for exploration. From Market Square, you can walk south through beautiful **Kaivopuisto Park**, where many embassies are located, go north and east to the **Uspenski Cathedral**, or west to the shopping area. **Mannerheimintie** is the main street of Helsinki, running at an angle through the center of town. At its southern end, it is a rather formless jumble of office and shopping complexes, but as it runs north past the Parliament House and Finlandia Hall, it broadens into a graceful avenue.

In little more than a hop or a skip, you can get to the recreational islands of Helsinki as well. And there are several other pleasant short day or even half-day trips outside the city.

GETTING THERE

Finnair and **Delta** fly nonstop from New York's Kennedy airport to Helsinki, but Delta only has three flights per week each way, with an additional flight in summer. **SAS** flies from New York, connecting either through Copenhagen or Stockholm.

GETTING AROUND

When you arrive at the Helsinki Airport, you will be about 12 miles outside town. Buses depart approximately every 15 minutes for Helsinki, stopping at the Hotel Inter-Continental and at the terminal just behind the Railway Station. Buses and trams run frequently to most of the destinations the tourist will want to visit. Tram #3T passes the major sights in its circle of the center of the city and features a four-language commentary on a ticker board above the tram driver's seat. The **metro system** is efficient, but not yet complete. It is handy for getting to the east side of Helsinki and to the outskirts. For information on **buses**, **trams** and the **metro**, ☎ *4722 252.* You can purchase 10-trip tickets at City Transport Offices and at R-kiosks. **Taxis** can be hailed on the street or you can go to one of the taxi stations around town, or call one by looking under Taksiasemat in part I or at the beginning of part II of the Helsinki phone book. For advance bookings, ☎ *1824* between 3:00 p.m. and 8:00 p.m. of the day before you need the taxi. The base charge is 14FIM and includes tip.

WHAT TO SEE AND DO

Helsinki is an easy place to see in a limited time, but that does not mean it has little to offer. Most of its major points of interest are located within a small area, easy enough to get around on foot. Within the radius of central Helsinki, the visitor can decide just how detailed a tour he wants to make. For the zealous tourist, the **Helsinki Tourist Office** has an excellent booklet, See "Helsinki on Foot," with six detailed walking tours. If you have time, it is worthwhile to take these. Otherwise, follow the suggestions below for more abbreviated tours of the major points of interest. At the tourist office, you can also pick up various brochures and maps, and a listing of suggested programs, which is drawn up daily. To get to most of the starting points for your sightseeing adventures, you can take tram #3B or #3T. The latter is the one that offers a commentary telling you what you are passing. You can get off either tram at any spot you wish. Another will be along shortly. If you want a good general introduction to the city, ride the tram all the way around. Or for a fine overview, try going up to one of the high vantage points from which you can overlook all of Helsinki. The **Olympic Tower**, which is 72 meters high, offers a terrific panorama, as do the various hotel-top restaurants. With apologies to our male readers and to the management of the **Torni Hotel**, who will probably put out a contract on the life of this guidebook writer, we have to say that the best view in town is from the ladies' room of the top-floor bar at the Torni. But ladies, please, out of kindness to the hotel and concern for this writer's life, at least buy a drink at the bar before you take your sightseeing excursion to the ladies' room. If you prefer something more organized, there are bus and boat tours available from Market Square, Olympic Harbor and the bus terminal, some of which are free with your Helsinki

Card. Inquire at the **City Tourist Office**, or call **Ageba Travel Agency**, ☎ *669 193*. Several of these include lunch.

SIGHTSEEING TOURS

Most tours can be booked at the Ageba Travel Agency in Olympia Harbor. ☎ *669 193*. The **Sightseeing Tour of Helsinki** is a 24-hour tour with a multilingual guide. The tour includes Senate Square, Market Square, Kaivopuisto Park, Sibelius Park and Monument, the Olympic Stadium and the Tempelliaukio Church, as well as the garden city of Tapiola. The tour leaves from the Silja Terminal, and there is also pick-up at the Hotel Kalastajatorppa, the Inter-Continental, Marski, Vaakuna, Hospiz and Helsinki. Check with hotel and tourist office for departure times. **Sightseeing by bus and boat** departs every day from the beginning of June through August. **Helsinki from the Sea** leaves daily June–August at 11:00 a.m., 1:00 p.m. and 3:00 p.m. (a 14-hour trip). A tour of **Historical and Eastern Helsinki** includes Senate Square and the wooden city area of Puu-Kapyla, which is the site of the original Helsinki. For those wishing to have lunch after the tour at the Chez Angelique in Itakeskus, free transportation is provided back to the center of Helsinki. A **do-it-yourself city tour**: Tram #3 passes most of the sights in central Helsinki, and has a ticker-board commentary in several languages, including English, overhead.

The **Hvittrask Tour** passes through Tapiola to Tarvaspaa, the home of Akseli Gallen-Kallela, and then to Hvittrask. Lunch at Hvittrask is included.

Taxi for Tourists: The first hour will cost 180FIM, and after that you will be charged in four-hour increments of 90FIM. You may design your own tour, and the rate will be the same for one or two persons. Buy a voucher at Ageba Special Travel Service offices. Limousine Tours at 660FIM for one or two people for 24-hours city sightseeing, and 725FIM for three to four people are available at the same offices.

THE MARKET SQUARE AREA

For the most colorful introduction to Helsinki, head first for Market Square, which is located at the harbor. The market gains much of its distinction from its surroundings, the pastel neo-classical buildings and the gracious Pohjoisesplanadi. In summer, the market is a bustling place, splashed with the brilliant colors of the flower and fruit stalls, and the glistening phalanxes of freshly caught fish. Even in winter, there is daily activity at the market, though the vegetables are mainly root vegetables and the main attractions seem to be the fur stalls, where the selection ranges from hats and gloves in adventurous colors to full-length coats. Fish stands are mainstays of the market both summer and winter, and even on the bleakest days, one or two flower stalls offer a welcome burst of color against the gray-white, icy landscape. The location of the Market leaves it open to the elements. It is battered by the rain and the snow that blow in from the Baltic, but on a pretty summer day, the atmosphere is festive, and it is the perfect place to start your exploration of Helsinki. The Market is open Monday–Saturday from 7:00 a.m. to 2:00 p.m. On summer evenings, the cafes in the square remain open, and the scene is as lively as the ever-bright evening sky.

You might want to stop first at the **tourist information office**, *Etelaesplanadi 4*, or at **Helsinki City Tourist Office**, *Pohjoisesplanadi 19*, just by Market Square, to pick up maps and brochures. From the tourist office, walk toward the harbor. To orient yourself once you are at the market, look toward the **Havis Amanda fountain**, a landmark of Helsinki. In summer, the flower and fruit stalls are clustered around this end of Market Square. And on **Vappu Eve**, April 30, students drape the statue with garlands of flowers and a huge white cap. The next day, May Day, is a national holiday and heralds the end of winter. Nearer the east end of the Market Square stands the Czarina's stone, an obelisk crowned by a double-headed eagle. Carl Engels designed the sculpture in 1835 in commemoration of the 1833 visit of the czar and czarina to Helsinki. The double-headed golden eagle, the symbol of Imperial Russia, was struck down during the Russian Revolution of 1917, but was saved and eventually placed atop the obelisk again in 1972.

Now, though the lively harbor with its splendid ships and brightly painted fishing boats might beckon, save that walk for another day (see "Kaivopuisto Park") and turn, instead, to **Pohjoisesplanadi** with its parade of stately, pale-colored 19th-century buildings. These house government offices. As you walk east along the Pohjoisesplanadi, you will see the **City Hall** designed by the German architect Carl Engels, who seemed to have a hand in every building constructed or renovated in Finland in the 19th century. Originally built as a hotel, the building became the City Hall in 1913. To the east of the City Hall stands the **Swedish Embassy**, and next to it, the **Supreme Court**. At the east end of that block of neoclassical buildings, you will see the **Presidential Palace**, which was built in 1818 as a private residence. In 1843, the ubiquitous Mr. Engels redesigned the residence to make it fit for a king or, in this case, for the Russian czar who used it during his stays in the Russian Grand Duchy of Finland. In 1919, the palace became the official residence of the presidents of Finland. Just beyond the Palace is the **Guard House**.

As you head east, appropriately, you will cross a bridge leading to the **Uspensky Cathedral**, with its dark brick exterior crowned by 13 golden onion domes. The Finnish insist on referring to all such cathedrals as Greek Orthodox, although they were built by the Russians for their soldiers during the years when Finland was a Grand Duchy of Russia. This Greek Orthodox Cathedral, dedicated to the sleep of death of the Virgin Mary, dominates the waterfront. It was designed by A.M. Gornostajev in 1868 and is the largest Orthodox church in Scandinavia. You can climb the hill to see it, but remember that it is closed on Saturdays, and that on Sundays, the services are not tourist attractions. To get to the Cathedral, cross a small bridge over the Katajonokka Canal. If you have time, the island of **Katajanokka**, where the Uspenski Cathedral, the hotel Grand Marina and the new congress center are located, is pleasant and interesting. You can get a fine view of the north harbor and the Finnish ice-breaker fleet, which is tied up there for the summer. You might even glimpse a Russian ship. The booklet "See Helsinki on Foot," which you can pick up at the tourist information office, offers a detailed walking tour of this island.

SENATE SQUARE

(*This walk is of special architectural interest. Designed by Carl Engels,* **Senate Square** *is the last purely neoclassical square built in Europe.*) During the 17th century, Senate Square was the site of a church, a town hall and the provincial governor's headquarters. However, as with so much in Finland, the wars and fires of the 18th century destroyed the buildings and the square was rebuilt, mainly by merchants who erected their private homes here. The former church and the town hall were torn down. A plaque in the cobblestones of the square now marks the site of the former church.

The statue in the center of the square is of the popular ruler Czar Alexander II. He and Alexander I were the only czars the Finns admired enough to commemorate. The sculpture was created by Walter Runeberg in 1894.

At the north end of the square, you will see the **Cathedral**, designed by Carl Engels, of course, who unfortunately did not live to see the completion of his plans. The building was finished in 1852 by E.B. Lohrmann, who added four smaller towers around the central tower for support and built two pavilions to carry the weight of the church bells. At one time, Lohrmann also added a row of columns along the front of the Cathedral, but these were later moved to the Main Guard Post.

The interior of the cathedral is rather spare, but it is brightly lit, and its pale walls and neoclassical details are pleasantly simple. The painting above the altar is by the German-Russian painter T.K. Neff. The statues are of the Reformation leaders Luther and Melanchthon. Until 1959, the church was called Nicholas's Church after the patron saint of trade and seafaring, and after Czar Nicholas I, who ordered the statues of the apostles added to the roof in the fashion of St. Isaac's Cathedral in St. Petersburg. When Helsinki became a diocese in 1959, the church was renamed the Cathedral. It is a center for important State events as well as for concerts and exhibitions, and it is the place where crowds gather to welcome the New Year.

On the west side of the square are the buildings of the **University** including, a little to the north of the main building, the **library**, considered one of Engels's finest achievements. The library is open to the public and well worth a look inside. In design and proportion, the University mirrors the Council of State, and makes this square one of the most perfect neoclassical squares in Europe. Gradually, the University began to take over the entire block on this side of the square, and housed, in addition to much of the important art of Helsinki, the main concert hall of the city. But most of this was destroyed in an air raid in 1944. (Though the hall was rebuilt in 1948, Finlandia Hall is now the main concert hall of Helsinki.)

Across the square from the University are government offices. On the east side of the square is the **Council of State** building, also considered one of Engels's finest creations. Completed in 1822, it was originally the meeting place of the Imperial Senate of the Imperial Grand Duchy. Now it is the seat of the Finnish Government. The Prime Minister's office is on the first floor on the corner of Aleksanterinkatu. Inside the building, above the main entrance is the Empire-style **President's Room**, formerly the Throne Room. Unfortunately, the public is not allowed into this room.

At the southern end of the square, you will find the houses that belonged to merchants during the 19th century. Some of the cellar vaults date from the 17th century. The oldest brick house in Helsinki, the Sederholm House, is here, and next to it is the Lord Mayor's Residence.

If all this sightseeing has worn down your feet and worked up your appetite, try the **restaurant Amadeus**, which specializes in game. *It is located at Sofiankatu 4.* At lunchtime, the best values are to be found on the à la carte menu. This is also a popular drop-in spot for pastry in the afternoon or after a concert. It's a good idea to reserve ahead.

KAIVOPUISTO PARK

Start this tour at **Market Square**. From the *Havis Amanda* statue, take Etelarantu, the street that runs south from the square. Walk along Etelarantu toward the **South Harbor** to enjoy the splendor of the huge ships—Russians, Swedish, Norwegian—and the sprightly dance of the painted fishing boats that bob along the quay. As you walk, you will come to a red and white building that is the city's oldest **market hall**, built in 1888. You will also see a yellow brick building, which is the Olympic Terminal, built for the 1952 Olympics. Look across the water. The green and white building is the **Nylanska Jaktklubben**, open in summer as a restaurant. Turn toward **Tahtitorni Hill**. You will see Robert Stigell's *Statue to the Shipwrecked.* Farther along the water, you will come to the striking *Peace Statue*, created in 1968 by the sculptor Essi Renvall and dedicated to Finnish-Soviet amity. You can continue along the water here, or turn into beautiful **Kaivopuisto Park**, one of the prettiest parks in Helsinki. Largely residential, it is the place where most embassies are located. It was developed by Henrik Borgstrom, a businessman, in the late 1830s, when Helsinki enjoyed popularity as a favorite resort town for the Russian nobility. A building housing a spa and various salons for dining and entertainment was constructed in the park. Called **Kaivohuone**, that structure is now a restaurant. You will come to the French, British and United States **embassies**. If you turn north, you will find the oldest preserved villa in the park, built in 1839. Just north of this villa and a bit east, you will come to the **Mannerheim Museum**, located in the villa that Marshal Carl Gustaf Mannerheim occupied from 1924 until his death in 1951. And walking on a bit farther, you will reach the **Cygnaeus Gallery**. This villa was built by Fredrick Cygnaeus, a well-known art collector, in 1870. It is now a museum with works primarily of Finnish artists collected by Cygnaeus. Wander through the park and enjoy the tranquil beauty, stopping here and there to peer over a hedge or to guess which embassy you are passing. You can work your way back to the coast road, where you will find a cafe from which you can see the **Sarkka fortifications**, and farther on, the fortress islands of Suomenlinna. The odd constructions along the jetties do have a purpose. Families come down here in summertime to wash their carpets in the water—an old Finnish tradition. You might not want to stop to wash any carpets, so instead, head back toward Market Square and then take a leisurely stroll up Esplanadi, a wide boulevard ribboned down the center with a garden and stately trees.

ESPLANADI-ALEKSANTERINKATU-BULEVARDI

Begin this walk at the **City Tourist Office**, *Pohjoiseplanadi 19*. If you've got your walking shoes on and plenty of Finnish marks in your pocket, you can spend several hours strolling and shopping. The **Esplanadi** is the most elegant shopping area of Helsinki, with shops like **Arabia** and **Marimekko** and pleasant boutiques lining the streets that wind off the main boulevard. (The two sides of this wide street are called Pohjesplanadi and Etelaesplanadi.) At the west end of Esplanadi, you will come to a round building, which is the **Swedish Theatre**. If you want a quick, inexpensive lunch, the restaurant **Happy Days**, located in the building of the theatre, offers several dining options—self-serve, sit-down meals or a bar. At the Swedish Theatre, Esplanadi runs into **Mannerheimintie**, the main drag of Helsinki. From this point, you can take Keskuskatu up to Aleksanterinkatu, where the statue of the **Three Smiths** stands, and where you will find **Stockmann's**, Finland's largest and most ubiquitous department store. (If you have already walked along Aleksanterinkatu, you can cross Mannerheimintie at the Swedish Theater and continue to walk along Bulevardi.) At the corner of Keskuskatu and Pohjoiseplanadi you will find the **Academic Bookstore**, designed by Alvar Aalto. This is the largest bookstore in Europe, and it is a good place to find English-language books. But it is also a sight in itself, with its stunning central hall and graceful balconies. The cafe on the first balcony was designed by Aalto and bears his imprint on everything, from the chairs and tables to the glass vases.

Continue walking along Aleksanterinkatu to Unionkatu. Turn south on Unionkatu and you will find your way back to your starting point at Esplanade Park.

For a quick and informal bite, try the **cafe** in the Academic Bookstore or **Happy Days**, beside the Swedish Theatre. If you want a bit of old Helsinki atmosphere, try the **Esplanadikappeli** restaurant, Etelaesplanadi 1, which serves a variety of food, mainly self-service. For a more substantial meal, you might try **Kellarikrouvi**—an informal, intimate restaurant in a renovated old building—bricked and vaulted, the atmosphere is pleasant.

RAILWAY SQUARE-PARLIAMENT HOUSE-FINLANDIA HALL

Railway Square is the site of Eliel Saarinen's **Railway Station**, which is worth a visit, even if you aren't planning a train trip or subway ride. The station is a landmark of Helsinki, and is of particular interest to architecture buffs. One of Saarinen's most well-known creations, the station established him as the foremost Finnish designer, indeed perhaps the foremost international designer, of his time. Its red granite facades and functional design mark a significant development from the National Romantic or Jugend style of architecture predominant in the late 19th and early 20th centuries. The shopping complex under the station houses an assortment of rather utilitarian shops. These are open on Sunday, but they are not really worth an extra trip unless you are a die-hard shopper. Next to the station is the National Theatre in front of which stands the Waino Aaltonen statue of Aleksis Kivi, Finland's national writer.

If you have time and the day is pretty, you can detour through the **Botanical Gardens**. Otherwise, walk back to Mannerheimintie, where you will come to the

Ateneum Art Museum, the major art museum of Finland, housing the works of Finland's most renowned painters. As you continue north on Mannerheimintie, you will come first to **Parliament House** on your left, and, if you look farther left, just before Parliament House you will see the **Sibelius Academy**—a good location to note, since there are frequently concerts here. Parliament House is a splendid structure of red granite. Completed in 1930, it should be of interest to architectural students, who will detect in its design hints of the functionalist movement to come. As one of the last buildings to be constructed by hand, it represents the heart and energy of Finland in the quality of both the workmanship and the materials used. Its clean, imposing facade is a fine example of the Finnish gift for design, and the monumentality of this structure, the seat of the Finnish government, is a tribute to the reverence the Finns bear for their hard-won right to self-government. You can go inside the building, even attend sessions, and there are guided tours.

Continuing your stroll up Mannerheimintie, you will spot ahead of you on the right, **Finlandia Hall**, the main concert hall of Helsinki. Completed in 1975, it was designed, both interior and exterior, by Alvar Aalto. Just a bit farther north and on the other side of Mannerheimintie is the National Museum. Farther north along Mannerheimintie are two deluxe hotels, the Inter-Continental and the Hesperia.

The **National Museum of Finland** is a good place to absorb a bit of Finnish history. Its exhibits are beautifully designed to let you dip into Finnish culture, lore and history. The exhibits are extensive and well-displayed, encompassing the history of Finland from the earliest times until today. This is an excellent way to soak up some Finnish history, although the labelling of the exhibits is capricious. Some displays are explained in English and others are not. The furniture collections are particularly fine, with displays from many periods including a particularly beautiful original dining room of a chateau with a wonderful ceiling and muralled walls. There is also a Finnish smoke hut displayed here. The museum building itself is interesting. It was built in the National Romantic style, with that curiously successful blend of medieval motif and contemporaneity that characterizes the early 20th-century design of Finland. *Open Monday–Saturday from 11:00 a.m. to 3:00 p.m.; Tuesday, additional hours 6:00 p.m. to 9:00 p.m.; and Sundays, 11:00 a.m. to 4:00 p.m.*

ELAINTARHA AND TOOLO

For detailed walking tours of the **Elaintarha** and **Toolo** districts that lie behind Mannerheimintie, you can consult the "Helsinki on Foot" pamphlet. This is the area where many **museums**, the **zoo** and **Finlandia Hall** are located. It is a fine place to stroll, even on a snowy day, for the parks are lovely recreational areas where children play in tunnels and slides sculpted from ice, and even adults take an occasional sled run. The visitor with limited time, however, can simply begin by walking up Mannerheimintie.

OTHER IMPORTANT SIGHTS

The Sibelius Monument

Unless you are a hiker, you will probably want to take a taxi or bus to reach this monument, which is located in Sibelius Park, not far from the Olympic

Rowing Stadium. In some ways, it is most spell-binding in winter, when you trek across the snow-shrouded ground to this extraordinary monument for Finland's most renowned composer. Though the comparison of the stainless steel sculpture to the pipes of an organ is inevitable, the sculptor, Eila Hiltunen, insisted when it was unveiled in 1967 that it was simply a visualization of music, not any particular instrument. In deference to the sculptor's wishes, let us say that the stainless steel abstraction suggests a massive cluster of silvery icicles. The visitor does not have to look too closely to discern the relief of the composer's head, added to the sculpture in answer to the public outcry against the idea of an abstract monument to a human being. But the monument encompasses more than just the steel representation. It comprises, as well, the entire setting, the park with the trees, the rocks and the sea. It is a monument, not only to the man, but to the Finnish landscape that inspired his music.

The Temppeliaukio Church (the Lutheran "Rock Church")

Built as the result of an architectural competition in 1969, this unique structure is hewn from the rocks of a small hill in central Helsinki. The low, copper-domed interior of this earth-wrapped sanctuary is as awe-inspiring in its way as the loftiest Gothic naves. The great, coiled dome is made of 22 kilometers of copper, woven into a ribbon-like pattern creating a striking contrast of the warm, glowing copper against the cold, hard strength of the rock walls. The absence of Christian symbols in the church makes it rather ecumenical. The Finns, who do not make a habit of regular church attendance, come to this church because it seems at one with nature. Frequently, concerts are held here. Check your *Helsinki This Week* pamphlet for concert listings. Be warned, however, that tickets are expensive and sometimes the caliber of the musicians is not highly professional.

The Olympic Stadium

Located a few kilometers from the center of town, but accessible on foot for the energetic walker, the stadium was built in 1939 for the 1940 Olympic Games, which were then canceled. The 72-meter-high tower is a fine place for a view of the city. In front of the stadium is the statue of Paavo Nurmi, the great Finnish runner who won nine gold medals in the three Olympics held before WWII. Nurmi's athletic triumphs brought world attention to Finland. Any well-intentioned tourist should be certain to know the name of Paavo Nurmi as well as that of Matti Nykanen, the ski jumper who won the 1988 Olympics.

The Finnish National Opera

Finland has had a national opera company since 1873 but until 1993 it claimed as its home the *Alexandre Theater*, which was not designed for opera. Finally, 120 years after its founding, the Finnish Opera has a home of its own in a lovely setting beside the bay in the center of Helsinki.

OFF THE BEATEN PATH

The Amos Anderson Art Museum

20th-century Finnish art and European art from the 15th to 18th centuries is exhibited in the former home of Amos Anderson, an influential business-man who donated his home to the city. The museum also has important vis-iting exhibitions. Museum cafe. *Yronkatu 27, near bus station and Forum Center. Open Monday-Friday from 11:00 a.m. to 5:00 p.m.; Saturday and Sunday, noon to 4:00 p.m.*

The Arabia Museum

The museum houses an exhibit of the porcelain created by the Arabia fac-tory over a period of 110 years. *Hameentie 135.* Reach by tram 6 from the terminal or buses 71, 74, 76 from Railway Square. *Open Monday from 10:00 a.m. to 8:00 p.m.; Tuesday–Friday, 10:00 a.m.– 5 p.m; Saturday and Sunday, 9:00 a.m.–3:00 p.m.*

The Ateneum Museum of Finnish Art

The building, designed by Theodor Hoijer, is one of Finland's architectural treasures. Built over 100 years ago, it has just reopened after extensive ren-ovation. The collection of Finnish art encompasses works from the mid-18th century to the 1960s. International art on exhibit includes paintings by van Gogh, Gauguin, Modigliani, Chagall and Munch, and sculptures by Rodin. The building is also temporarily housing the works which will even-tually be placed in the Museum of Contemporary Art now under construction.

The Cygnaeus Gallery

Located in Kaivopuisto Park in a former mansion, the gallery houses the art collection of the 19th-century millionaire art collector, mainly works by Finnish artists. *Open Wednesday–Sunday from 11:00 a.m. to 4:00 p.m. and Wednesday evenings, 6:00 p.m. to 8:00 p.m.*

Museum of Finnish Architecture

Photos, records and reference library for contemporary and historic Finnish architecture. *Kasarmikatu 24. Open Tuesday–Sunday from 10:00 a.m. to 4:00 p.m. The archives are closed Sunday.*

The Helsinki City Art Museum

Finnish and French art of the 20th century. *Tamminiementie 6.* Bus 18 from Railway Square or tram 4. *Open Sunday–Friday from noon to 4:00 p.m., Thursday until 8:00 p.m.*

Oy Artek Ab

Alvar Aalto furniture and textiles. *Open Monday from 9:00 a.m. to 6:30 p.m.; Tuesday–Friday, 9:00 a.m.–5:30 p.m.; Saturday, 9:00 a.m.–2:00 p.m.*

Friends of Finnish Handicraft

Permanent exhibition and sales of textiles and rugs located in an old wooden cottage in Meilahti. The association was established in 1879 and has been instrumental in the development of the Finnish *ryiy* rugs. Some of Finland's greatest artists, such as Gallen-Kallela and Eliel Saarinen, have designed for the association. *Open weekdays from 9:00 a.m. to 4:00 p.m.; Saturday, 9:00 a.m. to 3:00 p.m.*

The Burgher's House

This is the oldest wooden house in Helsinki. *Kristianinkatu 12. Open every day except Saturday from noon to 4:00 p.m.*

The Helsinki City Museum

Next to Finlandia Hall. History of the city of Helsinki. Cafe. *Open every day except Saturday from noon to 4:00 p.m.*

The National Maritime Museum

History of ship-building and maritime trade, archaeological findings, and fishing and pleasure boats. Located on island of Hylkysaari. You can reach the museum by boat from Market Square in summertime or by bus or footbridge. *Summer hours: 10:00 a.m.-3:00 p.m. daily; winter hours: weekends only.*

Urho Kekkonen Museum

At Tamminiemi. ☎ *480-684.* The late Finnish president lived in this house from 1956 until his death in 1986. The home is open to a limited number of visitors and all visitors must take the tour which is offered in several languages. *An English tour is usually scheduled for 1:30 p.m., but call first.*

FOR SPORTS FANS

The **Sports Museum** is located in an extension of the Helsinki Stadium where the 1952 Olympics were held. In addition to the permanent exhibit of the history of sport in Finland, there are two temporary exhibits each year. Here too are medals and photographs, as well as a special section containing the museum's most treasured possessions: Paavo Nurmi's gold-coated running shoe and his stopwatch; Hannes Kolehmainen's spiked shoes and withered laurel crown from his 1912 Olympic victory in the 5000 and 10,000 meter races; and the ice-skates worn by Clas Thunberg, "the Nurmi of the Ice," when he won the 1924 and 1928 Olympics. Many other sports mementoes are here, and visitors can also make use of the library and enter the archives, where more than 50,000 photographs cover Finnish sport from the 1870s to the present day. *Open all year from 11:00 a.m. to 5:00 p.m. on Monday, Tuesday, Wednesday, and Friday, and from 11:00 a.m. to 7:00 p.m. on Thursday. Weekends from noon to 4:00 p.m. Free with Helsinki Card.*

HELSINKI'S ISLANDS

The four "tourist islands" are accessible by boat from Helsinki. In summer, guided motorboat tours of the archipelago are available from the Market Square and Hakaniemi piers. The boat clubs of the islands provide dock space for visiting sailors.

Korkeasaari is the site of Finland's largest **zoo**. Open year-round, the zoo is famous for its snow leopards. On the nearby island of **Hylkysaari** you will find the **National Maritime Museum**. Both islands are accessible in winter by footbridge from Mustikkamaa. Take bus 16 or 58 to Mustikkamaa and walk from there. In summer, boats run from Market Square.

Pihlajasaari is actually made up of two islands. This is the location of a **recreational park**, which offers a varied terrain from lush forests to sandy beaches.

There are picnic spots, kiosks, outdoor cooking facilities and bathing-huts available. Reach the island by 15-minute motorboat ride from Laivurinkatu during the summer.

Seurasaari Island is the site of the **open-air museum**. It offers visitors a glimpse of past life in rural Finland, with buildings that have been transported from many parts of the country. Worship services are held in the 17th-century, wooden Karuna church during summer months. This island is also the site for concerts and the traditional midsummer celebrations. Seurasaari is also a good spot to cross-country ski in winter. Get there by boat from Market Square in summer, or by bus 24 from Erottaja, next to the Swedish Theatre, anytime of year.

Suomenlinna is the site of an enormous 18th-century **fortress** built as the main defense of Finland. Most of the fortifications make up a museum. See especially the **King's Gate** and the **grave monument** of Augustin Ehrensvard, the builder of the fortress. You will find as well a church, art gallery, summer theater and restaurant. The island can be reached by boat from Market Square winter and summer.

RECREATION

SAUNAS

The sauna is, of course, the great Finnish tradition, and you should try a genuine Finnish sauna at least once. Many hotels have saunas available for their guests, and several have swimming pools as well. The most sensational sauna is at the new **Strand Intercontinental**. The **Hotel Hesperia** also has one of the best saunas, with a scrubwoman and an Olympic-size pool. For a true Finnish adventure, try the **Finnish Sauna Society** at Lauttasaari, an island reachable by a road just outside central Helsinki. Call ahead to book, ☎ *678 677*. Open for men every Tuesday, Wednesday, Friday and Saturday afternoons; for women on Thursday afternoon. You will find a genuine smoke sauna here, and chances are that someone will lend you his/her birch branch to stir up your blood. No swimming pool; instead, an ice hole cut in the Baltic offers, to those brave enough to try it, an unforgettable experience and plenty of material for impressive conversation once you get back home; in summer, of course, the swim in the sea is much easier to take. Lounge with fireplace and refreshments. Scrubwoman. Bus 20 from Erottaja and a short, lovely walk from the bus stop. The Helsinki card features the Sauna Society.

SPORTS

Though the Finnish taste for outdoor activities inclines to less formal, organized sports, the Finns are beginning to discover golf. There is an 18-hole **golf course** outside Helsinki at Tali Manor, 7 kilometers from the city center. The **swimming stadium** is the place to go if you want to swim in a pool. Otherwise, there are plenty of **beaches** around the city. Try **Pihlajasaari Island** in particular, or any of the other islands near the city. **Bicycle rental** is available from the youth hostel at the Olympic Stadium, and your Helsinki Card will get you half price. If you are in Helsinki in wintertime, try **cross-country skiing**, the Finnish pastime, or **ice-skating**. Inquire at the City Tourist Office for particulars. **Row**

boats are available for rental at the Rastila camping site. For information on **fishing cruises**, ask at the Helsinki City Tourist Office.

SHOPPING

The **Esplanade**, along with **Aleksanterinkatu** and **Kaisaniemenkatu**, forms the heart of the shopping area. Here you will find the shops bearing the names that have put Finland on the international design map. Senaatti Square is a center for **Finnish Handicraft**, located, as you might suspect, in Senate Square. Do not underestimate **Stockmann's Department Store**. It offers a wide selection of Finnish goods including furs, and will happily and efficiently ship your purchases home tax-free. The **Forum** on Mannerheimintie is a vertical shopping mall with a huge variety of shops and eating places. Fredrikinkatu and Korkeavourkatu are good streets on which to find smaller boutiques. The **Railway Station** has underground shopping open till 10 in the evening on week nights and from noon to 10:00 p.m. on Sundays when everything else is closed, but the shops are rather utilitarian and dull.

Shopping hours: Shops are generally open weekdays from 9:00 a.m. to 5:00 p.m. and Saturday, 9:00 a.m. to 2:00 p.m. The large department stores remain open until 7:00 p.m. or 8:00 p.m. on weekday evenings, and in the summer some shops do remain open on Sunday afternoons.

Best Buys: Finnish glass and ceramics and textiles. The names you'll recognize are **Iittala** for glass, **Arabia** and **Pentik** for ceramics and **Marimekko** for home and fashion textiles and designs.

Tax-free shopping: As in most Scandinavian countries, you can make use of the tax-free arrangement if you spend a certain amount in one store. Be sure to inquire at the store. It's a simple procedure, and you will be able to redeem your tax-free check at the airport or border, or on a ferry boat when you leave Finland. The only requirement is that you show your passport at the shop when you make your purchase and that your package remains sealed until you leave the country.

FURS

Finland is the place to buy furs as both the quality of the fur and the design are first rate. Just be sure that the coat was made in Finland. Among good bets are **Tarja Niskanen**, which is a fine, established furrier that has been in business for years. The shop is located at *Unioninkatu 30*. For more up-to-the-minute styles, try **Grunstein** in *Senaatti Center*. And do not forget about **Stockmann's Department Store**, which has a vast selection and a good one.

JEWELRY

Bjorn Weckstrom, at *Unionin katu 30*. The artist was known first for his sculptures in glass, marble and acrylic, and there is definitely something sculptural about his jewelry.

FINNISH WARES

Aarikka on Pohjoisesplanadi sells Finnish designed wooden jewelry. **Arabia**, also on Pohjoisesplanadi, is good for glass, porcelain and ceramics. **Artek**, located at *Etelaesplanadi 18*, is the best source for furniture and housewares designed by Aalto. **Marimekko**, on Pohjoisesplanadi, is one of Finland's most famous design names, with textiles for fashion and home furnishing, clothing and accessories. **Annikki Karvinen**, at *Pohjoisesplanadi 23*, sells clothes and textiles and features articles made in the old Finnish "poppana" technique. Mentioned above under museums, **Friends of Finnish Handicraft** is also a sales outlet for Finnish handicrafts, especially rugs. Among the items for sale in addition to rugs are textiles, domestic linens and embroidery. Located at *Tamminiementie 3 in Meilahti*. **Kalevala Koru**, at *Unioninkatu 25*, sells jewelry modelled on designs from ancient Finnish burial grounds.The jewelry designs date from the period of the *Kalevala*, the Finnish national epic poem. Many of the pieces contain precious and semiprecious stones. **Kankurin Topa, Finnish Design and Handicrafts**, *at Mannerheimintie 40 and in the Hotel Kalastajatorppa*, has works by over 100 artists.

For hungry shoppers: Not far from the corner of Pohjoisesplanadi and Kluuvikatu, is **Fazer**, a cafe and bakery with a variety of delicacies to tempt you. You can simply, or not so simply—given the treasure trove of pastries available—have tea, or a sandwich, or even a heartier meal.

WHERE TO STAY

Because of a recently more favorable exchange rate, hotel prices are not quite so high as they were, and many hotels offer much lower rates.In Helsinki, I prefer some of the hotels in the expensive category to the very expensive, as the former have more charm and offer many of the amenities of the more expensive ones.

VERY EXPENSIVE

The Strand Intercontinental
John Stenberginranta 4 • Helsinki's newest and most glittering jewel. Brand new and ultra-modern, it offers all the amenities and comforts you could wish for. The sauna section is magnificent.

The Hesperia
Mannerheimintie 50 • A modern hotel that is commercial, but with a Finnish flavor. The rooms are comfortable, though a bit small. Excellent health club with Olympic-size pool, saunas with scrubwoman, sauna bar and several restaurants. A Helsinki Card will get you an appreciable discount here and at the Intercontinental.

The Intercontinental
Mannerheimintie 46 • Another large, commercial hotel. The rooms here are beautiful, freshly decorated in bright colors and larger and lighter than most Helsinki rooms, but there is nothing distinctively Finnish here. This is a luxurious American-style hotel. It is located next door to the Hesperia. The pool and sauna facilities are excellent. No charge for the pool, but a nominal fee for the sauna. Two restaurants, the Brasserie and the more formal Galateia, a seafood restaurant.

The Kalastajatorppa
Kalastajatorpantie 1 A beautiful setting overlooking Laajalahti Bay, just five kilometers. out of downtown Helsinki. Designed to blend into the land-

scape, it was built in 1937, but has been extended and renovated since then. The rooms are sleek and comfortable. Hiking trails, boating, tennis, fishing and swimming. Sauna section with indoor pool. Its restaurant, overlooking the water, is a glamorous dining spot.

SAS Royal Hotel
Runeberginkatu 2 • Brand new and in keeping with the SAS tradition of comfort and luxury; 260 rooms, all with private bath, TV, minibar. There are saunas, squash courts and a fitness room.

The Ramada Presidentti
Et. Rautatiekatu 4 • Located in central Helsinki, the public spaces are sleek, but dark and commercial. However, the rooms are large and comfortable. Restaurant, cafe open all night, bar and nightclub. Indoor pool, sauna.

The Palace
Etelaranta 10 • The hotel occupies a prime harbor location with an unprepossessing but friendly lobby, and spectacular views from the rooms facing the water. Gourmet restaurant on the 10th floor. Sauna, bar and restaurant.

EXPENSIVE

The Klaus Kurki
BulevaDrdi 2 • This is my favorite. Housed in a turn-of-the-century building that has been renovated inside and out, this is a warm, intimate hotel with 135 pretty and cozily comfortable rooms. There is a lively pub-style wine and beer cellar, a bar and a pleasant restaurant that is a member of the Chaine des Rotisseurs. The staff is young and lively. The hotel is located on Bulevardi, one of the most attractive streets in Helsinki, close to the shopping area. Sauna.

The Rivoli Jardin
Kasarmikatu 40 • A new, small hotel with great style. It is owned by a woman and, at the risk of sounding sexist, it does demonstrate the woman's touch in its brightly airy rooms and large, efficient bathrooms. A small, beautifully appointed sauna and solarium are available at no charge to guests. TV, minibar and hair dryers. A delectable breakfast buffet is served in the winter-garden breakfast room. Since the hotel caters to business travelers, most rooms are singles, but the atmosphere is anything but commercial.

Grand Marina
Katajanokanlaituri 7 • Just opened in February of 1992, the hotel is beside the Marina Congress Center. As might be expected, this is a large hotel with 462 rooms.

Lordhotel
Lonrotinkatu 29 • Located in a beautiful old building, this smaller hotel has lots of appeal. Its elegant restaurant is a popular attraction for Helsinkiites as well as travelers. A small modern annex holds additional rooms. All the rooms have private bath, TV and minibar.

Seurahuone Socis

Kaivokatu 12 • This 150-year-old landmark hotel is long on atmosphere, though many of the rooms are not exceptional. I prefer the rooms in the old section of the hotel, which have a quirky old-world charm. Each one is different, and some are much nicer than others, decorated with antiques, brass beds and pretty fabrics. These older rooms are also very big, and the bathrooms are all renovated. Room 205 is especially attractive, as it is decorated in lighter colors than many of the other rooms. All rooms have private bath and TV. The location of the hotel, overlooking the railway station, is excellent, as the Railway Square is one of the most impressive sections of Helsinki. The Cafe Socis, located off the lobby, is a famous gathering spot in town, a good spot for lunch or tea, with wonderful pastries. There is a more formal restaurant and a nightclub.

The Marski Hotel

Mannerheimintie 10 • Situated right in the heart of Helsinki. The lobby is dark, serviceable and modern. The rooms are large and comfortable, with nothing to distinguish their decor, but the new executive wing is definitely a three-star place to stop. Four restaurants and a bar make this a lively place. Marski Gourmet is the formal restaurant, but Marski Cellar is the most popular place, with reasonably priced meals served late in casual surroundings. Rooms have TV and refrigerator. Sauna.

The Torni

Yronkatu 26 • You can spot this hotel by its tower, a controversial landmark in Helsinki since before the second World War. The rooms are a bit down-at-heel but they are comfortable. Avoid rooms in the tower, as they are excruciatingly small. Two bars, one on the top floor with a fine view. The attractive Parilla Espanol restaurant serves Spanish food for lunch and dinner every day at moderate prices. The more formal restaurant is the Knight Restaurant, which serves dinner only. It and the Parilla Espanol are among the few hotel restaurants open on Sunday. Well-located near Stockmann's department store. Four saunas available at a slight charge.

The Vaakuna

Asema-Aukio 2 • This hotel is also located on Railway Station Square. It is modern, but like so many Nordic hotels, it is very dark. The rooms are comfortable, but charmless, and they vary greatly in size. The hotel caters to businessmen and groups with an executive floor which has its own check-in.

MODERATE

Helka Hotel

Pohjoinen Rautatienkatu 23 • This older hotel has been renovated and provides comfortable, if somewhat somber rooms, all with private baths. The restaurant is known for its traditional menu as well as a French bistro-style offering. Its bar is one of Helsinki's most popular. Excellent location in the center of town.

Hospiz

At Vuorikatu 17 • This hotel is known for its friendly service. It has been recently renovated, and is well-located in the center of town. Most rooms with private bath. No alcohol is served on the premises. A double with private bath will run about 400FIM.

The Hotel Haaga

Though I have not seen this hotel, it is well-recommended for travelers who wish to stay outside of town at a moderately priced hotel: It has an indoor pool and sauna, and all rooms have private baths. Since this is a hotel school, the service might not be perfect, but it is a comfortable place, popular with large groups who need conference facilities. A double will cost about 400FIM.

Cumulus Kaisaniemi

Kaisaniemenkatu 7 • The hotel occupies an old house and has been completely renovated in the past two years. The rooms are comfortable and the rates moderate. The location is very central. Bar, restaurant, rooms for non-smokers.

WHERE TO EAT

The food in Helsinki tends to be more Continental than Finnish, but there are a few places for traditional and new Finnish cuisine. Russian food is also almost a Finnish staple in this city that has lived so long under the shadow of Russia. (See below for a list of Russian restaurants.)

Insider Tip

Many restaurants in Helsinki close on Sunday, even those in the hotels. The following are open, but you should check ahead: Karl Konig, Marski Cellar, the Brasserie in the Hotel Intercontinental, Saslik. Others might have changed their policy by now, so inquire at your hotel.

FINNISH SPECIALITIES

Piekka Finnish Cuisine

Mannerheimintie 68 • This is one of the best places in town to find genuine Finnish specialties. It is designed in the best of the new Finnish tradition, with pale birch furnishings and sleek lines. This is the place to try reindeer, if you are so inclined. A dish combining a filet of veal with strips of reindeer topped with cloudberry sauce is a good introduction to that Scandinavian delicacy. Appetizers include Finnish-style Baltic herring or various smoked fish, or for the adventurous, smoked bear steak in Karelian pastry. In addition to the above mentioned veal and reindeer, lamb, pork and game make up the meat entrees, and there are several fish offerings as well. The menu is in English as well as Finnish and includes detailed descriptions of each item. A three-course dinner will run about 200FIM without wine.

INTERNATIONAL CUISINE IN THE CENTER OF TOWN

Havis Amanda

Unioninkatu 23 • One of Helsinki's landmark dining spots, Havis Amanda is considered the finest fish restaurant. It is quietly elegant, too quietly for my taste, in fact, and a little staid. But the food is exquisite and you cannot go wrong on any selection. Try king crab flamed with brandy and pernod, or the melange of three fish in white wine sauce. This is one of the most expensive restaurants in Helsinki and one of the best, but I think that there are more interesting places to spend your money.

Konig

Mikonkatu 4 • Konig has been a presence in Helsinki for almost a century. It was established by Karl Konig in 1892 as "a meeting place for gourmet gentlemen," and attracted the artistic, intellectual and political cream of Helsinki. It was a favorite haunt of Sibelius. Though its interior has been kept much as it was, the gentleman's club atmosphere has largely disappeared and it is a popular spot among tourists as well as Helsinki residents. The only drawback to this restaurant is that it draws quite a few tourists, but then, that's what we all are at some point. It is one of the few places open on Sundays; at least it was at the time of printing, but check. Reservations suggested.

Savoy

Etelaesplanadi 14 • One of Helsinki's gastronomic stars, Savoy was designed by Alvar Aalto in the 1930s. Aalto's innovative free-form vase was first used here. Perched over Esplanadi Park, the restaurant offers a fine view of a pretty part of Helsinki. A specialty is *vorschmack*, said to be the recipe of the great Marshal Mannerheim. Other selections vary from nouvelle cuisine to Finnish specialties.

Amadeus

Sofiankatu 4 • This is a relative newcomer to the restaurant picture in Helsinki, but it is situated among the oldest houses in town, in the Senate Square area. I have not eaten a meal here, but it is a fine place for tea or after-concert snacks, as the desserts are quite special. Game is a specialty and for economy's sake, you will be better off with a set menu meal in the evening. At lunchtime, diners do better with the à la carte menu.

Palace Gourmet

This restaurant has a deservedly good reputation. Situated on the ninth floor of the Palace Hotel, with a fine view of the harbor, it is pleasant and unaffected. The chef is one of Finland's most renowned, and he has created two menus, *one cuisine moderne*, with lighter, more innovative dishes, and the other *cuisine traditionelle*, with classic offerings. Expensive. Reserve ahead.

Kappeli

Etelaesplanadi 1 • The tourist in Helsinki cannot avoid this beautiful landmark, which looks more like an English folly than a downtown restaurant. The restaurant has occupied its place on the edge of Esplanadi park in the middle of Helsinki since 1867, when it started off as a kiosk. The food is not always as enchanting as the looks of this spot, so you might prefer to try a snack in the Cafe Manta, a popular gathering place for artists and writers, in the same building. You can eat lightly here, mainly sandwiches and pastries. A pub has just opened in the cellar of the kappeli.

RUSSIAN RESTAURANTS

Alexander Nevski

Pohjoisesplanadi 17 • This is the newest star on the Russian cuisine scene. Alexander Nevski is located above Havis Amanda, and has the formal elegance of French-influenced Russian decor of the late 19th century, with light colors and graceful furnishings, and a pillared corner called the Winter Garden. The menu offers a mix of traditional Russian dishes and newer creations. Roast bear, which is a kind of bourguignonne served under rye crust, is a specialty, but you need not be quite so adventurous. Fish and fowl are on the menu, as well as more familiar beef dishes. There are sumptuous desserts and a special house tea, served from a charcoal samovar, with waffles and jam. A three-course meal with wine will cost you about 250FIM.

Bellevue

Rahapajankatu 3 • By the harbor, near the Uspenski Cathedral, this has always been a place where Finns come to celebrate special occasions. Beautiful, with the air of an old Russian aristocratic house, it has recently been redecorated but retains its charm. The piped-in music, which other Russian restaurants seem to favor also, either adds atmosphere or is annoying, depending on your attitude about such things. Bellevue is expensive, running about the same as Alexander Nevski for a three-course meal with wine.

Troikka

Caloniuksenkatu 3 • A good choice for a somewhat less expensive venture into Russian dining. It is small, one long room, partially divided in half, with vaulted ceiling and lace curtains, and waitresses in Russian dress. Among the specialties are the chicken Kiev, vorschmak, and stroganov Zakuski, traditional Russian hors d'oeuvres are served on a tray, including such items as pickles in honey and sour cream, gravlax, a bulb of garlic marinated in red wine and beet juice, and the list goes on. The food is excellent and a three-course meal with a half-bottle of wine will run about 200FIM.

Saslik

Neitsytpolku 12 • Heavy on atmosphere with its various rooms, all different sizes and shapes, this is a place you can snuggle into red velvet comfort among heaps of Russian antiques. Game is featured here, but the most popular dish is the Georgian pepper steak, which comes with cabbage and potatoes and lots of spicy garlic sauce. The portions here are hearty, so you really do not need to order a first course, although the blini with sour cream, caviar and the usual garnishes is excellent. A two-course meal with vodka and half-bottle of Georgian wine will be about 200FIM.

FOR LESS EXPENSIVE DINING

Kosmos

Kalevankatu 3 • This is a lively place, a gathering spot for journalists, artists and neighborhood regulars, where the camaraderie and the conversation is more important than the food. The menu is extensive, and the prices very reasonable.

Elite

Et. Hesperiankatu 22 • This is another big, bright and lively meeting place for artists. Everyone seems to know everyone in this jolly spot, so it makes for good people watching, if you enjoy that. You can eat reasonably, though not cheaply, here, but you can linger over an Irish Coffee or a beer for hours.

Kellarikrouvi

Pohjoinen Makasiinkatu 6 • An attractive cellar restaurant with an upstairs bar near Market Square. Brick walls and rough plank floors make it a pleasant retreat. A light snack menu offers enough for a good lunch, and children's items are available for about 25FIM. For more substantial meals, appetizers are between 40 and 50FIM; main courses between 60 and 100 FIM; and desserts between 30 and 40FIM.

Lyon

Mannerheimintie 56 • Not far from the Hesperia Hotel, this small restaurant offers a selection of Finnish and international cuisine at moderate prices. The food is good, the service friendly and quietly efficient, and the restaurant attractive.

Kellaritonttu

Hallituskatu 3 • This cellar restaurant attracts a young crowd, and you always have to wait at the lively, noisy bar. The food is good, though not outstanding, but it is a reasonably priced spot.

Marski Cellar

There are three different sections to this restaurant in the *Marski Hotel,* two of which are slightly formal, and one quite casual. It is not especially attractive, but neither is the much more expensive Marski Gourmet, and the prices here are considerably lower. You can have a three-course meal here for about 150FIM. Also in the Marski Hotel is the nightclub, Fizz, which is the most attractive of the public rooms in the hotel, and which serves light snacks late.

Sipuli

Formerly the Golden Onion, this attractive restaurant overlooks the Uspenski Cathedral.

Happy Days

Plenty of choice here for casual, inexpensive dining. While the food is not exceptional, the moderate prices make this an attractive place in this expensive city.

Cafe Socis

In the Seurahuone Hotel • A good place for afternoon tea. During lunchtime hours, selections are rather expensive, though some items, like the baked vegetables and the pepper steak, are more reasonable. Later in the afternoon, a less expensive, abbreviated à la carte menu with offerings like Finnish salmon soup or pikeperch in sour cream is available.

OUTSIDE TOWN

The Kalastajatorppa Round Room

Located in the Hotel Kalastajatorppa, this restaurant overlooks the bay. The kitchen of the Kalastajatorppa is a member of the Chaine des Rotisseurs Gastronomic Society.

Hvittrask

Located at the country house of Finland's three famous artists and architects, the restaurant is a cozy spot serving Finnish specialties. (Look in the "What to See" section of Helsinki for more on this studio/museum.)

SUMMER RESTAURANTS

Several restaurants by the water are open only in summer. **Seurasaari** serves traditional Finnish food. **Walhalla**, in the Suomenlinna fortress, is elegant, but its location inside the fortifications means that there is no view of the sea. **Sarkanlinna** or Sarkka island offers a spectacular view of the open sea.

NIGHTLIFE

The **Hesperia** and the **Grand Marina** have nightclubs. In the **Ramada Presidentti**, try the nightclub **Pressa**. There is also a new casino in the hotel. **Marski Fizz** in the Marski Hotel is a pretty spot that serves late-night snacks. For discos, try the one in the **Adlon**, near Senate Square, or the **Helsinki Club** in the Hotel Helsinki. Dance restaurants are popular in Helsinki, and a new dance restaurant, Fennia, at Mikonkatu, has just opened and is very popular with the 20s and 30s crowd. Many of the hotels have live music in their main dining rooms. At **Vanha Maestro**, a kind of dance hall, ballroom dancing begins at 4:00 p.m. and continues until 1:00 a.m. It starts to get crowded around 6:00 p.m. On Wednesdays, it is ladies' choice only, and many women prefer to go at that time, since they can then select their partners. This is a very acceptable practice and women need not feel at all uncomfortable going to one of these nicer dance restaurants.

A new opera house will have just opened as of this printing, so there will be yet another place for music lovers to spend their evenings.

EXCURSIONS FROM HELSINKI

HVITTRASK

The home and studio complex of the Finnish architects Herman Gesellius, Armas Lindgren and Eliel Saarinen are open to the public. If you have the time, try to fit this excursion into your schedule. The train ride will take you past some industry, and then into the country where the typical wooden Finnish houses are veiled by delicate birch trees and stands of pine. Even the train stations are attractive, pastel wooden buildings with a touch of gingerbread here and there. The house is gracious and livable; you will be able to imagine the life conducted here, with the artists working together and the families living in houses around the central courtyard. The rooms, with much of the furniture designed by Saarinen, might be old-fashioned to your eye, but in their time they were revolutionary.

Somehow, Saarinen managed to create a sense of both warmth and airiness in spite of the frequent use of the dark woods and colors. In the living room, dark, warm colors predominate, with an enormous red-tiled stove, a timbered ceiling painted black to lessen its height, and the famous Gallen-Kallela Flame rug draped over the sofa. This is where the architects, Gallen-Kallela and other artists, musicians, and the composers Mahler and Sibelius gathered for long evenings over a few bottles of Scotch. The rings attached to wooden pillars by the fireplace are reportedly for the drinkers to grab hold of. When someone could no longer hold himself upright even with help of the ring, he was sent, or carried, to bed.

The vaulted ceiling of the dining room was stencilled by Gallen-Kallela. Above the dining table is a stained-glass window depicting the Hvittrask "scandal." The painting is called *The Courtship at Hvittrask* and refers to the criss-cross romances of the residents of Hvittrask. Gesellius fell in love with Saarinen's wife, Matilda, who divorced Saarinen to marry him. Saarinen then married Gesellius's sister and life went happily on. Saarinen's second wife, Loja, was an accomplished artist herself and made many of the rugs in the house, the most notable of which is the *Fairy Tale Carpet*, which covers the sofa in the dining room and illustrates the tales she used to tell her children. The bedrooms, though simply furnished, house interesting photographs of the families and friends who came here. Of special note is the breakfast room, furnished with Saarinen's remarkable *White Suite*. And everywhere, from every window and from the balcony that hangs in the trees, one is in touch with the landscape—the filmy woods and the lake.

The building across the courtyard from the main house was Gesellius's house, and it has been made into a restaurant. Lindgren's house burned down and was replaced by a building that is used mainly for small conferences. In what must be the apotheosis of Finnishness, a sauna on the grounds is open to the public. An excellent guided tour is available on request.

Reach Hvittrask by bus 166 from the Bus Station, platform 62, or by train to Masala and taxi from Masala. The taxi trip from Masala could be a little "iffy," as there is a taxi stand at the station, but it always seems a miracle that a taxi actually shows up there. You can get off the train at Luoma instead, and walk about three kilometers to the house. This is a lovely walk, and you will get a good view of some charming Finnish country houses, but you should be aware that the last part of the walk is uphill and could be a little difficult for some travelers. *Open Monday–Friday from 11:00 a.m. to 7:00 p.m.; Saturday and Sunday until 6:00 p.m. There is an excellent restaurant on the premises, which is open Monday–Saturday from noon to 10:00 p.m., and Sunday until 6:00 p.m.*

THE GALLEN-KALLELA MUSEUM

Located slightly outside town in Espoo, the artist designed this Jugend-style studio/house by the sea for himself. The studio houses a changing exhibit of Gallen-Kallela's paintings and graphics hung in the midst of the artist's tools. Be sure to notice the cupboard with the carving of *The Tree of Good and Evil* and a Polish renaissance armchair, which was a gift to Gallen-Kallela from Marshal Mannerheim after the Civil War in 1919. Across from the studio, in which was the artist's home, there is a cafe. *Open Tuesday–Saturday from 10:00 a.m. to 4:00 p.m. (later in summer) and Sunday, 10:00 a.m. to 5:00 p.m.*

AINOLA: THE HOME OF JEAN SIBELIUS

Located in Jarvenpaa, about 25 miles from Helsinki, this is a compulsory stop for any music lover. And even if you're not a music fanatic, the beauty of the setting makes this a more than worthwhile journey. If you're not totally jet-lagged and luggage burdened when you arrive in Finland at Helsinki Vantaa Airport, you could go straight to Ainola, as it is only about a 10-mile taxi drive. Otherwise, take Bus No. 1 from the Helsinki bus station or a train. Get off at the sign, Ainola, and walk for about five minutes. Overlooking Lake Tuusula, on a wooded hill, the villa was the residence of the composer and his wife from early in the 1900s. Named after the composer's wife, the country home evidently provided the right atmosphere for creativity, as Sibelius wrote more than 150 works, among them five symphonies, in this tranquil retreat. *Open from May-September from 10:00 a.m. to 6:00 p.m., Wednesday, noon to 8:00 p.m. Closed Monday.*

IF YOU WANT TO STAY IN THE AREA

Hotel Rivoli

Asemaaukio, ☎ *011 3580 27141*, is a modern hotel with plenty of comfort amenities, including private saunas in the more expensive rooms.

Hotel Krapi

Rantatie, ☎ *011 3580 251 501* is a more bucolic hotel on the grounds of the Krapi Manor estate.

The rooms, which are in the converted dairy barn, are of contemporary Finnish design. There are also an 18-hole golf course and tennis courts on the grounds. A restaurant is located in the farmhouse.

PORVOO

Tourist Information Office: *Rauhankatu 20, 06100 Porvoo. Open Monday–Friday, 8:00 a.m.–4:00 p.m.; Saturday, 10:00 a.m.–2:00 p.m. May 15–August 15. An information office by the Old Town Hall Square is open every day from 10:00 a.m. to 6:00 p.m.*

Porvoo, one of Finland's four remaining medieval towns, is a very short trip from Helsinki, just about 30 miles. Actually, the only medieval building there is the **Cathedral**, but there are several noteworthy 18th-century buildings preserved in this town, which grew up at the mouth of the River Porvoo around the year 1200 and was granted a town charter in 1346 by the Swedish king. Porvoo has attracted artists and writers. The home of the national poet, J.L. Runeberg, is located here as well as an art museum dedicated to the works of Ville Vallgren and Albert Edelfelt, two prominent Finnish artists who came to Porvoo to work. One of the largest publishing firms in Finland, **Werner Soderstrom**, is headquartered here.

GETTING THERE

Porvoo is an easy drive or bus ride from Helsinki, but the most entertaining approach is by boat. The *J.L. Runeberg* sails from Market Square in Helsinki to Porvoo on Wednesday, Friday and weekends in the summertime. Purchase tickets at **Ageba Travel Agency** at the Olympia Terminal in Helsinki.

WHAT TO SEE AND DO

Old Porvoo is the place to head for. Stroll through the narrow lanes with its old wooden houses, some dating from the 16th century, and then head for the riverfront to see the old storehouses.

Porvoo Cathedral

The Cathedral, as it looks now, was completed in 1418 and is today the center of the Porvoo Diocese, to which all Finland's Swedish-speaking congregations belong. The Cathedral was also the place where, in 1809, Czar Alexander I promised to make Finland an autonomous Grand Duchy of Russia, thereby allowing the country to keep its own language and religion.

Old Town Hall

Built by the townspeople between 1762 and 1764 with the addition of a clock tower in 1771, it now houses the Porvoo Museum, which contains displays of the cultural history of the area.

Holm's House

Next to the town hall, this 18th-century house is the art museum with the paintings of Albert Edelfelt and sculptures of Ville Vallgren.

Home of J. L. Runeberg

Finland's national poet lived in this house from 1852 until 1877. It has been restored to reflect the way it looked when the poet lived here. *Open May–August, Monday–Saturday from 9:00 a.m. to 4:00 p.m.; Sunday, 10:30 a.m. to 5:00 p.m. The rest of the year, it is open Monday–Saturday from 10:00 a.m. to 3:00 p.m.; Sunday, 11:00 a.m. to 4:00 p.m.*

Walter Runeberg Sculpture Collection

Next door to the Runeberg house is the building housing the collection of sculptures by the poet's son, Walter Runeberg. *Open May–August, Tuesday–Saturday, 9:30 a.m.–4:00 p.m.; Sunday, 10:30 a.m.–5:00 p.m. During the remainder of the year, the museum is open Wednesday–Saturday, 10:00 a.m.–4:00 p.m. and Sunday, 11:00 a.m.–5:00 p.m.*

The Old Cemetery

Here, devotees of J. L. Runeberg can visit the poet's grave.

WHERE TO STAY

If you are looking for a room, the **Haikko Manor Hotel** is located just a few kilometers from Porvoo. The main building of this hotel, spa and conference center was built around the turn of the century, but the original manor on the spot was built in the 14th century under the auspices of the nearby Dominican Monastery. There are only a few rooms in the main building, all with a raggedy charm and some with lovely views of the water. The newer conference center has more up-to-date accommodations. There is an outdoor pool and a health treatment center here as well. This is one of the premier spas in Finland, so if you are looking for that kind of a holiday, this is a good choice. Remember, however, that these spas are not like the ones in the United States.

Author's Observations

ON THE WAY EAST: *If you are heading east toward Lappeenranta and the lake district,* **Kotka**, *a small town 134 kilometers east of Helsinki, about halfway between Helsinki and Lappeenranta, is a worthwhile stop. There is bus and train service from Helsinki, Tampere, Turku and Lappeenranta. A nice drive would take you from Helsinki to Porvoo and then on to Kotka.*

KOTKA

Kotka Tourist Office: *Keskuskatu 17, 48100, Kotka. Open June–August, weekdays from 8:00 a.m. to 4:00 p.m.; Saturday, 9:00 a.m. to 1:00 p.m. The rest of the year, weekdays only from 8:00 a.m. to 4:00 p.m. The office can arrange guides, sightseeing and accommodations.*

At Kotka, set beside the Langinkoski Falls on the River Kymi, is the former **imperial fishing lodge** of Czar Alexander III. Built at the end of the 19th century, the lodge is now part of a nature reserve and is open to the public as a museum from May through September. The Langinkoski Falls were at one time the premier salmon fishing spot in Finland, one year yielding 7000 kilograms of salmon from a 600-meter stretch of water, and the czar was an ardent fisherman. The lodge was built for the czar by the Finnish government according to the czar's instructions calling for a simple dwelling using Finnish materials. The porcelain came from the Arabia factory, which had just been established; the textiles were from Tampere and the furniture from Kotka. The lodge is built of logs in a Slavic Karelian style, and has one large main room on the ground floor with small bedroom above. The kitchen is large, with some of the original equipment still there, but there has never been running water in the lodge. It is thought that the czar and his family spent the days at the lodge, but at night would be rowed to their boat, the *Zarevna*, which had running water. The czarina, Danish by birth, was said to have enjoyed preparing meals at the lodge herself. She and the czar both looked on this rustic dwelling as a retreat from the hectic pace of St. Petersburg. The lodge was used during World War I as a drying out spot for overindulgent Russian officers. Later, Queen Dagmar opened Langinkoski as a recreational spot for war victims. The lodge was deserted for many years after the war and was on the verge of demolition when it was saved by the Kymenlaakso Museum Society. The buildings and grounds have been restored to their original condition. The oldest building here is the **Orthodox Chapel**, which was built in 1809 by the monks of the Valamo Monastery when the czar rewarded them with the fishing rights at the falls. The monks spent time here praying and working, and catching large quantities of salmon to send to St. Petersburg. The building of a dam in the Kymi river and the pollution from the timber industries decimated the salmon population during the 1950s and '60s, but efforts since then have resulted in a gradual return to the glory days of salmon fishing at Langinkoski.

THE WEST COAST AND THE ALAND ISLANDS

Turku is the largest and oldest of the medieval towns.

TURKU/ABO

Tourist Information Office: *Kasityolaiskatu 3, 20100 Turku. Open June, July and August, Monday–Friday from 8:00 a.m. to 5:00 p.m.; September–May, Monday–Friday, 8:30 a.m. to 4:00 p.m. An information office at the harbor is open daily from 7:30 a.m. to noon and from 6:00 p.m. to 9:30 p.m.*

DIRECTORY

Car Rental • Avis, ☎ *921 315 411*; Hertz, ☎ *921 500 175.*

Emergency • ☎ *000*; ambulance, ☎ *006.*

Private medical service • ☎ *601 601.* Dental service, ☎ *517 500.* University Pharmacy, ☎ *324 516.*

Railway timetables • ☎ *044.*

Shops • Most shops are open from 9:00 a.m. to 5:00 p.m. On Saturday, stores close at 2:00 p.m. Many department stores remain open Monday and Friday evenings until 8:00 p.m.

Taxis • ☎ *041 333 333.*

The largest and oldest of the medieval towns, Turku, or Abo as it is called in Swedish, has had a difficult history. Work was begun on Turku Castle in the late 13th century in order to establish a stronghold at the mouth of the River Aura. The cathedral was dedicated in the year 1300. But throughout its long existence, Turku has been caught between the two powers of Sweden and Russia, and has been devastated several times by fire. During Finland's years as a Grand Duchy of Russia, the city lost its position as the capital when the czar, considering it too close to Sweden and too far from St. Petersburg, established a new capital in Helsinki. After a fire destroyed the university in Turku, that too was moved to Helsinki. Turku residents, upset by these losses, built their own university; in fact, they built two, a Swedish and a Finnish one because, at that time, there was great rivalry between the two populations and frequent fighting, even rioting, especially among the students. Now both universities appear to coexist peacefully. The fire of 1827, which resulted in the loss of the university as well as just about everything else in Turku, brought the ubiquitous Carl Ludwig Engels, who seems to have put his finger into every architectural pie in Finland, to Turku in order to plan the rebuilding of the city. Engels designed the elegant Market Square and many of the houses around it. So zealous was he in his pursuit of neoclassical purity that he wanted to tear down the few remaining houses in central Turku and put up neoclassical buildings, but fortunately he was overruled, more because of money than from any real sense of preservation. The private homes near the cathedral, which are now part of the Swedish University, bear Engels's stamp as does the steeple of the cathedral, which was the only wooden portion of that structure and so was lost in the fire.

Today's Turku is a blend of old and new. The castle, though damaged in World War II, still stands and has been restored. The cathedral remains in the center of town not far from the large, gracious Market Square. Along the river is the contemporary Sibelius Museum. Two universities and a school of economics and business administration have reestablished Turku as a center of learning, and industry, from shipbuilding to the production of textiles and jewelry, has contributed to the town's prosperity. The Turku running track in Turku Sports Park is supposedly the fastest in the world, an appropriate distinction, since Turku is Paavo Nurmi's hometown. Turku harbor is one of Finland's major ports. Travelers can sail from Turku to Stockholm on one of the overnight or day cruises that are so popular with Scandinavians.

GETTING THERE

SAS flies to Turku from Stockholm. The airport is just 7 kilometers from town. Trains and buses run regularly from Helsinki and Tampere.

SIGHTSEEING TOURS

Guided tours of Turku leave from in front of the Town Hall at 1:00 p.m. every day from mid-June until the end of August, except for Midsummer Eve and Day. Boat tours of the Turku islands are available also. Inquire at the Tourist Information Office. At the City Tourist Office, visitors can pick up a pamphlet with two **walking tours** of Turku. The tour of the old town will take you through the older sections of town, to the **Sibelius Museum** and the **Cathedral** and as far as the **Handicrafts Museum**. The other tour is a walk along the River Aura past the statue of Paavo Nurmi to the harbor, the **Waino Aaltonen** Museum, and the sailing ship Sigyn. The SS *Ukkopekka* is the last Finnish steamship still sailing. It offers a relaxing way to see the Turku archipelago. There is a playroom for children, and the restaurant on board serves traditional Finnish specialties. Several choices are available, among them a cruise to Naantali, a cruise to Uusikaupunki, a luncheon cruise in Turku, a weekend holiday, a luxury holiday at sea, midsummer in the archipelago and many more. The steamship runs from June 1 through the end of August. *For booking and information, contact: Bookingcentre: Ageba, Passenterterminals, SF 20100 Turku,* ☎ *921 302 457.*

WHAT TO SEE AND DO

Turku Castle

The castle was begun in the 13th century and work continued on extensions of it until the middle of the 16th century, when the banqueting halls were added to the top story of the structure. As the strategic importance of Turku was yielded to Helsinki, the castle fell into disrepair and was further damaged during WWII. From 1946 until 1961, however, careful restoration was conducted, and the castle is once again an impressive sight, playing a central role in the life of the city. In addition to several permanent collections of the **Provincial Museum**, the castle also hosts frequent festivities and special exhibitions.

Turku Cathedral

Portions of the cathedral, which is considered the most important medieval church in Finland, date from the 13th century. Among the treasures housed here are the paintings illustrating, among other things, the writing of the first *Bible* in Finnish—only the *New Testament* at the time, because Michael Agricola, the gentleman who translated it and who is depicted in the painting, died before he got to the *Old Testament*. The picture here shows the presentation of this first Finnish translation of the *New Testament* to King Gustav Vasa. The completion of this book was a most significant occasion for Finland, for until that time, there was no written Finnish language and most books were written in Swedish or Latin.

One of the **side altars** is dedicated to St. Henry, the patron saint of Finland, who came with King Eric to christianize Finland in the 12th century, and who met his death when a Finnish farmer, thinking the stranger had stolen food, murdered him. The **tomb of Catherine Mansdotter** is located here and has been the subject of some mild bickering between Finland and Sweden. Catherine's husband was poisoned by his brother in a dispute over the Swedish throne. The brother subsequently exiled his sister-in-law to Finland where she lived out her life. Now the Swedes would like to have Catherine's remains returned to Sweden to be buried beside her husband, but the Finns refuse to relinquish their adopted daughter, though they have made it clear that they would welcome her husband's remains in Finland.

As in many Scandinavian churches, you will see the beautiful votive ship models hanging from the ceilings. These are the gifts of wealthy families often donated in gratitude for a rescue at sea, or just to remind worshippers of the sailors and the sea in their prayers. Sailors still face these ships as they pray, and many believed (and perhaps still do) that they could forecast the wind by the way the votive ship moved. The boats are almost always models of actual ships.

Luostarinmaki Handicrafts Museum

This open-air museum is situated on a hill just outside the center of town. The area was first developed after the fire of 1775, when a plan was established for extending the town beyond its original limits. Building continued from late in the 18th century until the early 19th century. The people who inhabited this area were primarily artisans, masons, carpenters and stonecutters. It is thought that many of these residents came to Turku from other places in Finland and brought with them old timber from their former homes. These simple houses, mainly one story, are of irregular shapes, suggesting that their design was made to fit the available old timber. Luostarinmaki was spared from the fire of 1827 and, along with the castle and the cathedral, is all that remains of Turku before 1827. However, the Luostarinmaki area was looked down upon after the citizens of Turku became accustomed to the newly found elegance of their rebuilt city, and so these old wooden houses fell into disrepair. After a lengthy struggle, however, Luostarinmaki was declared a preserved area, and, over time, the houses and workshops were restored as a museum. Here you will find a variety of old houses and workshops furnished as they were in the 19th century. Several of the buildings house demonstrations of old crafts.

Market Square

Another design of Carl Ludwig Engels, the square is dominated by the stately Greek Orthodox Cathedral.

The Market Hall

This is a lively place, filled with fresh fruits and vegetables, breads and pastries and a few stalls with handcrafted items. During Christmas season, the butchers of the market serenade shoppers with carols. *Open Monday–Thursday from 8:00 a.m. to 5:00 p.m.; Friday, 8:00 a.m.–5:30 p.m.; Saturday, 8:00 a.m.–2:00 p.m.*

The Waino Aaltonen Museum

The museum contains sculptures and paintings, as well as the archives of this most famous Finnish artist, who lived and worked in Turku early in his career. There are also exhibits of other modern Finnish artists. *Open Tuesday–Sunday from 11:00 a.m. to 7:00 p.m. Closed Monday.*

The Sibelius Museum

The museum houses musical instruments and memorabilia of Sibelius and other Finnish composers. *Open weekdays from 11:00 a.m. to 3:00 p.m. and, in addition, from 6:00 p.m. to 8:00 p.m. on Wednesday, when there are frequently concerts. Check with the tourist office for weekend hours.*

Qwensel House

This house on the banks of the river is thought to be the oldest wooden building in Turku. The middle-class residence houses the **Pharmacy Museum**, with shop, laboratory and a restoration of an 18th-century house. *Open May–September every day from 10:00 a.m. to 6:00 p.m.; October–April, 10:00 a.m. to 3:00 p.m.*

The Museum Ship Sigyn

This ship is permanently moored in the Aura River. *It is open from early May–August, Tuesday–Friday and Sunday, 10:00 a.m. to 3:00 p.m.; and Saturday, 10:00 a.m. to 5:00 p.m.*

WHERE TO STAY

EXPENSIVE

The Hamburger Bors   ★★★★

Kauppiaskatu 6. Located right in the center of town at the Market Square, this is a popular hotel, especially for businessmen. The modern, rather somberly decorated rooms are large and very comfortable. The sauna complex on the top floor, with a large indoor pool overlooking Market Square, is first rate. The hotel has several restaurants, bar, nightclub, and casino. A lively place. Rates for a double room will be about 600FIM, though weekend rates and some discount packages may be available.

The Hansa Hotel   ★★★

Kristiinankatu 9 • Situated in the Hansa Shopping Center just beside Market Square. Luxurious and modern, this hotel, with just 66 rooms, is another star on Turku's ever-expanding hotel scene. The hotel has a winter-garden restaurant, lobby bar and sauna facilities accommodating up to 20 guests.

The Park Hotel   ★★★

Rauhankatu 1 • The Park Hotel occupies a turn-of-the-century art nouveau building, constructed in 1904 as a private residence. Each of the 20 rooms is different, ranging from the Captain's Room to the Hunter's Room. On the upstairs landing is a lounge area with a stone fireplace. A separate building contains the sauna. The Jugend Room is the more formal dining room, but meals are also served in the breakfast room.

Sokos Hotel Seurahuone   ★★★★

Humalistonkatu 2. The word Socis is really Swedish slang for Societhuset, denoting exclusive restaurants and hotels for the wealthy. The original Seurahuone moved to this location in 1928 and, in 1988, underwent one of the most extensive renovations imaginable. Now it is sumptuous, with a lavishly decorated lobby and restaurant, and luxurious rooms. It has, in its transformation, lost all traces of Finnish distinctiveness, but it is a beautiful hotel and extremely comfortable. A double room will be about 700FIM. Summer rates are less than half that so be sure to request the lower price.

Marina Palace ★★★★
Linnankatu 32. On the water, this hotel has both an indoor and outdoor pool and is less business oriented than the Hamburger Bors. The hotel was built in 1973 and renovated in 1986. It has a restaurant, bar and sauna. Double rooms will be about 700 FIM.

MODERATE

The Cumulus Turku ★★★
Eerikinkatu 28. A centrally located, strikingly modern hotel just a few blocks from Market Square. The hotel has four restaurants, a large sauna complex and a pool. A double room will be about 550FIM.

Hotel Julia ★★
Eerikinkatu 4 • This modern hotel situated in the center of town is a smaller, less expensive alternative to the other large, centrally located hotels;. 118 rooms, all with private bath, TV, minibar. There is a sauna in the hotel. The Hotel Julia's restaurant was named "Restaurant of the Year" for 1993 by the Finnish Gastronomic Associates.

WHERE TO EAT

Pinella
This is the oldest restaurant in Turku, established when Nils Henrik Pinello, an Italian, built a refreshment pavilion in the park, serving tea and light food. When a statue was to be erected on the site, the restaurant was moved to its present location on the banks of the Aura River. During the 19th century, the pavilion attracted the artists and writers of Finland. The place continued to grow, with Mr. Pinello's son taking over, extending the building and offering music on Tuesday and Friday evenings. The fishermen used to stop here for a beer in the morning after coming in from fishing. The restaurant has been nicely renovated, with an eye to keeping its rustic charm. Diners have several choices here: a pub, a dining room that faces the park and a terrace. Open only in the summer when lunch and dinner are served every day. *Moderate.*

Brahen Kellari
Known for its game and fine wine list, the restaurant is divided into several small, cozy rooms. The food is excellent. Since this is a place that caters to the business traveler, it is closed on weekends. *Moderate to expensive.*

Samppalinna
Yet another interesting location for a restaurant. This one is in an old house that belonged to a wealthy importer. There are two terraces in addition to the main dining room. Dancing every night.

Calamare
>   In the Marina Palace Hotel, this is a popular, reasonably priced seafood restaurant.

Svenska Klubben
>   The name means Swedish Club, and that is what this restaurant originally was. Now it is open to the public. Excellent food. Reasonable.

Ristorante Foija Cafe
>   The cafe is located under the Swedish Theater in a building that is over 150 years old. It offers pizza, steak and fish at reasonable prices.

In addition to the above restaurants, the **Hamburger Bors Hotel**, the **Seurahuone** and the **Cumulus** also have several restaurants to choose from.

NIGHTLIFE

The hotels are probably the best bet here. The **Hamburger Bors** has a lobby bar and a large nightclub. The **Cumulus** offers a lively nightclub, and in the **Marina Palace Hotel** is a dance restaurant.

EXCURSIONS FROM TURKU

NAANTALI

Tourist Office: *Tullikatu 12, SF 21100 Naantali.*

A convent, a spa and a pair of socks, or rather about 30,000 pairs of socks. Those are the secrets to Naantali's continued existence. The town owed its birth to the building of the convent of Saint Birgitta in 1443. Even before it was built, the church had decreed that the site of the convent would be called the **Valley of Grace**, or *Nadendal*, in Swedish. So the town of Naantali sprang up simply because of the convent, and it soon realized prosperity from the number of pilgrims who journeyed to this peaceful seaside town. The Reformation put an end to this rather short-lived heyday, and the convent was demolished as the Swedish king not only wanted to be rid of the Catholic Church, but needed the money and materials from those churches. Through the next three centuries, Naantali suffered a declining economy; at one time, a proposal was made to move all the residents to Turku, but the townspeople stood firm and turned to their own resources. One skill that had been handed down from the nuns was the knitting of socks with turned heels, and this cottage industry brought in enough to keep the town going. Everyone knit socks virtually all day long. Men, women and children could be seen in their houses, in the streets and by the water, knitting and knitting. At times, as many as 30,000 pairs of socks were exported. But it was not until 1863, when a spa was opened here, that Naantali came back into its own. International travelers flocked to the health resort, of which only the Kaivohuone and Merisali restaurants remain. In 1922, Naantali also became the second government seat of Finland, with Kulturanta, the summer residence of the president, located on Luonnonmaa Island just across the bay.

GETTING THERE

Most travelers come to Naantali from Turku and while one can drive, it is more fun to take the steamboat, which runs between the two towns every day in summertime.

WHAT TO SEE AND DO

The **Old Town** was originally built in the 14th century around the walls of the convent with no particular plan. Although fires destroyed almost all of medieval Naantali, the town was rebuilt along the same streets, with new houses built exactly on the sites of the old ones. So it is easy to imagine Naantali in the Middle Ages. All that has really disappeared are the old windmills and the cottages along the shore. The houses in the old part of town date from the late 18th and early 19th centuries. One third of the buildings are preserved as architectural and historical church examples, and 20 of them are national monuments. The houses are wooden, in the thatched-cottage style with two living rooms separated by an entrance hall. In most of them, you will notice a decorative gate with a nameplate that usually dates back to the original house name.

The Church of the Convent of St. Birgitta

The 15th-century church is the only remaining structure of the convent. In the church, you will find items from the old convent; among these are needlework (remember, it was the nuns who taught the town to knit socks) and the crown the novices wore when taking their vows. *Open daily from mid-May to August, noon–6:00 p.m. In July, it is open from 11:00 a.m. to 7:00 p.m.; and in winter, Sunday only, noon–4:00 p.m. Guided tour every day at 5:00 p.m., except Sunday.*

Kultaranta

The summer residence of the president of the republic is situated on an island across the bay. The house was built by Alfred Kordelin, a self-made millionaire and a bachelor, who left the house and garden to the state. Though the house is not open, visitors can walk through the gardens on Friday evenings from May through September. Of special interest is the rose garden, with literally thousands of roses.

The Naantali Museum

Situated in three of the old wooden houses with other outbuildings from the 18th and 19th centuries, the collections in the museum are displayed in 10 different rooms, representing different periods in Naantali's history. *Open mid-May to August from noon to 6:00 p.m. daily.*

The Yacht Harbor

Located in the center of town. Even if you are not a boat owner, it is fun to walk around here. For sailors, there are moorings and other services and there is a restaurant here also. This is an excellent harbor for small boats, and many sailors come here from Germany and Sweden.

The Naantali Music Festival

The festival, held in June at midsummer, is fast becoming an international event. The focus is on chamber music and, in addition to Finnish artists, a visiting orchestra and internationally known musicians are invited to perform. Concerts are held in the convent church, in buildings by the yacht harbor and on the outdoor stage on the island of Kailo. Some concerts are also given in churches around the Naantali area. Each summer, the kick-off for the festival is a music cruise to an interesting destination. In the past, the cruise has sailed to Leningrad and Gotland.

WHERE TO STAY

The **Naantali Spa Hotel**, completed in 1984, is truly a spa and health treatment center with steam baths, pools, sauna and beauty programs; however, it is not a resort hotel and is not of particular appeal to the young and healthy. In the past, there were many permanent clients and many war veterans, but these are declining. It is possible to spend a spa day that includes sauna and steam baths, use of the recreational and Roman pools, a mud treatment, half massage and lunch or dinner for about 300FIM. **Cafe Antonius**, mentioned under "Where to Eat," also has a few rooms available.

Apartment rentals: The tourist office can help visitors with rental of apartments in some of the old wooden houses by the water.

WHERE TO EAT

Merisali is one of the restaurants remaining from the old spa. Here you can have a relatively inexpensive lunch or dinner right on the water. **Kalatrappi** is a fish restaurant, well-recommended. **Cafe Antonius**, *located on Mannerheiminkatu*, is a popular cafe with sandwiches, pastries and plenty of atmosphere. There are also a few rooms here, all with private showers. They are old–fashioned and decorated in a charmingly quirky way. Owner Lilja Ahtiainen makes all the pastries and sandwiches, and she has crammed the house and cafe areas with Victorian memorabilia and furniture, some antique, some just second-hand, but all appealing. The house is as stuffed as you will feel when you finish one of Lilja's fabulous doughnuts that bear no resemblance to the ones of the "dunkin" variety.

RAUMA

Tourist Information Office: *Etelakatu 7, 26100 Rauma. Open June–August, Monday–Friday from 8:00 a.m. to 5:00 p.m.; Saturday, 10:00 a.m. to 2:00 p.m. The rest of the year, it is open weekdays from 8:00 a.m. to 4:00 p.m. The office will help travelers with guides and sightseeing tours, hotel bookings and motorboat tours.*

The town was founded in 1442, but in 1550 all inhabitants were forced to move to Helsinki in order to populate that new city. In addition, extensive fires and exorbitant taxes kept Rauma from developing as it might have. The last serious fire was in 1682, and since then it has been rebuilt, with several of the old wooden buildings dating from the late 16th and early 17th centuries. But most of the structures in Old Rauma were built in the 18th and 19th centuries, and these reflect the prosperity the town enjoyed when Rauma came into its own as a maritime center during the era of the great sailing vessels. Now it is undergoing a third rebirth as a thriving port and industrial town. It is also known for its lace-making.

GETTING THERE

Rauma is 92 kilometers from Turku. Bus service is available between the two towns. There is also bus and train service from Helsinki and Tampere.

WHAT TO SEE AND DO

Old Rauma, which is located south of the canal, is one of the largest and best preserved areas of old wooden houses. Though the town plan was devised in the 16th century, and there are a few houses from that period, most of the structures are 18th and 19th century.

The Old Town Hall

Built in 1776, this is now the home of the **Rauma Museum**, with collections related to maritime life and lacemaking. *Open Tuesday–Friday, 10:00 p.m.–4:00 p.m.; additional hours for Tuesday, 6:00 p.m.–8:00 p.m. Open Saturday, 10:00 a.m.–2:00 p.m.; Sunday, 11:00 a.m.–5:00 p.m. Lacemaking demonstrations are given Sunday, 2:00 p.m.–5:00 p.m.*

Pinnala House

Built around 1795, the **Art Museum** is located here with exhibits of 19th- and 20th-century Finnish painting. *Open Tuesday–Friday from 10:00 a.m. to 6:00 p.m.; Saturday, 10:00 a.m.–4:00 p.m.; Sunday, noon–6:00 p.m.*

The Marela House

Located on Kauppakata, this museum is furnished as the home of a shipowner at the turn of the century. *Open every day but Monday. Check with tourist office for hours.*

Kirsti House

The house serves as an example of the way more humble craftsmen might have lived in the 19th century. Nearby, a lace shop offers demonstrations of lacemaking. *Open only in summer months.*

The Church of the Holy Cross

A 15th-century church originally part of a Franciscan monastery. *Open in June, July and August.*

The Ruins of the Church of the Holy Trinity

The church was built in the 14th century as a monastery before Rauma was granted a town charter.

THE ALAND ISLANDS

Tourist Information Office: *Storagatan 18, 22100 Mariehamn. Open June through mid-August every day from 9:00 a.m. to 6:00 p.m. The rest of the year, Monday–Saturday from 10:00 a.m. to 3:00 p.m.*

DIRECTORY

Banks • Open weekdays from 9:00 a.m. to 4:15 p.m. Currency exchange also at the tourist information office.

Emergencies • ☎ *000* for ambulance; ☎ *17008* for doctor on duty.

Chemist • Centralapotek, *Skarpansvagen 24,* ☎ *11 655.*

Police • *Strandgatan 27,* ☎ *15 444.* Alarm ☎ *002.*

Holidays • Christmas and Boxing Day; New Year's Day; Good Friday, Easter
Day, Easter Monday; May 1st, Ascension Day, Whitsun Eve and Whitsunday, Aland's Autonomy Day on June 9th, Midsummer's Day, All Saints'
Day, Independence Day, December 6th. Restaurants are open on these
days, but shops are closed.

Aland is wide bays, wooded islands, red frame houses and green
meadows. It is quiet and restful, a fine place to walk or bicycle, to
explore and to soak up the tranquillity. The Aland islands are a kind
of anomaly in Finland. Though they are Finnish, they enjoy autonomy on every matter except foreign policy, with their own parliament
and a chairman. All taxes are paid to Finland, and these are subsequently returned to Aland within the limits of a budget. Often called
a bridge between Finland and Sweden, the culture and landscape of
Aland seem at times more Swedish than Finnish, and the islands are
Swedish-speaking. Both Swedish and Finnish currency are accepted.
Caught between Russia and Sweden during the wars of 1808 and
1809, Aland was ceded, along with all of Finland, to Russia. The
Russians, after the Crimean War, promised not to fortify Aland, a
promise they kept until 1915, when a fortress was constructed. During WWII, the fortifications were bombed, and none have been built
since. There is no military in Aland except for the coast guard. The
sea has always been the source of Aland's livelihood. Viking graves
are testimony to the ancient seafaring heritage of the islands, and, in
the days of the great sailing ships, Aland was in its glory. Even today,
half of the Finnish merchant fleet is from Mariehamn. Aland is also
known for its midsummer poles, which vary in color and composition from village to village. The ones you will be most likely to see
are those in Sund and around Mariehamn, and these are usually yellow and red, the colors of the sun and of love. The poles are often
left up for quite some time.

GETTING THERE

There are regular flights from Stockholm, Helsinki and Turku, but more fun
is to come by boat from Stockholm, Turku or Naantali, a trip of from four to six
hours on one of the large cruise ships. Board the boat in Stockholm, enjoy a
pleasant dinner, buy whatever duty-free items you wish, and get off at Mariehamn. You can follow a similar schedule if you are coming from Turku or Naantali. **24-hour cruises from Stockholm**: Packages are available for boat trip and
overnight accommodations on the cruise ship or at a hotel in Mariehamn. Inquire of the shipping lines listed under "Where To Stay."

GETTING AROUND THE ISLANDS

Once you are on the islands, you can get around by interisland ferry. The larger islands are linked by bridges. **Cruises in the archipelago**: several boats are available for charter on excursions through the islands. They often cruise the inner waters in the evening, so there is no worry about rough water, but schedules can be adjusted. Cruises to Kastelholm, Bomarsund and Kvarnbo are among the choices, but others can be arranged. Boats are also available for fishing with a guide. The fishing boats are owned by fishermen, who run the boats and know where the fish are. They will take you through the calm inner waters and they fish the "American Way," as they call it, trolling and waiting for the fish to swim up to them. Book through **Archipelago Cruise Line**, *Alandsvagen 33, SF 22100 Mariehamn, Aland Islands.* Your travel agency may also have information on these charters. **Bicycle packages** are also available and include maps, accommodations, meals and a bicycle. The tourist office has information on these. Some tours can be designed around special interests such as history or nature. Bicycles and boats can also be rented in the east harbor, which is the harbor where the ferries land.

SIGHTSEEING TOURS

Sightseeing tours by motor coach are available from mid-June to mid-August, and leave from the **Aland Tourist Information Office**. The tours are in Finnish and Swedish only. Each day a different tour is available. Among them are a Northern tour, which includes the Finstrom church, Dano, Saltvik and Sund; an archipelago tour; a rural tour; and a western tour. Most of these last about five hours, though there is a "quick tour" on Saturdays of only two hours. Inquire at the Tourist Information Office. Even though they are not in English, these tours offer a good way to get around to the major sights on the islands if you do not have a car.

MARIEHAMN: THE CAPITAL OF ALAND

Though as far back as the 16th century, King Gustav Vasa expressed interest in developing a town in the Aland Islands, Mariehamn did not come into being until 1861, after the Crimean War and the destruction of Bormasund Fortress, when Czar Alexander II established a town in the area on the narrow peninsula between two harbors. He called the town Mariehamn, after his wife, the Czarina Maria. Until that time, the only settlement on Aland was Skarpnost, a small community outside Bormasund Fortress, which was burned in order to allow for more fighting ground around the fortress. Because of its situation on the long peninsula, Mariehamn is laid out with a very long main boulevard, which is broad and tree-lined, and joins the Aland Self–Government House at one end with the museum ship *Pommern* and the Maritime Museum at the other. Mariehamn church stands on the boulevard halfway between the two harbors.

WHAT TO SEE AND DO

The Aland Museum

For an understanding of the culture, history and geography of Aland, this museum is first-rate. Clearly presented, thoughtfully detailed exhibitions have brought it citations as one of Europe's best museums. Exhibits covering 6000 years of habitation are organized thematically rather than chronologically, and include displays on the earliest inhabitants of Aland, the peasant culture, the maritime life, the town of Mariehamn, the government of Aland and the topography and geology of the islands. *Open Tuesday–Sunday from 11:00 a.m. to 4:00 p.m.; additional hours Tuesday from 6:00 p.m. to 8:00 p.m.*

The Museum Ship Pommern

The *Pommern* was originally built for a German shipping company in 1903. When the German fleet was divided up after WWI, the *Pommern* was bought by Captain Gustaf Erikson, Aland's most prominent ship-owner, who owned the largest shipping fleet in the world. As part of Captain Erikson's fleet, she was a grain ship, carrying wheat from Australia to England. In the "grain ship" races that used to occur on the route, the *Pommern* acquitted herself well, winning one race and an overall fifth place, averaging 108 days for the voyage from Melbourne to Liverpool. Anything under 100 days was considered fast, but one ship took 165 days to make the journey. The crew on board the *Pommern* numbered 26 men, not a large number for the amount of work required. During WWII, the *Pommern* remained in port at Mariehamn. In 1952, the Erikson family presented the ship to Mariehamn as a museum ship. The *Pommern* is the only steel four-masted ship to be preserved intact. The only change is that the figurehead is a copy of the original, which is in the Aland Maritime Museum. Some of the old-time sailors from the windjammer fleets work on the boat now, making new sails for her. *Open June–August daily from 9:00 a.m. to 5:00 p.m.; all other months, 10:00 a.m. to 4:00 p.m.*

The Aland Maritime Museum

Exhibitions on the seafaring life of the Aland Islands. *Open weekdays from 9:00 a.m. to 5:00 p.m.; Sunday, 10:00 a.m. to 4:00 p.m.*

The Aland Art Gallery

Exhibits on art in Aland from the 1840s to the present. Open the same hours as the Aland Museum.

THE DISTRICTS OF ALAND

Aland is divided into districts, some comprising entire islands, others making up part of the main island. Among the more interesting ones are those listed below. There are many medieval churches in the outlying districts of Aland; the 14th-century castle of Kastkelholm is another point of interest as is Bormasund Fortress. In addition, there are many sites of Viking settlements and graveyards that can be explored, and beyond the sights, Aland is a beautiful place to bicycle or drive just for the pleasure of the landscape.

SUND

Sund, northeast of Mariehamn, has a concentration of interesting sites.

The Jan Karlsgarden Open-Air Museum

A complex of several old buildings brought to this site from all over Aland. The centerpiece of the exhibit is an 1850 farmhouse with exceptional interiors: a formal parlor with beautiful wall paintings, a charming kitchen, furnished as it would have been, a family bedroom and an informal sitting room. *The buildings are open from the beginning of May through September every day from 9:00 a.m. to 7:00 p.m. The grounds can be visited at other times.*

The Vita Bjorn Crown Jail

Just across the road from the museum is the old prison building. It is a small structure, with attached quarters for the warden. Each of the four cells is furnished according to a period in the long history of the prison. It was in operation from around 1775 until 1975. It is interesting to note the changes in living conditions, from a small cell, furnished with one bed but intended to accommodate as many as six prisoners, to the cell from the mid-20th century, when prison reformers had managed to require that only two prisoners occupy a sizable cell. *Open May–September from 10:00 a.m. to 5:00 p.m. daily.*

Kastkelholm Castle

This 13th-century ruin is located near Jan Karlsgarden and can be seen from the outside, but it is closed to the public during restoration.

Bormasund Fortress at Sund

The ruins of the fortress built by the czars. It was blown up by British and French forces during the Crimean War. The view from the north tower is especially beautiful. Open at all times. At Prasto Pilot Station in Sund is an exhibition on the fortress, which includes some of the finds from the site. *Open June–August, Tuesday–Sunday from 10:00 a.m. until 3:00 p.m.*

FINSTROM

This is one of the largest districts of Aland and lies in the center. The village of **Godby** has shops, cafes and a hotel and is the second largest town of Aland. The **Finstrom Church** is of particular interest, dating from the 12th century.

HAMMARLAND

The ride from Mariehamn through Hammarland and on to Eckero is a pleasant one. Hammarland is a farming district with **St. Catherine's Church**, another granite church from the Middle Ages, and one of the few remaining church stables in Aland. **Skarpnato** is an especially scenic area, with a homestead museum and crafts shop. From there, you can take the bicycle ferry to Geta.

ECKERO

This is the westernmost district, not only of Aland, but of Finland. It was to Eckero that the mail was taken by rowboat and sailboat between Aland and Grisslehamn in Sweden. Now, every year at the beginning of June there is a mail service race with the old-style boats. **The Post and Customs House** in Storby was designed by C.L. Engels and completed in 1828. There is also a small mail-boat museum and a homestead museum, Labbas, at Storby, which is open June–

August, Tuesday–Sunday from 11:00 a.m. to 1:00 p.m. The 13th-century church at Eckero is a very pretty one.

SALTVIK

North of Jomala and Finstrom, Saltvik is an agricultural district with beautiful scenery and many traces of ancient settlements. The higher hills in Saltvik are good places from which to get an idea of the geological history of Alands. The sea was once several meters above its present elevation so many of these rocky hills were, in fact, islands or island fortresses, made safe by the natural formations of rocks. One warning to would-be picnickers: Though the rocks look like a great place for a picnic, they are often ant-infested, even without the temptation of food, so picnickers might be chewed up before their food is.

JOMALA

Situated beside Mariehamn, Jomala boasts **St. Olof's**, one of the oldest churches in the islands, and a nature preserve, **Ramsholmen**, with rare plant and bird life. At Mockelo is a beach and camping site.

LEMLAND

Lemland sits across the Lemstrom Canal from Jomala. In Lembote, visitors will find a restored **seafarers' chapel** that is thought to be one of Finland's oldest buildings. There is also a medieval church here.

FOGLO

Foglo is a large outer island to the west of central Aland. At Degerby is one of the most well-equipped **marinas** in the area. The main street of the village is charming, with several impressive old houses, an inn and a cafe. In the old **courthouse**, visitors can get a meal and a room. The church is from the 14th century.

LUMPARLAND

Here you will find one of the four **wooden churches** in Aland. Its date is in dispute, some saying 1638 and others placing it as late as 1720, but it is a very appealing structure whatever its date of birth.

VARDO

Vardo, one of the outer islands, has attracted some of Aland's most well known writers. The 15th-century granite church is impressive, and the last kilometer of the old mail road has been left unchanged and is marked with milestones. The **Seffers homestead museum** at Lovo is open only by prior arrangement.

KUMLINGE

Kumlinge is the only outer island district with an inn and an airfield. Its 15th-century **St. Anne's Church** is of special interest because of the well-preserved murals depicting scenes from the Bible.

WHERE TO STAY

Visitors can choose to stay in town at a hotel and make excursions out into the countryside, or to stay in a pension or rent a holiday cottage in the countryside. Cottage rental can be done through a local travel agency or through the shipping companies that operate ferry service to Aland. Try **Alandsresor Ab**, *Box 62, SF 22101 Mariehamn;* **Viking Line**, *Storagatan 2, SF 22100 Mariehamn;* **Silja Line**, *Samseglingsagenturen, Torgatan 10, SF 222100, Mariehamn;* **Birka Line**, *Storagatan 11, SF 22100, Mariehamn.*

MARIEHAMN

The Park Alandia Hotel   ★★★
In the center of town, the Park Alandia is a pleasant, modern and comfortable hotel with a friendly atmosphere. Sauna and pool.   *Moderate.*

The Pommern   ★★★
The hotel was expanded and renovated in 1987, and all its 54 rooms are comfortable and pleasant. The restaurant here is excellent. Sauna, outdoor and indoor pool.   *Moderate.*

The Hotel Arkipelag
Located along the water, on Strandvagen, this is a modern, attractive spot that seems bigger than the other hotels in town, though it has only 86 rooms. Everything is up to date here. There are a restaurant, casino and sauna.   *Moderate to expensive.*

The Hotel Adlon
Situated just outside of town. The 54 rooms all have private bath but no TV. There is a sauna and indoor pool.   *Moderate.*

WHERE TO EAT

The best bet in town is the **Pommern Restaurant** in the Pommern Hotel. The specialty here is fish, elegantly and deliciously prepared in attractive surroundings and with friendly, unpretentious service. For a casual meal in a jolly place on the water, try A.S.S. It is boat-ey, cozy and fun.

TAMPERE AND THE CENTRAL REGION

Tampere is an industrial city disguised in surrounding greenery.

TAMPERE

Tourist Information Office: *Verkatehtaankatu 2, PB87, 33211 Tampere. Open June, July, and August, weekdays from 8:30 a.m. to 8:00 p.m.; Saturday, 8:30 a.m.–6:00 p.m.; Sunday, noon–6:00 p.m. All other months, weekdays only, 8:30 a.m.–4:00 p.m.*

TAMPERE CARD

Available from June 1 through August 31. The card entitles holders to free bus transportation, entrance to city sight-seeing and admission to several museums. Purchase at the City Tourist Office, the local traffic information office, Tampere Camping Harmala, VR travel service and hotels. Good for 24 hours. **Sarkanniemi Tourist Center** now has a tourist card, available between April 30 and Sept. 3. With the card, visitors gain admittance to six of the major attractions, including the Amusement Park, the Aquarium, the Sara Hilden Art Museum and the Children's Zoo.

DIRECTORY

Banks • Open Monday–Friday, 9:30 a.m.–4:30 p.m. On Saturday, money can be exchanged at the City Tourist Office.

Bicycle rental • Urheiluruutu, *Itsenaisyydenkatu 25*, ☎ *553 751* or Kauppahuone Maailmak, *Tammenlanpuistokatu 23-25*, ☎ *611 622.*

Car rental • Budget, **Tehdaskatu 4**, ☎ *532 588.* Hertz, **Pyynikintie 13** (Rosendahl), ☎ *113 341.*

Hotel Booking • *Puutarhakatu 16 B, 5th floor,* ☎ *133 155.* Open June–August weekdays from 9:00 a.m. to 5:00 p.m.; Saturday, 10:00 a.m.–2:00 p.m. September–May, weekdays, 8:00 a.m.-5:00 p.m.

Cottages • Tampere Provincial Tourist Organization, *Verkatehtaankatu 2.* ☎ *124 488.* Mailing address: *P.O. Box 87, 33211 Tampere.*

Taxi • ☎ *041.*

Tampere, an old weaving and textile center, hangs between two lakes on a narrow isthmus slit by the Tammerkoski rapids. Surrounded by green parks and woods, the city successfully disguises the heavy industry that has made it into one of the most prosperous and largest inland cities in Scandinavia. Tampere is a "summer city," with boats plying the lake routes, and the beautiful Pyynikki Ridge offering woods and trails from which to view the city. In addition, there are several major festivals that bring visitors to town. The center of Tampere is, of necessity, small, since it is built on a narrow piece of land with a river running through the middle. Along the river, the old factories are being converted into apartment houses and shops, so there is little evidence of the industrial side of Tampere.

GETTING THERE

Tampere-Pirkkala Airport. Bus and train service from Helsinki and Turku.

SIGHTSEEING TOURS

Daily sightseeing tour: *June–August at 2:00 p.m. from the City Tourist Office.*

WHAT TO SEE AND DO

The Cathedral

Designed in 1907 by Lars Sonck, the cathedral is a fine example of the National Romantic style that developed as a statement of liberation from Russia and a love for Finland. The style draws on medieval forms of Finnish architecture and is characterized by the use of stone and by carvings of animals and flowers on the facades. This style is still quite old-fashioned, though one can glean some indications of the art nouveau style, which was to develop under the leadership of Eliel Saarinen. This Lutheran church—as are all the national churches of Finland—is a friendly, almost cozy place. The space is defined by curves, arcs and apses, and is decorated almost merrily, or at least optimistically, with bright frescoes. The painting above the very simple altar was done by Magnus Ecknell, a well-known Finnish painter of the time, and is a representation of the Resurrection with, instead of the figure of Jesus, a procession of people of different races walking, or perhaps marching forward.

The other paintings in the church are the work of Hugo Simberg, another prominent Finnish painter. Along the length of the nave Simberg painted a fresco of twelve boys dancing, a garland intertwined among them. The twelve boys, of course, represent the apostles. But beyond that, they represent the Finnish people and the ways in which they meet life. This painting caused quite an uproar at its unveiling, not just because its representation of the apostles as young frolicking boys was controversial, but also because the paintings were representations of actual children of the congregation. The painting of death is also unconventional and, in its way, positive. Death is depicted as a gardener, tending delicate green shoots, nurturing life so to speak. There is even the homely touch of a towel on which one of the gardeners seems ready to wipe his hands. *The church is open May–August, every day from 10:00 a.m. to 6:00 p.m. The rest of the year, it is open from 11:00 a.m. to 3:00 p.m.*

The Kaleva Church

This church was built in 1966 according to a design by Reima and Raili Pietila, who also designed the city library. Its white-bricked exterior, with a series of curved facades, is intended to reflect the purity of the Scandinavian light and the eternity of the landscape. But the visitor who takes the trouble to step inside will be rewarded with the astonishing interior that seems to be a contemporary, Finnish interpretation of a Gothic cathedral. The church is arresting in the splendid austerity of its light-filled space, which rises high, carrying the eye, the imagination and perhaps even the soul upwards.

Pispala

Walk through this hillside area of higgledy-piggledy topography on which residents have built a charming assortment of pastel-colored frame houses, now in various states of repair (and disrepair). Once an area for artists and older people, Pispala is enjoying renewed popularity. Residents are renovating the old houses and building new ones in the style of the old. In summertime, it is pleasant to walk here, as there are paths and steps that wind between the houses and down the hill. You need no guide and no printed walking tour. Just set out, comfortably shod, and let your feet and curiosity lead the way.

The Sara Hilden Museum

Located in the Sarkanniemi Park, this attractive, contemporary structure houses a fine permanent collection of modern Finnish and international art, and is often the host to major traveling exhibitions. The heart of the collection was donated by Sara Hilden, and contained primarily works by Erik Enroth; but with the establishment of the Sara Hilden Foundation, the collection has been expanded to include major modern European works by Henry Moore, Alberto Giacometti, Paul Klee, Joan Miro, Picasso, Leger and Juan Gris. Several sculptures are situated in the grounds of the museum, and the design of the building incorporates the beautiful outdoor scene so that from within, the visitor can look out and see some of these sculptures against the natural backdrop of the lake and the trees. *Open daily from 11:00 a.m. until 6:00 p.m.*

Sarkanniemi Park

One of Tampere's primary summer attractions. In this area, you will find an amusement park, a zoo, an aquarium and a planetarium. The Nasinneula **observation tower**, 551 feet high, has an observation platform with a revolving restaurant. *The tower is open May–August from 10:00 a.m. to 8:00 p.m. The rest of the year from 10:00 a.m. to 5:30 p.m.* The **planetarium** *has performances every hour on the hour from May to August between 10:00 a.m. and 7:00 p.m.; all other months, between noon and 5:00 p.m.* The **aquarium** *is open from May to September every day from 10:00 a.m. until 8:00 p.m. The rest of the year it is open from 10:00 a.m. until 5:30 p.m.* The **dolphinarium** presents a half-hour show several times a day. In addition there are over seven areas of rides and games, *open in summer from noon until 8:00 p.m., and in May and the end of August, on weekends only.* It is possible to pick up vouchers for discounts on activities in the Sarkanniemi area from travel agencies in town.

Tampere Hall

This brand-new hall, Finland's largest conference site, is a spectacular modern design with the capacity to stage several events at one time. Managed by the former manager of Finlandia Hall in Helsinki, the center attracts the best and most important performances available.

The City Library

This stunning contemporary library is a community center as well as a library, but it would make a reader out of the most reluctant student with its sleek blue, black and white interior, its open spaces and inviting nooks. Designed in the shape of a bird, the building is astonishing both inside and out. If you cannot read the Finnish books on the shelves, there is a well-stocked section with books in English, or you can relax in one of the listening chairs in the music library, have a coffee in the cafe or just watch the people of Tampere as they enjoy this beautiful facility. In the library, a permanent exhibition of the original illustrations of the *Moomin Valley*, by Tove Jansen, includes three-dimensional tableaux and a completely furnished Moominhouse with balconies and secret passages. *The exhibit is open from noon until 6:00 p.m. during May, June, July and August, and the rest of the year, Wednesday–Sunday from noon until 6:00 p.m. All departments of the library are open from June 1 through August 31 weekdays from 9:00 a.m. to 7:00 p.m. and Saturday from 9:00 a.m. to 3:00 p.m. Closed Sunday. During the rest of the year, it is open on weekdays until 8:00 p.m. and Saturday to 3:00 p.m. The reference library and reading room are open weeknights until 9:00 p.m., Saturday, 9:00 a.m. to 3:00 p.m., and Sunday, noon to 6:00 p.m.*

The Pyynikki Open Air Theater

This theater is something to see because of its revolving auditorium, unique in Scandinavia, and its beautiful setting. Each summer a different play is put on. Though performances are in Finnish, there is a summary in English. *No performances on Monday.*

Hameensilta Bridge

In the middle of town, this bridge is adorned with four statues by Waino Aaltonen.

Amuri Workers' Museum

In displays of 25 homes, two shops and a bakery, the museum depicts the living conditions of the workers of Tampere between the years of 1880 and 1970. *Open mid-May to August, Tuesday–Sunday from noon to 6:00 p.m.*

The Lenin Museum

A small two-room museum in the Tampere Workers' House. The exhibits trace Lenin's work and activities in Finland.

The Tampere City Museum

Located in the main house of the former Hatanpaa Estate. It offers exhibits on the history of Tampere. *Open Tuesday–Friday, noon–6:00 p.m. Closed Monday.*

Haihara Doll Museum

In a former manor house located about four miles out of the center of town. In addition to exhibits of dolls, which are housed in the old stables of the house, the main house of the manor contains a costume museum and an exhibit of furniture and room interiors showing what life used to be like in a manor house. *Open May–October every day from noon to 6:00 p.m. Closed Midsummer Eve and Day. The rest of the year, it is open from noon to 4:00 p.m. every day but Friday.*

The Laura Viita Museum

The childhood home of this well-known Finnish writer. Even if you have never heard of Laura Viita, you might be interested in coming to her house, as it is located in Pispala and offers a good chance to get inside one of the houses in that picturesque area.

The Iittala Glass Works

Located 60 kilometers outside Tampere, on highway 3 in the direction of Helsinki. You will find a glass museum, factory shop and gift shop, as well as a textile and pewter shop and a restaurant. *Open May–August from 9:00 a.m. to 8:00 p.m., and the rest of the year from 9:00 a.m. to 6:00 p.m.*

LAKE CRUISES

The Finnish Silverline makes several trips between Tampere and Hameenlinna. The old steamer, *Tarjanne*, sails to Virrat, 70 miles north, along the "Poet's Way," which got its name from the fact that Finland's national poet, J. L. Runeberg, praised the beauty of the area when he spent the summers at Ruovesi. The boat stops at Ruovesi, where you can visit the 18th-century wooden church and the local history museum, and then goes on to Virrat where it moors for the night. In Virrat, the woods, lakes and cliffs lend themselves to hiking. If passengers do not wish to spend the night on the boat, they can travel one stretch of the route by boat and the rest by bus. There are also shorter cruises on both the lakes of Tampere.

SHOPPING

Tampere has some fine museum-quality handicraft shops with exhibits and sales. The two main centers, Verkaranta and Kehrasaari, are located in the center of town along the rapids.

In the **Verkaranta Center** there is an exhibition hall, the **Pirkanmaa Kotityo** shop and a cafe. In the shop, Finnish handcrafted articles, rugs, knitted goods and Finnish traditional costumes are sold. In the **Kehrasaari Center**, you will find **Marian Kamari**, selling wooden toys as well as men's, women's and children's wear. Also in the center is the shop of **Aarikka**, which sells wooden jewelry and gift items as well as handicrafts.

There are several other boutiques in the centers, and these are pleasant places to browse as well as buy. For porcelain, glass and wood articles, try **Arsopi** at *Nasilinnankatu 29* or **Arvin Kauppa** just a few doors down the same street, with Finnish glass, woodcraft and sauna accessories. **Marimekko** designs are available at the shopping center **Koskikeskus**. English books are available at **Akateeminen Kirjakauppa** at *Tuomiokirkonkatu 28*. There is also an **indoor food market** at *Hameenkatu 19* that sells **reindeer meat** and Finnish cheese, and outdoor markets every morning on weekdays. Many factories also have shops. **Finlayson** sells fabrics and bed linens; **Junotex** sells leather jackets and gloves.

For more, inquire at the Tourist Information Office.

WHERE TO STAY

The Hotel Ilves ★★★★

Hatanpäänvaltatie 1 • The most luxurious place in town. This is a deluxe hotel with three restaurants, a bar and nightclub, as well as a beautiful pool and sauna center. The rooms are large, typically commercial, with nothing distinctively Finnish about them. But this hotel is oh-so comfortable. It adjoins the Koskikesus Shopping Center with about 80 shops and several cafes and restaurants. The hotel itself has several restaurants, none of which is anything special. There is also a nightclub and disco. Finncheques and weekend rates apply. *Expensive.*

The Cumulus Koskikatu ★★★

Koskikatu 5 • In the center of town beside the Tammerkoski Rapids, the Cumulus has 230 rooms, 60 of which are non-smoking rooms. Three restaurants and a bar add to the activity here. Indoor pool and saunas.

The Hotel Rantasipi ★★★

Yliopistonkatu 44 • Not far from Sorsapuisto Park. Winter-garden restaurant, summer terrace, a Turkish sauna, two Finnish saunas and seven rooms with private saunas, whirlpool. The rooms are bright and modern.

The Hotel Rosendahl ★★★

Pyynikintie 13 • This is a deluxe hotel situated in Pyynikki Park. There are four restaurants, including the **Catalina Rosa** gourmet restaurant as well as a pub and a nightclub. Skiing and jogging are available on trails in the park. There are also squash and tennis facilities, as well as saunas, a pool and a small beach. *Expensive, moderate weekend prices.*

The Sokos Hotel Tammer ★

Satakunnankatu 13 • This hotel is an old war-horse, built in 1910 but renovated not too long ago. The lobby is venerable and Victorian, with a shiny bar. The rooms could use some freshening up, but they are comfortable and all have private baths, TV and minibar. There is an informal restaurant, a pub, a nightclub and a summer terrace. Located in the center of town. *Moderate.*

Sokos Hotel Villa
Sumeliuksenkatu 14 • A new hotel built in 1991 next to Tampere Hall; a popular, busy place. The restaurant is run in connection with a restaurant school, which means that the food is interesting and good.

The Hotel Tampere
Hämeenkatu 1 • Another old standby in town across from the railway station. The rooms are small but were renovated several years ago and are in good condition. This is a popular place with plenty of activity. There is a café-restaurant, a lobby bar, a terrace restaurant and a night pub, as well as a new shopping arcade built around a courtyard. *Moderate to expensive.*

The Pyynikki Residential Hotel
Apartments are available here by the day, week and month. The building dates from 1916, but has been completely renovated into one- and two-room apartments or three-room suites, all with kitchens. There are also two saunas for the guests. *Moderate.*

The Hotel Victoria
Itsenäisyydenkatu 1 • Not far from the center of town, this modern hotel does not look like much from the outside, but it has comfortable, if rather plain, rooms. All have private W.C., and most have private baths or showers and TV. The room rates include a morning sauna and swim as well as breakfast. There is a Chinese restaurant nearby. *Moderate.*

Motel Härmälä
Located on the outskirts of Tampere about five kilometers from the city center. Good bus service from town. Situated near Lake Pyhäjärvi and the Tampere Fair and Exhibition Center. Fully licensed restaurant with beautiful views over the lake. This is a simple and inexpensive spot.

WHERE TO EAT

Finlaysonin Palatsi
Situated in an old mansion, this grand old landmark lives up to its popularity. In addition to several dining rooms and private rooms, there is a sauna and a pleasant three-acre park where an outdoor restaurant is open in summertime.

Klingendahl
Located in a big, old factory building that also houses boutiques and apartments, this is a fine spot frequented by residents of Tampere.

Mona Lisa
The restaurant of the Cumulus Hotel serves light food.

Ohranjyvä
A popular spot with journalists, this place is appropriately smoky, but the food is good and the ambience lively.

The Rosendahl

Located In the hotel of the same name, this restaurant serves fine food in a beautiful setting. Try the pub in the hotel for a moderately priced meal.

Expensive.

Näsinneula

This revolving restaurant on the top of the sight-seeing tower is expensive, but if you have the money and time, it is a good way to get an overall view of the city.

Tiiliholvi

Situated in the brick vaults of a former bank. Good food. *Expensive.*

Suomalainen Klubi

A traditional Finnish buffet lunch is offered every weekday in this centrally located restaurant.

Salud Bedega

Famous for steaks and Spanish food, the restaurant has a buffet lunch Monday–Friday.

Gasthaus Berlin

An inexpensive restaurant with Finnish home cooking located in the **Tullintori** shopping center.

Kinjakahvila Into

This vegetarian restaurant is located in the old library building in the center of town.

Myllarit

The restaurant occupies an old mill near the conference and concert center.

Rosso Koskipuisto

A casual pizza and pasta place with a summer terrace beside the river.

Koruna

This moderately priced restaurant serves Finnish and international cuisine in its picturesque National Romantic building in the center of town.

NOTE: *Hotels and restaurants that seemed expensive two years ago are now moderate or inexpensive due to the devaluation of the Finnish mark and resulting drop in prices.*

NIGHTLIFE

Hotel Ilves *nightclub is open every night except Sunday from 10:00 p.m. to 4:00 a.m.*

Tiffany *in the Cumulus is open from 8:00 p.m. to 4:00 a.m.*

Cabare Oscar *has a disco on the first floor and a live orchestra on the second. Open Monday–Saturday from 7:00 p.m. to 2:00 a.m. and Sunday from 9:00 p.m. to 2:00 a.m.*

Joselin's in the Arctia Rosendahl offers live music *Tuesday–Thursday from 9:00 p.m. to 3:00 a.m., Friday and Saturday from 9:00 a.m. to 4:00 a.m. It is closed on Sunday.*

Dores *is a rock disco open every night from 10:00 p.m. to 4:00 a.m.*

ON THE WAY NORTH

For a novel way of getting to Hameenlinna, see "Lake Cruises." Art lovers headed to Jyvaskyla, in the town of **Mantta**, about midway between Tampere and Jyvaskyla, will find a treasure in the **Gosta Serlachius Museum of Fine Arts**. The museum contains one of Finland's finest private art collections. G.A. Serlachius, a pharmacist and owner of a paper mill, was an early patron of Akseli Gallen-Kallela and other Finnish artists, not only giving them financial support but acting as a kind of coach, urging them on, telling them to work harder and aspire more. The patron established a Fine Arts Foundation in his home town of Mantta and the collection fostered by this foundation is on display at Jokiniemi, the manor house of Gosta Serlachius in Mantta. The exhibit contains major works by some early Finnish painters as well as modern ones. In addition, the museum possesses some fine European art. Two paintings from the museum were selected several years ago as illustrations on UNICEF Christmas cards. There are 130 works by Gallen-Kallela, making this the most important private collection of his work in Finland. The museum occupies the library of the manor, and a steward's house has been made into a cafe and restaurant. The mansion is interesting in itself, with a beautiful view of the lake. *Open from the beginning of May to August every day, except Monday. In winter, it is open weekends only. Check for hours. Guided tours in English are available on request.*

JYVASKYLA

Tourist Information Office: *Vapaudenkatu 38, 40100 Jyvaskyla. Open June, July and August weekdays from 8:00 a.m. to 6:00 p.m. Weekends from 10:00 a.m. to 6:00 p.m. The rest of the year, weekdays only, from 8:00 a.m. to 4:00 p.m. In the same building, Central Finland-Vacation Finland will assist with reservations for hotels, holiday chalets and farmhouse vacations.* ☎ *(9) 41 610 866.*

GETTING THERE

Bus and train from Helsinki, Turku and Tampere. Boat service to and from Lahti from early June to early August.

About 100 miles north of Tampere, Jyvaskyla, a university town, is of particular interest because it boasts several buildings by Alvar Aalto. For travelers wishing to study the works of that renowned Finnish architect, this is the place. There are enough buildings here, within walking distance of one another, to provide a definitive view of the designer's work. Among the Aalto-designed structures are a 1920s renovation of a traditional wood cottage, the city theater, which was completed in 1982, and the police headquarters. But the real treasure trove is the university, where the dining rooms, gymnasiums and classroom buildings are Aalto designs. Walking distance from the university is the Alvar Aalto Museum with Aalto's sketches and furniture.

Sightseeing cruise: A two-hour cruise through Paijanne Lake is available at about $12 per person. Inquire at tourist office.

WHERE TO STAY

Rantasipi Laajavuori ★★★★
Located amid forests and lakes, the hotel is about four kilometers out of town. Many of its 176 rooms contain Aalto-designed furniture. There are saunas, an indoor pool, boating, tennis and golf nearby. In winter, the ski trails are lit. Three restaurants, a nightclub and a bar. A double will run about 600FIM.

The Cumulus Jyvaskiyh ★★★
Located in town in two modern buildings containing 238 rooms in all. There is a sauna section with a pool, a restaurant and a Viennese cafe. A double room will be about 425FIM.

Hotel Sokos Alexandra ★★★
In the middle of town, this is a new hotel with modern, comfortable rooms. There is a no-smoking floor in addition to a business-class section. Restaurant, bar and sauna. Double room from 550FIM.

Restaurant suggestion: Katinhanta serves traditional Finnish food with entrees averaging about $22 per person. Among the specialties are reindeer in a wild mushroom sauce, snow grouse, and an assortment of appetizers that includes smoked reindeer and smoked and salted salmon.

LAHTI

Tourist Information Office: *Torikatu 3 B, PB 175, 15111 Lahti. Open June–August weekdays 8:00 a.m.–5:00 p.m.; Saturday and Sunday 10:00 a.m.–2:00 p.m. Rest of year, weekdays 8:00 a.m.–4:00 p.m. The tourist office will help you with guides, hotel bookings and holiday cottage accommodations.*

South of Tampere, Lahti is the winter sports center of Finland, having hosted the World Ski Championships in 1978 and again in 1989. Its ski stadium is considered one of the world's best.

GETTING THERE

Bus or train from Helsinki, Turku, and Tampere. Between Lahti and Heinola there is both boat service and an **old steam locomotive** that runs in summertime on Sundays. Travelers can go one way by boat and return by the train.

In addition to the sports attractions, stop by to take a look at: **The Town Hall**, designed by Eliel Saarinen in 1912. **The Church of the Cross** was designed by Alvar Aalto and built in 1978. *Open daily 10:00 a.m.–3:00 p.m.* **The Lahti Sports Center** includes a ski stadium, three ski jumps, an ice stadium and a multipurpose sports hall. *The sightseeing platform on top of the 90-meter ski jump* *is open in June and July, Monday–Friday from 11:00 a.m. until 6:00 p.m., on Saturday and Sunday from 10:00 a.m. to 5:00 p.m. There is also a 50-meter-high lookout tower with a cafeteria open every day from 10:00 a.m. to 9:00 p.m* **The Lahti Art Museum** displays primarily Finnish art. **The Lahti Historical Museum** in Lahti Manor has exhibits on the cultural history of the area in addition to a Karelian collection from the Viipuri Museum, and French and Italian art and furniture from the 13th to the 18th centuries. *Open Tuesday–Sunday from noon to 4:00 p.m., also Tuesday from 6:00 p.m. to 8:00 p.m.*

SIGHTSEEING TOUR

A two-hour tour of the city is given on Wednesdays and Saturdays from June through August.

WHERE TO STAY

Seurahuone

This is a good choice, with 121 rooms, a restaurant, bar, sauna and pool. All rooms have TV and video. A double will be about 450FIM.

Hotelli Musta Kissa

A smaller hotel with just 67 rooms. All rooms have private baths. No restaurant, but a bar and sauna.   *Moderate.*

Sokos Hotel Ascot

This is the biggest of the hotels listed with 144 rooms, two bars and three restaurants. There is a sauna and indoor pool. A double will be about 475 FIM.

Mukkulan Kartano

An old manor house a few miles out of Lahti that has been converted into an inn. The 15 rooms are all simple but airy and attractive. Not all have private baths.   *Moderate.*

Messila Holiday Center

Situated on spacious grounds, seven kilometers outside Lahti, this is a good choice for travelers wanting to take their time and enjoy the leisure life in Finland. An excellent golf course and ski area as well as horseback riding and swimming make this an attractive resort both summer and winter. In addition to the hotel, there are self-catering cabins, a hostel and campgrounds. Three restaurants are located on the premises, one in the turn-of-the-century manor house, another in the converted 1920s stable, and a third, the Market Place restaurant, occupies the attic of what was a cowshed. Also on the grounds are handicraft workshops where visitors can watch Finnish craftsmen at work. Write **Hotel Messila**, *SF–15980 Messila, Finland.* ☎ *(918) 531 666.*

HAMEENLINNA

Tourist Information Office: *Palokunnankatu 11, 13100 Hameenlinna. Open June 1 to mid-August, Monday–Friday from 9:00 a.m. to 6:00 p.m.; Satur-*

day 9:00 a.m.–2:00 p.m.; Sunday noon–3:00 p.m. Rest of year, weekdays 9:00 a.m.–4:00 p.m. and in May also Saturday, 8:00 a.m.–1:00 p.m.

Hameenlinna was founded in 1639 on the site of the **Hame** tribal community. The people of the Hame region are said to be silent and shy, and the area is known for its breads, grains and porridges, so the hungry traveler will find many small bakeries offering warm, freshly baked bread. The medieval **Hame Castle** and **composer Jean Sibelius's childhood home** are the two drawing cards here. But the beautiful Aulanko Park is also a reason to make the short trip from Helsinki or Tampere.

GETTING THERE

Bus or train from Helsinki, Tampere, Turku and Lahti.

SIGHTSEEING TOUR

An eight-hour sightseeing cruise leaves every Thursday from June 4 to August 18. Passengers will sail from Hameenlinna to Visavuori to visit the studio home of Emil Wikstrom, the Iittala Glassworks and the Kanajarvi Peasant Museum. Return is by bus. The price of approximately $57 includes lunch on board the boat and a snack at the museum.

WHAT TO SEE AND DO

Hame Castle

Construction on this 700-year-old castle, on the shores of Lake Vanajavesi, began in the middle of the 13th century when Birger Jarl of Sweden came to Finland and ordered it built to serve administrative and strategic needs. Construction occurred in three stages, in the 13th, 14th and 18th centuries, and there are obvious differences in the building materials and techniques. Interestingly, more restoration had to be done on the later sections because the mortar of the 18th century was softer than that of the 13th. The castle, one of just three surviving medieval brick buildings in Finland, has served as a garrison, a granary and a prison. Now the King's Hall and the Queen's Chamber, so named for the visit of Gustavus II Vasa and his queen in 1614, are used for chamber concerts and banquets. The small chapel serves for marriages and baptisms, and in the old constable's chamber there is a restaurant. The former bakery is now the site of a summer cafe. *Open May–August every day from 10:00 a.m. to 6:00 p.m.; the rest of the year from 10:00 a.m. to 4:00 p.m.*

Sibelius's Childhood Home

Simply furnished and supplied with plenty of interesting photographs and some musical instruments, this little house in the middle of town was the birthplace of Finland's most renowned composer. From time to time, concerts are given here. *Open May–August every day from 10:00 a.m. to 4:00 p.m. The rest of the year, weekdays noon–4:00 p.m.; Sunday noon–4:00 p.m.; closed Saturday.*

The Hameenlinna Art Museum

Located in a former granary which was designed by C.L. Engels and completed in 1838. The permanent collection is composed of Finnish art as well as changing exhibits.

The Fredrika Wetterhoff Cottage Industry Teachers' College

Located next to the bus station, containing an exhibition of Finnish textiles. There is also a shop here selling textiles, woven goods, jewelry, and wooden items. *Open weekdays 9:00 a.m.–5:00 p.m.; Saturday, 9:00 a.m.–1:00 p.m.*

Aulanko Park

This large, beautiful park and nature preserve owes its existence to the generosity of Captain Hugo Standertskjold, a wealthy weapons manufacturer who wanted to leave something to the people of the area. The Captain, who was not married, was an outgoing, altruistic man. He imported foreign trees and plantings for the park, built a tower from which visitors can get a good view of the surroundings, and set up a school for his employees. In the park by the lake are a golf course, a riding school, tennis courts and boats and bicycles for rent. A camping area has 31 cabins, about one third with showers. All have heat, electricity and kitchen facilities. The camping area is open May to mid-September. Later than that it becomes too cold in Hameenlinna for camping, even for the rugged Finns.

Music in Hameenlinna

One would expect the birthplace of Jean Sibelius to resound with glorious music, and Hameenlinna does. All year long there are concerts in the Sibelius home, the Town Hall and the art gallery, as well as the concert hall.

Iittala Glassworks

Finland's most famous glass company has its factory and shop on Highway 3 north of Hameenlinna. Guided tours of the works and glass blowing are available. A new museum has just been completed, and several shops are located on the premises. There is a restaurant here also. *Open daily May–August from 9:00 a.m. to 8:00 p.m.*

WHERE TO STAY

Hotel Rantasipi Aulanko

Set in Aulanko Park by the lake, this spacious hotel has a large, airy dining room that serves excellent Finnish food. From the hotel, there is access to horseback riding, tennis, golf, boating and windsurfing. In winter, the park lights its skiing trails.   *Expensive.*

The Cumulus Haneenlinna

In the center of Hameenlinna. Pleasant and modern, with newly renovated rooms. Sauna with fireplace and pool.   *Moderate.*

Sokos Hotel Vaakuna

Possentie 7 • Well located in the center of Hameenlinna, this brand new hotel has 123 rooms, all with private bath, TV, minibar. There is also a sauna and a restaurant.

WHERE TO EAT

The Rantasipi Aulanko serves some of the best Finnish food in town. Twice a week, the hotel offers a Finnish buffet, and twice a week the Captain's Russian Buffet. The **Restaurant Pauliina** is located in the city. Its international and Finnish cuisines are excellent.

EASTERN FINLAND AND THE SAIMAA LAKE REGION

Saimaa is the largest lake area in Europe.

The Finns are so proud of their beautiful lakes that they have actually tried to count them. They call their country the land of a thousand lakes, but the number researchers have come up with is 187,888 bodies of water. If the assignment of counting them all seems monotonous to you, you have not seen the glorious lake areas of Finland, which would be worth a bit of tedious counting just to have the excuse to visit them. Saimaa, the eastern lakeland of Finland, is the largest lake area in Europe with some 33,000 islands and more than 31,000 miles of shoreline. Here are silver lakes and shimmering islands, fringed with lush green forests.

Along the shores of the lakes of eastern Finland are towns of varying sizes and sophistication, many incorporating the rich Karelian culture with its complex history and its unique hospitality. Karelia, the easternmost region of Finland, is rich in its own unique culture and heritage and in its tragedy, for much of Karelia was ceded to Russia after World War II. The loss of Karelia was particularly ironic and tragic, because Finland had earlier, during the Winter War of 1939 and 1940, succeeded in pushing back Russia's advances when Russia invaded Finland, expecting a quick and easy victory. The Finns, though outnumbered and with little artillery, fought valiantly, using whatever weapons were at hand. The snow was to their advantage, and the dramatically effective "ski troops" fought a guerrilla-type war in the forests, appearing out of nowhere, white against the white snow. But in the fighting that ensued during WWII, Russia demanded a high price, annexing a large portion of Karelia, including the important city of Viipuri. Few Karelians wanted to be Russians, so many moved back across the border and Finland accepted over 400,000 of her own citizens into the now shrunken borders. In the History Museum of Lappeenranta, there is an extraordinary model of Viipuri, which was the second largest city in Finland until it was bombed during the war and then annexed by Russia. Now men and women who used to live there come to this model to remember, with tears, what once was.

Hotels are listed below by town. If you wish to rent a cottage in a holiday village or a self-catering cottage, contact the **Lappeenranta** or **Savonlinna Tourist Services** or Saimaatours/Kirkkokatu 10, *53100 Lappeenranta,* ☎ *(9) 53 17 772* for rentals in South Karelia. *The North Karelian Tourist Office, Koskikatu 1, 80100 Joensuu.* ☎ *(9) 73 201 363* will arrange rentals in North Karelia.

LAPPEENRANTA

Tourist Information Office: *Bus station, P.O. Box 113, 53101 Hupeenranta. Open first three weeks in June and August, weekdays from 8:00 a.m. until 6:00 p.m.; Saturday 9:00 a.m.–1:00 p.m. From the end of June through the end of July, weekdays 8:00 a.m.–8:00 p.m.; Saturday, 9:00 a.m.–1:00 p.m. and Sunday from 10:00 a.m. until 3:00 p.m. There is a tourist information office in the fortress open from June 1 through the middle of August, weekdays 9:00 a.m.–7:00 p.m. and weekends 10:00 a.m.–6:00 p.m.*

Lappeenranta, on the southeastern shore of Lake Saimaa, is the administrative and cultural center of South Karelia. Lappeenranta does not look like a town with major industry, but all through the lake area, industry based on timber abounds, and you will find sawmills and paper mills. Unfortunately, paper mills create substantial pollution, both of the lakes and the air, and though steps are being taken to counter this damage, your nose will tell you when you are nearing one of them. However, in the town of Lappeenranta, which is the wood processing center of Finland, visitors will not be at all aware of the industry lurking beyond the lovely lakes and forests. Lappeenranta is a gracious, pretty town, lake-bound and linden-lined. Though it is a modern city, its wooden church, leafy parks and the casino by the lake give it the air of an old-fashioned European resort, which it was during the 19th century when it enjoyed popularity as a spa town, attracting visitors from all over Europe, among them the czar himself.

The idyllic, lakeside town gives no hint of its embattled history, when it was juggled between Sweden and Russia. Founded as a market town in 1649 at just about the point where the fortress ruins now stand, Lappeenranta, in its early history, came into glory only once a year on the occasion of the large market gathering. During the period of Swedish rule, earthern ramparts were constructed as part of a larger system of fortifications throughout southeastern Finland. But when Finland was partitioned after the peace treaty of 1743, the border between Sweden and Russia was moved to the river Kymi, leaving Lappeenranta in Russia as part of what was called Old Finland. The later fortifications were constructed under the order of Catherine the Great and were once again planned as part of a chain of defenses through eastern Finland. Major Alexander Suvorov, a colorful Russian officer who spoke Finnish and was very popular with the Finns, oversaw the construction of the Lappeenranta fortress. It was during the 19th century that Lappeenranta became a popular resort attracting international visitors who flocked here for the health spas. Even the czar visited. In the course of the Winter War, Lappeenranta was almost completely burned, but the old part of the town can still be seen, not as it was in 1649, but somewhat as it was when Lappeenranta was a garrison town late in the 18th century.

GETTING THERE

The airport is just a mile out of town, and the flight from Helsinki takes 30 minutes. Bus and train service from Helsinki, Turku and Tampere. Boat from Savonlinna via Puumala.

CRUISES ON LAKE SAIMAA

Several choices from two-hour to two-day trips are available from Lappeenranta. It is possible to go by boat from Lappeenranta to the Saimaa Canal at the Russian border or to Vyborg. Cruise through the archipelago on a summer evening, or take one of the summer-night dancing cruises offered on Saturday nights in July from 9:00 p.m. until midnight. Most of the lake steamers have fully licensed restaurants, and some even have saunas on board.

For information and booking, contact any Finnish travel agent or **Matkapalvelu Travel Services/Saimaa Lines**, *Raatimiehenkatu 12, SF 53100 Lappeenranta. Also* **Lomamatkat Lomatours**, *Kalevankatu 56, SF 00100 Helsinki. FAX 648 355.*

WHAT TO SEE AND DO

IN THE OLD TOWN

The Fortress

One street of the old garrison remains much as it was, with the houses that were once the quarters of the soldiers, officers and staff of the fortress. It is here that many of the interesting sights of Lappeenranta are found, and in addition to the museums listed below, there are also pottery and handicraft workshops in the fortress. In summertime, the fortress is also the scene of an outdoor theater.

The South Karelian Museum

At the end of the street is the building that houses both the historical and the art museum. The building itself was a storehouse for the garrison in the 19th century. The collections of the South Karelian Museum have been gathered from the former city museums of Viborg (Viipuri), Kakisalmi and Lappeenranta. Here one can see actual rooms of Karelian peasants that were brought to the museum and furnished with Karelian objects. The bedroom has an unusual stenciled wall, and the plate of food (plastic) on the kitchen table is intended as an illustration of a typical Karelian meal. There are also rooms of the Jugend period, which ran from 1880 until about 1900, roughly corresponding to the Victorian era of England. Many of the furnishings here are quite typically Russian. In the center of the hall is the beautifully constructed model of Viborg, which belonged to Finland until the end of WWII. It was an international city of sophistication and culture, where it was said that four languages were spoken. The everyday language of the people was Finnish, of the government Swedish, of the business community German and of the military Russian.

In the other wing of the building is the **South Karelian Art Museum**, devoted primarily to paintings from Viborg. The statue of the anguished young woman is an allusion to the tragic fashion of years ago when young Finnish women, and occasionally men, would go to Imatra to jump off the bridge over the rapids. *Both museums are open in summer, weekdays 10:00 a.m.–6:00 p.m. and weekends 11:00 a.m.–5:00 p.m. In winter, they are open Tuesday–Sunday 11:00 a.m.–5:00 p.m. and Thursday 11:00 a.m.– 8:00 a.m.*

The Orthodox Church

This is Finland's oldest Orthodox Church, dedicated in 1785. Only the barrel vaults and the nave date from the 18th century; the rest was added in 1903. The church has recently been completely restored. *Open in summer only, Tuesday–Sunday 10:00 a.m.–6:00 p.m.*

The Cavalry Museum

Housed in the oldest building in town, which served as the guardhouse of the fortress, the collection includes pictures and paraphernalia of the Finnish and Uusimaa dragoon regiments and of the Hame cavalry regiment. There is still a Uusimaa dragoon battalion whose band, dressed in the traditional costumes, plays at important occasions. *Open in summer on week-*

days 10:00 a.m.–6:00 p.m. and weekends 11:00 a.m.–5:00 p.m. In winter, Tuesday and Wednesday 11:00 a.m.–3:00 p.m.; Thursday 11:00 a.m.–8:00 p.m.

Lunch break: The Cafe Majurska, just across the street from the Cavalry Museum, serves meals and wonderful, homemade Karelian pastries in an interesting, renovated old building. The name of the cafe means the Major's Wife, appropriate since the owner is indeed married to a soldier. She has painstakingly renovated the house and collected a potpourri of antiques and quirky finds that make this a most pleasant place to stop.

LAPPEENRANTA CENTER

New Town Hall

The center of town is a blend of old and modern with the old Lappee Church and the impressive new city hall and conference-and-concert center. Step inside the city hall just to see the interiors of birch and granite, and the beautiful textiles, which are the work of Laura Korpikaivo, a well-known Finnish textile artist who has a museum in Lappeenranta.

The Lappee Church

The 18th-century wooden church stands in the central park in what was once a wooded area. This is the only church in Finland built on a double-cross plan. The blue-and-white wood interior with its beautiful chandeliers makes it particularly attractive. It was built between 1792 and 1794 by a peasant named Juhana Salonen who could neither read nor write and who was not licensed as a carpenter or builder. But when he demonstrated, in his less important endeavors, his great talent, he was allowed to design and build this church. His son, who helped him on the church, became a skilled designer and builder in his own right. *Open every day in summertime from noon until 5:00 p.m.*

The Market Place

Located on Oksasenkatu, in the middle of town, the market is a lively place, where you will find Karelian specialties like the fish-filled bread from Kuopio called *kalakukko*. It is rye bread stuffed with smoked whitefish and pork or with salmon and potatoes. There is also a Karelian bread sold here that was originally made at the monastery in Viborg. This comes in various sizes and is shaped somewhat like a pretzel. In addition to the breads, there are meat, cheeses, fruits and vegetables. Goods are displayed outside in the square as well as in the market hall. *Open Monday–Saturday 7:00 a.m. to 1:00 p.m. and also in summer from 3:00 p.m. to 7:00 p.m. on weekdays.*

Laura Korpikaivo-Tamminen's Museum for Textile Handicrafts

In 1979, the artist donated her house and her collection of handmade textiles to Lappeenranta with the understanding that the town would build a museum for handicrafts on the vacant lot next to the house. The building was opened in 1983. In addition to Korpikaivo-Tamminen's contemporary work and exhibitions on the weaver's art, the collection includes textiles from the artist's childhood home as well as some of her early needlework. *Open in summer 10:00 a.m.–6:00 p.m. weekdays; 11:00 a.m.–5:00 p.m.*

weekends. *In winter, Tuesday and Wednesday, 11:00 a.m.–3:00 p.m.; Thursday, 2:00 a.m.–8:00 p.m.; Sunday, 11:00 a.m.–5:00 p.m.*

WHERE TO STAY

The Sokos Hotel Lappee

The building stretches out instead of rising high, so you sometimes have a long walk to your room, but the halls are light and airy and the rooms the same. With 211 rooms, this is a good-sized hotel, but it has a pleasant, friendly air about it. There are several restaurants and a nightclub, in addition to a swimming pool and sauna area with sauna bar. A double room will be about 500FIM.

The Cumulusm Happeenranta

Also in the center of town. Comfortable rooms, pool, sauna, two restaurants and a cafe, in addition to a lobby bar. It will be about the same price as the Lappee.

WHERE TO EAT

The Kasino

A lively place, with several choices of rooms to dine in and plenty of activity. It is open only in summer and is a good choice because it is right on the lake. As you might expect, the fish is a specialty but there are meat dishes as well. Live music.

Majurska Cafe

(see "Old Town" section) • *Open only from 10:00 a.m. to 6:00 p.m.*, it is probably more convenient for lunch or tea when you are in the area of the fortress than for dinner.

FOR KARELIAN COOKING

Lemi, just about 15 miles west of Lappeenranta, is the place to go. Lemi is known for its potatoes, especially a variety called "Lemi's red," and for a dish called *sara* made of mutton and potatoes. The meat and potatoes are baked in a wooden trough called a *sara*, hence the name. The **Restaurant Kippurasarvi**, located in Lemi, is known for its *sara*. Book ahead. ☎ *(953) 827 57*. *Sara* is also served in the restored **Sara Cabin** which is part of the Lemi Museum and in the **Sara Hut** at Korpi-koulu.

EXCURSIONS FROM LAPPEENRANTA

THE SAIMAA CANAL

Because there was no natural waterway from Lake Saimaa, the largest lake area of Europe, to the Gulf of Finland, a canal was built over 100 years ago to link those waters. The present canal, which was under construction from 1963 until 1968, is 43 kilometers long, with eight locks. Twenty-three kilometers are in Finland and the Finnish are the principal users, followed by the Russians and the Germans. Travelers wishing to see the canal can go by boat from Lappeenranta or by car. The drive along the canal is pleasant and it is always fun if you are lucky enough to see a ship, especially one of the big Russian ones, go through one of the locks. The canal is closed during the coldest part of the winter.

NUIJAMAA

Just a few kilometers from Lappeenranta, right at the Russian border, is the village of Nuijamaa. Nuijamaa lost much of its territory to Russia and is now only half the size it once was. Even part of the center of town was lost to Russia. Now the town has fallen into difficult economic times, and by the time you read this, the village may have been incorporated into Lappeenranta.

The center of town is just a small green with the church, bell tower, cemetery and library. The soil of Nuijamaa is especially excellent for growing berries and apple trees, and there are several medium-sized fruit farms here. Some Finnish farmers live within the border zone but can travel freely in and out on the Finnish side. The border seems to cause no problems nowadays, though it was responsible for a tragedy in WWII when the Nuijamaa church organist climbed to the top of the bell tower in order to look over into Russia. The Russian soldiers spotted him and fired on him, killing him and setting fire to the church.

The new Nuijamaa Church was given by American Lutherans to Nuijamaa after the old church was burned. The interior of the church is of dark pine with plenty of windows to lighten the space. If you walk down the road to the border station, you will come to a small patrol station where a guard will hand you a sheet entitled, "Instructions concerning movement and stay in frontier zone." Among the activities listed as "offending the integrity of the frontier and the peace of the frontier" are photographing the frontier; shouting over the frontier or speaking to the frontier authorities or civilians of the neighboring country; throwing or delivering objects, documents, newspapers or the like across the frontier; and casting light on the frontier or the area of the neighboring country. In spite of these restrictions, residents say the border is a peaceful spot, adjoining, as they put it, "two vastly different peoples." Nuijamaa is a good destination if you are driving along the Saimaa Canal, and it is an important place to see for an idea of just what Finland lost to Russia.

IMATRA

Tourist Information Office: *Imatran Seudun Matkailu, Tainionkoskentie 68, PB22, 55121, Imatra open September–May, Monday–Friday, 8:00 a.m.–4:00 p.m.; June 1–August 31, Monday–Friday, 9:00 a.m.–5:00 p.m:. Open all year Monday–Friday, 8:00 a.m.–4:00 p.m. Tourist information for Eastern Finland, hotel and holiday cottage booking, guides. In summer there are also tourist information centers at the center of Imatrankoski and on road 6 both north and south of town. All three are open from June to August 16, 10:00 a.m.–8:00 p.m. daily.*

Imatra, which shares a 19-kilometer border with Russia, is the oldest tourist area in Finland. As long ago as the mid-17th century, the first inns were opened in the area, and in 1772 Catherine the Great of Russia came to Imatra to see the rapids. The rapids used to be the scene for the suicides of young women who chose death over a life without love. In 1903, the State Hotel, Imatran Valtionhotelli, was built on orders from the Imperial Finnish Senate, in order to accommodate the tourists who flocked here just to see the rapids, which are no longer quite so rapid; in fact, they are almost nonexistent as they are "turned on" for only 20 minutes on certain days or evenings.

GETTING THERE

Regular air service is available between Helsinki and Lappeenranta airport. Taxis run several times a day from the Valtionhotelli in conjunction with flights. There is bus and train service from Helsinki, Turku and Tampere.

SIGHTSEEING TOURS

Tours depart from Inkeri Square after the rapids show on Sundays at 3:30. The ferry *Hopeanorppa* leaves from the pier by the Hotel Vuoksenhovi or from the main post office in Imatrankoski and offers a watery perspective on Imatra and the surroundings.

WHAT TO SEE AND DO

Imatra is an area for active travelers more than for sightseers. The surroundings lend themselves to hiking and boating, and there is an 18-hole golf course here. Cross-country ski trails and the Mellonmaki Ski Slope are an attraction in winter. It is helpful to have a car here as there are three city centers. The rapids and the Valtionhotelli are in the part of town called Imatrankoski.

The Crown Park and the Rapids

The park, which was established under orders from Czar Nicholas I in 1842, is the oldest nature park in Finland. It is divided into four parts: the **Park of the Rapids**; the **Park of the Dam**, where you will see the sculpture the *Maid of Imatra*; the **Park of the Ancient Riverbed**, where the "devil's churns" are testimony to the time when the rapids churned out of these cavelike holes; and the **Park of the State Hotel**. *Guided tours are available on Sundays in summertime. For the best times to see the rapids, check with your hotel or the Tourist Information Office as the days and hours when they are released change. At last report, they were "on" for Wednesday and Friday at 7:00 p.m. and Sunday at 3:00 p.m.*

River Vuoksi

The river cuts right through the center of Imatra and is surrounded by the woods of the Crown Park. Walk along the river to the **War Memorial** and **Imatrankoski Church**, whose bell, altarpiece and communion cups belonged to the town of Jaaski, which is now part of Russia. The river is known for its salmon. The **Imatran Valtionhotelli**, located beside the park, is a sight in itself so even if you do not stay there, you should get over to see it. (See "Where to Stay.")

The Karelian Farmhouse Museum

Farm buildings from the area have been brought here to reproduce the environment of a 19th-century Karelian farm. *Open May–August, Tuesday–Sunday from 10:00 a.m. until 6:00 p.m.*

The Industrial Workers' Housing Museum

Exhibits illustrating the lives of the industrial workers of the area from about 1890 until 1960. *Open May–August, Tuesday–Sunday from 10:00 a.m. until 6:00 p.m.*

The Church of the Three Crosses
Designed by Alvar Aalto.

The Orthodox Church Chapel
Built in 1962 according to a design by Toivo Paatela.

The War Memorial
Built by Kalervo Kallio, it is situated near the heroes' cemetery.

RECREATION

The Imatra Leisure Center at Ukorniemi
Here, visitors will find the largest marina on Lake Saimaa in addition to opportunities for a variety of outdoor activities like jogging trails, skiing, horseback riding and tennis. There is a campsite here with 35 cabins. It is from the harbor here that travelers can pick up cruises on Lake Saimaa. There is also a spa in the area.

The Imatra Golf Course

From this 18-hole course on the shores of Lake Immalanjarvi, you can look across to the Russian side of the lake. Two-day golf packages that include hotel, one meal and greens fees are available at reasonable rates. Golfers who have a handicap or belong to a golf club can pay a greens fee for one day and play. Book golf packages through the Imatra travel service, who will even make your tee time and pair you with another golfer.

FESTIVALS

Summer in Imatra is bracketed by two festival weeks: the **Big Band Festival** at the beginning of the summer and **Imatra Festival Week**, with an international motorcycle road-racing competition for either the World or European championships at the end of the summer. During Imatra Festival Week there is also a carnival and various traditional Karelian events more cultural than motorcycle racing. In the autumn, **Imatra Art Week** occurs.

WHERE TO STAY

The Imatran Valtionhotelli (State Hotel)
Rising like an enchanted castle in the woods beside the Crown Park, the Imatran Valtionhotelli is the place to stay if you want to soak up the atmosphere of turn-of-the-century Imatra. When the hotel opened in 1903, it attracted the aristocracy of Europe. Even Czar Nicholas II was a guest at the popular Grand Hotel Cascade, as it was called. During WWII, the hotel was used as a hospital and administrative center for the Finnish army. It was badly damaged during this time, and though it was used again as a hotel, it was in disrepair. In 1982, the Arctia hotel chain bought it and returned it to its early splendor. The hotel is a fine example of the National Romantic Style of Finland, made famous by Eliel Saarinen and inspired by both the medieval concepts of architecture, and art nouveau. The exterior is distinguished by towers and balconies and stone or brick trim, and the interiors,

by the use of stained glass and painted wood trim. The main lobby is remarkable for its deep red, ornately decorated walls, tile floor and unusual fireplace. But throughout the hotel, in out-of-the-way corners, on the landings of the wide staircase and in the halls, you will find arrangements of art nouveau furniture creating museumlike tableaux. The newly refurbished rooms are varied in decoration with either pale colors or art nouveau-style wallpaper and fabrics that reflect the original designers' choices. The rooms are large and airy, most with small, rather shaky balconies. There is also a **Congress Hotel and Conference Center** across the lawn from the old hotel, but while it is comfortable and modern, it lacks the charm and fun of the old hotel. Request a room in the old hotel but avoid the fourth floor, as you will find yourself under the eaves in rooms that may be charmingly garret-like, but that are too warm in summer with their tiny windows. The hotel has saunas and an indoor pool.

The Vuoksenhovi Hotel

A new hotel by the River Vuoksi with comfortable and modern, though rather charmless rooms and a pleasant restaurant with an outdoor terrace. The boat *Hopeanorppa* belongs to the hotel, and it is easy to arrange a cruise on the river in summertime.

The Imatra Spa

This is a serious spa, offering health treatment and facilities for the handicapped. The rooms are comfortable, and most guests come here for several days of treatment.

WHERE TO EAT

In the **Valtionhotelli**, diners have two choices. The **Castle Room** is the beautiful art nouveau-style main dining room of the hotel, with a gracious enclosed veranda where meals are also served. This is a large dining room, and it is the place where breakfast is served, so if you are staying in the hotel, you might prefer the smaller and more intimate **Tsar's Room**, which, as you might guess, serves Russian food.

The Buttenhoff Cafe Restaurant, in town, is an informal, cozy restaurant decorated in Karelian style and serving Russian food in addition to Finnish and international selections. For late nighters, **The Castle Cellar** in the Valtionhotelli is a bar that stays open late. **The Castle Inn** is a more casual spot, also in the hotel.

SAVONLINNA

Tourist Information Office: *Puistokatu 1, 57100 Savonlinna. Open early June to mid-August, 8:00 a.m.–10:00 p.m daily. Open May and mid-August through September, 8:00 a.m.–6:00 p.m. daily. Open October–April, Monday–Friday 9:00 a.m.–4:00 p.m. The tourist office will arrange guides and accommodations in hotels and private homes, as well as sightseeing tours.*

DIRECTORY

Bicycle rental • Kesport Vepsalainen, ☎ *136 80*; Intersport Urheilupirtti, ☎ *222 84*; Polkupyorakorjaamo P. Markkanen, ☎ 239 77.

Boat Hire • Reissuvene, Savonlinna, ☎ *296 55.*

Boat Service • Visitors' Harbor, ☎ *130 90.*

Car Rental • Inter-Rent Oy, ☎ *289 61*; Europcar, ☎ *221 02*; Budget, ☎ *248 80.*

Emergencies • Ambulance, ☎ *000*; Pharmacy and doctor on call, ☎ *008*; Health clinic, ☎ *132 12*; Police, ☎ *5721 002.*

Opera Festival Office • *Olavinkatu 35, 57130 Savonlinna, Finland,* ☎ *226 84*; in July, ☎ *244 84* or *244 86.*

Taxi • ☎ *08.*

Savonlinna is a small town that packs a big punch every summer with its internationally renowned **Opera Festival** held in the haunting ruins of the Olavinlinna Fortress. The town of Savonlinna was established in 1639, but the history of Savonlinna is really the history of the fortress, which was built over 500 years ago, around 1475, in order to secure Eastern Finland. The records of Savonlinna go back to 1323, when the borders between Sweden and Russia were established. These borders divided the area of Savonlinna between the two nations and inevitably gave rise to a long period of struggles and eventually to the construction of the fortress. In 1743, Savonlinna surrendered to Russia and in 1812 became, along with the rest of Finland, part of the Grand Duchy of Russia.

GETTING THERE

The Savonlinna Airport, with flights from Helsinki, is 13 kilometers from Savonlinna. Flying time between Helsinki and Savonlinna is 50 minutes. Bus and train service is available from Helsinki, Turku, and Tampere. The trip by rail from Helsinki takes about five hours. Buses from Tampere also go to Mikkeli and Lahti, so travelers can get here from those cities. From mid-June through mid-August, there are boats from Kuopi and Punkaharju, and during the month of July, from Lappeenranta.

SIGHTSEEING CRUISES ON LAKE SAIMAA

Lake steamers, all bearing suitably operatic names, like *Figaro, Fidelio* and *Faust,* leave regularly from the passenger harbor in the town center for 1-1/2-hour cruises on the lake. Daily one-hour cruises also go to Punkaharju, Kerimaki, Sulkava and Rantasalmi.

WHAT TO SEE AND DO

Olavinlinna Castle

Though there have been several stages of construction in the history of the castle, the entire structure works as a whole, thanks to the painstaking attention of the builders and architects who have, since the 15th century, had a hand in the development of this extraordinary monument. Erik Axelsson Tott, who was governor of Viipuri and the Eastern Provinces in the 15th century, ordered the original construction, which consisted of three towers and a courtyard enclosed by a wall and flanked with three smaller towers. Wings for living quarters were built inside the walls. Early in the 16th century, the main towers were heightened with the addition of bricks made at the castle, and other alterations were made. By the middle of the 17th century, the fortress was virtually completed with the addition of **Kijl's Tower** in the northeast corner. At the end of the 18th century, the Russians, who had taken over the castle, embarked on major reconstruction, repairing sections that had been damaged by fire and replacing one of the towers with a larger structure called the **Thick Bastion**. The **Adjutant's Apartments** in the courtyard of the main castle and the **Suvorov Fort** on the eastern edge were added at this time. When the Russians left in the middle of the 19th century, taking all the furnishings with them, the castle became a prison for a brief time and was subsequently restored and opened to the public.

Because the castle has been in continuous use throughout its history, it has grown with the needs of Savonlinna and of Finland. The latest restoration, designed to make the castle a viable part of the community and a center for activities and festivities, has been minimal and skillful, with care taken to make obvious what is old and what has been restored. The furnishings are modern but appropriate, as one would expect of the Finns with their extraordinary sense of form and design. Part of the castle is now used as a **Congress and Concert Hall**, seating 200 people. Now the **King's Hall**, which was once the church, is a setting for banquets. The **medieval chapel** which was Roman Catholic, then Lutheran, is now an ecumenical place of worship.

But the main attraction of Olavinlinna is the **Opera Festival** held in July, which draws opera lovers from all over the world. Performances are given in the tent-covered courtyard, certainly a dramatic setting. It is fun also just to wander through the castle, admiring the restoration, stealing spectacular glimpses of Lake Saimaa through the frames of the round windows in the towers, and imagining 500 years of life within the thick stone walls.

Naturally, in the course of 500 years, many stories about the fortress were bound to evolve, tales of imprisonment, escape and the usual castle gossip. The legend repeated most often is of a young woman who was hidden in the wall of the small courtyard during one of the many battles here. Whether she was simply hidden there for safety or imprisoned as a traitor has never been clear, but those responsible for stashing the maiden in the wall and who, therefore, knew where she was, perished in the battle, leaving the young maiden to die alone and forgotten. Not long after her death, however, the survivors noticed a mountain ash growing from a crack in the wall where she was said to be buried. The tree was destroyed in a storm in the 1950s, and you might well ask how it was determined that the lost maiden was indeed buried at that point in the wall, but such is the stuff of legends.

Located on an island in the Kyronsalmi Sound, the castle is easily reached by a bridge. There are **two small museums**, one with relics from the castle, the other an Orthodox Museum with interesting icons. A cafe is located in the ground floor of the Thick Bastion. *The castle is open June 1–late August, daily from 9:00 a.m. to 5:00 p.m. The remainder of the year, it is open daily from 10:00 a.m. to 3:00 p.m.*

Pyrri Art Center

Situated at the Piispanmaki school in the center of Savonlinna.

Suruton

This restored villa on Kasinonsaari Island houses an exhibition on the Savonlinna Opera Festival. *It is open during the festival every day from 10:00 a.m. to 6:00 p.m.*

The Savonlinna Museum at Riihisaari

Three museum ships are on exhibit here. *Open June, July and August from 10:00 a.m. to 8:00 p.m. The rest of the year it is open Tuesday–Sunday from noon to 6:00 p.m.*

THE SAVONLINNA OPERA FESTIVAL

An event of international dimension, the festival is held every year in July. Performances are given in the courtyard of Olavinlinna Castle, a most dramatic setting. For tickets and information, contact the Opera Festival Office. The numbers are listed in the "Directory" of this section.

EXCURSIONS FROM SAVONLINNA
KERIMAKI

Kerimaki Church

Located 16 miles from Savonlinna, this is the largest wooden church in the world, seating 3300 people. It is worth seeing for the beauty of its design, as well as for its size. This enormous church, completed in 1847, took three years to build, and is a fine example of the old wooden churches of Finland. The Jugend-style chandeliers were designed specifically for the church. The organ is Finnish, from about 1894. The church, which is used only in summertime because there is no heat, acts as a concert hall during the Savonlinna Festival. *Open June–August, Monday–Friday from 9:00 a.m. until 8:00 p.m.; Saturday, 9:00 a.m.–6:00 p.m.; Sunday, 11:00 a.m.–8:00 p.m.*

On the Hyterma Islands, near Kerimaki and accessible by boat from the church, are a **nature preserve**, **outdoor museum** and an interesting **collection of stoneworks**. Also at Kerimaki are the **Keriland Holiday Home Exhibition** and a domestic animal park.

RAUHALINNA

Built around the turn of the century, Rauhalinna was the summer home of a general in the czar's army. Now the wooden villa has been restored and converted into a hotel and restaurant. (See "Where to Stay.") With a sauna by the lake and a resident ghost, this is a picturesque spot, full of atmosphere. Even if you do not choose to stay here, you should come out to see this gracious, old world manor by the lake. About 12 miles from Savonlinna. There is bus and boat service from Savonlinna, and a pleasant excursion is to come out here for lunch and return by boat. Check for opening hours.

PUNKAHARJU

The **Punkaharju Ridge**, formed during the Ice Age, is a place of rare natural beauty. In addition to the landscape, the major attraction is **Retretti**, a most extraordinary museum with a cave-like complex of exhibition halls. The caves were dug out of Finnish bedrock, more than 25 meters deep, and afford the visitor the chance to look inside one of the oldest geological formations in the world. The Finnish landscape is the central theme of the exhibits and of the museum itself. The displays, which change each year, are more like "happenings" than like ordinary museum exhibits, often bringing light and sound into play along with the works of art. Recent exhibitions have been on surrealism in art and film, glass sculpture and light in art. There is also a pretty sculpture garden as well as an underground restaurant and a concert hall that is used during the Savonlinna Festival for chamber operas and concerts. In June, July and August, an old steamer makes the trip to Retretti from Savonlinna twice daily. The bus from Savonlinna makes regular trips here. *Opening hours vary throughout the summer, so be sure to inquire.*

Visit also the Jugend-style **railway station**, which has become a sculptor's studio with an exhibit of wooden pieces illustrating the *Kalevala*. The **Valtionhotelli Hotel**, Finland's oldest hotel, built during the time when Finland was a Grand Duchy of Russia, is also of interest.

GETTING THERE

Punkaharju can be reached by boat from Savonlinna.

WHERE TO STAY

The hotel situation in Savonlinna is deplorably inadequate. Although the new Tott Hotel is now open and the Seurahuone has been renovated, there is still a lack of good rooms for the numbers of tourists coming here in July. Travelers with cars might consider staying out of town, at Kerimaki or Rauhalinna, or at the Valtionhotelli in Punkaharju.

The Hospits
I have not seen this hotel. It is a newer, small hotel with just 21 rooms, a dining room and a summer cafe.

Hotel Tott   ★★★
Just renovated in 1988, it is a good choice. The rooms are up-to-date, all with private baths, TV and video. There is a sauna, an indoor pool, and an outdoor bar on the roof, which is protected by a glass enclosure. Sauna and indoor pool. Double rooms are between 550FIM and 700FIM.

The Spa Hotel Casino   ★★★
Just across a foot bridge from the town center and the lake, this is a complete spa with treatments and a fitness center, saunas and pool. It was built

in the 1960s but renovated in the early 1980s and is a modern, airy complex with comfortable rooms. Double rooms run between 500FIM and 690 FIM. Restaurant.

Hotel Seurahuone

Newly renovated with a rooftop terrace overlooking the lake, the location of this hotel makes it the best bet in town if you request a room in the new addition. The older rooms have been renovated, but they are small. There is a restaurant here and a sauna.

Hotel Herttua   ★★★★

At Kerimaki, this hotel is right on the lake, a pleasant spot with tennis, marked ski trails and a complete spa with a fitness center, saunas and an indoor pool looking onto the lake. There are several bars and a lake view from most rooms. The hotel was renovated in 1987, and all rooms have private baths, TV and video channel. There are some rooms set aside for allergy sufferers. In addition to skiing and tennis, there is a skating rink nearby, and boating and fishing on the lake. The area is also a good place for hiking and biking.

The Hotel Rauhalinna

The hotel is open only in summer and has very few rooms, so it is essential to book far in advance. Charming and in beautiful surroundings, it has just been renovated, but not all rooms have private baths. There is a sauna beside the lake. Beautiful restaurant. I have not assigned stars to this hotel because its great attraction is its ambience and charm, and I have not seen the renovated rooms. For atmosphere and setting alone, it would be my first choice, but it is several miles from the center of Savonlinna.

Punkaharju Valtionhotelli

In the park at Punkaharju Ridge • The hotel is cozy and endowed with an old-fashioned Finnish charm. The rooms are simple, but comfortable, though not all have private baths. Nevertheless, the setting in this most beautiful part of Finland makes up for a lack of amenities.

For holiday villages and farmhouse holidays, consult the Savonlinna Tourist Service.

WHERE TO EAT

The Rauhalinna Hotel

A top choice for lunch or for an early dinner. (See "What to See and Do" section.)

The Wanha Kasino

Located next to the Spa Hotel Casino in one of the few wooden buildings to have survived the fire that destroyed much of Savonlinna and the first Spa Hotel. Open in June, July and August. This is also a dance restaurant.

Majakka

A cozy, informal spot by the harbor with good fish from the lake, as well as meat dishes.

The Restaurant Ship Hopeasalmi

The boat is moored in the harbor in the center of town and serves a variety of offerings from snacks to full meals all day and until 1:00 a.m. in the morning.

Ravintola Snellman

Offering Finnish dishes like whitefish in sour cream or cloudberries with whipped cream. *Moderate to expensive.*

JOENSUU

Tourist Information Office: *Koskikatu 1, 80100 Joensuu. Open mid-June to mid-August weekdays from 8:00 a.m. to 6:00 p.m.; Saturday, 8:00 a.m.– 2:00 p.m. Closed Sunday. The rest of the year, it is open on weekdays from 8:00 a.m. to 4:00 p.m.*

Joensuu, the capital of North Karelia and a center for Karelian culture, was established in 1848 as a market town beside the Pielisjoki River. It is a university town with little industry beyond a plywood factory, a sawmill and one of the largest dairies in Scandinavia.

GETTING THERE

The airport is just about eight miles from town. Bus and train service from Helsinki, Turku and Tampere.

SIGHTSEEING TOURS

A two-hour **city bus tour** on Wednesday. On Tuesday, a seven-hour trip to the Valamo Monastery is available. For other tours, inquire at the tourist office. All bus trips leave from the tourist office. **Horsedrawn carriages** will also take tourists on a tour of the town.

WHAT TO SEE AND DO

City Hall

Designed by Eliel Saarinen and constructed in 1914, the city hall bears a marked resemblance to the Railway Station of Helsinki. In the city hall are a theater and one of Joensuu's best restaurants.

The Joensuu Art Museum

The museum contains Finnish art, both from the 1950s and 1960s, and from the last century. There are also small but impressive collections of ancient Greek and Chinese objects as well as some rare Russian Orthodox icons. The building itself, an old school, is rather interesting for its mixture of styles.

The Orthodox Church of St. Nicholas

The oldest church in Joensuu, it was completed in 1887. It is the second largest Orthodox church in Finland after the cathedral in Helsinki.

The Karelia House

Also known as the Northern Karelia Museum, the Karelia House contains exhibits on the history and culture of North Karelia, including textiles, crafts, and folk art. Located on **Ilosaari**, a tiny island in the river whose name means island of joy. Ilosaari is a lively place with much activity including a three-day rock festival in summertime. *Open Tuesday, Thursday and Friday from noon to 4:00 p.m.; Wednesday noon–8:00 p.m.; Saturday 10:00 a.m.–4:00 p.m.; Sunday 10:00 a.m.–6:00 p.m. There is an excellent restaurant here serving Karelian dishes.*

Kotiteollisuus Asema

A weaving center where weavers can rent looms. Upstairs in this old building there is usually a display of regional art and weaving of which much is for sale. The items here are of exceptionally fine quality as a rule.

The Market Place

Every day but Sunday, winter and summer, there is a market here. Five times a year, a *huge* market, with vendors from all over Finland is held here.

Rantakatu

On this street that runs along the river are the best examples of the 19th-century architecture of the early town. Most of the buildings here were built for the wealthy merchants of Joensuu. Today many of these have been renovated and now house offices. At *Rantakatu 2* is a sales **exhibition of local handicrafts**.

The Joensuu Song Festival

The festival is held every summer for one week in June, and it brings choral societies and choirs from all over Finland and often from other European countries to this river city. The construction of the **Joensuu Bowl**, an outdoor amphitheater, has facilitated the performance of other productions in conjunction with the festival. The festival is built around a different theme every year, and new choral music or a new opera is premiered.

WHERE TO STAY

The Sokos Hotel Kimmel ★★★★

The glamour address in town, and a lively place with steak restaurant, a dance restaurant, disco, pool and sauna. A double room will run abut 550 FIM.

The Atrium ★★★★

The newest hotel, a pleasant, family establishment with comfortable rooms and a small restaurant. All rooms with private bath, TV/video and minibar. The hotel is known for its breakfast. A double room was 450FIM at last check.

The Arctia Hotel Kuopio

Immaculate and cozy, it sits beside the lake in the center of town. A good choice for families with its sauna department and swimming pool and lovely views.

The Sokos Hotel Vaakuna

I have not seen this hotel but it comes well recommended.

WHERE TO EAT

Karjalan Talo on Ilosaari serves Karelian food at moderate prices. The **Kimmel Hotel's** restaurants are among the best in town, both a steak house and a main dining room with live music on some nights. The **Teatteriravintola** in the City Hall is one of the best restaurants in town, serving Karelian and other dishes. Expensive.

EXCURSIONS FROM JOENSUU

LAKE PIELINEN

The area with the towns of **Nurmes**, **Lieksa** and **Koli** is easily accessible from Joensuu by boat or car. There is regular boat service from Joensuu. Here are forests for hiking, small villages and plenty of cottages and boarding houses, as well as campsites. In the restaurants, you will find Karelian specialties. Guided trips on the Ruunaa Rapids are available.

FOR INFORMATION ON THE AREA

Lieksan Matkailu Oy, Pielisentie 7, SF 81700 Lieksa.☎ *(9) 75 205 00. Or Loma-Nurmes Oy, Kirkkokatu 12, SF 75500 Nurmes.* ☎ *(9) 76 217 70.*

At **Lieksa**, the **Pielinen Museum** has an open-air museum as well as an interior exhibition hall. The open-air museum consists of about 70 buildings with farm houses from each of the last four centuries, as well as a fire-fighting section and a lumber camp. *Open mid-May to mid-September every day from 10:00 a.m. to 6:00 p.m. Closed on Midsummer Eve and Independence Day.*

About 30 miles south of Lieksa, in the direction of Koli, tourists can visit the **woodcarving studio** of Eva Ryynanen, who uses Karelian pine for her sculptures of animals, children and nature. *Her home and workshop are open every day in summertime, on weekdays from 11:00 a.m. to 7:00 p.m. and on weekends from noon to 6:00 p.m.*

Nurmes is called the town of birches, and its birch-fringed streets are lined with old wooden houses. The **Bomba House and Karelian Village** at Nurmes, on the shores of Lake Pielinen, is a reconstruction of a house originally built in 1855 in the district of Viipuri. The house has been reproduced here with all the careful attention to detail that characterized the first structure, a spacious wooden manor entirely constructed of wood. In keeping with the Karelian style of building, no nails or other metal parts were used. The Bomba House serves now as the center of the reconstructed village and contains a restaurant, offices and an information desk. In the village, there are also an Orthodox prayer house and a conference center.

WHERE TO STAY

Accommodations are available in the various buildings that make up the Karelian village. Each room has its own name. Two saunas are located by the lake, and there are also an outdoor theater, a summer cafe and a souvenir shop. The village is reached by car or by train and also by regular boat service.

ILOMANTSI

For tourists interested in the *Kalevala*, the Finnish epic, Ilomantsi is a center of the Kalevala tradition, located about an hour's drive from Joensuu. At the **Ka-levala House**, visitors will find a display of translations of the *Kalevala*. There is also a restaurant here. Visit the **Cabin of General Raappana,** who commanded the 14th division, during what the Finns refer to as the Continuation War in the early days of WWII. A foundry museum is located in Mohko where you will also find **Mohkon Manta**, an old houseboat that is now a summer cafe. Take time to stop at the **open-air museum** at Kakonaho. Throughout the area, visitors will find battlefields and war memorials as Ilomantsi and its surroundings were wracked many times by political and religious battles.

THE VALAMO MONASTERY

For information and booking: *Contact Valamo Monastery/Reception, SF 79850 Uusi-Valamo.* ☎ *(9) 72 61 911 or 72 61 959. Booking hours are on weekdays 8:00 a.m.-4:00 p.m.*

Originally established on the island of Valamo in Lake Ladoga over 800 years ago, the monastery grew to hold the most important position in the spiritual community of Karelia. In 1940, during the Finnish-Russian Winter War, the monks of Valamo were forced to move to a new location at Heinavesi. The new Valamo monastery is now the only monastery in Finland and, as such, is once again a center for the Greek Orthodox community of Finland. Many tourists, as well as pilgrims, make the journey to this most beautiful and tranquil spot, so do not be surprised to see a few tour buses and a souvenir shop. But there is nothing touristy about Valamo.

Guests come here simply for a quiet day or two spent in beautiful surroundings, for a religious retreat or perhaps to learn something more about the Orthodox religion. Short courses for guests are offered on a variety of subjects such as the Orthodox faith, herbal gardening and iconography. Many of these are given in English.

In the white, golden-domed main church is the great medieval treasure of the Orthodox Church of Finland, the **icon of the Mother of God of Konevitsa**. The other icons and sacred objects are from the Old Valamo Church, and most date from the 18th and 19th centuries since, in the long history of the monastery, much was lost. In addition to the church, there is an old wood-panelled building with many icons, which served as both church and dining hall when the monks first came here from Lake Ladoga. A large library and an exhibition hall, which has visiting exhibits, most often of religious art, are also located on the grounds. Visitors can enjoy a pleasant walk to the cemetery, which is situated on a hill among birch trees. It was restored in the early 1980s in the tradition of Orthodox Karelia, and a wooden chapel was built there as well.

About 15 monks and novices live at Valamo. In addition to their studies and prayers, the monks do much of the work of the monastery and the grounds themselves. The patron feast of the church is celebrated on August 6, a day on which many pilgrims come to the monastery. The celebration includes a procession to the lake for the Blessing of the Waters.

GETTING THERE

The monastery is situated four kilometers off the main road between Joensuu and Varkaus. Regular bus service from Helsinki, Varkaus and Joensuu stops at the Uusi-Valamo crossing just outside one of the entrances to the monastery. A bus connects with the Turku train to Varkaus. In summer, boat trips can be arranged to the convent of Lintula.

WHERE TO STAY

Accommodations on the grounds are available either in comfortable guest rooms or in a hostel. The rooms are sparely furnished and do not have private baths, but they are immaculate and peaceful, situated in the tree-fringed meadows of the monastery grounds.

The cafe-restaurant **Trapesa** offers self-service meals with a special Russian Tea Table consisting of traditional Russian dishes, including a salty pie of salmon or mushrooms and sauerkraut, pickles served with honey and sour cream and honey cakes with raspberry jam. In summer, there is also a cafe in a small red frame building on the grounds. In the past two years, the facilities have been expanded. This has had both pluses and minuses since the expansion now means more people can be accommodated, but that brings more activity and does infringe on the tranquillity of the place.

KUOPIO

Tourist Information Office: *Haapaniemenkatu 17, 70100 Kuopio. Open June until the last week of August, weekdays from 8:00 a.m. to 6:00 p.m.; Saturday from 8:00 a.m. to 2:00 p.m. The rest of the year, weekdays only from 8:00 a.m. to 4:00 p.m.*

Kuopio, located on the shore of Lake Kallavesi, is the largest city in Eastern Finland, founded in 1782 by King Gustav III of Sweden. There is a university here, the youngest one in Finland, and the city is also the center of lake traffic.

GETTING THERE

The airport is just 18 kilometers from town. Bus and train service is available from Helsinki, Tampere and Turku.

WHAT TO SEE AND DO

The Orthodox Church Museum

The museum's extraordinary collection of icons, liturgical textiles and other sacred objects dating primarily from the 18th and 19th centuries, with a few icons from the Middle Ages, make this one of the most important reminders of the significance of the Eastern Orthodox faith. *Open May–August, Tuesday–Sunday from 10:00 a.m. to 4:00 p.m. The rest of the year, Monday–Friday, noon–3:00 p.m.; weekends, noon to 5:00 p.m.*

Kuopio Open-Air Museum

Buildings illustrate life in Kuopio from the late 18th century until the 1930s. Many of the buildings have been brought here from the area, but others are on their original sites. *Open from mid-May to mid-September, Tuesday–Sunday, 10:00 a.m. to 5:00 p.m., and Wednesday until 7:00 p.m. At other times, it is open from 10:00 a.m. to 3:00 p.m. every day, except Monday.*

Market Square

In the square is the **Town Hall**, which dates from 1884. The market is also the place where you can buy Kuopio's special fish and pork pie called *kalakukko.*

Puijo Tower

A 75-meter-high observation tower with a revolving restaurant on top. *It is open June–August every day from 8:00 a.m. to 11:00 p.m. and May, 9:00 a.m. to 6:00 p.m. The rest of the year the tower is open from 10:00 a.m. to 6:00 p.m.*

A **Finnish Farm** is situated 20 kilometers south of Kuopio. *Open mid-May through August. Open daily from 10:00 a.m. to 8:00 p.m.*

The **Finland Ice Marathon** attracts almost 1000 skaters. The **Kuopio Dance and Music Festival** is the major dance festival of Finland with performances of classical ballet and modern dance in addition to classes, seminars and competitions. The **Puijo Winter Games** are held every winter on Puijo Hill.

WHERE TO STAY

The Arctia Hotel Kuopio   +★★★★

Set beside the lake and the park, this is a sister hotel to the Rivoli Jardin of Helsinki and carries on that hotel's modern, airy theme. Many of the rooms have lake views, and the gourmet restaurant is one of the best in town. There are an indoor pool, tennis court, saunas and a jogging track. A double room will be about 570FIM.

The Rauhalahti Spa   ★★★★

Also situated just outside the center of town on the lake. With a large restaurant, an extensive sauna section and pool, tennis courts, and boats for hire, this is a good choice if you do not have to be right in the center of town. Rates are about the same as the Cumulus.

The Hotel Cumulus   ★★★

A modern hotel with comfortable though uninteresting rooms. It is a lively place, with a popular bar and three restaurants, including a steakhouse that serves traditional Finnish food. The sauna section has an indoor pool and sauna bar. A double room at last check was about 450FIM.

Hotelli Lahti   ★★★

The inn has just opened and is the newest hotel in Kuopio. A family hotel in the center of town, all its rooms have private baths and TV. There are a bar, restaurant and sauna. There are some rooms for nonsmokers. A double room runs about 220 FIM.

Hotel Sokos Puijonsarvi

In the center of town, this is an older hotel, but the rooms are comfortable, all with private bath, TV/video. Some nonsmoking rooms. The hotel has been expanded and now occupies both sides of the street. The El Toro Espanol restaurant, two bars and a nightclub enliven the scene. Three saunas, fireplace lounge and good parking facilities. Doubles from 300FIM-400FIM.

WHERE TO EAT

Puijo Tower

A popular place atop the observation tower of Kuopio with a fine view of the surroundings. *Expensive.*

Musta Lammas

This cellar restaurant is considered the finest dining in the city. Specialties range from Finnish dishes like a cold Arctic bramble souffle to international cuisine. *Expensive.*

FINNISH LAPLAND

Lapland, the last frontier, occupies one-third of Finland.

Tourist Office: *Lapland Travel, Maakuntakatu 10, 96200 Rovaniemi,* ☎ *960 16052.*

Lying almost entirely above the Arctic Circle, Lapland is one of the last frontiers. In its wide open spaces and small villages, there is the excitement of the unexplored and undeveloped, and the beauty of solitude and tranquillity. Finnish Lapland is the largest of the Nordic Laplands and occupies one-third of the entirety of Finland. In spite of its vast space, however, there are only two people and two-and-a half reindeer per square kilometer. Of the human population, which was 200,000 at last count, 4500 are Lapps, or Sames, who were the original settlers of the area. The Sames are an integral part of Lapland and its culture. Though many are prosperous farmers and reindeer herders, living in modern wooden houses equipped with TVs, VCRs and computers, they have preserved their distinctive identity, culture and language, and have done much to give Finnish Lapland its singular character.

As in the northern areas of Norway and Sweden, the winters are somber and silent. This is the twilight time called, in Finnish, *kaamos*, illuminated only by the pale mystery of those Nordic jewels, the northern lights. But the summers are quick and exuberant, the endless sunshine spawning a bounty of flowers, berries and good times, with excellent fishing, miles of woods and fields for hiking, and fast-running rivers for rafting.

Finland has done more than the other Nordic countries to promote Lapland. Package tours to Lapland are available through
Finnair and the **Finnish Tourist Board**, and the tourist offices of Lapland have developed interesting attractions and activities to lure the
traveler. Reindeer safaris, downhill and cross-country skiing, Lapp
villages, river rafting and fishing, all draw the nature lover and the
seeker of adventure and beauty. The scenery changes quite dramatically between east and west Lapland, though the distances across the
region are not great. On the western side, the fells are more rugged
and higher than on the eastern side. South of Rovaniemi, the towns
of Kemi and Tornio, with rushing rivers and the Gulf of Bothnia,
offer plenty of outdoor activities. Farther north are the two areas of
Kittila and Enontekio, both of which have excellent ski facilities,
both cross-country and downhill. On the eastern side is Kemijarvi,
the center of the Arctic Fell region; and farther north, Sodankyla,
Luosto and the ski resort of Saariselka just south of Ivalo provide
wonderful opportunities for outdoor sports both winter and summer. The slopes are gentler here, but nowhere in Finland will skiers
find the kinds of challenges they would expect in the United States
or the Alps.

REINDEER OR SNOWMOBILE SAFARIS

Private guides lead safaris lasting from two days to a week through
the Finnish wilderness, stopping at wilderness huts or at the reindeer
farmers' houses. To ride through the snow, tucked warmly into a
sled behind a reindeer, is an extraordinary experience. It is a way of
getting in touch with the essence of Lapland, the vast, snow-blanket-
ed expanse stretching to the horizon, the frozen lakes, solid enough
for snowmobiles to cross, and the reindeer loping out of the birch
woods at feeding time, their antlers etched against the darkening sky.
Most of the farmers who take tourists out on these treks stop at a
Lapp hut in the wilds to warm up and have a cup of coffee brewed
over an open fire, with a bit of Lapp cheese to dip into that most welcome warm brew. All this, of course, is for the tourists, but it has its
roots in actual practice and it is one of those tourist activities that attracts people because it is so unforgettable. However, up above the
Arctic Circle in the middle of winter, the land is far from being overrun with tourists. If you are lucky, you might also be invited to the
herder's house for dinner, which will probably consist of reindeer in
some form and good bread and cheese.

For information on these trips, contact the Lapland Tourist Office
in Rovaniemi, the Finnish Tourist Board in New York, or the tourist

offices listed in the sections on individual towns and areas. Often your hotel will be able to arrange something for you.

DRESSING FOR THE COLD

The temperatures here hover around 0°F. or below. If you are planning to visit Lapland in wintertime, come prepared for the weather. Forget chic; leave the high heels or wing tips in Helsinki and put on your warmest, cloddiest, thick-soled boots and your puffiest down or fur coat. This is one place where furs are not yet frowned upon. Though the houses and hotels are warm, it is very cold when you are outside. Usually, the guide on the snowmobile or reindeer trips will provide you with additional wraps. On our reindeer safari, we were given mylar suits and moon boots that made us look like very pudgy astronauts, but we were very glad to have them.

The main towns and resorts have modern, well-appointed hotels with good restaurants (often dance restaurants with live music) and comfortable rooms. Holiday villages provide a pleasant alternative to hotel stays. Information about them is available through the Lapland Tourist Information Office listed above, and through **Lapland Travel Ltd**., *Maakuntakatu 10 96100 Rovaniemi,* ☎ *(9) 60 16 052, FAX 312 743.* There is also a network of overnight huts for skiers and hikers that can be reserved ahead and are maintained by the park service. The huts have dormitory-type sleeping arrangements, a fireplace and sauna. Visitors have to provide their own food and linens, and some of these huts are quite primitive, with benches for sleeping rather than beds. All are stocked with bread, salt and canned soups, as well as logs. If you use something, it is expected that you will replace it. Always sign the guest book and indicate where you are going next. In that way, others will know what hut will be occupied, and it is a safety measure as well, to let your whereabouts be known. Most of these huts are between 10 and 30 kilometers apart. Hikers and skiers are urgently advised to take a guide on these wilderness treks.

A program called **Lapland à la carte** provides a gourmet tour of Lapland by marking certain distinctive restaurants as members and offering set menus featuring Lapp specialties. There is more to Lapland than reindeer, though you certainly should not leave northern Finland without sampling some, unless those sweet, mild and shy creatures get to your heart before they get to your stomach. For kinder, gentler appetites, there is *ptarmigan* (snow grouse), salmon and the wonderful wild-growing delicacies like cloudberries and morels.

Northern Finland was more battered by WW II than any other part of the country. When the Germans retreated under the Russian advance, they burned whatever they could. What they did not destroy, the Russians did, leaving Lapland almost totally razed, a vast expanse of charred and smoking ruins. So almost everything the traveler sees is new. Visitors will find modern hotels with comfortable rooms and up-to-date amenities, but the towns are small and the spaces wide. You can drive for miles without seeing a house or even another car on the road.

GETTING THERE

The easiest route is by plane from Helsinki to Rovaniemi or to Ivalo. There are also airports in Kemi and Kittila with service from Helsinki. The flight to Rovaniemi takes about an hour and connects with transatlantic flights to Helsinki so that travelers can go straight to Lapland if they wish. Train and bus service is also available from Helsinki, Tampere and Turku. Sleeper service as well as room for your car is available on many of the trains. As with most of the Scandinavian trains, meals are available on board, but it is usually better to pack your own picnic. It is a good idea to reserve ahead especially at Christmas, Easter and Midsummer. Tourist tickets, valid for one month at a reduction of 20 percent, are available. There is no rail service beyond Kemijarvi.

GETTING AROUND

Once there, visitors really need a car. Bus service is fairly extensive, but driving makes it easier. For car rentals in Rovaniemi, contact: **Avis**, *Paljetie 3.* ☎ *(960) 311 501;* **Budget**, *Ahkiomaantie 5.* ☎ *312 266;* **Hertz**, *Paljetie 1.* ☎ *14550.*

The **Arctic Road** and the **Road of the Four Winds** are your passports through Lapland. The Arctic Road, over 1000 kilometers long, begins at Rovaniemi and goes through central and northern Lapland on its way to the Arctic Ocean. By following this road, tourists can see the best of Lapland's offerings, passing through Sodankyla and Ivalo to the North Cape of Norway. The Road of the Four Winds follows the Torniojoki River north through the fell country of Kilpisjarvi, across the Koli Mountains in Norway, and on to the Arctic Ocean. Even in winter, the roads in Lapland are kept in excellent condition, but motorists must look out for reindeer. It is a law that a motorist must report an injured or killed animal to the nearest police station.

ROVANIEMI

Tourist Office: *Aallonkatu 2, 96200 Rovaniemi,* ☎ *(9) 60 346 270; 322-2279. Open in summer, Monday–Friday from 8:00 a.m. to 7:00 p.m.; weekends 10:00 a.m. to 7:00 p.m. In winter, 8:00 a.m. to 4:00 p.m. weekdays. An information office is also open in June, July and August at the Railway Station from 7:30 a.m. to noon and from 2:30 p.m. to 6:00 p.m.*

Rovaniemi, the capital of Lapland and its largest city, sits amid four hills at the point at which the Kemi and Ounas rivers meet. After the war, only 12 houses were left standing in this town that had a population of 8000, but the feisty Finns rebounded quickly and engaged Alvar Aalto to draw up a town plan. The town was rebuilt in partial accordance with Aalto's plan in the shape of reindeer antlers and is now thriving, with several modern hotels and restaurants and a population of over 32,000. But the feeling here is of a frontier town, with open spaces, and low, mostly block-style buildings. What matters here is not the buildings but the land, the rivers and forests. The Finns love their outdoor sports, and even in the middle of this small city, they indulge their wish to be outside. You will see skiers gliding across the frozen river and children playing in the snow in the middle of town.

WHAT TO SEE AND DO

Tours

A sightseeing tour of two to four hours is given on Tuesdays and one of three to four hours on Sundays from June 15 to August 15.

Arcticum House

This remarkable new building combines the former Lapland Museum with an Arctic Museum. An important stop for any visitor to Rovaniemi.

Lappia House

Designed by Alvar Aalto, the building houses a theater, conference center and a library as well as the **Museum of the Province of Lapland**. *Open June–August, Tuesday–Sunday from 10:00 a.m. to 6:00 p.m.*

The Rovaniemi Art Museum

The Art Museum occupies one of the few houses that remained standing after WW II. It contains exhibits of modern Finnish art.

Ounasvaara Recreational Area

Five downhill slopes, three lifts and a summer toboggan slide. There is also a resort hotel here. (See "Where to Stay.")

Shopping in Rovaniemi

Lauri Tuotteet, at *Pohjolankatu 25*, is a handicraft shop with a cafeteria, all located in an attractive log house. *Open in summer, weekdays from 9:00 a.m. to 8:00 p.m.; weekends 10:00 a.m. to 4:00 p.m. In winter, weekdays from 9:00 a.m. to 5:00 p.m.; Saturday 9:00 a.m. to 3:00 p.m. Closed Sunday.*

WHERE TO STAY

The Rantasipi Pohjanhovi

Situated by the Kemijoki River, two kilometers from the Rovaniemi train station, the rooms here are all renovated in bright, light decor and all have private bath and TV. The gourmet restaurant, Valkoinen Peura, overlooks the rapids. There is another restaurant, which features live music most nights, a bar, a disco and a beautiful sauna section and pool. Doubles run about 600FIM. The price includes morning sauna, swim and breakfast.

The Hotel Ounasvaara

Located just outside town on a hill with cross-country and downhill skiing, hiking trails and a summer toboggan slide, this is a resort hotel. For aspiring Matti Nykanens there is a 90-meter ski jump. Many of the ski trails are lighted. In addition to the 40 rooms, there are 12 holiday apartments, all with private sauna and kitchen. The Panorama restaurant overlooks the ski slopes. The rooms are comfortable and airy, all with private bath and TV/video. Double rooms run about 500FIM.

The Gasthaus Ounasvaara

A family-style guesthouse with a small living room, kitchen and private sauna. This is a fine place for skiers. A good restaurant is on the premises.

Hotel Polar

The rooms in this midtown hotel are comfortable, all with private bath and TV. There is a restaurant and a bar as well as a pub and a sauna section. Doubles are about 600FIM.

The Hotel Gastof

A modern box of a hotel in the center of Rovaniemi. The rooms are small and simple, but attractive, and all have TV, private baths, and some even have waterbeds. The hotel's restaurant, Pecktopah, serves Russian food. Doubles are about 400FIM.

Karhunpesa

A luxurious wilderness lodge with accommodations for 12 people and dining facilities with full restaurant service for 40. The lodge is managed by the Arctia Hotel Polar. There is a sauna, shower, telephone, TV and video here. Wilderness excursions, hiking, skiing, campfire evenings and fishing can be arranged through the Hotel Polar. The hotel is located about 30 kilometers north of Rovaniemi on a lake. Double rooms with bath will be about 700 FIM.

The Lapponia

One of the newest hotels in Rovaniemi. 170 rooms, all with private bath, TV, minibar. There is a sauna on the premises and swimming nearby. Restaurant, nightclub with dancing. I have not seen this new hotel yet, or the **Sokos Hotel Vaakuna**, but I have heard nothing but good reports.

Sokos Hotel Vaakuna

Another new addition to the hotel scene in Rovaniemi. The hotel has 157 rooms, all with private bath, TV, minibar. There is a sauna, squash and tennis courts, restaurant, nightclub with dancing.

Ounasvaaran Pirtit

This is nice for visitors preferring cottage-type accommodations.

WHERE TO EAT

The best bets are the hotels:

Valkoinen Peura

Located in the Pohjanhovi, and my first choice for its well-conceived menu of Lappish specialties and the lovely view overlooking the river. Some of the Lappish delicacies served here are glowfried salmon, snow grouse, creamed morels and Lappish breadcheese with cloudberries. A three-course dinner without wine will cost about 200FIM.

Restaurant Lapponia

At the Hotel Polar; has a pleasant dining room offering well-prepared Finnish specialties such as reindeer, salmon and snow grouse, in addition to beef. A three-course dinner will be about the same or a bit less than at the Valkoinen Peura.

Ounasvaara Hotel

Here you can dine overlooking the ski slopes and the forests of Lapland. This restaurant is also known for its Lappish cuisine. Several nights a week there is dance music. A full meal will run about 150FIM to 175FIM.

Peckopah

Choose this restaurant in the Hotel Gastof for more moderate dining. Though it is low on charm, this might be a good choice if you have had enough Lapp food and are interested in trying Russian cooking.

EXCURSIONS FROM ROVANIEMI

AT THE ARCTIC CIRCLE

Sightseeing buses and local buses leave regularly from Rovaniemi for the Arctic Circle, just 10 kilometers north of Rovaniemi. In summer, river cruises lasting about one-and-a-half hours are available. Inquire at the City Tourist Office.

Santa Claus's Workshop Village on the Arctic Circle

Located 10 kilometers north of town on highway E4. If there really is a Santa Claus, this is where you will find him. Right at the Arctic Circle in a beautifully designed wood and glass complex, Santa Claus's Village is about as free of tourist claptrap as one could expect in such a spot. There is a pretty cafe and shops with various Finnish goods, toys, handicrafts, jewelry, furs, clothing and gourmet foods. Visit Santa in his office, where he and his elf assistants are busy answering letters from children all over the world. If you enter a child's name on the list, the child will receive a letter from Santa at Christmas time. *Santa Claus's Village is open June, July and August every day from 9:00 a.m. to 8:00 p.m. and the remainder of the year from 9:00 a.m. to 5:00 p.m. except, of course, Christmas Eve and Christmas Day, when Santa is otherwise occupied.*

Arctic Circle Glass Shop and Factory

I include this only to tell you that it is not all it promises to be. It is a barn-like shop of various Finnish items, mostly glass, but the prices are not particularly low and the selection is limited. The glass-blowing demonstration is disappointing and the thrust is definitely commercial. Located next to Santa Claus's Village.

Devil's Churns

At Hirvas, 21 kilometers from Rovaniemi, on the way to Kemi. These are pits from the glacial era. The deepest one is almost 60 feet down.

THE RANUA WILDLIFE PARK

Located a few miles southeast of Rovaniemi, past miles of unoccupied land, woods and lakes, this is the northernmost zoo in the world. Its concept is different from other zoos you have seen. The zoo is part of the woods, and the animal enclosures are enormous, allowing animals like the lynx or the bear or wolves to wander almost freely. Visitors feel that they are walking through the woods, coming upon animals in their natural habitat. The animals here are all indigenous to Scandinavia and there is quite a variety of them, from birds to bears and mice to moose. It is a pleasure simply to walk through the spacious, forested grounds, with natural paths cut through the trees and animal enclosures that are in keeping with the surroundings. A nature trail challenges the visitor to identify the vegetation and wildlife. An entry card can be bought at the ticket office, and there are prizes to the winners. There is a playground here, and a children's zoo. A campsite is situated on the shore of Lake Ranuanjarvi. In addition to caravan sites, there are cottages, saunas and eating and cooking facilities.

The wildlife park grew because of an apparently insoluble plight that befell the town of Ranua. Ranua was a religious farming community, but as agriculture declined, residents began to move away. The town could attract few newcomers, nor did it seem possible even to develop a tourist industry here because the town was a strict religious community with laws forbidding alcohol. Ranua appeared doomed until the idea of the wildlife park arose. Now there is the park, Murrr-murrr Castle, which is a glorified toy store, and a hotel; and the area is thriving in spite of the fact that there are no licensed bars. Some industry is moving into the area, the largest of which is the Fazer company, which makes all its marmalade here. There are also some special events at Ranua, including the Portimo-jarvi reindeer races, the Cloudberry Fair during the first weekend in August, border-to-border ski excursions across Northern Finland, and the Golden Trout Fishing Competition at Simojarvi around the last weekend in July. *The wildlife park is open in May and September every day from 10:00 a.m. to 6:00 p.m. Open June through mid-August, every day from 9:00 a.m. to 8:00 p.m.; October–April, 11:00 a.m. to 4:00 p.m. every day except Christmas Eve, Christmas Day and Boxing Day. There is a restaurant serving excellent meals here, as well as a cafe. In summer, an outdoor hamburger and hot dog stand stays open until 9:00 p.m. every evening.*

By the time you read this, travelers to Ranua will be able to take a ride on a submarine below the surface of Lake Simojarvi. Trips last about one hour with a maximum diving depth of 20 meters. The submarine will make nine trips daily between 9:30 a.m. and 9:30 p.m. during June, July and August. For bookings, contact **Finnish Submarine Tours, Ltd.**, *SF 97700 Ranua, Finland,* ☎ *385 60 52088; FAX 358 60 52166.*

Near Simojarvi is the Soppana outback camp, which is known for its salmon fishing.

The Hotel Ilveslinna at Ranua provides comfortable accommodations in 33 double rooms, all with private baths and TV. The hotel is not impressive from the outside, but the rooms are modern and the restaurant attractive. At last check, a double room was 350FIM, probably more by now.

KEMI AND TORNIO

Tourist Information Office: Kemi, *Kauppakatu 22, 94100 Kemi. Open June, July, August, weekdays from 8:00 a.m. until 6:00 p.m.; Saturday 10:00 a.m.–6:00 p.m. The rest of the year, weekdays 8:00 a.m.–5:00 p.m.; and Saturday 9:00 a.m.–2:00 p.m. In* **Tornio**, *the tourist office is located at Lukiokatu 10, 95400 Tornio. Open daily from June to mid-August 8:00 a.m.–9:00 p.m. The rest of the year it is open weekdays 8:00 a.m.–4:00 p.m.*

Southwest of Rovaniemi are the cities of Kemi and Tornio, situated at the edge of the Gulf of Bothnia. Kemi's position between tributaries of the Kemijoki River has made it the timber center for northern Finland. Tornio is just next door. A trading center since the 14th century, it was chartered as a town in 1621. Now it is a jumping-off spot for tourists headed for Sweden.

The area here is a sports center, with cross-country and downhill skiing, fishing, riding and river rafting. There is a visitors' harbor for small boats. Reindeer and snowmobile safaris can be arranged through the tourist office or your hotel. Inquire about a snowmobile trip, which includes dinner in a Lapp tent. From Kemi, visitors can take sightseeing cruises on the **Icebreaker *Sampo***, which operates on the Gulf of Bothnia. This old icebreaker has been newly remodeled by Vuokko Laakso, who has designed the interiors of many of the Silja Line cruisers. Take a ride on this hardy liner that churns through the ice with tourists aboard in December and January and again from mid-March to May. From mid-June until mid-August, there are daily cruises on the M/S *Tuuletar* from the inland harbor.

GETTING THERE

There is an airport at Kemi. Buses and trains also come here from Helsinki, Turku and Tampere.

WHAT TO SEE AND DO

The Aine Art Museum

In Tornio, this museum displays Finnish art. *Open Tuesday–Friday from noon to 7:00 p.m. and weekends 11:00 a.m. to 5:00 p.m. In summer, it is also open Monday from noon until 7:00 p.m.*

The Torniolaakso District Museum

In Tornio, this museum has exhibits of handicrafts, furniture and ethnological material. *Open Tuesday–Friday from noon until 7:00 p.m.; weekends noon–5:00 p.m.*

Just north of Tornio are the **Kukkolankoski Rapids**, which are the largest unharnessed rapids in Finland.

Green Zone Golf Course

The course is located on the border between Finland and Sweden, with nine holes in each country. No customs officers or passport checks will keep you from retrieving lost balls, although an errant shot might cause you to lose an hour as well as a ball, since there is an hour's time difference between the front and back nine. The location, just below the Arctic Circle, means that avid golfers can play all day and all night. The course is about a half-hour's drive from the KemiTornio airport.

The Kemi Art Museum

At the Cultural Center, the museum has collections of older and modern Finnish art, with special emphasis on the art of northern Finland. *Open June–August, Tuesday–Friday from 10:00 a.m. until 5:00 p.m.; Saturday, 10:00 a.m.–2:00 p.m.; Sunday, 2:00 p.m.–6:00 p.m. The rest of the year, it is open Tuesday–Friday from 10:00 a.m. to 7:00 p.m.; Saturday, 10:00 a.m.–5:00 p.m.; Sunday, noon–7:00 p.m.*

Kemi Museum

An open-air museum in Meripuisto Park. Consult tourist office for hours.

The Gemstone Gallery

This gallery has displays of gold and jewelry and replicas of famous pieces such as Marie Antoinette's necklace. *There is a shop here as well. Open in summer every day from 10:00 a.m. to 8:00 p.m.; in winter, Tuesday–Sunday 10:00 a.m.–6:00 p.m.*

WHERE TO STAY

IN KEMI

The Hotel Merihovi   ★★★

Seventy-one rooms including nine with private sauna. The rooms are comfortable and attractive, and all have private bath and TV/video. Rooms for nonsmokers are available. There are two restaurants, a bar and saunas. The main restaurant, Merihovi, is a member of the gastronomic society, the Chaine des Rotisseurs, and the restaurant Ankkuri on the ground floor is a well-known gathering spot. Doubles will be about 500FIM.

The Hotel Cumulus   ★★★

A large modern hotel, built in 1982. In addition to comfortable rooms, some of them for allergy sufferers, there is a sauna section and pool, a dance restaurant and another restaurant and bar. A double will run about the same as at the Merihovi.

IN TORNIO

The Kaupunginhotelli   ★★★

Renovated in 1987, this hotel is situated in the center of town. Of the 101 rooms, several have been set aside for allergy sufferers and nonsmokers. All rooms have private bath, TV and minibars. There is a large dance restaurant and a small gourmet dining spot called *Bothniae*. In addition, the Discotheque Nelson is a popular spot. There is also a Pub and a Tahiti Music Bar. Three saunas and pool. Double rooms are about 500FIM.

KITTILA

North and a little west of Rovaniemi, the municipality of Kittila lies amid woods and gentle fells. The Kittila airport has service to and from Helsinki. This is a recreational area with several resorts and downhill as well as cross-country skiing. Remember that the fells, which are Finland's version of mountains, are not very high; nor are they precipitous. They are gently rounded slopes, well-suited to easy downhill and challenging cross-country runs. Expert downhill skiers would soon be bored, but for beginners and chickens like some of us, it is just right. The lifts are all T-bars, no chairs. Ski rental is available. In the area of Kittila are about 30 fells, the principal of which are Pallas, Levi, Katka, Aakenus and Kumpu. **Levin Safarit** in Sirkka will arrange snowmobile and reindeer safaris, cross-country ski treks, or fishing trips. Packages can be arranged that include lunch or coffee in the wilderness. *Contact* **Levin Safarit**, *99130 Sirkka*.

At **Kaukonen**, about 20 miles south of Kittila, is the **home and studio museum** of the late Reidar Sarestoniemi, one of Finland's most popular contemporary artists. A visit here is quite extraordinary. The home and studio are presided over by the artist's brother Anton Sarestoniemi, who speaks no English, but if you come with a Finnish-speaking friend, Mr. Sarestoniemi will tell you all about his and his brother's lives here, and about his brother's work. The artist studied in Helsinki and then St. Petersburg, and finally returned to his birthplace. The house in which both brothers were born and where Anton has lived his entire life (except for his years in the army during the war) was built in 1768, and was renovated 108 years ago when the Sarestoniemi family moved here. When Reidar's first studio burned, the artist engaged the architects Reima and Raili Pietila to design a new studio and house. This building is remarkable, with a swimming pool and sauna on the second floor overlooking the wood-panelled gallery, where the brilliant bursts of color that characterize Sarestoniemi's paintings illuminate the rough pine walls. Shortly after the painter's death, the art organizations of Finland saw the need for a memorial, and Sarestoniemi's childhood home, where he returned as a grown man to live and work, seemed the most appropriate spot. Plans are underway to extend the museum buildings and to add a cafe, but the place is really just right the way it is.

Levitunturi Spa

This hotel and spa is literally and figuratively the splashiest spa around. The spa has saunas and steambaths, and a huge swimming pool that might be called a swimming environment, with waterfalls and whirlpools. This is an excellent family hotel with some rooms that are large enough to accommodate a whole family. All rooms have private baths, color TV. An annex houses an activity center with toys and games for children, and, for adults, a golf simulator, billiards, slot machines and a cafeteria. The restaurant here participates in "Lapland à la Carte." A typical set menu might consist of *vol-au-vent* stuffed with creamed morels, reindeer steak and assorted ice creams of sea buckthorn, spruce shoot and angelica. Double rooms at last check were about 500FIM.

The Hotel Sirkantahti

The hotel opened in winter of 1988, so the rooms are modern and comfortable. Many of the rooms have their own sauna. The pleasant restaurant has live dance music most nights, and the hotel also has two bars. The restaurant is moderately priced and has a pizza menu in addition to its traditional fare. There is also a self-service table where guests can eat lightly and quickly between 5:00 p.m. and 7:00 p.m.

The Hotel Kittila

Located 18 kilometers from Levi Fell. Guests of the Hotel Kittila are given privileges at the Levi Spa. The rooms here all have private baths and TV with video channel. The rather plain restaurant has dance music several nights and serves Lapland specialties in addition to other offerings. Another, smaller restaurant is a bit cozier and less formal. The hotel has two saunas and a pool.

KEMIJARVI

Tourist Office: *Rovaniementi 6, 98120 Kemijarvi. Open June 15–August 15, Monday–Friday, 8:00 a.m. to 7:00 p.m. The rest of the year, weekdays from 8:00 a.m. to 4:00 p.m. In summer months, there is also a tourist information office at the camping site Hietaniemi.*

Kemijarvi lies east and just a little north of Rovaniemi. Though its population is only 13,000, Kemijarvi is the largest town in terms of area in Northern Finland. The area has been inhabited since the 16th century and, because of its location on the River Kemijoki, it became an important market center in the early 18th century. In addition to industry, which Kemijarvi successfully disguises, the town is a center for outdoor activities. The Pyhatunturi Fell National Park, one of Lapland's principal National Parks, has five fells, the highest of which is 540 meters.

WHERE TO STAY

The Hotelli Suomu

Located just out of town at the foot of the Suomuntunturi Fell. All rooms with private bath, TV. There are six ski slopes here with three lifts and a lake nearby. Double rooms between 300FIM and 600FIM. The restaurant here is good. The hotel does close for some weeks in off-season so check ahead.

The Sokos Hotel Koilliskunta

Forty-nine rooms, all with private baths and TV. There is an indoor pool, sauna and tennis courts. A double room will be about 400FIM.

Mestarin Kievari

A simple family hotel in the center of town. All rooms have private baths and TV. The restaurant is pleasant and serves good Finnish food; salmon, reindeer and ptarmigan are usually on the menu. Double rooms were between 250FIM and 300FIM, though that probably has changed by now.

KUUSAMO AND THE KUUSAMON TROPIIKKI SPA

Kuusamo is located in the far eastern corner of Lapland, an easy drive from Rovaniemi. The spa lies near Highway 5, and is only a 90-minute flight from Helsinki. The new four-star spa, a year-round "tropical" resort, is one of the major attractions of Kuusamo. Fine accommodations and plenty to do at the spa and in the surroundings make this an ideal spot for a family or an adult get-away. Kuusamo is a good center for outdoor activities both summer and winter. Downhill skiing is available at Ruka Felll, just 20 kilometers away, and at Kuusamo, cross-country skiing, tennis, golf and horseback riding are right there. It is also a wonderful spot for fly fishing and white water rafting, and there is downhill skiing just 20 kilometers away at Ruka Fell.

WHERE TO STAY

Kuusamo Tropiikki *(mailing address: Kylpylatie 93620 Kuusamo).* Double rooms in high season are 600FIM and in normal season 550.

Kuusamo

Sokos Hotel Kuusamo *Kirkkotie 23 A, 93600 Kuusamo.* ☎ *358 989 859* 20. The 186 rooms all have shower, minibar, color TV. There is a pool, sauna and restaurant and bar.

Rukapulkka Resort *689 Pulkkajarvi, 93999 Juusamo.* ☎ *358 989 859 8811.* Log cabins with kitchen, sauna, fireplace, color TV.

SODANKYLA

Tourist Office: *Sodankylan Matkailu Oy, Jaamerentie 9, 99600 Sodankyla. For reindeer safaris and even more exotic trips, contact* **Pomoretket Oy**, *Poromiehenkatu 19, 99600 Sodankyla.* **Korvatunturin Matkat** *(Santa*

Claus Safari) at Ahkiotie 1, Sodankyla also organizes adventures through Urho Kekkonen Park and to the "secret home" of Santa

North of Rovaniemi, Sodankyla is situated at the edge of the Urho Kekkonen National Park and is near two major tourist centers, **Luostotunturi** and **Pyhatunturi**, which work together in arranging ski treks. Hikers and cross-country skiers will find wilderness huts here in addition to good accommodations in hotels and holiday villages. Both centers have downhill skiing as well with several illuminated runs and lifts. There were signs of life as long as 2000 years ago along the Kitinen and Luiro rivers, but by the beginning of the 19th century, the old Lapp settlements had disappeared and the Lapps had melded into the general population. Now the population is 10,500, and 350 are Lapps.

In town, visit Sodankyla's old church, built in 1689, one of the oldest wooden churches in Finland. Sodankyla also has a local history museum and an exhibit of Lapp culture at the Sodankyla Center.

In the northern part of Sodankyla municipality is the **Tankavaara Gold Village**, where gold was discovered in 1934. There is a gold museum here and accommodations in 12 gold digger-style bungalows with kitchens and open fireplaces. A few hotel rooms, all with private bath, are available in another building. The **Gold Diggers' Cafe** serves reindeer steak in a gold pan. At Tankavaara, tourists will find the guide center and main entrance of **Urho Kekkonen State Park**. This is the point where campers and hikers should start.

The largest and northernmost Finnish army base is located at Sodankyla. The young Finnish soldiers are very much a part of the community. One of the things they learn in the army is to dance, so do not be surprised when you walk into the dining room of the Arctia Hotel Sodankyla and see the Finnish army sitting at one or two long tables there. You might even get a chance to dance with a soldier, as they like to practice their dancing and their English. Leave it to the Finnish to teach their soldiers to dance.

WHERE TO STAY

Arctia Hotel Sodankyla
A pleasant, modern hotel with just 53 rooms, all with private bath. There are two saunas and a swimming pool, bar and dance restaurant. The hotel also has a children's playroom, game machines, billiards and roulette.

The Arctia Hotel Luosto
The hotel has standard rooms and bungalows in addition to a holiday village. The hotel building houses a sauna, two bars and a dance restaurant serving Lapp dishes.

Luosto Holiday Cottages and Tankavaara Cottages

Accommodations can be booked through Sodankylan Matkailu Oy, ☎ *134 74.*

SAARISELKA, IVALO AND INARI

Ivalo and Inari are situated close to the top of Finland, on the edge of Lake Inari. These are small towns, almost outposts. **Inari** has, with an open-air Lapp museum displaying Lapp costumes, a herders' community and a fishing village. *Open June to mid-September from 9:00 a.m. until 4:00 p.m. every day.*

Also in Inari is the Samekki **Handcraft Workshop and Shop**. Beautiful Finnish objects are made and sold here by a master craftsman and silversmith who runs the whole operation himself. Fine silver jewelry and decorative items, bone handled knives and leather and wood products.

Reindeer Herder Into Paadar takes visitors by snowmobile across a frozen lake to feed his herd and to have coffee and Lapp cheese in a Lapp tepee by an open fire. Visitors can also drive their own reindeer and receive their reindeer driver's license. You can write **Inarin Poro-farmi**, *Kaksamajarvi, 99870 Inari*, or arrange through the Lapland Tourist Office in Rovaniemi. Since Mr. Paadar does not speak English, it is probably more advisable to go through the tourist office. For **Dogteam Tours**, contact **Kamisak Ky**, *Kakslauttanen PPA 2, SF 99800 Ivalo.*

South of Ivalo is the excellent recreational area at Saariselka with cross-country and downhill skiing and Finland's longest illuminated ski track. There are 12 downhill slopes and six T-bar lifts, including one for children. Ski treks, reindeer safaris and sledge dog trips can be arranged through the hotels. Farther north, the towns of Inari and Ivalo sit on the edge of Lake Inari almost as far north as one can get in Finland.

GETTING THERE

Ivalo Airport has service from Rovaniemi and Helsinki. Bus service runs to Saariselka from the Rovaniemi airport.

WHERE TO STAY

AT SAARISELKA

The Hotel Riekonlinna

A new, modern, beautifully designed hotel with light, airy rooms. All with private bath, TV and minibar. Some rooms have private saunas; several are large enough to accommodate a family, and a few rooms for allergy sufferers are also available. A dance restaurant and lobby bar with an open fireplace are both popular after-ski spots. Saunas, playroom. Rooms range in rates from 480 FIM to 700 FIM. Breakfast and sauna are included.

The Hotel Riekonkieppi
The sister hotel across the road. It is more rustic but still modern in decor. The rooms here are cozy and attractive. All have private bath and TV. There are large rooms for families and rooms for allergy sufferers. This is more of a family hotel, while the other is geared a little more toward groups and conferences, though both hotels have family rooms and conference facilities, so they aim for the whole tourist spectrum. The restaurant at the Riekonkieppi serves Finnish and Lapp specialties. Both hotels have frequent bus service to the ski area.

The Saariselka Spa
The northernmost spa in Finland offers a variety of spa amenities and pampering. There are tennis, squash and volleyball as well as the usual pool and sauna complex. Added attractions include both downhill and cross-country skiing plus more exotic adventures like reindeer and snowmobile safaris.

Luppoloma
"The Cabin At The Hill," has 12 one-room apartments and one two-room apartment for four people. Each apartment has its own private entrance, complete kitchen facilities and private bath. Breakfast at nearby Rauni's Cottage is included. Rauni's also sells homemade food and will pack box lunches. Luppoloma has a sauna for the use of its guests. The cabin is situated near the Saariselka resort.

IN IVALO

The Hotel Ivalo
On the river, in the midst of wooded land, the hotel has comfortable rooms all with private bath and TV and rooms for nonsmokers. There are a restaurant and bar, also a sauna. Doubles were about 400FIM at last check.

Kultahippu is a participant in *Lapland à la Carte*. The menu here is varied. In addition to the Lapp specialties, there are steaks and pork, hot sandwiches and a children's menu.   ***Moderate.***

IN INARI

Inarin Kultahovi
A simple but comfortable hotel that has been newly renovated. The rooms are very simple but immaculate and comfortable. All the rooms have private bath. Situated on the water, the hotel has a bar and restaurant and a sauna by the river. This is a gathering spot for Inari residents so the bar fills up late at night with reindeer herders and fishermen. Double rooms are about 350 FIM.

Lemmenjoki Cabins
Situated between Ivalo and Inari near Lemmenjoki National Park. The cottages accommodate from two to four persons, but standard hotel rooms are also available. Sauna and cafe-restaurant.

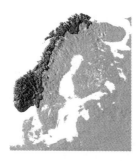

NORWAY

Fjords of Norway top the list of tourist attractions.

AN INTRODUCTION

The long, thin arm of Norway wraps around the top of Finland and Sweden, and opens its palm toward Denmark. Within its embrace are 13,000 miles of coast, the lifeline of the country. The waters of the seas and the fjords beat the rocky shores or wander through green valleys, joining the many communities that would otherwise be isolated by rugged terrain and impassable mountains. This long country—about 1300 miles from top to bottom—is also very narrow. A traveler can cross it in eight hours by train from Oslo to Bergen, even with the slow going on tracks that twist over and around some of the most rugged country ever to challenge a railway. But the railway does not extend all the way north, nor can it service the coastal towns efficiently, so the coasts, with the coastal steamers and ferries, provide communication between towns and link Norway with the rest of the world. And it is the coastal industries—fishing, shipping and offshore oil drilling—that have brought Norway her prosperity and her prominence in international commerce.

Because the topography and landscape are so varied, it is really necessary to travel through all of Norway in order to know it. Along the east coast north of Oslo, green farmlands slope gently down to shining lakes and rivers. But as you travel west—and there is no better way to do this than on the spectacular Oslo-Bergen railway—the change is abrupt. The mountains become steeper and rockier until, at one point on the railway line, you find yourself atop the glaciers, with their icy promontories and churning waterfalls. But once past these, you will find the lush rain-washed hills of Bergen and the blossoming orchards of the Hardanger fjord. The west coast is warmed by the Gulf Stream and its infamous rain is a gentle one, coming and going as capriciously as a troll, but not nearly so menacing. If you journey to the North Cape through the small but charming cities and past the mysterious, mist-shrouded Lofoten Islands, the landscape changes yet again. For as you travel north, you move above the timberline to the dramatic, rocky terrain of the North Cape. No trees to soften this scene—just low-growing grasses and mosses which, as early as August, are already changing color, painting the rocky vista a pale amber against the gray sea.

Most visitors come to Norway with a checklist of things to see and do. The fjords top the list. The attraction of these deep, water-filled slices between the precipitous mountains is irresistible. Nowhere else is there anything quite like this scenery. Next on most travelers' lists is the Midnight Sun. Though all the Scandinavian countries enjoy long days and short nights in summertime, Norway has more hours of daylight each year than any other country in the world, and she has become the queen of the Midnight Sun, with thousands of tourists trekking to the North Cape to see the red glow of the sun at midnight. Unfortunately, many of those thousands trek back in disappointment, for more often than not the sun at the North Cape is obscured by fog and clouds. But still, it is the idea that matters and, in Norway, in any town above the Arctic Circle, the visitor can experience 24 hours of daylight with all the psychological and physical chaos that goes with having "to go to bed by day." (Remember that

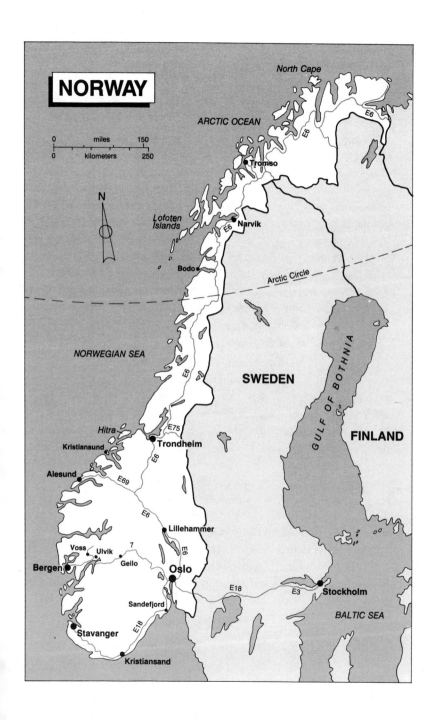

NORWAY

North Cape

ARCTIC OCEAN

E6

0 miles 150
0 kilometers 250

N

Tromso

Lofoten
Islands

E6 Narvik

Bodo

Arctic Circle

NORWEGIAN SEA

E6

SWEDEN

GULF OF BOTHNIA

FINLAND

Hitra E75
Kristiansund Trondheim

E6

Alesund

E69

E6

Lillehammer

Voss Ulvik 7
Bergen Geilo E6 Oslo

Stockholm

E18 E3

Sandefjord

BALTIC SEA

E18

Stavanger

Kristiansand

old Robert Louis Stevenson poem? How would you like to grapple with a four-year-old's bedtime in daylight every night from April until August?)

Up there along with the Midnight Sun comes its corollary, the days of darkness, when during a period that in some places lasts from November to February, there is virtually no daylight beyond a pale rosy glow for an hour or so, reminding you of the sun that isn't there.

Travelers journeying north are often surprised to find that, unlike many northern towns in the other Scandinavian countries, the cities above the Arctic Circle are neither barren nor undeveloped. They are not sterile outposts of civilization, but rather lively cities, surrounded in summer with green hills and sparkling fjords. The snow and gloom is there as well, of course, especially in Finnmark where the long nights, deep snow and frigid temperatures might even make the polar bears shiver; and for a truly arctic landscape, you can visit Svalbard/Spitzbergen, the group of islands west of the mainland in the Arctic Ocean where the icy remains of winter stay around for most of the year. Here, only a few inches of the ground ever thaw. But even with that, you will still find, in the brief summer, many varieties of plants thriving in the frigid soil.

Norway is a country of sheer beauty and infinite variety, from the deep, shining fjords and precipitous cliffs to the wide slopes and green meadows; from the pine-fringed hills to the stark, rocky landscape of the North Cape. But there is more to Norway than mere beauty. The ruggedness of the land has spawned a people who are, on the surface, deceptively simple and fun-loving but who have, since the days of the Viking adventurers, proven themselves equal to any challenge. Their art, literature and music and their colorful history are testimony to the individualism and complexity of the Norwegians. The stereotype of the mournful Nordic countenance, the strong silent Norseman is, however, just that—a stereotype. Norwegians are for the most part outgoing, warm people with easy smiles and quick laughter, an exuberant, even zany, sense of humor, and a heartening earthiness and willingness to see the fun or at least the irony in life.

THE CULTURAL SIDE

In preparing for a trip to a foreign country, it is helpful to read something of its literature, to listen to its music and to look at examples of its art. The accomplishments of Norwegians in literature (three Nobel Prize winners), art and music have done much to enrich our understanding of the Norwegian character and landscape.

So the dedicated traveler might pick up a volume of Henrik Ibsen's plays to read of the social and moral issues that were very much a part of the Norwegian 19th-century consciousness. It is in Ibsen's plays that we gain an understanding of the puritanical rigidity and tension that constricted life in Norway and that was one of the reasons for the wave of emigration that swept over Norway in the latter half of the 19th century. For a vivid picture of medieval Norway, Nobel Prize-winner Sigrid Undset's *Kristin Lavransdatter* is unequaled. Read also the brooding novels of another Nobel laureate, Knut Hamsun, whose works are often infused with a lyrical romanticism that seems at odds with his more searing social commentary and his Nazi sympathies. Or locate an anthology of folk tales and learn of fantastical creatures like the one-eyed, many-headed trolls, who often removed their single eye and lent it to a less fortunate troll; or the blond *hulder*, mythical women whose beauty was marred by the possession of a cow's tail, which would only fall off if she married a human man in a church. The hulder also were known to steal unchristened children. Of a more kindly nature were the *nisse*, little old men dressed like Santa's elves who, when so inclined, could be of great help to a farmer; and there were also the *Fossegrimen*, river-dwelling musicians who instructed students in the complexities of the Hardanger fiddle. Even today, figures of trolls abound in Norway, standing guard at a restaurant entrance, enticing visitors into a shop. The legend of *Peer Gynt*, the boastful farmer from Gubrandsdalen who was both foolish and cunning, cowardly and bold, has not only been Norway's most famous cultural export, but has had a profound influence on the Norwegians as well. Many Norwegians claim that the example of Peer's daring exploits and swaggering self-confidence has inspired them to their own achievements, and when those achievements include the accomplishments of explorers like Fridtjof Nansen or Roald Amundsen, we can't really dismiss old Peer too readily.

In music, the name of Edvard Grieg overshadows all others. His songs, the incidental music for *Peer Gynt*, and his symphonic works evoke the beauty and splendor of the Norwegian landscape and the mystery of the Norwegian spirit. Travelers can make an Edvard Grieg "minitour," which would include a visit to Loftus in the Hardanger fjord region where the composer spent several summers in the tiny hut that is now on the grounds of the Ullensvang Hotel and also, and most important, a visit to Troldhaugen, Grieg's house, in its wooded setting just outside Bergen.

No discussion of Norwegian culture, no matter how brief, can leave out Norway's two major artists, Edvard Munch and Gustav Vigeland. The tormented, twisted figures of Edvard Munch's paintings embody all that ever need be said about the melancholy Scandinavian. Strange and evocative, the paintings are haunting and often depressing. Fine collections of Munch's paintings can be found in many museums in Norway, but it is the Munch Museum in Oslo that has the definitive collection of Munch paintings and memorabilia.

The spirit and body of Gustav Vigeland's sculpture are the antithesis of Munch's paintings. Robust and energetic, these huge figures populate the remarkable Vigeland Park in Oslo, creating a kind of sculptural Everyman in the hundreds of figures, representing human life in all its stages and moods. The park represents his life work, and he was subsidized by the government for the lifetime it took him to complete his monumental task.

RELIGION IN NORWAY

The state religion of Norway today is Lutheran, but Norway's religious history reaches back to the Vikings and to their concept of Valhalla with the great gods Thor, Odin and Ullr. But it was also the Vikings who brought Christianity to Norway. In the course of the pirating forays and trading expeditions to Western Europe, these maritime marvels managed to spread their influence throughout Europe, to father an ancestor of William the Conqueror and to bring back sizable plunder from the lands they visited. But they were most impressed by their introduction to Christianity and, indeed, it was their zeal for the new religion that brought the end of the Viking era. These warring chieftains, once they found religion, could not resist spreading the word, by force when necessary, to their countrymen. So Christianity brought the end of the interest in expansion and exploration, and fostered instead a focus on national unity as the bearers of this new religion carried the word of it throughout Norway.

The Norwegian converts of those early years of Christianity left a unique legacy in the form of the **Stave Churches**. At one time there were 3000 to 4000 of these odd wooden structures, built with huge posts or staves to anchor them. During the Reformation, the interior decorations were torn away, but the exteriors remained the same and the churches weathered the ages and the storms of both nature and religion. The one thing they could not withstand was the bad judgment of the parishioners who, in the 18th and especially in the 19th centuries, tore down most of these treasures in order to replace them with bigger and more lavish places of worship. Now there are only some 30 stave churches remaining in Norway as fascinating displays of architecture, craftsmanship and religious art. The shapes of the roofs, with their scale-like shingles, are almost oriental. Oddly angled peaks and gables and figures of mythical creatures testify to the tentative faith of these early Norwegian Christians. They were not quite ready to give up all semblance of their pagan beliefs and so retained a few symbols—just in case. Hedging their religious bets, so to speak. The stave churches might even stand as a metaphor for the Norwegian spirit. Sturdy enough to endure the hardships of the weather and the rigors of history, the churches sought, in their dark interiors, to offer the light of faith to those early worshippers. Just as the northern regions emerge from winter darkness to endless daylight; just as beyond the melancholy, brooding spirit represented so often in their literature and art, the Norwegians have an exuberant sense of the fun of life; so do the stave churches with their sturdy, quirky exteriors and their snug, dark sanctuaries offer the promise of light out of darkness.

Two of the most accessible stave churches for travelers are the one at the Folk Museum in Oslo and the Fantoft Church outside Bergen. If possible, visitors should try to see at least one of these, if not both, as they are very different, and each quite wonderful in their own way.

THE MONARCHY

When Norway finally won independence from Sweden in 1904, it was time for the constitution, which had been drawn up in 1814, to be put into effect, and since that constitution had called for a monarchy, the order of the day was to find a king. Because Norway's nobility had been decimated by the Black Plague of the 14th century—even the young noblewomen had to look to Denmark and Sweden for husbands—there were few men to choose from in Norway. But in anticipation of this, leaders of the government had already conferred with the Danish Prince Carl, grandson of Christina IX, who once he was assured that the Norwegian people did indeed prefer a monarchy to a republic, accepted the offer to become their king. In 1905, Prince Carl was crowned King Haakon VII of Norway at the Nidaros Cathedral in Trondheim, the traditional coronation church for Norwegian kings. King Haakon VII became a very popular monarch, commanding both the love and respect of all Norwegians. He married Queen Maud, the daughter of Edward VII of England, and their son Olav V was the much-beloved successor to his father, ruling Norway until his death in January 1991. He was a highly esteemed and beloved king, very much a man of the people who skied on the Norwegian Olympic team and could often be seen on a fine summer's day sailing in races around Oslo. Olav's son, King Harold V, has succeeded his father.

TRAVEL ESSENTIALS

Norwegian Tourist Board: *655 Third Ave., New York, NY 10017,* ☎ *(212) 949-2333.*

GETTING THERE

SAS flies nonstop to Oslo from Newark and via Copenhagen from Chicago and Seattle. From Seattle, **British Air** has service to Oslo through London. Icelandair connects through Reykjavik, Orlando and New York's JFK.

GETTING AROUND

Air service is available between most of the major cities and several of the smaller ones. Air fares are high, but if you book nonrefundable seats with certain other limitations, the fares can be greatly reduced. Senior citizen discounts are in theory available only to Norwegian citizens, but sometimes the regulations slip through the cracks and Americans have been able to obtain a reduced fare. Youth fares are also available to anyone under 26 years of age. For these fares, you can usually only book 24 hours ahead of your flight. The three carriers operating in Norway are: **SAS, Brathenes S.A.F.E.** and **Wideroe**.

The Norwegian Railway System is generally efficient and pleasant and something of a miracle of engineering. There are two classes of service, but there is almost no difference, so most travelers choose second class. Almost all trains have food service of some sort. The dining car, when there is one, is not as elegant as you might hope. Usually, it is a small cafeteria serving a few hot items, nothing very elegant. Hostesses push carts with coffee, cold drinks and snacks through the cars. If you are leaving by train from Oslo, I recommend picking up sandwiches in the bakery-cafe, which is right in the terminal. The brie sandwich on homemade dark French bread is especially delectable. You can pick up some fruit at one of the newsstands in the terminal and you will probably have a better lunch than one you would buy on board. The ride from Oslo to Bergen is one of the world's most beautiful train rides. It takes eight hours and leaves twice a day. It makes sense to take the morning train so that the trip is made in daylight, though If you are going in June, July or the beginning of August, darkness is, of course, not an issue. In summertime, the evening express which leaves Oslo at 3:45 p.m. and arrives in Bergen at 10:20 p.m., has dining car service but you must make a reservation. One thing you should take along for the ride is a good map of Norway so that you can follow the route and learn a bit of geography.

Because the train does not go all the way north, you might find yourself turning to **buses**. The service is good and connects efficiently with scheduled ferries for travel through the fjord areas. See "Bergen" section for a listing of several bus/ferry/steamer trips through the fjord areas.

Driving yourself can be an adventure on roads that rival an amusement park thriller ride. Try the road up to Stalheim with its 24 hairpin turns, but don't look at the scenery while you're maneuvering those curves. The going is slow through Norway because the roads are tortuous, though usually in good condition. Be advised that many roads are closed in wintertime.

Coastal steamers and ferries are inescapable in Norway, and who would want to escape them? The service is efficient and the ride enjoyable; and you haven't really seen a fjord until you've actually been on the water looking up at the mountains and feeling appropriately insignificant against the splendor of those sheer granite walls. There are express boats between many of the west coast cities and ferries between smaller towns. And then there is the coastal steamer, a 12-day trip from Bergen to Kirkenes and back. You can pick up the boat and leave it at any spot along the way, but it's fun to take it for at least a couple of days. A word of warning: these steamers fill up a year in advance for the full twelve-day trip, so if you do want to go, you must book well ahead, even a year if you possibly can. More details about the trip are given at the end of the "Bergen" chapter. For information: **Bergen Line, ☎** *(800) 323-7436.*

MONEY MATTERS

Though it has the reputation of being one of the most expensive countries in Europe, most of the others have caught up with Norway, and generally the hotels and restaurants are not quite so highly priced as those in Sweden and Denmark. Like all the Scandinavian countries the standard of living is high and taxes are astronomical. Especially if you take advantage of the special summer and weekend rates, hotels, even the best ones, can be affordable. There is a tax figured into the cost of all goods and services, so restaurant and bar bills can be very high. The tax on retail items is refundable to visitors taking the goods out of Norway (see "Tax-Free Shopping"). The kronor, or krone, written as NOK, is the currency of Norway. At the time of this writing, the exchange rate was approximately 6.7 kroner to the U.S. dollar.

TAX-FREE SHOPPING

As in all the Scandinavian countries, you can get your tax back on items above a given amount, usually around $50. Remember to ask for a form when you make your purchases and then turn this in at the airport when you leave the country. You will receive your refund on the spot, in Norwegian kronor.

HOLIDAYS

Christmas, New Year's and Easter are national holidays. In addition, everything stops on May 17, Norway's independence day. Also May 4, and May 14 and 15, Ascension Day and Whitsun are national holidays in all Scandinavian countries.

SPECIAL EVENTS IN 1995

March 7–8, Lillehammer: World Cup Ski Jumping

March 11–12, Lillehammer: World Cup Alpine Skiing

March 16–19, Lillehammer: World Cup Biathlon

May 24–June 4th, Bergen: International Festival

July 18–23,. Molde: International Jazz Festival

August 25–Sep 1, Haugesund: Norwegian Film Festival

December 10, Oslo: Nobel Peace Prize Presentation

HOTELS AND OTHER ACCOMMODATIONS

The train station in Oslo has a hotel booking center where you can make hotel reservations and also get a list of small pensions and private accommodations. In other cities, the tourist information center can provide you with information on available accommodations. A minimum standard for any hotel in Norway has been set by the Hotel Law of 1983, and you can count on any hotel being clean and well-managed. The terms *Turisthotel* and *Hoyfjellshotell* (Mountain hotel) are carefully regulated. Such designations usually mean that the hotels so named are of the highest standard for the area. Sometimes, the terms *Fjordhotel* or *Hotell* are used instead, but the hotels still measure up to the minimum standards and usually exceed these. *Motell* could be the same as a hotel, or it might have self-catering units.

HOTEL RATES

For Norwegian hotels, the price categories in this book are arranged as follows, but remember that summer rates can dramatically reduce the prices at even the most expensive hotels.

Very Expensive:	**More than 1200NOK double room ($175 or more)**
Expensive:	**1000-1200NOK double room ($150 to $175)**
Moderate:	**600-1000 NOK double room ($100 to $150)**
Budget:	**Less than 600NOK double room**

In Norway, almost every hotel includes breakfast in the price of the room.

Summer Rates: Although hotels in Norway are very expensive, the wise traveler can often cut his hotels bills in half. In summer, in most city hotels, even the most deluxe, summer rates are available at great reductions. You can only get these if you contact the hotel directly, not through their U.S. booking offices. These rates mean that you can stay in a deluxe hotel for just about what you would pay in a less expensive one. Passes are also available. The **Fjord Pass** is a very useful one to have. Many hotel chains have their own pass that you can use throughout the country at hotels belonging to that chain. You can obtain these passes through the Norwegian Tourist Office in New York City or through your travel agent. Hotel rates almost always include a buffet breakfast with plenty to choose from. In most hotels, children are given a discount of almost 50 percent if they occupy the same room as their parents.

LANGUAGE

Almost everyone in Norway speaks English, and very good English at that. English is a required course in the schools from the fourth grade on. In some of the more remote areas, particularly in Finnmark, you might find some places where only Norwegian is spoken, but this is rare.

WEATHER

The umbrella should be the national symbol of Norway. It rains and rains and rains, especially on the west coast. But it is a gentle precipitation, not the hair-raising, wind-whipped rain of Denmark. The weather is capricious, so even on the sunniest day, it is probably a good idea to take an umbrella. In central and northernmost Norway, it gets very, very cold in winter. But the west coast is surprisingly mild because of the warming influence of the Gulf Stream. It is rarely uncomfortably warm anywhere in Norway, and even in summertime, visitors will be happy to have a warm sweater and a waterproof wrap.

FOOD AND DRINK

Fish, fish and more fish. If you don't eat it here, you shouldn't eat it anywhere. The fresh fish glisten on carts in the market squares of all the coastal towns, newly hauled in from the sea and the fjords. The Norwegians practically invented herring and sardines, so you will find plenty of these, especially on the breakfast buffets which are included in the price of almost every hotel room. Salmon in all forms abounds. Be sure to try *gravlaks*, which is a variation on the ubiquitous smoked salmon. The salmon is marinated raw and served with a honey mustard sauce. But Norwegians also like their meat, particularly wild game, and beef and lamb as well. So if you tire of fish, there is relief available. The *koldtbord*, which means cold table but which often includes hot dishes as well, is standard in many restaurants for lunch, and the price and quantity of offerings vary. Because of the high cost of restaurant dining in Norway, it is usually a good idea to have a big lunch and eat more lightly for dinner. The koltbord will provide you with enough nourishment for a week and the prices are not outlandish considering the amount of food served. In most restaurants, there is a daily menu for lunch and dinner, which is the best buy.

Quenching your thirst is expensive in Norway unless you drink the wonderfully pure water that is found in most cities and towns. As in all Scandinavian countries, the tax on liquor and wine is astronomical. Even beer is not as cheap as you might expect. And Norwegian beer will be a disappointment if you're accustomed to the Danish variety. But in Tromso, above the Arctic Circle, you will find the **Mack Brewery**, which puts out the best beer in Norway.

THE OUTDOOR LIFE—HIKING, FISHING AND SKIING

Many travelers to Norway plan to spend their time hiking, fishing or skiing. **The DNT touring organization** *(Den Norske Turistforening)*, with headquarters in Oslo at *Stortingata 28*, can help you plan your hiking itinerary and give you maps with the locations of huts and the ranked difficulty of the trails. **Fishing** is available in every fjordside or seaside town. Contact the local tourist offices for information. Be advised that if you bring your own fishing equipment, you must have it sterilized in Norway before you can use it. Any local veterinarian will do this for you. While there is quite a bit of alpine skiing in Norway, **cross-country skiing** is the national sport. Lighted trails are a necessity in wintertime, even around Oslo, because of the early darkness. Just outside Oslo you will find some of the best cross-country skiing in Norway, and a bit farther south is Telemark, where the Telemark style of skiing was developed. There are at least a thousand **campsites** in Norway, and most are of high standard. The Norwegian Tourist Board in New York City can give you a list of these. In addition to campsites, most of these areas have huts of varying degrees of comfort.

OSLO

Oslo Harbor offers castles, museums, shopping and boat tours.

OSLO: THE TOP TEN

The sights listed below are the most popular attractions for tourists and if you get to all of them, you will have scurried all about town and learned something of the city in the process. The following are described in detail in the appropriate sections of "What to See and Do."

- Akershus Fortress and the Resistance Museum
- City Hall
- Fram-huset
- Holmenkollen
- Karl Johans Gate with the National Theater, Parliament
- Oslo Cathedral
- Kon-Tiki Museum
- Munch Museum
- Norsk Folkemuseum
- Vigeland Park
- Viking Ships Museum

Norway Information Office: *Vestbaneplassen 1.This is the main tourist information center for Oslo and Norway, offering a vast array of brochures, maps, calendars and video cassettes. There is also an exchange office here.*

Open mid-May to mid-September from 9:00 a.m.–4:00 p.m. The rest of the year opening times are shortened so check ahead.

Oslo Central station: *Jernbanetorget 2 N-0154.* ☎ *22 17 11 24. FAX: 22 17 66 13. This office is set up specifically for Oslo. You can book hotels, pensions and private accommodations through this office, either on the spot or by mail or fax in advance. Open daily all year 8 a.m.–11:00 p.m.*

OSLO CARD

You can pick up a card at hotels, travel agencies, Norwegian State Railway offices and the Tourist Information Offices. It is valid for one, two or three days, at the price of 110NOK for adults and 55NOK for children for one day. A two day card will be 190NOK and 85NOK, and a three day card is 240NOK and 110 NOK. The card is almost a must in this museum-rich, and very expensive city. The booklet you receive with your card lists the myriad activities available to you at a discount—too many to list here, but among the things you should know:

The Oslo Card entitles you to free rides on all public transportation within the Oslo area. This includes ferries as well as trains, subways and buses. If you purchase your Oslo Card at one of the Norwegian State Railway offices outside Oslo, you can obtain a 30 percent discount on train travel to Oslo from other places in Norway. Quite a few hotels offer discounts to holders of the card. And another bonus—since many films are in English with Norwegian subtitles, a great way to pick up a smattering of the language—the Oslo Card offers you a discount on movies.

DIRECTORY

American Embassy • *Drammensvn. 18, 0255 Oslo 2,* ☎ *44 85 50.*

Banking hours • *Monday–Friday, 8:15 a.m.–3:30 p.m. Thursday 8:15 a.m.– 5:00 p.m. In summer, the banks close at 3:00 p.m., except for Thursday.*

Currency exchange • Most hotels will exchange money at a rate comparable to that which banks offer, but check. You can also change money at the Oslo Central Station. *From the beginning of June through September the exchange at the station is open from 8:00 a.m.–11:00 p.m. every day. Oct. 1–May 31, Monday-Friday, 8 a.m.–8:30 p.m. Saturday 8 a.m.–2:00 p.m. Closed Sunday. There is an exchange in the bank at Fornebu Airport, open Monday–Friday, 6:30 a.m.–9 p.m., Saturday 7:30 a.m.–7:00 p.m., Sunday 7:00 a.m.–10:00 p.m.* The main post office also has an exchange as do the branches. Two camping sites, Oslo S. Ekeberg and Bogstad Camping, have exchanges.

Car Rental • **Avis**: ☎ *84 90 60. And at Fornebu Airport,* ☎ *53 05 57.* **Hertz**: *SAS Scandinavia,* ☎ *20 01 21. At Fornebu Airport,* ☎ *53 36 47.* **Budget**: *in Oslo Spektrum.* ☎ *22 17 10 50.*

Church Services in English • American Lutheran Church. *Fritznersgt. 15. 0264 Oslo 2,* ☎ *44 35 84.* St. Edmund's Anglican/Episcopalian Church, *Mollergt. 30, 0179 Oslo 1,* ☎ *55 24 00 or 12 04 50.* Synagogue: *Det Mosaiske Trossamfunn, at Bergstien 13.* ☎ *22 69 65 70.*

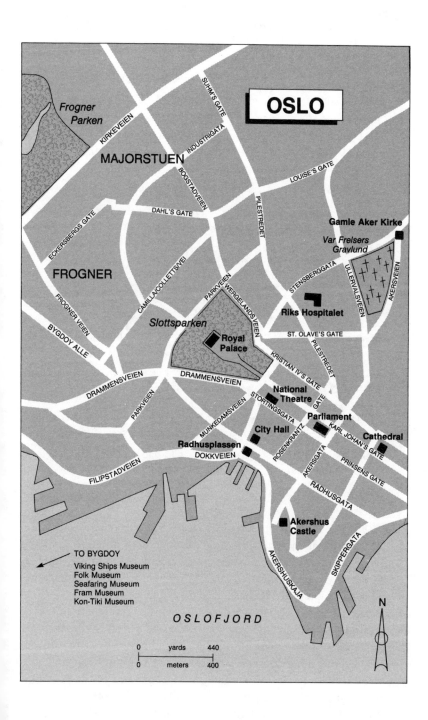

OSLO

Frogner
Parken

SUHM'S GATE

KIRKEVEIEN

MAJORSTUEN

INDUSTRIGATA

BOGSTADVEIEN

LOUISE'S GATE

DAHL'S GATE

PILESTREDET

ECKERSBERGS GATE

Gamle Aker Kirke

Var Frelsers
Gravlund

FROGNER

CAMILLACOLLETTSVEI

STENSBERGGATA

ULLEVALSVEIEN

AKERSVEIEN

PARKVEIEN

WERGELANDSVEIEN

Riks Hospitalet

FROGNER VEIEN

Slottsparken

Royal
Palace

ST. OLAVE'S GATE

BYGDOY ALLE

PILESTREDET

KRISTIAN IV'S GATE

DRAMMENSVEIEN

DRAMMENSVEIEN

National
Theatre

GATE

PARKVEIEN

MUNKEDAMSVEIEN

STORTINGSGATA

Parliament

DRAMMENSVEIEN

City Hall

KARL JOHAN'S GATE

Cathedral

ROSENKRANTZ

Radhusplassen

AKERSGATA

PRINSENS GATE

FILIPSTADVEIEN

DOKKVEIEN

RADHUSGATA

Akershus
Castle

SKIPPERGATA

TO BYGDOY

Viking Ships Museum
Folk Museum
Seafaring Museum
Fram Museum
Kon-Tiki Museum

AKERSHUSKAJA

N

OSLOFJORD

0   yards   440
0   meters   400

Emergency numbers • Police. ☎ *002*. Fire and accidents, ☎ *001*. Ambulance, ☎ *003*. Automobile Breakdown, Falken Bil-og, ☎ *23 25 85*. NAF Alarmsentral, 24-hour service, ☎ *42 94 00*. Viking redningstjeneste, 24-hour service, ☎ *60 60 90*.

Emergency medical service • ☎ *70 20 10 90 or 17 09 50*.

Dental services • Oslo Kommunale Tannlegavakt: Toyen Senter, *Kolstadgata 18, 0652 Oslo 6,* ☎ *67 30 00*. Hours are very limited. Call first.

Hotel Booking • Private accommodations, hotel, bed and breakfast can be booked at Tourist Information Office Oslo S in the Central Station and at the Tourist Information in the City Hall. A booking fee is charged.

Laundry • Self-service. (Majorstua Myntvaskeri) • *Vibes gt. 15, Oslo 3,* ☎ *69 43 17*.

Left Luggage • *Airport Bus Terminal at Oslo Harbor side.*

Pharmacy. Jernbanetorgets apotek • *Jernbanetorget 4 B, Oslo 1,* ☎ *41 24 82; FAX: (02) 36 34 10. Open 24 hours.*

Post Office • (Oslo Central Post Office) *Dronningensgt. 15. Oslo 1.* (Entrance on corner of Prinsensgt.) *Open Monday–Friday, 8:00 a.m.–8:00 p.m. Saturday, 9:00 a.m.–3:00 p.m. Closed Sunday and holidays.*

Tax-free shopping • As in all Scandinavian cities, most shops participate in the tax-free program.

Taxis • For advance booking (at least one hour in advance), call Oslo Taxicentral, ☎ *38 80 90*. Otherwise, taxi stands are plentiful in the center of town or, if you are dining in a restaurant, just ask the staff to call a taxi for you. They come promptly and the drivers all speak excellent English. Tipping is not expected, though a few kronor are always accepted graciously.

Telecommunications • Telefax, telephone, telex and telegrams. *Kongensgt. 21. (Entrance Prinsensgt.) 0153 Oslo 1. Open 8:00 a.m.–9:00 p.m.*

Telephone • The telephone code for Oslo is 22. Within the city, you need not dial the code.

Oslo is a coquette among cities. Seen from the air in summertime she is a distant jewel, set against the sparkling water of the Oslo Fjord and colored by the abundant greenery of parks and suburbs. But once you come down to earth, you might be initially disappointed in this capital city. Railway travelers arrive in an unfortunately unattractive section of the city and even the very center of town, around the National Theater and Parliament, lacks the beauty of Stockholm or the charm of Copenhagen. But give Oslo a bit of time. She will reveal her treasures slowly, and she might just win your love forever. Take the time to wander and to get out of the center of town. The suburbs are charming and I know of no other city where it is so easy to get a peek at the residential areas. Look especially at the houses on the island of Bygdoy—a quick ferry ride from Radhus Square. Frogner and Majorstuen are also pleasant urban living areas. What you will begin to understand as you walk through the residential areas and browse in the museums is that Oslo is an eminently livable city, a comfortable place with plenty to see and do. Pray that your weather will be as splendid as it can be in midsummer, but always take an umbrella. Oslo is a tease and moody. She will greet you in sunshine and then change her mind, glowering sullenly from beneath black skies.

Oslo's position at the top of the fjord had already made it a successful trading center by the time King Harald Hardrade and Queen Ellisiv established a royal residence there in A.D. 1050. In addition to its importance as a mercantile center, Oslo afforded a strategic location for forays to Denmark and for protection from invaders. But it was not until the early 14th century that King Haakon V Magnusson built Akershus Fortress on a promontory above the sea, a short distance from what was then the center of Oslo. The fortress established Oslo as a European capital worthy of attention and attracted the German merchants of the Hanseatic League who fostered the commercial golden age of Oslo. The glory was short-lived, however, for the Black Plague soon took its toll, rampaging through Norway as aggressively and cruelly as any political enemy. Devastating fires followed upon disease and by the end of the 14th century, the fortunes and the population of the city, indeed of the entire country, were decimated. It was finally King Christian IV of Denmark, after Oslo's great fire of 1624, who brought Oslo back to life. The architect/king saw the logic of centering the city around the fort. After bribing the citizens with promises of free land, he persuaded the inhabitants to rebuild the city closer to the fortress instead of at its original location. The old city was still called Oslo, but King Christian named his new city Christiana, a name that remained in use until 1924.

GETTING THERE

SAS flies to Oslo nonstop from Newark and via Copenhagen from Chicago and Seattle. **Icelandair** connects through Reykjavik from Baltimore, Orlando and New York's JFK.

GETTING AROUND

Fornebu Airport is only a 15-minute ride from Oslo center. A taxi should cost you between 80 and 90NOK (at last check about $12). The **Flybussen** airport bus runs regularly to and from the airport. You can get it at the Oslo Central Station, the airport bus terminal at harbor side, the National Theater or the SAS Scandinavia Hotel. The fare is 30NOK. Gardermoen Airport, which services charter and military flights, is about 35 miles from Oslo. Bus service is available from the airport bus terminal at Oslo Harbor.

Though Oslo is small, several of the attractions require a car or public transportation; but Oslo's buses, ferries and its minisubway are very accessible and easy to use, so visitors should not be afraid to venture from the center. Buses and trams run frequently to most of the spots you'll want to visit and the museums on Bygdoy are accessible by frequently running ferries. Information is available at the information center, Trafikanten, at Jernbanetorget. The subway is not very extensive but it is easily managed. There are eight lines, which converge at the *Stortinget* (Parliament) Station. Four run west from there through the Majorstuen Station and four run east through Toyen Station. Ferries for Bygdoy Peninsula and sightseeing boats leave from the harbor just across from the Town Hall.

Driver beware! Parking can be a problem in central Oslo. The maximum time allowed is three hours Monday through Saturday, and only in indicated spots. Longer hours are available at the Central Station. After 5:00 p.m., or 2:00 p.m. on Saturday and all day Sunday, parking is free. Outside the center, you will find three kinds of parking meters. Maximum time indicated by color. Yellow—1 hour. Gray—2 hours. Brown—3 hours.

WHAT TO SEE AND DO

Oslo is a city of museums and fascinating ones at that. But don't confine yourself to them. Take the time to catch the spirit of the city as well. For the purposes of efficiency and ease, I have divided the city into four sections and listed the sights within each of those. The center of town is the stretch of two main streets, **Karl Johans Gate** and **Stortingsgata**, which run parallel to one another from Parliament to the Royal Palace on either side of a tree-lined mall filled with cafes and fountains. Here stands the National Theater at the very heart of Oslo. The next area for exploration is the **harbor**, with Akershus Fortress, the City Hall and Aker Brygge. From there, you can catch a ferry for a quick ride to Bygdoy Peninsula, where several museums are located. And then there is the area just west of the center, known as Frogner, where you will find the extraordinary Vigeland Park. So if you allow two days and see two of these areas a day, you will have a fairly good introduction to Oslo, though there's plenty more of interest and Oslo is a pleasant place to take your time in. If you have more time, you will be able as well to take the short ride to Holmenkollen Park or even to ride the train to Lillehammer, site of the 1994 Winter Olympic Games.

SIGHTSEEING TOURS

Several sightseeing tours are available, all leaving from the harbor in front of Radhus Square. The boat cruises have limited departures at the beginning and end of the season, so check with tourist information at the Radhus.

The Fjord Cruises depart daily in summer from pier 3 or 4 at the harbor by the Radhus. These last two hours and take you through the islands and sounds where you will glimpse Oslo residents enjoying the swimming and sailing that are so much a part of Oslo summer. The same cruise, with a stop for lunch at the restaurant Najaden, leaves daily at 10:30.

Mini-Cruise, 50-minutes on the fjord, affords a view of the harbor and the inner part of the Oslofjord. It departs daily on the hour from May 20 to August 20. From June 23 to August 15, you can take a two-hour evening cruise, which includes dinner at the famed Najaden grand maritime buffet. Check with the tourist board for changes in times. Several of these cruises are available at a discount with your Oslo Card.

Selected Oslo Sightseeing takes you by bus to Holmenkollen, Vigeland Park, the Viking Ships and Kon-Tiki museums. *Everyday at 11:00 a.m. From June through August, an additional tour departs at 1:30 p.m.*

Great Oslo Sightseeing is a seven-hour bus tour. *Summer only from June 1 through August 31. The trip departs daily at 10:00 a.m. and returns at 6:00 p.m. It allows an hour's stop for lunch, which is not included in the ticket* ☎ *22 20 82 06.* Tours by boat or bus run from City Hall everyday in the morning and afternoon. ☎ *22 20 07 15.*

A Safari in Oslo might sound a little strange, but visitors can take this Norwegian-style safari through the woodlands of Oslo. Travel through pine and birch forests, past mountains and lakes. Instead of leopards and lions, you will see black grouse and ptarmigan and a seasonal sampling of the more than 1000 varieties of wild flowers that blanket the Norwegian woods. Half-day (five-hour) and full-day (10-hour) tours are available. Lunch in a forest chalet or tent is included in the package and participants can also choose to catch and grill their own trout. Safari Land Rovers depart from the Oslo City Hall. Tickets can be purchased at the Tourist Information Office in City Hall.

In addition, you can take the following walking tours by yourself:

TOUR # 1: THE CENTER OF TOWN

The National Theater

This building stands at the heart of Oslo's center, so we will start there. The small park in front of the theater is called Studenterlunden, and the two statues you see here are of Norway's literary lights, Henrik Ibsen and Nobel Prize-winner Bjornestjerne Bjornson. *The theater offers guided tours Monday at 6:00 p.m. all year round and every day from June 15 until July 8.* ☎ *41 27 10 for information.*

The University

Across Karl Johans Gate you will see the neoclassical, terra cotta colored facade of the old University, which nowadays houses mainly administrative offices rather than classrooms.

The Historical Museum

Behind the University, to the northeast on Frederiks Gate, is the Historical Museum with its Antiquities Collection of artifacts from prehistoric Norway.

The National Gallery

Just behind the Historical Museum on Universitesgata, this is Norway's principal art museum with exhibits of Norwegian and international art.

The Royal Palace

A bit farther west, set in yet another park, actually two parks, as the one to the north of the palace is called Slottsparken and the one to the south is Dronningparken. *The changing of the guard occurs here at 1:30 p.m. every day.*

If you walk in the other direction on Karl Johans Gate or Stortingsgata, toward the Stortinget or Parliament, you will be in the primary shopping area and the place where the deluxe hotels are located. The scene here is lively, even late at night.

The Stortinget

The yellow brick facade of this impressive, rather somber building suggests solidity and substance rather than the road to Oz. But inside there are some striking contemporary murals.

Oslo Cathedral

Continue on past the Parliament and you will come to the cathedral, fronted by Stortorget, a large square with a fruit and flower market. The cathedral was consecrated in 1697, and boasts the oldest working tower clock in Norway. It was installed in 1718, though the tower itself was rebuilt in 1850. As you enter the cathedral, take special note of the bronze doors. They are the work of Dagfin Werenskiold and illustrate the Sermon on the Mount. Perhaps the most striking aspect of the interior of the cathedral is its blend of old and new and dark and light. The heavy wooden altarpiece beneath the bright colors of the contemporary ceiling paintings; the elaborately carved pulpit and the massive, beautifully decorated 18th-century organ illuminated by the stained-glass windows of the 20th century. The cylindrical pulpit was the first of its kind in Norway and, like the altarpiece, inspired a new style of decorative church art. The stained-glass windows in the chancel are the work of Emanuel Vigeland (not the sculptor Gustav Vigeland of park fame), and the 16 windows in the transepts were done by Borgar Hauglid. They were a gift from the Norwegian-American commander, J. A. Gade, in memory of those killed in WWII. Perhaps the most striking features of the cathedral are the ceiling decorations, the work of Hugo Lous Mohr, from 1936 to 1950.

TOUR #2 THE HARBOR AND AKERSHUS FORTRESS

Though the area around the National Theater is touted as the center of town, there is more to Oslo than this and my suggestion is to "get thee to the water," as Oslo's heart beats to the luff of sails and the putter of the fishing boats' motors.

City Hall

You might head first for the City Hall or Radhus, an easy walk from the National Theater, where you can pick up an Oslo Card if you haven't already done so and find other information on the city. Though the Radhus may not be your idea of an architectural gem, take the time to explore the interior and to see the splendid paintings by some of Norway's finest artists, which decorate the hall. The building itself was designed by Arnstein in

Arneberg and Magnus Paulsson and was almost 20 years in the making. If you enter through the main door, which is on the opposite side of the building from the harbor, you will see the splendid murals, the work of some of Norway's most esteemed artists. These murals, begun in the 1930s, but not completed until the late 1950s because of the war, depict life in Oslo and include illustrations of the Nazi occupation.

Akershus Castle

Exit the Radhus by the entrance on the harbor. This is the entrance by the tourist information office. Walk along the water toward Akershus Castle, which sits at the edge of the harbor in medieval majesty, its sweep of lawn an irresistible temptation to sunbathers. If there is sun, you might want to yield to that seduction yourself. Take a moment to sit on the ramparts of the castle and look out to the fjord to get your bearings. Just below you, from your vantage point at the castle, you will see fishing boats, many heaped with freshly caught shrimp you can buy right from the boat. Here, too, are the sightseeing boats and the ferries to Bygdoy, the peninsula you can see across the harbor. Just across from where you sit, looking a bit to the right, you will see a complex of new glass and old brick buildings. This is **Aker Brygge**, a waterfront shopping and restaurant center. But you can't loll around forever, as pleasant as it is. Akershus Castle is really worth exploring, so pick yourself up and head for the castle. King Haakon V built this castle/fortress in the 14th century to command and protect the harbor of Oslo. In the 17th century, with the encouragement of King Christian IV of Denmark/Norway, the great builder king, the fortress was renovated as a Renaissance Palace. Since that time, the castle weathered periods of neglect punctuated by sporadic interest in restoration until the 1930s, when the architect Arnstein Arneberg, who was one of the designers of the Town Hall, oversaw a carefully researched renovation. As with the Town Hall, the project was interrupted by WWII and was not completed until 1963. The grounds have also been restored according to early plans and drawings. Now open to the public, the castle and its surroundings are an inviting and fascinating prospect the tourist can explore independently or with a guided tour. *Tours at 11:00 a.m., 1:00 p.m. and 3:00 p.m. on weekdays and at 1:00 p.m. and 3:00 p.m. on Sunday. The tour lasts about 45 minutes.*

If you prefer to wander on your own, among the spots to notice: the **Maiden Tower**, where the original main entrance and drawbridge were located; the **Christian IV Hall** with its 17th-century tapestries; the **Romer-ike Hall**, which served as the offices of the 17th-century governor Hannibal Sehested, and in subsequent years saw both lofty and mundane service, falling from the grandeur it enjoyed as the Lord Chamberlain's room to the indignity of serving as a granary. The **Margaretha Hall** is the room named for Queen Margaretha, the young wife of Haakon VI. At the age of 18, the queen, residing at Akershus during her husband's absence, wrote to him of the hardships of life at the castle—the lack of food, the bitter cold. It is thought that she gave birth to her son, Olav Hakonsson, in this room. Look also at **Henrik Wergeland's office**, occupied by that gentleman and poet who was appointed head of the State Archives in 1840, and as such was the first keeper of public records in Norway. One of the most impressive chambers is the **Olav Hall** with its massive, timbered ceiling, last restored in 1976 for the celebration of the 75th anniversary of King Olav V. The chapel contains the tomb of King Haakon VII.

The Resistance Museum

This museum is located on the grounds of the fortress, just beside Akershus Castle, which served as one of the most brutal of the German prisons during WWII. Its exhibit is a thoughtful and detailed presentation of the events in Norway during the German occupation. Allow plenty of time for this museum. *Open Monday–Friday, 10:00 a.m.–4:00 p.m., Sunday 11:00 a.m.–4:00 p.m.*

Aker Brygge

As yet this new shopping and restaurant complex at the harbor is a bit lean on the shopping side, but there are several good eating spots, including the lovely restaurant **D/S Louise**, as well as cafes and lunch places offering a variety of ethnic choices and seafood. So if you didn't think to pinch a roll and some cheese and sausage from the breakfast buffet at your hotel for a picnic, you could head to Aker Brygge and pick up something there—either to eat on the spot or to bring back to a picnic on the castle lawn.

TOUR #3: BYGDOY PENINSULA

In winter, take Bus #30 from the National Theater. In summer, **ferries** leave frequently from the harbor, pier 3, just in front of City Hall, for the brief ride to Bygdoy, where some of Oslo's most interesting museums are located. You can ride free with your Oslo Card. The ferry will leave you off within an easy walk of the museums. Get off at the first stop if you are going to the Folk Museum or the Viking Ships Museum. The second stop will take you right to the Maritime Museum, the Fram and the Kon-Tiki museums. But you can also walk from the museums at stop #1 to those at the second stop. The way is well-marked and interesting, as this is one of Oslo's nicest suburbs. Several embassies are located here, but the private homes are also lovely. You'll get a glimpse of Norwegian home life—upper crust or upper middle-class—and begin to understand why Norwegians like to spend so much time at home. They are house-proud, and these immaculately painted houses, mostly white frame with black tile roofs and charming gardens, are enticing.

Stop #1 on Bygdoy:

As you disembark, you will see a restaurant at the pier, **Lanternen**, where you can stop for a snack or lunch. If you continue up the street, you will come to signs directing you to the Viking Museum. On your right as you walk, you will see a small antique shop called **RomAntique**. It occupies a small house and garden, both cluttered with a variety of interesting old Norwegian pieces—worth a look. The address is *Huk Avenue 20*, in case you slip by without noticing it the first time.

The Viking Ships Museum

The museum contains three ships in a building designed to show them off perfectly. The ships were used as funeral ships and so were better preserved than many, because they were buried in soil that acted as a protection for the wood. As you enter the museum, you will see directly in front of you the *Osebergskibet*, which is the best preserved and the most extensively restored of the three ships on display. The visitor cannot help but be struck by the grace and majesty of this lovely ship, excavated in 1904. It was an exceptionally luxurious ship, with a burial chamber amidships for the burial of two women of high station.

Because a very tightly sealed barrow was constructed above ground for the preservation of many objects, the relics from this burial spot are extraordinary. In particular, carvings of human figures, very rare in Viking art, were found here. Excavators also found funeral sledges in very good condition, with some of the rope used to tie the bodies to the sled. The ship itself was in fragments upon excavation, but the timber was well-preserved, and so almost 90 percent of the rebuilt boat is constructed from the original timber.

The next boat on display, the *Tuneskibit*, is really just fragments, but it will give you a good idea of the enormous task of rebuilding these ships. The final boat is the *Gokstad*. Be sure, in looking at all three boats, to climb the steps to the balconies which overlook the ships so that you can look down into the boats. *The museum is open daily 10:00 a.m.–4:00 p.m. in summer. Other times during the winter are varied so check before you go.*

The Norsk Folkemuseum

The largest museum of cultural history in Norway offers excellent indoor exhibits as well as the interesting old buildings brought here from various regions of the country. You can spend many pleasant hours here, wandering through the lovely grounds and numerous buildings and exhibits that have been collected from the towns and countryside of Norway. Gamle Byen is a collection of old townhouses, while the open-air museum consists of farmhouses and buildings with sod roofs. Other buildings house the museum's collections of furniture, costumes and art, in addition to a Sami (Lappish) culture exhibition. You can also visit Henrik Ibsen's study, reconstructed with its original furniture. Don't miss the Stave church from Hallingdal, built around the year 1200.

If you are hungry: Just outside the grounds, but easily accessible, you will find a restaurant that serves sandwiches and typically hot Norwegian dishes at reasonable prices. You must keep your museum ticket when you exit the gates to go to the restaurant as you will be required to show it to get back inside the grounds. *The museum is open in summer on weekdays from 10:00 a.m. to 6:00 p.m. and on Sunday from 11:00 a.m. to 6:00 p.m. Winter hours are 11:00 a.m. to 4:00 p.m. and on Sunday, noon to 3:00 p.m.*

Stop #2 on Bygdoy:

The ferry will let you off at the point where three seafaring museums have been constructed.

The Framhuset

This A-frame structure houses the polar ship *Fram*, the ship used by Fridjof

Nansen in his crossing of the polar seas 1893–1896. Later, famed polar explorer Roald Amundsen used it for his expedition to the South Pole. The exhibit offers excellent text on Nansen's two expeditions, but the material on Amundsen has not yet been translated into English. However, the main interest of this museum is the boat itself, and you can climb aboard and crawl all over it, exploring its decks and depths, using your imagination to put yourself on the icy seas. The skis propped in the cabins and the fur-trimmed parkas will suggest just what these expeditions must have entailed. In one of the officer's cabins, a violin is propped against a wall—imagine for a moment the sound of a violin piercing the arctic stillness. *Open May 16–August 31 daily 10:00 a.m.–5:45 p.m. At other times of year, the museum opens at 11:00 a.m., and its closing hours vary from 2:45 p.m. to 4:45 p.m., so be certain to check.*

The Kon-Tiki Museum

Dedicated to the explorations of the anthropologist/explorer Thor Heyerdahl, who set out with five men in 1947 to prove his theory that the pre-Inca inhabitants of South America could have sailed to Polynesia, the museum houses Heyerdahl's two boats, the beautiful reed boat *Ra II* and the *Kon-Tiki* raft. But there are other items of interest, in particular, the giant statues from Easter Island, a reproduction of an Easter Island family cave and various objects collected from Thor Heyerdahl's exotic anthropological expeditions. *Open May 18–August 31, 10:00 a.m. to 6:00 p.m. At other times, the museum opens at 10:30 a.m. and its closing hours vary between 4:00 p.m. and 5:00 p.m.*

The Norwegian Seafaring Museum

Scholars of nautical history will find here the definitive exhibit of the maritime culture and history of Norway. All facets of maritime life are included here, from boats to crafts, to art and antiques. Outside, you will find the *Gjoa*, the boat Roald Amundsen used in his search for the Northwest Passage.

Restaurant Alert: There is an excellent restaurant, **Najaden**, right here in the midst of these three museums at Bygdoynesvn. 37. Its nautical ambience is just the thing for your outing on Bygdoy, but stand forewarned that while the open sandwiches available at lunch are affordable, the à la carte items are more expensive than you might expect in a museum restaurant. *Open every day 11:00 a.m. to 9:45 p.m.*

TOUR #4: THE WEST END

Several major attractions are located a bit outside of town, to the west of central Oslo, but it's easy to get there. Tram #2 from the National Theater will take you to the main entrance of Vigeland Park. Both the City Museum and the Vigeland Museum are located here as well.

Vigeland Park

This pleasant, spacious park contains the fruit of sculptor Gustav Vigeland's lifetime labor. The theme of the sculptures is human life and human relationships, with an emphasis on the family. The sculptures depict parents and children at play, at rest, in contemplative and even angry poses. The most well-known is the monolith, the giant obelisk of entwined human figures, which dominates the park. My favorite is the mother who is being ridden by her children like a horse. She appears to enjoy her tasks, though the burden is obvious. The park is a pleasant place to spend a few hours. There is a small playground, but children prefer to climb on the sculptures themselves rather than on the jungle gyms. You will find several kiosks selling ice cream and cold drinks. In summertime, an outdoor cafe is open.

The Vigeland Museum

Located across the street from the park, this building was constructed by the city of Oslo as a home and studio for Gustav Vigeland. In return, he promised to donate all his works and original casts to the city. The sculptor lived here from 1924 until his death in 1943. In 1947, it was opened to the public as a museum. This is a monumental building, large enough to house 1600 sculptures, many of them massive, in addition to thousands of drawings. The original, full-sized models for the pieces in the park are here, and it is an overwhelming experience to see them indoors. You will realize just how huge they are and what an enormous undertaking the park must have been. It is interesting to study the development of Vigeland's style and to follow the creation of some of the works from the initial sketches to the completed piece. *Open May–Oct.,Tuesday–Sun. 12:00 p.m.–7:00 p.m. Remainder of year, open Tuesday through Sunday 1:00 p.m.–7:00 p.m. The museum is closed on Monday.*

The Oslo City Museum

At Frogner Manor on the grounds of Vigeland Park. The main building, open only in summer, was built in 1790. It contains an exhibit of home interiors. Other exhibits, which include part of the city's art collection, center on the cultural and commercial history of Oslo. *Open June–August Tuesday–Friday, 10:00 a.m.–6:00 p.m.; Saturday and Sunday 11:00 a.m.– 5:00 p.m. Earlier closings in winter. Closed Monday.*

The Henie-Onstad Foundations (*Hovikodden Kunstsenter*)

Situated a few miles west of Oslo. The museum contains the largest collection of international art in Norway. The museum was developed by Sonia Henie and her shipping magnate husband Niels Onstad as a way of sharing their extensive art collection with the public. The building and its site, by the fjord, are attractions in themselves. In addition to the permanent exhibits, the museum offers concerts, films and traveling exhibits. Take any of the following buses: 151, 153, 161, 162, 252, 261 and get off at Hovikodden. *Open Tuesday–Friday, 9:00 a.m.–9 p.m.; Saturday–Mon. 11:00 a.m. to 5:00 p.m. June–August, the museum remains open until 7:00 p.m. on Saturday and Sunday.*

THE MUNCH MUSEUM

Because it is located in the east end of Oslo, a visit to the Munch Museum has to be a trip in itself. The museum is a 10-minute bus ride (bus #29) from the square in front of the central railway station, or you can take the subway to Toyen. Visitors will find the definitive collection of Edvard Munch's paintings, those bleak, haunted creations that are the most palpable manifestations of the Scandinavian melancholy. The anguish of these elongated, grief-laden figures is almost audible. This is not a museum to visit if you are depressed, but you will emerge with a solid understanding of the artist, of both his psyche and his artistry, and of the development of his style. Be sure to go downstairs to see the portraits of the artist's family and drawings of his childhood home. Concerts are held here frequently throughout the year. *Open daily May–September from 10:00 a.m. to 8:00 p.m. From Oct. through April, the museum is closed on Monday and its closing hours vary from day to day.*

HOLMENKOLLEN

A 30-minute subway trip (of which only the first few minutes are underground) from the National Theater will bring you to Holmenkollen. This is a pretty ride that, just outside Oslo, begins a gentle climb through the trees and offers glimpses of suburban life as you pass perfectly kept white frame houses with neat gardens. This area, part of the Oslo Forest, has more cross-country ski trails than anywhere else in Norway. Many of the trails are lighted for night skiing, since night falls early in wintertime here. In summer, the area is a lovely place for hiking.

Tryvannstarnet (the Tryvann Tower)

Take the above mentioned ride from the National Theater to the end of the line at *Voksenkollen* and walk the rather rigorous way to the tower, the highest point in the Holmenkollen range. An express lift will take you up to a most spectacular panoramic view. The tower's opening hours vary from month to month, but it is generally *open from 10:00 a.m. to 5:00 p.m.* with *longer hours during July and August and earlier closing times from Oct. through April.*

The Holmenkollen Ski Jump and Ski Museum

If you've gone to Tryvannstarnet and are ready for another hike, you can walk down to the ski jump, site of the world-famous **Holmenkollen Ski Festival**. If you chose to skip Tryvannstarnet, you can get off the train at Holmenkollen stop. It's just a short walk up the hill to the jump and the museum. An elevator will take visitors almost to the top of the jump, but you do have to climb some stairs to reach the point where you will see where the skiers stand, steadying their nerves (maybe they don't even have such things) for that plunge of thrill and skill. At the base of the jump is the **Ski Museum**, which traces the history of skiing in Norway from the earliest evidence of cave paintings showing figures on skis through the polar expeditions of Nansen and Amundsen. *Open daily 10:00 a.m.–5:00 p.m. in May and September, 10:00 a.m. to 7:00 p.m. in June and August, and 9:00 a.m. to 10:00 p.m. in July. Earlier closings Oct.–April. There is a small cafe and outdoor terrace here.*

The Holmenkollen Park Hotel

Really a sight in itself. (See "Where to Stay.") Visitors can have a sumptuous and expensive cold buffet lunch there in its famed **De Fem Stue Restau-**

rant, or they can walk farther down the hill to the **Holmenkollen Restaurant**, where you can have a lunch buffet for 140NOK. There is also a **cafeteria** for a less expensive meal.

OFF THE BEATEN PATH

Once you've done the *must-do's*, you will find plenty to occupy your remaining time.

Hoymagasinet

At Akershus • For a dip into Oslo history, visit the multimedia exhibition, *Christiania, a City in Europe*, presented daily on the hour from *June 1 through September 15*. This exhibit describes the development of Christian IV's renaissance city, now part of the center of Oslo.

Gamle Aker Kirke (*Old Aker Church*)

Erected in 1100, this is the oldest stone church still in use in Scandinavia. The cemetery just around the corner is the burial spot of many illustrious Norwegians, including Henrik Ibsen. *The church is open Monday–Thursday from noon until 2:00 p.m. It is closed Friday and Saturday, and on Sunday the service is at 11:00 a.m. You can also arrange to visit the church by appointment. Guided tours are available.* While you are in the area, take the time to explore the surrounding streets. This is one of the oldest areas in Oslo and one of the few places with any remaining old wooden houses. **Telthusbakken**, just by the church, is filled with such houses.

The Kunstindustrimuseet

Oslo's Museum of Applied Art is right in the neighborhood of Gamle Aker Kirke, at *1 St. Olav's Gate*. Its most important attraction is the 13th-century **Baldishol Tapestry**, but there are many other exhibits of interest such as collections of crafts and industrial design, and a royal costume exhibit. *Open Tuesday–Friday, 11:00 a.m.-3:00 p.m. and Saturday and Sunday noon–4:00 p.m. It is open also on Tuesday from 7:00 p.m.–9 p.m. Closed Monday.* Bus #17 to Nordahl Bruuns g. or the subway to the Sentrum stop.

The Theater Museum

Located on the lower level of the Gamle Radhus Restaurant, in one of the oldest buildings in Norway. The museum traces the history of the theater in Oslo from the 19th century to the 1950s. *Open Monday and Tuesday from 11:00 a.m. until 3:00 p.m., Sunday from noon till 4:00 p.m.*

Skating Museum

If you are especially interested in skating, you might want to take Tram #2 to Frogner Station. Its hours vary, but you can always get in if you schedule an appointment. ☎ *61 11 10.* For an exhibit and sales of Norwegian art and crafts, visit the **Kunstnerforbundet** at *3 Kjeld Stubs gata*, near the Radhus. *It is closed on Sunday from September 1 through January 9. Otherwise it is open every day Monday–Friday, 10:00 a.m.–5:00 p.m.; Saturday, 10:00 a.m.–3:00 p.m.; and Sunday, noon–4:00 p.m.*

WHERE TO SHOP

The main shopping area is in and around **Karl Johans Gate** and **Stortingsga-ta**. As you work your way up Karl Johans Gate, you will come to the large department stores. The old stables that encircle the cathedral are now shops as well. Stortorvet, the square in front of the cathedral, has an open-air market every day. The more elegant stores are on **Stortingsgata** and on streets that run off it, especially **Tordenskjoldsgate**, where you will find fine antique shops and particularly high quality ladies' wear. **Aker Brygge**, the new waterfront complex, is still struggling to establish itself as a shopping center and the shops here come and go most unpredictably. The **SAS Scandinavian Hotel** is a shopping center in itself. **Oslo City** appeals more to young people. This is a vertical shopping mall near the railroad station with plenty of inexpensive shops and fast-food places.

Shopping hours: Shops are usually open Monday–Friday from 9:00 a.m. to 5:00 p.m. and many stay open until 7:00 p.m. on Thursday. Watch for summer hours, however, when shops tend to close at 4:00 p.m. During winter and summer, most stores close at 2:00 p.m.

NORWEGIAN CRAFTS AND DESIGN

Norway Designs (*Stortingsgata 28*), has beautiful handcrafted pieces from all of Scandinavia. Here you will find sweaters, weavings, glass and ceramics. **Den Norske Husfliden** is the name given to shops that carry exclusively Norwegian handcrafted pieces. You will find these shops all over Norway and one of the largest is at *Mollergata 4*. Everything including all the Norwegian sweaters you might ever want to see. Go upstairs to see the display of regional Norwegian costumes. If you're "crafty" yourself, you can buy fabric and wool here and do your own thing. **Glas Magasinet** is the major department store where you will find gift items of Norwegian design. **Heimen at Rosenkrantz Gate 8** is another source for Norwegian handcrafts, especially good for regional costumes.

GLASS

The major Norwegian glassworks is **Hadeland**, which is about 45 miles from Oslo in the direction of Lillehammer. You can get there by bus from Gronlands Torg, leaving every hour on the hour. *The glassworks has a shop, restaurant and museum open weekdays from 9:00 a.m. to 6:00 p.m.; Saturday, 10:00 a.m.– 5:00 p.m.; and Sunday, 11:00 a.m.–6:00 p.m. The glass blowing is done weekdays from 9:00 a.m. to 3:00 p.m.; Saturday, 10:30 a.m.–2:00 p.m.; and Sunday, noon–4:00 p.m.* Hadelands glass can be purchased in Oslo at many shops. The **Glasmagasin** has a very complete inventory. It also offers tours to the glassworks. **Porsgrunn Porselen** *on Karl Johans Gate* has a nice selection of Hadelands.

SWEATERS

If you're in the market for typically Norwegian sweaters, you will have no trouble finding them, as they seem to be hanging in every window and on every corner. The quality and price vary greatly. For the best selections, try the **Husflidens** and the **Oslo Sweater Shop** *in the SAS Scandinavian Hotel.* There are other beautiful sweaters available in Norway if you don't happen to care for the particularly Norwegian style, but look carefully at the labels. Many of these other sweaters are not made in Norway.

ANTIQUES

Kaare Berntsen at (*Universitetsgaten 12*) has a dazzling display of European antiques. It's just across the street from the Savoy Hotel.

JEWELRY

David Andersen (*Karl Johans Gate 20*) is the place. This internationally renowned jeweler offers all sorts of enticements, from contemporary designs to carefully wrought copies of traditional pieces. The jeweler is especially known for pins and bracelets of silver and enamel in the form of flowers and butterflies. These make beautiful, if costly, souvenirs.

CLOTHING

Oslo has several shops with fine ladies' and men's clothing of international design. **Ferner Jacobsen** is the Brooks Brothers of Oslo. *Located on Stortingsgata* just down from the Continental Hotel, this venerable clothing store has been in business for years. The Ferners, both father and son, are Harvard educated and seem to have brought a taste for Ivy League fashion to Oslo. The ladies' shop is next door.

BOOKS

The best selection of books in English is at **Erik Quist** *on Drammensveien*, a few blocks from the National Theater.

WHERE TO STAY

VERY EXPENSIVE

The Continental   +★★★★

Stortinsgate 24-26 across from the National Theater • This hotel wins my vote as the place to stop and flop if money is no object. And even if money is the object, you might be better off than you imagine as there are weekend and summer rates available at considerable savings. The Continental has the best location in town for those who really want to be in the center of things—right across the street from the National Theater. It also has its owner, Ellen Hansen Brochmann, and her daughter Elisabeth Caroline Mellbye, who carry on a family tradition of hotelkeeping started in 1900, when Ellen Brochman's grandparents managed and later bought the new Hotel Continental and Theater Cafeen. The rooms are large and pleasantly decorated in pale, fresh colors. The bathrooms are about the best around, with nice touches like heated floors and Braun hairdryers; the staff is excellent and accommodating. The restaurants here provide a variety of dining choices from the reasonably priced Tivoli Grillen to the chic, noisy Theatercafeen and the serenely elegant Annen Etage.

The Bristol   ★★★

Kristian IV's Gate 7 • The lobby of this hotel is a particularly lively and rather exotic spot, with its *fin de siècle*/moorish decor. The rooms are comfortable, and most doubles are large. All have been renovated and redecorated in fresh, light colors. The hotel has a rich history, having served at the turn-of-the-century as the beacon for the elite of Oslo, who gathered here regularly for tea and dancing. It is the place where members of NATO and the Norwegian Parliament meet for official dinners. The library bar, just off the lobby, is an attractive spot. There is a Grill Room, a disco and a cellar restaurant called El Toro.

The Grand   ★★★

Karl Johans Gate 31 • The Grand has held sway over Oslo since 1874, playing host to such Norwegian luminaries as Henrik Ibsen, Edvard Munch and Roald Amundsen. Its rooms are large and comfortable, and all have been recently renovated. The hotel boasts a very attractive rooftop pool and bar, as well as several restaurants. It's a busy place and does not manage quite so intimate an atmosphere as the Continental, in my opinion. I find its much-extolled rooftop restaurant, L'Etoile, a rather unimaginative spot, but the views are beautiful.

Royale Christiana

Biskop Gunnerus Gt. 3 Biskop Gunnerusgt 3 • Located near the Railway Station, this is the completely renovated and enlarged edition of what was the Sara Hotel Oslo. With 400 rooms, this is one of the larger of Oslo's hotels. I have not seen the rooms, but it is reported to be comfortable, attractive and, of course, up-to-date.

Reso Oslo Plaza   ★★★★

Sonja Henies Pl. 3 • A tall icicle of a building, the newest addition to Oslo's hotel list boasts the dubious distinction of being the largest hotel in Northern Europe. It is slick and posh and its large, comfortable rooms offer magnificent views of the city. With its indoor access to Oslo Spectrum, the new conference center, and its high tech amenities, it is designed to attract the business traveler more than the tourist. Its location near the Railway Station makes it convenient, though the area around the station is not particularly attractive or desirable.

The SAS Scandinavia Hotel   ★★★

Holbergs Gate 30 • Of the filing-cabinet school of architecture, this is a big, commercial, rather charmless hotel, but it offers every comfort and convenience one could imagine—as well it should at the highest prices in Oslo. It has been redecorated in the last year, so the rooms are fresher and more pleasant than they were. Its restaurant is considered quite good by Oslo-ites who know. The abundance of shops in the hotel's lower arcade draws shoppers from all over town.

Holmenkollen Park Hotel Rica   ★★★★

This historic hotel is located at Holmenkollen, a half-hour train or car ride from Oslo. It is a resort hotel, offering the beauty of the Oslo forest, wonderful cross-country ski trails and an indoor swimming pool. The main building, built in 1896 in the Dragon style, has been renovated and contains the restaurant De Fem Stue, whose unpretentious, rustic decor belies its very sophisticated, urban prices. Also in this building are conference rooms that have been restored under the supervision of the Chief Inspector of Ancient Monuments and Historic Buildings. These rooms were the original hotel rooms but are so large that it is impractical, in fact prohibitive, to use them as such now. They are worth taking a peek into as the renovation is exquisite and it is fun to see what life used to be like for the privileged traveler. The new wings are completely modern and house the guest rooms, swimming hall, sauna, lobby and bar.

EXPENSIVE

Hotel Nobel   +★★★

Karl Johans Gate 33 • This small hotel in the center of town will run you about 200 NOK less than the aforementioned hotels. All the rooms have been refurbished, but the second-floor rooms, which have been converted from offices, are especially large and attractive. The hotel itself has an intimate charm with antiques in the corridors and a wonderful, sweeping stairway. Weekend rates for singles are about the same as the Continental, so the choice in that case is largely a question of individual taste. This hotel has only 85 rooms. To be blatantly subjective, I would choose this over either the Grand or the Bristol because of its size and charm.

The Scandic Crown

Parkveien 68 • This hotel deserves mention only because, as the saying goes, "It's there," which means that travelers will hear of it and want to know about it. Until recently, it was the K.N.A. Hotel. At the time I visited, the hotel was in the process of renovation, so one would hope the rooms will be comfortable and modern. The renovation looked promising as far as I could see from the lobby, but both times I tried to see a room it seemed too much for the very harried and apparently overworked staff. That does not bode well for the service, and since I never did get to see a room, I can't give this hotel a rating. However, it is pleasantly located—down a street off Drammensveien, which runs alongside the Royal Palace and the park.

The Europa

St. Olavs Gate 31 • A rather utilitarian, charmless but comfortable hotel, it is popular with businessmen probably because of the nicely sized single rooms.

The Ambassadeur Best Western   +★★★★

Camilla Colletts Vei 15 • Here is a charming small hotel near Frogner in an area where many embassies are located. It is privately owned, and many of the antiques and artworks in the public rooms belong to the owner. The rooms are newly decorated in one of six different motifs: Roman, Captain's Cabin, Osa, London, Amsterdam and Shanghai. A small swimming pool and sauna are located on the lower level. The hotel also has the restaurant Sabrosa, recently opened by the chef of Feinschmecker, one of Oslo's most popular eating spots.

MODERATE

The Bondeheimen Hotell

Rosenkrantz Gt. 8 • The hotel represents exceptional value. The rooms are freshly and tastefully redecorated in a very Scandinavian contemporary style, and the prices are reasonable. The Bondeheimen is located on Rosenkrantz Gate, which is in the center of town just behind Karl Johans Gate.

The Carlton Hotel

Parkveien 78 • On a quiet street near the Royal Palace, the hotel is a friendly, cozy place with small, rather stuffy, but comfortable enough rooms. The restaurant, Park Lane, is attractive and reasonable.

The Rainbow Hotel Stefan ★

Rosenkrantz 1 • The Stefan is a mission hotel that seems to attract young people. The staff is friendly and the lobby attractive. The rooms are small, but pleasantly decorated. Bathrooms are adequate. While the hotel is centrally located, it is across from what will soon be a parking garage, not the greatest view. The lunchtime buffet is justifiably famous.

The Inter Nor Savoy

Univesitetsgt. 11 • The Savoy offers rates considerably lower than the above two hotels, but the rooms are rather stuffy and the corridors extraordinarily dreary. The bathrooms are surprisingly modern, however, and if you get Room No. 520, you could accommodate an entire family in the sumptuous marble bathroom. The lobby is cozy and the location excellent. The restaurant Martini is popular and the Savoy Bar is a well-known gathering spot.

The Gabelshus

Gabelsgate 16 • Here is another of those hotels located in the west suburbs of Oslo. The Gabelshus is enchanting from the outside, and the public rooms are delightful and cozy in the English style. The rooms themselves are pleasant, though some are a bit small. Reach this hotel and the Ritz (listed below) by Tram No. 9.

The Ritz

Frederik Sstansgate3 • Located just behind the Gabelshus, and owned by the same people, the hotel is priced just a bit lower, but not enough to count. It is pleasant and comfortable, but the Gabelshus would be my first choice between the two.

The Norum ★★

Bygdoy Alle 53 • Similar to the two hotels above, but on a somewhat busier street so it could be a little noisy. The rooms vary quite a bit, and some, like No. 324, should be avoided. Corner rooms are large and airy, but noisy. Of course, if you are staying in the center of Oslo, you will find noise aplenty, but those who choose to stay out of the center are probably looking for a quieter spot.

WHERE TO EAT

Dining out is something of a problem in the larger Norwegian cities because the restaurants are very expensive and the quality is not consistent with the prices. The top-of-the-line dining spots are excellent but exorbitant, and even in the relatively less expensive restaurants, you will pay more than you should for a rather ordinary meal.

In most restaurants, you can order the daily menu consisting of two or three courses at a lower price. It is often less expensive to eat your larger meal at lunch and just have a light evening meal.

You should book ahead at most of the restaurants, even the informal ones like the Theatercafeen and the Tivoli Grillen, as they crowd up quickly, even on weeknights.

RESTAURANTS IN THE CENTER OF TOWN

3 Kokker

Drammensveien • Diners are almost in the kitchen at this attractive restaurant, which takes its name from the fact that it has three chefs, all very much in sight and in hearing of restaurant patrons. The unselfconscious provincial decor and extremely friendly service make this a most pleasant dining experience. The menu is original, featuring Norwegian ingredients and traditional foods treated in a most imaginative way. Some might object to the noise from the open kitchen, while others find it fun to watch the cooks in action. The three-course daily menu and wine will run upwards of $50.

Blom

Karl Johans Gate 41 B • ☎ *42 73 000.* This has been, for over 100 years, a gathering spot for artists, journalists and politicians. It is an institution in Oslo, so much so that when the surrounding buildings were razed to make way for a new shopping complex, care was taken to preserve the core of the restaurant and to number and catalogue all elements of the original structure for restoration once the complex was built. That restoration was completed in 1985, and the restaurant reopened with its distinctive character intact. It is beautiful, with its heraldic shields and fine paintings. Unfortunately, however, Blom seems to be resting on its rather wilted laurels. The staff seems downright indifferent and the service is careless. ***Expensive.***

Stortorvets Gjestgiverie

Grensen • This is a popular spot with tourists. Its more formal upstairs dining room is charming, but guests might be put off by the dingy stairway entrance and the somewhat unsavory surroundings. Several other eating spots—a cafeteria with courtyard, a pub and a nightclub—occupy the same building.

Annen Etage

In the Continental Hotel, ☎ *41 90 60* • This sedate, elegant dining room is a favorite spot for Oslo residents to celebrate grand occasions, and you will frequently find gatherings of Oslo's upper crust, spiffily turned out.

Theatercafeen

In the Continental Hotel, ☎ *33 32 00* • This busy, noisy, and stylish cafe/restaurant is an Oslo landmark and attracts the young smart set of Oslo. One goes here more to see and be seen than for the food. It's crowded, smoky, and lively, and is definitely the place to be. *Moderate to expensive.*

Tivoli Grillen

In the Continental Hotel • This informal restaurant offers simple fare at reasonable prices. Children's menu available.

L'Etoile

Karl Johansgate 31, ☎ *42 93 90* • The potential here is great with the wonderful view over Oslo from the top floor of the Grand Hotel, but I find this a rather unimaginative spot. You can spend your kronor better.

The Grand Cafe

In the Grand Hotel, ☎ *42 93 90* • Henrik Ibsen loved it, and when you first walk in, you'll love it too, this turn-of-the-century cafe of the Grand Hotel with its wonderful 19th-century mural and its piano music. But take a peek and walk out. The service is poor and the food mediocre. Save your kronor or settle for a coffee or a beer and find another spot to eat.

Mamma Rosa

Ovre Slottsgate 12, ☎ *42 01 30* • An Italian restaurant might seem a curious choice in Norway, but you will find the natives of Oslo dining here, as they love Italian food and get enough Norwegian fare at home. On the second floor of a building overlooking the walking street end of Karl Johans Gate behind Parliament, this is a lively place. A meal can run up to $30 per person, which might seem a bit steep for a plate of pasta, but this is Oslo.

Holberg's Arstidene

In the SAS Scandinavia Hotel • The chef in this gourmet restaurant won Norway's chef-of-the-year award in 1987, so if you're after gastronomic excellence, this hotel dining room will be of interest to you. *Expensive.*

D/S Louise

Aker Brygge, Stranden 3, ☎ *83 00 60* • A snappy maritime atmosphere coupled with excellent food makes this a top choice.
Moderate to expensive.

Gamle Raadhus

Near Akershus Fortress in the old City Hall • Heavy on atmosphere, but relatively light on the pocketbook, Oslo's oldest restaurant has a dark and cozy elegance that is anything but stiff or formal. Seafood is the specialty, but you can order meat as well. Although a full-course dinner is expensive, you can eat more reasonably in the very attractive bar. This is a good spot for a big lunch as well. A fixed price lunch will run you about $15.

FOR LIGHTER FARE IN THE CENTER OF TOWN

Cafe Felix

Next door to 3 Kokker on Drammensveien • The cafe is owned by 3 Kokker and the food, though simpler and less expensive, comes from the 3 Kokker kitchen. It has little to recommend aesthetically but it's a good spot for a late snack. The kitchen closes at 10:30 p.m., but you can get pita sandwiches and baguettes after that. The cafe remains open until 3:00 a.m.

Cafe Frolich
Drammensveien • Life begins late at this pleasant cafe that serves Norwegian fare, steaks, sandwiches and pasta. It's another place to keep in mind if you want a late bite, as its kitchen remains open until 12:30 a.m.

Fru Blom
Next to the restaurant Blom on Karl Johans Gate • This dark, cozy place looks a bit dusty and tired, but you will find a limited menu at prices much more reasonable than Blom.

FOR BUDGET WATCHERS

The Stefan Hotel
A good bet for its lunch smorgasbord. The buffet will cost you about $25 but it will fill you up for the rest of the day and maybe part of the next, so in the long run it's a bargain.

Kaffistova Storstua
In the Bondeheimen Hotel • An inexpensive and good cafeteria. It closes at 7:30 p.m. weekdays and even earlier on weekends, so check ahead.

Vegeta Vertshus
In the basement of 3B Munkedamsveien • This vegetarian restaurant, located in the area between the National Theater and City Hall, offers a self-serve, all you can eat buffet for 90 NOK. Among the choices are pizza, soup and various hot and cold dishes.

Peppe's Pizza
4 Stortingsgata and in the west end at Frognerveien 54 • You'll find these popular spots all over Norway and, again, this is where you'll find the Norwegians who love pizza as much as Americans do.

RESTAURANTS IN THE WEST END

Feinschmecker
Bernt Balchens Gt. 5 • Distinguished by an unpretentious but most attractive decor and friendly service, this is one of Oslo's best dining spots. Many Oslo residents think this is the best spot in town. ***Expensive.***

Bagatelle
Bygdoy Alle 3, ☎ *44 63 97* • This is Oslo's claim to culinary fame since the restaurant has been awarded a Michelin star. Its ambience is cool and sleek, and its prices stratospheric. If you are after Michelin-caliber dining, this is probably the spot for you, but I find it lacking in atmosphere and while the food might be imaginative, the decor is rather sterile. ***Very expensive.***

Hos Thea
Gabelsgate 11, ☎ *44 68 74* • You must book far ahead to get one of the few tables in this charming, tiny restaurant located in the same neighbor-

hood as the Gabelshus and Ritz hotels. Here too you can watch the cooks in action. The menu is imaginative and varied and the ambience is homey-chic which might sound like a contradiction in terms. It will not be as expensive as Bagatelle or 3 Kokkor.

Sabrosa

Located in the lower level of the Ambassadeur Hotel • This is a plushly cozy spot, artfully designed to disguise the fact that you are, indeed, sub-rosa, in the basement of the hotel. Run by the same team as Feinschmecker, this restaurant serves fine international style meals.

Kastanjen

Bygdoy Alle 18, ☎ *43 44 67* • An elegantly austere restaurant with service to match. The menu is varied and interesting.   ***Moderate to expensive.***

De Fem Stuer

Kongveien 26, ☎ *14 60 90* • This is the main dining room of the Hol-menkollen Park Hotel. It is worth a trip out here just to see the restored dragon-style interior. Gourmet dining with somewhat contrived but attractive rustic charm. Its lunchtime buffet is sumptuous and costly. ***Expensive.***

LIGHTER FARE ON THE WEST SIDE

Cafe Elise

Behind the Norum Hotel • This is a tiny neighborhood cafe, good for lunch or a light supper. It is a very simple place, which attracts the locals and is fine if you are in the area and don't want to splurge on any of the above mentioned spots.   ***Inexpensive.***

NIGHTLIFE

Oslo is lively long into the night, especially in the summer. Oslo residents seem to enjoy just being out, so the cafes on Karl Johans Gate are busy most of the time. Most of the pubs and jazz spots in central Oslo attract a young crowd. For the young, **Gamle Christiania**, in the same building as the previously mentioned Stortorvets Gjestgiverie, is very popular. My objections have to do with the area, which is not particularly attractive or comfortable. For those wanting a quieter scene, the major hotels, notably the Grand and the SAS Scandinavia, have bars and discos that stay busy late.

Insider Tip

ON THE WAY WEST: *If you are heading to the west coast from Oslo, the train from Oslo to Bergen is one of the most spectacular rail trips in Europe. If you are driving, Lillehammer, the site of the 1994 Olympic Winter Games, is on the main road to the west. Lillehammer also makes an easy one- to two-day excursion from Oslo. You can include a drive along the legendary Peer Gynt Road, an easy drive from Lillehammer. See the chapter, "Oppland and Rondane: Eastern and Central Norway."*

THE OSLOFJORD DISTRICT

If you want to venture farther along the Oslo fjord, several towns are within a few hours of Oslo and you can make a day trip out of a visit south.

GETTING THERE

Trains run regularly from Oslo's central station; however, you might run into schedule problems if you try to make a trip to both sides of the fjord.

GETTING AROUND

The two towns of major historical interest, Tonsberg and Fredrikstad, are on opposite sides of the fjord, but if you are driving, you can get across by boat from Moss to Horten and then travel south.

FREDRIKSTAD

For centuries there has been a town on this site, but these municipalities repeatedly fell victim to devastating fires, and so never lived up to the potential that the location on the estuary of an important river offered. But in 1663, when Norway had to cede the province of Bohuslan with its major fortress to Sweden, a fort was built at Fredrikstad. The fortress made Fredrikstad a major strategic location, and the area thrived until the fort was assaulted and forced to surrender to Sweden in 1814. The old fortified town (**Gamelbyn**) can be reached by the ferry, which departs from Fredrikstad and will take you across the river to the fortress. Guided tours of the old town are available. **Kongsten Fort** is another, smaller fortification built in the 1680s on Gallows Hill, just east of town. It was originally known for its underground passages and chambers. The fort was decommissioned, along with the main fortress, in 1903. It is now a national monument. Also stop to see **Glemmen Church**—a stone church from about 1100. At **Oltidsveien** (Highway of the Ancients), the section of Highway 10 running between Fredrikstad and Skjeberg, archaeology buffs will find a wealth of archaeological treasures—among them a series of 3000-year-old carvings.

HORTEN AND BORRE

In the center of the Viking relic-rich area of Norway, these are neighboring towns that offer much for the student of Norwegian history and culture. (From Horten, you can take the ferry across the fjord.) **Lovoy Church** was built about 1200 beside an ancient spring that, before the Reformation, attracted hordes of pilgrims for its healing powers. The church, which fell into ruins, was reopened in 1950 after extensive renovation. Because excellent documentation of its history was available, this church has become one of Norway's most well known and important religious landmarks, offering a very complete account of the religious history of Norway from the Viking era to the present. A visit to the church is rewarding in particular because of its unique and ancient treasures. The altarpiece is the original one, created when the church was built. The pulpit was added in 1600. Of special interest is the font, which is lowered from the ceiling in the hands of a christening angel. Also worth a visit are the **Borre Burial Mounds**, the largest collection of such mounds in Scandinavia. The mounds at Borre contain the graves of the Ynglinge clan, the forerunners of the great kings of Norway.

At **Asgardstrand**, an artist's colony and seaside resort, you can visit the summer home of Edvard Munch, the house that the melancholy Munch called "the only pleasant house I have lived in." *The house is open to the public from May to September.*

TONSBERG

Tonsberg is the capital of Vestfold county and the oldest city in Norway. In his saga of King Harald the Fairhaired, Snorre Sturlasson says that Tonsberg existed as a self-governing town before the battle at Hafrsfjord, which occurred about the year 872. Recent excavations are expected to yield more information on the age of Tonsberg; but it is known from earlier discoveries of burial mounds and funeral ships (the *Oseberg*, now to be found in the Viking ships Museum at Oslo, was one) that the royal family of Vestfold, descended from the Ynglinge clan, lived here in luxury and carried on successful commercial ventures with other nations. At one time, Tonsberg was the capital of Norway as well as of Vestfold. The great king of Norway, Hakon IV Hakonsson, who reigned as absolute monarch of Norway from 1217–63, was descended from the Tonsberg kings. King Hakon Hakonsson built the largest medieval fortress in Norway, **Castrum Tunsbergis**, on the hill called Slottsjfellet, and was responsible for the excavation of the canal to make it navigable for large ships and for the construction of a Franciscan monastery in the city. The city was ravaged by plague and fires and in 1536 it was completely burnt. Its fortunes ebbed and flowed with the fluctuations in the trading powers of Europe. But in the mid-19th century, it was once again established as a major maritime commercial center, with its whaling and ship-building trades bringing it international importance. Tonsberg was also the home of Count Jarlsberg. His estate at **Sem Royal Court** was rebuilt in Empire style in 1812 and contains the largest farm in Norway. It is not open to the public.

You will want to see **Sem Church**, the oldest church in Vestfold, a Romanesque-style stone church built around 1100. Two stories involving red-hot iron and claims to the throne center on this church, for it is said that in 1129 Harald Gille walked across fiery hot plowshares to prove that he was the half brother of the king. And in 1204 Chief Erling Steinvegg carried red-hot bars of iron to prove his right to the throne.

Slottsfjellet and the Castrum Tunsbergis ruins, built by King Hakon Hakonsson, was Norway's largest medieval fortress. Its ruins are among the oldest in Europe. There is a fine view from the tower, which is open only in summer and for limited hours.

The **Vestfold County Museum** contains archaeological exhibits as well as shipping and whaling displays. In a separate building, you will find exhibits depicting Vestfold cultural history of the last century and outside there is a farm section with buildings from rural areas of Vestfold. In summer, you can have lunch at the Seter cafe, which serves the regional seter porridge in addition to other fare. *Closed Saturday all year. Open Sunday from noon to 5:00 p.m. For other hours, check with the tourist information office in Oslo.*

At **Haugar** (Mill Hill), in the middle of town, is the burial place of King Harald the Fairhaired and his sons Olav and Sigrod. **Nordbyen** and **Fjerdingen** are the old sections of town, where you will find many restored wooden houses. The **Sjobod** quarter has preserved store houses which have been converted into shops. The **Oseberg Mound** is the spot where the Oseberg Viking funeral ship was excavated. The excavation of the ship yielded evidence that two women of the upper class were buried there around A.D. 850. It is thought that the younger woman was Queen Asa, the grandmother of Harald the Fairhaired.

SANDEFJORD

Fifteen miles south of Tonsberg on the same side of the fjord, you will come to this resort town. It is a pleasant place just to loll about in, enjoying its beaches, boating and fishing. Once a popular spa town, it attracts many Norwegians who have summer cottages in the area. But it was also an important whaling center, and the whaling monument, which greets you at the harbor, is an appropriate symbol of the town. You could just stretch out on the beach or putter around in a boat. There are 37 miles of coastline here and Sandefjord has a pleasant marina and several parks and playgrounds, as well as a swan lake and a golf course, which is located seven miles from town. The **Royal Burial Mound** at Gokstad is the place the *Gokstad* ship, now in the Viking Ships Museum in Oslo, was found.

At **Commander Chr. Christensens Whaling Museum**, the big attraction is the replica of the monumental blue whale, but there are other exhibits as well, all centering on the whaling trade of Sandefjord. **The Sandefjord Town Museum** contains exhibits on the history and culture of Sandefjord and its surroundings. The museum is located at Pukkestad, a preserved farm from the late 18th century. *In Sandefjord, all the museums are open the same hours: 11:00 a.m.–4:00 p.m. weekdays during May–September, Sunday 11:00 a.m.–5:00 p.m.; Oct.– April, Sunday only, noon–4:00 p.m. The whaling museum is also open every Thursday, winter and summer, from 4:00 p.m. until 7:00 p.m.*

WHERE TO STAY

The best bet, if you do want to stay overnight in the area, is the **Park Hotel** at Sandefjord, which was built on the site of the former spa buildings. The hotel has its own guest harbor and pool.

TELEMARK

If the name is familiar, it might be because this is the area that gave its name to the classic method of cross-country skiing. And, as you might expect, this is the place for the sport. The terrain is unexcelled for both cross-country skiing in winter and hiking in summer. Telemark lends itself to a relaxed pace, to outdoor sports like hiking, fishing and skiing, more than to hectic sightseeing, though there are several spots of interest listed. You can get around it most easily by car, but bus service is good and you are limited only by your own time and interests. I've just listed a few highlights for the traveler interested in getting an idea of the area without spending a great deal of time. However, if you want to settle in and enjoy the natural beauty, you could stay for several days, hiking, fishing and camping. Check with the tourist office in Skien: *Skien Reiselivslag/Kongensgt. 31,* ☎ *(03) 52 82 27.* Or write to them at *Postboks 493/ 3701 Skien.*

GETTING THERE

You can reach Bo, the center of Telemark, by train from Oslo and then take a bus through the scenic countryside. Buses and railways have junctions in Bo and at Lunde; trains connect with canal boat service. At Nordagutu, connections can be made for other parts of the country. In addition, the airport at Skien has service to Oslo, Stavanger, Haugesund, Bergen and Trondheim. Also from Notodden airport, travelers can fly to the west coast.

GETTING AROUND

Two of Norway's major highways cross Telemark: the E18 crosses the southern portion of the area and the southwestern coast, while the E76 runs through the middle of Telemark and all the way beyond to Hardanger and Haugesund. The railway comes through as well, stopping at Nordagutu, Bo and Lunde. For an offbeat mode of travel in summertime, try the old steam cruisers, *Victoria* and *Vildanden*, on the Telemark canal. The cruise from Skien to Dalen takes a full day. You can also take a bus, which takes you from Skien through lovely country, and past Lake Norsjo to Bo.

For those who wish to see stave churches, there are two in Telemark. The **Heddal Stave Church** at Notodden is the largest of the stave churches; it dates from the middle of the 13th century. Next to the church is the **Heddal District Museum**, with buildings from the area. At **Eidsborg**, not far from Dalen, you will find yet another **stave church**.

SKIEN

Travelers will get a good feel for the area if they head for Skien, an old town, which like most others, has suffered through the ravages of many fires. Archaeological excavations have shown, however, that Skien is the only city in Norway that has been continuously inhabited since the Viking Era. At **Brekke Park**, there are several interesting exhibits including the **Historical Museum** and **Sondre Brekke**, an old manor house furnished with period pieces from the Renaissance to the Victorian age. You will find also an old **book shop, apothecary**, and **barber shop**, and several other old buildings from the Telemark area that have been rebuilt in this location. There is also an exhibit of Henrik Ibsen memorabilia. **Snipetorp** is an old street with early 18th-century buildings. Visit **Ibsengarden**, at #27, where Henrik Ibsen lived for a time. A little farther from town is **Venstop**. Henrik Ibsen's father moved his family permanently here, to

what had been their summer home, after the family fortunes fell into ruin. This is where Henrik grew up, and knowledgeable readers will recognize shadows of this place in Ibsen's plays. The farm buildings have been restored so that they are the way they might have been when the Ibsen family lived here. The farmhouse is filled with possessions of the Ibsen family. **Ibsenhuset** is a cultural center built at Venstop. At **Kapitelberget**, the church ruins from 1100 are the site of the oldest crypt church in Norway and the most important monument to the powerful Dag family who ruled Skien in the middle ages.

BO

Visit the **Old Church**, a Romanesque stone church dating from the middle of the 12th century. Dedicated to St. Olav, the pulpit of the renaissance interior is of particular distinction. The **Bo District Museum** is actually made up of two museums, the **Aheim General Store Museum**, a store dating from the early 1900's, and the **Polen Museum**, with displays of Bo's history, at Oterholt Bridge. At **Osterli Farm**, visitors can glimpse into the rural life of the past. **Telemark Summerland** is a family entertainment park with attractions like the Plunger, the longest water-slide in Norway. Children can also visit Fairy Tale Land, Tarzan's Jungle and the Old Wild West, as well as a Prehistoric Park where you can meet a dinosaur face to face.

WHERE TO STAY

BO

The Bo Hotel
A modern hotel in a rural setting. It boasts a heated outdoor swimming pool, indoor spa, table tennis, minigolf. All rooms with private bath, TV.

The Lifjell Turisthotell
Set in the woods, the hotel has both indoor and outdoor swimming pools. It is about five miles from the Bo center. It was modernized in 1982, but a few single rooms do not have private bath and toilet.

SKIEN

The Hoyers Hotell
This is an older hotel situated in the center of town. All rooms have private shower and toilet as well as TV. Solarium.

The Rica Ibsen Hotel
A comfortable hotel built in 1979 in the center of town. All rooms with private bath and color TV. Indoor swimming pool and solarium.

FOR SKIERS AND HIKERS

The Rjukan Gaustablikk Hoyfjellshotell
At the foot of Mt. Gausta near Lake Kvita; makes a good base for cross-country skiing. The hotel was built in 1970 and offers a host of activities. It has indoor and outdoor pools, sauna, tennis and badminton courts. And beyond that, it has three ski lifts, plus a children's ski tow, six slalom slopes, and a total of 8000 meters of marked and groomed cross-country ski trails.

The Skinnarbu Hoyfjellshotel
Set on Lake Mosvatn, this lodge was renovated in 1979. In addition to an indoor swimming pool, sauna and fishing, there is a ski lift and about 60 miles of marked ski trails.

EASTERN AND CENTRAL NORWAY

Lillehammer is the principal city of Oppland.

Here is a land of thick forests, rolling hills laced with cross-country and hiking trails, rushing streams and mountains high enough for some of the best downhill skiing in the country. It is an area that lends itself to a slow pace, to hiking and fishing or sailing. In the county of Oppland, the two principal cities are Lillehammer and Gjovik, both located on Lake Mjosa. In the county of Oppland, you will find the vast Rondane National Park. Futunheimen Mountain range opens a window onto more dramatic scenery, giving you a preview of the landscape that characterizes western Norway.

GETTING THERE

The express train from Oslo takes two hours and 20 minutes. A slower train, taking about three hours, stops at Hamar and Eidsvoll. As the site of the 1994 Winter Olympic Games, Lillehammer came into its own with international media attention unveiling the beauty and charm of this still unsophisticated town. Vestiges of the Olympics remain as tourist attractions so we ordinary mortals can play at the sites of the Olympians' victories and defeats. But there is more to eastern Norway than Olympic excitement. As you head north from Oslo, you will find some of Norway's richest farmland and most welcoming terrain.

Gudbrandsdalen—Norway's longest valley, a great sweep of green fields sloping down to dark lakes, holds the huge Lake Mjosa and the Peer Gynt Road in its far-reaching embrace. The area is a fine spot for hiking and fishing (be sure to pick up a license at a sporting goods store or at the post office) and for ski touring. You can drive, a good idea since you need a car for exploring the Peer

Gynt Road, or you can sit back and leave the driving to the Norwegian Railroad, which does this trip in fine style—a clean, comfortable train passing through lovely towns and lush farmlands.

LILLEHAMMER

Lillehammer Tourist Office: *Sturgaten 56,* ☎ *062 51 098.*

The Lillehammer Card: The card will entitle you to discounts on meals, hotels, sights and some shops.

DIRECTORY

Banks • Open weekdays 8:30 a.m.–3:00 p.m.; Thursday 8:30 a.m.–4:30 p.m.

Buses • Departures from bus terminal at railway station. ☎ *062 50 630.* Open weekdays: 8:30 a.m.–4:30 p.m.; Saturday 8:30 a.m.–1:00 p.m.

Car rental • **Avis**—*fina Service A/S, Storgaten 136,* ☎ *062 55 311.* **Hertz**— *Stavseth Bilutleie Industrigt. 24–26,* ☎ *062 53 145.*

Chemists • **Mesna Apotek,** *Kirkegt 55.* ☎ *062 50 160.* Open weekdays 8:30 a.m.–4:30 p.m.; Saturday 8:30 a.m.–1:00 p.m.; Sunday 5:00 p.m.– 7:00 p.m.

Emergency • **Police**: *Storgaten 120,* ☎ *062 58 800.* **Fire**: ☎ *003.*

Doctor • ☎ *062 51 450.*

Post Office • *Kirkegt 70.* ☎ *062 58 111.* Open weekdays: 8 a.m.–4:30 p.m. Thursday 8 a.m.–5:00 p.m.; Saturday 9:00 a.m.–1:00 p.m.

Shopping • Shops are open Monday–Friday from 9:00 a.m. to 4:30 p.m. with Thursday closings at 6:30 p.m.; Saturday 9:00 a.m.–2:00 p.m.

Taxis • ☎ *062 53 100.*

Lillehammer is the principal city of Oppland and a good headquarters for further exploration of the area. It is also on the main road from eastern to western Norway. From here, you can take excursions into the hills to visit the summer farms. A note of literary interest: this is **Sigrid Undset** territory. The Nobel Prize- winning author lived in Lillehammer at one time in her life, and the summer farms she wrote of in her novels are modeled after those in the nearby hills.

And for sports enthusiasts, even though the 1994 Olympic Games are now only a snowy memory, travelers can still enjoy the benefits of Lillehammer's brief moment in the spotlight, for many of the venues are now open to the public, and you can even take a bobsled run in summertime—on wheels.

GETTING THERE

Train service runs regularly from Oslo to Lillehammer. Gardmoen Airport is situated between Oslo and Lillehammer. If you plan to fly into Gardmoen, you can rent a car and drive from there. The drive from Oslo is approximately 120 miles along either the east or west side of Lake Mjosa. The west route is more scenic and has less traffic.

WHAT TO SEE AND DO

Maihaugen: the Sandvig Collections

The slogan of this open-air museum is, "You have to know about the past to understand the present," and in a country that seems to take that philosophy to heart with open-air folk museums in almost every town, this is one of the best. It touts itself as a miniature replica of the Gudbrandsdal Valley, but with 130 historic buildings and 95 acres of ground, it is not really miniature at all. The heart of the exhibit is the collection of antiques, old houses and art that Anders Sandvig brought to Lillehammer early in this century. The collection is constantly extended. You will find farm exhibits, trades and crafts displays, and a museum building containing folk art, silver and glass. Be sure to visit the old workshops. The **Garmo Stave Church**, which Anders Sandvig brought to this location, has been rebuilt but its roots go back to St. Olav's time. A guided tour is included in the admission fee, but you can also wander on your own. *Open May 15–September 15. June–August, it is open from 10:00 a.m. until 5:00 p.m. In May and September, hours are from 10:00 a.m.–4:00 p.m. Two cafes are located on the grounds; the Kirkestuen, open June 15–August 13, 11:00 a.m.–5:30 p.m. serves Norwegian dishes as well as snacks and sandwiches.*

The Lillehammer Municipal Art Gallery

At the turn of the century, Lillehammer was an artists' colony. Einar Lundy, a well-to-do merchant, became a patron of sorts for these artists, exchanging clothing from his shop for paintings. The result was an admirable collection of art, which Mr. Lunde donated to the city of Lillehammer in 1927. In later years, other gifts, most notably Oscar Johannessen's donation of the Dusseldorf Collection, expanded the collection and made this museum one of the largest in eastern Norway outside Oslo. The works here are all by Norwegian painters, many of whom painted in Lillehammer. The Dusseldorf Collection is made up of the works of several Norwegian painters who studied and painted in Dusseldorf, but their works all center on Norwegian themes. The collection is impressive, with works of Edvard Munch, J. C. Dahl, Henrik Sorenson and Eilif Peterssen. There is always a visiting exhibit as well as concerts and lectures. *Open Tuesday–Friday, 11:00 a.m.–4:00 p.m.; Saturday 10:00 a.m.–2:00 p.m.; Sun noon–4:00 p.m.*

Skibladner

The world's oldest paddle steamer still in use. The roundtrip from Eidsvoll to Lillehammer takes 12 hours, but you can get off along the way. The steamer travels to and from Lillehammer Tuesday, Thursday and Saturday, from June 15 until August 15.

Hunderfossen Family Park

An amusement park just a few miles outside Lillehammer features the Fairy Tale Grotto designed by Ivo Caprino, the film and puppetry artist who also created the dioramas at the North Cape Museum. *Open May 27–September 3.*

The Glassblowers' Hut

A small working exhibit of glass blowing at the Mesna center in Lillehammer with demonstrations and sales. If you haven't had a chance to visit a glassworks in Scandinavia, this will give you an idea of how it is done, but it is not a substitute for a visit to the larger works in the Glass District. Demonstration and sales. Don't forget that the **Hadlands Glassworks** is in Oppland. (See "Oslo" for details.)

The Museum of Vehicle History

Mesna Center in Lillehammer. Norway's only museum of vehicle history traces the development of transportation from sledges and wagons to automobiles.

The Digerasen Mountain and Dairy Farm

Here, outside town, you can watch cheese made in the traditional method. There is also an exhibition of arts and crafts.

Skarsmoen Farm

This is also open to visitors for conducted tours. Inquire at the tourist office in Lillehammer for information on both these farms.

Lake Sjusjoen

The lake area about 15 miles north of Lillehammer. Ski buses run between Lillehammer and Sjusjoen. Or you can drive and include a few other stops. Some tourists choose to stay in this area, enjoying the tranquil beauty at one of the simple but pleasant mountain hotels that are suitable for families and quite a bit less expensive than the places in town.

Rustad Hotell and Fellstue

A simple, family mountain hotel in a beautiful setting on Lake Sjusjoen with a bathing beach.

Sjusjoen Hoyfjellshotel

Situated in the forest belt with views of the mountain and the lake. It was last restored in 1983. Good hiking and skiing terrain. Indoor and outdoor pools. Watersports, riding, ski school.   *Moderate to expensive*

WHERE TO STAY

For a town its size, Lillehammer offers a good selection of hotels, with three fine, first-class hotels in addition to a very pleasant guest house.

EXPENSIVE

The Inter Nor Hotel Lillehammer   +★★★★

Located just a bit out of the center of town, this lovely, big hotel has the air of an old-fashioned resort with its park-like grounds and heated outdoor pool. The public rooms are large but cozily furnished and there is a pleasant, clubby bar and a restaurant that belongs to the prestigious Chaine des Rotisseurs gourmet society. Indoor pool in addition to the outdoor pool. Nearby is the Lillehammer ski center with downhill as well as lighted cross-country ski trails. An orchestra plays every night but Sunday for dancing. The hotel can arrange excursions throughout eastern and central Norway.

For the slight difference in price between this and the other first-class hotels, this would be the choice unless you want to be right in town. It's about a 10-minute walk from the hotel to town. Double rooms run about 1000NOK, but weekend rates are available.

MODERATE TO EXPENSIVE

The Oppland Hotel
A smaller, 75-room hotel located right on the lake. The sunny dining room and cozy sitting rooms have beautiful views. The lunch buffet is excellent, and it's especially pleasant to dine overlooking the water. Rooms are not up to the standard of the Lillehammer, but the location on the lake and in town might be more appealing to some. Indoor pool. The better rooms are almost as high as the Lillehammer, but lower-priced rooms are available. Double rooms 920NOK in winter; 645NOK weekends and summer. Dancing every night but Sunday.

The Rica Victoria Hotel
Another hotel that is right in the center of town, but this one is not on the lake. In an old building, its rooms have been recently renovated and are very pleasant. Some larger family rooms are available as well. The drawback might be that its location on the main street of Lillehammer could make it noisy. Lively disco here. Double rooms are 995NOK; weekends 750NOK. The hotel's open-air restaurant, Terrassen, just across the street, is considered one of the nicest outdoor restaurants in Norway.

Hammer Home Hotel
This is a new addition to the Lillehammer hotel scene with just 35 rooms. I have not seen it, but it has been recommended by those who have. While not elaborate, it does have a sauna and solarium, and is fully licensed, though with no restaurant. TV and phones in the rooms.

INEXPENSIVE

The Ersgaard Guesthouse
This simple but lovely inn is situated in the mountains just a mile from town in a most picturesque setting, with easy access to skiing and riding. Not all rooms have private baths. There is a pleasant dining room and terrace.

The Dolaheimen Hotel and Kafeteria
Charmless but adequate, it is next to the railway station. All rooms have private toilet and shower or bath.

WHERE TO EAT

The best bets here are the hotels. **Lillehammer Hotel** has a gourmet restaurant serving a buffet lunch in wintertime. In summer, the buffet is served at dinner, and the noon meal is three courses. This restaurant belongs to the Chaine des Rotisseurs gourmet society. The **Hotel Oppland** has a pleasant dining room overlooking Lake Mjosa, and serves an excellent buffet lunch. At the **Rica Victoria Hotel**, there are several choices. In addition to the main restaurant, guests in summertime can eat at the outdoor **Terrassen Restaurant**. Victoriahjornet is a lively pub in the hotel, and there is also a disco called Victor. In town, try **Scala**

Spiseri or the Chinese restaurant, **Ming Garden**.Lundegarden Brasserie & Bar on Storgaten offers bistro fare with one of the house specialties being filet of venison with lingonberries.

EXCURSIONS AROUND LAKE MJOSA

Several opportunities for day trips are available from Lillehammer. Eidsvoll and Hamar are on the railway line between Oslo and Lillehammer, and there is bus service as well. Eidsvoll is also the starting point for *Skibladner*, the old paddle steamer on Lake Mjosa. Round trip, stopping at Hamar and Lillehammer, takes 12 hours, but you can, of course, take it half way. It's a beautiful trip and a most enjoyable way to get to Lillehammer. And besides all the gorgeous scenery, the real come-on is the salmon and strawberries that are served on board. *Operating summers only on Tuesday, Thursday, Saturday. Call Skibladner office, ☎ 062 58 560 for schedule and booking information.*

EIDSVOLL

At the southern end of Lake Mjosa, this town is of historical interest as it is the birthplace of Norwegian independence. It was here, in May 1814, that Norway's constitutional assembly convened to draft Norway's first constitution at Eidsvoll Hall, the mansion of Carsten Anker, a wealthy landowner and industrialist. Norway had been ceded by Denmark to Sweden in 1814, but in 1813, anticipating this possibility, the Danish king had sent his cousin, Prince Christian Frederik, as regent to Norway. When the Treaty of Kiel officially ceded Norway to Sweden, elections for the constitutional assembly were held, and, at those elections, Norwegians declared they would "defend Norway's independence and sacrifice life blood for their beloved native country." The assembly convened and drafted the constitution, and, on May 17, 1814, the constitution was adopted and Christian Frederik was elected king of Norway, establishing Norway as a free and independent realm.

HAMAR

It was to this town and the eastern shore of Lake Mjosa that King Haakon VII and his government withdrew just ahead of the German occupying forces on April 9, 1940. And it was at Hamar, later on the same day, that the king and his government declared a state of war. Hamar is a pleasant lakeside town with the ruins of an ancient stone cathedral. It is a stop on the *Skibladner* paddle steamer route. Hamar is part of the so-called Mjosa City, a grouping of 11 cities, the largest being Hamar, Gjovik, and Lillehammer. They are linked by bridges and act as a network center for commerce and communications. It is this municipal network that worked together to organize the 1994 Winter Olympic Games.

GJOVIK

Gjovik is an attractive commercial and resort city nicknamed "the white town" of Lake Mjosa, because of the preponderance of white frame buildings. You can take a round trip drive from Lillehammer—Gjovik-Minnesund-Hamar, 140 miles—or choose to stay in Gjovik.

Rica Hotel Gjovik

A resort hotel in the center of town, with a heated outdoor pool and an indoor pool. It is also close to skiing, water-skiing and boating. Glasshylta restaurant, disco, pizzeria.   *Moderate*

The Gjovik Hotel

Also in the center of town. It has an outdoor pool and tennis courts. Grill restaurant and Torvetten restaurant.   *Moderate.*

INTO THE MOUNTAINS

The wilderness area of eastern Norway is popular for camping, farm holidays and holiday huts. For information on renting cabins in the Valdres and Gudbrandsdal valleys, contact the following: **Nordisk Hytteferie**, *Storgaten 8, N-2600 Lillehammer,* ☎ *062 54 900.* **Den Norske Hytteformidling**, *A/S Kierschowsgt 7/N-0462 Oslo 4,* ☎ *02 35 67 10.* **Valdres Turistkontor Hytteutleie**, *N-2900 Fagernes.* ☎ *063 60 400.* In addition, **DNT, Den Nordiske Turistforenning**, which has its office at *Storgatan 28 in Oslo*, will map out hiking tours with a network of wilderness huts and chalets where you can stay.

THE PEER GYNT ROAD

The Peer Gynt Road runs through the land of the real and legendary character, Peer Gynt. Actually, a farmer of similar name did live in Gudrandsdalen and had a reputation as a boaster and spinner of yarns. It was this character who was apparently the inspiration for Henrik Ibsen's play and, of course, for Edvard Grieg's music composed for the play. The road runs between Lillehammer and Vinstra, crossing the mountains on the west side of Gudbrandsda from Skei, over Rauhogda, along the Gola and Fefor lakes to Dalseter. You can make a day trip or choose to settle in at one of the hotels or mountain lodges along the way. The central section of the road, the most mountainous, is closed in winter, but travelers can get to most of the hotels by cutting in and out from the E6.

Near Gausdal, visit **Aulestad**, the home of Bjornstjerne Bjornson, Norway's Nobel Prize winning poet. *Open from May 18 to September 17. May and September 11:00 a.m.–2:30 p.m.; June and August 10:00 a.m.–3:30 p.m.; July 10:00 a.m.–5:30 p.m.* Also in the Gausdal area, you can go to Hell and back if you're so inclined. The giant potholes known as *Helvete* (Hell) are found at the gateway to the Espedal Valley. For three kronor you can make a trial expedition to Hell and come back with a certificate to prove you've been there and lived to tell about it. And if you want to have it all, you can go to Paradise as well, for that is the name given to a beautiful hiking path along the Skei River in Eastern Gausdal. Peer Gynt's grave is located near Vinstra, where he lived.

WHERE TO STAY

ALONG THE PEER GYNT ROAD

Hotels designated as Peer Gynt Hotels are first class, but there are also smaller inns and lodges. All these hotels are moderate to inexpensive.

The Peer Gynt Hotel Gausdal

Near Skei, this is a modern hotel and conference center.

Skeikampen

At Skei, this is a tastefully designed hotel with cozy touches that belie its identity as a conference center. Indoor pool.

The Skei Apartments

These have cooking facilities, and guests can use the facilities of the above hotels. Downhill skiing with seven ski lifts.

The Peer Gynt Gola Hoyfjellshotell

At Gola, this is a complex of cottages and a hotel. Plenty of activities are available including watersports, tennis and both downhill and cross-country skiing.

The Peer Gynt Hotel Fefor

At Vinstra, on Fefor Lake, it has cottages as well as hotel rooms. It offers a cozy ambience with traditional Norwegian interiors.

The Peer Gynt Hotel Espedalen

At Espedalen, this small, homey mountain hotel is located near the potholes known as Helvete. Illuminated ski track. Cross-country ski instruction. Apartments are also available within the hotel and larger holiday cabins on the premises.

RINGEBU AND THE RONDANE NATIONAL PARK

Otta Tourist Office • *P.O. Box 94, N-2671 Otta,* ☎ *47 62 30 244.*

Ringebu Tourist Office • *Open all year round on weekdays 9:00 a.m.–4:00 p.m. From mid-June to mid-August it is open Monday–Saturday, 9:00 a.m.–7:00 p.m. and on Sunday 10:00 a.m.–6:00 p.m.,* ☎ *062 80 533.*

Rafting on the River Sjoa • *Call Norwegian Wildlife and Rafting.* ☎ *066 29 794 to arrange a tour—day trips and overnights available.*

Guided walking tours • *Monday, Tuesday, Thursday, Friday from mid-June to mid-August. Leave at 9:30 a.m. from Venabu Fjelhotell. Apply a day in advance at the hotel or the Ringebu Tourist Office.*

The center of the northern region is **Otta**. Travelers can drive to Otta on the E6 or go by railway. The **Rondane Hotel** will arrange to pick up guests at the train station. In the Rondane area visitors will find many mountain hotels and excellent cross-country skiing.

The **Rondane National Park** is a vast expanse of protected land with loads of outdoor activities: horseback riding, fishing and canoeing. Tours are organized around themes like wild reindeer or Ice Age geology. **Ringebu center**, called Valebru by the locals, is the smallest "town" in Norway. It was built in 1890 in accordance with a carefully drawn-up plan and is distinguished by its art nouveau architecture. At the old **baking house**, you can see the Norwegian crispbread baked in the traditional method. The **Ringebu Stave Church** is a 13th-century church at Ringebu. **Myfallene**, with its three waterfalls, is a two-mile walk along a marked path from Venabu on the Ronde Road #220.

WHERE TO STAY IN THE AREA

Hovringen Hoyfjellshotell

A traditionally designed, family hotel about half an hour north of Otta at the national park. Hovringen itself was once a summer farm community. Now it is a tourist center in the midst of splendid countryside with excellent, well-marked hiking and ski trails. *Inexpensive.*

Rapham Hoyfjellshotell

Situated in the mountains, with a beautiful view of Rondane and Gudbrandsdalen, is another good base for cross-country skiing and hiking, fishing and boating. Indoor pool. *Moderate.*

Rondane Hoyfjellshotel

At Mysuseter, located in a cluster of summer farms near Otta in the midst of mountains and lakes. Indoor pool. Fishing, boating and cycling nearby. The area of Rondane lends itself particularly to huts, farm holidays and camping.

Hammerseter Camping

N2656 Leirflata, ☎ *47-62 34 950.* Offers nice campgrounds with some cabins, and has space for 100 caravans with electricity. Close to the River Sjoa. The Heidal area has more protected farm buildings than any other district in Norway, so, as you might expect, it's a good center for farm holidays. Many of the farmhouses are available for rental, and while they retain their traditional style, they offer modern comforts. Contact Otta Tourist Office.

VALDRES

Valdres is the valley on the eastern rim of Oppland. The Valdres publicists extoll the glory of the landscape, the variety of the terrain—suitable for old and young alike, for the rugged climber and the Sunday stroller—the purity of the water, and the freshness of the air. These same "PR" folks urge the tourist to exert himself, to "Use your body—give yourself time for the sights and smells"...and to "get things into perspective." It's good advice for all of Norway, for this is landscape that does put things in perspective, makes one see oneself as a mere sojourner, an ephemeral guest at nature's infinite and eternal party.

GETTING THERE

The road to Valdres, E68, was the old post road between Oslo and Bergen, and as you drive along it, you will sense the difference between the landscapes of eastern and western Norway. Here you should do exactly what those taskmasters at the tourist board tell you—exert yourself! Hike, sail, fish and breathe deeply. Enjoy the landscape. You can base yourself in several places. My suggestion would be Fagernes or Beitostolen. If you can take time out from your physical exertion to exercise your mind a bit, try the **Valdres Folklore Museum**, which has 61 buildings to trace the rural life of the area from centuries ago to the present. Especially outstanding is the costume exhibit, the largest in Norway. **Beitostolen** is the place for true mountaineers, for the mountains here are about as high as you'll find in Scandinavia. **Bitihorn** is a popular challenge to hikers and climbers, or the imaginative adventurer can try to follow Peer Gynt's path along the precipitous ridge of **Besseggen**. The steamer *Bitihorn* sails twice daily from Bydin to Eidsbugarden at the foot of the Jotunheimen mountains. In **Beitostolen**, you can hike, horseback ride or even cycle if your lungs and legs are up to it.

WHERE TO STAY IN VALDRES

The Inter Nor Fagernes Hotel

Located near Strandefjorden, offers watersports including windsurfing, boating, tennis and an indoor pool. Close to Valdres Alpine Center, it also has miles of cross- country ski tracks and a disco. *Expensive to moderate.*

Beitostolen Hoyfjellshotel

A lively, modern center for skiing, hiking, riding and all the attractions of Valdres. The hotel is newly renovated. In addition to hotel rooms, there are seven deluxe cabins, each sleeping 10.

Beito Hoyfjellshotel

The names of these two hotels are so close that it's easy to confuse them. They are also located very near one another. This one, with its taller building, its larger capacity and indoor pool, is a bit slicker than the Beitostolen.

Bitigrenda Luksushytter

Excellent holiday cabins. ☎ *063 41 033*. These cabins, furnished in traditional Norwegian style, have all the amenities, including fireplaces, television and stereo, and even a dishwasher. Easy access to all the outdoor activities of the area.

TRONDHEIM

Tourist Office: *In the Hornemann Building on the market square (Torvet).* ☎ *73 92 94 05. Open from June 1 until late August, 8:30 a.m.–8:00 p.m. on weekdays; Saturday 8:30 a.m.–6:00 p.m.; Sunday 10:00 a.m.–6:00 p.m. The rest of the year the office is open Mon–Friday, 9:00 a.m.–4:00 p.m.; Saturday 9:00 a.m.–1:00 p.m.; closed Sunday.*

DIRECTORY

Car Rental • **Avis**, *Munkegt. 10,* ☎ *52 69 15. Also at Vaernes Airport,* ☎ *82 53 03.* **Budget**, *Royal Garden Hotel and Vaernes Airport,* ☎ *94 10 25.*

Emergency • General Emergency medical ☎ 73 99 88 00 **Fire**: ☎ *001.*

Police • ☎ *002.*

Ambulance • ☎ *003.*

Chemist Emergency Service • *St. Olav Vaktapotek,* ☎ *52 31 22.*

Norwegian Automobile Association • *Information concerning road conditions, routes, etc.,* ☎ *96 62 88.*

Taxis • ☎ *52 76 00.*

Trondheim, the third largest of Norway's cities, is yet another wellspring of Norwegian history and an important political site. It is here in the Nidaros Cathedral that the kings of Norway are crowned. This northern city, with its wide boulevards running into the spacious central square, its river fronted by old wharf houses and its meandering backstreets, has the air of a sophisticated river town. The people of Trondelag were the first Norwegians to accept Olav Tryggvason (Olav I) as their king. This great grandson of Harald Fairhair was the son of a local king of southeastern Norway. When he had gained acceptance in the Trondheim area, he established a town at the mouth of the river Nid and built himself a palace there. Thus, Trondheim, the city King Olav I built, became the capital of Norway.

After King Olav's death, Norway was split once again by political and religious factions, and fell to foreign rulers. Then, in 1015, another descendant of Harald Fairhair, another Olav, in fact, appeared like a savior to restore Norway to its former power. This Olav II, Olav Haraldson, is best known, however, by another name, which indicates his central role in Norway's history. For after his death in battle against Norwegian adversaries in the district of Trondheim, he became Olav the Saint. It is as Norway's patron saint that he is remembered today. His canonization was brought about by the miracles that seemed to surround his burial place: After the fateful battle, Olav's body was carried secretly to Trondheim and buried along the river. It appeared that hope for a strong, independent and reunited Norway had died with him, but not long after his death, reports of holy water gushing from his burial place began to crop up. His body was exhumed and placed above the altar in St. Clement's church, and he was canonized as a martyr in the cause of liberty. In death rather than in life, King/Saint Olav became a symbol of national spirit and unity, drawing the people of Norway together. Saint Olav was worshipped not just by Norwegians, but all over Europe where churches in his name were built. Trondheim became a center for pilgrims visiting his shrine, and in 1300, a new cathedral worthy of the saint, was dedicated as his shrine. The church, the **Nidaros Cathedral**, is Norway's largest medieval structure, and it is the place where since the middle ages the kings of Norway have been crowned.

GETTING THERE

Vaernes airport is 35 kilometers north of town and offers good connections all over Norway. A direct flight to Copenhagen leaves every day but Sunday. Buses to and from the airport connect with scheduled SAS and Brathanes S.A.F.E. flights. The buses stop at the Trondheim bus terminal and the SAS Royal Hotel.

The Coastal Steamer stops twice a day at Trondheim. There are day and night trains to Oslo and Bodo, and a day train to Sweden.

WHAT TO SEE AND DO

From June 1 to about August 20, a two-hour sightseeing tour, **Trondheim and its Outskirts**, leaves daily at noon from the Market Square by the tourist information office for a trip through Trondheim and its outskirts. You can also ride an old 1920's tram around the center of Trondheim while a guide gives you a brief history of the city and the tram. From June 15 until September 10, every day but Monday, a **boat tour** of Trondheim from the sea leaves from Ravnkloa at 1:00 p.m. The two-hour trip follows the city along the water and includes a 1/2-hour stop at Munkholmen Island.

A **day trip on Trondheim fjord** leaves from Fosen Quay by the railway station. A catamaran takes passengers past the villages along the Trondheim fjord. On Monday and Thursday, passengers on the early boat may disembark at Brekstad on the return trip and pick up the later return. *May 1–August 31 Monday–Friday, 9:00 a.m., returning at 3:15 p.m.; and 1:45 p.m., returning at 7:00 p.m*

Nidaros Cathedral

Built as a shrine to Saint Olav, this is Norway's coronation cathedral and its largest medieval building. What you will notice first is the elaborate stone carving on the facade. It would take hours to study it all thoroughly. Once inside, you will be most struck by the beautiful rose window. The church employs 35 artisans working in the traditional medieval methods of blacksmiths, joiners, glassmakers and stone carvers in the continuing maintenance and restoration of the cathedral.

The oldest part of the cathedral, the southern transept, was begun in 1130. The northern Romanesque transept was built around 1150. For several centuries, the cathedral fell into disrepair, and most of the restoration was completed in the early 1900s. The icon on the wall of the southern transept is a 16th-century Russian one, a gift on the occasion of Saint Olav's jubilee in 1930. The altarpiece, which stands at the place where Saint Olav was first buried after the battle of Stiklestad, was completed in 1872. It is a replica of the original, which was removed during the Reformation. The baptismal font next to it and the statues on the choir walls are the work of Gustav Vigeland. The well is at the place where the pilgrims drew the holy water on their pilgrimages here during the Middle Ages. Notice also the altar font, depicting the death and canonization of Olav Haraldson. It is possible to go up into the tower in the summer months. Also on display, from June 1 until sometime around the 20th of August, are the Norwegian crown jewels. Be sure to allow some time to stroll through the park surrounding the cathedral. As is the case with most churches in Norway, the cathedral is open only at scheduled hours. These vary quite a bit with the different times of year. *From mid-June through August the church is open on weekdays from 9:30 a.m. until 5:30 p.m.; Saturday from 9:30 a.m. until 2:00 p.m.; Sunday from 1:30 p.m. until 4:00 p.m. Check with the tourist information office or at the church for hours during other times of the year. A guide is always on duty. The cathedral is a parish church, so services are held regularly. During most of the summer, organ concerts are given at 1:00 p.m. every weekday with a brief service. At other times of the year, a regular Saturday concert is held at 1:00 p.m.*

The Archbishop's Palace

This is the oldest secular building in Scandinavia, dating from the 12th century. It was built as the residence of the Archbishop, and remained as such until the Reformation. For about 100 years after the Reformation, it served as the residence for the Danish governors. Now it is used for government receptions. *Unless it is in use for an official reception, the palace is open from June 15 to August 15, 9:00 a.m.–3:00 p.m. weekdays; 9:00 a.m.–2:00 p.m. Saturday, and noon–3:00 p.m. Sunday. Guided tours are always available.*

Stiftsgarden

The large, mustard-colored frame building on Munkegate, near the market square, is the residence of King Olav when he is in Trondheim. *From June 1 through August, guided tours are given every half hour between 11:00 a.m. and 2:00 p.m. on weekdays.*

Gamle Bybro

The old bridge is on the site of the first one, built in 1681. The present bridge and gates were built in 1861.

The Trondelag Folk Museum at Sverresborg

The museum is built around the ruins of the 12th-century palace of King Sverre. Various types of buildings have been brought here from the Trondelag district. A ski museum is located in the old chemist's shop. The old inn, called **The Tavern**, which dates from 1739, is now a restaurant. There is also a cafe in the bishop's house. *Open from around May 20 until August 31 from 11:00 a.m.–6:00 p.m. every day. Guided tours in English at 11:15 a.m., 1:00 p.m., 3:00 p.m. and 4:30 p.m.*

The Ringve Music Museum

This is the only music history museum in Norway. The remarkable collection includes musical instruments from the world over. The instruments are displayed in period rooms in the 18th-century **Ringve Mansion** at Lade, and they are played on request by the guides. Be sure to visit the gardens as well. The outbuildings of the mansion now serve as concert halls. There is an outdoor cafe in the courtyard. *Visitors may go through the museum only on a guided tour. Guided tours in English are given from around May 20 to June 30 at noon and 2:00 p.m., July 1–August 15 at noon, 2:00 p.m., and 4.00 p.m., August 16–September 30 at noon and 2:00 p.m. The remainder of the year Sunday only at 1:30 p.m.*

The Trondheim Sjofarts Museum

Situated in a 1725 building next to the Royal Garden Hotel, the museum is devoted to exhibits on fishing, whaling, and shipping. *Open daily all year 9:00 a.m.–3:00 p.m.; Sunday noon–3:00 p.m. Closed Saturday in winter.*

The Trondheim Art Museum

Down the street from the cathedral, the museum houses painting and sculpture of Scandinavian origin. Several works by Danish sculptor Bertel Thorvaldsen. The museum is pleasant and manageable, and the collection is very well displayed with good light and plenty of space. *Open weekdays 10:00 a.m.–3:00 p.m.; Thursday, 10:00 a.m.–7:00 p.m.; Sunday noon–4:00 p.m.*

The Handicraft Museum (*Kunstindustrimuseum*)

On Munkegate, near the cathedral. Here are displayed both old and new crafts. The focal point of the exhibit is an extensive display of tapestries woven by Hannah Ryggen.

Our Lady Church (*Var Frue Kirke*)

The original church on this site was constructed in the 13th century. It was extensively restored in 1739, but parts of the walls are original. *Open June–August weekdays from 10:00 a.m.–2:00 p.m. and Saturday from 11:00 a.m.–2:00 p.m. It is closed to sightseers during services.*

The Island of Munkholmen

Benedictine monks built a monastery on this island in 1125, hence its name, Monk's Island. But in addition to its religious role, the island has worn many faces—as an execution ground, a prison fort and then as a customs house. Today it is a recreational island with beaches and a restaurant. *Boats leave from Trondheim in good weather from the end of May until the beginning of September, every hour on the hour 10:00 a.m.–5:00 p.m.*

The Trondheim Library

Though you most likely will not be taking out a Trondheim library card, this building is worth a visit. During excavations for the construction of the library, an old church and several graves were unearthed. The building plans were somewhat altered in view of these findings, and now the design is such that the graves and the old church foundations are visible. The incorporation of the ruins into the contemporary marble, pine and birch interior is stunning. A small museum with the 13th-century relics from the Olav's church is built over the old foundations. The museum also has an exhibit of the history of the church and the town hall. There is a cafe here as well.

A Walk to the River

Be sure to walk the town, especially along the river where you will find the old 18th-century wharf houses, and toward the canal where the buildings are even older. You can walk from Torvet down Kongensgate to the river where you will cross the old bridge. If you turn right off the bridge and walk along Bakklandet, you will be able to slip between the houses and glimpse the cathedral spire rising above the river. Spend a little time here. It's an old part of town that is gradually being restored, and the shops and houses are interesting and attractive. Back across the bridge, turn right and walk along Klopmannsgate until you come to the Sjofarts Museum and the Royal Garden Hotel. If you turn left at Fjordgate, past the Sjofarts Museum, you will come, after a few minutes' walk, to **Ravnkloa** at the bottom of Munkegata, where the fish market is located. The boats for Munkholmen leave from here. What is possibly the northernmost synagogue, the Trondheim synagogue, just three degrees below the Arctic circle, occupies the former municipal railroad station. Dedicated in 1925, 50 years after the first Jewish settlers had come to Trondheim from Lithuania and Latvia, the synagogue was in constant use except for five years during which it served as a German army barracks. For visitors planning to attend services, remember that sundown varies extremely in such a latitude. Candles can be lit as early as 2:00 p.m. in winter and as late as 11:00 p.m. in summer. There is also a war Victims Memorial in the Jewish cemetery in honor of the 60 Jews of Trondheim killed by the Nazis.

SHOPPING

The shopping and restaurant complex, built in conjunction with the new concert hall, Olavshallen, is an attractive modern structure with several elegant shops. The other shopping areas are in Olav Tryggvasonsgate, Nordregate and Dronningensgate.

HANDKNIT WEAR AND NORWEGIAN CRAFTS

Husfliden in *Olav Tryggvasonsgt 18*. As in all Husfliden shops, Norwegian handicrafts are on sale here. **Trondheim Brukskunstforening**, *in the Olavshallen complex*, has beautiful hand-knit and highly styled women's clothing, as well as household and decorative items like pillows and ceramics. **Sjoberg**, *at Nordre Gate 16*, sells Norwegian knitwear and a particularly good selection of hats. **Arne Ronning**, at *Nordre Gate 10*, carries the popular Dale Knitwear.

SILVER

Henrik Moller Silvershop and Silversmith at Munkegata 3. has been in business since 1720. A Trondheim landmark.

CRYSTAL AND CHINA

Andreas Moe at Olav Tryggvasons gate 29–31.

WHERE TO STAY

Reso Royal Garden   +★★★★
Kjopmannsgate 73 • The first choice of most visitors who can afford the more expensive hotels here. The Royal Garden is modern, lively and, true to its name, filled with sunlight and greenery. Its two main restaurants are considered among Trondheim's best. **The Prince Olav Grill** is sedate and sleekly nautical. **Cicignon** is less expensive and livelier with dance music most nights. A nightclub is located on the lower level and piano music enlivens the glass and vine-entwined lobby throughout the day. Indoor pool. Expensive, but worth it. Check on summer rates.

The Grand Hotel Olav   ★★★★
Kjopmannsgaten 48 • This newest addition to the Trondheim hotel scene might give the Royal Garden a run for its money. Slick and perhaps a bit glitzy, the rooms are sumptuously comfortable. It is located in the

Olavshallen complex, which will be a draw for some and a turn-off for others, as it's a busy place. All the rooms are well-decorated and big. Room 223, which at last count went for a healthy 1480NOK per night, is particularly beautiful. ***Expensive.***

The Britannia ★★★

Dronningensgate 5 • A gracious dowager with old-world charm, the Britannia draws the upper class of Trondheim for lunch in the winter-garden courtyard, Palmehave, where the fountain splashes and the violins sing. The rooms are modernized with TV and video in every room. Expensive, but summer rates available.

The Hotel Residence

Torvet. Its central location on Torvet makes it a busy place, and in summer its terrace and glass-front cafe attract a noisy crowd. Inside, the dining room is lovely and serves an excellent buffet lunch. The rooms have recently been renovated, but the old art nouveau facade and public rooms have been maintained. The hotel is associated with SAS and offers the services common to SAS hotels, such as flight check-in and ticket office in lobby. All rooms have TV/video, minibar and safe. Expensive in winter, but very reasonable in summer.

The Prinsen

30 Kongensgate • The Prinsen has been around a long time and commands a certain unexplained prestige among tour operators and guidebook writers. However, I would steer you away from this spot. Your money—and it will be considerable—will be better spent elsewhere. Even the hotel's very friendly and accommodating staff cannot compensate for the drawbacks. The Prinsen charges first-class rates and offers only the most ordinary of accommodations. The rooms are in need of freshening and the noise and ventilation problems are significant. ***Expensive.***

Larssens Hotell ★★

Thomas Angell's Gate 10 • Here is a most pleasant small hotel with reasonable rates and a family atmosphere. The rooms are modest with few amenities, but all have private baths. The dining room serves very good, home-style Norwegian food, but you do have to arrange in advance if you want to have dinner. The hotel is licensed for beer and wine.

The Augustin Hotel ★★

Kongensgate 26 • A small hotel built in 1920 but frequently and recently renovated, the Augustin is across the street from the Prinsen so it could also be noisy, but the rooms are fresh and pleasantly decorated in light colors. The bathrooms are completely modernized. This hotel has endured something of a blight since it was used as Nazi headquarters during the occupation. This will not bother everyone, but those who might be troubled by it should know. That dark past is long gone, though not forgotten, but the brightness of this hotel does its best to overcome those shadows. All the rooms have cable TV, minibar and hair dryers. Nonsmoking rooms available. The hotel serves breakfast only, and there is no alcohol. An affiliation with the Residence Hotel makes it easy to dine there.   *Moderate.*

The Trondheim Hotel   ★

15 Kongensgate • The rooms here are quite varied and some tend to be rather small but they are all renovated and pleasant.   *Moderate.*

For rooms in private homes, contact the Tourist Information Office. No advance booking is possible for these accommodations.

WHERE TO EAT

The Prince Olav Grill

In the Royal Garden • This is one of the top choices in town. A sleek, masculine decor, nautical in motif.   *Expensive.*

Palmehaven

The palm court of the Britannia Hotel has a *fin de siècle* flavor with columns and arches around a central fountain. Popular with well-heeled locals, the atmosphere is lively and the food good.

Restaurant Cicignon

In the Royal Garden • Less expensive than the Prince Olav Grill, the attractive dining room serves excellent food and also has dance music every night.

The Residence Restaurant

In the Residence Hotel • A warm, paneled room, where an excellent lunch buffet is served daily. This is also a pleasant choice for dinner.

Havfruen

Kjopmannsgata 7, ☎ *56 26 26* • The premier fish restaurant in town. Located in one of the old warehouses along the river, it is an inviting spot. You will find the menu interesting and the food excellent. The budget conscious might want to try it for lunch rather than dinner. Reservations are a must.   *Moderate to expensive.*

Theatergrillen

In the Hotel Prinsen • This landmark restaurant has long enjoyed some renown in Trondheim. It is an informal place, divided into several small, cozy rooms. The food is traditional Norwegian.

Hos Magnus

Kjopmannsgata 63. On the second floor of an old warehouse on Kjopmannsgt., the street running along the river. • The style of this restaurant is contemporary Norwegian country with tables of pale birch and pretty pastel fabrics. The menu is interesting, with the accent on Norwegian specialties.   *Moderate.*

Dickens

Kjopmannsgata 57. • Situated in a very old building, this informal, popular spot is darkly rustic, more like a pub. Salads, pizza, beer.   *Inexpensive.*

Bryggen

Ovre Bakklandet 66. Just across the old bridge • The owners of this casual restaurant, Mr. and Mrs. Skogseth, will welcome you themselves on most evenings. Mr. Skogseth has gained some renown in Norway and other spots for the excellence of his cuisine. The restaurant is large and airy, with an open kitchen. Dinners will run you about $40 per person if you want more than the bare minimum. *It is not open for lunch and it does close for two weeks in the middle of July.*   **Moderate to expensive.**

Egon

Ths. Angell's gts. 8 • A popular, inexpensive and informal gathering spot in the heart of the city; serves pizza, beef, and salads.

Jonathan's

Next to the Britannia • This is a kind of coffee shop for the hotel, but it's pleasant and inexpensive.

Also try **Olavshallen**, the complex containing the new concert hall. You'll find several choices for light, inexpensive dining.

NIGHTLIFE

Studio Hjorten, *in the Royal Garden Hotel*, is the drawing card for late nighters. Disco and live music. *Open every night but Monday from 9:00 p.m. until 2:30 a.m. Cover charge about $8*. The **Kjellerkro No. 50** is a cellar pub across from the Royal Garden. It serves beer (23 different kinds) and wine from 5:00 p.m. to noon Monday–Friday, and Sunday. Saturday it remains open until 1:00 a.m.

The Bistro, *on the lower level of Olavshallen*, serves light food from 3:00 p.m. until 2:00 a.m.

ROROS

Roros Tourist Information: *On Bergmansplassen*, ☎ *074 111 65.*

A smelting hall and slag heap might not be your idea of tourist attractions, but Roros has won a place on UNESCO's World Heritage List by dint of the excellent preservation of this old wooden mining town that began mining copper in 1646. Roros has mountains as well as mines, however, and makes a good base for enjoying and exploring the region. It is worthwhile to walk along **Bergmanns-gata** to see the old miners' houses. **Olav's Mine**, which was in operation until 1972, is open to the public, and **Bergmannshallen**, in the depths of the mine, is now the site of local performances every summer evening. **Roros Church** was once the only stone building in Roros. **Smelthytta** is the old smelter, which has now been transformed into a museum. The **Eidet Smeltehytte** is one of the best-preserved ruins in northern Europe. **Odden Tunet** is an old house devoted to exhibits on regional agriculture.

At **Ratvolden**, visitors can see two farms: Trondalen, the birthplace of journalist Johan Falkberget, and Ratvolden, where he lived as an adult. A writer's museum is located here. The **Fjell-Ljom Newspaper Museum** boasts the oldest newspaper printing press in Scandinavia. This is where journalist Johan Falkberget started his career. If you plan to stay in the area, there are only a few choices:

Bergstadens Hotel

Located right in the center of the old mining town. All 78 rooms have private bath, TV/video and minibar. Indoor pool, live music six nights a week. Restaurant and bar.   *Moderate.*

Inter Nor Hotel Roros

Above the town, it allows for fine views. This is a large hotel with 148 rooms, all with private bath. Ten of the rooms are in a motel-type building. All have TV/video. Indoor pool, fitness center. Disco/ nightclub.

Expensive

STAVANGER AND THE SOUTHWEST COAST

Swords in the Stone, Stavanger, pay tribute to Vikings.

Rogaland, the region of western Norway south of Bergen, was one of the first inhabited areas of Norway, with evidence pointing to life here almost 12,000 years ago. It was the place from which the Vikings set their sails towards the rest of Europe, and it was at a point not far from Stavanger that the decisive battle resulting in Harald Fairhair's unification of Norway occurred. The climate of Rogaland, in spite of the North Sea coast, is quite mild, thanks to the warming influence of the Gulf Stream; the sandy beaches are among the best in Norway, and the area has much to offer the nature lover, the fisherman and the hiker. Traditionally, farming and fishing have been the major industries, but the off-shore oil enterprises have brought even greater prosperity to the area.

The history buff will find plenty to pique his interest. Archeological digs in 1984 at Gjesdal yielded material from the New Stone Age and Early Bronze Age. Throughout 1985 and 1986, excavations established evidence of an even older Stone Age settlement, in fact, the oldest known inland settlement in Norway, dating back almost 9000 years.

STAVANGER

Tourist Information Office: *At the harbor across from the fish market. Open June–August, weekdays from 9:00 a.m.–6:00 p.m.; Saturday until 4:00* *p.m.; Sunday 10:00 a.m.–4:00 p.m. The rest of the year it is open weekdays 9:00 a.m.–4:00 p.m.; and Saturday until 1:00 p.m.*

From the Iron Age to the oil age, there have been life and commerce in Stavanger. The foundations of an Iron Age farm found just outside the city center give testimony to the existence of ancient agriculture communities, and Stavanger's commercial importance goes back to the days when the Vikings used this harbor as the departure point for their forays to other lands. Historically, Stavanger could be considered the birthplace of the first united Norway, for it was here, at a point just three kilometers from the present center of the city, that Harald the Fairhair united Norway in the year A.D. 872. However, soon after Stavanger was declared a town in A.D. 1125, the fortunes of the city began to decline for a while—seven centuries, in fact. By 1880, the city counted a population of just 2000, though it had a solid fishing industry. But by 1900, what one might call the Sardine Age dawned, and those curious and tasty creatures brought new life to the city. Stavanger claimed its place as the sardine canning capital of the world. In 1960, the city entered yet a new phase, the flourishing of the oil industry, and Stavanger's strategic position on the North Sea brought it new prosperity. Economic success and international stature have now made this harbor town on the North Sea a small-scale cosmopolitan city.

One would expect Stavanger, the off-shore oil drilling center of Norway, to be a dreary industrial complex, and, in fact, the giant oil rigs that stand in the North Sea on the approach to the city are rather grim sentinels. However, Stavanger is anything but a steel-and-concrete jungle. It is a charming city of immaculately preserved old white frame houses and buildings, green-clad hills and sandy beaches.

The fourth largest city in Norway, it claims to be the most international, for the oil industry has brought business interests from all over the world. Eight percent of the population is foreign. Stavanger has met the new demands imposed on it with grace and has managed to retain its charm and beauty even with those great hulking oil rigs standing guard. Here is an industrial city with the pleasures and amenities of a resort town.

GETTING THERE

You can get to Stavanger by air, boat, train or car. The E18 road from Sweden ends here. Stavanger is seven hours by train from Oslo. Flights arrive daily from the major European cities, usually routed through Copenhagen, London or Amsterdam. The airport is 15 kilometers from the center of the city. Ferries sail several times a week from Stavanger to England and Denmark. There's frequent service by express boats to Norwegian destinations. The express boat from Bergen takes about four hours and is a comfortable way to get to Stavanger. The boat has a small snack bar and airplane-style seats, and will give you a nice view of the coast between Bergen and Stavanger.

GETTING AROUND

A **Stavanger Card** is yours free for the asking at your hotel. It entitles you to reductions on museums, NSB buses, city buses, Clipper Fjord Sightseeing, Interrent car rental, some concerts and theater.

SIGHTSEEING TOURS

The center of Stavanger is small and most of the things tourists want to see are within easy walking distance, but sightseeing by both bus and taxi is available. A sightseeing bus leaves daily from Stavanger Cathedral at 1:00 p.m. You must reserve by 11:00 a.m. on the day of departure. The trip lasts two hours. *Available mid-June through mid-August.* Inquire at the tourist information office at Stavanger harbor by the fish market. You can also engage a taxi for a city tour, which lasts one hour, or a more extensive two-hour trip, which includes the surroundings of the city as well. Inquire at the tourist information office or at Taxisentralen, ☎ *52 60 40.*

FJORD SIGHTSEEING

Listed here are sightseeing tours of a few hours. See the section "Excursions from Stavanger," later in this chapter, for more details on where to stay if you wish to remain in any of these places overnight.

By boat to the Lysefjord and Pulpit Rock. The trip lasts 2-1/2 to 3 hours. *June–August every day but Wednesday and Sunday at 10:30 a.m. July through mid-August, an additional afternoon departure at 3:00 p.m. is available. On Wednesday and Sunday, the boat departs at 5:00 p.m.*

A more extensive trip through the Lysefjord and the Pulpit Rock to Lyseboth includes a visit to the hydroelectric plant and a return to Stavanger by *Clipper* boat. The trip lasts six hours. *Departs June–September on Wednesday and Sunday at 10:30 a.m. In May, the trip runs only on Sunday, 10:30 a.m. departure.* For rugged, independent types who enjoy hiking on their own to the Pulpit Rock, the *Clipper* boat leaves on Monday and Saturday at 10:30 a.m. from Skagenkaien for Meling, where you will meet up with a bus for the trip to Prekestolen cabin. From there, you will go on foot to Prekestolen. The walking tour is independent and will take approximately four hours. The entire trip lasts eight hours.

Fishing tour to Ryfylke. Passengers can rent fishing equipment. Purchase tickets at the pier 10 minutes prior to departure, or book in advance by calling ☎ *04 52 02 67.* This trip is subject to filling a minimum of 10 seats. See section, "Excursions from Stavanger," for information on where to stay in this area if you wish to do more than a one-day tour. *June–August on Tuesday, leaving at 6:30 p.m. from Skagen quay.*

WHAT TO SEE AND DO

Stavanger Cathedral

Construction began early in the 12th century, but the cathedral was extensively damaged by fire in 1272. By the beginning of the 14th century, however, it had been rebuilt in Gothic style and retains that style today. Among its treasures is its baroque pulpit, carved by Andrew Smith.

Old Stavanger

Beautifully preserved, this old part of town has more than 150 frame houses from the 17th and early 18th centuries. One might call this a living museum, since the houses are still occupied. This means that sightseers cannot go inside them; nevertheless, you will have a true sense of active life as you stroll through the narrow cobbled streets and notice what the residents have done within the restrictions of the preservationists to beautify their homes and gardens.

The Maritime Museum

Exhibits on shipping and ship building include a sailmaker's loft, a ship owner's office and a general store.

The Canning Museum

One would expect to find such a museum in the former canning capital of the world. The museum is in a reconstructed sardine canning factory. *Open mid-June to mid-August from 11:00 a.m. until 3:00 p.m., every day but Monday. The rest of the year, it is open only on Sunday from 11:00 a.m. to 4:00 p.m. Closed in Dec.*

Ledaal

Large old homes and mansions are rare in Norway, for much of the wealth used to be in Danish hands, and those Norwegians who amassed fortunes tended to spend most of their time in Denmark. But Stavanger has two lovely old mansions across the street from one another. Ledaal was built as a summer house in 1799 by the family of poet Alexander Kielland, and is now the royal residence and a part of the Stavanger Museum. *Open to the public from mid-June to mid-August, Tuesday–Sun. from 11:00 a.m. until 3:00 p.m. The rest of the year it is open on Sunday only from 11:00 a.m. to 4:00 p.m. It is closed in Dec. and Jan.*

Breidablikk

Breidablikk was built in 1880 by the shipping magnate Lars Berentsen. His three children never married and lived here until their deaths. Throughout their lives, they changed little in the house, so it is virtually as it was when it was first built. It was given by the last Berentsen to the city. The garden is especially beautiful in May, when its spectacular rhododendrons are in bloom. *Open the same hours as Ledaal. For visits outside opening hours, contact Mrs. Lengauer, Eiganesveien 38, ☎ 52 50 85.*

The Stavanger Museum

Visitors will find displays of arts and crafts, as well as zoological and historical exhibits from Rogaland. *Open mid-June to mid-August, daily 11:00 a.m.–3:00 p.m. Closed Monday and in Dec. The rest of the year it is open only on Sunday from 11:00 a.m. to 4:00 p.m.*

The Utstein Kloster

At Mosteroy • Considered Norway's best preserved medieval cloister, this has been a royal residence, a cloister and a manor house. It has been extensively restored and is used for seminars and conferences. Take a boat from Fiskepiren to Askje at Mosteroy, and then a bus to the cloister. From June 1–August, a ferry leaves Stavanger at 12:15 p.m. and connects with the bus to Utstein. Return bus leaves Utstein at 2:40 p.m. On Sunday, the schedule is different, so check with tourist information. *Open to the public daily from May through Oct., 1:00 p.m.–4:00 p.m.*

Ullandhaug

This reconstructed Iron Age farm with a beautiful view of the Hafrsfjord lies just outside town. The farm has been rebuilt on the excavated foundations of the original farm, which dates from 350–550 A.D. The site is also that of the battle that united Norway 1100 years ago. A striking monument of three towering swords rises alongside the fjord to commemorate that moment in history. **Ullandhaug Tower** provides a wonderful view of Stavanger and its surroundings. You cannot drive all the way up to it, but you can park your car and walk up the hill.

TRACE YOUR ROOTS

The **Norwegian Emigration Center**, *Bergjelandsgata 30,* ☎ *52 07 08*, is the place to go to search the archives for your ancestors. *Open Monday–Friday, 10:00 a.m.–2:00 p.m. Saturday 9:00 a.m.–1:00 p.m. Monday also 5:00 p.m.–8:00 p.m. except during school holidays.*

PARKS AND RECREATION

Lake Breiavannet, in the middle of town, provides a tranquil, pastoral retreat with gardens surrounding it. **Kongeparken**, at Lagard, is a recreational center with bathing facilities, a skateboard pipe, a wild-west mining town, a model of a farm and various other attractions. Children will love climbing over the huge figure of Gulliver, who lies strapped to the ground ready for the onslaught of 20th-century Lilliputians.

SHOPPING

Stavanger was the first city in Norway to create traffic-free walking streets, and these are very pleasant, with none of the somewhat honky-tonk cheap stores that seem to be inevitable along most of the Scandinavian walking streets. Most of the shopping is right in the center of town on pedestrian streets that run up from the harbor and fish market.

WHERE TO STAY

For a city of its size, Stavanger has a remarkable number of excellent hotels, and the good news is that most of the first-class hotels listed as expensive offer very reasonable summer rates and end up, in summer, being no more expensive than budget hotels of much lower quality. You do have to book directly in order to get those rates, but what you spend on a phone call is more than compensated by the savings.

The Skagen Brygge Hotel   ★★★★

This hostelry calls itself the "Charmhotel," and that is not a misnomer. The Skagen Brygge is one of the most tasteful and delightful uses of old wharf houses that you will find. It is located behind the white frame facades of five old wharf buildings, and it manages to combine contemporary comfort with old-world charm to give you the amenities of a first-class hotel with the hospitality of a family pension. The 110 rooms almost all vary slightly. In one wing, the ubiquitous Laura Ashley has found her way and decorated 13 rooms in her hallmark cozy fashion. A small spa is available for guests, with sauna and whirlpool. The hotel serves breakfast but has no restaurant. However, the management has a unique arrangement with many of the restaurants in Stavanger, and you can look at the menu from the comfort of your hotel room, make your reservation and even order your dinner before you go.   *Moderate to expensive.*

The SAS Royal   ★★★★

The same high standard of comfort that one finds in almost all SAS hotels exists here, but this hotel has the feeling of more intimacy than many members of this chain. Each floor has a different decorating motif—American, Oriental, Italian and Scandinavian—and some of the rooms are really pretty spiffy. The hotel is built around an atrium which houses one of its restaurants. At lunchtime, the atrium restaurant serves a buffet.   *Expensive.*

The Reso Atlantic   ★★★

A big modern hotel set between the lake and the harbor. This is a lively place, especially at night. The rooms are air-conditioned and have video as well as TV. There are three restaurants and bars, and the Cobra Club is a very popular night spot.   *Expensive.*

The Reso KNA Hotel   ★★★

Though it is a five-minute walk from the center of town, the KNA is still quite well located. The modern facade belies the traditional interior with its panelled lobby and clubby furniture. Many of the floors here have been renovated, and the rooms are of very high quality. The seventh floor is particularly nice. The hotel has four restaurants, one of which is a member of the gourmet society Chaine des Rotisseurs. Roof garden with dancing nightly.
                                    Expensive.

The Grand

I have not seen the rooms here; however, the hotel is well recommended by residents in Stavanger, and is somewhat less expensive than any of the above.

The Inter Nor Victoria   ★★★

Much like the Grand Terminus in Bergen. The Victoria is an older hotel in a building dating from 1900, and it is Victorian to its core. Renovated in 1985, the rooms are comfortable and pleasant. Good location in center of town by the water. Dining room.

The Scandic Hotel Stavanger ★ ★ ★

Modern, with conveniences like video in the rooms and an indoor pool. Close to the new conference center of Stavanger. Near golf and tennis and watersports. (1.5 kilometers from center of town.) *Moderate.*

WHERE TO EAT

The restaurant scene in Stavanger is lively and ever changing. A few good ones you can count on being there for a while are:

Sjohuset Skagen

A salty old landmark with loads of atmosphere and good food in an 18th century warehouse at the harbor.

Straen

In a pleasant setting near the harbor, this restaurant is known for its fish and is popular with Stavanger residents. It houses a disco and cafe as well as the restaurant.

Jans Mat og Vinhus

A gourmet restaurant owned and run by one of Norway's finest chefs. In a wood-paneled and stone interior, with beamed ceilings and Victorian chandeliers, chef Harald Osa conjures up regional as well as international specialties.

The KNA

The gourmet dining room of the hotel is a member of the Chaine des Rotisseurs, and you will enjoy a fine meal in style.

Prinsen

In the Victoria Hotel • The specialty here is steak.

NIGHTLIFE

Cobra Club

The most popular disco and bar is in the Hotel Atlantic. Visitors pay a cover charge of about $7. Members go free. Open 9:00 a.m.–3:00 a.m. Tuesday–Friday and Saturday till 4 a.m. Closed Sunday and Monday.

Amadeus

Also in the Atlantic, a more restrained place for dancing. Hotel guests are admitted free; otherwise there is a cover of about $7.

Taket

A rooftop nightclub in the SAS Royal.

EXCURSIONS FROM STAVANGER

All around Stavanger you will find charming spots with nice family-run inns, good fishing, hiking and lovely beaches. Listed below are the primary areas for outdoor recreation.

RYFYLKE

Ryfylke is the commune containing the districts of Forsand, Strand, Hjelmemeland, Suldal and Sauda. The Suldalslagen (Suldal River) teems with salmon.

In fact, if a count were made, it might be found that salmon outnumber the people of this rural stretch of river and wood. On Road 13 from Ryfylke you can visit a salmon "studio" on the Suldal River, where the salmon are visible through a glass window. This is fishing country, so you should bring your own equipment (remember the disinfecting requirement) or arrange in advance for rental.

WHERE TO STAY

The Sauda Fjord Hotel

Saudasjoen, N-4208, ☎ *047 78 12 11.* A charming, old, English style hotel in a beautiful white manor house. It is known for its good food and friendly atmosphere.

The Sand Fjordhotel

4230 Sand, ☎ *04 79 75 01.* A very pleasant, well-recommended hotel.

The Sand Gjesteheim

N-4230 Sand, ☎ *04 79 74 54.* This is a pension, well recommended by Stavangerites.

Lindum Ferie og Kurssenter

A camping center with 10 modern cabins equipped with showers and toilets, plus six small older houses in addition to the campsite.

THE JAEREN NATURE PRESERVE

Take the coast road to this protected coastal area that has something for every variety of nature lover. At **Orrestranda** the nature center houses exhibitions about nature conservation and outdoor life. You will also find grave mounds from the Iron and Bronze ages, and restored boathouses built upon the foundations of those from the Iron Age.

For ornithologists: At the **Kjor Nature Reserve**, the puffin is one of the protected species. **Revtangen** is a popular spot for watching spring and autumn bird migrations. You will find nesting birds as well as off-shore birds and waders.

For horticulturists: The sand dune vegetation is of special interest. Marram Grass is the most important vegetation, for it binds the sand with its roots and thus helps the formation of new dunes. The **Ogna Botanical Reserves** harbor rare plants like the Marsh Orchid, and along the pebble beaches you will find Oyster Plant, Bladder Campion and spear-leaved Fat Hen Saltbush. On the rocky coast Common Thrift, Sea Aster and European Seaside Plantain grow.

NOTE

As in all nature preserves in Norway, free access is not always permitted. Tourists must not trespass on farmland unless it is covered by frost or snow. And because of the fragility of the dunes, hikers should follow designated trails only. For that reason also, the use of motorized vehicles is forbidden, and horseback riding is allowed only on designated trails. No hunting is permitted within the bird sanctuaries, and dogs must be kept on a leash. Flowers and plants must not be removed.

LYSEFJORD

This is the beautiful fjord running northeast from Stavanger. If you choose to drive, you will probably want to venture along the contorted road (27 hairpin turns) down to Lysebotn, situated at the head of the fjord. The Stavanger Tourist Board has a tourist cottage here that serves well for travelers wishing to start out from this point for trips on the Lyse and Sirdal moors. You can also get here by boat from Stavanger.

Preikestolen (the Pulpit Rock) is well worth visiting. See "Sightseeing Tours" for day trips to this landmark. If you wish to stay overnight, you will find the Preikestolen cabin, located 3 kilometers from road #13 at the point where the climb up to Preikestolen begins. *Open from June 1 to September 1 for overnight accommodations, meals and information.*

Just north of Stavanger, near the Pulpit Rock, you can stay at:

Vagen Fjordhotell
    N-4100 Jorpeland, ☎ *04 44 88 78.*

HAUGESUND

The Haugesund Tourist Information Office: *In the town center, it is open during June–August. At other times, visit the tourist office at Smedasundet 90.*

Northeast of Stavanger, Haugesund is a fishing center and shipping port on the North Sea. From the water, you will see the blend of the old herring warehouses and the new buildings, among them the Rica Maritim Hotel with its outdoor restaurant. Haugesund is the site of the annual Norwegian Film Festival, held in late August, and is now billing itself as the "Nordic Cannes." Insofar as the quality of the films is concerned, this is not a misnomer. The film festival is certainly a first-rate event, always organized around a theme, and attracting high-quality films and well-known actors. While you won't find the sizzling sun of the Riviera here, Haugesund is a lovely, tranquil spot with a touch of the cosmopolitan, and it has much to offer as a gateway to the mountains and fjords of the North Sea. Haugesund is a stop on the express boat line from Bergen to Stavanger. You can also fly here from Bergen, Oslo and Stavanger. The airport is on Karmoy Island.

A stone obelisk, **Haraldshaugen**, just about two kilometers out of town, marks the spot where Harald Fairhair is thought to be buried. This impressive national monument was built in 1872 at the spot historian Snorre Sturlason visited in 1217. Snorre reported that a small church stood near Haugesund, and that in the churchyard were the headstone and burial mound of King Harald Fairhair, who died of the plague at the royal residence at Augvaldsnes. The church Snorre mentioned was a small stone one, whose ruins were still standing in 1872 when the monument was erected. The **Haugesund Town Hall** is one of the most well-known public buildings in Norway. It was commissioned by the shipowner Knut Knutsen and inaugurated in 1931. The pretty park that adjoins the town hall was completed in 1949. The building is a lovely pale pink, odd perhaps in a municipal building, but it has a rather charming elegance and inside are an abundance of paintings and other decorations. The **Dokken Museum** contains exhibits on life in Haugesund during the herring fishing boom of the 19th century.

The Rica Maritim Hotel

This hotel, one of the liveliest places in town, sits beside the water, convenient to watersports and deep-sea fishing. All rooms have TV/videos. Rates for a double will run between $125 to $200, but summer rates are available and are very inexpensive.

The Rica Park Hotel

This hotel will cost you slightly less than the Maritim, but not appreciably so. It does have an indoor pool and TV and videos in the rooms.

The Rica Saga

Built in 1959 and renovated in 1984. It will be less expensive yet, but will still run you over $100 a night during winter.

KARMOY ISLAND

Nearby Karmoy Island is a lovely, unspoiled bit of the past and a mecca for fishing enthusiasts. It is also the source of the copper from which the Statue of Liberty was cast. Travelers can get to Karmoy by bus from Haugesund and by ferry from Stavanger. Daily tours of Karmoy leave from Karmoy. At the southern tip of the island, you will find Skudeneshavn, a beautifully preserved old fishing village, with immaculate white skippers' houses. Walk up Soragada for an idea of life in the days of "Captain Worse," a character from a well-known book by Alexander Keilland. The book was made into a film for which **Skudeneshavn** was the setting. Also on Soragada is **Maelandsgarden**, a museum in a preserved old building. Next door is an art gallery. *Open June 1-August 31, Monday–Saturday from 11:00 a.m. to 5:00 p.m. Sunday from 1:00 p.m. to 6:00 p.m.*

Look too at **Derekhuset**, a restored house. To get there, follow R-511 for about 1 kilometers., turn left at Vik, and go another kilometer. *Open early June to early August from 3:00 p.m. until 6:00 p.m.*

Akrehamn, on the western side of the island, is one of the largest towns on Karmoy. This is where you should head if you are in search of good beaches and fine fishing. There is also a fishing museum here. *Open on Sunday only from mid-June to August 31, 2:00 p.m. until 6:00 p.m.*

For sailors, a guest harbor is available at Kopervik, the administrative center of Karmoy on the eastern side of the island.

Historical monuments abound on Karmoy. **St. Olav Church** was built by King Hakon Hakonsson in the middle of the 13th century. It was considered one of the most beautiful churches in Norway, and was certainly one of the largest. Because of its proximity to the royal residence at Avaldsnes, it was a royal chapel. The restoration of the church took place early in the 19th century and was completed in this century. Next to the church is the memorial stone, **The Virgin Mary's Needle**. The monument leans toward the north side of the church, and a legend claims that if the stone ever touches the wall, it will be the end of the world.

At **Ferkingstad**, you will find stone monuments; at **Hoyevarde** is a grave from the Bronze Age. Visit also the five monoliths known as the **Five Bad Virgins** at Norheim and the burial mounds, **"Rehaugane"** at Avaldsnes.

For a secluded beach, drive along the R 14 from Skudeneshavn to Sandvesanden. Here, in addition to the beach, is a small fishing harbor. Continue along R 14 to **Ferkingstad**, which has many fishing shanties that are interesting to see, as well as the stone monuments mentioned above. R 14 will also take you to **Akrehamn** and **Akrasanden**, one of Norway's nicest beaches, and to **Vedavag** where the **Fishing Museum** is located. R 511 from **Kopervik** to **Skudeneshavn** is a pretty drive passing sheltered bays and quiet woods.

WHERE TO STAY

The Karmoy Hotel

At Kopervik, this hotel has recently reopened with totally renovated rooms and a top floor addition. All rooms will have satellite TV and video, minibar and hair dryer. There is also a bar and dining room and a sauna. I have not seen it, but it should be a most comfortable, first-class spot.

Camping Sites and Overnight Huts:

Ferkingstad Rorbucamp, ☎ *82 01 54.*

Sandve Camping, ☎ *82 07 30 Sandhaland V/S.*

Sandve Vandrerhjem, ☎ *82 01 91.*

Norneshuset, ☎ *82 91 72.*

BERGEN

Bergen seems to float amid the fjords at Norway's western edge.

The Tourist Information Center: *Located on Bryggen. Open May–September, weekdays 8:30 a.m.–9 p.m. and Sunday 10:00 a.m.–7:00 p.m. The rest of the year it is closed on Sunday and open weekdays 10:00 a.m.–4:00 p.m.*

BERGEN CARD

A one day card is 100NOK for adults and 50NOK for children under 15. A two day card in 150NOK and 75NOK. Pick up the card at the tourist information office or at you hotel.

DIRECTORY

Banks • Open Monday–Friday, 8:15 a.m.–3:30 p.m. except Thursday, 8:15 a.m.–6:00 p.m. *In summer, Monday–Friday, 8:15 a.m.–3:00 p.m.except Thursday, 8:15 a.m.–5:30 p.m.*

Currency Exchange • Tourist Information Center.

Car Rental • **Hertz,** *Nygardsgate 89 and at the airport* ☎ *55 32 79 20.* **Budget,** *12 Sverresgate* ☎ *55 90 26 15. At the airport,* ☎ *55 22 75 27.*

Church Services in English • The Norwegian Church offers English services in the Domkirken on Sunday at 9:30 a.m. June–August. At St. Paul's Roman Catholic Church, there is a mass in English at 10:00 a.m. on Sunday.

Emergencies • Police: ☎ *112.* **Fire:** ☎ *111.* **Ambulance:** ☎ *11.* **Emergency clinic:** *30 Lars Hillesgt (H3),* ☎ *32 11 20.General medical emergency:* ☎ *32 11 20.Open day and night.* **Emergency dental:** *At above clinic daily 10:00 a.m.–11:00 a.m., 7:00 p.m.–9 p.m.*

Holiday homes for rent • Den Norske Hytteformidling Bergen A/S. Fjordhytter, *13 Lille Markevei, 5005 Bergen.*☎ *23 20 80,* FAX *55 23 24 04.*

Hotel Booking • The tourist information offers assistance with accommodations.

Laundromat • Jarlens Vaskoteque. *17 Lille Ovregate (F2),* ☎ *32 55 04.*

Pharmacy • Apoteket Nordstjernen at bus station, ☎ *31 68 84.* 7:30 a.m.– midnight. Sunday from 8:30 a.m.–midnight.

Recreation • **Fishing**: Bergen Angling Association offers information and fishing permits. *37 Fosswinckelsgt.* ☎ *32 11 64. Open Monday–Friday, 10:30 a.m.–1:30 p.m. Wednesday 7:00 p.m.–9 p.m. Closed June 20–July 30.* **Golf**: Nine-hole golf course at Astveit, 15 min. north of Bergen on road 14. Asane bus from bus station, ☎ *18 20 77.* **Tennis**: Bergen Tennis Club at Arstad. Indoor tennis at Tennishallen, Ulrikdsal, ☎ *29 97 67.* Can get to both by Trolley #2. **Riding**: Sanviken Ridesenter. Contact Mr. Rune Asen, ☎ *32 22 44. Open Monday–Friday, evenings from 5:00 p.m. Saturday all day. Sunday from noon.* **Swimming**: Nordnes Sjobad. Near the aquarium, heated outdoor pool. **Horse racing**: Trotting track at Bergen Travpark, Haukas i Asane, ☎ *18 90 50.* **Walking**: Bergen Touring Club, 3 C. Sundtsgate. ☎ *32 22 30.* The club arranges walking tours and information on huts and mountain trails throughout Norway. *Open Monday–Friday, 9:00 a.m.–4:00 p.m. Thursday, till 6:00 p.m. Closed Saturday.*

Taxi • ☎ *99 77 10.* To order in advance, ☎ *99 77 10.*

Bergen nestles, there's no other word for it, at the feet of seven mountains on the clusters of land that seem to float amid the fjords at Norway's western edge. Everything about this second largest city in Norway is cozy, even its weather, which is, one must admit, rainy. But the rain is most often a comfortable one, gentle and misty. And the Gulf Stream is a warming influence, preventing the temperatures from ever reaching the lower depths of the more northern cities of Norway. In fact, on the west coast, one has to go up into the mountains, not a long trip, to find enough snow for skiing. To go to Norway without traveling to Bergen and the west coast is to miss Norway; beautiful as the east coast and east central regions are, it is the fjord region that most distinguishes this country.

Bergen itself is a particularly charming and interesting city, boasting more ancient beginnings than Oslo. The name, Bergen, is derived from Bjorgvin, which means "pasture in the hills," but the city's history is far from an idyllic pastoral. In 1070 or thereabouts, Olav Kyrre declared Bjorgvin a municipality, and the city, already a major port, became also an important stopping point for royal journeys. When in 1217, King Hakon Haakonson chose to be crowned in Bergen rather than in the great coronation cathedral at Trondheim, Bergen was really put on the map. After that, the fortunes of the city were zigzags of prosperity and disaster. For almost four centuries, the German merchants of the Hanseatic League controlled the trade out of Bergen and made the city into a major commercial power. But during and after those years, fires destroyed Bergen several times over. So what you see in Bergen, even the old wooden houses on Bryggen, are not as old as they should be, given the ancient beginnings of this city.

In fact, along Bryggen, you will see nothing built before 1702, the year of the great fire. However, because of careful and extensive archaeological excavations, and intelligent preservation efforts on the part of the city, the visitor can get a good picture of what life was like here. And Bryggen itself did manage to survive the last few fires, so unless you are yearning to see something earlier than the beginning of the 18th century, you will find it still very much intact and unchanged—and charming.

GETTING THERE

Frequent flights are available from Oslo, but the best approach to Bergen is by railway from Oslo. Billed as the most beautiful train ride in the world, the trip from the east to the west coast is spectacular and an easy lesson in geography and topography, as the train passes from the gentle undulations of eastern Norway, through the jagged claws of the glaciers, and down into the gulf-warmed landscape of the west coast.

GETTING AROUND

Transportation to and from the airport, 12 miles south of Bergen, is available via an airport bus, which leaves frequently from the SAS Royal Hotel, Braathens S.A.F.E. office at Hotel Norge and the bus station. The center of Bergen is easily and pleasantly walked in a couple of hours. City buses will take you to points slightly farther out. The buses are marked with destination and route number. Special tourist tickets for unlimited travel within 48 hours are available on board. For more far-flung sights, like Edvard Grieg's Troldhaugen or the Fantoft Stave Church, sightseeing buses are available.

WHAT TO SEE AND DO

The center of Bergen is located at the harbor. The two sides of the harbor, joined by a bridge, are a five-minute walk from one another and equally interesting and attractive. There is no "better" or "right" side. The fishmarket, open daily, is at the bridge.

SIGHTSEEING TOURS

Bergens-Expressen offers tourists a brief introduction to the center of town. Children will love this trainlike bus that takes passengers through central Bergen, past the fish market, along Bryggen with its old wooden buildings and up a portion of Mount Floien. Departures from Torgalmenningen. Tickets available at Tourist Information Center. Two companies offer a choice of three tours by bus, ranging from introductory one-hour tours, to two- and three-hour trips that include visits to Troldhaugen and the Fantoft Stave Church. Departures from Hotel Norge. **Bergen Fjord Sightseeing** offers the White Lady local fjord tours, departing daily from the fish market. There are four-hour fjord tours or one-hour harbor tours. A 1-1/2-hour evening archipelago tour is also available. Inquire at tourist information office. Some of these must be booked in advance.

THE BRYGGEN AREA

Most tourists head first for **Bryggen**, the wharf with its old wooden buildings. It is this section that seems to identify Bergen. Bryggen is included in UNESCO's World Heritage List as one of the world's most important monuments to the culture and history of medieval Europe.

The Hanseatic Museum

In spite of the many fires that repeatedly destroyed Bryggen, one building at the end of the wharf nearest the fish market has survived from the days of the Hanseatic League. It was the home of one of the German merchants who occupied the more luxurious houses on the wharf where they and their workers and apprentices lived and where business was conducted. This particular building now houses the Hanseatic Museum, beautifully restored to give visitors an idea of the way of life and the conduct of business in the days of the Hanseatic League. In addition to the merchant's house and offices, there are exhibits on the history and trade of Bergen under the Hanseatic League. *Open June–August every day from 10:00 a.m.–5:00 p.m.; May and September daily 11:00 a.m.–2:00 p.m.; off-season Sunday, Monday, Wednesday and Friday from 11:00 a.m.–2:00 p.m.*

The Bryggen Museum

Farther down the quay, just beyond the SAS Royal Hotel, you will come to the Bryggen Museum. It is a modern structure, built on the excavated ruins of old Bergen and designed to put you back in time and place. The major exhibit is of the excavations themselves, left just where they were. A glass wall opens the view to the cathedral, which was built in the 12th century and was part of the town whose excavations are in front of you. In this way, you have a sense of ancient time and place. You are standing precisely where the inhabitants of the excavated living quarters would have stood centuries ago, and you are looking at the cathedral they looked upon from their windows. In the other exhibits, you will find objects from the excavations, and a welldocumented, clear explanation of life in old Bergen. A walking tour of Bryggen starts at this museum. I recommend it as an excellent way to pick up a bit of history. The tour includes the Hanseatic Museum and Schotstuene. (See below.) With typical Bergen thoughtfulness, umbrellas are provided for tour goers. *Open May–August, Monday, Wednesday, Friday, 10:00 a.m.–4:00 p.m.; Tuesday and Thursday, 10:00 a.m.–8:00 p.m.; Saturday and Sunday, 11:00 a.m.–3:00 p.m. Rest of year, Monday–Friday, 11:00 a.m.–3:00 p.m.; Saturday, noon–3:00 p.m.; Sunday, noon–4:00 p.m.*

Schotstuene

This old guild hall of the Hanseatic days is an example of the communal halls of the Hanseatic League. Its name, which means "sea house," suggests that it was the most important of the guild halls, for the sea house, built facing the sea, was always the largest and wealthiest structure. The hall has been reconstructed to look as it did in the 16th century when the merchants on Bryggen used it as a meeting place and recreation center. Such structures were important, for they provided the only warm retreats in winter, as all forms of heating were forbidden in the warehouses themselves. The guild halls were also the centers of social life for the Germans since there were strict rules among the German community against socializing with the Norwegians. The halls served as schools as well, for lessons were given here to the young apprentices who came from Germany to learn the shipping business. There were also several kitchens in the guild hall, again a way of preventing fires in the tenements. *Open daily in summer from 10:00 a.m.–4:00 p.m. May and September 11:00 a.m.–2:00 p.m.; off-season: Sunday, Tuesday, Thursday, Saturday, 11:00 a.m.–2:00 p.m.*

St. Mary's Church

This is the 12th-century church behind Bryggen. Notice particularly the pulpit from the 17th century. This church was used by the Hanseatic merchants from the 15th century to the 18th century. You will find German graves in the churchyard. *Open weekdays 11:00 a.m.–4:00 p.m.*

Haakonshallen

At the far end of Bryggen, you will find this Royal Ceremonial Hall. Built in the 13th century by King Hakon Hakansson, it was inaugurated in 1261 on the occasion of the wedding of King Magnus the Lawmender. The hall was extensively damaged in the explosion of a German munitions ship in 1944 but it has been restored. *Open daily from middle of May to middle of September, 10:00 a.m.–4:00 p.m. Closed during the Music Festival. For opening hours at other seasons, check with tourist information.*

The Rosenkrantz Tower

Next to Haakonshalle • Originally a medieval keep, it was rebuilt in the 16th century by Erik Rosenkrantz, one of the Danish deputies who occupied the tower during the Danish rule of Norway. It too was destroyed by the explosion of 1944, and has been extensively restored. At night, it and Haakon Hall are illuminated and glow incandescently across the harbor. *Open mid-May to mid-September daily 10:00 a.m.–4:00 p.m. Guided tours every hour. Off-season, open Sundays: noon–3:00 p.m.*

Shoppers' Alert: In addition to attending to your history lessons by visiting all the museums at Bryggen, you should also allow yourself time to wander through the passages between the buildings. Dark and dank, and heavy with the atmosphere of Bergen in its heyday, these alleyways open onto cobbled squares with haphazard collections of shops and offices. The area behind Bryggen is not large, but you'll find several interesting shops here. At **Jenny**, *Finnegarden 3* (take the narrow passage beside the Hanseatic Museum), you will find hand-loomed garments of the traditional Bjudalshjerte black-and-white heart design. The items here, sweaters, skirts, dresses, hats, and scarves, are designed by Lise Skjak Braek, who takes the oldest patterns and mixes them, creating highly styled designs.

These are all quite special and are understandably more expensive than the ordinary souvenir sweaters and knit goods. Follow the signs pointing down another alley, off Bryggen Jacobsfjorden, to the restaurant **Tracteur Sted**. This historic pub and restaurant is not for all tastes (more about it in the restaurant section), but the passage leading to it and the open area around it boast several interesting spots. Look in at **Blonder and Stas** in the little wooden building in the middle of the passage. Here is a lovely collection of antique lace and embroidery, tablecloths, pillowcases, aprons and a few dresses. These items make very special souvenirs, since embroidery had always been an important craft in Norway. Each district, sometimes even each family, had its own particular pattern. In the same passageway, just beyond Blonder and Stas, is **Hetland's Atelier**. This small gallery devoted to the work of artist Audun Hetland is one of the most entertaining art galleries you can imagine. Mr. Hetland might be described as a stage artist, as he has done sets for various productions as well as decorated several restaurants. The focal points of this exhibit are the dollhouses with each room offering a glimpse into Hetland's sense of humor and whimsy. Here you can be an innocent voyeur, peeking in the windows and catching people at their human frailties—a maid dropping a tray, a lady preening as she tries on a hat, a woman undressing for the doctor, a gentleman taking a bath. The figures do not move, but Hetland has frozen them each at the perfect moment. This is fun, and if you have children who are museumed-out by this point, take them here for a break.

You will find many souvenir shops along Bryggen with varying degrees of quality. One of the better ones is **Regina** at *5 Bryggen*. This shop specializes in leather goods and sealskin. You'll find handbags and luggage, boots and slippers, as well as gifts and souvenirs.

LUNCH BREAK

Look at the restaurant section for a more extensive list and more detail, but right now you are very near two of Bergen's favorite spots, **Brygge Stuen** and **Brygge Loftet**. Both are excellent for dinner as well as lunch, but visitors could easily come here more than once, or they could try Brygge Stuen on the main floor once and Brygge Loftet upstairs the next time. **Tracteur Sted**, mentioned previously, has its pub open only at lunchtime, but that will do if you're just in the market for a beer. At dinner, a more extensive menu is available upstairs. If you don't mind a short walk back along Bryggen, **Michel's**, *Torget 7*, across from the fish market, serves a variety of ethnic food. The most reasonable bet is **Kaffistova**, also at the bridge. It has an upstairs and downstairs restaurant. Upstairs at lunchtime you can have a two-course daily menu featuring Norwegian specialties for 50NOK.

TORGALMENNINGEN AND SURROUNDINGS

From Bryggen, cross Torget (the square), taking time to check out the wares at the **fish market**. You may never again see such displays of fresh fish—glistening, silver-skinned salmon and huge, solid halibuts just swung in off the boats and not even sliced down into steaks yet. You can buy vacuum-sealed smoked salmon to take home with you. The fruits and vegetables are also tempting. It's hard to pass by without buying at least a bag of plums or apples from the orchards of nearby Hargander Fjord. Continue past the market and you will come to **Torgalmenningen Square**, which is the center of the other side of the harbor. You might already have been here if you've visited the tourist information office. In the square are many shops and department stores, and this is where the **Galleriet shopping center** is located. Behind the tourist information office is the **Norge Hotel** on Ole Bulls Place. This is the departure point for sightseeing tours.

The streets running off Ole Bulls Place and Torgalmenningen yield many pleasures and treasures, so you can really take off in any direction. Just to have a starting point, head northeast from the Norge Hotel, past the Grand Cafe toward the park. You will come to **Lille Lungegardsvann**, the little lake in the middle of town. If you take **Rasmus Meyer's Alle**, along the south edge of the lake, you will come to the gallery of that name. Here, there is a small, but excellent, collection of Norwegian paintings from 1814–1914, given to Bergen by Rasmus Meyer, a wealthy businessman. *Open May 15–September 15, weekdays from 11:00 a.m. to 4:00 p.m.; Sunday, noon–3:00 p.m. Off-season daily, except Tuesday, noon–3:00 p.m.* Beyond this building, you will come to Permanentan, where the **Vestlandske Kunstindustrimuseum** (museum of decorative and applied art) is located. Collections of European arts and crafts compete with antique Bergen silver and contemporary Norwegian ceramics, glass and furniture. The fishery museum is also here, and th**e Municipal Art Museum** is just beyond. And you will also see **Grieghallen**, Bergen's concert hall.

Now, if you go back to **Christies Gate** and take it south, you will come to the hill where the university is located. Up here are the **Natural History Museum**, the **Historical Museum** and the **Seafaring Museum**. Nygardspark runs in an easterly direction from these museums. The **Theater Museum** is on the way to the park. In the park, notice Vigeland's **Unicorn fountain**. Work your way back toward Ole Bulls Place. Checking your map as you go; you can weave in and out of the back streets till you arrive at the **National Theater**, which is actually just beyond the west end of Ole Bulls Place. In the garden, which fronts the theater, is Vigeland's statue of Bjornson. This theater, founded by violinist Ole Bull, became a crucible of Norwegian dramatic art, for both Henrik Ibsen and Bjorn Bjornson served as directors. Ludvig Holberg, a Bergen native and theatrical genius who has been nicknamed the "Molière of the North," gained critical acclaim and fame for his work here.

Far out on the point of this south side of the harbor is the **Aquarium**. This excellent aquarium, one of the largest in Scandinavia, has both indoor and outdoor exhibits. It will take you about 20 minutes to walk there from the center, or you can take Bus #4. *Open May–September, 9:00 a.m.–4:00 p.m. Rest of the year, 10:00 a.m.–6:00 p.m.*

ATTRACTIONS OUT OF THE CENTER OF TOWN

Gamle Bergen

The Old Bergen Museum is actually a park with a collection of 18th- and 19th-century buildings from Bergen. The grounds are open late in the evening all year round, but visitors can only go inside the houses on guided tours. The tours last about 45 minutes and are excellent. You will see four

or five houses on the tour. The interiors have been restored to approximate
the interiors of various shops and the homes of different classes of people in
the 18th, 19th, and early 20th centuries. *The museum buildings are open
from mid-May to mid-June, noon–6:00 p.m., last tour at 5:00 p.m.; from
mid-June to mid-August, 11:00 a.m.–7:00 p.m., last tour at 6:00 p.m.
From mid-August to September 10, noon–6:00 p.m., last tour at 5:00 p.m.
Guided tours are available every hour. The grounds are open all year. The
restaurant, on the grounds, is closed Saturday. Take Bus Nos. 1 or 9 from
the center.*

Troldhaugen

(Edvard Grieg's House) • Located on the edge of Lake Nordas a few kilometers east of Bergen, Troldhaugen (Troll Hill) was the home of composer
Edvard Grieg and his wife Nina for 22 years. By the time he moved here,
Grieg had already composed many of his major works, but he did compose
his *Violin Sonata in C Minor*, several minor songs and piano pieces, and the
Symphonic Dances for Orchestra here. The green-and-white frame house is
a blend of Victorian and Norwegian styles, and the bare timber interior
walls are evocative of the old Norwegian farmhouses. The house is open to
the public and has been left much as it was, with plenty of Grieg memorabilia and fascinating photographs. The composer and his wife, Nina, are
buried in a rock-bound niche high above the lake where they used to sit to
watch the sun set. Be sure to walk the path down the hill to the composer's
tiny studio set in the midst of the woods overlooking the lake. There is also
a small concert hall on the grounds. *Open May–October daily from 10:30
a.m. to 1:30 p.m. and 2:30 p.m to 5:30 p.m.* During the festival, it is open
only in the afternoon. Visitors can get to Troldhaugen either on one of the
sightseeing bus tours or by taking any bus for Fana from the bus station.
Buses leave every 20 minutes. Ride the bus to Hopsbroen (Hop Bridge).
When you get off the bus, turn right and walk 200 yards till you come to
Hopsvegen. Turn left and follow the signs for Troldhaugen. It will take you
about 20–30 minutes.

The Fantoft Stave Church

The original church was built in the early 12th century at Sognefjord, but
in 1883, when the congregants made plans to tear it down in order to build
a bigger church, the American Consul in Bergen, a Norwegian, bought the
church and had it moved to its present location. It was later purchased by
the family of the Norwegian shipowner, Jacob Kjode. Ironically, after centuries of survival against such odds, the church burnt down in June of 1992
and is now being rebuilt, using some of the original materials. The main
part of the church is completed and the entire structure should be open in
time for the 1995 tourist season. You can combine a trip to **Troldhaugen**
with one to this church. Get off the bus at Hopsbroen as you would for
Troldhaugen, or walk back from Troldhaugen to Hopsbroen, and follow
the main road E68 to the next crossroads, Paradis. Cross the main road and
turn right to Birkelundsbakken. A five-minute walk up the hill will bring
you to a sign for Fantoft Stavkirke. Take the path through the woods to the
church. It is not far. On the way back, you can get a bus at Paradis on the

right side of the road. Another route to the church is to take Bus #2 from the post office and ride to the end of the line. From there it is a 10-minute walk down the hill to Birkelundsbakken. *Open May 15–September 15, daily from 10:30 a.m. to 1:30 p.m. and 2:30 p.m. to 5:30 p.m.*

Ole Bull's Villa

(On island of Lysoen) • The home of the world-famous violinist is rather difficult to get to, but so exotic and situated so beautifully that it is worth the bit of extra effort. The violinist built the house in 1873 as a summer residence. He had paths made throughout the island so that the casual walker could enjoy the beauty of the spot. It is approximately 50 minutes by bus from the Bergen bus station. Get off at Sorestraumen where there is a ferry, the *Ole Bull*, which will take you across to the island. *Guided tours from mid-May through August, Monday–Saturday from noon to 4:00 p.m.; Sunday, 11:00 a.m.–5:00 p.m. Ferry service starts at noon weekdays and operates every hour on the hour until 3:00 p.m. On Sunday, its first run is at 11:00 a.m. and the last at 4:00 p.m. The last departure from the island is 4:00 p.m. weekdays and 5:00 p.m. Sundays.*

The Funicular to Floyen

The ride takes you 1050 feet above sea level. The funicular runs every half hour from early morning until 11:00 p.m. Check with tourist information for specific hours. Fjellveien, the mountain road, was built for walking, and there are many other excellent paths for easy walks through the wooded terrain.

The Cable Car to Mount Ulriken

Here, too, you will find footpaths. Take Bus 2 or 4 to Haukeland hospital, or go by car. See tourist information office for hours. At one point, there was talk of not running the cable car, so do check in advance. If you're a hearty soul or body, you can undertake the walk up, which is strenuous but rewarding.

ENTERTAINMENT AND CULTURAL ACTIVITIES

The Bergen International Festival

This major European event takes place during the last week of May and the first week of June, 12 days in all. Programs include concerts, ballet, drama, and folklore. Some concerts are held at Troldhaugen, others in Grieghallen, and various locations in Bergen. For tickets, contact the festival office in Grieg Hall, ☎ *55 21 61 00.* FAX *55 31 55 31.*

The Bergen Philharmonic Orchestra

The 225-year-old orchestra performs Thursday from September to June in Grieg Hall.

Concerts at Troldhaugen

In summer, concerts are held at Troldhaugen Wednesday and Sunday at 8:00 p.m. At other times, there are Sunday afternoon concerts. Check with tourist information center for schedule.

Fana Folklore

Spend an evening observing the old traditions and way of life of a rural Norwegian community just 20 minutes outside Bergen. The evening begins with a visit to the 800-year-old Fana church where the organist plays folk music of the area. Upon leaving the church, guests are taken to Rambergstunet where they are greeted by the fiddler and the master of ceremonies, who accompany them into the farm and to the long tables set for a traditional country festival meal. At dinner, dancers will demonstrate the dances of the village, and you are free to join in. You can purchase tickets at **your hotel or at A/S Kunst,** *Torgalmenning 9* you can or phone **Fana Folklore**, ☎ *55 91 52 40. Fana Folklore takes place Monday, Tuesday, Thursday and Friday, from June 9 to the end of August. Buses leave from Festplassen in the city park in Bergen at 7:00 p.m. and bring guests back to Bergen by 10:30 p.m.*

Bergen Folklore

A one-hour folk dancing exhibition at Bryggens Museum. *From mid-June to end of August, Wednesday at 8:30 p.m.; Sunday at 6:00 p.m. The program lasts one hour.*

SHOPPING

Shops are open weekdays 9:00 a.m.–4:30p.m.; Thursday until 7:00 p.m.; Saturday 9:00 a.m.–2:00 p.m. **Galleriet** and **By Stasjonen** at the bus station are open weekdays from 9:00 a.m. to 8:00 p.m. and Saturday from 9:00 a.m. to 4:00 p.m. Several of these shops have been mentioned in the tour of Bryggen, but I've included them again here.

NORWEGIAN GOODS AND SOUVENIRS

Regina on Bryggen: a good selection of souvenirs, leather and sealskin items. **Jenny** at *Finnegarden 3:* designer knitwear in the traditional black and white Bjudalshjerte patterns. **Husfliden i Bergen** at *Vagsalm 3:* across from the Banco Rotto. By now you know that Husfliden carries Norwegian hand-made items of high quality. This one has knitwear, ceramics, wooden objects, etc. **Blonder & Stas** offers antique linens and embroideries in the passageway leading to Tracteur Sted restaurant. **Brodrene Lie** at *12 Torgalmenningen* has a good selection of handknit Norwegian sweaters.

INTERNATIONAL FASHION FOR MEN AND WOMEN

Vincci at *Strandgaten 1:* mostly international designs but some Scandinavian.

JEWELRY

David Andersen, on *Radhusgatan* off Torgalmenningen. (Of the same fame as the one in Oslo.) **Theodor Olsens** at *7 Ole Bulls Place.*

GLASS AND PORCELAIN

Glasmagasin at *9 Olav Kyrresgt.* This is generally acknowledged as the place to go, but its selection is not vast.

BOOKS IN ENGLISH

F. Beyer on *Strandgaten*. On its second floor this shop has as many books in English as many American bookstores. If you're short on reading material, stock up here for the rest of your trip.

SHOPPING CENTERS AND DEPARTMENT STORES

The two major shopping centers are **Galleriet** on *Torgalmenning* and **By Stasjonen** at the Bus Station. **Kloverhuset**, on *Strandgaten*, was a traditional department store, but has been restyled into a shopping center with a fashion focus. Clothing, cosmetics, gifts and Norwegian wares. **Sundt & Co.**, *Torgalmenning 14* is Bergen's principal department store. **Hos Adelsten** in *Strandgaten* is the average run-of-the mill department store. **Hennes and Mauritz** (or H & M) is also on Strandgaten.

FOUL WEATHER AND SAILING GEAR

We hate even to suggest the possibility, but should you need something waterproof, **Blaauw Marine** has it all. *C. Sundtsgate 1*, near the Admiral Hotel.

GALLERY SHOPS

Prydkunst Hjertholm at *Torgalmenning*: works by Norwegian artists—ceramics, jewelry and weavings. **The Galleri Nikolai** at *Bryggen 7*: ceramics, jewelry and wearable art. There is also usually a temporary exhibit.

WHERE TO STAY

VERY EXPENSIVE

SAS Royal Bryggen   ★★★★

This is one of the nicest of the SAS hotels, as it has been built right at the end of Bryggen with such careful attention and respect for that wonderful area that it fits right in. The rooms are not large, and they are just about what you would expect from an SAS hotel: functional and comfortable but not heavy on charm. The Royal Club rooms are more attractive and are, of course, more expensive. But the general atmosphere of the hotel is much less commercial than most SAS hotels, and the location couldn't be better.

The Norge   ★★★★

4 Ole Bulls Place • Bergen's grand hotel is not one of those dowager empress types you find in so many European cities. The Norge, built in 1964, is a modern high-rise (at least high for Bergen—9 stories). Its lobby and restaurants, gathering spots for well-heeled Bergenites, are lively and attractive with good Norwegian fare. The rooms are comfortable, and many have lovely views of the mountains. The location on Ole Bull's Place and next to the park is excellent.

The Admiral   ★★★★

C Sundsgate 9 • A new hotel in an old building, the Admiral occupies what was an old warehouse across the harbor from Bryggen and uses this space ingeniously and attractively. Some of the rooms are quite small, but all are comfortable and well furnished. From many rooms, guests might look out their window and see an old fishing boat anchored in the canal below. The hotel is on a quiet street, five-minutes' walk from the market and Ole Bull's Place. Tiny, pleasant bar and attractive restaurant.

The Neptun ★★★

8 Walckendorffsgt • On a quiet street a few minutes from Ole Bulls Place, this hotel is the home of Lucullus, reportedly the best restaurant in town, though I haven't tried it. You are best off with a room on the fourth floor facing the park, which is hardly a park, simply a patch of grass and four trees; however, it is quiet on that side and the fourth floor has been very nicely renovated. There's a significant difference between the rooms on that floor and the other floors. The bar, called Ludvig, stays open till 1:00 a.m. The restaurant is pretty and expensive and closed Saturday and Sunday.

The Suitell Edvard Grieg

Located out of town at Sandsliasen 50 • Norway's only suite hotel opened in May of 1987. Each suite contains a bedroom and living room. Modern and comfortable, the hotel has a swimming pool, gym and sauna. Located three miles from Bergen Airport, 10 miles from Bergen center.

EXPENSIVE

Bryggen Orion

3 Bradbenken • A charmless but functional hotel not far from Bryggen. It is rather modern and appears (in its lobby) to be spacious, but the air somehow seems rather stale. The rooms, however, are comfortable and fairly large by Bergen standards. All have been recently renovated.

Grand Hotel Terminus

Across from the railway station • In spite of its location next to the railway station, this hotel is surprisingly quiet and inviting. It is a pleasant, old-fashioned hotel with generally large rooms in the manner of the older European hotels. The hotel was the first hotel in Bergen with private bathrooms. The rooms vary enormously, and the ones ending in 0 or 24 are the best. The latter are very nice doubles and will accommodate an extra person. There are also wonderfully large double rooms across the front of the hotel. These are not noisy. The lobby is clubby, with comfy corners to sit in and old photos on the walls.

The Hotel Rosenkrantz

I have not seen a room at this hotel, but Bergen residents speak well of it. It is in a good location behind Bryggen and is popular with small groups.

MODERATE

The Hotel Hordaheimen ★★

The exterior of this hotel belies its very pleasant rooms. The rooms have been recently renovated and are fresh and light. Some singles are quite small but cute. Most rooms have private toilet and shower.

The Augustin ★★

The hotel is friendly and homey, and the rooms were at one time charming, I'm sure, but they are badly in need of refurbishing. The old brown velvet, dusty Victorian decor has seen better days, and the rooms are small, which makes them seem stuffy. But the hotel is certainly adequate and not without charm. It is on the same street as the Admiral and the Hordaheimen and has a nice bistro restaurant that is open late, and also a lovely lunch and tea room, Augustus, with piano music—delightful and delectable.

WHERE TO EAT

The food in most of the restaurants of Bergen is rarely extraordinary, but often the ambience makes up for its lackluster quality. Several hotel restaurants are listed. These are usually consistently good, though rather expensive. My feeling is that if you have only a couple of nights in Bergen, you should try some of the moderate, typically Bergen informal restaurants, where you'll get good, if not great, food and enjoy the jolly, cozy Bergen atmosphere. Because Bergen is so small, I have listed the restaurants by price category rather than location.

EXPENSIVE

Lucullus

In the Hotel Neptun, ☎ *90 10 00* • Many Bergen residents consider this the best restaurant in town. It's very pretty, a bit more formal than most Bergen restaurants. The menu is varied. *Closed Saturday and Sunday.*

Enhjorningen

On Bryggen, ☎ *32 79 19* • Watch your step as you climb the narrow stairs and enter this old dining establishment, whose slanting floors are testimony to its authentic old-world charm. Fish is the specialty here. The service is, unfortunately, rather haphazard; and while the food is generally excellent, its quality is not always consistently high. However, you'll get a good meal if not an extraordinary one, and the atmosphere alone is probably worth the price. The other drawback to this restaurant is the fact that it is located above a pub, and as the evening wears on, the music from below gets louder. A seat in the back of the restaurant may help, but it is fun to sit by the windows and look out on the harbor.

Fiskekrogen

At Zachariasbryggen., ☎ *31 75 66, the newly developed complex of restaurants at the fish market* • This new fish restaurant is lovely looking, though more typical of newer Continental restaurants than of Bergen. The service is quietly friendly and efficient, and the food excellent.

The Grill Room

At the Hotel Norge, ☎ *21 01 00* • Diners will find this a gathering spot for Bergenites who want a fine meal.

Bellevue

9 Bellevuebakken, ☎ *31 02 40* • Though it endured some rough times, this once-shining star of the restaurant scene seems to be making a comeback. It is still beautiful, faithful to its name, and still offers one of the best views in Bergen. But it's too expensive to warrant the frequently poor service and often unexceptional food. You could try the inexpensive, casual **Bakken**, downstairs, which in addition to steaks and fish, is renowned for its hamburgers.

Bryggen Tracteursted

Bryggen, ☎ *31 40 46* • This is indeed a landmark of Bergen and Bryggen. It's in a courtyard reached by a dank passageway off Bryggen, but it's easy to find because a prominent sign points the way. Here you will find a limited but interesting menu specializing in Norwegian dishes. A downstairs pub serves lighter food. Upstairs, the daily menu will run you about 225 NOK. The decor of the upstairs restaurant is spare and rustic, with unpainted trestle tables in a barn-like, high-ceilinged room. It's a kind of uncozy, Shaker atmosphere, which might not be everyone's choice for the surroundings of an expensive meal. Also, the restaurant did have a problem at times with rowdy clientele. This is no longer the case, but you may find some Bergen experts warning you away. My advice is to take a look before you leap—you'll probably be in the area anyway—and then decide for yourself.

MODERATE

(Some of these overlap into the expensive category but they are included here because you can get a more reasonable meal if you order the daily menu, or if you eat here for lunch.)

Ole Bulls

In the Hotel Norge • The lunch buffet, which is sumptuous, will cost you 145 NOK, but you can stoke up for the rest of the day and perhaps the next.

INEXPENSIVE TO MODERATE

Brygge Loftet and Brygge Stuen

Bryggen, ☎ *31 06 30* • These two restaurants stand one above the other on Brygge and are everybody's favorite places. Upstairs, you can sit at a window table, observe the harbor scene and dine on fine poached salmon or a variety of meat dishes, including reindeer. Downstairs, the menu is similar and the ambience cozy, though missing the view over the water.

Wesselstuen

14 Engen, ☎ *90 08 20* • This rollicking pub-type restaurant is crowded with Bergen residents, especially young ones; but people of any age will feel comfortable here. The trout is excellent, but there are plenty of other choices. The service is jolly and friendly.

Dickens

8–10 Ole Bulls Plass, ☎ *90 07 60* • A Victorian-style, informal restaurant that, with a tiled-floor and hanging plants, looks like the Norwegian version of T.G.I.Friday's. Entrees range from hamburger to more formal fare.

Bakken

Mentioned previously in conjunction with Bellevue • A reasonably priced, casual restaurant with great hamburgers.

Augustin

The bistro restaurant of the Augustin Hotel offers nothing fancy, but you can get a good meal or a light snack at just about anytime.

Munkestuen

> *At 12 Klostergarden,* ☎ *90 21 49* • This one requires reservations because it's so small. Typically Bergenesque, popular with Bergen residents.

KjottBorsen

> *At 6 Vaskerelven,* ☎ *23 14 59* • A cozy, casual spot near the National Theater. It specializes in meat but fish is also on the menu, and there is a children's menu.

Three Musketeers

> *On Vaskerelven near Ole Bulls Place* • This appealing little restaurant is provincial in atmosphere with tiled floors and heavy wooden tables. You will find more meat than fish on the menu, so if you are fed up with fish, you might enjoy this spot.

INEXPENSIVE

Kaffistova

> *On Torget* • There are both upstairs and downstairs dining rooms, with self-service on the lower floor. The restaurant serves good Norwegian food at bargain prices. What you get is good food and a great view of the market. What you don't get is atmosphere.

Peppe's Pizza

> Here, there and everywhere it seems in Norway. But the price is right and the pizza's fine and this one is in Finnegarden, one of the passageways that run off Bryggen, so that gives it a bit more cachet than the usual pizza place.

LUNCH SPOTS

Most of the above restaurants serve lunch, but if you're looking for a light meal, you might also try **Augustus**, which is in two locations. One is at the Augustin Hotel; the other is in the Galleriet. **Baldakinen**, in the Norge Hotel, is a tea room where you can have tea with self-serve from the pastry selection. There is a somewhat meager salad-bar lunch for about 60NOK, or you can order from the à la carte menu, which will be more expensive.

For lunch buffets: try the one at **Ole Bulls** in the Norge or at the **Grand Hotel Terminus**.

NIGHTLIFE

The hotels are among the busiest spots for late night entertainment. The Norge has **Pandora** as well as Disken, both open for dancing on Friday and Saturday from 9:00 p.m. until 3:00 a.m. **The Bull's Eye Pub**, in the Norge has music on Wednesday, Friday and Saturday. **Engeln Discotheque** in SAS Royal, is open Wednesdays through Saturdays from 9:00 p.m. until 3:00 a.m. **Banco Rotto,** formerly a restaurant, is now a nightclub. It is a stunning space, worth the trip just to see it. **Rubinen**, *31 Rosenkrantzgate,* is a lively place with a variety of music. Tuesday–Saturday, 8:30 p.m.–3:00 a.m. Sunday 8:30 p.m.–2:00 a.m. **Maxime Club**, at Ole Bulls Plass offers music nightly from 9:00 p.m. until 3:00 a.m.

EXCURSIONS FROM BERGEN

SHORT FJORD TRIPS

Bergen is the departure point for exploration of the fjords. From here, it is possible to make trips of from one to 12 days, to travel a mere 100 kilometers to the nearby fjords or to journey all the way to the North Cape by coastal steamer. Of course, many cruise lines also include the fjords in their Scandinavian cruises, but for any but the most unadventurous, I recommend seeing the fjords somewhat more independently so that you can get into the countryside. On many of these independent excursions, you can disembark at the small towns and pick up the next ferry. Just be sure to check schedules. Tickets for most trips can be purchased at the Bergen bus station. My suggestion is to inquire at the Bergen Tourist Information Office, as there are several different trips, some of which include steamers on the fjords. Inquire at the Tourist Information Center for specific schedules.

NORWAY IN A NUTSHELL

This is a wonderful and easy way to take a day-long tour of the fjords and to travel up to the mountain plateau that separates eastern and western Norway. The trip includes a train ride to Flam, then a ride on the remarkably engineered Flam railroad from Myrdal to Flam, one of the most beautiful short trips you can find. For 12.4 miles, a 45-minute descent, you will travel through narrow passages and along the foot of the falls, stopping in spots for passengers to enjoy the view. At one point, you will be able to look back at three levels of track, which climb up the mountain. The train lets you off at the Flam station on the Aurland fjord. There is time for lunch before the steamer sails into the harbor to pick up passengers for the trip to Gudvangen. For **lunch** at Flam, there are three choices: a **kiosk** by the fjord with tables right at the water's edge, serving hamburgers and a few hot dishes; the **Heimley Cafe** on the other side of the fjord, just a five-minute walk; or the **Fretheim Hotel**, which offers a more substantial lunch, usually a buffet. The trip to Gudvangen lasts about two hours and takes you through the spectacular Naeroyfjord, or narrow fjord. At Gudvangen you connect, without a hitch, with the bus that will take you to Stalheim along one of the most harrowing and amazing roads you may ever see. The bus takes you back to Voss where you pick up the train for Bergen. This trip can also be incorporated into a package tour of three days from Oslo. Discounts are available to holders of Eurailpass and Nordturist tickets. Inquire at NSB offices or at tourist information offices.

DAY TRIPS TO THE HARDANGER FJORD

Hardanger is the name of the fjord area just west of Bergen. It is Norway's second-longest fjord, 179 kilometers. Day trips run from the Bergen bus station by way of Norheimsund. For details on what to see and where to stay, see the chapter on "The Hardanger Region."

If you want to spend more time, you can stay in Loftus or Utne for a night or two and explore the area from there, then follow the second part of the itinerary the following day. Just make sure when you purchase your tickets that they are good for more than a same-day return.

For more on Hardanger see the section of that name.

DAY TRIPS TO THE SOGNEFJORD

A day trip to the Sognefjord and Stalheim leaves Bergen harbor by express steamer at 7:30 a.m. daily from June 1 through August 31. Return from Gudvangen to Voss by bus and from Voss to Bergen by train. Another trip to Sognefjord and the Flam Valley leaves Bergen by express steamer, which will take you along the coast and up the Sognefjord into the Aurland fjord to Flam. The trip returns by train from Flam to Bergen. Departs June–August at 7:30 a.m. daily.

VOSS

Tourist Information: *Voss Turistkontor, Vansgate 81. Open June–August, Mon.–Sat. from 9:00 a.m.–7:00 p.m., Sunday from 2:00 p.m.–6:00 p.m.The rest of the year open Mon.–Fri. from 9:00 a.m.–4:00 p.m.*

SIGHTSEEING TOURS

Voss sightseeing leaves from the parking lot of the Park Hotel Voss. Check with tourist office for days and times. The tour lasts two hours and gives you an excellent view of the attractions of Voss. It includes a trip to the Lemme farm, 1500 feet above sea level, and to Nesheimstunet, the cluster farm. You also see the Tvinnefoss waterfall and have a half-hour guided tour of the Voss Folk Museum.

WHAT TO SEE AND DO

For maps and advice on hikes, visit **Nye Intersport Vossevangen A/S**, Utraagata, ☎ *56 51 11 66.* **S Endeve Sport A/S**, *Vangsgate 52* is a sporting goods shop which also has maps of walks for all western Norway. Voss Tourist Office also has information, particularly on less strenuous hikes.

Voss commune encompasses the mountain area of Mjolfell, the valley of Myrkdalen and Oppheim/Stalheim. Voss is a stop on the Bergen/Oslo railway line and a center for exploration of the western fjord area. Many of the day trips from Bergen to both the Sognefjord and the Hardangerfjord begin at Voss, and it is itself a pleasant place for a stay, as it is situated at the edge of Lake Vang and offers access to both summer and winter sports. Voss also enjoys some repute as the birthplace of Knute Rockne, and there is a Knute Rockne Memorial in town. Among other sights, visit **Vangskyrkja** (the Voss Church), a remarkable 13th-century stone church distinguished by its octagonal wooden tower. Notice the Renaissance pulpit and elaborate Renaissance and medieval artwork. The walls of the church are seven feet thick. **St. Olav's Cross** is the oldest historical relic in Voss, probably erected when the residents of Voss were Christianized in 1023. It is in Skulegata, between the Post Office and the Voss Comprehensive School. The **Voss Folk Museum**, on a hill overlooking the town, is a collection of old wooden farm buildings that were built over the years from 1600 to 1870 and were lived in until 1927. *Open May–August, 10:00 a.m.–5:00 p.m. daily; September, 10:00 a.m.–3:00 p.m.; Rest of year weekdays only 10:00 a.m.–3:00 p.m. Cafe serving coffee, waffles and pancakes is open daily June–August from noon to 4:00 p.m.* **Nesheimstunet**, a cluster farm, is a good example of the kind of farm common to the area in the 18th and 19th centuries. *Open mid-June to July weekends. Other times by appointment.* **Finnesloftet** is a 13th-century banqueting hall, one of the oldest secular buildings in Norway. *Open mid-June to mid-August.* The **Mangnus Dagestad Museum** is the home of the woodcarver and artist Mangnus Dagestad. Old Norse crafts are on exhibit. *The house and the small museum next to it are open June--August.* The **Troll-Taral Museum** is devoted to the troll pictures of the regional artist, Taral. *Open mid-May to mid-September.* At the **Voss Arts Society** (Voss Kunstlag), *Hestavangen 8,* visitors will find sales and exhibitions of local art. The **Knute Rockne Memorial** is a stone monument in memory of the famed football coach, who was born just across the street from this monument. **Myrkdalen** is a mountain dairy farm about a 30-minute drive from Voss in the direction of Vik.

RECREATION

HIKING

A cable car runs every day from the end of May through September. It is a four-minute ride from Voss center to the top of Hangur Mountain, where you can find many good hiking trails. There is a cafeteria. The chair lift will take you up another 800 meters.

RIDING

Riding at the Myrkdalen Valley at Helgatun Ungdomsheim is available from the end of June until about August 10.

SKIING

Skiing is an important attraction of Voss, and the area is beefing up its facilities. There are lighted cross-country trails and alpine skiing with chair lifts and cablecars. The ski school is inexpensive and good. Day care and children's ski program are available.

Trips from Voss:

Many of the fjord trips converge at Voss. For more details on the excellent one-day fjord tour, Norway in a Nutshell, which you can pick up in Voss or Bergen, see the "Bergen" section.

WHERE TO STAY

The Fleischer Hotel

The oldest hotel around these parts. It's got a kind of ragged charm; the rooms have all been renovated, and all have TV and minibar and cozy, quirky angles that add personality. Located right at the train station, it is central to everything. Expensive, but summer rates available. Impressive dining room, live music for dancing.

The Hotel Jarl

More modern than the Fleischer, it has an indoor pool, video films in the room, a sauna and a disco. Expensive but, again, remember to inquire about summer rates.

Vossestolen Turiststasjon

A family-run hotel situated by the lake and furnished in Norwegian style. It is about 20 kilometers outside Voss on the way to the Sognefjord and is rather special. A good place if you're going to settle in for a few days to enjoy the scenery and the outdoor life, as you can drive out from here.

The Voss Youth Hostel

Just two kilometers from the center of town, it is included here because it is generally judged to be the best youth hostel in Norway.

STALHEIM

Stalheim is one of the stops on several bus tours of the area. The road up to the top where the historic **Stalheim Hotel** perches like an eagle is a spectacular but harrowing engineering feat. The main attractions are the view and the historic Stalheim Hotel. The view speaks for itself—in a language everyone can understand. The hotel offers the best vantage points for drinking in the scenery and anything else you might want to slurp up. Just be sure that whoever's doing the drinking is not doing the driving. From the terrace, you will look over the Naeroy, Brekke and Jordal valleys, the Sible and Stalheim waterfalls, and the peak of Jordalsnuten. The first hotel on this site was completed in 1885, though there has been a lodging place at Stalheim since the 17th century, when this was a place at which the Royal Mail changed horses during its run between Copenhagen, Oslo (then Christiana) and Bergen. Early in the 20th century this was a popular resort for European aristocracy. Kaiser Wilhelm made 25 visits here. One family has owned and operated the hotel for the past 60 years and did so even during the years when the German army took it over. The hotel that you now find at Stalheim was built in 1960 and is the fourth hotel to be built on the site. The **Stalheim Museum** is located in a white frame house at the hotel. The museum is open by appointment.

A TRIP ON A COASTAL STEAMER

For travelers going north, either to Trondheim or even as far as the North Cape, the easiest way is on one of the coastal steamers from Bergen. These are actually the mail boats to north Norway and were at one time the main means of communication between northern Norway and the rest of the country. This coastal route has been a lifeline for Norway since Viking days. Because it is so narrow and so long, to know Norway is to know its coasts, and so most travelers will want to travel at least part of this route. But not only foreign tourists use the service. Residents of the towns along the coast sometimes take the steamer as a relaxed way of commuting. You will find businessmen and families on board, and often groups of schoolchildren accompanied by a teacher clamber noisily on board and ride for a while.

In 1838, the first paddle steamer, *Prinds Gustav*, made her maiden voyage from Trondheim north to Tromso. In the wake of that success, more steamers plied the waters north of Trondheim, and before long the service reached southward to Bergen. But these boats ran only in summertime and in daylight—which, of course, was plenty long enough. The first actual coastal express service was inaugurated in 1893 by the Vesteraalens Dempskibsselskab steamship company. This service ran day and night, year round, between Trondheim and Hammerfest. The coastal express was a great source of excitement and interest, and from the first attracted curious travelers, not just from Norway but from the world over. Now 11 of these boats make the 12-day, 1200-mile round trip from Bergen to Kirkenes, so you can choose your departure date quite freely, except that you need to do so a year in advance if you are planning to go in high season. These trips are very popular. They provide a comfortable, easy way to go north and a pleasant way to meet other people.

A couple of warnings: you may encounter some rough seas during the portion of the trip that is in the open sea, and your view from the lounges of many of the boats is not always great unless you choose to stand up, which can be a bit difficult when the going gets rough. The 11 boats are each slightly different, but all sail the same route and offer the same programs and amenities. Most were built between 1952 and 1964, but three were built in the 1980's and are larger. I sailed on the *Kong Olav*, which is one of the smaller wooden boats. Many prefer the ambience of these older wooden boats, but some choose the slightly more luxurious newer steamers. Generally it's a matter of which one sails on your schedule or which one you can get onto.

These boats are not luxury liners; the cabins are small but most have private showers. Don't take much luggage, as there's very little space, especially if two of you are sharing a cabin. But then you don't need much. There's no Captain's Ball or other such dress-up affairs. In summertime, a hostess is onboard to direct the side trips, to introduce passengers to one another, or occasionally to organize games for those so inclined, but it's all very casual. The trips are well planned, and time is allowed for disembarking in all the ports of interest so that you have time to explore. In addition, escorted side trips to the Geiranger fjord, the North Cape plateau, the Russian border at Kirkenes and guided tours of several cities are a frequent part of the program. These are optional and some require a nominal additional cost. You can pick up the boat at any stop and leave the trip at a place of your own choosing. So you may want to try it for just a few days if 12 days seems too long. For travelers taking the full 12-day journey, meals are included. For those booking only a segment of the trip, meals are paid for individually. There are two sittings in the dining room, and there is also a cafeteria for those who prefer that. The food is good and plentiful, but not elaborate.

Among the towns where you will stop are Alesund, Kristiansund, Trondheim, Bodo, Tromso and Kirkenes. Those are just a few of the stops, for the ships steam into 36 ports, towns and fishing villages. You will round the Orlandet peninsula and travel through the convoluted Stdfksund channel on your way to the Helgeland coast and then on to the Arctic Circle, past the Lofoten Islands, upward and onward to the end of Europe—the North Cape, the northernmost point of the European continent.

For more on the cities and towns of northern Norway, see the appropriate chapters.

THE HARDANGERFJORD REGION

Hardangerfjord is a good place to soak up the beauty of Norway.

Ullensvang Tourist Association: *Postbox 73, 5780 Kinsarvik,* ☎ *054 63 112.*

Eidfjord Tourist Office: *5783 Eidfjord,* ☎ *054 65 177.*

Hardanger is a joy to the senses. It is beautiful to behold, especially in May, when the blossoming fruit trees fringe the mountains and are reflected so clearly in the deep pure waters of the fjord that you may think you've been turned upside down. It is wonderful to smell, especially in summer when the scent of ripening apples is sweet and heavy in the air, and it even has its own song, the song of the Hardanger fiddle, the curious instrument that inspired the music of Edvard Grieg and of the great violinist Ole Bull. Hardanger is a fine place to relax and soak up the beauty of Norway. You can walk the mountain paths, row upon the fjord and fish in the deep clear waters.

Archeological findings indicate settlements in the area as long ago as the Bronze Age, which is usually dated from 1800 B.C. until 1500 B.C. In the 13th century, Cistercian monks from a monastery south of Bergen came to Hardanger to build a cloister. At Opedal, a farm above Lofthus, the monks planted fruit trees. The orchards have flourished ever since in this mild climate, tempered by the Gulf Stream. The steps the monks set into the mountain, the Monk's Steps, are still used by tourists climbing up to the plateau.

GETTING THERE

The express boat runs several times a day from Norheimsund to Loftus. It is also an easy trip from Bergen by bus and boat.

SIGHTSEEING TOURS

From most of the towns, you can arrange for boat trips and tours in a seaplane. Contact the tourist office. The ferryboat, *Turnus*, will take you to Botnen, an old farming community to which there is no access by road. The farm is at the innermost corner of Fykesund, caught amid mountains and waterfalls. The boat departs from Norheimsund and Oystese, connecting with buses from Bergen and Voss. The trip takes three hours. Coffee and Norwegian lefse are served at the farm. Another choice is a **minicruise** on the M/S *Oysterese* from the Hardangerfjord Hotel in Oystese. This trip takes you into the narrow Fykesund.

For another tour, leave Bergen by bus, connecting at Norheimsund for express boat to Utne. Utne is a tiny, fjordside village with one of the country's most delightful hotels and an excellent folk museum. You can continue on the boat along the Sorfjorden, if you like, for a view of the Folgefonna glacier.

THE ROSENDAL BARONY

Norway's only barony was established in 1678 when King Christian V of Denmark and Norway proclaimed the estate of Karen Mowat, Norway's wealthiest heiress, and her poor but aristocratic Danish husband, Ludvig Rosenkrantz, as the Rosendal Barony. As a baron, Rosenkrantz could levy taxes on his tenant farmers, and, since there were some 500 farms in his domain, this was a significant source of revenue. Certainly it is a bit of serendipity to find an elegant, Danish-style estate in the middle of this most beautiful of Norway's rural fjord areas. It may be a case of gilding the lily or overindulging in tourism delights, but my advice is to gulp it all in, gorge to your heart's content. The grounds here are a pleasure to walk through with their cultivated gardens brimming with roses and their sparkling ponds. The main building, the castle, is now a museum, preserved as a home as it was when the last owners left in 1927. Notice in particular the Gobelin tapestry in the library, the old Meissen and Royal Danish porcelain in the dining room.

GETTING THERE

Buses run from Bergen frequently. Check with Bergen tourist information.

UTNE

This might be your first stop if you come by express boat from Norheimsund. You can also come here by the same boat from Kinsarvik or by road from Oddan and Jondal. It's a tiny place but, with its wonderful old hotel, it makes a good stopping point.

As in all these towns, hiking is excellent and you can take off from here for the Folgefonna glacier by way of Jondal.

WHAT TO SEE AND DO

The Hardanger Folk Museum

There are several branches of this museum. The main one is here at Utne. It is both an open-air exhibit of old buildings from the area and an attractive, contemporary exhibition hall with displays of furniture, art work, handicraft and several temporary exhibits as well. The outdoor museum consists of many old buildings grouped as a cluster farm with all the equipment and furnishings that would have been typical of such a farm in the last century. You will find an old school building, with the school teacher's tiny living quarters, and the house of a crippled man who became the book binder of the village and who, in reading the books while he bound them, became a learned man himself. There are also three boathouses with the various types of boats belonging to the farm, including the church boat in which all the residents traveled to church. The general store of Utne, in service until a few years ago, is on the grounds with the items that were in stock when it closed.

Utne Church

Built in 1895, it is not as old as some of the churches in the area, but it's a very pretty white church and its situation overlooking the fjord is in itself inspirational. The artist Bernhard Greve designed and created the stained-glass windows. The altarpiece is the work of two local artists, Knut Utne and Per P. Utne. If this begins to sound like nepotism, just understand that many of the people you will meet around this area seem to be named Utne and are in some way related to the family for which this town was named.

Aga tunet

An ancient cluster farm, in use until the 1930s. The distinction of Aga tunet is that all the buildings are in their original location. They belonged to nine families who lived in houses grouped close together on a farm. This is one of the few surviving examples of this custom and one of the oldest, for some of the houses date from the 12th and 13th centuries. From archeological findings and written records, quite a bit is known about the inhabitants of the farm. Several of the farmers were prominent local politicians, and Johannes Aga was the first farmer in Norway to serve in Parliament. The jewel of this collection is the Judge's House, built, it is thought, before 1300 by a judge who was a prominent associate of King Eirik Magnusson. The house has changed over the years, but the foundations and some walls are original. The house is remarkable in that it is built on a basement, very unusual in medieval times. This house and the others were occupied until 1938, when the farmers agreed to redistribute the land in order to have larger tracts. The houses were in danger of demolition until some preservationists joined forces to form a trust, which now maintains the old buildings.

LOFTHUS

Lofthus is not so much a town as a collection of farms running north to south along the eastern coast of the Sorfjorden, an arm of the Hardangerfjord. A runic stone at Opedal, the oldest farm cluster, establishes the earliest habitation at around A.D. 600.

This is Edvard Grieg territory, for he spent several summers here, some of them in a little hut, which you can see on the grounds of the Ullensvangen Hotel. Lofthus perhaps belongs on the map also as the place where tourism in the area was born. A priest, named Herts-berg, who lived in Lofthus in the early 19th century, was the only resident to speak English, so he became the official greeter and guide of visitors and often invited the guests to stay at the monastery. Hans Utne became the other tourism pioneer when he opened a guest house of sorts in an unoccupied room of his boat house. The priest had more guests than Hans, perhaps because he had more room, and he began to spread the word of the delights of the area to other points in Norway. He produced what was the first brochure about Hardanger and worked through Norwegian consulates abroad to disseminate the information.

WHAT TO SEE AND DO

If you stay at the Ullensvangen Hotel, you can take a rowboat out on the fjord and you should take advantage of the opportunity. You haven't really seen a fjord until you are in the middle of one, in a simple rowboat, away from the noise of the express boat or the ferry. You will be amazed first by the stillness and then by the vastness. The loftiness of the mountain, the depth of the dark water, the clarity of the air, makes everything—the light, the silence, the smell of the apples growing in the orchards above the fjord—more intense.

Skredhaugen

A branch of the Hardanger Folk Museum about three kilometers from Lofthus on the old road. This open-air museum contains the old buildings and furniture collected by the artist Bernhard Greve. There is also a small building with an exhibition of Norwegian artists. Call ahead to arrange for a tour as the houses are much more meaningful when you learn a few details about the lives lived here. Museum director Anna Lutro is an excellent guide and will make the old houses come alive for you.

Ullensvang Church

A 13th-century stone church, lovely in its beautifully renovated simplicity. The name Ullensvang means "place of worship," and Ullin means the sacred one, so it is probable that there has always been a place of worship on this site, first a pagan temple and later perhaps a stave church. The church is mentioned for the first time in a document of 1390, but it was built sometime in the late 1200s. It has weathered the storms and high winds and sustained serious damage, but the foundations and walls have stood. In

1886, the church was enlarged and a tower was added, and in 1958 it was restored with white plaster over the walls, and a vaulted ceiling was added in place of the flat one that had been placed over the beams. The pulpit is old, from around 1536, the time of the Reformation, though it has been restored. The altarpiece dates from 1699, but the pews and other furnishings are new copies of the old ones. The stained glass in the chancel is the work of Bernhard Greve. The church is well known all over Norway because of a painting, *The Bridal Procession in Hardanger*, about which the poet A. Munch wrote a poem. In poems and songs, the church is called "Kirken pa Tangen," the church on the isthmus.

Grieg's Cabin

This is not much more than a hut, one small, log-walled room with a piano, but its story is long and eventful. Edvard Grieg had come to Lofthus one summer to compose. He rented the schoolhouse, which, of course, was not in use in summertime. The composer found the region so inspiring that he returned the following summer and took up residence once again in the schoolhouse. This summer was even more successful and he was deep in the throes of composition when the time came for the school bells to begin ringing once again. Grieg was desperate. He simply could not leave Lofthus and he had to find a place to stay. He took up residence at the Ullensvang Hotel, considerably smaller and less elaborate than it is now, and returned there for several summers, first simply renting a room, later commissioning a small hut to be built on the grounds. In spite of his reputed misanthropic disposition, tales survive of many evenings spent in the Red Saloon of the old hotel with Grieg playing the piano for guests who were often artists and distinguished Norwegians. Sometimes his wife Nina, a celebrated singer, would perform also, singing the songs her husband had written for her. Imagine, if you will, the old hotel, the red-walled saloon, white curtains moving gently in the breeze, the tiny, fierce-browed man playing the music that the fjord and the orchards and the mountains had sung to him. Eventually, the hotel life became too distracting for the composer. He needed more solitude and planned to move his hut down the road to a quieter spot. However, he could find no one to move the hut for him. His good friend Britta Utne, who with her husband owned the Ullensvang Hotel, suggested that he make a vat of beer and offer it to the local men in return for their service. Grieg did so and the hut was moved. But the composer had brewed so much beer that the movers were very drunk—so much so that it was something of a miracle that the hut arrived at the proper destination in one piece. They were a jolly bunch, but a pretty rough one, and when the composer became uncomfortable with the revelry and was anxious either to go into his hut or to escape back to the hotel, the revelers lifted him on their shoulders and begged him to play for them. But he protested. "There's no piano here, yet." He should have known better. Men who could move a house could certainly scavenge for a piano. They ran down the road and got his piano from the hotel where it had been left during the move. Then they lifted him through the window and placed him at the piano. The farmers, huge, hulking Norsemen, sat down on the ground outside the hut. You can imagine the scene, the farmers, their revelry silenced, listening intently to the music that flowed from the hut. But if you can't quite picture it, take a peek at the painting in the dining room of the Ullensvang Hotel.

KINSARVIK

Kinsarvik is the main center of Ullensvang, and it is the gateway to the largest mountain plateau, the Hardangervidda, in northern Europe. Kinsarvik was one of the early commercial centers of the region, attracting traders from eastern Norway who bartered iron and furs for the salt the farmers extracted from the sea. In the last half of the 19th century, Kinsarvik also became a woodcarving center due to the interest Lars Kinsarvik, an artist, fiddler and poet, took in reviving the craft. There is also a pewter factory in town.

WHAT TO SEE AND DO

For those interested in hikes of anywhere from a few hours to 10 days, Kinsarvik is an excellent starting point. Enjoy treks through the wooded Husedalen or climb to see the falls of the river Kinso. The tourist office will provide you with hiking maps and information on mountain huts and even a guide. A program of different daily guided tours, **Hardanger à la carte**, is available. Inquire at the tourist office or the Kinsarvik Fjord Hotel.

Kinsarvik Church

This church was completed in 1263, but it suffered several devastating fires. In the course of archaeological investigation, the ruins of an even older wooden church and graveyard were unearthed. Coins found near the church indicated a date of 1050 for the probable building of the wooden church, a date that would have put it in the reign of King Harold Sigurdson. The new stone church was built under the direction of Scottish builders. Remember that Norway at one time held the Shetland and Orkney islands, and the importing of European craftsmen and ideas indicates the influence of the rest of Europe on Norway in the middle ages. Several restorations of the church have taken place. The last, completed in 1961, restored the church as nearly as possible to its original interior. In the course of these restorations, the original frescoes from the 13th century were uncovered. You can see these on the walls of the church. Notice also the beautifully carved and painted choir and pulpit and the small model of the Scottish church from which the stone church was copied.

Hardanger Museum at Bu

The branch of the Hardanger Museum containing the collection of Aamund K. Bu, a resourceful entrepreneur who was a farmer, inventor, businessman, genealogist and inveterate scavenger. As a young boy, he was always picking up the old things other people threw away. At first he gave these objects to the Hardanger Museum, but then decided to develop his own museum. Here you will find two 18th-century open hearth houses with fireproof cellars. In the houses are the collections of furniture, costumes, weapons, coins, old tools and domestic items from the area. A trip to the Bu museum is a rather exotic experience because you really almost have to wade through the heaps of objects, discerning for yourself what is of value or interest. Aamund Bu found it all fascinating and that is perhaps the most interesting thing of all—the very perseverance and acquisitiveness of this unusual man.

Borstova

The building across the green from the Kinsarvik church sits on the site of St. Olav's Guildhall, which served as the guild meeting house in the 16th and 17th centuries. It was also the spot where the parishioners who came to church by boat warmed themselves before and after the chilly voyage. The current building is constructed partially from timbers of the original guildhall.

EIDFJORD

Eidfjord is the center of the county of the same name. It lies between the fjord and the Hardangervidda, at the western corner of the Eidfjord, a finger of the Hardanger fjord. Its major attractions are the spectacular Voringfoss Falls and the Sima power plant, which is powered by the falls. Here too, you will find excellent hiking and fishing. The tourist office in Eidfjord has boats, bicycles and fishing tackle for rent. Pick up the pamphlet entitled *Eidfjord Guide* for short walks and a description of the activities in Eidfjord.

WHAT TO SEE AND DO

The Voringfoss Falls

These attract hikers throughout the summer. You can walk up to the falls from the upper end of the Mabotunnel. If you follow the old road toward the river, you will come to a path which leads to the foot of the waterfall.

Kjeasen

This mountain farm is called the world's most isolated settlement. It nestles in the mountain almost 2000 feet above the Simadal fjord. You can get here by automobile through a tunnel or, if you're hale, hearty and not squeamish about heights, you can climb the old path up from the fjord. It takes about an hour to climb, and it is very steep.

The Sima hydro-electric power station

One of the biggest in Europe, it is open to the public. The plant itself is situated almost 700 meters inside the mountain and is large enough to accommodate a 14-story building.

The Hjolmodalen footpath

Cuts through the mountain at Upper Eidfjord and affords you spectacular views on your way up to the Asdalen cafe from where you can take a 20-minute walk to the overlook called "The Attic." Follow the marked trail to Vivelid tourist hut and to the Hardangervidda (about 1–1/2 hours).

ULVIK

Tourist Information Office: *Located in the town center on the main road.* ☎ *05 52 63 60. At the tourist information office, pick up information on two different nature walks of approximately six miles, starting from the center of Ulvik. Also ask for the booklet "Walks around Ulvik" for other walks and hikes. The tourist information office has bicycles for hire.*

At the top of the Hardangerfjord, not far from Eidfjord, Ulvik snuggles against the green slopes that run down from Hardanger glacier. Ulvik has a long tradition of tourism, one of the oldest in Hardanger, and it has a most pleasant place to stay, the **Ulvik Fjord Pension**. From here, you can take an excursion to **Finse**, the glacier-top village that was famous in its heyday as a ski resort for wealthy Europeans. Now the old hotel, still called the **1222** for the altitude measure of Finse, is a simple, undistinguished ski lodge, but if you want to get onto the glacier, this is a good spot. Finse is the highest point along the Norwegian railway, which runs from Oslo to Bergen. The polar explorers Scott, Amundsen and Nansen all trained here, and Sonja Henie's father chose this spot to build his daughter a practice rink.

WHAT TO SEE AND DO

Art Galleries and Handicrafts: The paintings and mosaics by the artist **Tit Mohr** are on exhibit in her house on the road to Osa past the Strand hotel. Inquire at tourist information for the hours. The paintings of **Sigurd Undeland**—portraits and Norwegian landscapes—are on exhibit in Sentrums-bygget across from the tourist information office. *Open July only, Monday–Friday, 1:00 p.m.–4:00 p.m.; Saturday and Sunday 3:00 p.m.–6:00 p.m.* The **Lekve Family Husfliden and workshops** offer exhibits and sales of woodcarving, weavings and stone artifacts, all made by members of the Lekve family. Open by appointment. Contact the tourist information office. **Vevstova-Systova** exhibits and sells woven items by the weaver Ranveig Lunestad and dresses created by Bente Sovik. **At the studio of Elleen Helen Upphelm**, demonstrations of the ancient Norwegian folk art of rose painting can be arranged. ☎ *52 66 60* (workshop).

RECREATION IN THE HARDANGER FJORD AREA

If you are planning to hike or fish, drop into or write ahead to the tourist offices for information. They have excellent trail maps for hiking and can help you with camping as well. There are also mountain huts hikers can use.

HIKING

HUSDALEN is the gateway to the Hardangervidda, the largest mountain plateau in northern Europe. There are four spectacular waterfalls within hiking distance of Kinsarvik. Guided tours on the Folgefonna glacier are also available. Contact the tourist office at Kinsarvik for information, maps and guide service. The tourist office also has an excellent pamphlet on Ullensvang with several easy walks in and around Kinsarvik, Utne and Lofthus. These include walks in towns as well as short hikes up to the waterfalls and to sites of old summer farms. From **Eidfjord**, there is fine hiking in the **Hardanger National Park** along well-marked trails. Tourist huts are available and the tourist office has excellent trail maps. From the old **Mabo farm**, a trail will take you up the Mabo mountain. It's steep, but there are 1500 steps and 125 bends to "ease" the way. You can also get to the **Voringsfossen waterfall** from here, about an hour's walk from the bottom. Another walk is on **Hjolmodalen**. A footpath leads from the top of this mountain to an overlook, Loftet and the **Valur waterfall**. It takes one-half to one hour to walk from the Asdalen Cafe at the top of the mountain. For all the above hikes, contact the tourist office for information and maps.

MOUNTAIN HUTS

You will find both staffed and unstaffed mountain huts. In the unstaffed, you will have to do your own cooking and cleaning. In the staffed, the huts are built around a central dining room/cafeteria and have a common lounge. All are modest, clean and comfortable. Contact the local tourist boards for lists of these. I've listed a few strategically located ones below:

Karins By og Hyttetun

5626 Kysnestrand, Jondal, ☎ *054 68 858* • New wooden chalets with a view over the Hardanger fjord, kitchens, no private baths.

Harding Motell og Hyttetun

5780 Kinsarvik, ☎ *054 63 182* • Chalet village by Hardangerfjord. Swimming pool sauna. TV in every cabin. Riding. Restaurant.

Eidford Hyttegrand

5783 Eidfjord, ☎ *054 65 340* • Five large, modern chalets overlooking Hardangerfjord. Bathroom with shower. Kitchen. Good spot for fishing. Book through Norske Fjordhytter in Bergen.

FISHING

Fishing permits are sold at the tourist office, hotels, camping sites and gasoline stations, as well as at some shops. Anglers bringing their own fishing rods from abroad must have them disinfected in Norway before using them. A local vet will take care of this task for you.

At **Eidfjord**, the Hardanger Plateau has literally hundreds of lakes teeming with mountain trout. Also the **Rivers Eio**, **Bjoreio** and **Simo** offer excellent salmon and trout fishing. **Ullensvang** also offers access to the lakes of the Hardangervidda and to the river Kinso in Kinsarvik. You can obtain fishing permits at the Tourist Office. There is free fishing in the fjord.

SKIING

Though the climate is mild, you will find skiing less than an hour away. Alpine center at Sejestad and cross-country at Maurset on the Hardangervidda. There is summer skiing at the **Folgefonna Glacier Summer Skicenter**, above Jondal.

BOATING AND SWIMMING

Boats and canoes can be rented at **Harding Camping** at Kinsarvik. The **Utne Hotel** in Utne and the **Ullensvang Hotel** in Lofthus also have rowboats available at no cost for guests. Brave souls and polar bears are welcome to swim anywhere in this purest of pure water, except near houses or piers. Incidentally, the water is so extraordinarily pure you can drink it freely. No need to order bottled water here.

FESTIVALS

As everywhere in Norway, May 17 is a great day for celebrations, as it is Norway's **Independence Day**. June 15 is the **Grieg Festival** at Lofthus. June 23 (or thereabouts) is the **Midsummer Festival**. Hardanger is the place to be for midsummer, for it is celebrated here with the **traditional child wedding** at Kinsarvik, in which two village children are chosen to enact the parts of bride and groom, and all the other children dress in the festive regional folk costume. The "bride" wears a special bridal crown, festooned with ribbons and embroidery, and there is a great parade for all the children. Stories still abound about the composer Edvard Grieg, who always used to join the parade with the children and who was just about their size. These were the few times he was seen to smile under those ferocious brows and mustache.

WHERE TO STAY IN THE HARDANGER AREA

UTNE

Utne Hotel

Built in 1722, this is the oldest hotel in Norway still in operation. It has been owned by the same family since 1787. The rooms are comfortable, all with private bath or shower and toilet, and they are decorated with simple, rural airiness. The reception area and bar, and the living room and dining room are charming and welcoming, full of family antiques and photos. Pull up a chair in the front window of the parlor and watch the boats come and go on the fjord or settle at the trestle table by the fire in the bar before dinner. You'll feel right at home and maybe will even wish it were your home.

LOFTHUS

The Hotel Ullensvang

The star attraction. Like the Utne, the hotel has been in the same family for generations. In fact, the family is also named Utne. What started as an extra room above a boathouse has grown into a large modern resort complex with indoor tennis and squash courts, bowling, a large indoor pool and a gorgeous setting—that was there from the beginning. Rowboats are available at no charge. Access to hydroplane and helicopter tours. There are new wings and old wings, but the rooms have all been renovated several times over and have every comfort, including TV and minibar. The hotel is also famous for its dinner buffet with countless varieties of dishes. Though it is no small operation, you will always find one of the Utne family on the premises, either Ellen Utne, the owner, or her son Edmund, both of whom always have time for a greeting and even a story or two about past and present days at the hotel. Take a few minutes to look around. Though it is thoroughly modernized, you will find little corners of history as you wander the corridors and public rooms. An old samovar in the dining room was brought from Russia by Ellen Utne's forebears. A jeweled belt in a display case was a gift from Nina Grieg to the Utne family in thanks for their hospitality. A cradle in the corner off the dining room is the old Utne family cradle, and the linens were embroidered by generations of the women in the Utne pattern. The pattern, incidentally, has been reproduced on the dining-room china. The hotel also has a small orchard across the road. The orchard is itself a family tradition from several generations back, when an Utne gentleman took a bride from the other side of the fjord. The bride was so homesick that her family sent her several fruit trees from her hometown, and those became the first trees of the Ullensvang Hotel's orchard.

Expensive.

The Ullensvang Gjesteheim

A small pension near the church. It is modest but clean and comfortable. There are no private toilets or baths. An old 16th-century log house is available for guests who request it. It sits by the falls and contains four short beds and one long table. The log house has no facilities, so you have to use those of the main building.

Kinsarvik Fjord Hotel

A modern, comfortable family hotel in the center of town. Almost all rooms have bath, shower and toilet. No TVs in room, but there is a TV lounge and a lounge with an open fireplace.   *Moderate.*

Harding Motell og Hyttetun

A very comfortable and complete chalet complex. (See under "Hiking.")

Inexpensive.

EIDFJORD

The Voringfoss Hotel

Situated at the edge of the fjord, the hotel has been in operation since the 1880s, with the last renovation completed in 1982. Most rooms have private toilet and shower or bath. There are a dining room and cafeteria. The murals by the Norwegian artist Nils Bergslien in the dining room are quite well known.   *Moderate.*

Ingrids Appartement

Rooms with kitchens. Four double rooms and four motel rooms with four beds. TV room.   *Inexpensive.*

Lyseth Penfjonat og Hyttetun

A mountain pension, 2500 feet above sea level and two kilometers from the Voringfoss waterfalls. There are also chalets containing three to six beds. All chalets have private toilet, some with private shower.   *Inexpensive.*

ULVIK

The Ulvik Fjord Pension

A delightful family-run guesthouse, impeccably white framed with a pleasant garden and comfortable rooms. 20 rooms, 17 with private shower and toilet.

The Brakanes Hotel
A first-class hotel on the fjord. Garden, small bathing beach, tennis court and miniature golf. Boats to rent.

GEILO

Geilo is not technically considered part of Hardanger, but it is included here because it lies east of the Hardanger glacier and at the edge of the Hardangervidda, halfway between Oslo and Bergen in the Halling Valley. It is Norway's largest and most well-developed winter sports center, with 12 chairlifts, T-bar lifts and 20 downhill runs. Geilo also has a very good ski school for beginning skiers. And the Geilo stadium is the place for ice skating in case you're not a skier. For cross-country skiers, more than 80 miles of marked and groomed tracks will lead you through spectacular scenery. In summer, enjoy hiking, fishing and horseback riding. A small iron and steel center, Geilo's best-known product, aside from its skiing, is the Geilo knife.

Check with the **tourist office** in the center of town for suggestions on activities. In addition to skiing and hiking, you can explore the area on horseback.

WHAT TO SEE AND DO

The **Geilo Riding Center**, at Vestlia, hires out horses for a day ride, or you can join a group for a longer trek across the Hardangervidda. Rent a bicycle and ride across the plateau on the old road, which was built to facilitate the construction of the Bergen-Oslo railway. The road is not open to cars.

At **Hol Village** you will find the 12th-century **Hol Old Church** with several old buildings around it. Here also is the **Hol Village Museum**. At Kleivi, watch and participate in the production of Hallingglass, handmade crystal. You can take part in a traditional Norwegian wedding on or around Aug. 5 at the **Hol Fair**. Sometimes the wedding is a real one, sometimes staged. After the ceremony in the Hol Old Church, the bridal procession of horses and carts, with a fiddler and guests dressed in traditional costume, travels along the Holsfjord to Hol Village Museum where the celebration continues with music and dancing. Also visit Tekjo, about 30 km from Geilo, where you will find 17 burial mounds dating back to the ninth century.

WHERE TO STAY

The Bardola Hoyfjellshotel
A 100-room hotel situated in quiet surroundings outside Geilo. Indoor and outdoor pools, health club and tennis courts.   *Moderate.*

The Highland Hotel
This hotel has both an indoor and an outdoor pool, and is located near tennis courts and a riding stable. A room will cost you about $100 a day.

The Romantik Geilo Hotel

A simple, family hotel near the railway station. Since 1876, there has been an inn on this site to accommodate the old mail coach. Now a new hotel has been built around the old mail-coach station, and the result is pleasantly quirky, maintaining its tradition of friendliness and excellent cuisine. It is a popular spot for skiers and summer travelers alike. The hotel has a nightclub and a pleasant lounge with an open fireplace.

THE JOURNEY NORTH

North Cape is 1300 miles from the North Pole.

The journey north along the west coast to the Arctic Circle provides an ever-changing landscape. Travelers will pass fertile green valleys and deep dark fjords; they will gaze out from rocky coasts to the open sea; and they will glimpse islands looming, mist-clad and eerie, as romantic and melancholy as a Turner landscape. If you make the trip in springtime, you will move through the blossomy spring of the more southern portion of the route to the not-yet-melted snows of the north. And, of course, if you choose to travel any time between May 23 and July 23, you will experience the Midnight Sun, that strange disruption of routine that is matched from December until February by the dark period.

One way to make the trip north is by coastal steamer. (See "Bergen" for more about these mail boats, which travel from Bergen to the North Cape and back in 12 days.) Some travelers choose to take the steamer in wintertime, to travel through that endless dusk that settles over the north. If that is your preference, you will not have as much trouble booking a cabin, but bring plenty of warm clothing.

ALESUND

The Alesund Tourist Office: *Located in the Town Hall. Open mid-June–mid-Aug. Mon.–Fri. 10 a.m.–6 p.m.; Sat. 9 a.m.–3 p.m.; Sun. noon–5 p.m. Rest of year Mon.–Fri. 9 a.m.–4 p.m.*

In January of 1904 a fire, fanned by a winter storm, grew so rampant and raging that it leaped across the sound and destroyed the entire town of Alesund. The town fathers planned carefully for the reconstruction, and the town was rebuilt according to a thoughtful plan in the Jugend or National Romantic or art nouveau style. It is one of the few preserved art nouveau towns in the world, and even if you don't find that style beautiful, you will certainly find it fascinating, with its colorful frills and furbelows.

Ride or climb to the top of Mount Aksla for a panoramic view of the entire area: the town, the islands and the sea. From that vantage point, you will see that Alesund is actually made up of two islands. The "sund" of its name means sound, and the sound runs right through the middle of town. The harbor is one of the world's largest export centers for *klippfish*, or dried cod, and you can pick up fresh prawns and fish right off the boats. Alesund also boasts relics of the Stone Age and Viking era and the 12th-century Giske Chapel.

GETTING THERE

The airport at Vigra has daily service to Trondheim and the north, to Oslo, Bergen, Stavanger and Kristiansand. Braathens SAFE and Wideroes fly to smaller coastal towns. Many tourists come on the coastal steamer. It is possible to drive from Bergen, about 11 hours. There are also bus connections to the Rauma Railway line.

WHAT TO SEE AND DO

Alesund consists of several islands linked by a network of tunnels, which makes it easy to get around.

Mount Aksla and the Fjellstua Tower and Overlook

At the Fjellstua restaurant at the top of Mount Aksla, you will get a fine view of Alesund and its surroundings. You can drive up the tortuous road or walk the 418 steps from the town park, and then reward yourself with a meal or a snack in the restaurant.

The Alesund Museum

The museum offers exhibits on commercial and daily life in Alesund before and after the fire of 1904, with attention to the history of the town, art nouveau architecture, local history and fishing. Outside the museum, the boat *Brudeegget* stands as the first example of a covered lifeboat. In 1904—a memorable year for Alesund—it sailed from Alesund to Boston. *Open weekdays 11 a.m.–3 p.m., Sun. 12 p.m.–3 p.m.*

The Town Park

You might wonder about the two statues in the lovely town park. The statue of Rollo (the Viking Chief called *Gangerolv* in Norwegian) was given to Alesund by the people of Rouen in commemoration of Rollo's establishment of the duchy of Normandy in 911. Rollo was not very popular in the region of Alesund where he was born and where he carried on fierce battles with other countries, thus exposing Norway to great danger from abroad. He was banned from Norway and made his way to France, where the local ruler, weary of fighting the Vikings, gave Rollo the county of Normandy. Rollo became, thus, an ancestor of William the Conqueror. The other statue is of Kaiser Wilhelm. He is commemorated here because of his generosity and efficiency in helping Alesund recover from the fire.

The Sunnmore Museum

At Borgundgavlen • This open-air museum contains nearly 40 old buildings from the area around Alesund. The farm clusters from Orsta and Stranda are of particular interest because of the irregular groupings of houses, characteristic of the region. The exhibit also includes boathouses and one of Norway's largest collections of wooden boats, including full-scale models of ancient boats and motor vessels of the 1930s, showing the shipbuilding accomplishments of Alesund. You will also find a collection of old files, photographs and manuscripts related to local history. *Open from about May 20 until June 20, Mon.–Fri. 11 a.m.–3 p.m., Sat. and Sun. 12 a.m.–3 p.m.; June 21–Aug., Mon.–Fri. 11 a.m.–4 p.m., Sat. and Sun. 12 a.m.–4 p.m.*

The Medieval Museum

Built on the remains of a 13th-century town, Borgundkaupangen, a center for trade 800 years ago, the display includes findings from the excavations here and, through the use of texts, photos and artifacts, constructs an exhibition designed to show how life must have been. *Open end of May–Aug. 31, Wed. 5 p.m.–7 p.m.,Sat. and Sun. noon–3 p.m.*

The Borgund Church

Rebuilt after the 1904 fire. If that is beginning to sound like the chorus of a song, it is because most Alesund residents measure history not in terms of B.C. and A.D., but in terms of before and after the "great fire." The oldest part of the church is from the late 12th century. The altarpiece is medieval and in the churchyard there are medieval gravestones. *Open June–Aug., 10 a.m.–2 p.m. Closed Mon.*

WHERE TO STAY

The Hotel Scandinavie

This landmark, art nouveau hotel was completely rebuilt in 1987, but the rooms have kept much of their quirky appeal because the angles and windows make each room a bit different. This hotel has the most atmosphere in town. Rooms have color TV and minibar. Restaurant and pub.

The Rica Parken Hotel

Located in town near Aksla, the hotel has comfortable, modern rooms with TV and minibars. Brasserie and dining room.

The Rica Hotel Alesund

Situated in center of town near the Coastal Steamer dock. Though it's not especially promising from the outside, the rooms were renovated as recently as 1987. All rooms have minibar, TV and video. Indoor pool. Restaurant, dancing.

The Hotel Havly

Small and unprepossessing, the Havly was renovated in 1987 and now offers comfortable rooms with TV, video, minibar and hair dryers. All rooms face the harbor. Restaurant serving traditional Norwegian cuisine. Cafe.

The Centrum Pensjonat

A good choice for modest accommodations at a very low price. It does not have private baths.

WHERE TO EAT

EXPENSIVE

Schobua Restaurant

A very pretty spot located in an old warehouse. You will feel as if you are on a boat, so close is this building to the water. The restaurant is tastefully informal with a cozy, nautical-style bar. Mr. and Mrs. Ove Fjortoft, the owners of the restaurant, were trained in France, and they keep a close watch on the proceedings in the kitchen and dining room, so you can count on the quality of the food and service.

Gullix Bistro

This cozy, rustic spot with stone walls and a small waterfall cascading in the corner is one of the most popular restaurants in town. Beef, pork and paella are specialties, and the accent is Spanish.

Fjellstua

At Aksla • The upper floor is all glass for a spectacular view of Alesund.

The Brasserie Normandie

In the Rica Parken • A French restaurant of good quality with a notable art collection consisting of work from some of Norway's outstanding contemporary artists. The cuisine is considered some of Norway's best. A specialty is the mixed seafood platter.

MODERATE

La Place Bistro

A popular informal restaurant built in the style of a French square around a fountain. Try the French onion soup and the scallops. In the same building are Fregatten Disco, which is not recommended, and Charlie's Pub.

Peppermollen

Bills itself as the only below-sea-level restaurant in Alesund. One story claims that the water actually broke through the walls to the amazement of the diners who applauded while the manager handed out rubber boots. Good seafood—it doesn't quite swim up to your table. Specialties include dishes with names such as "The Secret of Naftadjupet" or "Cousin Anton's Spiced Stew."

NIGHTLIFE

Nattklubben is an up-to-date disco popular with young people. The **Queen's Park Dancing**, in the Rica Park Hotel, is a first-class dance restaurant and bar, somewhat more sedate than Nattklubben. In the same building with La Place Bistro restaurant are three night spots. **Fregattan** is best stayed away from, but **Charlie's Pub** usually offers folk music, often by British singers. You might also want to try the **Piano Bar**.

EXCURSIONS FROM ALESUND

Giske Island is linked to the mainland by tunnels, one of which is among the longest in the world, nearly 12 km. Visit the 12th-century marble church, burial mounds and Makkevika, a preserved marshland area. You will find lovely sand beaches here as well. **Godoy** island has the Alnes lighthouse. On **Valderoy**, see the Stone Age community at Skjonghelleren cave. For a trip to the **Runde Bird Sanctuary**, inquire at the tourist office. The trip takes anywhere from two to four hours. The island is also reachable by car by means of two bridges. Runde is the home of the southernmost nesting cliff in Norway, and attracts over half a million birds of almost 40 different species. Bird life is active from March though mid-August. Visitors can follow marked paths around the reserve or observe from a boat. But from March 15 to August 15, landing at the preserve or walking within the protected area is prohibited. Sightseeing tours do take tourists around the island, and in good weather it is possible to get close by sailing into the Brandehol grotto. Nearby is the island of **Bergsoy** with a picturesque fishing village called Fosnavag and a small coast museum at Heroy.

HJORUNDFJORD—STORFJORD

The fjord area around Alesund can be reached by round trip bus tour from Alesund. This is a full-day tour, which takes you over the 600-meter-deep Storfjord leading into Geiranger. The bus stops at Orsta for a lunch break and then goes east to the village of Saebo, where passengers switch to the ferry to Standal. The trip resumes north by bus along the Hjorund fjord, which harbors legends of hidden treasure from the Viking Age. Inquire at tourist office for departure times and tickets.

ALESUND—TROLLSTIGEN

A half-day round trip coach tour takes passengers along the Romsdal fjord and up the Troll's Path, a twisting ascent to 852 meters above sea level. You will cross waterfalls and then drop to Valldal where, if it's the season, you'll probably smell the strawberries for which the village is known. Return to Alesund along the Storfjord through the peach and apricot orchard region. *The trip operates from mid-June to Aug. 31. In the past, the departures have been at 2 p.m. from Alesund, returning at about 9:30 p.m., but check with the tourist office.*

THE GEIRANGER FJORD

The tourist information office: *Just across from the spot where the ferry lands. Check with them on available tours. Open June–Sept. 9 a.m.–8 p.m.*

Daily tours to this spectacular fjord leave from Noteneset/Skansegata in Alesund at 9 a.m. The trip includes lunch in Geiranger. Inquire at tourist office.

R58, the Geiranger Road, was completed in 1889 and won a Gold Medal at the World Exhibition in Paris in 1900 for its technology. It took 300 men eight years to build the road. They worked only in the mild months from May through September, and the completion of this project was considered a most marvelous feat. Before the miracle of the road, however, Geiranger had begun to enjoy some renown as a tourist center. The first foreign tourist boat arrived in 1869, the first guest house opened in 1875, and by 1888 some industrious soul counted 39 tourists. Now more than a hundred years later, the numbers are considerably higher. Geiranger is one of the most popular of the fjord areas. It is harder to get to than the more southern ones, but that doesn't seem to cramp any determined traveler's style. *One warning: the road is closed all winter and does not open until June.*

A three-hour fjord cruise departs from Geiranger. This is a dramatic voyage, for the cliffs that border the fjord are as sheer as walls; the waterfalls, the **Seven Sisters** and the **Bridal Veil**, among others, are spectacular. Many consider Geiranger the most beautiful of all the fjords.

WHERE TO STAY

The Geiranger Hotel

A good choice if you plan to stay a few days. Though it has been in operation for 100 years, it has been transformed into a very modern structure with a pleasant contemporary rural interior and a lovely setting on the fjord. Outdoor heated pool, live music for dancing, a bar and restaurant. The hotel can arrange fjord trips and mountain tours. Ask for a room facing the fjord.   *Moderate.*

The Union Hotel

Built in 1890, it has been frequently renovated and expanded. Heated outdoor pool, indoor pool. Dance bar, dining room.   *Moderate.*

The Meroks Fjord Hotel

In the center of Geiranger, this hotel offers more modest accommodations than those above, but they are comfortable and reasonably priced, and some rooms look onto the fjord.

The Grand Fjord Motell

Located at the edge of the fjord with a garden sloping down to the water and a private jetty with rowboats for rent. A modest, reasonably priced family hotel. A few of the rooms have the bath in the corridor, but most have private shower. Cabins for two to seven people with private shower and toilet are also available.

MOLDE

Molde calls itself the city of roses, jazz, fjords and mountains, and that about says it all. Caught between the fjord and the open sea, surrounded by green farmland and gentle mountains, Molde is a gem of a town and frequently figures in the history and literature of

Norway. Both Henrik Ibsen and Bjornstjerne Bjornson spent time here.

GETTING THERE

Tourists can find their way to Molde by way of the coastal steamer, by train with a connection through Andalsnes, by car or by ferry. The drive from Alesund or Kristiansund is beautiful, an open landscape with mountains almost embracing the farms that lie at their feet in a patchwork of varied shades of green.

WHAT TO SEE AND DO

Head up to Varden for a splendid view of the 87 snow-crowned peaks. The **Molde International Jazz Festival** is the main event, occurring during the last week of July.

If you choose to come in the time of snow instead of roses and jazz, there is a large alpine center on the outskirts of town.

The Romsdal Museum

This regional open-air museum has 40 old houses all furnished according to their periods. Taken together they depict rural life from the 14th century to the 20th. Demonstrations of folk dancing. *Open June–Aug. 10 a.m.–2 p.m. weekdays and noon–3 p.m. Sun. From June 16 to Aug. 16 open from 10 a.m.–6 p.m. weekdays and noon–6 p.m. Sun.*

The Fisheries Museum

On the island of Hjertoya, popular for its beaches, this is the only such museum in Norway. Its open-air exhibit of buildings, boats and fishing gear centers on the life of the area fishermen during the last 100 years. *Open from June 1 to late Aug., weekdays 10 a.m.–4 p.m.; Sun. noon–4 p.m.*

The Rose Garden

The source of many of the roses for which Molde is known, on the roof of the Town Hall is the Rose Garden containing over 1000 roses including the Molde Rose, especially created for the town.

The King's Birch

It is here that King Haakon and the crown prince, the late King Olav V, took shelter early in World War II just before they left for England. For seven days, in fact, from April 22–29, Molde was the capital of Norway. It was, for this reason, heavily bombed during that time and has been almost totally rebuilt.

Molde Cathedral

A dramatic, modern white chalk structure built in 1957, the church is of interest also for its interior, elaborately embellished with stained glass and frescoes.

WHERE TO STAY

The Alexandra Hotel

A modern structure in the center of town with a rooftop terrace, fitness center and an indoor pool, the hotel commands fine views from the terrace.

Rooms have TV/video and minibars. Restaurant Gamle Molde; Bastian Pub. Expensive to moderate. Inquire about summer rates.

The Hotel Nobel

This old hotel has been completely renovated, so beneath the aging skin a young heart beats. There are just 42 rooms, all with private baths and TV/video. The rooms vary in size, shape and price.

The Hotel Romsdal

Located in the center of town, very near the marketplace and town hall, the hotel has been completely redecorated and all rooms have private bath and TV. This hotel is an adequate and functional place. And although it might lack some of the appeal of the other hotels, its more modern price makes it attractive.

The Knausen Molde

The Knausen Molde lies about three km out of town and is surrounded by green lawns with a view to the mountains and the fjord. No alcohol is served here. Rooms all have TV and are modern. There are also cottages.

The Rimo Hostel

Worth including here, since it is a very comfortable hostel, open only in summer as it is a dormitory during the school terms. No private baths, but all rooms have hot and cold water. Each flat has free kitchen facilities. You must provide your own cookware and dishes. In each flat there is a common room. TV in the reception area. The cafeteria is open for breakfast and dinner, and for lunch for groups on advance request. Coin-operated laundry. Babysitting service available.

WHERE TO EAT

Najaden Mat-og-Vinhus

This is generally acknowledged to be the best restaurant in Molde, the best, in fact, in the whole area.

Naust-Gryta

Overlooking the water, this is a simple spot with excellent seafood and an especially fine fish soup, which, along with some good Norwegian bread, makes for a very satisfying and inexpensive lunch. In summer, a terrace is open.

KRISTIANSUND

Tourist Information Office: *19 Kapten Bodtkersgate. Open all year Mon.–Fri. 8 a.m.–4 p.m.; Mid-June to mid-Aug. Mon.–Fri. 8 a.m.–5 p.m.; Sat. 10 a.m.–2 p.m. Closed Sun.*

Though Kristiansund is the mid-Norway base for off-shore oil, little evidence of this heavy industry is visible, and in spite of its location on the coast with the rough North Atlantic beating at its doorstep, it is a warmly welcoming town. The frequent hostility of the ocean is countered by the welcoming topography of the town itself, with its many parks and wooded areas.

This small city is actually made up of three islands that encircle a harbor. Almost entirely rebuilt after devastating damage in WW II, this modern city still retains an old-world charm.

Kristiansund has a long history going back perhaps as far as to the first Norwegians. Evidence points to settlers arriving in leather boats at the end of the last Ice Age. These pioneers called the place *Folgsn*, which means hiding place, and because of its situation on the sea with its safe, island-wrapped harbor, it has always attracted settlement and commerce. If Stavanger claims its fame as the place where King Harald Fairhair, who had sworn not to cut his hair until Norway was one nation, accomplished that unification, Kristiansund prides itself on being the spot where once the unification was complete, King Harald came to cut his fair and famous hair.

GETTING THERE

Separated from the mainland by the fjord, Kristiansund has begun serious efforts to improve access to the mainland. A monumental undertaking, the Krifast project will connect Kristiansund to the mainland by means of what will be Norway's longest underwater road tunnel and the country's longest suspension bridge. The airport is just seven km from the center of town. The coastal steamer stops here twice a day. There are bus connections to most of the surrounding cities. The buses drive onto the ferry and passengers can either remain on the bus or get off and walk around the boat.

GETTING AROUND

The life of the city is organized around its island structure. *Kirkelandet*, which means church land, is the center of city life with the highest population. At the end of the Ice Age, Kirkelandet and Gomalandet were two separate islands, but as the ice melted, the lowered water level revealed a strip of land connecting the two islands. **Nordlandet** (North land), is the airport island, just 10 minutes from the center of Kirstiansund. **Innlandet** (Inland) is the smallest of the islands and contains the oldest preserved section of Kristiansund. The islands are linked by *sundbaten*, a boat that scurries back and forth frequently. It is one of the oldest transport systems still in operation.

WHAT TO SEE AND DO

Kirkelandet Church
The church built in 1964 is sometimes called the Cathedral of the Atlantic. It is worth a visit to see its mosaic wall, made of 320 pieces of glass, grading from dark at the bottom to light at the top, a symbolic pull of the soul from darkness to light.

Varde Tower
At the top of Varde hill, the tower makes a fine lookout from which to view

the panorama of Kristiansund and its surroundings. The first tower on this site was built during the Napoleonic Wars. Then, in 1892, in honor of the town's 150th anniversary, a new tower was erected. The present monument was built in 1983.

The Nordmore Museum

Near the Atlanten Stadion in Kristiansund, the museum has exhibits showing life in the region from the early Stone Age settlements through the 19th century. Exhibit on klipfishing and agricultural life as well as marine archaeological findings. *Open Tues.–Fri. 10 a.m.–2 p.m., Sun. noon–3 p.m. Closed Mon. and Sat.*

Mellemvaerftet

Located near the center of town on the west side of Vagen bay, this old shipyard is now a working museum. Visitors can watch the restoration of old boats using traditional methods. There are no regular open hours, but drop by during normal working hours and you'll be sure to find something to watch.

Woldbrygga

On the east side of Vagen bay. Take the Sundbat from center of town to Goma. This group of buildings contains an old cooperage. *Open from last week of June until beginning of Aug., weekdays 2 a.m.–4 p.m., Sun. 1 p.m.–4 p.m. Closed Sat. This is part of the Nordmore museum.*

The Kristiansund Theater

Most visitors will see the theater, as it houses the tourist information office. But take the time to look around the structure, which was built in 1914 and survived the 1940 bombing with damage only to the roof. The beautiful ceilings have been restored, and the theater is an active place with concerts, plays and an opera festival held in February. Recently, the local ballet staged an original production about the process of klipfish production, probably a first in the annals of dance history.

Tingvoll Bygdemuseum

In Tingvollia • It's worth going out here just for the view of the Sunndal mountains. Take road 16 west from Tingvoll center, and you will find a sign to the museum. The museum was an old farm and will give you an idea of the rural way of life in the area. Several crafts are displayed, as well as a storehouse with old tools and equipment. Schoolhouse, sawmill, grinding mill and blacksmith shop.

Leikvin Bygdemuseum

Nine km east of Sunndalsora, five houses in their original setting make up this museum. The farm belonged to Lady Arbuthnot, who came from England to enjoy the beauty of the valley. Lady Arbuthnot's hunting cottage is in Grodalen. *The museum is open from June 1 through Aug., daily noon–6 p.m.*

Innlandet

The smallest island of Kristiansund has beautifully preserved old houses, and it is pleasant just to walk along the streets here. Stop to look at the out-side of the **Lossius Manor House**, built in 1780 by the Captain Torden-skjold, a wealthy ship captain. The house is still privately owned, so you cannot go inside, but it is simply a pleasure to stand outside enjoying the beauty of the house and garden, and imagining the grace of the life that must be lived within.

And if you've had your fill of museums, both indoor and open-air, of old houses, old boats and klipfish, simply take some time to walk through the parks and along the reservoir where the land surrounding it has been turned into a lovely park with paths for walking. Visit the **Fisherman's Stairs**, where the fish-ermen sell their catches fresh off their boats. As you walk through town, notice the various rather crudely executed stone monuments that have been built to commemorate people and events.

A Walk in the Park

Start at the Kirkelandet church. Nearby, you will come to the Brodkorp graveyard, a cemetery belonging to one of the wealthy merchant families of Kristiansund. This graveyard is near the Kristiansund church, where the Brodkorp family maintained a summer home. The graveyard is well main-tained and worth a visit. Continue your walk through the Vanndamman water park, where you can stroll along wooded footpaths by the reservoir. Continue to Varden, the hill tower from which you will have a spectacular panoramic view of Kristiansund and its islands.

WHERE TO STAY

The Rica Hotel Kristiansund ★★★

Located on the water, the Rica is the newest hotel in town. It is a sleek modern building with comfortable rooms furnished in light colors and woods. The restaurant is a good one, and in the hotel are a lobby bar, a pub called Endestasjonen, which has a railway station motif, and a nightclub. All rooms have TV and minibars. Expensive in season.

The Grand Hotel ★★★

This was the first building completed after the devastation of 1940. Its prices are a bit lower than the Rica, and its rooms, which vary in size, shape and decor, are not so brightly or freshly decorated. But they are comfort-able. The restaurant, Konsul, is lovely, and the food good. You will find two bars, a pub called Pub 1, and a nightclub with dancing, Gripsalen. All rooms have TV. Expensive but inquire about summer prices.

The Baron Hotel ★★★

This one gets my vote. With just 50 large rooms, each decorated a bit dif-ferently, the hotel has a distinctly intimate flavor. All the rooms have TV/video, hair dryers and minibar. The Baron Lobby serves light snacks and appetizers. The piano bar is a mahogany-and-leather, British-style spot. The only drawback is that it could make for a noisy time since the lobby is small and the music sometimes seems booming. The Baron Restaurant is attrac-tive and well recommended by Kristiansund residents. Your best bet here is the daily menu. The hotel is as expensive as the other first-class hotels in town, but inquire about summer rates and the Best Western "Go as you please" program for discounts.

Baron Hotel La Mer

Under the same management as the Baron Hotel, this is open only in summer. It is just two years old and is a small, cozy place with 50 rooms, all with private bath, TV/video and minibar. A small restaurant is next to the reception area.

WHERE TO EAT

The hotel restaurants mentioned previously are the best choices. While you are in Kristiansund, you should try the local specialty, which indicates the Continental influence that this fishing and shipping center has enjoyed over the years. *Bacalao* is a Spanish-style treatment of klipfish, the sun-dried cod for which Kristiansund is known. In this dish, the cod is cooked with tomatoes, potatoes, onions, olive oil and peppers.

EXCURSIONS FROM KRISTIANSUND

AVEROY

Drive the Atlantic road, which crosses islets and reefs, to arrive at this island community. The **Kvernes Stave Church** was built in the 14th century, although the interior dates from a slightly later period. The altarpiece is late 17th century and was built around a medieval triptych, which is thought to have been completed some time in the late 15th century. The pulpit is Dutch, and was presented to the church in 1640. Notice the decorations on the walls and ceilings.

The **Gamle Kvernes Bygdemuseum** has two sections. By the sea, you'll find a fishery museum with a fisherman's hut and boathouses. On the wooded mountain are old cottages and farm buildings. All the houses are furnished as they were. *Open May–Sept. Sun. 2 p.m.–6 p.m.*

If you are interested, you could also visit what I call Harald Fairhair's Barbershop. A green slope by the water is allegedly the spot where Harald cut his hair after unifying Norway. It is on the site of the estate of Ragnvald, the Earl of More, who was a close friend of the king. Harald retreated here after the battle for a bit of "R and R" and a beauty treatment. It is also possible to visit a salmon farm on Averoy.

KULOY

The **Kuli Stone** is the oldest Christian monument in Norway and the first where the name of Norway is written. The stone is thought to date from the year 1015. A copy of it is in the Norwegian Pavilion at Epcot Center. The **phallus stone**, also on Kuli, is an ancient fertility monument of an Iron Age religious cult.

You can get to all the above by car, boat or ferry.

GRIP

Almost 80 islands and reefs make up the island cluster known as Grip. In summer, boats make the trip every day from Kristiansund, about a 45-minute trip across the open sea. Bring your fishing rod if you're so inclined. You'll find fishing holes along the coast. Grip has been inhabited for centuries, the earliest settlers attracted by the plentiful fishing. After Norway was unified in the eighth century, the island was appropriated by the king, but later, the church and several wealthy families bought the land. In 1200, the Archbishop of Nidaros was the owner of Grip. The island reverted to the monarchy some time after that, but in 1728, King Frederik IV sold Grip once again to wealthy private citizens, many of whom maintained ownership until 1909. The island has had a checkered history of prosperity and poverty. At one time the population fell to 12, when the cod fishing was disastrously unproductive. Two catastrophic storms also wreaked destruction. In November 1796, a violent storm swept almost 100 houses into the sea. In February 1804, another storm brought more devastation. In the years that followed, the island was owned by various wealthy citizens of Kristiansund. The last owner was Ludvig Williamsen. It was he who, in 1909, sold the island back to its 200 residents. In 1964, Grip merged with Kristiansund. Over the years, the population, which ranged from as few as 12 to as many as 400, has dwindled. Now it is a summer colony, with the houses carefully tended by the families who still own them.

The **Grip Stave Church** is a rather undistinguished, painted wood building, but the interior, embellished with wonderful medieval wall paintings and an extraordinary 16th-century altar cabinet, is worth looking into. It is thought that the church, the smallest of the remaining stave churches in Norway, was built some time around 1470. Since 1621, when it was restored for the first time, it has been carefully maintained. If your timing is right, you may arrive in time for a concert or even a wedding.

Gripkroa Inn used to be the old schoolhouse. Now the inn is a good place to stop for a light snack. Rooms are available for overnight stays.

THE ISLAND OF HITRA

Located north of Kristiansund and Smola, Hitra is the largest island south of Lofoten and is an excellent fishing center. Plenty of watersports—diving, windsurfing and water-skiing. Travelers can also visit the Dolmen model village, the Dolm church, and the Hitra district museum. Of interest to conservationists is the wildlife preserve at Havmyran. There are ferry connections from Smola and Kristiansund. You'll find camping available here, and the **Hitra Pension**, N-*7241 Ansnes,* ☎ *074 40 546,* is recommended by several residents of the area. It is located on the water with seven double rooms and two singles, all with private baths. The pension is known for its good home-cooked food, and it is fully licensed. You can arrange for fishing trips through the pension and rent small boats as well.

BODO

Tourist Information Office: *Sjogata 21.* ☎ *081 21240. Open Mon–Fri. 9 a.m.–5 p.m. and 7 p.m.–9 p.m.; Sat. 10 a.m.–12 p.m.; Sun. 7 a.m.–9 p.m.*

You won't really know Norway until you have traveled to the top, to the end of Europe—the lonely plateau that unceremoniously caps off the continent. It's not so much the North Cape itself as the sur roundings and the approach that are extraordinary. Bodo, the gateway to the north of Norway, is the spot where the curtain goes up on the land of the Midnight Sun. During the deep days of summer, the sun never sets north of Bodo. This does not mean, of course, that there are 60 days of unmitigated sunlight from May 23 until July 23. It can rain here too, and all one need do is fly or take a boat to the **Lofoten Islands**, those mist-shrouded presences of the North Sea, to get a taste of Norwegian cloud cover. But it is light all day and all night, a phenomenon that certainly has its effect on residents and visitors alike. Even the natives find it disconcerting, many complaining that they can't sleep even when they're tired. Some people find themselves uncomfortably revved up, and conversely, in December and January during the "dark days," these same clock-spun residents complain that they are tired all the time, sometimes depressed and curiously without energy. However, the dark days are compelling to the traveler, and many visitors do come north in order to experience the day-long twilight and to see the spectral shadows of the mountains and the dusk-filled fjords.

Bodo was established in 1816, but like many northern Norwegian towns, it looks quite new because it was almost completely destroyed in one afternoon of bombing during WW II and has been almost entirely rebuilt since.

GETTING THERE

Bodo has an airport with service to and from Trondheim and other towns in Norway. The coastal steamer stops here. At last report, there was train service from Trondheim.

WHAT TO SEE AND DO

Saltstraumen

This maelstrom, the strongest and most well-known in Norway, is located outside Bodo. A maelstrom occurs when the difference in water levels between high and low tide forces huge volumes of water from one fjord into another or from the outer ocean to the inner fjord basins. Saltstraumen is about three km long and only 150 meters wide, lying between the inner Skjestad fjord and the outer Satenfjorden, and is the last outlet to the ocean south of Bodo. Within six hours, between 33 and 82 billion gallons of water rush through the strait at a rate of about 10 knots per hour. The force of the maelstrom varies with the tides and is most violent at the new and full moon. Some of the eddies or whirlpools, called cauldrons, are rumored to be bottomless. At the most turbulent moments, the water emits a kind of scream, adding to the mystery of the scene. Though there are many times when the signal station lights one red lantern to indicate the strait is not safe for passage, the area is popular for recreation with people coming to fish or merely to enjoy a few hours out of doors with the maelstrom churning and screaming in the background. When the tide is in, the current carries enormous numbers of fish. Buses depart five times a day from Bodo to Saltstraumen. *Check with the tourist office or bus station to find out when the maelstrom will be at its strongest.*

Svartisen

The second largest glacier in Norway. Check with tourist office for boat tours.

The Nordland County Museum

There are several branches of the museum in and around Bodo. At *Prinsensgate 116*, Bodo's oldest building, you will find the exhibits illustrating the daily life of the fishermen during the last century. At *Kjerringoy 15*, 19th-century buildings have been furnished as they were in this important northern trading center. A literary note: Kjerringoy appears as Sirilund in Knut Hamsun's novels. The open-air museum with a boat collection is located at **Bodosjoen**, four km from Bodo. Nearby is the Louis Philip chamber, a room in the main building of the Agricultural school. The chamber has been preserved since the 18th century, with rococo frescoes, tapestries and ceiling decorations from 1754.

Also visit the **Bodin Church**, an ancient church dating from A.D. 1242, and **Bodo Domkirke**, the cathedral that was built in 1956.

WHERE TO STAY

The SAS Royal

Storgatan 2 • Built in 1871, the hotel was renovated in 1982. All rooms have private bath and TV/video. Four restaurants, two bars and a coffee shop. The Marlene restaurant has a seafood buffet in summer at about 150 NOK.

The Diplomat Hotel

23 Slogaten • A relatively new hotel in the center of town by the harbor. All 84 rooms have private baths, TV/video, minibar and hair dryers. Bar, restaurant and nightclub. The nightclub stays open until 3:30 a.m. In summer, a "Nordland" evening can be arranged with folk dancing.

The Central Hotel

Prof. Schylles Gt. • Twenty double rooms and 25 singles, all with private bath, TV/video, minibar and hair dryer. *The Beef* restaurant, a bar and a wine bar; also a summer terrace.

THE LOFOTEN ISLANDS

Walled in by mountains alpine in their steepness, the Lofoten Islands sit atop the sea, separated from the mainland by the Vestfjorden. They are easily accessible from Bodo and are a summer attraction because their mountain walls protect them, their farmlands and their fisheries from the coastal elements. Writers have been drawn to the beauty and mystery of the islands, and artists flock here also because of the extraordinary light and the environment. At Svolvaer, a small artists' colony has developed. Lofoten also occupies an indelible place in history because of the commando raids on the islands during WW II. These raids were made in order to prevent the Germans from using the herring oil for glycerine in munitions. After the raids, many volunteers returned to England to strengthen the resistance movement.

GETTING THERE

Boat trips from Bodo to the Lofoten islands take about 4–6 hours, but it is only a 30-minute flight, and several flights come and go each day between Bodo and Lofoten. Steamers and planes also service the archipelagos of Rost and the island of Vaeroy, located south of the main cluster of the Lofoten islands.

Svolvaer is the capital of Lofoten and the center of the cod-fishing industry. Rost is of particular interest to ornithologists because of its bird sanctuaries. Cormorants and seagulls flock by the shore, and puffins nest near the ends of tunnels in the hills. On the high ledges above the sea, you will find auk and the sea eagle. Though it never gets terribly cold, the nearly 365 islands that make up the archipelago are frequently wind beaten or fog shrouded, and the sea can be violent. But it is certainly worth making the trip to any of these offshore islands. Steep mountains, grassy farmlands, beaches, birds and fish make these a nature lover's paradise. **Vaeroy** boasts **Sanden**, a beautiful beach sitting below a 1000-foot-high rock cliff. The deserted village of **Mostad** is shadowed eerily by the Mostad-fjell mountain, where more than a half million seabirds nest. The onion-domed **North Vaeroy** church was brought here from Vagan in 1799. Inside is a late medieval altarpiece, an alabaster relief that could date back as far as 1440.

WHERE TO STAY

The Hotel Havly

In *Svolvaer* • 50 rooms all with private bath. TV in rooms. Dining room, cafeteria. No alcohol served. *P.O. Box 115, N-8301 Svolvaer.* ☎ *088 70 344.*

The Norton Hotel Lofoten

In *Svolvaer* • A modern, white block of a hotel, sitting at the edge of the water. All rooms with private bath. Restaurant, bar and disco. Fully licensed. *P.O. Box 42, N-8301 Svolvaer.* ☎ *088 71 200. FAX 088 70 850.*

The Svolvaer Hotel Lofoten

In *Svolvaer* • Opened in June 1986, a friendly, comfortable hotel with pleasantly light furnishings. All rooms with private bath, TV/video. Eight rooms have kitchenette and minibar. *Austnesfjordgt. 24, N-8300 Svolvaer.* ☎ *088 71999.*

The Stamsund Lofoten Hotel

At *Stamsund* • All rooms with private bath. Bar and restaurant. Centrally located.   *Moderate.*

TROMSO

Tourist Information Office: *Tromso Arrangement AS, Storgata 61.* ☎ *10 000.*
Open June–mid-Aug. weekdays 8:30 a.m.–8 p.m.; Sat. 10 a.m.–4:30 p.m.;
Sun. noon–4:30 p.m. Rest of year, weekdays 8:30 a.m.–4 p.m.; closed Sat.
and Sun.

Fjord-wrapped Tromso lies across three islands, with the center of
town and most of the population on the largest middle island.
Tromso belongs to an association called Warm Winter Cities, an
oxymoron that does not refer to temperature, but rather to the climate of friendliness, liveliness and welcome. In that sense, Tromso,
even in the darkest days of its long, long winter, is certainly one of
the warmest of cities. But it is also not as cold as its location parallel
to northernmost Alaska would lead one to expect. The warming effects of the Gulf Stream moderate the temperature to an average of
26 degrees F. in winter, though just 50 miles inland the temperature
may drop to 40 degrees below zero.

A story, most likely perpetrated by the tourist board, claims that at
the turn of the century, a French tourist, on first seeing Tromso, ex-
claimed, "This must be the Paris of the North." He could not have
been referring to any Champs Élysée or Louvre, and surely he was
not likening the Torvet at the harbor to the Place D'Étoile, but
Tromso could possibly challenge the city of light in its nightlife offerings. Tromso counts more restaurants per capita than any other
town in Norway, and the restaurants are good—perhaps not Michelin-starred, but generally excellent and most pleasant. And while
Paris has its wines, Tromso has its beer, Mack Beer, probably the best
beer you'll find in Norway. Mack is the northernmost brewery in the
country and the only family-owned brewery in Norway. One tradition is to serve the beer with seagull's eggs. The quality of the beer is
due primarily to the extraordinary purity of the water here. In fact,
Tromso is the only place in the world where the Coca-Cola bottler is
not required to distill the water before using it.

Tromso is the capital of northern Norway and is also a university
town, with the University of Tromso, which offers courses in medicine, science and less conventional subjects like fishery technology
and Lapp languages. Tromso was the starting point for many polar
expeditions. Roald Amundsen ate his final meal here at Peppermollen (more on that later) before starting on his last, doomed voyage.

The visitor will find an outstanding selection of hotels here, as well
as some interesting, somewhat offbeat museums. And for outdoor
life, you need only cross the long bridge connecting the center of

Tromso to Tromsdalen, the island on which the Arctic Cathedral is located. Here, you can take a funicular up the mountain for beautiful views of Tromso and easy, pleasant hiking trails.

GETTING THERE

Langnes Airport is 10 minutes from the center of Tromso with frequent flights from Oslo, Bergen, and Trondheim. An SAS bus goes between the airport and the SAS Royal Hotel. It is scheduled to coordinate with most incoming and outgoing flights, but on Sundays, there is no service before 2:10 p.m. The coastal steamer stops here and there is also bus and ferry service from various towns. If you drive, you can get here on Highway #6 from southern Norway.

WHAT TO SEE AND DO

The center of Tromso is a lively place, with a market by the harbor and a cultural center with the theater of Tromso and Finnmark nearby. Tromso is included in most of the concert tours that swing through Norway.

The Tromso Museum

Located just a few minutes outside the center of town, the museum houses extensive exhibits on Lapp culture and on the wildlife and geology of northern Norway. One word of warning: the text accompanying the exhibits is not in English, but English tours may be available, so inquire. *Open June-Aug. daily 9 a.m.–6 p.m. Rest of the year 8:30 a.m.–3:30 p.m. The aquarium is open summer only from 10 a.m. until 5 p.m. daily.*

The Northern Lights Planetarium

This is the only planetarium in northern Norway, and the only one of its kind in the world. The program is given in English at 3 p.m. every day, but check with the information number, ☎ *10 000 or 76 000, for schedule changes.* A cinema-in-the-round film on the northern lights and the midnight sun is informative even though it is not in English. The beauty and eeriness of the northern lights and of the dark period is fascinating, and there is little need for dialogue. Much of the midnight sun footage was shot at Spitzbergen, which you can visit on an organized tour from Tromso.

The Tromso City Museum

Located in an 18th-century customs house on the site of Tromso's 13th-century fortifications, the museum offers exhibits on the culture and history of Tromso. English guides available. *Open June–Aug. daily 11 a.m.–3 p.m. Rest of year weekdays only 11 a.m.–3 p.m.*

The Polar Museum

Exhibits on polar life and the polar expeditions are displayed in a 19th-century customs/warehouse. *Open May 15–Sept. 15, 11 a.m.–3 p.m. daily. Rest of year daily 11 a.m.–3 p.m., closed weekends.*

The Tromso Folk Museum

Mortengarden. A fishing and agricultural farm with its original 18th-century house. *Open June–Aug. daily 11 a.m.–3 p.m.*

The Arctic Cathedral

The themes of northern Norwegian nature, culture and faith come together in this frosty white structure that rises above the town in icy splendor on the island of Tromsdal. At night, when all alight, it is particularly compelling. The large stained-glass windows are of interest. *Open June–mid Aug., Mon.–Sat. 10 a.m.–5 p.m.; Sun. 1 p.m.–5 p.m. The remainder of the year, open to the public on weekdays only from 10 a.m.–12 p.m.*

Tromso Cathedral

The wooden church you see west of the harbor, built in 1831 and one of Norway's largest wooden churches.

Fjellheisen

The cable car will carry you high above Tromso on Mount Floya for a fine panoramic view and good skiing and hiking. The funicular will take you up 420 meters, beyond the timberline. There is a restaurant up here as well.

Skavberg and Kvaloya (Whale's Island)

Near Straumhella, about 17 miles south of the center of town • Ancient stone carvings, some almost 4500 years old, illustrate the history and culture of the Samis (Lapps).

The Sami Land Folk Museum

Lapp souvenirs, handicrafts and silver. In a typical Lapp tent, by an open fire, you can sample reindeer soup and dried reindeer meat.

RECREATION

FISHING

Every Wednesday during June and July at 4:30 p.m., a 2-1/2-hour cruise will take you to fish in the water around Tromso and Kvaloya. Inquire at your hotel or through **Tromso Arrangement**, *Storgate 61.* You can rent fishing equipment at Straumhella, Kvaloya. There is a restaurant here open June–Aug. 4 p.m.–10 p.m. Mon.–Sat., and from noon until 10 p.m. on Sun. Cabins available for rent.

RENT BICYCLES

At **Barske Glaeder**, *Amtmannsgata,* ☎ *90 026.*

A THREE-DAY HIKING TRIP

The trip to Ovre Dividal departs Thurs. Day trips at Kvaloya go every Mon., Tues. and Wed. in the summer. Contact Tromso Arrangement at above address.

WALKING

You can pick up a guide to walking tours of Tromso at your hotel or at Tromso Arrangement. Good for the body and soul is a stroll across the long bridge connecting the center of town with Tromsdal. Especially breathtaking at night, with the Arctic Cathedral glowing like a beacon.

For something a little different, you can visit the **beer hall** in the Mack Brewery. It used to be a gathering spot for sea captains and sailors, and you can still get a beer as early as 9 a.m. and anytime until 5 p.m.

SHOPPING

Tromso has a number of fine shops. Maybe that's where it got its nickname, Paris of the North. For furs, try **Paul Figenschaus**, *Storgata 64*. A good selection with particular attention to Arctic furs and Lapp handicrafts. The **Veita Senter** is an enclosed shopping complex on Storgata. The **Husfliden** across from the SAS Royal Hotel is an excellent one.

WHERE TO STAY

The SAS Royal

This hotel is a deservedly popular spot. It is a lovely hotel, with all the amenities SAS hotels offer, but with a pleasant intimacy as well. The Charlotte Lobby Bar serves an inexpensive lunch. Charley's Bar and Grill is the main dining room of the hotel and one of the mainstays of the restaurant and nightlife scene in Tromso. The bar is extraordinarily pretty and stays open until 4 a.m. The disco is open six nights a week. Half the rooms overlook the water. There are nonsmoking rooms available. Rates will run about 1200NOK for a double. Royal Club rooms are only about 75NOK more than a double, and these have added amenities like turn-down service, use of Euro-Class check-in, and a separate breakfast room which is also open at night for complimentary coffee and soft drinks. Summer prices available.

Hotel With

One of the most charming new hotels I've come across. It was built in 1988 and is nautical and Norwegian in theme, with white walls and wood trim, and neat, ship-shape rooms. Nice touches like books in the room (most in Norwegian) and a beautiful spa with wood-burning stove make this a most welcoming place. The hotel has no restaurant, but breakfast is served every morning, and on weekdays a light cold table is available in the evenings. Summer rates.   *Moderate to expensive.*

The Hotel Saga

Another lovely but simple hotel, right in the center of town, near the harbor. The rooms are comfortable and bright with TV, coffee percolator and minibar. No alcohol is served. But the restaurant serves excellent food with the emphasis on Norwegian cuisine. At lunch a substantial cold buffet is available, as well as lighter fare at a cafeteria line.   *Moderate.*

Scandic Hotel

Near the airport • A modern hotel with an indoor pool and fitness center. A bright, new hotel, good for families. The Sea Gull restaurant is a good one.   *Moderate.*

The Grand Nordic Hotel

The rooms here vary, but most are spacious. Some are fresher and brighter than others. It's a lively place with the popular Papageno Disco and several restaurants. All rooms have TV, minibar and hair dryers. Twenty nonsmoking rooms are available. Expensive but with the Bonus Pass, you can get a room for even less than summer rates.   *Expensive.*

The Polar Hotel

An economy bed and breakfast hotel with modest rooms, all of which have TV and private bath. The Toppen Bistro on the top floor is a popular, moderately priced restaurant.

WHERE TO EAT

Tromso claims to have more restaurants per capita than any other city in the world, including Paris. I haven't even scratched the surface of this vast offering, but the ones I visited were excellent.

Peppermollen Mat & Vinhus

A fine fish restaurant in the house where Roald Amundsen stayed before he embarked on his last voyage. Pictures of Amundsen and other polar explorers crowd the walls in the dining room, which is decorated in a turn-of-the-century motif.

Arctandria

There is a downstairs pub and a more elegant upstairs dining room, which serves excellent fish as well as reindeer and lamb.   *Moderate.*

Brankos Mat & Vinhus

A cozy jumble of Yugoslavian decor. The food is, as expected, Yugoslavian and very good. A fine supply of Yugoslavian wine is also available. It is suggested that you book ahead.   *Moderate.*

Napoli

A reasonable and good Italian restaurant.

The Sea Gull

In the Scandic Hotel, this restaurant offers an international menu and a good view.

Caravelle

The gourmet restaurant of the SAS Royal Hotel. A member of the Chaine des Rotisseurs, it lives up to the demands of that gourmet society. Elegant and expensive.

Charley's Bar and Restaurant

In the SAS Royal Hotel, it is more casual and less expensive than Caravelle.

The Grand Restaurant

In the Grand Nordic Hotel, this is an old standby. Elegant and formal. The emphasis is on northern Norwegian specialties.

Grillstova

In the Saga Hotel, it is modest in appearance but the food is tasty with a focus on Norwegian specialties.   *Moderate.*

NIGHTLIFE

Plenty to do after dark or in the light, as the case may be, up here in the land of the midnight sun. It seems that each of the spots listed below enjoys a different night of popularity.

Tuesday is the night for the **SAS Royal**. But it's a lively place every night and
both the disco and Charley's Bar are open late Mon.–Sat. **Boccaccio/ Boccon-
cino** is a discotheque and nightclub and is open most nights till 2 a.m. and on
Fri. and Sat. until 4 a.m. On Mon. nights it is the place to be. The **Grand Nordic**
has a nightclub with dancing as well as a popular pub. It's the place to be on
Thurs. **Skarven's** ground-floor pub is popular with students. Often, European
performers appear here. **Prelaten** is another popular gathering spot. It is open at
lunch as well as late into the evenings. Frequent live entertainment. **Pingvinen**
(Penguin) is the Scandic Hotel's nightclub.

SPITZBERGEN

Spitzbergen is not for the faint of heart or body. Tourist boards and
guide books will warn you of harsh storms and the ever-present
threat of polar bears. Few accommodations aside from camping are
available, and the landscape, even in summer, is overshadowed by
snow-topped glaciers and frequently gray skies. But there are those
true adventurers who cannot resist this exotic spot, so if you are one
of that breed, risk it. It will be memorable.

Spitzbergen probably was discovered as long ago as 1194 by Icelanders but then neglected for centuries until, in 1596, the Dutch
explorer Willem Barents came upon this cluster of islands, writing
home that, "The climate is so harsh that the animals are completely
white." The whaling frenzy of the 17th and 18th centuries wreaked
havoc on the whale colony, and, in the late 19th century, a sea captain brought a load of coal from Spitzbergen to the mainland. A coal
rush began, attracting a breed as rough and violent as the Americans
who ran west for gold at nearly the same time. Finally, in 1904, a
gentleman from Michigan, John M. Longyear, came to Svalbard as a
tourist and saw the potential. It was Longyear who, with his Arctic
Coal Co., brought order and efficiency to the coal chaos.

The winter here is the longest and darkest of Norway. The dark period lasts from Nov. 14 to Jan. 29. But residents also are rewarded
with four months of sunlight from April 19 until Aug. 23. Only
three feet of the ground thaw in summer, yet almost 160 different
plant species thrive here. Picking the flowers is a serious violation
that could land you in jail, so resist the temptation and take home
photos instead.

Politically, Spitzbergen is unique. Forty-two countries share com-
mercial rights here thanks to the Norwegian Count Fritz Wedel
Jarlsberg who, as a delegate to the Paris Conference in 1925, gained
Norway complete sovereignty over the region of Svalbard, of which
Spitzbergen is a part. The 42 nations who signed the Svalbard Treaty
agreed that the land would not be used for military purposes and

that all 42 countries possess equal rights for the mining of minerals on the island.

The farther north you travel along the coast, the more spectacular the scenery becomes. See in particular the Kongsfjord with its three peaks, the Three Crowns, which hover over the monumental King's Glacier.

GETTING THERE

Flights depart from Tromso three times weekly. For accommodations and other information, contact Tromso Arrangements. Address given above.

THE NORTH CAPE

Tourist Information Office: *Nordkapphuset, Honningsvag.* ☎ *01 01 31 12. Also information available at the Kafjord ferry station.*

The trip, as you've come north from Bergen, has been so varied and extraordinary, that the North Cape itself may seem anticlimactic. It is, after all, simply a plateau, jutting out into the ocean just a bit farther than any other piece of land on the European continent, though if the truth be known, there is actually a little wisp of land that straggles about a fingernail's length farther. However, the North Cape is the piece of land that points directly north. From here it is about 1300 miles to the North Pole and the same distance to Oslo.

By the time you arrive at the North Cape or at Honningsvag, the town that serves as the gateway for the North Cape, you will be beyond the timber line. The most dramatic approach is by air. A small, but very sturdy Wideroe Air prop plane makes the flight from Tromso via Lakselv, taking the passenger from a landscape thick with pine and birch to one of naked rock and slopes only scantily clad with low growing brush. If you fly to Honnigsvag, the gateway to the North Cape, you will have flown over the eerie, mist-clad mountains and islands of the North Sea and its fjords, over scraps of land that float upon the water, over mountainous heaps of crumpled, snow-covered rock. The trees thin out and become smaller until from the air they look like moss, and then it is just moss—amber even in late August. You will see dark mountain lakes bordered like tea cups by the saucers of the mountains surrounding them. The flight takes the cape-bound travelers to Lakeselv, where they change to a 20-seat propeller plane for the flight to Honnigsvag. It's just a half hour flight, but it seems eons away from the rest of the world. Alternatively, you can take a bus or drive from Alta to Kafjord and then catch the ferry to Honnigsvag.

It is here in Finnmark that the largest Lapp population of Norway is found. Actually, it is the largest Lapp settlement in Scandinavia since two-thirds of the Samis (Lapps) live in Norway.

KARASJOK AND ALTA

Karasjok and Alta are the jumping-of spots for exploration of Finnmark and the Lapp country, and Alta, in particular, makes a good stopover point if you are driving to the North Cape. From here, you can drive or get a bus to Honningsvag, the town nearest the North Cape. You can also make an excursion to Kautokeino, one of the few remaining truly Lapp villages in Norway. Bus service is available. The Alta River is considered one of the world's great salmon rivers. For information on excursions to Lapp villages and on fishing, contact the tourist office.

WHAT TO DO

Karasjok is the center of Sami culture and politics. Visit the new museum which houses exhibits on Sami life and history. Reindeer sleigh rides, visits to a Sami camp and even dinner in a sod roof house can be arranged through Karasjok Adventures, *P.O. Box 912, 9/30 Karsjok, Norway.* ☎ *67400, FAX—(believe it or not)—66900.*

WHERE TO STAY

S.A.S. Karasjok Tourist Hotel
 9730 Karasjok, Norway; ☎ *67400; FAX 66408.*

The Alta Hotel
 A contemporary white cube of a building, centrally located near the North Cape Road, #6. It has been extensively renovated in the past two years. All rooms have private bath, TV/video. Restaurant, dance bar, lobby bar and disco. **Moderate.**

The Altafjord Turisthotel
 Has 68 modest rooms with private bath and TV. There is a bar and a restaurant in the hotel. **Moderate.**

Frokosthotellet
 Near the North Cape Road also, and located in a new shopping center. It is a simple, small hotel with five single rooms and five doubles, all with private bath and TV. **Moderate.**

HONNINGSVAG

The town of Honningsvag huddles in the embrace of the mountains on the island of Mageroy. Here, above the timberline, there is little to soften the landscape, but residents love the barren land that sweeps down to the sea. The population has swelled and ebbed in the years since 1900 when Honningsvag grew to be the center of the island. There are now about 4500 inhabitants. Fishing is the major industry and, of course, tourism, as thousands of tourists make the trek north in order to see the midnight sun at the top of Europe.

GETTING THERE

Flights from Tromso or Lakeselv, or buses from Alta, Lakselv, Hammerfest and Kirkenes via a ferry connection at Kafjord. Travelers coming from Finland can take a bus from Karasjok. A *word of warning*: Though there are usually three different ferry connections running from Kafjord in summertime, you may find quite a crowd. If you take a ferry departing Kafjord between 7:15 a.m. and 12:45 p.m., the lines may be shorter. The coastal steamer also stops at Honningsvag. Once here, visitors either take a bus or drive the 22 km road to the plateau. The road is excellent but narrow and at times runs quite high above the sea with several sharp bends. You should always be on the lookout for reindeer and ready to encounter strong sidewinds.

WHAT TO SEE AND DO

The North Cape is the major attraction, and the drive here is fascinating in itself. Buses leave from Honningsvag four times a day in summer. Check with FFR Honningsvag or FFR Hammerfest for schedule. The landscape is different from anything you've yet seen in Norway, and you will feel that in some way you are indeed at the end of the world, though of course you're not. You still have 1300 miles to go to the North Pole. On your way to the plateau, you will pass signs pointing to **Gjesvaer**, a small fishing village where you can take a boat to the bird mountain nearby. Those so inclined can detour to **Tufjord** to search for **whalebones** in this remnant of a 17th- and 18th-century whaling station. A few kilometers to the east is Skarsvag, the northernmost fishing village in the world. It is a popular camping spot.

The North Cape Hall

You should understand that your view of the plateau can be obscured by fog, which is not uncommon, and in order to get the best vantage point, you must enter the North Cape Hall. It is from here that you will view the lonely promontory that points due north and rises 307 meters from the Arctic Ocean. Here is the cliff that sailors long ago described as "a fortress which defended the continent of Europe against the mighty ocean..." and so it seems to do. A North Cape fee of about $12 for adults, $4 for children is required of all visitors to the plateau. Visitors are not allowed outside the building onto the plateau, so the only way to see it, except from the road as you approach, is from the hall. But there is quite a bit to see in the hall itself. The hall is built so that part of the plateau is exposed inside the building and forms a wall. Dioramas that recreate moments in Norwegian history and in the history of the North Cape are the work of Ivo Caprino, a very gifted artist and filmmaker whose work has enlivened stages, outdoor parks and museums throughout Norway. Also in the hall is the tiny Thai Museum, created in honor of the 1907 visit of King Chulalongkorn of Siam to the North Cape. The centerpiece of the exhibit is a rock on which the King's signature and the date of his visit are inscribed. It is the only item found from his entire European trip.

A 15-minute *supervideograf* film on the changing seasons of the North Cape is shown every half-hour, running continuously. You can become a member of the North Cape Royal Club, a pretty exclusive group since it's limited to people who have actually come to the North Cape. Among its privileges is the chance to have a drink in the northernmost bar in Europe. You will get a "diploma," commemorating your initiation, and you will come away with snazzy looking stickers and a little lapel pin. The subscription fee helps pay for maintenance of the cape and the hall.

At the hall, you will find a souvenir shop and a post office, from which you can mail cards with the exclusive North Cape postmark. The Compass restaurant here, with a panoramic view of the cape and the Arctic Ocean, is excellent. It's a fine place to have dinner in the summer, but you must book ahead.

The Nordkapp Museum
At Honningsvag, this contains exhibits on the cultural and commercial history of Finnmark. In summer there is usually an art exhibit and sale of Norwegian artwork.

Skarvberget
One of the longest tunnels in Norway.

Tana Solv
A silver workshop where you can buy jewelry and souvenirs. Located one kilometer south of Skarvberg tunnel. You will also find exhibits of old fishing equipment.

Repvag Camping and Cafeteria
The camping center has rowboats for hire.

Nordkapp Boatservice
Arranges photo safaris around the North Cape to Skarsvag. The trip lasts four hours. Other excursions are available as well, but you must book ahead. ☎ *47 84 72 008.*

WHERE TO STAY

The SAS Royal
Modest by SAS standards, but clean, comfortable and pleasant. Built in 1957 and last renovated in 1985, it has 174 rooms which vary greatly. Because so many visitors come as part of a group, the hotel makes a point of treating those individuals who come on their own quite specially, so that they will not feel overwhelmed or left out by the larger forces of group tours. There are a few nonsmoking rooms. In addition to the Caroline Restaurant, a small bistro offers table service to individual travelers in summertime. The hotel also has a nightclub.   *Moderate.*

Lagunen Motel and Camping
Cabins accommodating four-to-six people are simple, clean and cozy and all but five have private baths. No cooking facilities. The motel is located on

a gentle slope by a small pond. Restaurant and, in summer, a nightclub.

Moderate.

The Sifi Sommerhotell

On the water, a simple lodging with clean, modest rooms, most without private shower. Restaurant serving northern Norwegian food.

Moderate.

SWEDEN

City Hall is Stockholm's premier landmark.

AN INTRODUCTION

Clean, austere and dignified, Sweden is among the most civilized of countries with much to offer the tourist, from Stockholm, the beautiful capital, to the tranquil lake country or the mysterious and compelling island of Gotland with its 12 haunting church ruins rising above the sea. In the cozy southern region of Skane, the thatched cottages and lively residents are testimony to the centuries of Danish dominion, and the kingdom of glass is yet another lure for the tourist.

It is possible to get a sampling of all the faces of Sweden as air and rail travel are efficient and extensive. The visitor can fly or take a train from Stockholm to the upper reaches of Lapland in little more than an hour. And anywhere you can't go by plane, you can get to by boat. Boats are ubiquitous in Sweden. Almost every self-respecting Swede has a boat, and it seems that all of them are out in the Stockholm archipelago on a summer Sunday afternoon. But you too can be on the water, for the sightseeing tours from Stockholm extend far into the archipelago. And from Nynashamn, about 30 miles south of Stockholm, you can get a boat that will take you on a full-day trip through the islands or all the way to Gotland.

A SMALL DOSE OF HISTORY

Today it is easy to forget that Sweden, the country that embraces neutrality, was once an aggressive world power, which, under the leadership of Gusta Vasa, overthrew Denmark and routed the German Hanseatic League. In fact, the history of Sweden often seems to be an account of continuing battles with Denmark, occasionally interrupted by skirmishes with Norway and Finland. The chronicle is far too long and complex to cover here, but it is helpful to the tourist to understand at least something of Sweden's heroes and to recognize a few of the names he will encounter as he traipses through the castles and cathedrals of Sweden. So here is a capsule chronicle that will leave serious historians shaking their heads, and tourists at least a little more able to untangle the various *Gustavuses* they encounter.

Sweden's Viking conquests are well known and well chronicled. But after its glorious years as a Viking power, Sweden faltered during the Middle Ages under weak leaders and foreign influence. A brief golden age glittered for all Scandinavia during the Kalmar Union, which was established in 1397 under the regency of the extraordinary Queen Margaret. But the Union itself sowed the seeds for later trouble by opening Sweden to Danish domination; in addition, Queen Margaret's nephew, King Eric, squandered the political legacy of his aunt, leaving Sweden to the rapacious grip of foreign powers. It was Engelbrekt Engelbrektsson, the son of well-to-do German miners from Dalecarlia, who, in 1434, led a battalion of peasants, armed with scythes and pitchforks, through Sweden, successfully deposing King Eric and establishing a revolutionary council, the Riksdag, or People's Parliament. The Riksdag, meeting near Stockholm in 1435, elected Engelbrekt regent of Sweden and established the principle that all subjects of the king had both the right and the responsibility to establish and maintain law and order.

The peace that Engelbrekt achieved was short-lived; fewer than 100 years later, King Christian II of Denmark marched into south-western Sweden and on to Stockholm, finally declaring himself King of Sweden. His coronation took place amid days of celebration, which concluded with an invitation to the nobility of Stockholm to assemble at Stockholm Castle for what was to be, as one historian put it, "a banquet of another kind." Within hours, 82 people, most of them aristocrats and bishops, had been executed in the square of the Old Town. The next day, similar procedures were followed in provincial towns.

Soon after the Stockholm massacre, the young Gustavus Vasa, who had been kidnapped and imprisoned by King Christian, escaped and returned to Sweden only to hear that his own father had been executed by the king and his estates confiscated. The young man made his way to Dalecarlia where he embarked on a campaign to rouse the peasants in a rebellion. In the towns of Mora and Rattvik on the shores of Lake Siljan, Gustavus Vasa carried his cause to the people, who were disappointingly apathetic. In spite of his fervor, the peasants remained intractable, and Gustavus, in despair, set off on foot for Norway.

In the meantime, word came that King Christian was preparing to march on Dalecarlia and to carry his murderous tactics north, setting up a gallows in front of every aristocratic manor of the region. The terrified peasants quickly sent runners in snowshoes to overtake the young man who had promised to lead them against the Danes; and Gustavus Vasa returned to Mora to address the people of the province. The peasants, armed with scythes and pitchforks and with their proclaimed "King of the Dales and of Sweden" at their head, marched to Stockholm, meeting the Danes at the Dal, an estuary 75 miles northwest of Stockholm. The Danes, hearing of the ruggedness of these peasants, lost their confidence. Archbishop Trolle, who was leading the Danish forces, observed that "men who can eat wood and drink water will not yield to the Devil himself," and within a short time the Danes had withdrawn. It took two more years, but in 1523, Gustavus Vasa had succeeded in routing the Danes and in June of 1523, he was crowned king of Sweden.

Gustavus Vasa ruled over a Sweden that did not include the southern regions of Skane, Blekinge and Halland, which were Danish, nor the territories of Bohuslan, Jamtland and Jarjedalan, held by Norway, which was at the time under the aegis of Denmark. It was not until 1660 that King Charles X crossed the ice between Sweden and Denmark, surprising the Danes and forcing them into a treaty yielding the provinces of Skane, Blekinge, Halland and Bohuslan to Sweden. This treaty gave Sweden back her rightful territories and expanded her boundaries to the sea.

Gustavus Vasa's son Eric, who was crowned in 1561, brought a dubious fame to Sweden with his spurned pursuit of Queen Elizabeth of England. He also tried his luck with Mary Queen of Scots, who might have been well advised to take his offer. Eric's exploits at Kalmar Castle are usually gleefully recounted by the guide if you happen to make a trip there. Among other descendants of the Vasa line, Gustavus Adolphus is largely credited with developing modern military techniques in his successful campaign to add the German territories to his holdings in the Baltic. It was his daughter, Queen Christina, who abdicated in a dramatic gesture at Uppsala. Her cousin, Charles X, ascended the throne in her place. But it was Charles XII who was perhaps the most dashing of the Swedish kings, gaining fame over all of Europe for his Great Northern War, in which he conquered Poland and Latvia before embarking on a disastrous campaign against Russia. Though at the end he had bankrupted Sweden and lost most of her holdings, Charles XII was mourned desperately by the subjects who had worshipped him.

The Vasa dynasty endured until 1877 when the last of the line, the son of Gustavus IV, died without male heirs. His father, Gustavus IV, had abdicated in disgrace, largely responsible for the loss of Finland to Russia, and had lived out his life under an assumed name in Switzerland, dying impoverished in 1837. But the Gustavus who is perhaps best remembered after the great Gustavus Vasa is Gustavus III. He dreamed of raising Sweden to the cultural heights of the central European countries and modelled his court after Versailles. It was during his reign that the Swedish Academy was established, and it was Gustavus III who founded the Royal Opera and the Royal Ballet as well as the court theater of Drottningholm. And finally, it was Gustavus III whose assassination, by a young aristocrat during a fancy-dress ball at the Stockholm Opera House, was the inspiration for Verdi's opera *The Masked Ball.*

The Bernadotte dynasty was established by King Charles XIV John, Napoleon's marshal who had gained favor with the Swedish army because of his fair treatment of prisoners. It was also thought good policy to have a close associate of Napoleon on the Swedish throne in view of Sweden's desire to recover Finland from Russia. Charles XIV John came to Sweden in 1810 with his wife Desiree and their son Oscar, as regent for the aging Charles XIII, but Bernadotte, seeing that the king was too distracted and weak-willed to rule effectively, soon took over the day-to-day agenda of government. As king, Charles XIV John found himself fighting his former countrymen when he signed a secret treaty with Russia for help in acquiring Norway from Denmark. In return, the Swedish king promised to aid Russia in Germany against the French army. For the Swedish king the tactic was successful. Norway was ceded to Sweden in January of 1814, and did not really gain its independence again until this century, when it elected its own king, albeit a Danish one.

Finally, in this century, King Gustav V, who reigned until 1950, brought back the Vasa line through his wife, Victoria, who was the great-granddaughter of Sophia, the daughter of Gustavus IV. Today the king of Sweden is King Carl XVI Gustaf. He and his wife Queen Sylvie are among Europe's most popular monarchs.

The Constitutional Reform Act of 1974 makes the king a ceremonial head of state only. Another change in the Constitution in 1980 introduced a new right of succession, with the throne inherited by the eldest child regardless of sex. Government is left in the hands of the prime minister and a Parliament made up of five parties.

THE SWEDISH PEOPLE AND THEIR CULTURE

While not every Swede is like the angst-ridden, silent characters of the Ingemar Bergman films, the Swedish do tend to be a serious people. The Swedes are industrious and organized, and they reap the benefits of that diligence in a high standard of living. As with the other Scandinavians, much of the Swedish social life centers around the home and no one depicted the Swedish home more invitingly than Carl Larsson, Sweden's most popular painter and probably its most well-known, who painted scenes that were far from the melancholy images sometimes associated with life in Sweden. Larsson's frescoes for the foyer of the National Museum in Stockholm and the ceiling paintings in the Royal Opera House are substantial works. But Larsson gained more international recognition through the publication of a series of watercolors titled *A Home*. These paintings depicted the family life of the artist, his wife and their eight children at their home in Sundborn, and they have often been discounted as a kind of Swedish Norman Rockwell vision of life. The paintings, however, were not intended to be a chronicle of idyllic Swedish country life; instead they were the artist's vision of what life should be like. Growing up impoverished in the poor section of Stockholm, Larsson was all too well acquainted with the realities of life in Sweden in the latter half of the 19th century. His frequent bouts of depression were probably the result of the early deprivation, and perhaps his painting was an attempt to make life better than he knew it could be. But the paintings in *A Home* were important in another way, for they were also to become a major influence on the changing style of Swedish design. Larsson and his wife Karin, a textile artist, hated the dark interiors that were common in Swedish houses of the 19th century. The Larssons' light-filled house with its simple furnishings and white walls was a revolution to the Swedish eye, accustomed as it was to dark panelling and heavy tapestries. Much of what we think of as the Scandinavian country look was a direct result of Larsson's work. If it is possible, travelers should make a trip to Sundborn, Larsson's house outside Falun in the province of Dalarna. This is the house that was the inspiration and model for the collection *A Home*.

Another artistic pilgrimage can be made to the home of Anders Zorn at Mora on the shores of Lake Siljan. Zorn was a large, self-confident man with none of the self-doubt and melancholy that plagued Carl Larsson. Born to a family of substance in Mora in 1860, Sorn enjoyed early success with his portraits and was able to travel to Europe and the United States, earning commissions to paint portraits of Presidents Taft, Cleveland and Teddy Roosevelt, as well as Andrew Carnegie. However, Zorn remained attached to Sweden and particularly to Dalarna, where he and his wife built a house called Zornsgarden. The Dalecarlian influence is evident in his paintings of local life, endowed with a remarkable sensitivity for light and space. In his glowing, robust paintings of nudes, Zorn rejected the idea of melancholy and of moral degradation which seemed to pervade much of the spirit of 19th-century Scandinavia, and infused his subjects instead with what he called a "strong, healthy sensuality."

The works of playwright August Strindberg, on the other hand, corroborate all our preconceptions of the Swedish spirit. Brooding and pessimistic, his plays and his famous novel *Red Room*, named for the red room (which has recently reopened at the Berns Salonger in Stockholm), pick at the fabric of upper-class Swedish life. His characters are tormented and degraded, much as he himself was when he finally lapsed into madness. Another writer, Nobel Prize winner Selma Lagerlof (who was the first woman to win the prize), has succeeded in painting a more rounded picture of the Swedish soul, though the settings of her novels are largely confined to her native Varmland. Lagerlof's *The Story of Gosta Berling* has become a modern epic for Sweden and has recently been staged as a stunning ballet that epitomizes everything Swedish, from the spirit of the story to

the music, to the staging and set design. If it is performed while you
are in Stockholm, be certain to see it.

The poet Carl Mikael Bellman, who was a frequenter of the court
of Gustavus III, has become a kind of national institution, though
his reputation rests more on his legendary drinking prowess and on
the impromptu verses he created while making the rounds of Stockholm's pubs and bars with his friends than on memorable poetry.
Bellman has been called the Robert Burns of Sweden, perhaps because he set many of his poems to music and sang them to his own
accompaniment on the lute. Because they are virtually untranslatable, little is known of Bellman's work outside Sweden, but his is a
name the visitor should recognize, mainly because it crops up so frequently as the name of restaurants or bars. It might not have been
the way Bellman himself would have chosen to be remembered, but
he has at least achieved a certain immortality.

In science, the name of Anders Celsius is familiar even to those of
us who live with the Fahrenheit thermometer scale. Karl von Linne
(Carolus Linnaeus) was the botanist who came up with the system of
classifying plants that is used to this day. His house and garden in
Uppsala are open to the public. Emanuel Swedenborg started his career as a scientist in the field of natural history, but his philosophical
mind turned to loftier concerns and, with the publication in 1745 of
his book *Culture and the Love of God*, he resigned his position as as-
sessor of mines and began writing on church doctrine, asserting that
his words were direct revelations from God. After his death, the
Swedenborgian Church was established.

But perhaps Sweden's most significant contribution to intellectual
pursuit is the Nobel Prize. In 1895, Alfred Nobel made a will, which
declared that a prize was to be awarded in each of five disciplines:
chemistry, physics, medicine, literature and peace. The winners were
to be selected by the Royal Swedish Academy of Sciences (chemistry
and physics), the Nobel Assembly of the Karolinksa Institute (medicine), the Swedish Academy (literature), and the Norwegian Nobel
Committee, Oslo (peace). In 1968, the Bank of Sweden established
an additional prize for economics in honor of the 300th anniversary
of the bank. With the exception of the Peace Prize, which is given in
Oslo, all prizes are awarded in Stockholm on December 10th, the
anniversary of Alfred Nobel's death. A banquet in the City Hall follows the awards.

TRAVEL ESSENTIALS

Swedish Travel and Tourism Council: *655 Third Ave., New York, NY 10017,* ☎ *(212) 949-2333. Most of the towns listed in this book have tourist information offices at central locations. To write ahead to those offices for which mailing addresses are not given here, consult the Swedish Tourism Council in New York.*

GETTING THERE

SAS flies to Stockholm nonstop from Newark and from Chicago and Seattle, with connections through Copenhagen for Stockholm and Gothenburg. **American Airlines** offers nonstop service to Stockholm from Chicago. **Delta** flies from JFK in New York through Copenhagen. And **Finnair** flies from New York JFK to Stockholm via Helsinki. Another possibility is **British Air** from Seattle with a connection in London.

GETTING AROUND

Air and rail service is extensive throughout Sweden. **Linjeflyg** (LIN) and **SAS** fly the domestic routes in Sweden. From the US, book LIN flights through SAS or any travel agent. **Swedish State Railways** (SJ) is the state-operated railway system. The major routes are: Stockholm–Gothenborg four and a half hours (or just three hours if you take the new high-speed train); Stockholm-Malmo six and three quarters hours; Gothenborg–Malmo four hours; and Stockholm–Kiruna 19 hours.

Boat services run regularly on the lakes and canals between the mainland and the islands. For reservations to Gotland, contact the **Bergen Line,** ☎ *(212) 986-2711,* or make the booking through your travel agent. The Swedish Tourist Board has a schedule of all boat traffic. The **Gota Canal** links Gothenborg on the west coast with Stockholm on the east. The canal steamers have become a very popular way to make this journey. See the section in this book on Gothenborg for information on the steamers. In addition, boats ply the waters between islands and towns, and there are boats going back and forth daily between Stockholm and Finland. (These are discussed in more detail in the introductory sections to Finland.)

Bicycles can be rented in most towns, and the Swedish Touring Club sells bicycle packages, which include bicycle rental, overnight accommodations and meals in several different areas. Bikes may be taken aboard trains at the cost of no more than $8 to any destination in Sweden. Swedish Touring Club, *Box 25, S-101 20 Stockholm, Sweden,* ☎ *(08) 227200.*

Car rental can be arranged in advance from North America and ready for pickup in Sweden, or rented in Sweden. Speed limits are 110, 90, or 70 kilometers per hour outside urban areas and 50 kilometers per hour in cities and towns. Slower limits are posted in some areas. Expressway speed limits are 110 kilometers. *Heavy penalties are imposed on drivers under the influence of alcohol or drugs. Permissible blood-alcohol levels are so low that two cans of beer can put a driver over the legal limit. Swedes do not drink at all if they are going to drive.* Seat belts are required and headlights must be on day and night. In case of accidents, the emergency number for motorists throughout Sweden is ☎ *90000*. This is to be used only for accidents. For breakdowns, motorists should call the local number of Larmtjanst, the organization which provides 24-hour service nationwide.

MONEY MATTERS

Sweden's recent economic woes are no secret. For the tourist, this means that raging inflation and increased taxes have compounded to make this one of Europe's costliest countries to visit. However, as of this printing, the exchange rate has become quite a bit more favorable for Americans. In addition, SAS has reduced its domestic full fares by six percent, not an incredible savings, but better than before. SJ, the Swedish railroad, has slashed its fares by eight and a half percent, and the ferry line to Gotland, Gotlandslinjen, has cut its low-season fares by 18 percent and its in-season by 10 percent. Taxis in Stockholm have also reduced their charges, and the RESO and Countryside Sweden hotel chains have cut their rates. The Swedish Krona, written SEK, is the currency of Sweden. At the time of this writing, the exchange rate was 7.4SEK to the U.S. dollar. The value added tax, MOMS, adds over 18 percent to all bills, whether for clothing, food or hotel. Service is included in restaurant bills, but in Sweden, it is customary to leave a little change if the service has been good. Taxi drivers expect an eight to 10 percent tip. Banks are open in Sweden from 9:30 a.m.–3:00 p.m. Monday–Friday, with additional hours on Thursday from 4:00 p.m.–5:30 p.m. Banks and money exchanges at railroad stations and airports usually keep longer hours.

TAX-FREE SHOPPING

This works the same way as in the other Scandinavian countries. Many shops selling glass will ship your purchases home tax free. There is a minimum amount required to qualify for tax-free shopping. Be sure to bring your passport when shopping at a tax-free store. Refunds are paid at airports, ship terminals and on board ships leaving Sweden, as well as at Copenhagen, Oslo and Helsinki airports, but they must be obtained before leaving Scandinavia.

HOLIDAYS

Banks, post offices, government offices and most businesses are closed on New Year's Day; Epiphany; Good Friday; Easter Sunday and Monday; the first of May; Ascension Day; Whit Sunday and Monday; Midsummer Day; All Saint's Day; Christmas Day; and Boxing Day.

HOTELS AND OTHER ACCOMMODATIONS

Visitors arriving in Stockholm with no reservations can check with the tourist information center at Sweden House or at the **Accommodations Service Center** in the Central Station. Hotels in the big cities are expensive, but once you are in more rural areas, the rates go down.

For youth hostels, contact *Hostelling International American Youth Hostels, P.O. Box 37613, Washington, D.C. 20013.* ☎ *202-783-6161.*

Discount passes at many hotel chains and groups are available throughout Sweden. Travelers purchasing **Scandinavian Bonus Passes** before coming to

Sweden can receive a 15-to-40 percent discount off the rates at many hotels. You can purchase Scandinavian Bonus Passes through your travel agent or through ScanAm World Tours, ☎ *800-545-2204* or Eurocruises ☎ *800-688-EURO.* Best Western Scandinavia Hotel Cheques in Sweden offer flat rates in double rooms for holders of the **Best Western Cheques**. These can also be purchased through travel agencies or through ScanAm World Tours. **Scandic Hotel Cheque** allows you to make reservations ahead and the rates are per room rather than per person. Contact Holiday Tours of America ☎ *800-677-6454.* **The** Reso Hotels have a plan for family discounts which allow a family of four to stay in a double room for a very reasonable rate which includes breakfast. Contact Delta Supranational Hotels ☎ *800-843-3311.* In Sweden, the number is ☎ *011-46-08-720-88-80.* **Countryside Sweden** is a group of 33 hotels or manor houses throughout Sweden. For information and booking, contact ScanAm World Tours or Scantours ☎ *800-223-7226.* For manor house stays, contact Scantours ☎ *800-233-SCAN* or Romantik Hotels ☎ *800-826-0015.* Another option is vacation villages, which are apartment complexes, something like condominiums. Often there are swimming pools and other recreational facilities. Each unit has a kitchen and four–10 best. There is usually a restaurant on the premises or nearby. Contact ScanAm World Tours ☎ *800-545-2204* or Scantours ☎ *800-223-7226.* For Farm House Holidays and bed and breakfast accommodations, contact Borton Overseas ☎ *800-843-0602.* The same outfit can also book you into holiday homes and cottages which are usually located by the water or in the mountains. These are popular with Scandinavians so book early.

I have classified the hotels in Sweden according to price as listed below. In small towns and rural areas, I have tried to give an approximate idea of the rates for a double room, but these are, of course, subject to change. The rates are based on an exchange rate of 6.36SEK to the US dollar.

Very Expensive: -------------------- More than 1400SEK

Expensive: --------------------------------- 900-1395SEK

Moderate: ----------------------------------- 600-800SEK

Inexpensive: ---------------------------- Less than 600SEK

LANGUAGE

Swedish is the most universal of the Scandinavian languages, so if you wish to learn a few phrases that will serve you in all the countries, Swedish is the language to choose. Almost everyone in Sweden speaks excellent English, so you need not worry aside from learning a simple *tak* for thank you.

FOOD AND DRINK

The **smorgasbord** is the great culinary contribution of Sweden. The other Nordic countries have their versions of this buffet, but Sweden is the originator. Instead of heaping your plate with all the different items, it is customary to make several trips to the buffet table, taking first the cold fish, of which there are variations of herring, salmon and other smoked and marinated fish. Next, return for the salads, cold meats and cheeses. Then try the hot dishes, and finally have some dessert. For each course, you take a clean plate. Actually, *smorgas* is the word for the open sandwich that the Swedish eat at any time. These are not as elaborate as the Danish smorrebrod, but rather a slice of bread with butter and a slice of cheese or sausage. The Swedes eat smorgas with morning coffee, or as a quick lunch or between-meal snack.

Crayfish are the national obsession of Sweden. During the month of August, more than three million tons of these tiny, lobster-like creatures are caught, boiled, and served to virtually every Swede in the nation. The crayfish season is legislated by the Riksdag, the Swedish Parliament. It begins at midnight on the second Wednesday of August and is usually finished by the end of the month, though it is permissible to sell crayfish until December. Crayfish are served cold in the dill, vinegar and salt in which they were cooked, and it is customary to suck out all the juice and then eat the meat. If you can get yourself invited to a *kraftskiva*, by all means go to this most Swedish of celebrations. These are crayfish parties held outside under paper lanterns with heaps of the tiny delicacies to munch on, along with aquavit and beer, bread and butter and cheese. The custom is to down a shot of aquavit after eating each claw. Lingonberries are another Swedish favorite, usually served as a jam accompaniment for pancakes and waffles, but also with meat dishes.

Swedish beer is classified according to alcoholic content. Klass III is the strongest; Klass I the weakest. Wine and liquor are exorbitant in Sweden, as they are in all Scandinavian countries. The government owns the liquor stores, and the taxes on alcohol are very high. Even the restaurants purchase most of their wine and liquor through the state-owned monopoly, so their cost is passed on to you with, of course, a sizable mark-up.

MIDSUMMER CELEBRATIONS

Midsummer is celebrated throughout Scandinavia, but the Swedes seem to have invented it. Celebrations begin in the morning of Midsummer Eve when Swedes decorate their houses, cars, churches, virtually everything that stands still and a few that move, with flowers and branches. In the afternoon, they gather around the maypole in the center of the village, and once the pole is raised, the dancing begins and goes on and on. Dalarna is particularly known for its Midsummer celebrations, and thousands of tourists flock there. An easier place to celebrate, if you are not planning to go as far as Dalarna, is at Skansen, the park in the center of Stockholm. Midsummer meals consist of various kinds of pickled herring, boiled new potatoes with dill and for dessert, fresh strawberries. The traditions associated with Midsummer revolve around its supernatural attributes. Midsummer is supposed to be a night of magical events. The dew and some plants are thought to possess properties that will cure illnesses. It is said that ferns bloom only on Midsummer Eve. And to discover whom you will marry, pick a bouquet of seven or nine different flowers from that number of meadows or ditches and put it beneath your pillow. The person you dream of will become your spouse. If you don't want to gather posies, try eating "dream herring" to achieve the same effect.

STOCKHOLM

The Royal Palace houses several museums, royal apartments and the Hall of State.

STOCKHOLM: THE TOP TEN

Stockholm has more to see and do than any tourist can ever hope to cover. And if it is a gloriously sunny day, you might want to scrap everything and head out into the archipelago. But for the diligent sightseer, here is a list of the major attractions. Don't just settle for these, however. You will not know Stockholm until you have wandered the quirky streets of Gamla Stan, sat on a bench in Kungstradgarden, or hopped in a boat for a quick trip to anywhere. These sights are described in detail under "What to See and Do."

- City Hall
- Drottningholm Palace and Court Theater
- The Kaknas Tower on Djurgarden
- Kungstradgarden
- Gamla Stan with the Royal Palace, the Cathedral and Stortorget
- Millesgarden
- The National Museum of Art
- The Royal Opera House (and a performance if possible)
- Skansen Open-air Museum
- The Wasa Museum

Stockholm Information Service, *Sweden House, Kungstradgarden. Open weekdays from 9:00 a.m.–5:00 p.m., weekends from 9:00 a.m.–2:00 p.m.* Call them for updates on prices, sightseeing tours, etc. Information: ☎ *(46)8 789 24 90, FAX: (46)8 789 24*91. For bookings with the Excursion Shop: ☎ *(46)8 789 24 15; FAX (46) 8 789 24 91.*

STOCKHOLM CARD

At the Tourist Information Office in Sweden House, pick up a Stockholm Card and the booklet that accompanies it. The Stockholm Card entitles the holder to discounts on just about every sight and amusement in town as well as unlimited free travel on the efficient and immaculate subway, on buses and some trains. Two free sightseeing trips are also part of the package.

WHAT'S ON TODAY

For information on activities in Stockholm, ☎ *08 22 18 40.*

DIRECTORY

American Embassy • *Strandvagen 101,* ☎ *(0) 8 783 53 00.*

Banks • In Stockholm banks are generally open Monday–Thursday from 9:00 a.m.–5:30 p.m. and Friday from 9:00 a.m.–3:00 p.m.

Car Rental • Avis at *Sveavagen 61,* ☎ *34 99 10;* **Hertz** at Master *Samuelsgatan 67,* ☎ *24 07 20;* **Europcar**, *Birger Jarlsgatan 59,* ☎ *23 10 70.*

Currency Exchange • Try to exchange currency at banks rather than at your hotel as the hotels pass on the fee that they must pay the banks. There is an exchange office at the Central Station open every day from 8:00 a.m.–9:00 p.m. American Express at *Birger Jarlsgatan 1* changes money and some post offices have exchanges.

Emergencies • For police, ambulance and fire, ☎ *90 000.* For car towing, Larmtjanst, ☎ *24 10 00.*

Hotel Booking • Hotellcentralen in the Central Railway Station. Open daily 8:00 a.m.–9: p.m., ☎ *24 08 80.*

Medical Help • Tourists can obtain medical help at the hospital in the district in which they are staying. For information, call Medical Care: ☎ *44 92 00.*

Parking • Parking is allowed at marked spaces on weekdays from 8:00 a.m.–6:00 p.m.

Pharmacies • For 24-hour service, C.W. Scheele, *Klarabergsgatan 64,* ☎ *24 82 80.*

Taxis • To order a taxi, ☎ *15 00 00.* To reserve in advance, ☎ *15 04 00.* There is a 25 kr. charge for the trip to pick you up. And taxi drivers expect an eight-to-10 percent tip. It can be difficult to get a taxi in Stockholm, so allow plenty of time.

Temperature • The average temperature in Stockholm in January is 26°F and in July, 64°F.

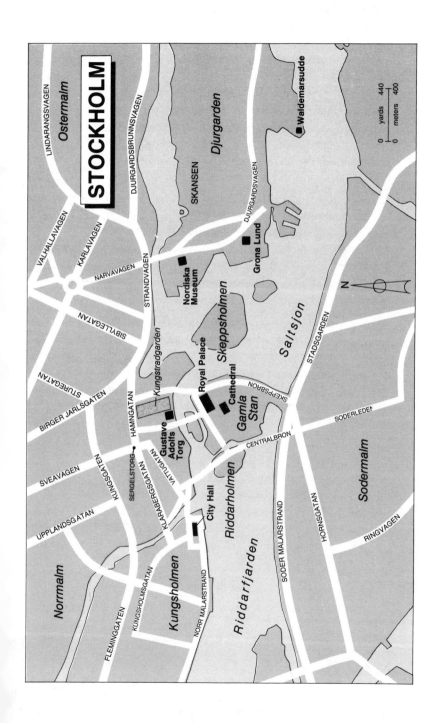

STOCKHOLM

Ostermalm

LINDARANGSVAGEN

DJURGARDSBRUNNSVAGEN

Djurgarden

Waldemarsudde

SKANSEN

VALHALLAVAGEN

KARLAVAGEN

NARVAVAGEN

STRANDVAGEN

Grona Lund

DJURGARDSVAGEN

Nordiska Museum

Skeppsholmen

SIBYLLEGATAN

STUREGATAN

Kungstradgarden

Saltsjon

STADSGARDEN

Royal Palace

BIRGER JARLSGATAN

HAMNGATAN

Cathedral

SKEPPSBRON

SVEAVAGEN

KUNGSGATEN

SERGELSTORG

Gustave Adolfs Torg

Gamla Stan

SODERLEDEN

VIATTUGATAN

KLARABERGSGATAN

CENTRALBRON

UPPLANDSGATAN

City Hall

Riddarholmen

HORNGATAN

Sodermalm

RINGVAGEN

Norrmalm

KUNGSHOLMSGATAN

Kungsholmen

NORR MALARSTRAND

Riddarfjarden

SODER MALARSTRAND

FLEMINGGATEN

N

0   yards   440
0   meters   400

Tipping • The cloakroom charge runs from four–six kr. All other service charges are included in the bill except as mentioned above for taxis. It is always appreciated if you leave a bit of change for the waiter, however.

Many European cities are beautiful in their uniformity: the gray stone facades and mansard roofs of Paris; the biscuit-colored buildings of Florence. But Stockholm is lovely in its variety. Modern block-and-glass structures sit beside dark stone buildings, ancient red-washed houses and a persimmon-tinged cathedral. Spires, onion domes, pointed roofs and curved gables punctuate the skyline. At ground level, the water laps the stone banks and rushes under the bridges.

Called "the Venice of the North" or "the City that Floats on the Water," Stockholm is a city of elegant beauty, a city in which almost every building seems important, or at least appears to have been constructed with care. From the pink facade of the 16th-century **Riddarhus** to the baroque **Opera House**; from the orange stucco of **St. Jacob's Church** to the sternly elegant facade of the **Royal Palace**, the beauty of Stockholm is extraordinary, and of infinite variety.

Stockholm yields its mysteries to the walker and explorer who delights in following the winding streets and crossing the hundreds of bridges. The streets, no matter how convoluted, can only go on for so long before they—or you—wind up in the water, so it is not hard to find your way. And somehow, higgledy-piggledy as it might seem, this division into islands lends a kind of eccentric pattern to the whole place.

In 1187, King Canute I of Sweden built a wooden fort on a small island at the point where **Lake Malaren** pours into the Baltic Sea and named it Stockholm. It was Birger Jarl who, in the 13th century, established Stockholm as the principal city of Sweden. He built a fortress on the island now known as Gamla Stan and effectively stopped the invasions from the Baltic coasts, which had until then wrought havoc on the city. Finally, in 1523, Gustavus Vasa established Stockholm as the capital of Sweden.

GETTING THERE

SAS flies direct to Stockholm from New York, Chicago, Los Angeles and Seattle. American Airlines flies direct from Chicago. Arlanda Airport is the airport that serves both domestic and international traffic. Its location 45 kilometers north of Stockholm makes for an expensive (around 250SEK) cab ride into town. An economic alternative is the airport bus, which will take you to the center of Stockholm, near the Central Station, and which at last check was 30SEK. There is a subway at the Central Station and also, at last check, a shuttle bus to several hotels from the station. There is, of course, a cab stand also at the station, but travelers should be aware that it can be difficult to get a taxi in the center of town, especially on a holiday or a pretty day. Another option is to take one of the private car services offered by SAS and several private companies to and from the airport. These will run about 185SEK for the first person. The second person to or from the same stop goes for half. Incoming passengers can pick up the service at the limousine counter in the arrival hall. Your hotel can arrange the car on your return flight.

GETTING AROUND

The subway system is immaculate and efficient, and your Stockholm Card entitles you to free rides. Some of the stations are attractions in themselves, with interesting artwork and innovative design. The line from Kungstradgarden to Alkalla and Hjulsta is called the world's longest art exhibition. Among other stations of note are Kungstradgarden T-Centralen, Radhuset, Fridhemsplan and Solna Centrum. All lines converge at T-Centralen. Buses and boats also provide easy ways of moving about this city of islands. And your feet will also serve you well as most of the places of major interest are within walking distance of one another.

SIGHTSEEING TOURS

Stockholm offers a cornucopia of sightseeing tours. Tourists would do well to take at least one and possibly two in order to get an idea of the layout of the city and to have a few hours on the water, which is as much a part of the city as the streets. You can choose from boat and bus tours, most of which are excellent. The only trip I think is a bit of a waste of time is Under the Bridges of Stockholm. You will cover much of the same territory on other tours and get farther. From October–April, an excellent bus tour leaves every morning from the **Sweden House** and picks up tourists at the Grand, Sheraton, Continental, Royal Viking and Sergel Plaza hotels. Check with the hotel for time of departure. Other bus tours available all year long are those run by **City Sightseeing** at the Royal Opera House. These are given every day from late March until early November and on weekends the rest of the year. One, leaving at 9:30 a.m. from the Royal Opera, includes a short walk through the Old Town, a visit to the cathedral and city hall. The other, which departs at 1:30 p.m., includes a visit to the State Apartments of the Royal Palace and a trip to Millesgarden, the residence-museum of sculptor Carl Milles. Both tours leave from in front of the Royal Opera House, but they also offer pick-up at several hotels. Check with your hotel or with the City Sightseeing Office at the Royal Opera, ☎ *11 70 23* or *21 20 06.*

Stockholm Sightseeing *at Skeppsbron 20,* ☎ *24 04 70,* also offers bus and boat tours as well as boat trips to Drottningholm and through the archipelago. Tours are also available to Sigtuna, Skokloster and Uppsala. (see "Excursions from Stockholm.")

The Tourist Line or **Turistlinjen** bus has 14 stops near the major attractions, so you can fashion a do-it-yourself-tour. In summer, buses run daily every 10 minutes, and in winter on Sundays only every 20 minutes. A similar service by boat runs in summertime. The Stockholm Card allows holders free rides on both.

In June and July, the **Stockholm Municipal Museum** sponsors guided walks and boat tours in various parts of the city. Inquire at the museum or at the tourist information office. The **Old Town Guide Group** is an organization of licensed Stockholm guides who lead evening walks through the Old Town of Stockholm. These tours, which are conducted in English, leave every evening at 6:30 p.m. from the Obelisk on Slottsbacken in Old Town. The cost is 30SEK for adults.

The **S.S. *Blidosund***, a 1910 steamer, offers various cruises ranging from music cruises on summer evenings to Christmas tours with smorgasbord. The restaurant serves Swedish fare. For information, contact the S.S. *Blidosund*, *Hamngatan 4*, ☎ *08 11 71 13* or the Stockholm Service, ☎ *08 789 20 00*.

WHAT TO SEE AND DO

The list of sights is endless. Stockholm has a museum for every esoteric and quirky interest imaginable, from a tobacco museum to a teenage museum. A bit of editing is necessary unless you plan to spend your life here, which you might want to do once you have seen this glorious city. Don't get carried away, however. Word has it that the wait for an apartment in the city is 200 years. For the sake of your friends and relatives who might be expecting you back home within the next few years, I've whittled the list down to the absolute "must do's," followed by a few suggestions for "ought-to-do's" if you have the time.

As Stockholm is a city of islands linked by bridges and canals that are easily accessible to the walker, I have listed the major sights by island to facilitate the sightseer's task. At the end of each sightseeing section, you will find one or two suggestions for places to eat. A more complete listing of restaurants is found in the "Restaurants" section of this chapter. For those so inclined, there are many beaches in the Stockholm area. The tourist office will give you information on those.

TOUR NO. 1: NORRMALM AND OSTERMALM

Head first for Kungstradgarden, which is the center of life in Stockholm. **Sweden House** is located here. You can enter from either Kungstradgarden or Hamngatan. This is the place to pick up all your information on Stockholm. It is pleasant to linger in the park here. In winter, an ice-skating rink is set up in the middle of the park. In summer, the area around the fountains draws office workers and mothers with children to soak up the summer sun and enjoy the lively scene. Outdoor cafés line the park, and on weekends there is usually a band concert or some other form of entertainment. Nearby is the **Royal Opera House**, where there is usually a ballet or opera so that non-Swedish can have an evening's cultural entertainment. From Kungstradgatan, you can stroll along the water in order to reach two of Stockholm's principal art museums.

The National Museum of Art

Located within walking distance of Kungstradgarden, along S. Blasie Holmshamnen • The building, little more than a century old, is of interest in itself, designed to take advantage of its waterside location, its loggia-like entrance and wide staircase decorated with frescoes by Carl Larssen. As you climb the stairs, stop and turn around to look out through the tall windows onto the waterfront scene. The excellent collection of Swedish painting and sculpture is on the second floor, along with a sizable display of the great masters, including fine representations of Rembrandt and the Flemish painters and several impressionist paintings. The department of drawings and graphic arts contains over 100,000 pieces. Many of the old masters' drawings were brought to Sweden by architect Carl Gustaf Tessin. The graphics collections contain pieces from the 15th century to the present, with emphasis on the 17th and 18th centuries and contemporary Swedish works. My favorite exhibits are the applied arts collections on the first floor. The museum possesses a fine collection of 16th-century tapestries, the largest collection of European porcelains in Scandinavia (including Meissen and Sèvres), a majolica pottery service from Urbino, and many examples of Swedish glass and silver. The 20th-century collections include glass and ceramics, works by Alvar Aalto, Tyra Lundgren, Simon Gate, and Edvard Hald. There is no contemporary painting or sculpture in this museum since that collection was moved to the Museum of Modern Art, nearby. *Open Tuesday 10:00 a.m.–9:00 p.m., Wed–Sunday 10:00 a.m.–4:00 p.m. Closed Monday.*

The Museum of Modern Art

On Skeppsholmen, just across the bridge from the National Museum • The museum is not large, but it has a solid collection of the big names of the 20th century. There is a pleasant self-serve cafê. *Open Tuesday–Friday 11:00 a.m.–9:00 p.m.; Saturday and Sunday 11:00 a.m.–5:00 p.m. Closed Monday.*

If you are hungry: Along Kungstradgatan, you will find several casual restaurants with outdoor terraces. The **Cafê Opera** in the Royal Opera House is a less extravagant, but still not inexpensive, alternative to the opulent **Operakallaren**. **Vau de Ville**, on the corner of Kungstradgarden, is a popular place for Stockholm residents. The menu is varied and prices moderate to expensive. Farther along Hamngatan is **Martini**, a lively, upgrade bistro with a covered terrace and an indoor restaurant. Good salads as well as heftier entrees. My favorite for lunch is **KB** at *Smalandsgatan 7*. It is located in the House of Artists, and the walls were decorated years ago by the artists who frequented the restaurant. The selection is varied, and the prices moderate to expensive. Fast food has come to Stockholm also, but you need not settle for MacDonald's if you are in a hurry. **Matpalatset**, which means food palace, offers a wide choice in attractive surroundings. It is located near Norrmalmstorg. Here, in addition to Swedish fare, you can have Mexican, Italian or just about anything that strikes your fancy. Beer and wine are available. Self-service. Inexpensive. In Ostermalmshallen, the old market, which you should visit, are two popular, casual lunch spots, **Gerda's** and **Lisa Elmqvist**. Hungry shoppers crowd around the shared tables, slurping up shrimp, herring and other offerings from the sea.

TOUR NO. 2: KUNGSHOLMEN

This is a small island that boasts a big attraction, the extraordinary **City Hall** of Stockholm. Visitors can only go through the city hall on the tour which is given at 10 A.M. every day and also at noon on Sunday. This square-towered hall, which seems to float on the water, is Stockholm's premier landmark, and the place where the Nobel Prize Awards Banquet is held. If you see no other sight in Stockholm, you must see this.

Construction of the building, which was designed by Ragner Ostberg, began in 1911 and was not completed until 1923, when the hall was inaugurated in conjunction with the 400th anniversary of Gustavus Vasa's entry into Stockholm. The three crowns that top the tower are the crest of Sweden. On the south facade, you will see the Engelbrekt column, which was created by Christian Eriksson after the architect, Ragner Ostberg, rejected Carl Milles' design. Milles' model for the statue is at Millesgarden. Inside the hall, the tour will take you through the Council Room, where the City Council of Stockholm sits, the Prince's Gallery and the Blue Hall. But the most glorious chamber is the extraordinary Golden Hall, paved from floor to ceiling with 19 million golden mosaic tiles. The fresco on the north wall is of the Queen of Lake Malaren. You can rent out the Golden Hall if you wish for several thousand kronor. It would make a splendid setting for a wedding, and you can order any of the menus from the past Nobel Prize Banquets. *The tower, which houses a museum and offers a splendid view of Stockholm, is open from May through the first two weeks in September from 10:00 a.m.–3:00 p.m.*

If you're hungry: All this talk of Nobel banquets might set stomachs grumbling. The restaurant that caters the Nobel banquet is located in the cellar of the city hall. Called **Stadshuskallaren**, it is a lovely, rather elegant place. The prices are high, but the food is good. Check to make sure that it is open for lunch on the day you plan to be there.

TOUR NO. 3: GAMLA STAN

Just across a bridge from Norrmalm, is Gamla Stan or Old Town, the site of the Royal Palace and Stockholm Cathedral as well as of the Stock Exchange and the Swedish Academy, where the Nobel Prize judgments are made. Gamla Stan's narrow, winding streets with interesting antique shops, boutiques and restaurants make this a popular spot for Stockholm residents as well as tourists. Take time just to walk through the narrow cobbled streets here.

Stortorget

This is the main old square lined with colorful and eccentric ancient buildings. In 1520, this square was the site of Danish King Christian II's "bloodbath of Stockholm," in which more than 80 members of the Swedish nobility were executed. The white stones on the facade of the red house in the square are said to mark the number of victims. The large, shell-colored building is the Stock Exchange. Walk down Vasterlanggatan, the main street of Old Town with shops, restaurants and offices.

The Royal Palace

The present palace was built in the 18th century over a period of more than 60 years after the original palace was destroyed by fire. The design was initiated by the architect Nichodemus Tessin the Elder, and was completed, after his death by his son. The main attraction is the **royal apartments** with their fine furnishings, tapestries and portraits. The vaults that were used as the foundations of Birger Jarl's original fortress still stand beneath the

present royal palace and within them are several museums. Visit the **Treasury** with the crown jewels. *It is open May–September, weekdays and Saturday from 10:00 a.m.–3:00 p.m., and Sunday from noon–4:00 p.m.* **The
Royal Armory** houses a collection of coaches, weapons and coronation
dresses. The display is aided by light and sound effects, and is a great attraction for children. *Guided tours weekdays except Saturday, at 2:00 p.m. On
Sunday there is a tour for children at 2:00 p.m. and for adults at 3:00 p.m.
Open May–August, weekdays from 10:00 a.m.–4:00 p.m. and on weekends
from 11:00 a.m.–4:00 p.m.* **The Palace Museum** is built on the ruins of
the former 12th-century castle. It contains the items that were found when
the new castle was built. *Open June-August from noon until 3 P.M. every
day.* **The Museum of Antiquities of Gastav III** holds the king's collection
of Roman sculpture. *Open from noon–3:00 p.m. every day during June-
August.* **The Hall of State** contains the silver throne and is the location
used by the king to read his State of the Nation address before the opening
of Parliament. *Open May-September from noon–3:00 p.m. every day, and
in October, weekends only from noon–3:00 p.m.* One caution: The palace
is sometimes closed without notice due to official occasions. Check with the
tourist information office about the best times to visit.

The Changing of the Guard takes place at the royal palace *on weekdays at
noon, on Saturday at 12:10 p.m. and Sunday at 1:10 p.m.* If you want to
catch the guards along the way to the palace, their route goes from the
Army Museum along Riddargatan and Artillerigatan, to Strandvagen, and
on to Hamngatan and Kungstradgatan; via Stromgatan to Gustav Adolfs
torg (where the Royal Opera House is located); across Norrbro bridge to
Skeppsbron in Gamla Stan, and finally up to the palace. Actually, if you are
walking in central Stockholm at midday, it seems you can hardly miss this
impressive parade as the route covers most of the spots tourists like to see,
but check with tourist information on hours and days, as well as the route
of the parade, as they are subject to change according to the time of year.

The Great Cathedral of Stockholm
Built in the 13th century, the cathedral's most notable treasure is the
wooden sculpture of St. George and the Dragon, carved from wood in
1489. The golden royal pews are 330 years old, and the silver and ebony
altar was made in 1652. Notice also the huge painting of the Last Judgment. It is the oldest preserved painting in Stockholm, and also one of the
largest paintings in the world. This is the coronation church, as well as the
place where the kings of Sweden are christened and married. It was from
this pulpit that the Lutheran reformers ranted against the Catholic church.

Riddarholm
This is actually another little island which has now been joined to Gamla
Stan by a wide street. If you walk down Storykirkobrinken from the cathe-
dral, you will come to the main square of Riddarholm dominated by **Rid-
darhuset**, the House of the Nobility, which was built in the 17th century.
Main interest here are the shields of the Swedish noble families. The hall is

often the site for concerts. *Open Monday–Friday from 11:30 a.m.–12:30 p.m. only. Closed on weekends.*

Riddarholm Church

The church was built in 1270 as a Greyfriars Monastery, but it soon became the burial place of kings. Within its ancient brick walls and beneath its distinctive spire, lie many of the most renowned monarchs of Sweden, including Magnus Ladulas who wrote the first laws giving rights to women. Gustav III was buried here after his assassination, which became the basis for Verdi's opera, *The Masked Ball.* Charles XIV John, Napoleon's field marshall who founded the Bernadotte dynasty, is also buried here in the Bernadotte chapel. His wife, Desiree, lies beside him. The last king buried here was King Gustav V, who died in 1950. His successor, Gustav VI Adolf, is buried at Haga Park. Between the Gustavian and Bernadotte chapels is a marked stone thought to be the grave of Karl Nilsson Farla, who was purportedly murdered in front of the altar in 1381 by the Lord High Steward, Bo Jonson Grip. *The church is open from May–August, Monday–Saturday from 10:00 a.m.–3:00 p.m. and Sunday from 1:00 p.m.–3:00 p.m.*

The Swedish Parliament (Riksdag)

The parliament was built at the turn of the century on its own island, the Island of the Holy Spirit, just across from Gamla Stan. In 1980, the Riksdag was totally renovated to accommodate the 349 members of the one house parliament that was created in 1971. *Open from late June through August, from noon–3:00 p.m. every day but Sunday. The rest of the year, it is open on weekends only from noon–4:00 p.m.*

If you're hungry: Kristina, at 66 Vasterlanggatan, has a delectable display of pastries, but you can also get a meal. This is a cozy, old tea room with panelled walls and plenty of the Gamla Stan appeal. Several of the finest restaurants in Stockholm are located in Gamla Stan. (See "Where to Eat.")

TOUR NO. 4: DJURGARDEN

The recreational island boasts several major museums in addition to the amusement park Grona Lund and miles of paths to walk or bicycle along. You can rent bicycles at the bicycle hire shop on the Djurgarden side of the bridge from Strandvagen.

The Kaknas Tower

The highest structure in Scandinavia. Ride up by express elevator for a spectacular view of Stockholm and much of the Stockholm archipelago. There is a restaurant at the top and also a cafeteria and tourist information center. If you wish to have dinner, it is suggested that you book ahead. *Open every day of the year; from May through August, 9:00 a.m.–midnight. In April and September, 9:00 a.m.–10:00 p.m. Rest of the year 9:00 a.m.–6:00 p.m.*

The Wasa Museum

On August 10, 1628, a beautiful Sunday afternoon, the new pride of King Gustav II Adolphus' war fleet, which had been under construction for two years at the spot where the Grand Hotel now stands, left the quay at Lodgarden, near the site of the present royal castle. A large crowd had gathered to watch the proud ship as she set out under four of her sails. The breeze blew, the sails swelled, and the *Wasa* heeled, righted itself, then heeled again, water rushing into her open ports. Within minutes, the warship *Wasa* sank. The museum holds the resurrected ship, the oldest, fully preserved warship in the world. Visitors can get a good look at the exterior of the boat with its elaborate heavy carvings—no wonder it sank—and then study the exhibit chronicling the effort to get it up from the water, which is as interesting as the boat itself. Every hour, a film on the salvaging of the ship is shown. A cafeteria run by the owners of K.B., in the center of town, offers museum visitors a very good lunch for about $18 per person. *In summer, guided tours are given after the film. In winter, guided tours are given on weekdays at 12:30 p.m. and 4:30 p.m. and on weekends at 10:30 a.m., 12:30 p.m., 2:30 p.m. and 4:30 p.m. Open every day, June–mid-August from 9:30 a.m.–7:00 p.m.; the rest of the year every day from 10:00 a.m.– 5:00 p.m.*

Waldemarsudde House

The elegant home of Sweden's painter prince, Prince Eugene, the great grand uncle of King Carl XVI Gustav, is open to the public as a museum. Prince Eugene studied art over the objections of his parents and became a respected exponent of the National Romantic school of painting at the turn of the century. The prince engaged the prominent architect Ferdinand Boberg to design this home for him on Djurgarden at the tip of the island jutting out into Lake Saltsjon. Prince Eugene lived here until his death in 1947, after which the house was opened to the public. It has been maintained just as it was in his lifetime, and has an air of livability with masses of flowers from the gardens arranged in all the rooms. The collection includes Nordic art as well as the major examples of the Prince's work. Temporary exhibitions of contemporary Swedish art are also staged. Visitors are free to walk through the park and exquisite gardens that overlook the water. The kitchen of the house has been turned into a most attractive câfé, with light snacks and pastries. The small gift shop sells a cachepot that is available only here. On Sundays, the museum is crowded so try to plan another day for your visit if possible. *Open June–August every day, but Monday from 11:00 a.m.–5:00 p.m., and also from 7:00 p.m.–9:00 p.m. Tuesday and Thursday. The rest of the year it is open Tuesday–Sunday from 11:00 a.m.–4:00 p.m. Closed Monday and in November and December. Check with tourist information for the exact dates.*

The Thiel Gallery

Built by the banker Ernest Thiel to house his enormous art collection, the gallery, at the tip of Sodra Djurgarden with panoramic views of the archipelago, became a gathering spot for artists and writers in the first quarter of the 20th century. When Thiel declared bankruptcy in 1924, the state bought the gallery. In the collection are works of early 20th-century Nordic artists, among them Edvard Munch, Carl Larsson and Anders Zorn. *Open all year Monday–Saturday from noon until 4:00 p.m., Sunday from 1:00 p.m.–4:00 p.m.*

The Nordiska Museum

This looming, sprawling building is the major museum of Swedish cultural history with displays ranging from the 16th century to the present. *Open June-August from 10:00 a.m.–4:00 p.m. on weekdays and from noon–5:00 p.m. on weekends.*

Skansen

The vast open-air museum contains a reconstructed Nordic village, a zoo and an aquarium, as well as restaurants, theaters and art exhibitions. The park was opened in 1891 at a location that was, at the time, on the outskirts of Stockholm. Now it, and all of Djurgarden, serves as an oasis in the middle of the urban center of Stockholm. The park covers approximately 75 acres devoted to various exhibits and recreational facilities. It contains about 150 buildings from all the areas of Sweden, and there is a Lapp Camp that portrays Lapp life of the earlier part of this century. Be sure to visit the Rose Garden by the Swedenborg summer house, and the herb garden which has, in addition to the usual spices, plants for medicinal purposes and those that were used in witchcraft. Skansen also affords visitors the chance to attend the early morning Christmas service at the Seglora Church. Visitors can celebrate the bonfires of May Day Eve, go to the midsummer festivities or attend the festival of St. Lucia in December when Sweden's "Lucia" for the year is crowned. If you are in Stockholm at Christmas time, be sure to attend the Christmas Markets at Skansen. New Year's Eve is celebrated with a fireworks display. In the zoo, visitors will find Scandinavian animals, in particular those threatened by extinction. Situated on a hill, Skansen also offers fine views of Stockholm. Plan to spend some time here and be sure to pick up the small guidebook which is available in English, and which you can buy at the main gate. *The park of Skansen is open daily from 9:00 a.m.–10:00 p.m. in summer and from 9:00 a.m.–5:00 p.m. in winter. The old buildings are open from 11:00 a.m.–5:00 p.m. in summer. In winter, only certain buildings are open from 11:00 a.m.–3:00 p.m. Guided tours are offered every day from mid-June–August at noon, 2:00 p.m. and 4:00 p.m.*

TOUR NO. 5: SODERMALM

Sodermalm is the southern, hilly island where the workers used to live. Now there are many restored wooden houses, so-called houses of culture, which are leased from the city to people who appear to be responsible enough to care for them properly. Years ago, when rents were low, Sodermalm was the hang-out for artists and writers, but rents are no longer low, so the struggling artists have to look elsewhere for housing. **Alfred Nobel's house** is located on this island, and there is also a park where one can rent canoes for a paddle on the canal. The wooden posts which stick up from the water were supposedly placed there to keep the people of the archipelago from rowing in without paying customs duties. Puckeln, the Hump, is the main street of art galleries here and the main attraction.

ATTRACTIONS OUT OF THE CENTER OF TOWN

Millesgarden

At the former home and garden of sculptor Carl Milles and his wife, visitors strolling through the park-like surroundings are treated to the works of Sweden's most well-known sculptor, as well as to spectacular views from the terraced gardens cut into the cliffs of Lidingo. In addition to a vast exhibition of Milles's own sculptures, his collection of ancient Roman and Greek art is on display. The gardens are built on three levels—the upper, middle and lower terraces. The entrance is on the upper terrace, where you can also visit the Small Studio, an addition to the main building used primarily for temporary exhibits. The main building was the Milles's home until they moved to the United States in 1931, where Milles taught at the Cranbrook Academy of Art in Michigan. The Milles's donated the house and their art collections to the city. Now the main house is a museum with a gift shop that sells bronze replicas of many of the works. Upstairs is the breakfast room with collections of glass, china and old Swedish pewter. The wooden cupboards were painted by Olga Milles. Visitors can visit the marble gallery, the main studio, the music room, the Red Room and the Monk's Cell.

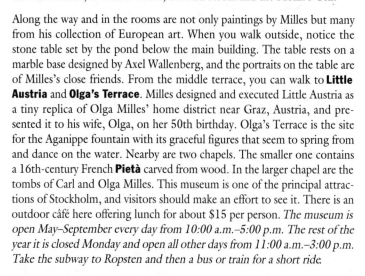

Along the way and in the rooms are not only paintings by Milles but many from his collection of European art. When you walk outside, notice the stone table set by the pond below the main building. The table rests on a marble base designed by Axel Wallenberg, and the portraits on the table are of Milles's close friends. From the middle terrace, you can walk to **Little Austria** and **Olga's Terrace**. Milles designed and executed Little Austria as a tiny replica of Olga Milles' home district near Graz, Austria, and presented it to his wife, Olga, on her 50th birthday. Olga's Terrace is the site for the Aganippe fountain with its graceful figures that seem to spring from and dance on the water. Nearby are two chapels. The smaller one contains a 16th-century French **Pietà** carved from wood. In the larger chapel are the tombs of Carl and Olga Milles. This museum is one of the principal attractions of Stockholm, and visitors should make an effort to see it. There is an outdoor câfé here offering lunch for about $15 per person. *The museum is open May–September every day from 10:00 a.m.–5:00 p.m. The rest of the year it is closed Monday and open all other days from 11:00 a.m.–3:00 p.m. Take the subway to Ropsten and then a bus or train for a short ride.*

Drottningholm Palace and Court Theater

Drottningholm was the summer residence of the Swedish Royal Family, but King Carl Gustav and Queen Sylvie have now chosen to make this their year-round home. The 17th-century palace was built as a miniature Versailles, designed by Nichodemus Tessin the Elder, who died before he could complete the work. His son, Nichodemus Tessin the Younger, finished the design and planned the French garden. Over the years, changes in the interiors were made by the various royal tenants, from the 17th through the 19th centuries. Restoration is a continuing effort, and the most recent efforts have resulted in returning the baroque garden and the Grand Staircase to their original splendor. Worth special attention are the Hall of State, redecorated in 1850 as a *salle contemporarie* with portraits of the reigning king of Sweden as well as other contemporary heads of European states, and King Oskar's Hall, which was added by King Oskar in the 1890s. *The Palace is open from May to August every day from 11:00 a.m.–4:30 p.m. and Sunday from noon–4:30 p.m. In September, it is open weekdays from 1:00 p.m.–3:30 p.m. and on weekends from noon–3:30 p.m.*

Also on the grounds, the **Drottningholm Court Theater** dates from 1766 and is the oldest theater in the world that still uses its original stage machinery. From May to September, opera and ballet are performed here. The theater and park does crowd up on weekends, so if you can go during the week, it might be more pleasant. *The theater is open to the public May–August during the same hours as the palace and in September daily from 12:30 p.m.–3:00 p.m. Guided tours are given every 30 minutes starting 1/ 2-hour after opening.*

The Chinese Pavilion is Sweden's answer to Marie Antoinette's Le Hameau at Versailles. This small palace, designed according to the Swedish conception of a Chinese palace, is the spot where King Gustav III and his court used to while away the sunny summer hours. Next to the palace is a miniature 18th-century village called Kanton, where the attempt was made to grow silkworms until the larvae froze to death in the Swedish winter. Visitors can get to Drottningholm by boat, which is the nicest way to come, or by subway to Brommaplan and then a bus. *Open April, September and October daily from 1:00 p.m.–3:30 p.m. and May–August from 11:00 a.m.–4:30 p.m.*

Haga Park with the Pavilion of Gustav III

The park is just north of the Stockholm city limits. The palace here was the retreat of King Gustav III and his family. The story of the king's assassination begins here with the assassin peering in the windows of the pavilion, plotting the murder of the king. Guided tours are given on the hour. *Open May-August, Tuesday–Sunday from noon–3:00 p.m. Closed Monday. In September, open on weekends from 1:00 p.m.–3:00 p.m.*

OFF THE BEATEN PATH

For visitors with plenty of time, Stockholm offers a variety of small, special-interest museums. For a more complete list, consult the booklet, *What to See and Do in and around Stockholm*, which is available at the tourist information office at Sweden House.

The August Strindberg Museum

This was the playwright's home from 1908 until 1921, and has been reconstructed with authentic furnishings. There is a library with photo and newspaper archives. In addition, the museum often hosts literary and theatrical events and concerts. *Open all year, Tuesday from 10:00 a.m.–4:00 p.m. and from 7:00 p.m.–9:00 p.m.; Wednesday–Saturday from 10:00 a.m.–4:00 p.m. and Sunday from noon–5:00 p.m.*

The Eldh Studio/Museum

Here you will find the only working art studio in Stockholm with its origi-

nal furnishings preserved. In the studio and museum are most of the works
of the sculptor Carl Eldh, who lived from 1873 until 1954. The building
was designed by Ragnar Ostberg, who designed the Stockholm City Hall.
Open May–September, Tuesday–Sunday from noon–4:00 p.m.

The Postal Museum

In the Old Town at *Lilla Nygatan 6* • The museum contains two of the rare
Mauritius Post Office stamps. In addition to stamps, the museum displays
include a railway mail car, mail boats and all kinds of postal paraphernalia.
*Open Tuesday–Sunday from 11:00 a.m.–3:00 p.m. and Wednesday until
9:00 p.m.*

The Museum of National Antiquities

(also called the National History Museum)
Narvavagen 13–17 • The museum houses treasures of the Viking expeditions and displays of life in the Viking era. This is one of the leading museums of Viking life in the world, and the opening of a new room, The Gold
Room, in October, added significantly to its collections. Gold and silver
artifacts from the Viking era and the Middle ages are housed here in this
7,532 square foot underground vault. There is a câfé here. Take the subway
to Karlaplan. *Open Tuesday–Sunday from 11:00 a.m.–5:00 p.m. and on
Thursdays until 8:00 p.m.*

SMALL PALACES IN AND AROUND STOCKHOLM

Although Drottningholm was the official retreat, it seems that every monarch
felt the need to build his own getaway from the rigors of Stockholm life. Consequently, there are several small palaces in and around Stockholm that make
pleasant outings for the traveler with time.

Rosendal Palace

In Djurgarden • Built by King Carl XIV John in the early 19th century for
his queen, Desiree, the interiors are just as they were when Queen Desiree
occupied the palace. *Open June–August from noon until 3 p.m. every day
but Monday. In September, weekends 1 p.m.–3 p.m. closed all other times.*

Rosersberg Palace

The palace, which was constructed around 1800, is furnished much as it
was during the reigns of Charles XIII and Carl XIV John. *Open only from
mid-May until mid-September, Tuesday–Thursday from 11:00 a.m.–4:00
p.m. and Sunday from noon–4:00 p.m. Guided tours are given every hour
on the hour.*

Svindersvik Manor

This is an 18th-century summer house, not a royal one. The original fur-
nishings of the house are still here with some additions from the Nordiska
Museum. The house is only open to visitors taking guided tours. *Open
Sunday 1:00 p.m.–4:00 p.m., mid-May to mid-September.*

Bellman Exhibition

A new museum in an 18th-century manor house, this exhibit is dedicated
to the 18th-century poet, Carl Michael Bellman. The manor house, **Kall-**

halls Gard, is located on Langholmen Island, an appropriate site for this monument to the poet who, in spite of great popularity, favor with the royal family and marriage to a wealthy woman, died in debtor's prison, though not in the prison on Langholmen which has recently been converted into a hotel and youth hostel.

SHOPPING

The thing to buy in Sweden is, of course, glass. If you are going into the glass district, you should wait to buy at the glassworks, though many of the factory shops sell only seconds. These usually appear perfect to the unschooled eye and are available at quite a savings, but if you want the pure, unflawed product, buy in regular retail outlets. Prices are about the same everywhere, and most of the retailers run similar specials, but you might save a few kronor by shopping around a bit. You need not worry about buying in any of the shops in central Stockholm. They are all reputable. Most shops will mail your purchase home tax-free, and this is a big help, since carting around a heavy package of expensive glass is pretty cumbersome. This also relieves you of the hassle of getting back your tax at the airport. Swedish handicrafts are also the thing to buy if your tastes run to the homey rather than the elegant.

Shopping hours: Usually shops in central Stockholm are open weekdays 9:00 a.m.–4:00 or 5:00 p.m. and Saturdays 9:00 a.m.–2:00 or 3:00 p.m. The department stores stay open Monday nights until 7:00 p.m. and until 4:00 p.m. on Saturday. NK and a few others are open on Sunday from noon–4:00 p.m. and later on Saturday in the winter.

Most of the shopping is in the center of town. **Drottninggatan** is a long pedestrian mall, which is still somewhat under construction. Many of the stores are large department stores and utilitarian shops, but as more places move in, that should change. The department stores, **Nordiska Komapniet (NK)**, **Ahlens City**, and **PUB** are all located nearby. Of these, NK is the finest, with high-quality merchandise and a vast selection of all the big names in Swedish design. They also have a handicraft and glass collection in the basement and a good selection of furs. In Hamngatan, you will find the enclosed shopping complex, **Gallerian**.

Lunch suggestion: Alavarium in Kungstradgarden is a popular lunch spot with the focus on fish in about any form you can think of. The more expensive shops are located on **Birger Jarlsgatan** and **Biblioteksgatan**, a pedestrian-only street that runs off Birger Jarlsgatan. Also in this area is the wonderful market, **Saluhallen**, at Ostermalmstorg, where you can stop for a bite or buy a sumptuous picnic to take to Djurgarden or to eat by the water. A shopping mall, the **Stuer Mall**, opened in March of 1989 with shops, restaurants and cafés. The mall occupies the same building as the venerable Stuer Baths, which have also reopened with their former splendor restored. The baths are open to anyone. The shops of the Stuer Mall remain open until 9:00 p.m. and the restaurants until midnight.

Gamla Stan has many antique shops and off-beat boutiques. Most of these are located on Vasterlanggatan and Stora Nygatan, as well as Osterlanggatan.

GLASS

Svenskt Glas on Birger Jarlsgatan is a prime source for all the glass you might ever want or need. A range of quality and prices is available and you will see items here that are different from the usual. **Rosenthal Studio Haus**, located down the street from Svenskt Glas, sells porcelain and other up-market housewares as well as crystal. **Nordiska Kristall**, at *Kungsgatan 9*, has some beautiful art pieces from Kosta Boda and Orrefors and one-of-a-kind objects from artists and craftsmen. While the prices are not particularly bargain level, the display and the limited inventory makes it easy to look carefully. The **Sheraton Hotel** has a glass shop with a good selection. **NK** and **Ahlens** department stores also have excellent glass departments with all the major names. They ship home tax-free. **Casselryds** is a popular name, plastered over magazines and signs throughout the city, but it does offer excellent bargains and good selection. It caters to Americans with prices given in US dollars as well as kronor, and all the prices include insurance and shipping. It is located outside Stockholm at the **Skarholmen Indoor Mall**, but the shop offers free rides both ways, if you call them at ☎ *08 7105116*. **IKEA**, the popular and popularly priced home furnishings store is also at Skarholmen, in Barkarby, so you could make a day of it. The largest **flea market** in Stockholm is located in the same area. The **Gift Shop of the Royal Palace** has an excellent selection of gifts in silver, pewter and crystal which you will not find elsewhere. *Open Tuesday–Sunday from 10:30 a.m.–4:30 p.m.*

FURNITURE

IKEA home furnishings are well-known in Sweden and abroad for their good design and low prices. As mentioned previously, the store is located outside Stockholm and has acres of furniture, carpeting, fabrics and lighting, in addition to glassware and china. *Buses leave from Regeringsgata 13, across from Fritzes Bookstore every hour on the hour from 11:00 a.m. and return from IKEA every hour on the half hour starting at 11:30 a.m. IKEA is open weekdays from 11:00 a.m.–8:00 p.m.; Saturday 10:00 a.m.–5:00 p.m.; Sunday 11:00 a.m.–5:00 p.m.*

SWEDISH HANDICRAFTS

Stockholms Lans Hemslojdsforening, at *Drottninggatan 18–20*, sells country crafts, pine furniture, textiles and pottery. **Svensk Hemslojd** at *Sveavagen 44* is another source for handcrafted items. **Hantverksbutiken Klockargarden**, at *Kungsgatan 55*, sells textiles and other homemade items in additional to Swedish national costumes. **Konsthantverkarna**, at *Master Samuelsgatan 2*, is a permanent exhibit and shop run by artists who are discriminating in their selection of merchandise.

Foreningen for Nutida Svenskt Silver (The Association for Contemporary Silver) at *Karlavagen 59*. Permanent exhibition of handmade silver. **Handarbetets vanner** (Friends of Handicraft) *Durgardsslaten 82–84*. This shop sells hand-woven textiles and embroidery. It is closed in July. Otherwise it is open weekdays from 11:00 a.m.–3:00 p.m. **Sameslojen** specializes in Lapp handcrafted items. It is located at *Sjalagardsgatan 19* in Gamla Stan.

FURS

The best place for furs is Helsinki, but if you are not including Finland in your itinerary and are determined to buy a Scandinavian fur, try **Sophie Ericsons**, *Master Samuelsgatan 45*. This is the largest furrier in Sweden and the selection is vast, with special emphasis on SAGA mink. **Rune Landert**, at *Nybrogatan 29*, one of the streets running off Ostermalmstorg, is a small, very exclusive fur shop with beautiful selections at top prices, but not overpriced. If price is no object and style and quality are, this is the place. **Amoress**, at *Norrlandsgatan 5*, is at the other end of the spectrum from Rune Landert, with a large selection of mass market furs. The prices are low but you get what you pay for. There are some more expensive coats here also and a terrific display of eccentrically and brightly dyed furs.

BOOKS

Akademibokhandeln, at *Master Samuelsgatan 32*, has an excellent selection of American and English books.

GALLERY HOPPING

Hornsgatspuckeln (The Horn Street Hump) is located on Sodermalm and offers a series of art galleries where artists and craftsmen sell their work. If you start *at Hornsgatan 34* at the **Galleri Origo**, you can get instructions on where to go next, and learn a little about the "hump." *Take Bus 55 to Mariatorget. Monday–Thursday 11:30 a.m.–5:30 p.m. Friday–Sunday noon–4:00 p.m*

WHERE TO STAY

Stockholm has an ample selection of excellent hotels in all price categories, but the hotel rates in Stockholm are the highest in Scandinavia—even a moderate hotel might cost over $100, and a very expensive one can near the $300 mark. As in other countries, weekend and summer rates are often available, and if you cannot book those rates ahead, ask when you arrive. Hotelcentralen, on the ground floor of the Central Station can book hotels and hostels. This can be done on the day of arrival or in advance. ☎ *08-24-08-80, FAX 08-791-86-66.*

VERY EXPENSIVE

The Victory Hotel   ★★★★★

In Gamla Stan at Lilla Nygatan 5 • This is my favorite: a small, friendly, and impeccably run deluxe hotel that has been designed in the most stylish and ingenious manner, from its ship-shape lobby with mahogany and brass that dazzles the arriving guest, to the attractive guest rooms, which put a minimum of space to a maximum of comfort and attractiveness. The hotel occupies an exquisitely renovated ancient house, which was itself built on the foundations of an old defense tower. In the 18th century, the owners of the house buried an immense fortune in silver beneath the foundations. The rooms are decorated in white and pale blue and each has its own treasury of framed memorabilia, old photos of the sea captain after whom the room is named, ship models and other seaworthy items. Every amenity is available, from robes to hair dryers, and the biggest complimentary chocolates you will ever see. The owner of the hotel is a devotee of Lord Nelson, as the names of his other two hotels in Gamla Stan suggest. They are called the Lord Nelson and the Lady Hamilton. The Victory, named for Lord Nelson's boat, is appropriately the flagship of the three. In the lobby and in display cases in the hallways, you will find Nelson memorabilia. The restaurant here, Leijontornet, is one of Stockholm's best, and has won a Michelin star. The history of the building and of the excavations that yielded buried treasure is fascinating and available in a pamphlet at the hotel. Be sure to inquire about summer rates as they should be available and are substantially lower.

The Grand Hotel ★★★★★

Blasieholmshamnen 8 • This is the *grande dame* of Stockholm, sitting by the water like a ship in full sail, under the colorful flags that fly from the roof. The hotel offers the old-style elegance of large, airy rooms and formal public areas. With 335 rooms, one could hardly call this place intimate, but in summer its location, overlooking the water and an easy walk from most of the major attractions of Stockholm, is unbeatable. The Grand Câfé is a popular gathering spot for visitors and natives. The Grand Veranda is a pleasant dining area overlooking the water and the sightseeing boats. A set menu at lunch is 165SEK; at dinner, 215. The more formal French dining room also overlooks the water. The Cadier bar is cozily elegant and also has a veranda-type section overlooking the water. This is another hotel which offers significantly lower rates in summertime.

The Berns Hotel ★★★

Norrmalmstorg • This brand-new, small hotel, with just 63 rooms, each of which is different in size and design, is a unique addition to Stockholm's hotel scene. Of the 62 rooms, four are suites, one with a private sauna. The hotel occupies three floors above the famous Berns restaurant, one of Europe's largest restaurants, where Josephine Baker and Marlene Dietrich used to perform. The hotel offers SAS EuroClass check-in at the SAS Strand Hotel, which is nearby. EuroClass passengers also get a 10 percent discount on regular room rates.

The SAS Strand Hotel ★★★★

Nybrokajen • The hotel offers all the service and convenience that SAS hotels provide, with flight check-in and a limousine service, for a charge, for business-class travelers. Built in 1912 for the Olympic games, the Strand was under renovation from 1980 to 1983. The public rooms are only minimally attractive, but the service is friendly, and the hotel is convenient and highly comfortable. The guest rooms, while not exceptional, are for the most part large and comfortable, but they do vary. If it's in your budget, try one of the extraordinary deluxe tower rooms. A step down from those are the Royal Club suites and rooms, which are lovely. The hotel is built around an atrium housing an informal restaurant. There is a formal dining room here as well.

The Hotel Diplomat ★★★

Strandvagen 7C • Located on the most beautiful part of Strandvagen, the Diplomat was first an elegant apartment building and then an embassy, first for Romania, then Iran, and finally Canada. It still retains its old-world charm and manages a personal touch with several small public rooms where guests can relax with a cup of coffee. The rooms vary a great deal in size and design, but all are comfortable with TV and video channel, minibar and, of course, private bath. The hotel has a sauna, available at no extra charge. *The Diplomat Tea Room is a popular spot for lunch and tea, and also serves dinner Monday–Friday, lunch only Saturday.*

The Royal Viking

Next to the Central Railway Station • This is a giant, commercial hotel with 319 large, ultra-comfortable rooms. The hotel offers SAS flight check-in, free sauna and an indoor pool. This is a big, busy, rather impersonal spot with nothing distinctively Swedish about it, but it is bright and lively and attractive in a commercial way.

The Sergel Plaza

Brunkebergstorg 9 • This one tops the Royal Viking in size with 407 rooms. It is a beautiful, modern hotel with every convenience imaginable. The rooms are as nice as you will find. For those who like their glamour up-to-date, this might be the choice over the Grand, though, again, there is nothing distinctively Swedish about this, and the location, while convenient, is not in the prettiest part of this beautiful city.

The Sheraton

Near the Railway Station • The Sheraton is the Sheraton is the Sheraton. What else can one say? Sheratons are predictable, but they are comfortable and modern and filled with plenty of busy travelers. This one is located in the center of town near the Central Station.

EXPENSIVE

The Anglais Hotel

Humlegardsgatan 23 • The fine location, overlooking the pretty Humlegarden park, is convenient to shopping and entertainment with cinemas, nightclubs and restaurants all around. The hotel has 211 comfortable and attractive rooms. Request a room on the park. The piano bar is a popular late night spot. Restaurant and rooftop terrace.

The Sara Hotel Reisen +★★★

In Gamla Stan on the water • With 113 rooms, it is a family hotel and, as with most hotels in Gamla Stan, sports a nautical motif. Two salons from a boat form part of the public and conference rooms. The guest rooms vary, but most of the doubles are good size. Two restaurants, a more formal *Quarterdeck*, and the casual *Clipper Club Grill.*

The Lady Hamilton

In Gamla Stan • This is another of the group of salty hostelries, which includes the Victory Hotel. The Lady Hamilton is small and nautical with comfortable rooms that are not quite up to the luxury of the Victory, but are certainly attractive and comfortable. The decor is, like the Victory, enhanced by antiques and nautical details. Plenty of brass, mahogany and good Swedish antiques in the corridors and lobby. All the rooms have private baths, minibar and cable TV, and there is a sauna for the guests. Plenty of charm and Old Town atmosphere. The hotel does not have a restaurant, but the small breakfast room serves sandwiches and drinks. The Lady Hamilton belongs to the Romantik Hotel Organization, a group of hotels which have been selected because they offer something a little different in atmosphere and service.

The Lady Hamilton Hotel owns and manages a small apartment building with charmingly decorated apartments complete with modern kitchen and, in some of the rooms, tiled stoves. Breakfast at the Lady Hamilton Hotel is included in the price, along with cleaning twice a week. For information on rates, contact the Lady Hamilton Hotel, *Storkyrkobrinken 5, S-111 28 Stockholm,* ☎ *(8) 23 46 80.*

The *Malardrottningen*
Moored off Riddarholm • *Malardrottningen* is a luxury yacht that has been turned into a hotel. Built in 1924 for an American millionaire, the boat was bought by heiress Barbara Hutton. In 1982, it was converted to a hotel with 60 rooms and three suites. The boat is moored off Riddarholm in view of the City Hall. If you like something different, this is your place, especially in summertime when you can enjoy the view of Lake Malaren from the deck. The rooms are snug and comfortable, but they are cabins and, as such, are very small. A double is a tight squeeze for two, no matter how cozy you might want to be. All rooms have private bath and an ingenious shower arrangement. A sauna is available to guests at no additional charge. Prices are lower in summer, especially after Midsummer, and on weekends. The restaurant is an excellent one and very attractive with fine views of Lake Malaren. In summer, an outdoor grill is set up on deck.

Clas Pa Hornet
On Surbrunnsgatan • Here is something a little different. Located rather far from the center of town in a residential neighborhood, this 200-year old house has the ambience of the home of a country gentleman. The inn is known more as a restaurant than as a hotel, but there are a few charming rooms here also.

MODERATE

The Lord Nelson
In Gamla Stan • This is the third member of the Victory group. It too has all the seafaring flavor and charm of the others. Its rooms are scaled down just a little from those of the Lady Hamilton, with rather small bathrooms, but are nonetheless very comfortable and pleasant. And the rates are a little lower than at the Lady Hamilton. All rooms with private bath and TV and plenty of nautical decorative touches. The rooftop terrace overlooking Gamla Stan is justifiably popular in summertime. The hotel is part of the Romantik Hotel organization.

The Hotel Continental
Near the Railway Station • The hotel has just been renovated, so I was

unable to see it in its new shape, but the remodeling looked promising and the location is convenient.

Karelia   ★★

Birger Jarlsgatan 35 • The hotel, which was owned by Finns, will be under new ownership by the time of publication so I do not know what will happen. Prior to this, it has been a pleasant, recommendable place, with clean, comfortable rooms, a real Finnish sauna and two restaurants, one Russian and one with dancing.

The Castle Hotel   ★★

Behind the Dramatiska Teatern • Perhaps because of its proximity to the theater, the Castle draws many musicians. The hotel is new, but in an old building. The rooms are small, but well designed. A double runs about 1100SEK, which is a bit high for this spot but then, this is Stockholm.

The Esplanade

On Strandvagen near the Diplomat • The Esplanade enjoys a rather inexplicable popularity, especially with Swedish-Americans. I include it in the expensive/moderate category, because the four large double rooms, which are the only nice rooms, go for 1300SEK. Smaller doubles start at 950SEK, but these are rather ordinary and, I think, charmless. The hotel occupies one floor of an office building and commands beautiful views of the water. Perhaps it is the quiet, intimate atmosphere and the location that please the guests.

The Central Hotel   ★★★

Vasagatan 38 • If the Central Hotel keeps its rates down, it will be one of the best buys in town. Located just far enough from the Central Station to be out of that hubbub, the hotel has recently moved across the street from its former location into a modern, light-filled structure with 93 rooms. It is geared to the business traveler, so most of its rooms are singles and they are small, but extremely attractive and comfortable. Each room has cable TV, private baths and hair dryers. At last check, rooms begin at 725SEK for a single; 850 for a double.   .

The City Hotel   ★★

On Slojdgatan • Because it is run by the Salvation Army, the hotel does not serve alcohol on the premises, but this is a very good spot for its price, which at last check was under 800SEK. The location, near the shopping district, is convenient. The rooms have been recently renovated.

Hotel Terminus   ★★

Across from the Railway Station • The lobby is not encouraging, but the 155 rooms are fresh and clean, and in spite of its location, it seems to be a rather quiet place. There is a sauna, but the pool that is advertised is just a plunge pool. The hotel has been owned by the same family for 70 years. Two restaurants, the Câfé Terminus and Kaspar, are popular spots.

The Scandic Crown Hotel

At Slussen on Sodermalm • The hotel has only recently opened. I have not seen the hotel, but its advance notices are good. The hotel has two restaurants, an indoor pool, sauna and solarium.

INEXPENSIVE

Anno 1647

On Sodermalm • The name refers to the date in which the hotel was built. Though the buildings are old, the rooms have been modernized and are very pleasant, some even with a tiled stove. Not all rooms have private baths.

The Adlon

On Vasagatan • This is a rather dreary place and though it falls into the inexpensive category, it has little to recommend it beyond comparatively low price. And at 700–1100SEK, it still will run you over $100. Prices fall dramatically in summer and on weekends, however. The rooms are very small, and though two of the floors have been renovated, the breakfast room and kitchen are located on one of those floors, so rooms there could be noisy. All rooms have private baths and include breakfast.

The Langholmen Hotel

On Langholmen Island • A former prison turned youth hostel and hotel. You serve time in fairly comfortable if slightly cramped cellular style. The hotel cells/rooms have shower, TV and telephone. The hostel rooms are more like dormitories with two to five beds and two cells share a bath. *If you bring your own linen and clean your own room, the hostel price is even lower.*

OUTSIDE TOWN

Radisson

Situated 10 minutes from the center of town on the park-like grounds of the 19th-century Haga Castle, this new, first-class hotel has 202 rooms, two restaurants and a bar.

The SAS Arlandia Hotel

A modern, 300-room first-class hotel for business travelers, just four minutes from Arlandia Airport. All rooms have TV/video, hair dryer and minibar. There are two restaurants and a bar in the hotel, and a Sports Club, which includes a heated pool, sauna, tennis court and jogging track. The hotel has a Royal Club and an "office for a day" service. Airline check-in at the hotel and hotel check-in at the airport, for the best of all worlds.

The Stockholm Globe Hotel

The Globe Arena is a mammoth structure opened in February of 1989. With this vast arena, Stockholm can host events of major international importance. In June of 1989, Pope John Paul II celebrated a Mass for 16,000 people. In conjunction with the Arena, a hotel, the Stockholm Globe, with 300 rooms opened in March of 1989. The hotel rooms are minisuites, with the beds in a raised alcove opening onto a sitting area. The sleeping area contains ample workspace with special lighting. A Business

Services Office offers fax and telex in addition to other facilities. Sauna and steam bath complex. Two restaurants.

A SPECIAL YOUTH HOSTEL

af Chapman

On Skeppsholmen • An old sailing vessel turned youth hostel. Anchored in the heart of the city with wonderful views, this is a unique hostel. It is open from March–December.

WHERE TO EAT

It is not difficult to eat well in Stockholm, but it is difficult to eat inexpensively. Stockholm has more Michelin star restaurants than any other Scandinavian city, and in addition to those that have been singled out for acclaim, there are many pleasant, unpretentious places with excellent food. Unfortunately, most restaurants, even the casual ones, will cost at least $30 per person if you want more than the most minimal meal. As in all of Scandinavia, this is partly due to the MOMS tax which is figured into the cost of everything. For budget-minded diners, eat your big meal at lunch taking advantage of the daily lunch special, which is available in most restaurants for about 50SEK. Then eat a light meal at dinnertime.

RESTAURANTS IN THE AREA OF NORRMALM AND OSTERMALM

Operakallaren

In the Opera House • Some Stockholm residents will turn up their noses at this famous and beautiful landmark because it is a tourist attraction, albeit a very up-market one. But, as with most tourist attractions, there is a reason for its popularity. It is glamorous, opulent and the smorgasbord, served only at lunchtime at a cost of about 150SEK, is one of the more reasonable ways to dine well in the city. Located in the Royal Opera House, the restaurant has been a landmark since its founding late in the 18th century. It was King Gustav III who decided that the Royal Opera House should have a cellar restaurant for the performers at the opera, but the restaurant soon attracted more than just actors and singers. Several fires, the first in 1892, have brought about changes through rebuilding, and now this is not a cellar restaurant at all. It has two dining rooms, a splendid main dining room, and just off it, a winter-garden that overlooks the water and the royal palace.

In 1955, the restaurant was bought by Tore Wretman, who set about reviving its reputation and bringing the smorgasbord back to the early splendor of the pre-war years. Though it has changed hands in recent years and is now owned by an Italian who has lived most of his life in Stockholm, the restaurant still puts on one of the best smorgasbords in town. The smorgasbord is served only at lunch. The only drawback to lunch here is that the Operakallaren is frequently a stop on organized tours. If you request a table on the enclosed veranda, which is just as pleasant as the more formal dining room, especially on a pretty day, you might avoid some of the chaos of those caravans of tourists. ***Expensive.***

The Câfé Opera

Also in the Opera House • This is the place to be for lunch or dinner and
after theater. Its vast central room's unusual painted ceiling and spectacular
chandeliers vie with more contemporary elements to make this a unique
spot. The main room and the glassed-in veranda are jammed with the
young, chic population of Stockholm at both lunch and dinner. The menu
offers lighter meals, as well as full dinners at moderate prices. The food is
good, though not outstanding, but it is a less expensive alternative to dining in the Operakallaren, and its atmosphere is just as unique. Reservations
are accepted for lunch, and it is a good idea to make one if you do not want
to stand in line. At dinner, however, you have to take your chances, and pri-
ority is given to holders of a Câfé Opera Card, so arrive early, especially if
you plan to eat here before attending a performance at the opera. At midnight, dancing begins. There are two other appealing spots in the opera.
Bakfickan has counter service with a varied selection of Swedish home cooking at reasonable prices. The Operabaren is the turn-of-the-century bar,
which still retains its art nouveau and clubby atmosphere. It is most popular
for lunch and cocktails.

Franska Matsalen

In the Grand Hotel, S. Blasieholmshamnen 8. • This is the Grand Hotel's
very grand dining room. The cuisine here is "Swedish modern," but features international as well as classic Swedish dishes.   ***Expensive.***

Riche and Teatergrillen

Birger Jarlsgatan 4 • These are two parts of the same restaurant. Riche is
the more formal of the two, almost English with roast beef served from silver trolleys. The food is good. A two-course meal with a glass of wine will
be about 200SEK. The Teatergrillen caters to the after-theater crowd. It
used to close for the month of July, so check.

Birger Bar

Also on Birger Jarlsgatan • A lively, informal spot, the restaurant serves
hamburgers, pasta and Swedish dishes. A simple meal, perhaps pasta, salad
and a glass of wine, will be about 125SEK.

Vau de Ville

Hamngatan 17 • The bistro-style restaurant offers a variety of selections for
lunch and dinner. It is crowded at lunchtime, and you sometimes have to
wait, but the food is good and the prices reasonable, though not cheap.

K.B. or Konstnarshuset

Smalandsgatan 7 near Norrmalmstorg • (If you want to try all those
tongue-crunching letters, the full name means house of artists.) One of
Stockholm's Michelin star restaurants, this is a friendly, intimate spot with
the walls decorated by the artists in payment for their drinks. Try the mus-
sels, but everything here is good.   ***Expensive***

Martini

Norrmalmstorg • The food in this popular, stylish restaurant is mostly Ital-

ian. The dining room is pretty and sophisticated, and there is also a covered
terrace.   *Moderate.*

Paul & Norbert

9 Strandvagen next door to the Diplomat Hotel • Popular with the residents of this posh neighborhood, this tiny restaurant serves fine food with a minimum of fuss and has won itself a Michelin star.

Per Olsson

On Grev Turegatan, not far from the Castle Hotel • Another neighborhood restaurant, this one with simpler fare. The menu consists of traditional Swedish dishes and the restaurant bakes its own bread twice a day. The restaurant is furnished in a simple, rustic style with rough wood panelling hung with farming tools.   *Moderate.*

Rolf's Kok (Rolf's Kitchen)

Tegnergatan 41• This is a very simple and rather unconventional spot, where diners can watch the activity in the open kitchen and where the cooks serve the food as well as prepare it. The food is traditional Swedish.
                                                                               Moderate.

Eriks Bakficka

Fredrikshovsgatan 4 • The name means Erik's backpocket, suggesting a hidden, understated treasure trove, and that's just what this is. Related to the Michelin-starred Eriks in Osterlanggatan, this is a neighborhood spot where you will see more locals than tourists. The menu features homey Swedish fare at reasonable prices. In summer, there is an outdoor terrace. In winter, meals are served in two small, peasant-style rooms.   *Moderate.*

Clas Pa Hornet

Surbrunnsgatan 20 • Though it is also a hotel (see "Where to Stay"), it is as a restaurant that the Clas Pa Hornet is best known. The food is fine, and the atmosphere elegant, but not formal, in a beautifully restored old house of the last century. Swedish dishes, for the most part, are moderate to expensive. An attractive, tiny bistro offers less expensive food than the dining room.

Berns Salonger

Near Norrmalmstorg • An historic restaurant and music hall, Berns hosted performers like Josephine Baker and Marlene Dietrich. It has just been refurbished and brought back to its original splendor. The restoration was a meticulous and slow process, working through years of the grime of cigarette smoke to get down to the original colors. Now the 700-seat restaurant, which sits beneath huge gleaming chandeliers and graceful balconies, is in business again. In addition to the large dining room, the Hall of Mirrors is a small gourmet restaurant with just 40 seats. There is also the Red Room, which was celebrated by August Strindberg in his novel of the same name. Patrons wanting just a cup of coffee or a beer can sit on the balconies and overlook the 700 seat restaurant below.   *Moderate.*

Wedholm's Fisk

Nybrokajen 17 • The restaurant has won a well-deserved Michelin star. As its name suggests, fish is the focus here. In fact, fish is the only offering, served with few garnishes but exquisitely prepared. The turbot is a specialty. Dinner for two with wine will be around $170.

RESTAURANTS IN GAMLA STAN AREA

Leijontornet

Lilla Nygatan 5 • This stunning restaurant is located in the basement of the Victory Hotel, but it has to qualify as the most elegant cellar restaurant in Stockholm, with an austere mix of medieval and contemporary decor. The foundations of the ancient watchtower, which first occupied this spot centuries ago, and for which the restaurant, whose name means Lion Tower, is named, are visible through a glass case that has been built around them. The menu includes selections of fish, game, beef, and fowl, all beautifully and imaginatively prepared. **Very Expensive.**

A small bistro is located on the ground floor of the hotel and serves lighter, simpler fare. It, too, is excellent.

Eriks

Osterlanggatan. Yet another Eriks. This one has won a Michelin star. In addition to the excellence of the food, the restaurant is notable for its cozy elegance. The bar downstairs serves lighter fare while the upper level focuses on seafood. A simple meal with a glass of wine downstairs will run about $50 a person, but upstairs a full meal with wine will near the $200 mark.

Aurora

Munkbron 11 • A beautiful restaurant in a 17th-century building, Aurora serves Swedish and international dishes. **Expensive.**

Fem Sma Hus

Nygrand 10 • The name means five small houses and, as you might guess, the restaurant occupies five small, and old, houses in Gamla Stan. The menu offers a wide range of selections at very high prices. This is a popular spot with tourists, which is no reason to avoid it since there is good reason for its popularity, but some travelers shy away from such places, so this is fair warning.

Kallaren Diana

Brunnsgrand 2 • Another fine cellar restaurant. The cuisine is of the new Swedish style and features quite a bit of game. **Moderate to expensive.**

Den Gyldene Freden

Osterlanggatan 51 • Sweden's oldest restaurant, it has been named an official cultural treasure. The restaurant opened in 1720, and continued through good times and bad until 1986, when it was forced to close rather then undertake the necessary extensive and expensive repairs. Now, the company Stockholm-Saltsjon has restored the restaurant and is managing it. There are three sections: a street level restaurant serving simple meals;

the Bellman Suite; and the cellar vaults for more festive and formal occasions.

Fredsgatan 12

Located on ground floor of the Academy of Art near the Parliament Building, this moderately-priced, lively restaurant serves food with a Mediterranean accent.

PA & Co.

Riddargatan 8 • A trendy, bistro restaurant, very popular. Try the Swedish meatballs with mashed potatoes. Moderate by Stockholm standards.

There are a few less expensive restaurants that you will walk by every time you stroll through the streets of Gamla Stan. Of these, **Rodolfino,** at the corner of Stora Nygatan, specializes in Italian food, though there are other items on the menu. Both outdoor and indoor service. Reasonable. **Cattelin** always seems to have a crowd sitting at its window seats. It offers bistro-style French food, which is not particularly recommendable. **Zum Franziskaner** on Skeppsbron is a Gamla Stan landmark. Inside, the atmosphere is pub-like with a German touch. The food is adequate, though not exceptional.

RESTAURANTS ON SODERMALM

Nils Emil Backficka

Folkungagatan 126 • A favorite place for those in the know. In this charming, unaffected, thoroughly Swedish restaurant, you will find some of the best Swedish cooking around. *Try his mother's meatballs.*

Expensive to moderate.

Pelikan

The place to be on Thursday nights for pancakes with lingonberry jam, and pea soup with Swedish punch.

RESTAURANTS OUTSIDE TOWN

Ulriksdals Wardshus

Norrtull, Solna In Ulriksdals Slottspark • This is a special place that travelers will find worth the slight effort to get to. The restaurant is a beautiful old inn set in a lovely park. The smorgasbord, served Saturdays and Sundays, is the claim to fame, but all the food is good. Come for lunch on a pretty summer Sunday. *Expensive.*

Fjaderholmarna

On Lilla Vartan • In summer, you can come by boat to this restaurant at the point where the archipelago begins. Seafood is the specialty. Moderate. Pick up the boat from the Grand Hotel or Slussen.

Edsbacka Krog

Sollentunavagen 220 • Northwest of the city, this Michelin-starred country restaurant offers a tavern-like atmosphere with fine food, some of which is Lithuanian in origin. *Expensive to moderate.*

NIGHTLIFE

Café Opera is a popular place, often with a line waiting to get in.You can also try the Opera Bar, just beside it. The cafe becomes a disco after 10:00 p.m.**Borsen** is Stockholm's biggest nightclub, with a variety of first-rate international entertainment and late-night dancing. **The Daily News Café**, in Kungstradgarden, is crowded at all hours. **Fasching**, at *Kungsgatan 63*, is the place for jazz. **The Hard Rock Cafe**, on *Sveavagen*, is just what you would expect if you've frequented these spots elsewhere. No self-respecting European city is without this staple of the rock scene. As in other cities, this one draws crowds that line up around the block. This is not just a night spot. The câfé opens at 11 a.m. and serves a varied menu all day, and until closing at 2 a.m. Sturehof is one of the best places for a variety of music, blues as well as jazz. **Jazzpuben**, in Gamla Stan, is the most popular jazz spot in Stockholm. Across the street, **Cattelin** draws the overflow. **Zum Tiroler**, also in Gamla Stan, is a moderately priced restaurant more popular for its music than its food. Most of the large hotels have lively bars and nightclubs. The piano bars at the **Hotel Anglais** and the **Sergel Plaza** are popular spots. And the **Royal Viking** is always lively with its Diademe nightclub on the top floor.

Performances at the Royal Opera

Since most of the events at the Opera House are either concerts or ballet, even non-Swedish speakers can enjoy these, and it is fun and interesting to attend a performance here. As opera houses go, this one is almost intimate and cozy. Because it is small, the house sells out quickly, so buy tickets well in advance if you can.

Cinemas

Films in Sweden are not usually dubbed and many of them are American or English.

EXCURSIONS FROM STOCKHOLM

A variety of boat tours leaves from the pier in front of the Grand Hotel as well as from city hall. Several of these go into the archipelago. A quick trip into the archipelago takes you to Fjaderholmarna, about 25 minutes from the center of town. There is an aquarium here as well as an outdoor theater and swimming. If you're hungry, pick up seafood at the Smoke House or eat more formally and more expensively at the Fjaderholmarnas Krog. My preferences on the other boat tours are the one to Drottningholm Palace; the archipelago cruise, which lets you off at Vaxholm where you can have lunch and return on a later boat; and the Stockholm tour, which combines a bus and a boat tour. If you have seven hours, you might consider the Coastline: Archipelago of Sodertorn, which lands at small fishing villages and seaside towns and allows you time for a swim. There are also boat and bus tours to Sigtuna, Skokloster and Uppsala along the Royal Water way, one of Sweden's most beautiful water routes. For Uppsala, it is necessary to change boats. *Contact Stromma Kanalbolaget, Skeppsbron 30, or Stockholm Sightseeing at Skeppsbron 20.*

VAXHOLM

Vaxholm is about an hour's boat ride from Stockholm, and many of the sightseeing cruises come here. The town is filled with wooden buildings adorned with gingerbread carving. There is a Folk Art Museum depicting the way the Vaxholm fishermen used to live, and the Vaxholm fortress is now a museum exhibiting military memorabilia. There is a direct boat connection from Stockholm to the fortress, which is open every day from mid-May through August from noon to 4:00 p.m. Vaxholm also has a pleasant hotel and restaurant, where you can dine with a view of the harbor and the fortress. Accommodations in the archipelago: Visitors can rent chalets in the archipelago for $500–$700 per week. *Contact Stockholm Information Service, Box 7542, 10393 Stockholm,* ☎ *789-200.*

GRIPSHOLM CASTLE

The castle is located in Mariefred, about 65 kilometers south of Stockholm, an easy drive along E3. A steamer also leaves from the city hall every day at 10:00 a.m. during June, July and August. This is a most pleasant trip. The boat ride is fun, the 16th-century castle beautiful and interesting and the town of Mariefred charming. It is also possible to travel one way by boat and to make the return trip by train, an advisable course since the train ride is only a little over an hour while the boat trip takes four hours. Tickets and information for boat and train are available at Sweden House. The castle houses the Swedish State Portrait Collection and the Court Theater. *Open May–August every day from 10:00 a.m.–4:00 p.m.; September, October, March and April from Tuesday–Friday 10:00 a.m.– 3:00 p.m. and weekends from noon–3:00 p.m.; in January, February and November–December, open weekends only from noon–3:00 p.m.*

SIGTUNA

Tourist Information: *Drakegarden, Stora Gatan 33.* ☎ *8-592-50020*

In season, boat tours from Stockholm come here and to Uppsala. Some also include a stop at Skokloster Castle. Sigtuna was founded in 980 and its main street, Stora Gatan, claimed to be the oldest street in Sweden, still runs along the same route as the original 11th-century street. Besides just soaking up the idyllic atmosphere and doing a little shopping in the gift store, which is stuffed with up-market gifts for your friends at home, you can stop in to see the **church ruins** of St. Per's, Sweden's oldest church; visit the country's smallest **Town Hall**, just as it was in the 18th century; and see the **Maria Church** from the 13th century. Sigtuna is something of a cultural center with the **Sigtuna Foundation**, a church-sponsored center that offers courses, mainly of a philosophical or religious nature, and also houses a library and conference center in addition to a guesthouse. Visitors are welcome to stay in the guesthouse if arrangements are made ahead of time. Writers often come here to work in a quiet, inspiring atmosphere, surrounded by gardens and fountains. The Foundation, which hosts conferences on religion, is religious in the spiritual rather than the denominational sense.

WHERE TO STAY

The **Stadshotellet** in town is an adequate overnight spot with a pleasant restaurant.You can also arrange accommodations at the Sigtuna Foundation. Contact Tourist Information for other lodging possibilities.

SKOKLOSTER CASTLE

The castle is located 70 kilometers northeast of Stockholm and about 15 kilometers northeast of Sigtuna. This 17th-century, white baroque castle was built by Field Marshal Carl Gustav Wrangel, and is furnished with an extraordinary collection of tapestries, paintings, weapons and furniture, the bounty of his successful campaigns. The collection offers a good lesson in the history of Sweden's glory days. There is a Motor Museum containing Sweden's largest collection of old cars and motorcycles. Several boat tours from Stockholm stop here as well as at Sigtuna and Uppsala. *The castle is open every day from 11:00 a.m.–4:00 p.m., May–August. Visitors must take a guided tour. The Motor Museum is open every day from 11:00 a.m.–4:00 p.m.*

UPPSALA

Tourist Information: *Uppsala Turist & Kongress AB, Fyris torg 8, S-753 10 Uppsala. Turistbyra:* ☎ *018-11 75 00, 27 48 00. Guideservice:* ☎ *018-27 48 18. FAX 018-69 24 77.*

Uppsala is a university town, home of the oldest university in Scandinavian, founded in 1477. The city, the fourth largest in Sweden, is also the site of the historic, 500-year-old cathedral. The surroundings of Uppsala bear testimony to ancient religious practices. At Gamla Uppsala, which was the center of the old kingdom before the boats got too large for the river here, a large pagan temple once stood, and three burial mounds hold the remains of what were reputed to be Viking gods. It was at this place at Gamla Uppsala that the human and animal sacrifices of the old religion took place. Now the ritual most well known in Uppsala is the celebration of April 30, the Eve of May Day, when the students and alumni of the university sing and carouse all night, celebrating the end of winter and the coming of spring.

SIGHTSEEING TOURS

The M/S *Sagan*

A pleasure boat that travels in summertime between Uppsala and Skokloster, where you can visit one of Sweden's most interesting castles. (See "Skokloster Castle.") From Skokloster, it is possible to catch a boat for Stockholm via Sigtuna, or to make a return trip by train to Uppsala. *Departures of the Sagan are at 9:00 a.m. and 12:30 p.m. daily except Monday and Friday from around June 11 until the middle of August. The boat does not make the trip on Midsummer Eve or Day.*

For city sightseeing in Uppsala, Bus No. 700 makes a round trip of the city with optional guided tours at the major sights. *The bus departs from the Central Station every day, every hour on the hour, between 11:00 a.m. and 3:00 p.m. from late June–late August.*

WHAT TO SEE AND DO

Uppsala Cathedral

The first cathedral on this site was completed in 1150 and burned in 1250 and again in 1257. After rebuilding, it burned again in 1696, and was only completely restored at the end of the 19th century. Among the dignitaries, religious and royal, who are buried here are Gustavus Vasa; Erik the Holy, in a golden tomb; the parents of Saint Birgitta; and the philosopher Emanuel Swedenborg, whose brilliance seemed to touch every subject under and including the sun. The three main entrances of the cathedral are consecrated to the church's patron saints, St. Erik, St. Olof and St. Lars. *From the end of June through mid-August, a tour in English is given Monday–Saturday at 11:15 a.m. and 2:15 p.m. and Sunday at 1:15 p.m. and 2:15 p.m. During the last week of August and the first days of September, a sound and light show is given at the cathedral.*

Uppsala Castle

Offers an on-the-spot history lesson. Gustavus Vasa built this castle in the 16th century, and it was his daughter, Christina, who was its most dramatic occupant; for the young Queen Christina startled the nation when she abdicated her throne in order to go to Rome where she could pursue her religious vocation. Assuming the throne at the age of eighteen, and insisting that she be crowned *King* of Sweden, Queen Christina had surprised her subjects with her firm, confident hand and skilled diplomacy. She had brought a new interest in art and intellectual pursuits to her kingdom, even inviting the French philosopher Descartes, who it is said died of exhaustion from the rigors of the queen's intellectual demands. Then in 1654, the young queen, dressed simply in white, discarded her royal robes and crown and pronounced her cousin Prince Charles Gustavus her successor.

The castle has suffered several fires and boasts no exceptional architectural qualities except for its brick walls and the surrounding paths that bear a pinkish cast from the soil of the area. *Open daily from 11:00 a.m.–4:00 p.m. from May–September. Tours of the castle ruins and the Hall of State are given from late June through mid-August every day at 11:20 a.m. and 1:20 p.m.*

The House of Carolus Linnaeus

Carolus Linnaeus was an 18-century botanist who developed the system of botanical classification. His house is located near the University. Linnaeus taught at Uppsala University, and the house he lived in was the University residence for the head of the department of botany. The teacher and scientist laid out the garden himself. The garden and the house have been restored to the condition they were in when Linnaeus lived here. *Open mid-May to mid-September, Tuesday–Sunday from 10:00 a.m.–4:00 p.m. The gardens are open from the beginning of May through the end of August every day from 9:00 a.m.–9:00 p.m. In September, daily from 9:00 a.m.–7:00 p.m.*

The University Library

Called the Carolina Rediviva, the University Library possesses the renowned treasure, the Codex Argenteus, a fourth-century volume in which portions of the gospels, the earliest translations into Gothic, are written. The statue in front of the library is the work of sculptor Carl Eldh, portraying the young Prince Gustaf, who wrote the college song when he was a student here, and who died at the age of 22. *Open mid-June–August weekdays from 9:00 a.m.–7:30 p.m.; Saturday 9:00 a.m.–6:00 p.m. From June 1–September 15, the library is also open Sunday from 1:00 p.m.–3:30 p.m. The rest of the year it is open on weekdays from 9:00 a.m.–8:30 p.m. and Saturday from 9:00 a.m.–5:30 p.m. Guided tours of the university building, including the faculty rooms, the art collections, and the Augsburg cabinet, are given May–August (not at Midsummer) in Swedish and English at 1:30 p.m. and 2:30 p.m. daily.*

Gamla Uppsala

The old town is located about two kilometers from the center of Uppsala. There is an open-air museum, an old church, and a pleasant tavern where you can stop for a light lunch. This is also the site of the burial mounds mentioned above. It was to the pagan temple in Old Uppsala that the people of ancient Sweden came every ninth year to offer animal and human sacrifices.

Hammarby

The country house of Linnaeus which, with its grounds, is open to the public. Hammarby is reachable only by car or bicycle. *Open from mid-June through September from noon–4:00 p.m. daily.*

WHERE TO STAY

If you plan to spend the night in Uppsala, the **Hotel Linne**, near the Linnaeus Garden, is a pleasant, informal hotel with many of the rooms overlooking the gardens.

SMALAND AND THE BALTIC ISLANDS

Gotland is a sea-swept island off Sweden's east coast.

ON THE WAY TO THE SOUTH

If you are headed from Stockholm to Malmo and the southern part of Sweden, you can make a stop in the Kingdom of Glass. It is about a five and one half hour drive from Stockholm. In summer, Linjeflyg operates daily flights from Stockholm to Vaxjo in the glass district and there are also bus tours from Stockholm. The island of Gotland is also reachable by boat from Nynashamn, outside Stockholm, and by frequent daily flights from Arlanda Airport.

THE ISLAND OF GOTLAND

Tourist Office: *Burmeister House, Visby. Open April–September.*

GETTING THERE

Lygneflyg, the domestic arm of SAS, has 10 commuter flights daily from Stockholm to Visby. Ferryboats go from Nynashamn, south of Stockholm, and from Oskarshamn to Visby daily. Book these through **Gotlandsbolagets Bokningcentral**, *Box 2003, S 621 02 Visby,* ☎ *0498 119 00.*

GETTING AROUND

A car is almost essential here if you wish to see more of the island than the main town of Visby. This is also a cyclist's paradise.

SIGHTSEEING TOURS

A two-hour bus and walking tour leaves from the center of Visby every day at 11:00 a.m. from mid-June through mid-September. The tour hits the highlights of Visby and its surroundings.

The island of Gotland in the Baltic off Sweden's east coast is a sea-swept ellipse of rare and mysterious beauty. The town of Visby is the center of the island life, but the beaches and nature preserves farther out on the island are of great interest as well. Visby is somewhat of an anomaly. Its cozy, brightly painted, red-roofed houses nestle along narrow winding streets that seem welcoming and snug. Yet a glance upward in any direction yields the sight of the eerie towers of the 10 ruined medieval churches and the walls that rise above the city—silent sentinels to Visby's hectic past as a maritime center, a burger's haven and a Viking stronghold. Amid this heaping of cobbles, tiles and stone ruins, the roses grow in tangled disarray. Spilling from niches in the walls, from holes in the pavement, crawling up the door frames of the houses, they weave a web of color round the town. And from everywhere, through the gaping arches of the ruined churches, from the top of the winding streets, is the sea—clear and limitless, a blue rim around this rose-strewn picture-perfect town.

Visby is built on three levels. There is the area by the sea, then a bit higher the center of town and even higher, the newer houses, which do not look particularly new. You can easily get around the town by walking. A bicycle or car is a necessity if you want to go out from town to the beaches or the remarkable nature preserve, but in town, a bicycle could be a bit risky, as the streets are narrow and the drivers appear to be either suicidal or murderous.

Visby was a commercial center as long ago as the Iron Age. The Vikings and then the German merchants of the Hanseatic League appreciated it as an important stopping point on the shipping routes to the Black Sea and the Arab world. Visby was an international city with wealthy inhabitants who built beautiful homes and churches, but the town was prey to disaster, both natural and man-made. Fires and invasions left Visby a burned shell of its former self. The striking ruins that rise above the city are all that is left of the churches built by the German merchants who lived in Visby. The museum displays relics of these days, among them a valuable collection of gold coins from the Arab trade.

WHAT TO SEE AND DO

WALKING TOUR OF THE WALLED CITY

Start your tour of the walled city at **Almadelens**, the old harbor that is now a grassy park. In early times, when the island was lower, this area was water. But it became too shallow and so another harbor was found. Here, however, you will find the beginning of the wall at the **Gunpowder Tower**, which is still intact. Walk across the park toward the tower and through the arch into the walled city.

The Botanical Gardens

When you enter the walled city, you will be on Strandgatan, and if you follow this street you will arrive at the Botanical Gardens, with their extraordinary collection of plants from all over Sweden and from more exotic places as well. The soil of Gotland is low in acid, high in limestone and retains the heat. For these reasons, plants that cannot grow elsewhere in Sweden thrive here. In the gardens, you will find two mulberry trees from the Middle Ages; the poisonous Irish Spruce with which Gertrude allegedly killed Hamlet's father; a golden rain tree which is very beautiful, with its graceful yellow blossoms that are also poisonous, and which many cities have destroyed because of its danger for children. You will even find a Sequoia tree here, not so large as the California ones, but doing a fair job of remaining healthy. You might expect to discover some extraordinary roses here as well and you will not be disappointed. Hundreds of varieties, some extremely rare, are grown here.

Walk through the rose garden toward the northwest corner of the wall, which lies beyond the grassy meadow called **Pavilionsplong**. As you face the sea, you will see two low towers in the wall. The first you come to is the **Maiden Tower**, so called because it was in here that Karin, the young Swedish woman who befriended the Danish king when he was washed ashore on this island, was buried alive. The story is that a sailor was swept ashore, nearly dead, and taken to the home of a farmer to recover. The farmer's daughter—where have we heard this before—grew fond of the mysterious stranger and he revealed his identity only to her. He told her he was the king of Denmark, and he asked her to help him get the keys to one of the towers whereby he could gain entrance to the walled town. She did so and soon after he left, taking the keys with him. Some time later, he returned with a fleet of ships and many soldiers and attacked the city. While the Gotlanders were defending their city on one side, the Danish king took his keys and went round to the tower, gaining entrance to the town. The Gotlanders were vanquished but not so much so that they did not have the strength to seal up young Karin in the wall. If you look toward the north wall at this point, you will notice that there is an arched construction here, different from the west wall. At this point, the Gotlanders were adding height to the wall and learning more sophisticated building techniques as well. The arches demonstrate their understanding of basic structural theories.

St. Nicolai Church Ruins

Head back through the Pavilionsplong and take the small street called St. Nicolaigrand. This will lead you to the St. Nicolai Church ruins. There are 10 of these medieval ruins in Visby. Open to the sky and grass-floored, each seems to have its own aura and fascination. The ruins of St. Nicolai church serve as the stage for the famous *Petrus da Dacia*, the opera performed every summer in Visby. Take a few moments to look inside, as these ruins are particularly beautiful and reveal several styles of architecture illustrating the influences that came to Visby through its merchant trade.

St. Mary's Cathedral

Walk along Smedjegatan in the direction of the three towers of the cathedral. You will pass the church ruins of Helge Andsplan (the Church of the Holy Spirit) with its octagonal choir. Continue toward the cathedral, which is well worth a visit inside. It has been restored twice, once in 1905 and more recently from 1982 through 1987. The church was built by German merchants in 1225 and is the only church that was not burned, mainly because it was the German members of the Hanseatic League who came with torches to burn Visby and they did not want to burn their own church. However, this does not explain why St. Hans, another German church, was burned. Inside St. Mary's Cathedral are some of the medieval works of art that were removed from many of the churches during the Reformation. In Visby, much of this art has been saved and is well preserved because of the cool climate. You can see more of it in the Forlands Museum, but St. Mary's possesses some lovely pieces. Notice particularly the baptismal font. The altarpiece and fresco behind it are new. Be sure to visit the south chapel, which has been renovated with remarkable stained-glass windows. The organ in the chapel is interesting as well.

When you leave the cathedral, walk round to the south and you will see steps leading up to Nygatan. Take Nygatan to the left and follow it a few feet till you come to a grassy triangle. Cut left here and you will be on Norder Klint. Continue along this street to the end, and you will have a magnificent view of the town, the ruins and the sea. You will come out on Nygatan again, and if you go left a few feet to the spot where the cobbled street curves down into Nygatan, you will be on Norra Murgatan. Follow it back to the right. The houses here are tiny and flower-decked. The house at #38 is the smallest house in Scandinavia. Follow Norra Murgatan until it runs into Nygatan once more and follow Nygatan to Hastgatan. Now, all this careful instruction is not without purpose. At the spot where Nygatan runs into Hastgatan is a small square. There is a cafe here and also a fine ice cream shop **Cappucinobaren**. With ice-cream cone in hand—the pistachio is particularly good—take a short walk to the right just out of the ice cream shop. You will arrive at Osterport, the east gate of the walled city.

Beyond this is the newer town, with a pedestrian mall and the usual shops. It is to the credit of the Visby town planners that they have put most of this sort of thing outside the walls and so left the old city quite intact. There are a few hamburger spots that didn't know their rightful place was outside the walls, so occasionally you might come upon something less than appropriate in the old town, but for the most part the walled city is beautifully preserved, without artifice.

You could walk in the newer part of town, but for our purposes, I suggest you turn back down Hastgatan and cut off by the cafe down a short street called Smittensback, which leads to Sodra Kyrkogatan. Turn right on Sodra Kyrkogatan and you will come to **Stora Torget**, the main square. Just before the square, there is a small restaurant called **Masters**, where you can stop for lunch or a beer. There are three restaurants in Stora Torget as well. Whatever you choose, this is a good spot to end your walking tour and to have a snack or a meal. In summer, the **St. Katrins Rosengarden** has a lovely, rose-filled terrace where you can eat or have a drink and look at the ruins of the church. You will find pizzerias and hamburger places here as well. Unfortunately, the car park in the center of the square does not add to the ambience, but this is a lively center—a good place to come at night for the pubs and discos.

ALSO OF INTEREST

The Forlands Museum

The museum houses exhibits concerning the geological and anthropological history of Gotland. Among its most interesting displays are the treasures from sunken ships and Viking excavations.

ATTRACTIONS OUTSIDE VISBY

In addition to the attractions of Visby, the entire island of Gotland has much to offer the tourist who has a few days to take at leisure. You should get out onto the island either by bicycle or car. Because there are no hills, Gotland is an ideal place for cycling, and you can rent bicycles at the harbor. Buses operate from Visby across the island also, or you can arrange for an organized tour through the tourist bureau.

The **Lummellunda Caves** are a national attraction. Located north of Visby, these are the deepest caves in Sweden and are known for their stalagmites and stalactites. The **Karlso islands bird sanctuaries** off the coast of Visby can only be visited on an organized tour, which can be arranged through the tourist bureau. There are almost 100 medieval churches still in use on the island. Among the more interesting ones are: **Dalhem,** with its stained glass; **Gothem**, **Rone**, **Tingstade** and **Grotilingbo,** which has fascinating murals. The **Bunge Open-air Museum** displays houses and buildings depicting life on Gotland from as far back as the Iron Age. And the **Korumpu Fishing Village Museum**, near Klintehamn, houses a collection of fishing implements and boats from around the island.

SHOPPING

Visby is a fine place for handicraft enthusiasts. You will find several handicraft shops in Stora Torget and it is also worthwhile to walk to the **Gotlands Lans Hemslojd,** *St. Hansgatan 19.* This shop sells lovely items —textiles, ceramics and wood—made on Gotland.

WHERE TO STAY

If all this sounds too good to be true, or if you're saying, "Come on. It can't be this perfect," you're right. Gotland has one serious flaw—the hotel situation. There are very few adequate hotels. In town, the hotels are small and rather ordinary. If you are staying a week or longer, you can rent self-catering cottages through the tourist bureau. For holiday villages, contact the **Gotlandsresor AB**, *P.O. Box 2081, S 621 Visby,* ☎ *190 10.* For campsites and youth hostels, contact the **Swedish Touring Club**, *Gotlandsbokning. S 620 16 Ljugarn,* ☎ *46 498 912 20.* Once the season opens, call *Graboskolan,* ☎ *0498 169 33.*

The **Sara Hotel Snack**, near the airport, is modern and tastefully furnished, but a bit far from town. Some of the rooms are self-catering apartments, convenient if you are planning to stay several days and rent a car or bicycles to explore the island. *P.O. Box 1074, S 621 56, Visby,* ☎ *0498 600 00.*

If you want to be in a hotel in Central Visby, your best choices are: the **Hotel Lindgarden**, *Strandgatan 26,* ☎ *187 00;* or **The Strand Hotel**, *Strandgatan 34,* ☎ *126 00.* Both are adequate. **The Donnersplats Hotel**, across from Burmeister House, is more a rooming house than a hotel. Not all rooms have private baths. Though moderately priced, it is still a bit high for what it offers. But it is clean and comfortable enough. Its main virtue is that it is centrally located in Visby just across the street from the tourist office. ☎ *149 45.*

The Almedalens Lagenhetshotell
A good choice for visitors planning to stay a week or longer. Located right at the water in Almedalens, the site of the old harbor, this hotel has apartments available for two to four people for longer term rentals. Newly renovated and very pleasant. At the time I saw it, the owners were not certain what the minimum stay would be. It's worth looking into. *Strandvagen 8, 621 55 Visby,* ☎ *0498 718 66.* A restaurant is on the premises.

The Fridhem Pension and Guesthouse
Located about six kilometers from Visby, at the former summer residence of Princess Eugenie, King Oscar's consumptive daughter. This is a pretty, romantic spot, but the rooms do not have private baths or toilets. *S 621 98 Visby,* ☎ *654 00. P.O. Box 1183, S 621 58 Visby,* ☎ *640 10.*

Hotel Toftagarden
At Tofta • A small hotel with cabins as well as hotel rooms. It is located near the beach and a golf course. Not all rooms have private baths or toilets. *Tofta, S 621 98 Visby,* ☎ *0498 654 00.*

WHERE TO EAT

At one point during your stay, you should try the saffron pancake, a Visby specialty, made with 14 ingredients, seven of which are local, like milk, eggs and butter, and seven that were brought by the merchants from around the world: saffron, rice, cinnamon. The pancake is topped with mulberry sauce and sour cream.

Lindgarden
A beautiful restaurant in a charming setting but the food is somewhat overpriced. It is evidently popular, as it is usually crowded, and one should book ahead. The food is adequate but not up to the expectations set by the prices. The garden is an especially pleasant place, though it is not always open.

Rosengarden
Located on the big square, Stora Torget. A bit overpriced, but guests are served either in a very pleasant garden or the airy dining room.

Munkkallaren
In Stortorget, this is a lively, casual restaurant and pub. Try it for simple, inexpensive fare.

Gute Kalleran
Another informal restaurant in the main square.

KALMAR

Tourist Office: *Stortorget 36, Box 86, 391 21 Kalmar.*

Kalmar has enjoyed its prominence as a strategic, political and commercial center for centuries. In fact, the first mention of it was found south of Stockholm on a rune stone, dated 1067. Site of one of the finest medieval castles in Sweden, the 13th-century Kalmar Slott, Kalmar had a certain notoriety and experienced a bloody history. The castle, which stands today and is the main sight of Kalmar, and many of the area's churches along the coast were, in fact, built as fortresses. Today the city is a busy center for commerce, but it is also one of Sweden's most pleasant and interesting towns and has plenty to offer the tourist in terms of sightseeing, restaurants and excellent hotels.

WHAT TO SEE AND DO

The best way to see the sights of Kalmar is to take a walking tour. Because of its grid-like layout, it is easy to find your way, and it is small enough to get around on foot. The city is built on seven inlets, which are connected by bridges, and it was designed according to the Renaissance style, with parallel streets and quadrangles. Kalmar has won an award for its excellent maintenance of its historic buildings and its thoughtful renovation of its architectural treasures. One very obvious example of this is the brick water tower, which dominates the skyline of Kalmar. It has been converted into apartments that offer spectacular views of the city and the sea.

The following are suggestions for two walking tours that will give you close-up views of some of these buildings and unlock this city's considerable charm. Both tours begin at Stortorget, the central market square and the location of the cathedral. In addition, one can simply follow the city walls. This approach is particularly enjoyable when the lilacs are in bloom.

WALKING TOUR IN THE CENTER OF TOWN

Start at Stortorget, with the 17th-century **cathedral**, which was designed by Nicholas Tessin, the same gentleman who designed the Royal Palace in Stockholm. Take the time to look around the square. In the corner is the Dutch baroque-style former city hall, now the **Stadshotellet**. Your route will take you down Vastra Sjogatan toward the **harbor**, where many of the old warehouses have been renovated into shops, hotels and restaurants. At the corner of Olandsgatan and Lilla Torget, you will find the 17th-century house called **Dahm's House**. You can see the date, 1666, carved into the stone. Just across the street from this house is the home of the Kalmar County governor. Cate-corner from the Dahm's house is yet another 17th-century house worth a peek. Continue down to the water and stroll around the Guest Harbor, stopping perhaps for a coffee in the little yellow wooden cafe. From here you can see the bridge to Oland. At six kilometers, it is the longest bridge in Europe.

The Kalmar Lans Museum

As you continue your walk along Skeppsbrogatan, you will come to the museum, which is located in a beautifully renovated old flour mill. The exhibit of the findings from the Royal Ship *Kronan*, which sank just off Oland in 1676, is located here.

If you don't want to interrupt your walk at this point, add the museum to your list of things to return to. On your right, as you turn up Ostra Vallgatan, there is a large yellow stone building that was formerly the bath house when Kalmar was a watering spot for wealthy Europeans. It has also been turned into apartments. Now, as you continue on this street you will see a row of small wooden houses. These are Kalmar's treasures, dating from the last century. They too have been lovingly preserved. Continue past these houses, turning left at the corner onto Norra Langgatan, also fringed with these charming wooden houses. Follow this street and you will find yourself back at Stortorget.

WALKING TOUR TO THE CASTLE

From Stortorget, take Storgatan, the main shopping street of Kalmar and a pedestrian mall. This will lead you to the other market square of the city, where you will find the newly renovated theater of Kalmar. Occasionally, in summer, you might be lucky enough to catch a ballet or concert here, but the season ends in May. However, you can arrange through your hotel or the tourist office to go inside, even in off-season, if you wish. For now, though, continue walking past the theater and head toward the river and across the bridge. You will arrive at Slottsvagen, which you should take to your left. This is a broad boulevard, lovely and quiet. On your right, you will see the charming **Slottshotellet**, an old house that has been turned into a fine hotel belonging to the Romantik group of unique hotels.

You can continue straight on to the castle, but my suggestion is that you detour to your right and wander through some of the tiny streets that curve off the main street here. Take Molinsgatan, in which you will find a little ceramic and silversmith shop, where the two craftsmen who own it produce fascinating and fanciful creations that might not be to your taste but which you cannot help but find interesting and amusing. Look especially at the mechanical ceramics and the ceramic theaters. Once out of this shop, turn down Vasterlangaten and follow it, detouring momentarily onto Vasagatan to see the extraordinarily tiny houses from the late 18th and early 19th centuries. You can work your way back to Slottsgatan along the cemetery and through the park. The **Kalmar Art Museum** is located nearby.

Kalmar Castle

If you turn right on Slottsgatan, or just head through the park, you will come to the castle. This is your primary destination of the day. Take your time here. The castle was built as a fortress in the 12th and 13th centuries, and then rebuilt as a Renaissance palace by King Gustav Vasa and his sons Johan III and Eric XIV (who was known as the "pea soup king"). Look especially at King Eric XIV's State Room and the Grey Hall, which has an impressive coffered ceiling. Be sure to go into the chapel if it is not occupied by a wedding party. Also of interest in the castle is the museum gallery, which has a fine display of antiques and a maritime room. In fact, almost every room here is interesting for the architectural detail and the furnishings.

In the castle park, the **Byttan Restaurant** and cafe makes a good stop for hungry sightseers. There is a terrace, located by the water, or you can go inside and have an elegant meal at the restaurant.

WHERE TO STAY

Hotell Packhuset　　　　　　　　★★★★

Skeppsbrogatan 26, ☎ *0480 570 00* • The hotel occupies a beautifully renovated waterfront storehouse. The comfortable rooms retain the rustic flavor of the old building, but the furnishings and comforts are very up-to-date. This is a definite "thumbs up" recommendation.

Slottshotellet　　　　　　　　★★★

Slottsvagen 7, ☎ *0480 882 60* • A member of the Romantik Hotel Association, the Slottshotellet fulfills the standards of that organization in the unique charm of its rooms and its friendly, personal service. The main building was built in 1864, but the rooms are renovated and offer all the modern comforts one might wish. Each of the 35 rooms is individually decorated. All have private showers and toilet, telephone, radio, cable TV and video. Facilities are available for guests to cook their own meals. Conveniently located near the castle and the City Park.

Sara Hotel Witt　　　　　　　　★★★

42 Sodra Langgatan, ☎ *1 0480 152 50* • Built in 1972, the hotel is comfortable and modern with a fine restaurant, swimming pool and sauna.

Stadshotellet　　　　　　　　★★★

14 Stortorget, ☎ *0480 151 80* • Large, comfortable with newly renovated rooms and up-to-date amenities. Several restaurants, nightclub, pool and sauna.

WHERE TO EAT

Byttan is located in the City Park. You can eat in the airy, elegant dining room or on the terrace. The **Stadshotellet** offers gourmet dining in a dignified setting. For less expensive meals, try the above at lunch rather than dinner, or**Baronen,** *at 12 Skeppsbrogatan,* which serves dinner for about $14.

THE KINGDOM OF GLASS

Tourist Office: *Smalands Turistrad, Box 36, S 351 03 Vaxjo.*

It is not hyperbole to call the area between Kalmar and Vaxjo "The Kingdom of Glass," for the products of the Swedish glassworks are elegant in design and noble in execution. To watch the glassblowers at Orrefors or Kosta is to watch artists and heroes, dedicated to their craft and willing to endure great discomfort and difficulty in order to turn out their beautiful creations.

This glass area of the province of Smaland is also called the emigrant's region, for it is from here that almost 200,000 people from Smaland emigrated to North America in the middle of the 19th century. The thin, rocky soil of the region made farming difficult, and poverty and near-starvation drove many residents to America in search of prosperity and an easier life. Vilhelm Moberg's novel *The Emigrants* chronicles the hardships of these times. Moberg's childhood home has been torn down, but a stone marks the spot and his old school has been made into a museum. The farmstead of Klasa, in Langasjo, is the setting for the film of *The Emigrants*. Visitors interested in emigration can spend time at **The Emigrant Institute** in Vaxjo. This is a museum and research center for emigration from Smaland as well as other parts of Sweden.

If you wish to spend some time in the area, there are several choices, and one possibility is to base yourself in Kalmar and make excursions from there. Bear in mind that there is more than just glass in this region. Enjoy a swim in one of the sparkling lakes, hike through the forests or simply drive through the countryside, exploring the small roads.

GETTING THERE

In summer, Linjeflyg makes daily flights to Vaxjo from Stockholm. There is also bus service from Stockholm.

GETTING AROUND

The glass district is not far from Kalmar so a car is the best way to have the flexibility you will want if you're interested in seeing several glassworks. But there are bus tours from Stockholm if you simply want to come to the glass district and go no farther. Consult the Stockholm tourist office or the Smalands tourist agency.

WHAT TO SEE AND DO

THE GLASSWORKS

The best known glassworks, **Orrefors**, **Kosta** and **Boda**, are nearby and one can also visit the **Lessebo Hand Paper Mill**. At Nybro, the 19th-century buildings surrounding the old **Pukeberg** glassworks are preserved, and the glassworks operates as it did in the last century. These are all within an hour's drive from one another. You can watch the glassblowers every day until 3:00 p.m. at any of these. All these close for the month of July, but one demonstration workshop is usually open for visitors. Most of the glassworks have shops at which you can buy the products and arrange for your purchases to be shipped home duty-free. This is a highly reliable process, and the goods usually arrive much more quickly than promised. At Orrefors, you can buy only seconds, but the flaws are indiscernible. Of course, if you are looking for a collector's item or an investment, you would not want to buy these, but for the casual collector, there are some wonderful bargains and a vast selection. It bears repeating to remind readers that the glassworks shut down at 3:00 p.m. and that they take an early lunch break around 10:30 a.m., so plan your time accordingly. The shops and exhibition rooms stay open until 5:30 or 6:00 p.m. on weekdays and until 3:00 or 4:00 p.m. on Saturdays. Sunday hours are noon to 4:00 p.m. If you go late in the afternoon, you might be lucky enough to be able to stay around for the changing of a kiln. This does not occur every day, but it is quite a sight to see the glassblowers struggle with the red hot furnace, lifting out the glowing kiln liner and replacing it with a new, clean, white one.

Hyttsill, which means "glassworks herring," is a tradition in this area. Several of the glassworks cooperate in this effort and the hyttsill is conducted at different glassworks on different dates. This tradition grew from the time when the glassworks was a gathering place for all the people of the surrounding country. They met in the evenings for a bit of chatter and good cheer spiced with herring, prepared as it can only be done in a glassworks. This hyttsill is cooked in the fiery glass furnace, held on the glassblower's bar until the fish is baked crisply. Potatoes bake in the hot ashes of the furnace on a special glass-making tool that allows one to turn and shake the potatoes. These glassworks delicacies are further enhanced with homemade beer and aquavit—the ingredients of a lively evening of camaraderie and good food. In the old days, there was frequently a traveler or even a peddler who might spin a yarn or two. And present-day visitors to the hyttsill evening might be lucky enough to find among them just such a storyteller or to enjoy card games, old songs or just good conversation. Visitors can participate in a hyttsill evening by calling any of the following glassworks: **Bergdala** ☎ *0478 11650*; **Kosta** ☎ *0478 503 00*; **Orrefors** ☎ *0481 300-59*; **Pukeberg** ☎ *0481 137 20.*

OTHER SIGHTS

Among the most interesting of the old churches here are those at **Orsjo, Kraksmala** and the 13th-century wooden **Granhult Church,** the oldest wooden church in Sweden. The **Smaland Museum** in Vaxjo has the largest collection of glass in northern Europe. There are also museums at Orrefors, Kosta, Skruf, Johansfors, Lindshammar and Rosdala glassworks. At Strombergshyttan, there is a **Doll Museum** and at Kosta, a **Railway Museum.** The **Smaland Hunting and Fishing Museum** is located at Eriksmala. Northern Europe's longest **narrow gauge railway** runs from the glass district to the Blue Coast on the Baltic. Passengers can get off to visit the Rosdala Glassworks or to have a meal at one of the inns along the way.

WHERE TO STAY

If you are looking for a romantic place to stay, you will find an old inn near Varnamo. Located northwest of Vaxjo and easily accessible from Jonkoping or Granna if you have been in the lake district is the **Toftaholm Herrgardshotel**. With portions of the building dating from the 14th century, the Toftaholm Manor House is one of Smaland's oldest and largest estates. The legends claim that in 1552, King Gustav Vasa stole his bride from the south wing of the house, which is still standing. The hotel is beautifully situated in the middle of an inland wooded landscape and the terrace of the hotel overlooks Vidostern lake, where guests can swim, boat or fish. Winter sports are also available here, from ice-fishing and cross-country skiing to horse-drawn sleigh rides for the less athletic. The hotel has a fine dining room. *For information and booking, contact the manag-*

ers of Toftaholm, Jan and Lisbeth Boethius, Toftaholm, S 34015 Vittyard, Sweden, ☎ (0370) 440 55.

THE ISLAND OF OLAND

Tourist Office: *Olands Turistforening. Box 115, 387 00, Borgholm, Sweden,*
☎ *0485 123 40. The tourist office is located at the harbor in Borgholm.*

A short drive from Kalmar across Europe's longest bridge will
bring you to the island of Oland, a good spot to spend a few days enjoying the Swedish sunshine, the water and the beaches. Oland is a
fine place for cycling and is known for its bird sanctuary and nature
preserve as well as for its easygoing, friendly atmosphere.

The gregarious natives of Oland are proud of their island and are
delighted to show visitors the charm of their long, narrow beach-
rimmed paradise. This is a spot where one could settle for several
glorious summer weeks, baking on the beaches that are cooled by
gentle breezes, or cycling along some of the most varied landscapes
in Sweden. Oland is a haven for nature lovers. Meadows, white sand,
chalk cliffs and bird sanctuaries—the visitor will find them all on
Oland. In addition, one can scout out the evidence of Iron Age and
Viking settlements—rune stones, burial grounds, foundations of villages and strongholds.

Oland is a limestone plain—actually one single limestone rock that
was laid down 500 million years ago. The island was a popular health
resort at the turn of the century. Wealthy Europeans had villas here,
and the living was easy—and luxurious. The typical Oland houses are
wood above stone, and some of the more luxurious villas of Oland's
heyday are still standing—many of them serving now as pensions.

The **windmills** have become the symbol of Oland, and they sometimes punctuate the landscape in rows of as many as seven. Of the
original 2,000, approximately 400 remain. These are protected as
national monuments.

GETTING THERE

The easiest way to Oland is by car or bus across the long bridge from Kalmar.
From Stockholm, you can come by boat. There is also boat service from Travemunde in Germany via the Danish island of Bornholm.

WHAT TO SEE AND DO

One of Oland's most popular attractions is **Ottenby**, a bird station and museum on the southern point of the island. For the best sampling of Oland's trademark windmills, visit **Storlinge Kvarnar**, the longest row of windmills (seven in
all) on the island. Another landmark is **Lange Jan** (Long John), Sweden's tallest

lighthouse. **Solliden** is the royal summer residence of King Carl Gustav and Queen Sylvie. *From June–August, the park is open from noon to 5:00 p.m.*

Borgholms Slottsruin, the ruins of Oland's 12th-century castle, which was destroyed by fire in 1806, is a dramatic spot that serves as the setting for summer concerts. It makes for a most pleasant evening to listen to the music and the song of the swallows, and to watch the pink sky. **Stora Alvaret** is Oland's extraordinary treeless, limestone plain, where rare wildflowers grow in abundance. In early summer, the plain is covered with wild orchids. Also on the Alvaret is **Tingstad Flisor**, a series of stone formations.

Oland has several fortified villages tourists can visit. **Eketorps borg** is the site of the excavation and partial reconstruction of a fifth-century fortified village, and is perhaps the most interesting of those villages because of the restoration. **Graborg** is Oland's largest ancient fortress. Nearby are the ruins of the 13th-century **St. Knut's Chapel**. **Ismantorps borg**, an ancient fortress site with the foundations of 88 houses, was probably the site for a prehistoric cult. **Gardslosa Kyrka** is the best example of a medieval church on Oland. Here you will find 12th-century frescoes, and art objects of the 17th and 18th centuries.

There are many more burial sites with rune stones and more ancient fortresses and churches than I have listed here, so if you are interested in seeing more of these, consult the Oland Tourist Office for information.

WHERE TO STAY

Again, the tourist office can help you with reservations in pensions and summer houses.

The Halltorps Gastgiveri

A small inn with pleasant, cozy rooms and excellent food. The building was a farmhouse, and still retains a farmhouse charm. Specify a room with private bath. ☎ *0485 552 50.*

The Hotell Guntorps Herrgard

A charming manor house with newly renovated rooms and some apartments. It also has a swimming pool. It is within walking distance from the center of town. A definite "thumbs up" recommendation.

Hotel Borgholm

For a simpler, less expensive stay, this hotel is a lively place with adequate accommodations. Some rooms do not have baths. ☎ *0485 110 60.*

Villa Gattan 6

A lovely rooming house with large, airy rooms and a pleasant garden. For accommodations in this private house, contact the tourist office.

WHERE TO EAT

Backficken in the Hotel Borgholm is a deservedly popular gourmet restaurant. **The Halltorps Gastgiveri** serves exceptional food. It is expensive. **Robinson Crusoe** is right on the harbor. The food is excellent, expensive but not overpriced, and the setting, with an enclosed terrace overlooking the water, as well as a cozy inside dining room, makes for a very pleasant meal.

AUTHOR'S OBSERVATION

A culinary note: At some point during your stay on Oland, you should try "Oland flounder," which is served fresh or smoked with potatoes.

ON THE WAY

Travelers headed from Smaland to Skane can take the beautiful drive along the coast from Kalmar to Malmo. There are also direct flights between Kalmar and Copenhagen for those headed to Denmark.

SKANE: THE RICH SOUTHLAND

Skane was one of the last regions of Sweden to win its freedom from Denmark; and in its architecture, in its food and even in the character of its people, it seems almost more Danish than Swedish. Travelers can just about hop across the water from Malmo to Copenhagen or from Helsingborg to Helsingor. The villages of Falsterbro and Skanor, just 30 kilometers southwest of Malmo, are idyllic resort towns with nearly perfect beaches and enviable little flower-decked cottages. Helsingborg is the port city for departures to Denmark, and north of that is the resort town of Bastad, mecca for the chic set of Sweden. As well as being the breadbasket of Sweden, Skane is also the chateau country. The land is dotted with gracious manor houses and castles, some of which are open to the public. Going east from Malmo, you will drive to the historic and picturesque town of Ystad and on along the east coast of southern Sweden to idyllic fishing villages.

MALMO

Malmo Tourist Office: *Hamngatan 1, S-211 22 Malmo,* ☎ *040-341270. Open Monday–Friday, 9:00 a.m.–7:00 p.m.; Saturday–Sunday, 9:00 a.m.–3:00 p.m.*

MALMO CARD

Stop by the Malmo Tourist Office, 1 Hamngatan, to pick up this card, which entitles the bearer to discounts and free admission to many attractions in and around Malmo. With the card, you are entitled to travel free on the green ML buses within Malmo, and you receive a 50 percent discount on Pagatagen local trains. There is a 25 percent discount off the hydrofoil to Copenhagen. You can buy the card at ML kiosks, Pressbyran kiosks and at the Post Office.

DIRECTORY

Banks • Open Monday–Friday, 9:30 a.m.–4:00 p.m.; Thursday, 9:30 a.m.–5:30 p.m.

Car Rental • **Avis,** *Stortorget 9,* ☎ *040 778 30.* **Hertz,** *Skeppsbron 3,* ☎ *749 55.* **Budget/OK** *Biluthyrning, Baltzarsgatan 14,* ☎ *040 755 75.* **Europcar**, *Djaknegatan 2,* ☎ *040 716 40.* Avis, Budget/OK, **Interrent**, and Hertz all have car rental offices at Sturup Airport.

Currency Exchange • **Forex,** *Malmo Tourist Office. Hamngatan 1.* Open daily 8:00 a.m.–9:00 p.m., ☎ *040 124034.* **Hydrofoil Terminal,** *Skeppsbron 4.*

Open daily 7:30 a.m.–8:00 p.m. **Main Post Office**, *Malmo 1, Skeppsbron 1*. Open Monday–Friday, 8:00 a.m.–6:00 p.m., Saturday, 8:00 a.m.–noon.

Doctor on Call • ☎ *040 33 35 00*. Available 7:00 a.m.–10:00 p.m. daily and 10:00 p.m.–midnight, Monday–Friday, ☎ *040 33 10 61*. Other times, ☎ *040 33 1000*.

Emergency Number • ☎ *90 000*. Indicate fire, police or ambulance. Emergency calls are free from public phone booths.

Hotel Booking Service • ☎ *040 341268*.

Pharmacy • **APOTEK Lejonet,** *Stortorget 8*, ☎ *040 712 35*. Monday–Friday, 8:00 a.m.–6:00 p.m. Saturday, 9:00 a.m.–3:00 p.m. Day and night service. **Apoteket Gripen**. *Bergsgatan 48*, ☎ *040 19 21 13*.

Post Offices • Main Post Office. *Skeppsbron 1. Malmo 1*. Open Monday–Friday, 8:00 a.m.–6:00 p.m.; Saturday, 8:00 a.m.–noon. Post Counter, *SJ Railway Station*. Open Monday–Friday, 5:00 p.m.–9:00 p.m; Saturday, 10:00 a.m. to 2:00 p.m.; Sunday, 2:00 p.m.–6:00 p.m.

Telephone • The area code for Malmo is *040*. Local directory assistance is *000*. Within Malmo it is necessary to dial only the last five or six digits of a number.

Though Malmo is an industrial center, its many parks and canals, seaport and beaches, and beautifully preserved old town make it a pleasant stop for tourists in the south of Sweden. It is a city for the leisurely. No need to rush around trying to take in every sight at once. Rather, pace yourselves, as these southern Swedes do, and stroll through the fascinating streets of the old section, stop at one of the cafes in Stora Torget or browse at the market in Lilla Torget. Take a bus and your bathing suit to the beautiful beach at Falsterbro or explore the sailing harbor at Skanor, both towns just half an hour away from Malmo itself. And there are rewarding sights in Malmo proper as well.

Malmo's ideal location on a major navigational lane has made it an important seafaring and commercial center for centuries. Tossed back and forth among Denmark, the North German Hanseatic League and Sweden, it came first to Sweden as part of the dowry of the Danish Princess Sophia when she married King Valdemar of Sweden in 1260. It was recaptured by Denmark a century later, and both the Danish and German influences are still evident today. The City Hall and beautiful St. Peter's Church are certainly German in inspiration, but the Danish presence is reflected as well, both in the architecture and in the friendly, lighthearted atmosphere that pervades the city with its parks, gardens and outdoor cafes. Today it is

Sweden's third largest city, and it boasts the largest man-made harbor in the country.

GETTING THERE

SAS operates a hydrofoil between Copenhagen airport and Malmo several times daily. Other hydrofoils run regularly between downtown Copenhagen and Malmo. The trip takes less than an hour. Linjeflyg flies to Malmo from Stockholm and Goteborg. Sturup airport is located about 18 miles from the center of town.

GETTING AROUND

The center of Malmo lends itself to walking. For farther-flung jaunts, the tourist has several choices. For information on bus service, call the **ML. Green Buses, ☎** *040 29 25 10;* **Bus 999 Intercity, Lund-Malmo-Copenhagen,** **☎** *046 14 14 50.* **SJ Bus & Airport buses, ☎** *040 20 24 73.* There is frequent **ferry service** to Copenhagen and to Copenhagen airport. For information, **☎** *040 10 39 30.* The **Pagatagen** local trains operate between Malmo and the southwest area of Skane. They depart from the local train station, which is situated at the SJ Railway Station. Tourists can buy tickets at the machines on the platforms. This is an efficient way to get to nearby towns such as Lund. If you have a **Malmo Card**, which entitles you to a half-price ticket, simply push the button marked "halv" in the ticket machine for the child's fare.

SIGHTSEEING TOURS

Guided **bus tours** in Swedish and English leave Gustav Adolfs Torg and Varnhemstorget daily at 11:00 a.m. and 1:00 p.m. during June, July and August. Tickets can be purchased at the kiosk in the square. Your Malmo Card entitles you to a 50 percent discount. A guided **walking tour** of one and one half hours through the center of town is offered Tuesday and Thursday at 2:00 p.m. from June to August. It departs from the tourist office in Hamngatan. Inquire at the tourist office for details. The walking tour is free with the Malmo Card. **Boat trips** on the canals, through the old part of the city, the parks and past Malmohus Castle, leave on the hour from 11:00 a.m. to 5:00 p.m. from May to August. Departures from the Central Station. The boat trip lasts approximately 45 minutes.

WHAT TO SEE AND DO

A STROLL THROUGH THE OLD TOWN

The old town occupies the central section of the city, bounded by canals and crowned by Stortorget. The following walking tour will take you to the major points of interest. This walk begins at **Stortorget**, the large central square of Malmo. As you face east, you will see the **Town Hall**. This building was completed in 1546, but its appearance has changed over time. It was rebuilt in 1812 in neoclassical form, and then renovated in 1869 in the Dutch-Renaissance style. The sculptures on the facade represent Themis, the goddess of justice. There are also representations of the traditional occupations of Malmo: shipping, farming, crafts and trade. There has always been a tavern in the basement. Now it is a restaurant, called **Radhuskallaren**. The **Knuts Hall** and the **County Hall** are of interest as well.

If you need a little sustenance before starting your walk, the **cafe** on the terrace of the Radhuset is a popular, moderately priced spot. (The restaurant in the cellar is more expensive.) You will also find plenty of inviting cafes along the way, particularly in Lilla Torg. To your left as you face the Radhuset, you see a white building—actually two connected buildings. This is the residence of the mayor of Malmo. The equestrian statue in the center of the square is of King Carl Gustav X and was completed in 1896. At *No. 8 Stortorget* is the **Apotek Lejonet**, the oldest pharmacy in Sweden, built in 1571. *Open Monday–Friday, 8:00 a.m.–6:00 p.m.; Saturday, 9:00 a.m. to 3:00 p.m.*

Behind the Radhuset rise the towers of **St. Peter's Church**. Take the time to detour behind the town hall in order to see this 14th-century church that bears the mark of Malmo's German heritage. Designed in the Baltic-Gothic style, it closely resembles the Marienkirche of Lubeck. Notice particularly the pulpit, which was given to the church in 1599, the altar, the largest of its kind in northern Europe, the 15th-century merchants' chapel with beautiful murals, and a 17th-century sandstone font. On the outside of the chapel, look for the sculptures of the saints. These are among Malmo's oldest preserved sculptures.

Back on Stortorget, take **Sodergatan**, the walking street, south from the square. You can stroll along this street if you like, but for our purposes, you should take the little street called **Skomakaregatan** to your right, and you will come to **Lilla Torg**, a beautifully maintained 16th-century square. Take time to look at the lovely old buildings here. There are handicraft shops and galleries here, and you will find several cafes.

The **Form Design Center** occupies the 16th-century half-timbered Hedman House on Lilla Torg. The center offers changing exhibitions of Swedish design. There is also a shop, cafe and reading corner with design publications. Opening hours vary with the season, so check with the center or the tourist office. The Design Center is closed Sunday and Monday. Also at Lilla Torg is the **Saluhall**, or Market Hall. Take the time to go inside. It's a good place for browsing, especially if you're hungry. *Open Monday–Friday, 9:00 a.m.–6:00 p.m.; Saturday, 9:00 a.m.–2:00 p.m.*

Once out of the Saluhall, cross Engelbrektsgatan and turn onto **Jons Filsgatan**. The small houses on this street are beautifully restored and maintained. Follow this street to **Langgardsgatan**, which angles north. Take it north for just a short walk until you come to **Jakob Nilsgatan**. This is one of the prettiest and most nicely preserved streets in the area. It will lead you to **Slottsgatan**. Here you have two choices. If you are weary of walking and sightseeing, you can head back to the center of town. Turn right down Slottsgatan and you will come to Norra Vallagatan. Turn right on that street and you will be at one of the many canals of Malmo. Here is the railway station, which has an inexpensive but popular restaurant, and the Savoy Hotel, one of Malmo's finest, with an elegant restaurant, the cafe Savoy, and a less formal dining spot as well. The canal boat trips through town leave from this canal in front of the railway station. Your other choice, once you reach Slottsgatan, is to turn left, or south, and you will come to **Slottsparken** and **Kungsparken**, which make up the main park of Malmo.

Malmohus Castle

Located in the park, this 450-year-old castle has done service as a fortress, as the residence for the Danish kings visiting this outpost of their empire and even as a prison. The earliest portions of Malmohus were erected in the 15th century as a royal residence by Erik of Pomerania, who was instrumental in developing Malmo as a trade center. The residence later became the headquarters of the mint that made the coins used in Denmark. In the 16th century, King Christian III began work on a larger castle and fortress as an extension of the mint, and it is this castle, restored in 1932, which is the present Malmohus. Now it is Malmo's principal museum, housing six different museums inside its walls. Here you will find the **City Museum**, the **Art Museum**, the **Museum of Natural History** and the **Aquarium**. Even the restaurant, the **Wega**, is something of a museum itself with its turn-of-the-century furnishings. Nearby are the **Military Governor's House** and the **Technical and Maritime Museums**. *Closed Monday from September to June; open Tuesday and Saturday, noon–4:00 p.m.; Thursday, noon– 9:00 p.m.; Sunday and holidays, noon–4:30 p.m.*

OTHER POINTS OF INTEREST

The Limhamn Museum and Limhamn Yacht Basin

A haven for small pleasure boats. The little blue soldier's cottage located here is now a museum, furnished as it would have been for a fisherman. There are temporary exhibitions as well and a small archaeological exhibit. *Open all year, Wednesday from 6:00 p.m. to 8:00 p.m.; Saturday and Sunday from 1:00 p.m. to 4:00 p.m.*

Malmo Konsthall

The contemporary art museum of Malmo has exhibits of both Swedish and international art. Bookshop, museum cafe. *Open Tuesday and Thursday, 11:00 a.m.–8:00 p.m.; Wednesday, 11:00 a.m.–9:00 p.m.; Friday–Monday 11:00 a.m.–5:00 p.m.*

The City Theater

The theater, which was built in the 1940s, gained fame in the 1950s when Ingemar Bergman was its director. Considered one of Europe's finest theaters, it stages impressive and influential performances. The fountain in front of the theater shows figures of the world of comedy and drama. See if you can recognize any of them. A 50 percent discount on tickets are available to Malmo Card holders.

Mollevangstorget

Every Saturday, a market is set up in this square in the old working-class district of Malmo.

Pharmacy Lejonet

8 Stortorget • This is the oldest pharmacy in Malmo. *Open all year Monday–Friday, 8:00 a.m.–6:00 p.m.; Saturday, 9:00 a.m.–3:00 p.m.*

PARKS AND RECREATION

Malmo is the city of parks—14 large ones in all. **Kungspark**, mentioned above, in the west of Malmo is adjacent to Malmohus Castle. **Slottsparken** boasts the statue Pegasus by Carl Milles. Walking distance from the center of town is **Ribersborgsstrandsgatan**, where bathers can swim off the beach or the piers. The beach runs south to Sibbarp. Right in town, you can get your exercise by renting a paddle boat on the canal. If it's just fresh air and scenery you're after, take one of the canal boat cruises and leave the driving to someone else.

Limhamnsfaltet is the recreational area in the middle of the city. Nearby is Hylliekroken golf course, with six holes and a driving range. For fishing trips on the sound, contact the tourist office. *Daily departures Wednesday–Sunday.* Horse racing, both flat and harness, takes place at Jagersro.

SHOPPING

SHOPPING HOURS

Small shops are open Monday–Friday from 9:30 a.m. to 6:00 p.m., and department stores stay open until 7:00 or 8:00 p.m. On Saturday, most shops are open until 1:00 or 2:00 p.m., while department stores remain open until 3:00 p.m. Some department stores are open Sunday afternoon.

SODERGATAN

Running up from Stortorg through Gustav Adolfstorg, Sodergatan is the main pedestrian and shopping street of Malmo. But be sure to take some of the side streets that sprout off Sodergatan as well. **Lilla Torg** has many boutiques and handicraft shops, as well as a market. **Charlotte Weibull's Doll Center** is a must for anyone traveling with children, but you don't really need to have a child in tow for an excuse to explore this charming toy store. One can find traditional costumes of Skanor here also, and the gallery is filled with exhibits of crafts, folklore, and dolls.

GLASS AND HOME FURNISHINGS

Silverbergs is the place for cookware, Swedish glass and international furniture.

FURS

Mattson Pals, *Norrga Vallgatan 98*, has an outlet in the fur department in NK as well.

Obergs Pals, *Skomakaregatan 2.*

Osterlunds Pals, *Lilla Torg 1.*

MEN'S CLOTHING

Olsen's, *Gustav Adolfstorg 41.*

Cason's, *Gustav Adolfstorg 8.*

Olsen's for Women, *Sodergatan 21.*

JEWELRY

Detters, *Sodergatan 26.*

SHOPPING CENTERS AND DEPARTMENT STORES

Shoppers will find **NK, Ahlens** and **Domus** department stores here, as well as the **Gallerian Shopping Centre**, an enclosed center with more than 60 speciality shops under one roof. Here you will find expensive designer boutiques, as well as more moderately-priced trendy shops.

WHERE TO STAY

Malmo has several excellent hotels, worth the splurge if you're so inclined. Many of the hotels offer reduced rates in summer, so it's worth looking into some of the more posh spots.

EXPENSIVE

The Savoy
   62 N. Vallgatan, across from the railway station • This is an elegant, old-world hotel with nicely renovated rooms and a friendly ambience. Rooms at last check were running between 700SEK and 1000SEK. The Savoy cafe is one of the best restaurants in town.

The SAS Royal
   Ostergatan 8 • This new hotel lies in the heart of the old section and is ultra-modern, with rooms designed to appeal to the most spoiled of tourists. Each floor has a different motif, with one devoted to rooms decorated in the Italian high-tech style, another more Scandinavian in feeling, etc. As in most SAS hotels, there is a Royal Club floor with additional amenities. The restaurant here, in a renovated 16th-century townhouse, is lovely. Average room rate is 900SEK.

The Hotel Kramer
   Stortorget 7 • Another of Malmo's *grande dames.* With its lowest priced rooms at 600SEK, it's less expensive than the Savoy or the SAS Royal, but you can spend plenty here if you're so inclined, as the maximum double rooms go for over 1000SEK.

The Noble House
   Gustav Adolfs Torg 47 • The Noble is one of the most popular spots for tourists. It opened in 1986, and has very modern facilities. Rates run from 750SEK to 900SEK.

The Hotel Residens
   Adelsgatan 7 • This is also a good choice and a bit less expensive than the above-listed hotels. Rooms, at last report, ran between 750SEK and 850SEK.

MODERATE

The Anglais Fralsingarmens Hotel
   Stortorget 15 • This is a Salvation Army hotel, simple, but well run, immaculate and comfortable. Rooms run between 600SEK and 700SEK.

The Baltzar Hotel

Sodergatan 20 • The rooms range from 450SEK to 725SEK.

The Master Johan Lagenhetshotell

Isak Slaktaregatan 9 • Some rooms have kitchen facilities. The average rate is 900SEK and includes breakfast.

INEXPENSIVE

The Temperance

Engelbrektsgatan 16 • In spite of its name, it boasts a cozy bar. Rooms range from 500SEK to 675SEK.

The Hotel Tunneln

Adelsgatan 4 • Rooms with no shower or toilet go for under 300SEK. With shower and toilet, you will pay 495SEK.

Youth Hostel

STFs: Vandrarhem "Sodergarden," Backavagen 18. 55SEK, with a kitchen and washing machine available for guests.

Camping

Sibborps Camping, Strandgaten, ☎ *040 155165.* Open all year.

WHERE TO EAT

The Danish love and talent for fine cuisine seem to have floated across the Sound and pervaded the restaurants of Malmo. You will find plenty of fine dining here, and a zest for food that is more Danish than Swedish.

Kockska Krogen

Stortorget • This is as much a sight as a place to eat, as it is in the former home of the 16th-century mayor, whose name the restaurant now bears. The candlelit interior, with its thick walls and cozy vaulted rooms, is heavily atmospheric, and the food is excellent. *Closed Sunday and for Saturday lunch.* **Expensive.**

Olga's

In Pildammsparken • The setting of this rustic restaurant, by a willow-draped pond, is lovely. The food is hearty, well prepared and offers the best of Swedish cuisine. **Moderate to expensive.**

Pers Krog

A casually decorated restaurant with a pleasant though not particularly beautiful terrace; this is another good choice.

Moderate to expensive.

Arstiderna

Grynbodgatan 9 • This pleasant, airy, modern restaurant serves a variety of Swedish gourmet specialities. *It is open every day but Sunday for lunch and dinner.*

Radhuskalleren

Kyrkogatan 8 in the City Hall • A cozy cellar restaurant, with plenty of atmosphere. One of the dining rooms is known as the Witches' Cellar, because 19 women accused of witchcraft were imprisoned there. Though the menu is ambitious and the prices are not low, you can eat inexpensively at lunchtime by ordering the daily special, or *dagens ratt*, which will cost you about 35SEK. *Open daily for lunch and dinner.*

Casa Mia
12 Sodergatan • You can have a full meal, not the *dagens ratt*, for about 130SEK. As the name suggests, the focus here is Italian.

O'Yes
In the Borshuset, Skeppsbron 2 • This popular restaurant is located in the former stock exchange or *Borse*, which dominates the main canal in the area of the railway station.

HOTEL DINING

The Restaurant Thott
In the SAS Royal Hotel • A beautifully renovated 16th-century town-house that has been ingeniously incorporated into this very modern hotel. The food is excellent.   *Expensive.*

The Classic Restaurant
In the Savoy Hotel • An elegant dining spot with fine food and friendly service from courtly waiters. The restaurant serves dinner only and is open until 1:00 a.m. Expensive. Also in the hotel, just across the lobby is the **Grillen,** a cozy, plaid-wrapped pub-style restaurant that serves grilled meats and fish. It is open from noon until 1:00 a.m. The **Savoy cafe** is also open for lunch, and remains open until 2:00 a.m. with entertainment nightly. Both the Savoy Classic and the Grillen are moderately expensive, but you can order a set lunch in the Grillen at a more reasonable price. *Closed Sunday.*

EXCURSIONS FROM MALMO

The area of southern Skane around Malmo offers many enticements for day trips outside the city. For a quick dip into Skane's chateau region, two castles just outside Malmo make easy half-day or shorter trips.

Torups Castle
Open Saturday and Sunday in May and June only. Check with the Malmo Tourist Office ahead of time.

Svaneholm Castle
Just a 20-minute drive from Malmo. The original castle was built in the 14th century, but all traces of that have disappeared. The current castle is Gothic Renaissance in style and is now a museum containing exhibits on the past life at the castle. *The castle is open in summer from noon–5:00 p.m. on weekdays and from noon–6:00 p.m. on Saturday and Sunday. Winter hours are shorter. There is also a gourmet restaurant here, but check with the tourist office, as arrangements must be made in advance.*

FALSTERBRO AND SKANOR

Falsterbro Point is a beachy wisp of land with two charming harbor towns, Falsterbro and Skanor, just 40 minutes by bus from Malmo. A trip here from Malmo makes a pleasant outing, especially on a Sunday, when so many things in Malmo, as in most large cities, are closed. Here at the beach on Sunday, you will see the Swedish people at leisure, pursuing their favorite activities of sunbathing, swimming, and boating. It's a good chance to glimpse Swedish life with families, picnicking on the beach, and older couples out for a stroll. Falsterbro has one of Sweden's most beautiful white sand beaches, and the town itself is attractive as well. It's just about a kilometer from the beach and boasts the small **Falsterbro Museum**, which is open from June to August and has interesting historical exhibits of life in Skane. You can also investigate the 13th-century **St. Gertrud's Church**. **Falsterbro Point** is a nature preserve, with rare plants and birds. Skanor boasts a busy harbor and a charming inn.

Falsterbro is the place for **golf** enthusiasts. Its three courses, all classified as seaside courses, which means they present special challenges due to windy conditions, are well known to golfers all over the world. The Falsterbro course is 18 holes, as is Flommen, with particularly difficult water obstacles. Ljunghusen is a 27-hole course. Falsterbro, Hollviken and Vellinge all have fine **tennis** courts. Falsterbro is also a center for **horseback riding**. It is the site of the annual **Falsterbro Horse Show**. There are several stables and pleasant bridle paths in the area. Check with the Vellinge Tourist Information Center, ☎ *040 42 51 26. From June to August, you can also call the Hollviken office,* ☎ *040 45 01 87.*

For good country dining in the area: The inns of Skane are known for their excellent food. The **Gastgifvaregard** at Skanor is an especially delightful spot. It is a member of the Romantik Hotels and Restaurants, though it is a restaurant only. Considered one of Sweden's best and most enchanting restaurants, this is the spot to stop at for lunch or dinner in the area. For a less ambitious meal, try the **Shakespeare Pub** in Hollviken or **Kaptensgarden** in Falsterbro.

LUND

A university town just minutes by the Pagatagen train from Malmo, Lund is sometimes called the Uppsala of Skane. **The University of Lund**, founded in 1668, is the largest research institution in Scandinavia, with over 23,000 students. Its library houses a vast collection of books ranging from 12th-century manuscripts to contemporary works. Lund is an easy day trip from Malmo, but if you wish to stay longer, suggestions for hotels are included.

WHAT TO SEE AND DO

When you get off the train at the Lund station, head up the walking street in front of the station. This is a pleasant street with cafes and ice cream shops—a typical university town street. At the Hotel Lundia, take a right and head toward the Grand Hotel. This is Lund's premier hotel, and it is located on a pretty square with a pleasant park. From the Grand, you can walk along Klostergaten until you arrive at the cathedral.

Lund Cathedral

The cathedral, consecrated in 1145, is one of the finest examples of Romanesque architecture in Scandinavia. Its gray stone facade is a contrast to the red brick buildings of the university, which is directly behind it. Inside, notice the 15th-century altarpiece, the beautifully carved choir stalls and Joakim Skovgaard's mosaic of Christ in the apse. Be sure to go into the crypt, which was dedicated in 1123. Its pillars are carved with extraordinary reliefs depicting the legend of Lund and the Giant Finn who promised to build the cathedral, but who drove the ultimate bargain, demanding the sun, the moon and the eyes of St. Lawrence unless the saint could come up with the giant's name before the cathedral was completed. The giant's wife inadvertently revealed the name while singing to her children and when the saint confronted Finn with the correct name, the giant, enraged, threw his arms around a column in an effort to pull down the building. Finn's wife tried to help, but their strength failed and they were turned to stone. You can see that the columns of the crypt are entwined with their sculpted figures. The most popular attraction of the cathedral is the astronomical clock, which rivals the famous Strasbourg clock in ingenuity and whimsy. Constructed in the 14th century, it is the oldest such clock in Europe, and marks among other things, the celestial year, the solar, celestial, and synodic months, the day and night, the courses of the sun, moon and stars of the Zodiac. It rings at noon Monday–Saturday and at 1:00 p.m. and 3:00 p.m. Sunday. At the stroke of those hours, knights on horseback do battle, trumpeters play *In dulci jubilo* and the Magi parade past the Virgin Mary and Christ Child.

After you have seen the cathedral, stroll through **Lundagard park**, where you will come to the red-brick **Kungshuset**, built in the 16th century as a residence for Danish King Frederik II. It is now an annex to the university. The building by the fountain is the center of the university, and across Universitetsplatsen and Sandgatan, you will find the Foreign Academy, the Student Union building and the University Library. If you walk north on Sandgatan, you will reach the **Bishop's House**.

At the intersection of Sovlegatan and Finngatan is the **Lund Art Museum**, and farther along Solvegatan is the **Museum of Classical Antiquities**. Walk south to Biskopsgatan and then head southeast to the **Botanical Gardens**. Actually a part of the university, the gardens contain over 7000 varieties of plants from the world over. From the gardens, head for Stora Tomegatan. If you want to walk along what is called the prettiest street in Lund, you will have to do a bit of a backtrack here, going north on Stora Tomegatan until you run into **Adelgatan**.

Heading west on Adelgatan, you will come to the **Museum of Cultural History**, one of Sweden's largest open-air museums. Many of the old farm and manor houses that make up the reconstructed communities of the museum have been brought here from various spots in southern Sweden. Among other exhibits are Viking treasures and rune stones, collections of china, glass and textiles, an old grocery store and botanical gardens—the list is pretty long. You can buy an English guidebook to the museum.

From the museum, head south to Krafts torg and then down Kiliansgatan, which will take you to Martenstorget, where a colorful market assembles every morning. In the northwest corner of the square is **Krognoshuset**, a 16th-century stepped-gable house, which is an exhibition hall for art. Right beside it is the ultra-modern **Lunds Konsthall**, which exhibits Swedish and international art.

WHERE TO STAY

If you wish to base yourself in Lund, try the **Grand Hotel**, *1 Bantorget*, ☎ *11 70 10*, or the **Hotel Lundia**, *2 Knut den Storesgata*, ☎ *12 41 40*.

For less expensive accommodations, there is the **Concordia**, *1 Stalbrogatan*, ☎ *13 50 50*, or the **Ahlstrom**, *3 Skomakaregatan*, ☎ *11 01 74*. I have not seen the rooms in either of these two so I cannot vouch for them. The Concordia, I am told, is more modern, though it's in an old building. But the low prices of the Ahlstrom might justify taking that if your budget is pinching you by now.

A DRIVE ALONG THE SOUTHEAST COAST

The area southeast of Malmo is rich in castles, churches and lovely scenery. Ystad is an enchanting medieval town with a host of beautifully preserved, half-timbered houses. Farther east, the region of Osterlen touts itself as the least populated area of the most crowded province in Sweden. With its lush green landscape against the clear sea, it is a paradise for cyclists. The drive east along the coast from Ystad meanders past small fishing villages, thick forests, along sandy beaches. In the distance, across the rolling meadows, you will see from time to time a church spire rising, slender and graceful. You can base yourself in Ystad and drive on through the area of Osterlen, or you can choose another spot along the coast to settle for a few easy days of hiking, swimming and exploring. The distances are short, but this area of Sweden is well-suited to a slow pace. Drive southeast from Malmo to Dalby, then through Blentarp to Svarte on the coast and east along the coast to Ystad and on to Simrishamn and Kivik. At **Dalby**, you will find the oldest stone church still in use in Scandinavia. Built in the 11th century, it is a beautifully preserved structure, worth the short drive from Lund. **The Dalby Gastgifvaregard** is open for meals until 5:00 p.m. and in the evenings by appointment. The best way to get to Dalby is by car, but there is bus service by way of Lund. Check with the Lund tourist office. Farther along the road, at Svarte, you will find a **stone ship**—an arrangement of stones in the shape of a ship—which served as a burial mound in the Iron Age.

YSTAD

This is your primary destination of this leg of the journey. Stop at the **Tourist Office in St. Knut's Torg** to pick up the brochure on the sights of Ystad. A medieval trading center and port, this beautifully preserved town is a good base for traveling out to the chateau district of southern Sweden. Ystad deserves some time to explore its medieval town center, with over 300 restored half-timbered houses. Among the must-sees are: **Per Halsas Gaard**, which is a large block of medieval houses surrounding a central courtyard; and **Greyfriars Cloisters**, a 13th-century structure that houses the City Museum. *Open noon–5:00 p.m. Monday–Friday; 1:00 p.m.–5:00 p.m. Sunday; and during the summer, Saturday, 11:00 a.m.–3:00 p.m.*

Also, see **St. Mary's Church**, a Romanesque 13th-century church, the oldest church in Ystad.

For an excellent meal with plenty of atmosphere, try **Radhuskallaren**. The **Backahasten cafe** is a good place for lighter fare. Try the waffles with jam and whipped cream.

Back on the road, your next stop will be **Kaseberga**, site of an ancient stone Viking monument that is something of a cross between Stonehenge and a stone ship. The stones loom against the sea, stark and dramatic sentinels of the past. If you drive east, you will come to **Backakra**, Dag Hammerskjold's farm, which the secretary-general of the United Nations had planned as his retirement retreat. He died before his plans were realized, but the farm has been renovated much as he had planned it, and it is a meaningful monument to Dag Hammerskjold and to peace. *Open June–August 1:00 p.m.–5:00 p.m.* There is a youth hostel here as well. Continue driving along the coast to **Sandhammaren** on the southeasternmost tip of Sweden. Here you will find some of the best beaches in Sweden.

SKILLINGE

Skillinge is a busy harbor with a well-known restaurant, called **Hamnkrog**. There is a chapel for sailors here as well as a nautical museum, **Municipal House**, which has pictures and models of ships. A short distance inland, just before you get to Simrishamn, you will find the ancient fortress of **Glimmingehus**. The castle is open to visitors, and you can buy a guidebook there. *Open April–September, 9:00 a.m.–5:00 p.m. Closed Monday. Cafe.*

SIMRISHAMN

Simrishamn Tourist Office: *Tullhusgatan 2, ☎ 0414 106 66. Open Monday–Friday 9:00 a.m.–8:00 p.m., Saturday 11:30 a.m.–8:00 p.m.; Sunday 2:00 p.m.–8:00 p.m. At other times of the year, it is open Monday–Friday from 9:00 a.m.–12:30 p.m. and 1:30 p.m.–5:00 p.m. June 15-August 15. The rest of the year it is open Monday–Friday, but closes for lunch.*

Visitors can wander on their own or take a guided walking tour of this picture-perfect fishing village with its diminutive, pastel-washed houses. Among the houses to note particularly are: **Kockska Garden**; the **Bergengrenska** courtyard located on the southwest corner of Stortorget with a 100-year-old garden; the house at **Stora Radmansgatan 15**; and **Bjorkegrenska**, which is the Osterlen Museum. Be sure to see **St. Nicolai's Church**, built in the 12th century. The tower is a well-known landmark for sailors, and is made of the same sandstone that paves the streets of the town.

KIVIK

North of Simrishamn, Kivik has several claims to fame. The orchard of Sweden, with its abundance of apples and pears, it is the home of the biggest and most well-known market in Sweden. Kivik is also known for its herring and eel, and is the subject of many paintings. The most famous sight of Kivik is the **Royal Grave**, a huge tomb of the Bronze Age, covered with extraordinary carvings. *Open from May through August, from 9:00 a.m.–5:00 p.m.*

WHERE TO STAY

SIMRISHAMN

The Hotell Kockska Garden

☎ *117 55* • An old inn that has been renovated as a modern hotel. The courtyard is of special interest.

The Hotell Svea

Though it is unprepossessing from the exterior, the hotel is newly renovated and has a good dining room.

YSTAD

The Continental

A Romantik Hotel, this is the oldest hotel in town, dating from 1829. It has been thoroughly modernized and underwent its last renovation in 1984. The restoration succeeded in retaining the old style, while updating the decor with the use of fresh, light colors. All rooms have private bath and TV. The original dining room, a classically designed space of white and gold marble, offers a fine selection of international and Swedish fare, and also lighter meals.

YOUTH HOSTELS

STFs: vandrarhem, Skepparpsgarden, *Havang*, ☎ *740 71;* **Stjarnevallen**, *Gislov*, ☎ *251 82;* **Kopmanshuset**, *Garsnas*, ☎ *506 03;* **Bjorkhagens vandrarhem**, *Kivik*, ☎ *701 19;* **SiSu Taghem**, *Simrishamn*, ☎ *141 50.*

CAMPING

Vitemolla Camping, *Kivik;* **Kyhls Camping**, *Kyhls;* **Tobisviks Camping**, *Simrishamn.*

GUEST HARBORS

Kivik, Simrishamn, Skillinge. Inquire at the tourist office about self-catering cottages and boarding houses.

ON THE WAY NORTHWEST

It is easy to go on to Copenhagen from Malmo. Hydrofoils make the 40-minute trip frequently throughout the day. If you are heading next for Gothenborg on the west coast, the port city of Helsingborg and the resort of Bastad are good stopping points. (See"The West Coast.")

THE WEST COAST

Gothenburg is the major port city of Western Sweden.

GOTHENBURG

Tourist Office: *Kungsportsplatsen 2,* ☎ *10 07 40; Basargatan 10,* ☎ *10 07 40;*
Nordstadstorget, ☎ *15 07 05.* For Gothenburg Sightseeing ☎ *46-31-775-25-65.*

GOTHENBURG CARD

Pick up the Gothenburg Card at the tourist office, hotels, campsites and the Pressbyra kiosks. As with other city cards, in Gothenburg, you can use the card for free travel on buses, trams and boats within the Gothenburg limits. Among the free excursions offered are a sightseeing trip in Gothenburg, sightseeing on the Paddan boats, a boat trip to Elfsborg Fortress and a day trip to Denmark. In addition, there are free admissions to several nightclubs and to Liseberg Amusement park. Do check with the tourist office, as the dates of some of these offerings change. Most museums offer free admission to holders of the card. In addition, if you have a car, the Gothenburg card can save you quite a bit in parking fees as you can use any meter free of charge.

DIRECTORY

Banks • Open Monday–Friday 9:30 a.m.–3:00 p.m.

Car Rental • **Hertz,** *73 Engelbrektsgatan,* ☎ *810790;* at Landvetter airport, ☎ *946020.*

Currency Exchange • There is an exchange at the railway station, open Monday–Friday from 9:00 a.m.–7:00 p.m., and Saturday and Sunday from 9:00 a.m.–4:00 p.m.

Emergency Number • ☎ *90 000.* Indicate fire, police or ambulance.

Taxi • For taxis, ☎ *200400.*

Gothenburg is the major port city of western Sweden and a good jumping-off spot for trips up the west coast of Sweden or for Norway. The city is also the destination or the departure point of the popular Gota Canal Cruise. Gothenburg's charm is somewhat elusive. It is a commercial center rather than a tourist attraction, but the visitor can spend time strolling along the Avenyn (short for Kungsportsavenyn), the lively, leafy boulevard lined with cafes and shops, and visiting the harbor and market, and the popular amusement park, Liseberg, right in the heart of the city. One of the best of Gothenburg's attractions is the canal-boat ride which will slide you through the city's network of canals, designed and built by Dutch engineers in the 17th century. But beyond that, it is the people here who make the charm of this rather drab, commercial city. You will find the Gothenburg natives friendly, helpful and always courteous. So if you find yourself in Gothenburg for business or as a stop on your way elsewhere, you will certainly be able to amuse yourself with a bit of museum-hopping, shopping or, if the weather is pleasant, a stroll through the center of town. Gothenburg was a port of sorts as early as the 10th century, when the Vikings used the location at the mouth of the Gota River as their point of embarkation. Evidence of Stone Age settlements has also been excavated within the city limits, but the city of Gothenburg was actually established in 1621 by King Gustavus Adolphus. It is today one of Europe's largest ports and the principal port of all Scandinavia. Gothenburg is also the home of the Volvo automobile plant and Sweden's major shipbuilding center.

GETTING THERE

Gothenburg's busy Landvetter airport has service from many parts of Europe and North America through Stockholm. A bus runs between the airport and the Air Terminal near the Central Railroad Station with a stop at the SAS Park Avenue Hotel. A taxi from the airport will run about 150SEK. Boats from Germany and Norway come regularly to this major Swedish port. If you want to arrive in leisurely fashion, take the Gota Canal Cruise from Stockholm.

GETTING AROUND

It's easy to walk in Gothenburg, but it is also fun to take the trams and the **Paddan sightseeing boats**. Trams are rather unusual in Sweden, and here, in the summer, tourists have the added fun of riding on the vintage trams.

SIGHTSEEING TOURS

Paddan Boats

You will see the city from the water as you glide under the 20 bridges, through the canal to the harbor. After 2:00 p.m., the boat tours are free to holders of the Gothenburg Card. Tours run from 10 a.m.–5:00 p.m. in

May, June, September and October, and from 10:00 a.m.–6:00 p.m. in July and August.

Tour of Gothenburg

This 1-1/2-hour bus trip leaves from the Gothenburg Tourist Office at Basargatan 10. The tour takes in the major sights from the harbor to Slottskogen Park and Masthugget Church. The bus crosses Alvsborgsbron, one of the largest suspension bridges in Europe, to Hisingen and Ramberget. Back in Gothenburg, the bus goes to Avenyn, the city's main street and Gotaplatsen Square.

City-Harbor-Elfsborgs Fort

The 3-hour coach tour includes a boat trip through the harbor to Elfsborgs Fort and a guided tour of the Fort. It also leaves from the tourist office. The same tour is available with a stop at the harborside restaurant **Sjomagasinet** for an aperitif and a prawn supper.

WHAT TO SEE AND DO

Gotaplatsen

The monumental central square with Carl Milles' Poseidon Fountain. This is the cultural center of Gothenburg, as it houses the concert hall, the theater, and the art museum.

The Art Museum *(Konstmuseum)*

On Gotaplatsen • Gothenburg residents are justifiably proud of this impressive museum which houses the largest collection of Scandinavian art in Scandinavia. Most of the works are by late 19th- and early 20th-century artists.

The Art Gallery

Also situated on Gotaplatsen, the gallery offers temporary exhibits.

The Museum of Applied Art

(Rohsska Konstslojdsmuset) • Exhibits of Swedish porcelain and earthenware, silver, books, textiles and Swedish furniture. In addition there is a collection of Japanese and Chinese art and crafts. *All three museums are open Monday–Saturday noon–4 p.m.; Sunday and holidays 11 a.m.–5:00 p.m.; and Wednesday 6:00 p.m.–9:00 p.m.*

The Crown House

(Kronhuset) • Here in Gothenburg's oldest building, you can watch craftsmen of the Living Handicrafts Center ply their trades. The Dutch-style building, constructed in 1642, also contains part of the Gothenburg City Museum on the ground floor, which was a chamber of state during the time Parliament met in Gothenburg. There is a country store here, a pottery shop, gold- and silversmiths, a clockmaker, a glass blower and a copper beater. *The shops are open weekdays from 11 a.m.–4:00 p.m., Saturday 11 a.m.–2:00 p.m. Crownhouse City Museum is open Tuesday–Saturday from noon–4:00 p.m. and Sunday from 11 a.m.–5:00 p.m.*

The Antique Halls

A mecca for collectors, the halls house Scandinavia's largest permanent antique and flea market. More than 20 shops sell everything from glass to stamps. *Open weekdays 10:00 a.m.–6:00 p.m., Saturday 10:00 a.m.–2:00 p.m., Sunday in December only, from noon–4:00 p.m. Take trams no. 2, 3, 4, 6 or 7.*

The Market Hall

Built in 1888 because legislation was passed forbidding the butchering of meat in the open street, the market is a lively place and, though there are plenty of butchers' shops, you will not see any major violence. In addition to meat, you will find fish, cheese, fruit and vegetables for sale. Four cafeterias offer a variety of specialties. *Open Monday–Thursday 9 a.m.–6:00 p.m., Friday 8:00 a.m.–6:00 p.m., Saturday 8:00 a.m.–2:00 p.m.*

The Fish Church *(Feskekorka)*

This is neither a church nor a museum—it's a fish market, built in 1873 and 1874. The building itself, with its Gothic windows and steeply pitched roof, is well worth the visit. *Open Tuesday–Friday 9:00 a.m.–5:00 p.m., Saturday 9:00 a.m.–1:00 p.m. Closed Sunday.*

The Museum of Natural History

In addition to displays of Swedish flora and fauna, there is an ecology department. The Maritime Museum traces the development of sailing and fishing from the Viking Age to the present. There is also an interesting collection of figureheads and an aquarium.

Liseberg Park

Liseberg is the largest amusement park in Sweden and, as such, draws more visitors than any other attraction in the country. In addition to the usual amusement park attractions, Liseberg is a lively place at night, with restaurants and night spots. As in most European amusement parks, the landscaping and lights add to the enchantment, especially at night. Restaurant choices range from the Restaurant Paris to a Tyrolean cottage and the Wardshuset, modeled after a Swedish manor house.

The Harbor

Faced with 17th- and 18th-century buildings, most painted green and red, this is obviously a working harbor, lined with tankers and ferries and dotted with cranes. But it reinforces Gothenburg's continuing importance as a commercial port, and travelers should visit it, just to catch the rhythm of the busy life here. An early 20th-century ship serves as a museum here.

Goteborg Opera House

This brand new $80 million opera house just opened in October of 1994. The 1994–1995 season includes performances of Johann Strauss's *Fledermaus*, Mozart's *Don Giovanni* and *Le Nozze di Figaro*, and Wagner's *Flying Dutchman*. *For information, call the box office, ☎ (46 31)13 13 00.*

WHERE TO STAY

The **Gothenburg Package** is a way of cutting hotel costs in Gothenburg. The package is valid for two nights on all weekends, with Thursday occasionally included; on all major holidays and during the national sports holidays in winter; and through the summer from around June 20 until the middle of August. The package includes bed and breakfast and the Gothenburg Card.

VERY EXPENSIVE

The SAS Park Avenue Hotel

Kungsportavenyn 36-38 • This is considered one of the best, but it is rather commercial, and the rooms, though comfortable, are ordinary. For the price, 1200SEK for a double room, one might expect larger bathrooms and more and bigger towels at the least. The service is friendly, however, and the concierge most helpful. The gourmet restaurant, Belle Avenue, serves Swedish and French cuisine. The nightclub here is open every day except Sunday and Monday. Free admission for hotel guests, but you should book in advance.

The Sheraton

Sodra Hamngatan • The newest spot in town is one of the most attractive Sheratons I've seen, with a light, greenery-hung lobby, fountains and lobby restaurants. The hotel has a beautiful pool and fitness center. The rooms are spacious and luxurious. With 340 rooms, this is a large place, so don't expect an intimate atmosphere. The hotel is located in the old part of town. A double room runs between 1200 and 1300SEK. The Sheraton Towers is the business-class section of the hotel, with a separate check-in service and executive lounge. A double room in the Towers is 1460SEK.

EXPENSIVE

Rubinen

Kungsportavenyn 24 • Though it has 186 rooms, this seems like a small hotel, and its location puts it in the thick of the action. The rooms are bright and comfortable, though not large. There is a nonsmoking floor. The gourmet restaurant, Andra Vaningen, is well recommended and very pretty. There is also a bistro and a veranda, which overlooks Avenyn. At last check a double room was 1150SEK with a weekend price of 700SEK. This is a Reso hotel and, to my taste, the best choice in Gothenburg.

The Windsor

Kungsportavenyn 6 • As its name suggests, there is a rather English flavor here, with its mahogany reception desk and its wood-panelled brasserie. The old English aura disappears once you get into the guest rooms, which are simple but sleekly contemporary. With just 91 rooms, the hotel is an intimate spot, with friendly service. It houses the Brasserie Lipp, one of Gothenburg's most popular restaurants. Double rooms run from 1000 to 1100SEK. Breakfast is included.

MODERATE

Hotel Ekoxen

Norra Hamngatan 38 • This small hotel is in an old, rather unprepossessing building. The rooms are simply but pleasantly decorated in light colors and have all the amenities—TV, minibar, hair dryer. About a five-minute walk from the heart of Gothenburg. Double rooms from 1100SEK.

The Novotel Goteborg

At the harbor • The hotel is in a beautifully restored old warehouse. The rooms are enhanced by the original structure of the building. Double rooms were 800SEK, but may have gone up by now. A good buy if you don't mind being out of the center of things. The harbor is an industrial port, so it is not especially scenic though you can look out to the bridge and islands. But this is a convenient location if you are picking up a boat for other ports.

OUTSIDE TOWN

Tidloms Hotel and Restaurant

The hotel and restaurant occupy a turreted turn-of-the-century building that has been completely renovated on the inside. A member of the Romantik Hotel organization, the hotel offers a bit more charm and individuality than many of the accommodations in town. Each room is different, but all are comfortable and offer thoroughly modern convenience. The excellent restaurant occupies the old cellars and a glassed-in veranda. A double will be about 800SEK. Weekend and summer rates available.

WHERE TO EAT

Rakan

Lorensbergsgatan 16 • The name means shrimp and there's no better place to have them. Rakan wins the vote for the best fish in town. Salty atmosphere with a gimmicky delivery service by battery powered boat.
Expensive.

Westra Piren Restaurant

Sjoporten Eriksberg • Traditional Swedish food in a restaurant beautifully located on the waterfront in the central harbor. The restaurant is one of Goteborg's two Michelin-starred spots.   *Expensive.*

28 +

Gotabergsgatan 28 • The other Michelin-starred restaurant, this one serving French food, 28+ is one of Goteborg's most popular places, with a cozy, candlelit setting in a series of cellar vaults. Located close to Avenyn in the center of town.   *Expensive.*

Stallgarden

Kyrkogatan 33 • As its name suggests, the restaurant is housed in an old stable. It now contains several small, pretty dining rooms. The menu is varied with fish, veal and lamb as the primary offerings. A two-course meal will run between 260 and 300SEK. You can eat more reasonably for lunch with daily lunches ranging from 60 to 140SEK.

Rada Sateri & Gastgiveri

Rada Manor is an 18th-century manor house situated by Lake Radasjon, 10 km. from the center of town. Its excellent kitchen and pleasant service has made it a popular place. The menu is varied and interesting. A two-course meal without wine can range from 160SEK if you choose marinated herring with the Manor's home-baked bread as a starter and steak with fried onions for your entree, to 250SEK if you go with the house specialty of a fish platter as starter and tournedos with madeira sauce, or filets of sole with puree of morels for entree.

Tidbloms

In the hotel of the same name, located slightly out of town • The menu features well-prepared and creative seafood and game dishes.

Johanna

Sodra Hamngatan 47 • Excellent food in a cozy, clubby setting. This is one of Gothenburg's, indeed, one of Sweden's best restaurants.

Expensive.

Sjomagasinet

Klippans Kulturreservat • The restaurant is as notable for its setting as for its food. Located in the 200-year-old warehouse of the East India Company at the harbor, it offers great views of the activity there. You might forget to eat, with all there is to take in here, but don't. The food is good, with seafood the specialty.   *Expensive.*

Brasserie Lipp

The restaurant of the Windsor Hotel • Excellent location, in the center of town and activity. This is a lively gathering spot with a popular bar.

Weise

On Drottninggatan • Weise is the oldest restaurant in town. A traditional meeting place for artists and writers, the restaurant has retained its *bierstube* atmosphere and is popular with students and businessmen. Stained-glass windows and a huge wooden sideboard with elaborate carvings set the stage here for cozy, intimate dining. The food is varied, but as the name and decor suggest, German specialties are featured. Dishes like pea soup, baked beans and Wiese's famous hash, *Pytt I Panna*, are staples.

Hemma Hos

Haga Nygata 12 • The name means roughly "at home," and that's the feeling you'll have in this comfy-cozy spot, decorated with furniture from local antique shops.

Farbror Hjordis

Engelbrektsgatan 53 • In translation, the name is "Uncle Hjordis" a kind of a misnomer since Hjordis is a woman's name. But the crazy name is evidently intentionally a hint at the zany decor within. It's an intimate, and romantic, place, however, and very lively.

La Gondola

Covers the whole spectrum of Italian cooking from northern Italian cuisine to pizza. Located on Kungsportavenyn, it has an outdoor terrace for summer dining.

NIGHTLIFE

Liseberg is the place most people go for evening entertainment, but the main hotels have bars and the SAS Park Avenue has its **Lorensberg Nightclub**, which gathers a good crowd every night but Sunday and Monday. And the Sheraton offers the **Mirage Nightclub**. **Jazzhuset** is the place for jazz. The menu includes fish and seafood as well as salads and lighter fare. **Valand** is a restaurant and disco. Good food and reasonable prices make this popular with young people. **The Stora Teatern** in Kungsparken stages operas, operettas and ballets. Inquire at the tourist office for a schedule of performances.

EXCURSIONS FROM GOTHENBURG

For short jaunts out of town, take a day trip to Denmark on the Stena Line. The cost is 70SEK for adults and 35SEK for children. You can go free with your Gothenburg card, but you have to leave at 1:00 p.m. and return by midnight, and you cannot book ahead. Another choice for a day trip is to go south through the archipelago by taking tram #4 to Saltholmen and then catching a boat. Or go to the northern archipelago by catching bus # 24 from Nils Ericsonsplatsen to Hjuvik and then traveling by ferry. You can also go by boat to the islands of **Trollhattan** and **Lysekil**.

Kungsbacka and Tjoloholms Castle

This is a popular day trip destination. Kungsbacka is a market town dating from the 16th century and located about 40 miles south of Gothenburg. The castle is a Tudor manor built at the turn of the century. The house lies on a tip of land extending into the sea. On the grounds is a village with a village church, church and community hall and a carriage museum. There is also a cafeteria open from 11:00 a.m.–5:00 p.m. on the days the castle is open. *Open every day in June, July and August from 11:00 a.m.–4:00 p.m.; In April, May, September and October, weekends only from 11 a.m.–4:00 p.m.* Also in the vicinity are the 18th-century village of **Askhult** and the **Mansaby** mill.

The Bohuslan Islands

A sightseeing coach trip from Gothenburg will take tourists to the islands of **Tjorn** and **Orust**. The trip continues through the fishing villages of the West Coast and includes lunch featuring local dishes. The trip lasts about seven hours. *Advance booking must always be made at the Tourist Bureau the day of the tour.*

Marstrand

This is one of Sweden's smallest towns, situated on an island on which no cars are allowed. It is a fine place for fishing and swimming and is the site of an annual international sailing regatta. A 17th-century fortress still guards the island.

GOTA CANAL CRUISES

If you are heading to Stockholm from Gothenburg, and are not averse to slow, leisurely progress, the Gota Canal Cruise is one of the most pleasant journeys you can take in Sweden. Traveling between Stockholm and Gothenburg, these canal boats provide an easy way to glimpse some of the beauties of the Swedish lakes. You will be seeing the best of the Swedish lake district and will be treated to comfortable accommodations and fine food on the way. Start in Stockholm or in Gothenburg and spend three nights on board, passing through Lakes Vattern and Vanern in the heart of the Swedish Lake district, with stops at, among other places, Karlsborg, Vadstena and Motala. The first night out of Stockholm, passengers disembark at **Nykoping Castle** for a banquet. The cruises offer friendly and meticulous service. All the cabins are on the outside, with hot and cold running water but no private baths. There is a shower room on the main deck. The food is excellent; in fact, with the lack of exercise and the abundance of wonderful food, you will roll off the boat at your destination. The steamers carry a fine selection of wines and liquor. Lunch is a smorgasbord, a very weighty affair with more kinds of herring than you ever dreamed existed, gravlax, hot dishes, and plenty of other delectables to tide you over until the next meal. Dinner consists of three courses and will tempt you even though at lunch you thought you might never eat again. All the food is prepared on board, and the dining rooms of the steamers are usually cozily elegant. A salon provides a place for quiet pursuits. The Gota Canal Boats are members of the Romantik Hotel and Restaurant Organization, which means they offer something unique, a special ambience and excellence to the guest.

Special five-day cruise:

The five-day cruise is a relatively new addition and includes 12 stops. The cruise begins with a banquet at Nykoping Castle, and breakfast next morning at the Soderkoping Spa. Among the other stops are Vadstena, with visits to the castle, convent and abbey, and Granna, where passengers take the ferry to the island of Visingo for a fish dinner. There are only two five-day sailings as yet, and since this is a new cruise, its future might depend on its yet unproven popularity. Two-day cruises can also be booked. Cruises go from mid-May through mid-September and start at about $600 double occupancy per person. The price includes all meals and sightseeing. The steamship company will arrange for a rental car for your return trip. Discounts are offered on rail travel in connection with the cruises; and the company will also arrange hotels in Gothenborg and Stockholm at your request.

Information and Booking:

Rederiaktiebolaget Gota Kanal. P.O. Box 272, Hotellplatsen 2, S 401 24, Gothenborg, ☎ *46 31 17 76 15. For brochures,* ☎ *46 31 11 15 53. This is a 24-hour service.*

HELSINGBORG

Tourist Office: *Radhuset, S-252 21 Helsingborg,* ☎ *042 1203 10.* Open in June and August, Monday–Friday, weekdays 9:00 a.m. to 7:00 p.m., Saturday 9:00 a.m.–5:00 p.m., Sunday noon–4:00 p.m. In July, the hours are extended until 8:00 p.m. weekdays. The rest of the year, it is open 9:00 a.m.–5:00 p.m. weekdays and 9:00 a.m.–noon Saturday, and closed Sunday from September–May.

Situated south of Gothenburg on the west coast, Helsingborg is a port city and a large, commercial center. It is also a convenient departure point for Denmark.

WHAT TO SEE AND DO

The Keep
All that remains of Helsingborg Castle is this central tower, which dominates the town from its perch above the city. It is open to the public.

St. Mary's Church
The only other building to have survived the fires and wars of Sweden's past. In the 15th-century church, you will find a remarkable triptych from around 1450. The church's remarkable collection of silver is on display every day.

The Town Hall
This imposing structure, built in a neo-Gothic style in the late 19th century, has stained-glass windows that illustrate the town's history.

Fredriksdal Open-air Museum
Buildings have been brought to this site from the area of Helsingborg. There is an entire block of buildings from the old center of town, with shops and houses restored to their 19th-century condition. The Botanical Gardens and an open-air theater are also located here.

Sofiero
Once the summer residence of the late King Gustav VI Adolf, it is now a museum. The gardens, famous for the rhododendrons, are open to the public. There is a restaurant here. *Open from early May until mid-September.*

WHERE TO STAY

The Hotel Molberg
The oldest hotel still operating in Sweden, the Mollberg was renovated in 1986 and all its rooms have private bath, TV/video, minibar and hair dryer. The public rooms retain something of the grand elegance of the past.

The Grand
Located next door to and under the same management as the Molberg, the Grand has also been recently renovated. All the rooms have private bath, TV/video, minibar and hair dryer. Here too, the public rooms, particularly the dining room, are elegant and old world.

BASTAD

Tourist Office: *Stortorget, Box 1096, 269 01 Bastad.*

Bastad is the jet-set resort of Sweden, located on the Bjare peninsula north of Helsingborg. This is mecca for the young and beautiful, of which there are many in Sweden. But it is a lovely spot in itself, with woods, meadows and pretty, vine-entwined houses.

WHAT TO SEE AND DO

Walk down Agardhsgatan, with its old wooden houses, or take the walk along the beach that passes the harbor and delicate woods. You can visit the **Norrviken Gardens**, which are composed of several different styles, from Japanese to Renaissance. The church of Bastad is the 500-year old **St. Mary's**. Most people come to Bastad for **tennis**. It is the site, every July, of the internationally ranked Swedish Open Grand Prix, which is played at the Bastad Tennis Club. To arrange to play tennis here, contact the tourist office. *For tournament tickets, write; Tennisstadion, Box 1072, 26901 Bastad.*

WHERE TO STAY

The Grand Hotel Skansen

Located near the beach, it has just 52 rooms housed in what was a warehouse. The hotel has an excellent restaurant and houses the popular disco Grand Slam.

Hemmelovs Herrgardpensionat

A larger hotel, with 129 rooms, a heated outdoor pool and tennis courts. It is located in a 14th-century manor house.

WHERE TO EAT

The above hotels have excellent restaurants with dinners running about 150SEK or more for meals with wine. For a simple, inexpensive snack, try the **Solbackens Câfe and Waffelbruk,** located on Italienskavagen outside town. It has been serving Swedish waffles and other sweet treats since 1907. A terrace overlooks the water.

THE LAKE DISTRICT

Varmland is rich in forests, lakes, rivers and lore.

Of the many lakes that dot the countryside of Sweden, Lake Siljan, to the north, and Lakes Vanern and Vattern, farther south, draw the most visitors in search of tranquil beauty. The landscape here is peaceful rather than dramatic. Here you will not find the splendor of the fjord-ringed Norwegian lakes nor of the pine-fringed lakes of Finland. The lake district of Sweden is, like much of the Swedish landscape, understated and often similar to the quiet lakes of northern Michigan. While there are several old, charming towns like Vadstena and Granna on Lake Vanern, many of the towns are not particularly distinguished. This is an area for recreation more than for sightseeing.

DALARNA AND LAKE SILJAN

The Rattvik Tourist Bureau: *Torget, Box 90, 795 00 Rattvik,* ☎ *0248 109 10.*

The Mora Tourist Bureau: *Angbatskajen, S-792 00, Mora,* ☎ *0250 265 50.*

GETTING THERE

You can drive from Stockholm to Lake Siljan, the northernmost area of the lake district of Sweden, in about five hours. Several flights leave daily from Stockholm to Borlange and Falun. Train service is also available. Dalarna, with its gently rolling terrain, its graceful woods and its sparkling lakes, is the heart of the Swedish countryside. Distinguished by the typically Dalecarlian red timber farmhouses, and the folk art of the region, Dalarna is a pastoral enticement for both Swedish and foreign tourists. It is the center of many Swedish folk legends and traditions and is probably the spot to celebrate Midsummer Eve. The region is notable also for the Dalecarlian style of decorating, which entails the painting and stenciling of wooden surfaces—interior walls and furniture. Even the telephone booth in Tallberg is painted with folk figures and designs. The famed Dalecarlian wooden horses are also carved here at the town of Nusnas, about 15 miles from Rattvik.

The largest city of the area is **Falun**, but the resort area is centered around the towns of **Rattvik** on the east coast of the lake and **Mora** on the western side. However, the town, if it can be called that, of **Tallberg** is really the most attractive place from which to explore this territory. It seems to have sprouted on the hill above Lake Siljan solely for the pleasure of the tourists who wish to dally along the lake, enjoying the view and the tranquil, rural charm. The permanent population of Tallberg is only 250, but eight hotels provide quarters for more than 1000 visitors.

The lake area is rich in recreational facilities and opportunities to relax and enjoy the outdoors. Rent a bicycle and ride through the old villages. Enjoy windsurfing, fishing, tennis or golf. Take a lake cruise on the steamer, *Gustav Wasa*, which has been running on Lake Siljan for over 100 years. Stop at **Nusnas** to watch the production of the Dalecarlian wooden horses. Try the **water slide** at Rattvik, spend a day at **Sommarland Theme Park,** or simply enjoy the lake view from one of the hotels of *Toppen Tallberg*, which are situated on a small rise above the lake. The major attraction of the area is, of course, the lake and the pleasant countryside. But you should make the trip to **Carl Larsson's House**, in Sundborn, a delightful village that appears to have kept itself from the encroachments of tourism and the 20th century. Sundborn is located outside Falun and the trip to Carl Larsson's House is well worth the detour. Another artistic pilgrimage worth taking is to **Anders Zorn's house**, in Mora. *(For details on both these artists' houses, see subsequent headings.)*

The **Siljan Musikfestival** takes place every summer during the first 10 days of July. *For information, contact Musik Vid Siljan, Box 28, 795 00 Rattvik,* ☎ *0248 102 90.*

There are plenty of campsites, several youth hostels and cottages available for rent. The Rattvik Tourist Office has information on these.

MORA

Mora is a somewhat commercial city, but it was here that Gustav Vasa, when he was not yet king, tried to incite an uprising. In memory of this event, a major cross-country ski race, the Vasa Lopet, is held every winter. The race covers the same route (from the village of Salen to Mora, but in the opposite direction) Gustav Vasa took when he left Dalarna, discouraged at his failure to rouse the peasants to revolt. Anders Zorn's statue of Gustav Vasa, in the center of Mora, where the leader himself stood to incite the peasants to revolt, marks the finish line of the race. The most important stop to make at Mora is **Zornsgarden**, the former home of artist Anders Zorn. It is open to the public as a museum. The home is fascinating for the myriad possessions Zorn collected and for his highly original eye for design. The artist designed much of the furniture himself and panelled the living room with the wood that had been left on the junk heap when the church elders decided to remodel the interior of the town church.

After they saw the successful use of it in Zorn's living room, they wanted it back, but the artist refused, granting them, instead, the right to copy it for their own use. Zorn also brought back innovations in household comforts from his trips abroad. His was the first Swedish house to have hot and cold running water. A museum here contains many of Zorn's paintings.

FALUN AND CARL LARSSON'S HOUSE AT SUNDBORN

Falun is a rather large town or a small city, known for its copper mines, which you can visit if you are so inclined. The major attraction of Falun, and indeed of the Lake Siljan Area, aside from the lake itself, is **Carl Larsson's House** at nearby Sundborn. This is the house the artist immortalized in his collection of watercolors, *A Home*. It was here that Larsson and his wife Karin raised their eight children and set new standards for Swedish country design. The house is still owned by descendants of the artist, who open it to the public and very often conduct the tours themselves. Visitors can go through the house only on a guided tour, but you will not want to see it in any other way, because you will learn much about the house and its inhabitants from the guides, who are eager to share the stories of this extraordinary family. You will learn of the artist's poverty-ridden childhood and his effort to overcome the lack of education with voracious reading and traveling. He always wrote texts to accompany his paintings and, as a young man, illustrated many of the books of other writers.

Throughout the house, you will find little aphorisms painted here and there. One of my favorites is painted on the ceiling of the guest room, actually an old miner's house brought here by Larsson from a nearby village in order to preserve its extraordinary wall and ceiling paintings. Here on the ceiling are the words, "Really old is the only thing that is young forever." Less lofty is the greeting painted over the entrance to the house, which means, "Welcome to the House of Carl Larsson and his Spouse."

In the front entry, the walls are painted with portraits of the Larssons' four eldest children. The younger children's portraits adorn doors elsewhere in the house. The feeling of warmth and welcome and happy family life pervades every brightly painted, cozy room, each filled with antiques collected by the couple and with handicrafts made by both artists. Karin Larsson was a textile artist and sewed all the family's clothes, in addition to creating the costumes Larsson used in his paintings. In the studio, you will see her loom as well as several of Larsson's important works. *The house is open to the public May–September, weekdays and Saturday from 10 a.m. to 5:00 p.m.; and Sunday and holidays from 1:00 p.m. to 5:00 p.m. If you wish a tour in English, it is advisable to arrange ahead. Sundborn is an easy drive from Falun, or you can take a bus from the Falun bus station.*

WHERE TO STAY

FALUN

The Scandic Hotel

Just outside the city on the way to Sundborn. Modern and comfortable with an indoor pool, solarium, and sauna.

MORA

The Scandic Hotel

Another in this reliable chain of modern hotels, and a good choice if that is your preference over Dalecarlian charm.

The Mora Hotel

Comfortable. All rooms have private toilets, but not all have baths. Indoor pool.

RATTVIK

The choice is wide but not particularly good.

The Robbington

Unappealing and situated right in town, close to the lake. Certainly no idyllic retreat. Its lakeside situation offers easy access to swimming and recreation and all rooms have shower and private bath as well as TV.

The Motell Rattvikshasten

Also situated too much in the center of town for my taste, it boasts a swimming pool as well as private baths and showers and TV. Some rooms have four beds to accommodate families.

Gardebygarden

Set higher up and a couple of kilometers from the main part of Rattvik. Its main attraction is its view.

Hantaverksbyn i Ratvik

In a lovely location about 1-1/2 miles south of Rattvik center. In addition to hotel rooms, there are apartments available in newly built log cabins.

Youth Hostel: Rattviks Vandrahem

Near the railway station.

TALLBERG

Tallberg offers the best selection of accommodations.

The Klockargarden

The inn offers very individualized rooms located in a series of small buildings that the owner, Klockar Pelle Sandberg, has brought from various parts of Dalarna and restored as guesthouses. Klockar Sandberg and his wife have given personal attention to the furnishing of the rooms, and the result is pleasant, airy and comfortable. The inn also has a handicraft house that sponsors exhibits and sales of crafts. A cafe and garden and a restaurant make this a delightful spot to stay.

The Green Hotel

Situated at the highest spot in Tallberg, this is a large, busy, but pleasant place. The best rooms are those in the main building, fronting the lake. As with all the hotels in the area, rooms vary enormously, and here prices are adjusted accordingly. The Green offers a good buy for the money. Indoor and outdoor pools.

The Romantik Hotel Tallbergsgarden

A cluster of small houses, painted in the typical Dalecarlian red, centered around a main house. The hotel is enhanced by the presence of owners, Ulla and Brygt Bert Lindgren, whose interest and involvement keep the standards high. A smorgasbord is served at lunch every day, and on Sunday fiddlers dressed in Dalecarlian costumes entertain the guests.

The Dalecarlia

Another spot with a fine bird's eye view of the lake, this is not a top choice, but it is comfortable. The parlor and dining room are pleasantly decorated in homey Dalecarlian style, but the rooms are uneven in quality. If you do stay there, request one of the three rooms that face the water.

Langbersgarden

Very attractive, with its freshly painted red buildings and its magnificent situation above the lake; however, I was unable to see the rooms.

The Ackerblads Hotel

Has a pleasant dining room and serves up a very good set dinner every night. There is a tennis court on the property and the lake is nearby. This inn is highly touted by some, but its charm is a bit elusive, especially if you have a room in the main building. These are sadly in need of sprucing up. Even the wedding suite, which is the prize room of the main house, looks a bit like a Swedish interpretation of Miss Haversham's banquet hall. Request a room in the building called Lillestugan. Most of these are newly renovated and very pretty, and the suites are particularly comfortable.

VARMLAND AND ITS LAKES

Varmland Tourist Bureau: *Box 323, S 651 08, Karlstad,* ☎ *054 10 21 60.*

Filipstad Tourist Bureau: *Kyrkogatan 2, Box 303, S 682 01 Filipstad,* ☎ *0590 147 40.*

GETTING THERE

There are several flights daily from Stockholm to Karlstad.

Varmland is a land rich in forests, lakes, rivers and lore. It is the land in which Nobel prizewinner Selma Lagerlof set her 19th-century *Saga of Gosta Berlinger*—romantic, wild and compelling. **Lake Vanern**, at the southern end of Varmland, is Sweden's largest lake, and it is vast. The **Klaralv River** runs the length of Varmland and is a mecca for canoeists, fishermen and hikers. Bus tours run in summertime along the main road, or you can drive. The area around **Lake Fryken**, a small, picturesque lake, north of Lake Vanern, is a center for cross-country skiing and for hiking, with many fine walking trails available.

SUNNE AND MARBACKA

In the center of the Lake Fryken area is the village that reportedly served as the model for the village of Broby in *The Saga of Gosta Bjerling*. Visit the **Kinship Monument** here. At **Marbacka**, about 30 miles from Sunne, you will find the imposing, colonnaded manor house that was Selma Lagerlof's home. *It is open from mid-May to mid-September from 10:00 a.m. to 7:00 p.m. daily.*

Rottneros is the site of Rottneros Manor, the model for the manor house, Ekeby, in Lagerlof's saga. The house is not open to the public, but the gardens with their impressive sculpture collection are worth a visit. *Open from mid-May to September.* There is a restaurant and cafeteria on the grounds. **Tossebergsklatten**, which goes by the name Gurlitta Klatt in Lagerlof's story, serves up a spectacular view.

FILIPSTAD

Set by the Skiller River north of Lake Vanern, Filipstad is a center for cross-country skiing in winter, and in summer, a haven for canoeists. But Filipstad's major attraction for Americans is that it was the home and is now the burial spot of John Ericsson, builder of the iron-clad warship the *Monitor*, which defeated the *Merrimack* in that significant sea battle of the American Civil War. You can visit the town of **Langban**, a mining community, where John and his brother Nils were born.

KARLSTAD

Karlstad is the largest city of the area and the capital of Varmland. Located at the top of Lake Vanern, Karlstad is largely a commercial city, but it does offer interesting sights for the tourist, among them, the **Varmlands Museum**, which offers an overview of Varmland's culture and history, and **Almen**, the old town. Outside Karlstad, visit **Alsters Manor House**, the birthplace of the poet Gustaf Froding. The house is now a museum. **Kristinehamn** is a port city, which, with its islands, is a popular spot for summer tourists. Picasso's 15-meter-high sculpture serves as an extraordinary beacon for sailors. The 13th-century wooden church is located at **Sodra Rada**, south of Kristinehamn. Its ceiling and wall paintings date from the 14th and 15th century. On the western side of the lake, visit the **glassworks** at Liljedal, the oldest glassworks of Varmland.

WHERE TO STAY

FILIPSTAD

The Hennickehammars Herrgard
An 18th-century manor house, which has been converted to an inn.

KARLSTAD

The Stadshotellet
The grand old lady of the city.

The Sara Hotel Winn
A good bet for a more contemporary haven.

SUNNE

The Hotel Selma Lagerlof
A fairly new hotel in spite of its traditional style. Considering the high quality of its facilities and amenities, the hotel is rather moderate in price.

Lansmansgarden
The place for Selma Lagerlof readers. Each room is named after a character

in *The Saga of Gosta Bjerling*. At last check, rooms ranged from 300SEK to 400SEK.

LAKE VATTERN AND SURROUNDINGS

Ostergotland Tourist Bureau: *Box 176, S 581 02, Linkoping,* ☎ *013 22 76 00.*

Vadstena Tourist Bureau: *Radhustorget, Box 127, S 592 00, Vadstena,* ☎ *0143 151 25.*

Ostergotland occupies the area between Sweden's east coast and the eastern shore of Lake Vattern, Sweden's second largest lake and one of the most beautiful.

GRYTHYTTAN

One might easily miss **Grythyttan**. It is discernible on the map only with a magnifying glass, and you need to be looking for it to find it. It is not on any of the major lakes. Few guide books list it. There is little reason to visit it unless you are looking for a beautiful retreat. You won't find museums, town halls or palaces here. But you will find the **Grythyttans Gastgivaregard**, a delightful inn that boasts one of the finest cuisines in the nation and which attracts the great and the gastronomic to this out-of-the-way, postage-stamp town in the middle of nowhere. Even if you do not choose to spend the night in one of the Laura Ashley-designed guest rooms (Laura Ashley herself visited the inn to oversee the furnishings), at least stop for a meal. My suggestion, however, would be to stay over, so that you can enjoy the inn's cuisine and its marvelous wines with impunity, and then to head for Lake Vattern where there are several appealing lakeside towns and inns.

To drive from Grytthytan to Vadstena, leave Gastgivaregard by way of the parking lot behind the main building. Turn right and drive along the lake following the signs to Loka and then to **Karlskoga**, the town where Alfred Nobel lived. His house, **Bjorkborn**, is open to the public, but check ahead of time on the hours. From Karlskoga, follow the signs for Degersfors and then take 205 out of Degersfors towards Svarta and Askersund.

SVARTA

The main attraction here is the **Svarta Herrgard**, a lovely old manor house, now an inn, dating from 1782. It is set in a large garden beside a lake and a forest. If you don't choose to spend the night here, you might just stop for lunch. In the dining room, a smorgasbord is served daily.

On leaving Svarta, watch carefully for the turnoff to **Askersund**, a pleasant, lakeside town where you might stop for lunch. From Askersund, continue along the lake to Vadstena.

VADSTENA

The Vadstena Tourist Office: *Located at the City Hall (Radhuset)*. Open in the summer months. Information on guided tours of the town, accommodations and lake excursions is available. In winter, contact the Vadstena-Amberg Tourist Association, ☎ *0143 114 30.*

This ancient town on the shores of Lake Vattern is a delightful labyrinth of narrow streets and charming houses. Vadstena is known for its lace as well as for the castle, the church and the cloister, all of which attract many visitors each year. Vadstena is the birthplace of **St. Birgitta**, who was born to the aristocracy and who mothered eight children before she experienced the visions that led her to found the Birgittine Order. Though she died in Rome in 1373, her remains are buried in the church she had built in Vadstena. The main street, Storgatan, is a continuation of the National Highway 8 that comes into Vadstena from the north. Along Storgatan and in the streets running off it, tourists will find several old houses of interest. Along the east wall of the church, Lastkopisgatan is one of the area's oldest streets.

Vadstena Castle

Gustavus Vasa built this castle, with its fine Dutch Renaissance facade, between 1545 and 1620, and celebrated his wedding here in 1552. The castle/fortress has the distinction of never yielding to any enemy except, perhaps, time. It fell into disrepair in the 17th century and was at one time used as a granary, until it was restored in the 19th century. Tours are available. *Check with Vadstena Tourist Bureau for times.*

The Vadstena Abbey Church

The splendid Gothic-style church was designed by Saint Brigitta in the 14th century. As with most churches in Sweden, the simple interior, dating mainly from the Reformation, marks a change from the original design. The church's collection of medieval art is notable. The convent, part of which contains the original mansion where the nuns first lived, stands to the north of the church. Though the monastery to the south was restored and enlarged in the 18th century, portions of the original living quarters are still intact. There is a restaurant in the monastery for groups that book in advance.

The Vadstena School

In Stortgatan • This building is 500 years old.

The Bishop's House

Built in 1470 for the visiting Bishops of Linkoping.

If you wish to venture farther from Vadstena, **Omberg** is the sacred mountain of Ostergotland, offering fine views. At the southern end of Omberg is **Alvastra**, where you will find the ruins of a 12th-century Cistercian abbey. East of Omberg at the **Dagmosse bog**, a 4000-year-old settlement is under excavation. The **Rok Stone** is the most important rune stone of Sweden, and is located at the Rok church across Lake Takern from Vadstena.

GRANNA

From Vadstena, it is a beautiful, easy drive along Lake Vattern to Granna. You can enjoy the lake view here and stroll along the streets that slope down to the water, or, if you're looking for a bit more to occupy your time, try some of the museums. The **Vattern Museum** displays Iron Age relics that have been found in the area. In the **Andree Museum**, you will find memorabilia of the North Pole explorer Salomon August Andree, who tried unsuccessfully to cross the North Pole in a balloon. *Open only in summer.* **Visingo Island** is a 30-minute boat ride from Granna. On the island, you can see the ruins of **Visingsborg Castle** as well as those of the 12th century **Nas Castle**. There are several Viking burial grounds on the island.

WHERE TO STAY IN LAKE VATTERN AREA

The Grythyttan Gastgivaregard
A very special inn with charming rooms and a renowned cuisine. (See "Grythyttan.")

The Svarta Herrgard
There are 40 rooms, all with private bath. Since 1946, the hotel has been lovingly watched over by owners Nils and Marianne Frantzen. *For information and reservations, contact the Frantzens, 71011 Svarta,* ☎ *05 85 500 03 or 05 85 500 63.* (See "Svarta.")

The Gyllene Uttern
In Granna • A deservedly popular spot. Located right on the lake with a spectacular view, it could serve as a pleasant headquarters for exploration of this area. It is also a well-known retreat for honeymooners as it boasts a wedding chapel. A meal in the dining room overlooking the lake is a memorable experience.

SWEDEN'S NORTH COUNTRY

Reindeer safaris can be arranged in Lappland.

The northernmost districts of Sweden—Jamtland, Norbotten and Lappland—comprise about half of Sweden's total area. But in terms of population, the ratio is much lower. The region is sparsely populated, which makes it an ideal spot for those who like to get away from crowds. There are plenty of hiking trails, lakes, rivers and wilderness huts available to hikers. The **Swedish Touring Association** is the organization to contact for information on hiking in the area. Most Swedes shake their heads and wonder why anyone would want to go all the way north. Sweden, unlike Finland and Norway, does not promote its northern regions. But for the adventurers among you, here are the facts:

Swedish Touring Association (STF): *Jokkmokk,* ☎ *0971 11977.*

GETTING THERE

Though it is remote and wild, the northern portion of Sweden is easily accessible. There are airports at several towns, among them, Ostersund, Skelleftea, Lulea and Kiruna with service from Stockholm. In June and July, SAS offers a Midnight Sun tour from Stockholm to Kiruna, with transportation to the Norwegian coast to see the Midnight Sun. An express train makes the trip from Stockholm to the north in a day and a night. A train from Stockholm to Narvik, Norway makes a stop at Kiruna. For drivers, the E4 takes you straight from Stockholm to Haparanda on the Finnish border near Tornio.

The **Inlandsbana** is a railroad that chugs through 1300 kilometers of the back country of Sweden. The route runs from **Kristinehamn** in Varmland to **Gallivare** north of the Arctic Circle. Travelers can pick it up at various stops along the way. Part of the trip is made by coach. A package is available which allows you to pick up the train at **Mora**, with an overnight stay at the Hotel Mora, and takes you on to **Ostersund** with a stay at the Ostersund Hotel, and then to **Storuman** with a stay at the Hotel Toppen on Lake Storuman. The rate, at last check, was $295 per person, double occupancy. Along the way, local fiddlers and bands greet the train and there are excursions and concerts, as well as other activities planned for passengers.

Another package for the rugged traveler is a five-day hiking tour with stays arranged in tents or mountain huts. This is a loosely organized tour and allows you to select tents or cabins, to row or motor across the lakes and to choose, within limits, where to make camp. The package includes camping at selected sites, packet boat to Kebnats and a bus to Gallivare. The price is, or was, $155 per person. For either of these tours, ☎ *(800) 4444848*, or contact **Carlson's Viking Tours**, *12755 State Highway 55, Minneapolis, MN 55441*. The tours must be purchased with round-trip transatlantic air travel on KLM Royal Dutch Airlines to Amsterdam from any of the KLM gateway cities. Ask your travel agent for details. These packages are part of a group of tours called "50 Unique Reasons to Go to Sweden and Scandinavia."

JAMTLAND

OSTERSUND

Tourist Office: The office is located at *Rashusgatan 44*. Mailing address is *831 82 Ostersund,* ☎ *063 14 40 01 or 063 14 40 02.*

Located in the north central portion of Sweden in the province of Jamtland, Ostersund is almost a straight shot north from Lake Siljan. Swedes will tell you that you need not go north of Ostersund, as the areas here provide the best skiing in the country and give you a taste of everything you may see farther north. In addition to skiing, you will find the **Jamtl Open-air Museum** with an 18th-century house as well as Lapp huts, located a few kilometers from Ostersund. It is open only from late June to August. There are also a car museum and a brewery which offers a tour, with tasting. **The Hotel Ostersund** is the principal hostelry here, with a restaurant and nightclub.

ARE

Tourist Office: *Torget.* Or write *Box 53, 830 13 Are,* ☎ *0647 512 20.*

Are is the largest winter-sports center of the area, and once hosted the World Ski Championships, so you can count on the excellence of the downhill skiing. Hiking and fishing are the activities for summertime. Nearby are the "Dead Falls," so called because in 1796 the falls abruptly dried up. The largest active falls in Sweden are here also.

The **Diplomat Are** is a small hotel, open only from November to May, for the ski season. The **Aregarden**, with 84 rooms, is near the funicular and the railway station. The hotel has a sauna, a pool and dancing in the evenings. You can also rent ski equipment here. Apartments are available at **Are Fjallby**, which is a large complex with a pool, sauna and fitness center, several restaurants and dancing. **Sunwing Are** has apartments as well as rooms, a restaurant and nightclub, and a pool.

NORBOTTEN

LULEA

Tourist Office: *The Norbotten Tourist Board, Kungsgatan 5, Lulea,* will provide visitors with information on touring, camping and accommodations.

Lulea, on the east coast, is a starting point for many travelers on their way to Lappland. Lulea's appeal is its situation on the Gulf of Bothnia at the beginning of an archipelago of more than 300 tiny islands. The church here is a 15th-century one. You can also take the time to visit the Lapp museum.

The **SAS Lulea**, which has been recently spruced up, offers friendly service and many amenities. The rooms all have private bath, TV/video and even hair dryers. The hotel has the Amphion Restaurant; the North Bothnia Room, which is an 1850s style dining room; a nightclub; bar and the Cooks Krog informal restaurant. There is a health club with gym, sauna, bar and pool, as well as a business center "office for a day." SAS airline check-in is available at the hotel. The **Hotel Nordkalotten** is new, rustically designed and situated in a wooded area of Lulea. Cross-country skiing and hiking trails are right there, and downhill skiing is eight kilometers away. The hotel has an indoor pool, restaurant, bar and dancing, and TV in all the rooms.

LAPPLAND

ARVIDSJAUR

Tourist Office: *In the center of town at Skolgatan 8.* The office will help you with information on holiday villages or private accommodations and farmhouse holidays.

Arvidsjaur, which used to be an important trading center for the northern region, is located west of Lulea on Road 94. The train from Stockholm stops here, as does the inland railway mentioned previously, and you can also get here from Bodo, Norway by means of the "Silver Road," which passes through Arvidsjaur. With festivals and handicrafts, this is a center for Lapp culture. And it is a good spot as well for recreational activities. There are downhill slopes as well as cross-country trails. Mill festivals in summertime attract locals as well as tourists and offer a good opportunity to meet the inhabitants of this northern region. A music festival, called *Music in the Country of the Midnight Sun,* takes place during one week of July. The Lapp village here is the oldest surviving church village in Sweden, dating from the 18th century. There are about 80 Lapp houses. The church villages were the centers of activity of this sparsely populated area of Sweden. Here, festivals and worship gave the far-flung residents a chance to come together. **Lamburtrasket** is a nature reserve here, with many rare birds.

The **Hotel Laponia** is about the only choice if you want a hotel. A modern conference hotel, it is located on the lake and has an indoor pool, sauna and fitness center. There is a restaurant with dancing, and a bar. Downhill and cross-country skiing are within one kilometer, and the hotel will give you advice on dog sledding, snowmobile safaris and Lapp holidays.

JOKKMOKK AND SURROUNDINGS

Jokkmokk Tourist Information: *Porjusvagen 4.*

GETTING THERE

The town is linked to other villages by bus and to Stockholm via bus connections with the railway from Boden, Murjek and Gallivare. Jokkmokk is 170 kilometers from Lulea, 94 from Gallivare.

The name Jokkmokk means "bend in the stream," and the town was established on the Lulea River under decree of King Karl IX as the site for the winter market of the Sami people. The first market was held in 1605 and the first church constructed in 1607. The tradition of the winter market is all that has survived from those early days, and it is held on the first Thursday, Friday and Saturday of February. On Sunday of that market week, a special church service is held. To visit the market, it is necessary to arrange accommodations a year in advance, as this small town becomes overrun with visitors. Travelers should be warned that it can be very cold, at times down to 0-30°F. Jokkmokk also now holds an autumn fair at the end of August. Visit the old church, the pioneer museum and Storknabben, a hill from which the midnight sun can be seen for about 20 days. Lars Pirak, a Lapp artist, has a workshop and exhibition at *Jarregatan 4* in Jokkmokk. Watercolors and objects made of horn and wood are available.

HIKING, FISHING AND SKIING

Talvatis Hill near Jokkmokk offers about 20 kilometers of moderately easy hiking paths through rolling forest terrain. At the **Serri Nature Reserve**, there are 10–15 kilometers of marked trails, one of which is a wheelchair path with fishing from an excellent jetty. Fishing permits may be bought from *Jokkmokks Jakt och Fiske*. **Muddus National Park** has about 50 kilometers of trails with overnight cabins. Much of the park is closed between March 15–July 21.

Hotels are fairly basic. The three in Jokkmokk are the **Hotell Jokkmokk**, ☎ *0971 113 20*; the **Hotell Gastis**, ☎ *0971 100 12*; and the **Hotell Engelmark**, ☎ *0971 111 60*. The mailing address for all three hotels is *960 40 Jokkmokk*. All three have fully licensed restaurants. Surrounding towns also have hotel accommodations. Most of these are very simple also.

KVIKKJOKK

Situated 120 kilometers northwest of Jokkmokk at the end of Route 805, Kvikkjokk is the gateway to Europe's largest wilderness area. Sarek, Padjelant and Stora Sjofallet are the parks here, but travelers should be forewarned that these are remote areas with only a few trails. Padjelanta is the northernmost area, bordering Norway on the west boundaries. This region is a summer pasture for reindeer, and Lapps have summer quarters at various locations in the park. The Padjelanta Trail is a beautiful route with overnight cabins and a short boat ride. Its trails are moderately demanding according to those who know. For information on fishing and for permits, contact the **Jokkmokk Tourist Bureau**. Permits may also be purchased at some cabins along the Padjelanta Trail.

The Skabramaive ski area has an 800-meter illuminated run and a lift. **Bomyrberget** winter sports area near Vuollerim has a 550-meter and a 1000-meter run with lift. There is also an illuminated cross-country trail here. At **Kvikkjokk**, novices and experts will find varied terrain for cross-country skiing. Two-day trips to **Njunjesstugan** or **Partestugan** with stops at unmanned wilderness cabins are popular for the very rugged. You must come with full winter gear. At **Bjorkudden**, there is a holiday village that makes a good base for skiing in the forested and mountain terrain. *Contact Hjalmar Oberg 972 00 Gallivare,* ☎ *0973 410 15.* Pick-up service can be arranged.

KIRUNA

Kiruna Tourist Information: *Hjalmar Lundbomsvag 42.*

Kiruna is the world's largest city in area, if not in population. Its other claim to fame is the highest mountain in Sweden, **Kebnekaise**. Kiruna is not a resort town, but it is included here because it is an airport connection and a gateway to hiking and skiing in the area. It is also a stop along the North Calotte Highway, a beautiful route that runs north of the Arctic Circle from Rovaniemi in Finland to Narvik, Norway. The Swedish Touring Association maintains a station at Kebnekaise Mountain from where guided climbing trips to the peak can be arranged.

The Reso Hotel Ferrum is a comfortable, basic hostelry with 170 rooms, all with private bath and TV. A double will run about 650SEK. The **Hotel Kebne** has just 54 rooms, all with private bath and TV. Rates for doubles will be about 500SEK.

ICELAND

Reykjavik boasts urban sophistication and a population of 100,000.

AN INTRODUCTION

The emptiness is eerie; the ruggedness, awe-inspiring; and the variety of color and texture, unbelievable. It is as if Mother Nature has vented all her moods on Iceland: anger, melancholy, joy, calm. Treeless, windswept, lava -blanketed, the landscape of this island nation is raw and formidably beautiful. If your preference is urban sophistication, then you should not venture beyond the city limits of Reykjavik or perhaps not come at all. Iceland's tiny towns are spattered across the land like spots from a painter's brush, and between these far-flung enclaves of civilization runs a road which is at times a single-lane, unpaved challenge to even the most intrepid driver and the most rugged vehicle. With the exception of Reykjavik and Akureyri, most of the towns are scarcely big enough to deserve the name. Cossetted in a harbor or at the foot of brooding mountains, these towns can sometimes be charming but are often forlorn. Most have little more than a fishing harbor and a fish-processing plant, a video store and a rudimentary hotel with dancing on Saturday nights. But for anyone with the slightest interest in geology and the out-of-doors, Iceland is a paradise, offering the chance to observe the forces of nature in all stages, from the birth of an island to the renewal of ancient lava fields. To travel around the country is to be a witness to what the beginnings of the earth must have been like, and the landscape, ever renewing itself from geological disaster, is inspiring in its heartiness. From the most devastating destruction, the blackest of lava-covered fields, emerge green shoots of life. From seething caldrons beneath the sea, new islands are born. Here is testimony to nature's resilience.

THE ICELANDIC SAGAS

At the core of this wild land is a literary heritage which dates back to the 12th century when the great Icelandic Sagas, the tales of the daily lives and exploits of the leading Icelandic figures of the 10th and 11th centuries, were recorded. Written in Icelandic, the purest of the Nordic tongues, and translated into many languages, the sagas are still highly readable and constitute the backbone of the Icelandic culture. Of these often violent tales of life in a wild, untameable land, *Njal's Saga* and *The Laxdaela Saga* are the most widely read and are available in English. *Egil's Saga* another popular epic, which was probably written by the Norwegian historian Snorri Sturluson who lived in Iceland from 1179 until 1241, chronicles the life of Egil Skallagrimsson, the poet who was among the earliest and most original of the Scandinavian poets and who lived in West Iceland in the 10th century. In addition to the sagas, there are also the Eddas, some of which may have been written down as early as the 10th century. The *Poetic Edda* is the work of several poets and consists of both mythological and heroic poems. It is the basis for most of what we know about the heroes and gods of the Vikings. In fact, Richard Wagner drew on the Edda for his opera cycle *The Ring of the Nibelungen*. The original manuscripts of the Sagas, written on skin, were at one time all in Denmark, taken there by the Icelandic Professor Arni Magnusson, who had gathered a collection of Icelandic books

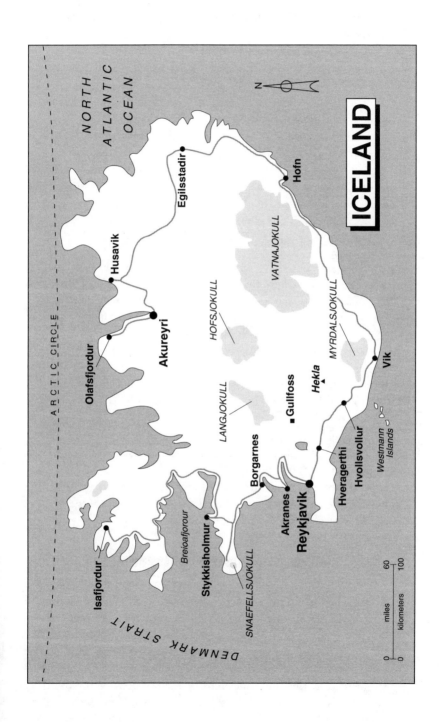

and who lived in Copenhagen in the late 17th and early 18th centuries. A fire destroyed much of his collection in 1728, but most of the Icelandic manuscripts remained intact and were then moved to the University Library in Copenhagen, which was also affiliated with the University of Iceland. In the years after the independence movement, negotiations were carried on to bring back the collection to Iceland, and finally, by 1985, most of the originals were safely ensconced in the Manuscript Institute at the University of Iceland in Reykjavik and they can be viewed there. All Icelanders are familiar with the sagas and in even the most simple and remote homes, you will find copies of these books, for Icelanders are avid readers. Indeed, Iceland, with a 100 percent literacy rate, publishes the greatest number of books per capita of any country in the world.

THE PERIOD OF SETTLEMENT: A.D. 870-930

Iceland's first settlers were Irish monks who sailed northwest in search of a place where they could worship in solitude, undisturbed by politics and dissent. This uninhabited island was the perfect spot. The monks' idyll was short-lived, however, and they fled in the wake of the Vikings' arrival in the ninth century. The Norsemen settled the land in the years between A.D. 870 and 930. That period of settlement is recorded in the remarkable *Book of Settlements*, which lists by name the four hundred earliest settlers. Iceland is, in fact, the only country in the world that can name its first settlers, and most Icelanders today can trace their roots back to these early pioneers. A Norwegian named Ingolfur Arnarson is said to be the first permanent settler of Iceland. He arrived by ship and, as was the custom, threw over his "chair pillars," the tall supports for the seat that were a symbol of his rank, and declared that he would stay wherever the pillars came to shore. They eventually washed up at the edge of a bay, whose steaming geothermal springs inspired Ingolfur to name the spot, "Smoking Bay," or Reykjavik.

THE SAGA PERIOD AND THE INDEPENDENT COMMONWEALTH: 930-1264

In A.D. 930 the Althing or Parliament was established at the great plain of Thingvellir. With this government, the Icelandic Commonwealth, an independent free state, consisting of 39 independent chieftains, came into being and lasted until A.D. 1262 when the Norwegian king declared power over Iceland. The Althing met every year on the great plain of Thingvellir where the Law Speaker stood to read the laws, one-third of them each year for the three years of his term. Judicial matters were discussed at the Althing and disputes settled as well. It has been estimated that at the end of the settlement period, the population in Iceland was between 60,000 and 80,000. Most of these settlers were of Norwegian or Celtic descent, with a few from Denmark and Sweden. But it was the Viking blood and culture that dominated and established itself permanently, even after the Viking era had ended. The early Norse language lived on, undiluted by new immigrants, and the literature and the Viking spirit of adventure continued as well.

ICELAND'S DARK AGES: A.D. 1264-1843

Life in Iceland began to decline under the Norwegian rule, primarily the result of natural and climactic disasters rather than of oppression. The resources of the country, particularly the fishing grounds and the forests (yes, there were once trees in Iceland) were drained. In A.D. 1380, when Norway and Iceland fell under Danish domination, Iceland's economy was debilitated by the imposition of the severe Danish trade monopoly. And in A.D. 1402, the Black Death, which was rampaging through Scandinavia, decimated Iceland's population. The years that followed were grim. Iceland's population in 1703 was counted at 50,000 and of those, it was estimated that 20 percent were beggars. Famine, smallpox and other natural disasters took further tolls and at the end of the 18th century, the Althing, which had stood since the 13th century, was dissolved.

TOWARDS FREE TRADE AND INDEPENDENCE: 1843-PRESENT

It was not until the middle of the 19th century, with the advent of a move towards independence led by Jon Sigurdsson, that conditions began to improve in Iceland. In 1843, the Althing was reinstated and a few years later, the Danish trade monopoly was entirely lifted. In 1874, on the occasion of Iceland's millenary celebration of its first settlement, the Danish king gave Iceland a constitution and complete control of its own trade. Home rule followed, but independence did not come until 1944. After occupation during World War II, first by the British and then the Americans, Iceland finally formed an independent state. On June 17, 1944, the anniversary of the birth of Jon Sigurdsson who is considered the liberator of Iceland, under a proclamation issued at Thingvellir, the country declared itself the Republic of Iceland.

THE POLITICAL SYSTEM

Since 1944, Iceland has been a democracy with a president who is elected every four years by popular vote. The Althing is a two house legislative body consisting of 63 members elected from eight constituencies. There are six political parties, one of which is the Kvennalistinna, or Women's List, a party which was formed in the 1970s with a women's general strike and which now commands the support of a substantial percentage of the electorate. Iceland's President, Vidgis Finnbogadottir, is the first woman to be elected president of the republic. She has served as president since 1980. Iceland is a welfare state, with a general insurance plan for all citizens and free education through the university level. There are no extremes of poverty or wealth in the nation, and the social system is completely egalitarian with no class distinction. As Professor Gwyn Jones explained in his article "My Noble Friends the Icelanders," "In a country where everyone can trace his ancestry back to his favorite settler in the ninth or early 10th centuries, how can one man be called an aristocrat and another a wage-slave?"

THE NEWEST LAND ON EARTH

In geological terms, Iceland is the youngest land on earth and one might say that it hasn't grown up yet. Of its two hundred volcanoes, thirty have erupted since the ninth century, which in geological measurements is very recent. In fact, the volcanoes are responsible for one-third of the lava that has spewed over the world in the past five hundred years. And as recently as 1963, a new island, Surtsey, near the Westmann Islands was formed by an undersea volcanic eruption. An eruption 10 years later on the island of Heymaey, also in the Westmann Islands, added yet more land to Iceland's dominion, for the size of Heymaey increased by one-sixth in the course of that eruption. But there's more to the landscape than volcanoes, and nature has been a friend as well as an adversary in this geologically hyper-active country. The many splendid waterfalls are the source of hydroelectric power for most towns, and the slight sulfuric odor you will notice when you first turn on the hot water faucet in your hotel room is due to the fact that hot water and central heating are provided from the many hot springs located throughout the country. So, though Reykjavik might mean "Smoking Bay," the capital city is in fact a smokeless city, and the wisps which Ingolfur saw were not smoke but steam, clean and soot-free from the hot springs.

TRAVEL ESSENTIALS

Iceland Tourist Board: *655 Third Ave., New York, NY 10017,* ☎ *(212) 949-2333.* There are also tourist information offices in Reykjavik, Isafjordur, Egilsstadir and Akureyri.

GETTING THERE

Icelandair flies to Keflavik airport outside Reykjavik from New York, Baltimore and Orlando. The flight, which is just four and one half hours from New York, is a most pleasant one, quick and comfortable, with extraordinarily friendly and efficient service.

GETTING AROUND

By air: Icelandair and **Islands Flag** are the domestic airlines, and between the two, travelers can get to most of the major towns by air. In general, domestic flights leave from Reykjavik City Airport and all are under one hour in length. But careful planning is necessary since not all flights go every day.

Bus service: Bus service around the country is excellent. Many of the buses also serve as sightseeing tours so you might find yourself listening to a well-informed guide and stopping at some of the sightseeing attractions on the way to your destination. The *Omnibus Passport* provides unlimited bus travel from one to four weeks, while the *Full-Circle Passport* is valid for a complete circuit of the country with no time limits. These tickets also entitle the holder to discounts on certain sightseeing tours and accommodations.

Driving: Driving in Iceland can be rigorous. The Ring Road, which is 1400 kilometers long, offers the traveler the advantage of circling the entire country, by way of the coast. But though it is the major highway, it is often only one and a half lanes wide, and there are segments which are not paved. Furthermore, towns and service stations are few and far between and there is little traffic, so if you have a problem you most likely will have to fend for yourself. The traffic that does appear generally comes shooting at you over bridges and around blind curves at speeds that threaten to break the sound barrier. But if you do have a problem and encounter an Icelander, he will be most friendly and helpful. All the major towns you will probably want to visit lie along the Ring Road, but it is possible to take detours off the road to sights which are a short distance away and then to rejoin the road.

Gas Stations: Gas stations are open Monday–Saturday, 7:30 a.m. until 8:00 p.m. Sundays (November 1–May 31) from 10:00 a.m.–8:00 p.m. Some remain open longer and most have vending machines which accept either major credit cards or bank notes of 100, 500, or 1000kr.

Speed Limit: The normal speed limit is 50 kilometers per hour for urban areas, 30 kph (kilometers per hour) in the center of Reykjavik, 70 kph in rural areas, and 90 kph on those rare paved roads.

Drivers are required to keep their car lights on 24 hours a day and drivers and passengers all must wear seatbelts. Very strict drunken-driving rules are enforced. A driver with a blood alcohol content of .05 percent will lose his license and be subject to a high fine. Because of changing weather conditions and the possibility of snow-blocked roads, it is advisable to check road and weather conditions through the local police before starting out for rural areas. The interior of the country is virtually impenetrable in any kind of vehicle. There are no roads or bridges over the glacial rivers.

Hiking: For experienced hikers, Iceland is a paradise, but there are many areas where it is highly unadvisable to go without a guide. Hikers are warned that it is particularly dangerous to hike across the interior, so travelers wishing to see more of Iceland than the coastal route should be advised to take guided tours. **The Touring Club of Iceland** offers over 200 different guided walking tours, ranging in duration from half-day to several days. Both Icelanders and tourists participate in these.

Tours: In other countries, you might feel that going on a bus tour is too "touristy," but in Iceland it is a wise choice. Tours range from half-day excursions out of Reykjavik to three-day tours of the Westfjords. There is also a one-day Icelandair tour to Greenland. (See "One- and Two-day Excursions by Air" in the Reykjavik chapter of this book.)

Full- or half-day hiking trips are also available on weekends all year round to Thorsmork, Landmannalaugar, Hveravellir, Veidivotn. *Contact the Iceland Tourist Board in New York or the Tourist Information Center at Bankastraeti 2 in Reykjavik for details and arrangements.*

For snowmobiling on the Snaefellsnes Glacier, contact Tryggve Konradsson, at *Ferdapjonustan Snjofell.,355 Arnarstapa, Snaefellsnes.* ☎ *93-56783.*

Valgard Halldorsson, ☎ *(354-1) 618000* will pick up your group by van from the airport or your Reykjavik hotel and drive you to Snaefellsnes, arranging whatever side trips you prefer.

Add-Ice, Icelandic Adventure, ☎ *(354-1) 676755* arranges jeep safaris on the Myrdals glacier, all the way to the top for a view of one of Iceland's most active volcanoes, Katla. In winter, snowmobiling and slalom-skiing behind a jeep are also available through this company. Add-Ice also operates fishing and riding expeditions.

Pony trekking: This is not really a way to get around the country, but rather a way to get out into the country for a few hours or even several days of fresh air and glorious scenery in a uniquely Icelandic form of exercise. The ponies are a breed found only in Iceland, brought over by the Vikings and never bred with any other strain. Their unusual gait is called the "tolt." Forty-one farms offer pony treks with a variety of tours to choose from. *Contact Iceland Farm Holidays for a complete listing. From the U.S.* ☎ *011-354-1-623640.* Another pony company is **Hestar**, ☎ *011-354-1-653044.* You can also inquire at your hotel.

Car Rental: Car rentals are listed in the guidebook under individual cities and towns. There are several car rental agencies in Reykjavik and Akureyri, but rental can be arranged in other towns as well and can be booked ahead from the U.S. Cars can also be booked through Icelandair and pickup arranged at either of the airports in Reykjavik or at your hotel. A V.A.T. tax of 24 percent is added to the rental rate. Gasoline is expensive, but keep your tank full as there are not many service stations in the rural areas.

MONEY MATTERS

The Icelandic Krona (kr.) is the currency of Iceland. At the time of publication the exchange rate was 67kr. to $1.00. As in other Scandinavian countries, a value-added tax is included in the price of everything, but you can often get some of this back upon leaving the country if you have the correct forms. Shops offering V.A.T. refunds display a sign in the window and will fill out the necessary papers for you to present at the airport.

HOLIDAYS

In addition to Christmas, New Year's Day, Good Friday and Easter Monday, most shops and museums are closed June 17—the anniversary of Iceland's independence—May 1, Labor Day, Ascension Day and Whit Monday.

HOTELS, GUESTHOUSES AND FARMHOUSES

Iceland's hotels are generally immaculate and comfortable though not often luxurious. With the exception of the major hotels in Reykjavik and Akureyri, many of the hotels have only a small percentage of rooms with private baths, so if that is important to you, book early and be very emphatic about your request for a private bath. Guesthouses are a less expensive alternative, but usually these too provide only a bathroom down the hall. Almost all hotels, guesthouses and farmhouses include breakfast in the room rate. The Iceclass chain of hotels offers a voucher system with reduced rates at participating hotels. Vouchers can be purchased in Iceland.

Summer Hotels: Many of these hotels are actually school dormitories which function as hotels in summertime. Operated by the Iceland Tourist Bureau, they are clean and comfortable though lacking in charm and luxury. But they are less expensive than the regular hotels. Most have dining service and many have a swimming pool. *For information contact the Iceland Tourist Bureau.*

Edda Hotels: These seventeen tourist class hotels are operated by the Iceland Tourist Bureau.The Open Edda Hotel Voucher can be used for rooms without private baths. Breakfast is included. The holder of the voucher can make a reservation for the first night, and after that, reservations are made from one hotel to the next. One telephone call per family is included in the price. You must inform the reception desk on arrival that you will be paying by Open Edda Voucher. The voucher does not guarantee a room.Contact the Iceland Tourist Board at *Skogarhilio 18, IS-101, Reykjavik.* ☎ *354-1-623300.*

Rainbow Hotels: A group of hotels which are open year-round have formed this association with a joint booking center. Contact Rainbow Hotels, *Raudararstigur 18, P.O. Box 653, IS-121, Reykjavik.* ☎ *354-1-620160.*

Farm Holidays: Staying at a farm is not the same as staying at a bed and breakfast. Your quarters are often part of the farmhouse itself and breakfast is taken with the family, more often than not at the kitchen table. In some farmhouses three meals a day can be provided on prior notice and some farms have separate cottages with cooking facilities. Your hosts will help you arrange whatever activities are available: pony treks, fishing, glacier trips, berry picking—the list is long and tempting. This is a wonderful way to get acquainted with Iceland and its people. *For information on farms, contact Iceland Farm Holidays, Baendahollin v/Hagatorg, 107 Reykjavik,* ☎ *(91) 623640.* They issue a booklet listing all farm accommodations. The booklet is also available through the Iceland Tourist Board in New York.

Youth hostels: Youth hostels are the least expensive option for accommodations, and there are also guesthouses which provide sleeping bag accommodations or "sbacc." *For more information, contact the The Icelandic Youth Hostel Association, Sundlaugavegi 34, 105 Reykjavik, Iceland.* ☎ *(91) 38110.*

The Touring Club of Iceland has a number of huts for hikers bringing their own sleeping bags and food, but first choice of these accommodations goes to people traveling with the Touring Club, so check ahead.

Camping: The best equipped campsites are in Reykjavik, Husafell, Isafjordur, Varmahid, Akureyri, Myvatn, Egilsstadir, Hella, Laugarvatn, Thingvellir, Jokulsargljufur, and Skaftafell. Be aware that in many places camping is restricted to marked areas and in others, campers must have permission from the farmer to camp on any fenced or cultivated land. In the nature reserves, camping is allowed only in the designated campgrounds.

HOTEL RATES

Very Expensive	More than 10,000kr.
Expensive	6,000-10,000kr.
Moderate	2,400-6,000kr.
Inexpensive	Less than 2,400kr.

WEATHER

In spite of its name and northern location, Iceland is not always snow-covered and freezing. The Gulf Stream is responsible for making the coastal areas a bit more temperate than one might expect, but the weather is highly unpredictable and you should always be prepared for wind, rain and cold, even in summertime. The average temperature in Reykjavik is 52°F in July and 30°F in January.

LANGUAGE

The Icelandic language is the purest of the Nordic languages and the closest to Old Norse, remaining basically as it was at the time of the settlement. Almost everyone speaks excellent English so you need not rush to sign up for a course in conversational Icelandic, but it is always polite to be able to use a few friendly phrases.

Thank you = *Takk*; good day and good morning = *godan daginn* (go-than-die-int); excuse me = *afsaekith* (af-sike-ith); goodbye = *bless*.

FOOD AND DRINK

Food and drink are both very expensive in Iceland but the recent inauguration of the "Summer Tourist Menu" can alleviate some of the hardship on your wallet. In many hotels throughout Iceland, the logo of a smiling sun wearing a chef's cap signals the special of the day. For a relatively reasonable price you can get a full meal at either lunch or dinner, with an additional discount for children. The tourist menu is available from June 1 to Sept. 15, and a list of hotels offering the menu is available from the tourist office in Reykjavik and at many hotels. Fish is, as one would expect, a staple of the Icelandic diet, but lamb, mutton and fowl, such as puffin and guillemot, are also served frequently and you will find beef and pork on many menus. Fresh fruit and vegetables are a delicacy since they must either be grown in greenhouses or imported. Aside from Reykjavik and Akureyri, most restaurants are small, almost snack-type spots, and the only place to dine is in the local hotel. But the food in these hotels is almost always good and, unfortunately expensive. Among the more interesting, if not the most appetizing, culinary quirks is the custom in the area of Lake Myvatn of eating rotten eggs for Thorrablot, a traditional feast held in January. The eggs are buried the previous spring in ashes, then hard-boiled. It is said that they taste like very ripe cheese. Another Myvatn specialty is *grassmjolk*, a milk-based dessert with Iceland moss. The liquor stores are all state run and, though less expensive than that purchased in restaurants, the prices on wine and liquor are very high. Iceland produces two very good vodkas. Until 1989, Iceland's beer was of lower alcoholic content, but now regular beer is sold. The local brew is Egils.

REYKJAVIK AND ITS SURROUNDINGS

Tourist Office: *Bankastraeti 2. Monday to Friday 10:00 a.m. to 4:00 p.m. There are also information centers in City Hall, Vonarstraeti,* ☎ *632005; at the Campsite Service Center, Sundlaugarvegur.* ☎ *686944; and at BSI Coach Rental, Reykjavik Bus Terminal,* ☎ *25035.*

REYKJAVIK TOURIST AND MUSEUM CARDS

The Reykjavik City Card offers unlimited travel on the city buses, admission to some museums and to the Municipal Swimming pool. Buy it at the City Hall information Desk or at the Tourist Information Center at *Bankastraeti 2*. A one day card is 400kr, 2 days are 500kr and a three day card will be 600kr. The Museum Card, which costs 300kr, admits you to the National Museum, the Icelandic Maritime Museum in Hafnarfjordur and the medieval collection at Nesstofa.

DIRECTORY

American Embassy • *Laufasvegur 21.* ☎ *629100.*

Baggage Storage • Baggage may be stored at the BSI bus terminal in Vatnsmyrarvegur. Monday to Friday 7:30 a.m. to 9:30 p.m.; Saturday 7:30 a.m. to 12:30 p.m.; Sunday, only in June, July and August, 5:00 p.m. to 7:00 p.m.

Banks • Hours 9:15 a.m. to 4:00 a.m. Monday to Friday.

Exchanges outside banking hours • Tourist Information Center at Bankastraeti 2 during June, July and August only. Monday to Friday, 4:30 p.m. to 6:00 p.m.; Saturday, 9:00 a.m. to 1:00 p.m. and Sunday 9:00–1:00. There is also an exchange at the airport for arriving passengers.

Emergency • Fire and Ambulance, ☎ *11100.*Police 1012 or 11166. Hospital, ☎ *696600.* Rescue Squads, ☎ *627111.* Medical help, ☎ *696600,* weekdays from 8:00 a.m. to 5:00 p.m. Also, ☎ *21230* on weekdays and weekends from 5:00 p.m. to 8:00 a.m. for non-emergency care.

Pharmacies • Open daily from 9:00 a.m. to 6:00 p.m. One pharmacy is open 24-hours on a rotating basis. See the newspaper for specifics.

Postal Service • Post offices are open Monday, Tuesday, Wednesday, Friday from 8:30 a.m. to 4:30 p.m.; The post office at the Bus Station is open Mon–Fri. from 12:00–6:00 p.m., and Saturday from 9:00–1:00 p.m.

News in English • From July to September, the news is broadcast in English at 7:30 a.m. on station 1, FM 93.5. Many hotels have television with access to round-the-clock news in English.

Reykjavik lies in a watery bed, embraced by mountains and warmed by the bright colors of its buildings and gardens. The high-

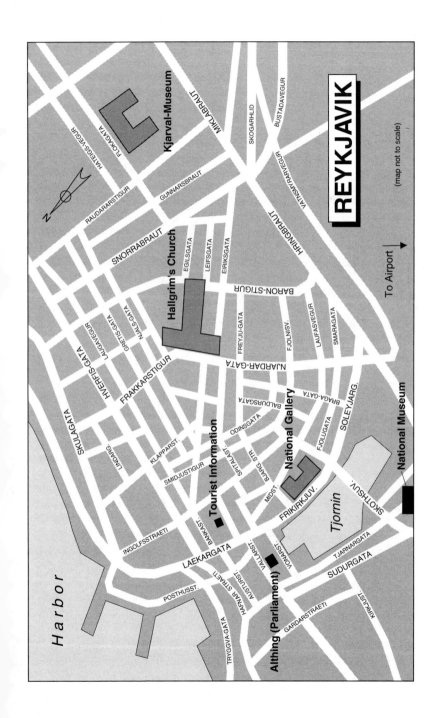

est point is the spire of its modern church which looms over the otherwise low buildings, a man-made pinnacle against the natural peaks of the surrounding mountains. The narrow streets lined with raucously painted houses built of corrugated tin and concrete make the city seem to be the creation of a slightly crazed child architect experimenting with shapes, materials and colors. Though it was founded in A.D. 874 by Ingolfur Arnarson who threw his chair pillars overboard and claimed that he would settle wherever they landed, Reykjavik did not come into its own until the late 18th century. Named for the steam which Ingolfur saw rising from the hot springs (Reykjavik means "Smoking Bay"), Reykjavik developed as a wool and ropemaking center. Gradually, the Althing (Parliament) and the Supreme Court, as well as the educational centers were established in the town. In 1911, the University of Iceland was inaugurated in Reykjavik and the population began to grow. After World War II, a great spurt of development occurred, and Reykjavik now counts about 100,000 residents, almost half the country's total population.

GETTING THERE

Icelandair flies from New York's JFK, Baltimore and Orlando airports to Keflavik airport, just 50 kilometers southwest of Reykjavik.

GETTING AROUND AND OUT OF TOWN

Reykjavik has two airports: Keflavik, which is for international service, and Reykjavik City Airport (referred to usually as Reykjavik Airport) from where most domestic flights depart. Buses run regularly between Keflavik and Reykjavik. They will drop passengers at the Hotel Loftleidir and the Hotel Esja year-round and at any Reykjavik hotel in summertime. The bus fare is 550kr. (about $8.00) and U.S. dollars are accepted. A taxi from the airport will cost approximately 4000kr. Bus service in and around Reykjavik is efficient, and the traveler can get to most of the points of interest by making use of the city transportation. There are two main bus terminals in Reykjavik, one at Laekjartorg in the center of town and the other at Hlemmur, which is about a 15-minute walk east along Laugavegur, the principal shopping street. Bus stops are marked with the signs SVR. At last check, fare was 55kr. Exact change is required. A package of tickets will cost you less and can be purchased at either of the two main bus stations.

Many domestic destinations throughout the country are reachable by Icelandair. No flight is more than 50 minutes. There are also excellent bus tours to points of interest outside Reykjavik. Driving is another choice for getting out of town and seeing the landscape, but travelers should be warned that the main road around Iceland, the Ring Road, is not exactly a super highway. In most places it is one and a half lanes and not always paved.

Car Rental: Avis, *Sigtun 5*, ☎ *(91) 25433*. **Europcar/InterRent**, *Skelfan 9*, ☎ *(91) 686915*. **Gullfoss**, *Smojuvegi 4e*, ☎ *(91) 67 04 55*. **Hertz**/Icelandair, *Flugvallarbraut*, *Reykjavik Airport*, ☎ *(91) 690500*. **Budget**, *Armuli*

1, ☎ *91-880880.*Most rental companies will pick up and deliver the car at your hotel.

WHAT TO SEE AND DO

For the energetic and curious, walking offers the best introduction to the city. Head for the harbor to catch the busy beat of the commercial side of town. Stroll around the lake and peek into the gardens. Take detours down the jumbled side streets, especially along the two blocks from the lake where the older buildings are located. It is difficult to get lost in Reykjavik, but if you do, you need not fear, even late into the evening, which of course in summer does not mean that it will be dark. Reykjavik is an extraordinarily safe town, and the people so friendly that if you stop to ask someone directions, he or she will probably walk along with you or drive you there, just to make sure you find your way.

The three long blocks on either side of Lake Tjornin afford the walker a good sense of the center of town. Another central starting point is the Hotel Borg in the center of the Old Town. Stop to take a look at the Althing (Parliament) and the gardens of the main square and then continue towards Lake Tjornin. As you walk you will be struck by the colorful houses, which from a distance look as if they are built of wood, but on closer inspection reveal themselves to be constructed of corrugated tin. Since timber is at a premium, i.e., just about nonexistent in Iceland, you will find few structures of wood. The tin houses date from the early part of the 20th century. Later in the century, the white concrete style developed, but even most of those have tin roofs. It is the tin houses, jumbled together in whimsical assortments of hues and shapes that give Reykjavik its coziness and its European cum frontier town atmosphere.

When you reach Lake Tjornin, take the time to stroll part way around the lake and try to see how many different birds you can spot. You will probably see eider ducks, mallards and certainly several arctic terns whose return every year from the Antarctic to Iceland is the first sign of spring. From the lake you can continue on to the National Museum.

Another convenient starting point, no matter where you are staying, is at Laekjartorg, where one of the city's two bus terminals is located. Across Laekjargata is one of Reykjavik's oldest buildings, originally constructed as a jail and now housing the offices of the president and prime minister. Heading north into Hafnaerstraeti, this curved street, one of the city's main shopping areas, will lead you to the harbor. Take a few minutes to look at the boats here. Vessels of all sizes from huge trawlers to two-men operations moor here. There is a fish market every morning and you might even glimpse a Russian fishing boat. Heading back from the harbor, you will find the Icelandic Handicrafts Center at Nos. 1–3 Hafnaerstraeti in an old building whose wooden falcons are a relic of the days when Icelandic falcons were raised here before being sent to the Danish king. Just off from this spot runs Adalstraeti, the city's oldest street. The house at No. 10 Adalstraeti is approximately 220 years old, the oldest house in Reykjavik. Adalstraeti runs towards the lake, but for the time being, and for the purposes of this walking tour, turn from Adalstraeti onto Austurstraeti, heading back towards Laekjargata. The row of houses across the street dates primarily from the 19th century. As you will notice, these now are occupied by shops, restaurants and a tourist information center. The large building to the south is the Reykjavik Junior College. The school, not the building, was established in the 11th century as Skalholt in southern Iceland. Among its illustrious alumni are Nobel Prize winners, Niels Finsen for medicine in 1903 and Halldor Laxness for literature in 1955. The short street running from the school is called Skolabru or School-bridge. Take it and at the corner of Skolabru and Laekjargata, turn right. You will see the Cathedral of Reykjavik and behind it the Althing or Parliament. Turn to the right onto Kirkjustraeti and as you walk along the side of the church, you will see Austurvollur or Eastfields, so named because it was situated to the east of Ingolfur Arnarson's farm, the first settlement in Iceland. The statue here is of Jon Sigurdsson, the leader of the Icelandic independence movement during the 19th century, a kind of Icelandic George Washington. At the corner of Kirkjus-traeti and Adalstraeti is the oldest churchyard in Reykjavik, the site of the local church until the cathedral was built in the 19th century. The statue represents Skuli Magnusson, an 18th-century industrialist whose wool-dyeing and rope-making factories were responsible for bringing more settlers to Reykjavik and developing it into a commercial center. Cross the street and continue until you reach Sudurgata. The National Museum will be straight ahead, but before you reach it, stop to enjoy the view of Tjornin. Once past the National Museum, or out of it, if you decide to make a visit there, walk through Tjornin Park. The octagonal building beside the bridge is the music hall, Hljomskalinn. You should take the time to stroll beside the lake. The discerning eye can find more than 40 species of birds here. Across the street is the Icelandic Gallery of Art. If you take Laekjargata again, back where you came from, on the right side of the street is a giant chess table where from time to time you might find a couple of chess champions battling it out. You are now back at your starting point in Laekjartorg which is walking distance from most hotels, or you can hop on a bus to take you back to your hotel or on to your next adventure.

SIGHTSEEING TOURS

City Sightseeing

This tour, which departs daily all year round at 10:00 a.m. and 1:00 p.m., covers the main cultural and natural points of interest in Reykjavik, including the Arbaer Folk Museum, the harbor and the shopping area. The afternoon tour also includes a stop at the National Museum. The tour lasts two to two-and-a-half hours and can be booked through most hotels and travel bureaus. ☎ *623020.*

Puffin Island and Videy Cruise

A two-hour cruise around Lundey island to view the thousands of puffins there, and then a one hour stop at Videy island, where you can wander at your leisure, viewing the bird life, the manor house and church. If you wish to stay and have dinner, you can catch a boat an hour later for just the cost of the transfer from the ferry to your destination in Reykjavik. *From mid-June to August, Monday, Wednesday and Friday at 5:00 p.m.*

(For sightseeing trips farther afield, see "One-and Two-Day Excursions" from Reykjavik at the end of this chapter.)

MUSEUMS AND GALLERIES

Arbaer Open-air Museum
A collection of old houses taken primarily from the center of Reykjavik. The oldest is Smidshus, built in 1820. In addition to the permanent exhibit, there are frequent special programs and exhibitions. A small restaurant, Dillon's House, is located in the 1835 house of the same name. The museum is too far from town to walk to, so you will either have to drive or take a bus, either Bus No. 10 from Hlemmur or No. 100 from Laekjartorg. *Open June–August, daily except Monday from 10:00 a.m. to 6:00 p.m. In September, weekends only. Closed October–May.*

Arni Magnusson Institute
Located at the University of Iceland, the institute houses a priceless collection of manuscripts. Here you will find a facsimile of the *Book of Settlement* which describes all the original settlers of Iceland. (Iceland is the only country in the world that can account precisely for all its original settlers.) There is also an extraordinary vellum copy of *Njal's Saga*, which is considered to be the richest and most beautifully written of the medieval sagas. *Open June 15–September 15, Tuesday, Thursday and Saturday from 2:00 p.m. to 4:00 p.m.*

Einar Jonsson Sculpture Museum
Collection of the distinguished sculptor's work. *Open June 1–September 30 from 1:00 p.m. to 4:00 p.m. daily except Monday; October, November, February and May, open weekends from 1:30 p.m. to 4:00 p.m. The garden is open all year from 11:00 a.m. to 5:00 p.m.*

Asmundur Sveinsson Museum
Freyjugata 41 • Both indoor and outdoor sculptures are displayed here. *Open June 1-September 30 from 10:00 a.m. to 4:00 p.m. daily; October 1-May 15, 1:00 p.m.–4:00 p.m. daily. The garden is always open.*

Gallery Borg
Located next door to the Hotel Borg, the gallery has exhibits and auctions of primarily Icelandic art. *Open Monday–Friday from 10:00 a.m. to 6:00 p.m. During special exhibits, it is also open Saturday and Sunday from 2:00 p.m.–6:00 p.m.*

Gallery Borg Grafik
This branch of the Galleri Borg displays and sells graphic art. Open during regular shopping hours.

Galleri 8
Austurstraeti 8 • The gallery exhibits and sells paintings, graphics and ceramics as well as silver, sculpture and textiles. *Open Monday–Saturday, 10:00 a.m.–6:00 p.m.; Sunday, 2:00 p.m.–6:00 p.m.*

Gallery of Icelandic Art
Vesturgata 17 • Exhibits of contemporary Icelandic art by members of the Gallery of the Artist Society. *Open Monday–Friday, 9:00 a.m.–5:00 p.m.*

Hallgrimskirkja

The tall church that dominates the city, hovering above the small houses and low buildings like a great mothering bird. This is the place from which to scan the whole of Reykjavik. Tourists can climb up the inside of the jagged, modern spire for a spectacular view and a fine orientation. *The tower is open Tuesday–Sunday from 10:00 a.m.–6:00 p.m. There is a nominal admission charge.*

Iceland National Museum

The largest in town features collections of historical, archaeological, and cultural interest. Definitely worth a visit to learn something of the history of Iceland. *Open May 15–September 15 every day but Monday, from 11:00 a.m.–4:00 p.m. Rest of the year, open Tuesday, Thursday, Saturday and Sunday from 11:00 a.m.–4:00 p.m. Reach it by bus Nos. 5, 6, 7, 13, 14, 16 or 100.*

National Art Gallery of Iceland

Iceland's premier collection of Icelandic art contains primarily paintings and some sculpture in its permanent collection but it also hosts several traveling exhibitions. There is a very pleasant cafeteria serving cold food and desserts. *Open daily except Monday from 11:00 a.m.–5:00 p.m.*

Natural History Museum

Hverfisgata 116 • A small museum with an impressive array of the treasures of Iceland's natural resources from rare minerals and stuffed birds, to a collection of jeweled birds eggs. *Open Tuesday, Thursday, Saturday and Sunday from 1:30 p.m.–4:00 p.m.*

The Nordic Center

Designed by Alvar Aalto, the center which is located near the University, houses special collections for Nordic studies and a library of modern Scandinavian literature, but even if you are not a Nordic scholar it is worth visiting the center simply for the architecture of the building itself. *The exhibition galleries are open from 2:00 p.m.–7:00 p.m. daily. There is a very good and reasonably priced cafeteria which is open Monday–Friday from 9:00 a.m.–7:00 p.m.; Saturday, 9:00 a.m.–7:00 p.m.; and Sunday, noon–7:00 p.m.*

City Hall

This new building is attractive enough to warrant a drop-in. Look at the huge map of Iceland on the floor. There is a nice little cafeteria here with a chef who seems to care about quality and who displays an amazing creativity, given the simple service and limited facility. It's a pleasant place for a quick lunch.

THEATER, SYMPHONY, CINEMA

Light Nights

Kristin G. Magnus is the actress who takes her audience on a multi-media journey through Iceland's history from the days of turf houses and Viking settlements. The theater is at *Tjarnargata 10e*, along the lake. Tickets can be purchased there on the evening of the performance or at the Hotel Esja, Hotel Saga and the Hotel Loftleidir. Performances from June 11–August 30, Thursday, Friday, Saturday and Sunday at 9:00 p.m. The show lasts almost two hours. At last check, admission was about $21.

Volcano Show

A two-hour film show of volcanoes and other natural Icelandic phenomena. Every night at 8:00 p.m. from June to August. The show is in English. It is advisable to book ahead. Ticket purchases at the Woolhouse, *Adalstraeti 4*, ☎ *269700*.

Icelandic Symphony Orchestra

For information, ☎ *22310*.

Icelandic Opera

For information, ☎ *11475*.

Cinemas

In addition to Icelandic films, foreign (that includes English and American) films are shown in their native language with Icelandic subtitles. Shows usually are at 3:00 p.m., 5:00 p.m., 7:00 p.m., 9:00 p.m. and 11:00 p.m. See entertainment section of newspaper.

SPORTS AND RECREATION

Swimming pools

In the Reykjavik area are three outdoor pools, all volcanically heated, and one indoor. All have saunas except for Sundholl. The hours given below are for winter. Patrons are allowed to remain in the pool for 30 minutes after closing time. Sundlaugin in Laugardalur near Hotel Esja, Bus No. 5, and Sundlaug Vesturbaejar, near the Hotel Saga, Bus No. 4, are outdoor pools which are *open weekdays from 7:00 a.m. to 8:30 p.m., Saturday, 7:30 a.m.–5:30 p.m., Sunday, 8:00 a.m.–5:30 p.m.* Sundlaug Fjolbrautarskolans is an outdoor pool in Breiholt, reachable by Bus Nos. 12 and 13. Its hours are the same as those above. Sundholl Reykjavik is an indoor pool near Hlemmur, Bus Nos. 1 and 17. *Open Monday–Friday from 7:00 a.m.–5:00 p.m.; closed 1:30 p.m.–4:10 p.m. Open Saturday, 7:00 a.m.–5:30 p.m.; Sunday, 8:00 a.m.–5:30 p.m. In summer, the hours are extended.*

Hiking

Two outdoor touring clubs, Ferdafela Islands, at Oldugata 3, ☎ *1 95 33* and Utivist, Grofin 1, ☎ *1 46 06*, offer day walking tours on Sunday and holidays in spring, fall and winter. In addition, both day and longer trips are available in summer time. The walking trips sometimes include one to three hours of driving time in addition to two to six hours of easy walking. Most have guides but no food is provided so be sure to pack a lunch. If you are looking for an easy hike on your own, you can drive or take a bus to the Heidmork Nature Preserve, just about 20 minutes south of Reykjavik on the way to the Blue Mountains. You will find hiking trails and roads and dramatic volcanic formations.

Ice Skating

If the temperature is low enough in winter, ice skating on Lake Tjornin is a popular pastime, but because of the warming effect of the Gulf Stream, the lakes in Iceland do not always freeze.

Mt. Esja

Reykjavik's own mountain offers the city visitor a chance to climb a bit without traveling very far. From the top, on a clear day, you will have a wonderful view of Reykjavik and the Snaefellsnes Glacier. Since the sun shines almost all night in summertime, you could do this at the cocktail hour and stop in at the Hotel Esja at the foot of the mountain for a drink on the way up or down. Icelanders like to climb at midnight on the night of the summer solstice.

The Blue Lagoon

Located about 40 minutes from Reykjavik and easily reached by bus from the BSI terminal, the geothermal waters which heat the water for the Reykjanes Peninsula flow into the lagoon whose startlingly luminous turquoise color is the result of the reflection of silica particles. The bus trip offered by Reykjavik Excursions affords you a good chance to see the tip of the Reykanes peninsula, including Hafnarfjordur (See "Quick Trips" in this chapter.) and also allows for about an hour at the lagoon so remember to bring your bathing suit. One word of warning: Though the moss-covered lava fields surrounding the lagoon appear benevolent, they are not safe to walk on. The moss disguises deep and dangerous crevices.

Pony Treks

It is worth the time to try this unique Icelandic form of recreation. The Laxnes Pony Farm not far from Reykjavik, offers three-hour pony treks departing at 10:00 a.m. and 2:00 p.m. daily from March to September. They will pick you up at your hotel. Riding across the valley, surrounded by mountains, you will feel that you are much farther away than just one-half hour from Iceland's capital. Ponies are sturdy and sure-footed and are assigned according to the rider's ability. ☎ *66 61 79.*

QUICK TRIPS

The Island of Videy

Located across Sundahofn harbor in the eastern part of Reykjavik, this island offers a capsule sampling of Iceland's wonders, with abundant birdlife, pleasant walking trails and an interesting history. There is an archaeological excavation underway and among its finds is a set of wax tablets dating from the period between 1450 and 1600. The extremely well-preserved tablets are inscribed in Latin, German and Icelandic. You might also look at the western side of the island where the American artist Richard Serra has erected 18 columns of Icelandic rock. The mansion, Videyjarstofa, which was built in 1755 as the home of the royal treasurer, Skuli Magnusson, houses a fine restaurant. There is also a cafeteria in the mansion. *Both the cafeteria and restaurant are open from June 1 to September 30, Thursday–Sunday. The restaurant is open from 2:00 p.m.–5:00 p.m. for coffee*

and cake and from 6:00 p.m.–11:00 p.m. for dinner. For dining in the restaurant, book ahead. ☎ 681045 or 28470. The ferry for Videy runs in conjunction with the opening hours of the restaurant and returns at 10:00
p.m., 11:00 p.m. and 11:30 p.m. The trip from Sundahofn takes about five
minutes.

Hafnarfjordur

Set in a lava field, the town of Hafnarfjordur just a 15-minute drive south
of Reykjavik is the third largest town in Iceland. Its excellent, and incidentally very beautiful; the harbor and its fishing industry made it an important
commercial center from its earliest beginnings, but the unusual setting in
the midst of ancient lava fields and its development on both sides of the
Laekurinn stream, which flows to the sea, make it of geological interest as
well. As early as the 15th century, Hafnarfjordur was an English trading
center. The English and the Germans battled for control of the harbor and
in the 16th century, the town was a kind of outpost of the Hanseatic
League. Early in the 17th century, the Danish king issued an edict prohib-
iting anyone except Danish citizens from trading with Iceland. This exclu-
sionary practice ended finally in the 18th century and nothing of those early
days is visible today. But there is an old town and you can visit three of the
oldest houses in Hafnarfjordur which have now been made into museums
and a restaurant. The Icelandic Maritime Museum, is a new museum
located in a 120-year-old warehouse. Next to the Maritime museum is the
oldest house in Hafnarfjordur. Built by Bjarni Sivertsen, who was known as
the "Father of Hafnarfjordur" for his entrepreneurial skills—he developed
the fisheries, built a shipyard and engaged in worldwide shipping—the
house now contains part of the municipal museum of Hafnarfjordur. In
turn, the building beside it is another old house which has been made into
a restaurant, **A. Hansen**. It serves fish, smoked puffin, and—unusual for
Iceland—steaks grilled on a hot slab. *The museums and the restaurant are
connected by a garden. The museums are open from June 8 to Sept. 30
every day but Monday from 2:00 p.m. until 6:00 p.m.* **Hafnarborg** is the
town's Institute of Culture and Art and hosts frequent exhibitions of Icelandic and international art as well as concerts. The galleries house a permanent collection which is open to the public. *The galleries are open every day
except Tuesday, from 2:00 p.m.–7:00 p.m. The cafe is open every day from
2:00 p.m.–7:00 p.m. If you have time, wander through Hellisgerdi, a
botanical garden set among the lava.*

SHOPPING

The thing to buy in Iceland is wool, wool and more wool. The woolen goods
are made from the wool of the miniature Icelandic sheep that you will see roam-
ing the countryside. Once you have exhausted the woolen supply, you can also
buy glass, ceramics and all sorts of handicrafts, in addition to two very good vodkas and wonderful Icelandic caviar at about a millionth of the price of Beluga.
But don't go home without some purchase of wool, in any of its various Iceland
forms from mittens to blankets and those wonderfully intricate sweaters.

Shopping hours in Reykjavik and most towns are 10:00 a.m.–6:00 p.m. from Monday to Friday, and 10:00 a.m.–2:00 p.m., 3:00 p.m. or 4:00 p.m. during Saturday, depending on the shop. Some supermarkets stay open later on Thursday and most shops, except for the woolen goods stores, close on Saturday during June, July and August. The shops at the Kringlen Shopping Mall are generally open later hours and on weekends.

The main shopping areas of Reykjavik are centered around the two main streets of the old town, Laugavegur and Skolavordustigur.

WOOLENS

The Handknitting Association of Iceland
Skolavordustigur 19 • Handknit as well as machine-knitted sweaters and blankets. The prices here are among the lowest in town though the selection is a bit limited.

Iceland Handcrafts Center
Hafnarstraeti 3 • A good selection of handmade sweaters and handicrafts

Alafoss
Posthusetraeti 13 • A fine source for woolens as well as other handcrafts and souvenirs.

BOOKS

Austurstraeti 18 • A good source for books on Iceland as well as maps and foreign newspapers.

HOUSEWARES

Habitat
Laugavegur • Household items of various designs including Finnish and Danish.

KRINGLAN SHOPPING MALL

About 10 minutes by car out of the old town on the main road, or by bus, with one transfer—inquire at your hotel or at the tourist information center. The shops here are open for longer hours and many on Sunday. There are several good woolen stores here as well as bookstores with books in English, but most of the shops are for practical items which might not be of interest to the tourist. It's worth going to if you want to shop at Rammagadin in off-hours, or if you have a burning desire to add the Hard Rock Cafe Reykjavik T-shirt to your wardrobe, that ubiquitous cafe has also found its way to Iceland and is located at the mall.

SHOPPING AT KEFLAVIK AIRPORT

You can leave all your shopping for the airport if you prefer not to drag packages around the countryside. The duty-free shops at the airport are wonderfully stocked with everything Icelandic from blankets to caviar. Incidentally, at last check the prices on Hermes scarves and French perfumes were about the best I'd seen. However, though the selection is excellent, the prices on woolens at the airport are not necessarily the best to be found in Iceland.

WHERE TO STAY

VERY EXPENSIVE

Hotel Esja

Sudurlandsbraut 2 • This is a large, rather commercial hotel, but the rooms are comfortable and the hotel offers every convenience from TV and mini-bars to shops and a hairdresser. The lobby is lively and bustling and the location, though out of the center of town, affords wonderful views of Reykjavik and Mt. Esja and is located near the largest swimming pool, but a little out of the center of town.

Hotel Island

Armuli 9 • The newest arrival on the Reykjavik scene is rather American in flavor, and the rooms are very comfortable with TV and minibar.

Hotel Saga

Hagatorg 1 • Though not quite in the center of the old town, the Saga's location, a 5- to 10-minute walk from the lake, the university and the National Museum, is convenient. The lobby of this large, modern hotel is stunningly designed in a kind of 1950s style and is a lively place with a lobby buffet and bar, and a shop selling Icelandic sweaters. There are several restaurants. The ballroom offers dancing and live entertainment on Saturday nights. The hotel also has a health club with a sauna, solarium and whirlpool. The rooms are comfortable with TV and minibar. Though the hotel was built in 1962, the lobby and many of the rooms have been renovated.

The Loftleider

With 221 rooms, this is a busy place. Since the hotel serves as a kind of terminal for bus service between Reykjavik and the airport, and for several Reykjavik Excursions tours, the lobby has the feel of Grand Central Station, Iceland style. Because the hotel is about three kilometers from the center of town, the main reason for staying here would be the convenience in getting to or from the airport. The rooms are functional and clean, but charmless, and the hotel has a rather plastic, utilitarian air about it. All rooms have private baths.

EXPENSIVE

Hotel Borg

Wonderfully located in the heart of the old town near the Althing, the Borg is a landmark and is probably Reykjavik's most well-known hotel. Newly renovated, all 30 rooms have telephone, cable TV, VCRs and coffeemakers. Request a room on the garden side as the disco, which is noisy until very late on Friday and Saturday, can be heard from the rooms near it.

Hotel Holt

Bergstadastraeti 37 • With 49 rooms, the Holt has the feeling of a small hotel and its location in the center of the old town is excellent. Its rather dark lobby is attractively Icelandic in feeling, and its restaurant, hung with stunning Icelandic art, is considered one of the best in town.

Hotel Odinsve

Odinstorg • A charming, small and friendly hotel right in the middle of the old town, the Odinsve is definitely a winner and my first choice. The 30 rooms are very comfortable and attractive, truly Scandinavian in flavor and all have minibars and TV. The restaurant is excellent, offering Icelandic specialties as well as several beef dishes—a rarity in Iceland.

Hotel Hofdi

This hotel, about a twenty minute walk from downtown along the main road of Reykjavik, is a most pleasant place with its 36 rooms furnished in a simple Scandinavian style. A few rooms do not have baths but all have TV and minibar. Request a third-floor room with a harbor view as these are definitely the nicest rooms in the hotel. Though there is no restaurant, light snacks are served and meals for groups can be arranged with advance notice. If you are staying out of the center of town, this would be my choice over the bigger, glitzier and more American-style Saga and Esja, but that is simply a matter of taste.

Hotel Reykjavik

Open since the summer of 1992, the hotel is fresh and light, with small but pleasant rooms and adequate bathrooms. There are two restaurants, and indoor parking for a nominal charge. The hotel is located about a 15 minute walk from the center of town and from the Kringlan Shopping Center.

Hotel Leifur Ericsson

Just opened in summer of 1991, the Leifur Ericsson occupies an old house in the center of old town, near the church. All 28 rooms have private baths, TV and minibar, and all are double rooms, but if possible, ask for No.207 or 407 as they are larger. One word of caution. The hotel is four stories high and there is no elevator.

MODERATE

Hotel Lind

Another relative newcomer, this simple, clean, modern hotel is situated near the bus station. All the rooms have private baths, minibars and TV.

INEXPENSIVE

Gestaheimilith

Kirkjustraeti 2 • The Salvation Army guesthouse offers rooms for two to six people plus space for sleeping bags at a lower rate. There are sinks in the rooms but no private bathrooms. A large breakfast room offers breakfast for an additional price. No frills, but it's one of the few budget spots in town.

AT THE AIRPORT

The Flug Hotel

Hafnargata 57, Keflavik • Since the airport is a 40 minute drive from Reykjavik, one would probably only stay here on the way in or out of town. The 39 rooms all have private baths, TV and minibar. There is a restaurant and bar as well as a travel agency, bank and car rental office on the premises.

APARTMENTS FOR RENT

The Arnfjord Hotel Apartments

Apartments in various locations in Reykjavik. The ones we saw were exceptionally lovely and in excellent locations. The rates range between approximately $90 per night and $250 for two people, with most of the apartments large enough to accommodate at least one extra person for an additional $30. For stays of more than two days, the rates can be negotiated. All the apartments have telephones, daily maid service and a free Continental breakfast provided in the refrigerator. A full breakfast can be delivered for $10 per person and the company will even arrange to deliver a restaurant dinner from any Reykjavik restaurant. The company meets guests at the first bus stop in from the airport and shows them the ins and outs of the ultramodern gadgetry with which many of the apartments are equipped. Apt. No. 250, at about $160 per night is a particularly attractive one, accommodating two-three people, and in an excellent location. Apt. No. 300, about the same size and price, is also a prime choice. Good location, great view. Apt. No. 100 is larger, with room for four to six people, but still just one bathroom. It is located in a beautiful, quiet section of Reykjavik, though somewhat far from the center. Contact: Sigurdur Magnusson. When calling from the U.S., ☎ *011-354-1 623030.*

GUEST HOUSES

Gisti-Inn

Soleyjaragotu 11, ☎ *(354-1) 613005, FAX 354-1-13005* • Occupying a 63 year old house, the Gisti-Inn is an airy, bright, pleasant spot, with just nine rooms, all decorated in Victorian style. Only one, #9, has a private bath, the rest have sinks, minirefrigerators and TV. There is a sauna and the two bathrooms which are for the use of the guests are modern and large.

Guesthouse Baldursbra

Laufasvegur 41, ☎ *(354-1) 26646, FAX 354-1-62664.* • This was formerly a youth hostel and, while it is not luxurious by any means, it is certainly a more than adequate place to stay. Though the double rooms will run about $95 in summer, there are very reasonable dormitory and sleeping-bag accommodations and the prices go down dramatically from November until the end of March and even in April, May and September.

Hotel Dora's Residence

Laugav. 140, ☎ *(91)623204* • Though located in a very unattractive street, the guesthouse has nine pleasant rooms and a sunny breakfast room. Once you get past the entry and the hallways, you will find the rooms comfortable and relatively large. All have private bath. Request one of the ones on the back, overlooking the garden. Reasonable rates include breakfast and tax.

WHERE TO EAT

In summertime, be sure to make reservations ahead, as much as two days for weekends. You will find that in most restaurants diners usually dress up a bit for dinner, coats and ties for men, skirts or dresses more often than pants for women.

Arnarholl

Hverfisgata 8–10 • Known for its chargrilled specialties of beef and game as well as for its fish entrees. Downstairs is the Operukjallarinn nightclub.

Fogetinn

Adalstraeti 10 • Situated in the oldest house in Reykjavik, the restaurant is worth visiting just for the location in this building which has served as home to many well-known Reykjavik leaders, most particularly the man who built the house in 1750, Skuli Magnusson Fogeti (sometimes called the second father of Reykjavik.) The menu includes fish, lamb and some game, but eating is secondary to drinking here, so you might just want to drop by for a drink and a bit of atmosphere.

Hornid

Hafnarstraeti 15 • You will come upon this restaurant frequently as it is right in the center of the old town. Its name means corner and that is exactly where it is. It's a good spot for families and casual meals and a convenient, pleasant place to drop into for anything from a snack to a full meal. The menu includes pasta and various "Icelandic style" pizzas and the prices are reasonable.

Jonathan Livingston Mavur

Tryggvagata 4-6 • Guess what "mavur" means in Icelandic? You're right! The location, which is actually just about two blocks from old town on the old wharf, offers a change of pace for those tourists who have stuck to the center of old town. Though the neighborhood might seem a bit forlorn, there's no need to be nervous here. The food is excellent. Seafood—not seagull—is featured, but there are other choices as well.   ***Expensive.***

Laekjarbrekka

Bankastraeti 2 • A lovely choice for quiet dining on Icelandic specialties. Located in a charming old house that was built in 1834, the building was the home of a prominent Danish shipbuilder who brought a Copenhagen baker to establish a bakery on the premises. The Danish flair for creative cuisine seems to have been bred into the walls of this house-turned-restaurant for the food here is excellent.   ***Expensive.***

Naust

Vesturgotu 6 • Another of Reykjavik's oldest restaurants—in fact, the oldest—Naust was once a fisherman's house and retains a nautical style with an emphasis on traditional dishes as well as a new, lighter line of offerings.

Moderate to expensive.

Cafe Opera

Laekjargata 2 • This is a popular and lively place where people come for anything from a bowl of soup to a full meal. Live music is played most evenings. The food is excellent and the menu varied, offering everything from Icelandic fish to game. The decor is funky but oddly stylish and in winter, with candlelight glowing in the little windows which look out onto a lively street scene, it's a cozy place. In summer, of course, the candles are superfluous, but the fresh flowers and congenial clutter make it a most attractive spot. It's a good idea to make a reservation. Next door is a piano bar called the **Cafe Romance**. Upstairs, you will find the quieter, Cognac Lounge.

Expensive.

Bumannskukkan (the Farmer's Clock)

Amtmannsstig 1 • This charming restaurant is located in an old house in the center of old town. The food is good and the atmosphere pleasant. Fish and lamb are the main menu items. *Moderate to expensive.*

Perlan

Reykjavik's newest elegant dining spot is also its most intriguing new structure. The name, as you might guess, means "the pearl," and the restaurant occupies a kind of flattened sphere atop the cluster of volcanic water tanks that heat Reykjavik. Visible from afar, it offers excellent views as it slowly revolves on its perch. The food is as good as the views. *Expensive.*

Thrir Frakkar

Baldursgata 14 • This tiny restaurant is situated in old town in an unprepossessing neighborhood, near the Hotel Holt and the Odinsve, and walking distance from the Saga. The menu features primarily fish, which is very good. *Prices are moderate. Reservations are a must.*

Vidtjornina

Templarasund 3 • Next door to the Althing, the restaurant is redolent with old Reykjavik charm and tradition. Its small dining rooms are furnished with antiques, and you will feel as if you are a guest in a private home. The food is as exquisite as the table settings with their old Icelandic linens and delicate china. This is a fish restaurant so do not go if you are craving meat, but if you want one wonderful seafood meal, this is the place to go.

Expensive. Reservations strongly suggested.

Videyjarstofa

On the island of Videy in Reykjavik Harbor. Situated in the old mansion on the island, the restaurant is elegant in a spare, Scandinavian way and the food is excellent. Again, fish is the specialty, though there are other items on the menu. This is a place where you can dress up if you feel like it. The ferry for Videy leaves Sundahofn Harbor at 6:00, 7:00, 7:30 and 8:00 p.m. and returns at 10:00, 11:00 and 11:30 p.m. The trip takes about five minutes. There is also a cafeteria in the mansion. Both the cafeteria and restaurant are open from June 1 to September 30, Thursday–Sunday. The dining room is open from 2:00 p.m. to 5:00 p.m. for coffee and from 6:00 p.m. to 11:00 p.m. for dinner. For dining in the restaurant, you must book ahead. ☎ *681045* or *28470*. *Very expensive.*

HOTEL DINING

The hotel dining rooms are generally excellent, certainly not a lesser alternative to independent restaurants. In fact, many Icelanders consider the hotels the best places to eat.

Grillid

In the Saga Hotel, Hagatorg 1 • Ask for a table overlooking the water in this very Icelandic "yuppie" elegant restaurant. This spot is a favorite with native Reykjavikites. For a less expensive, more casual meal, the buffet on the main floor of the hotel is excellent.   ***Expensive.***

Hotel Holt

Bergstradastraeti 37 • Considered one of Reykjavik's finest restaurants, the dark panelled walls of the dining room are hung with an excellent collection of Icelandic art, and the small leaded windows lend a cozy air to the whole place. But most important, the food on the table is as commendable as the art on the walls. Skuli Thorvaldsson, the owner of the restaurant, is the son of the man who opened the Holt and who was one of Iceland's most highly thought of restaurateurs. Icelandic dishes of fish, lamb and game, as well as pork, which is raised on the restaurant's own pig farm, are among the specialties.   ***Expensive.***

Hotel Odinsve

Odinstorg • A very pretty and inviting restaurant in this small, pleasant hotel. The food is first class and the selection interesting. At lunch time, a lighter, less expensive menu is offered.

NIGHTLIFE

Night spots usually open about 9:00 p.m. but things don't really get lively until 11:00 p.m. or even later. The cover charges in the discos are generally outrageously high, 700kr. at last check. And though the pubs do not charge a cover unless there is live music, the price of the drinks more than makes up for that little economy. But, on the plus side, there is no tipping.

Artun

Vagnhofdi 11 • The place for ballroom dancing attracts a crowd of all ages, but you will find more people of middle age and older.

Bjorhollin

Gerduberg, Breidholt • Not glamorous, but lively and popular with the beer-drinking crowd.

Cafe Hresso

Austurstraeti 18 • The bar opens at 6:00 p.m., but during the day this is a spot to relax over the newspaper or to observe the Reykjavikers who like to hang out here.

Cafe Straeto

Laekjargata 2 • A chic pub featuring Mexican and hard-rock music.

Casablanca

Skukagata 30 • Trendy and smart, the disco is popular on weekends. The intimate Maxim Gorku bar is open weekdays.

Danshusid i Glaesibae

Alfheimar • A spot for the older crowd. Live music.

Danshollin

> *Brautarholt 22* • A three-floor disco and cabaret. This one also attracts a slightly older crowd.

Duus-hus

> *Fischersund* •This is the place for jazz lovers on Thursday and Sunday nights. Because of its location near the harbor, you will find all types of clientele.

Operukjallarinn

> *Hverfisgata 10* • A wine bar with music from the 1950s to the present.

Sulnasaluar Mimisbar

> *In the Hotel Saga.* • This is the ballroom of the hotel and when it is not catering private parties, it offers a floorshow. Call for information, ☎ *29900.*

ONE- AND TWO-DAY EXCURSIONS FROM REYKJAVIK

While almost every tourist destination in Iceland could be visited as part of a one- or two-day trip from Reykjavik, if one chose to fly, the following trips are easily accomplished by bus or car in one to two days. You can drive yourself or take one of the bus tours from Reykjavik. To book those, contact **Reykjavik Excursions**, at the Hotel Loftleidir, ☎ *621011;* at the Hotel Esja, ☎ *688922* or **Travel City**, *Hafnarstraeti 2,* ☎ *623020.* Your hotel might be able to book these for you also and pick-up can be arranged for most hotels in Reykjavik.

THE GOLDEN CIRCLE

In a matter of ten to twelve hours, you can get a complete sampling of the variety of Iceland's natural wonders by either taking the bus tour of the Golden Circle, arranged through **Icelandair (TravelCity)** or **Reykjavik Excursions**, or by renting a car and driving yourself. A word of warning to drivers: though the drive from Reykjavik to Thingvellir takes just about an hour along a paved highway, the short-cut road degenerates after Thingvellir into a one lane, twisting nightmare which is not only unpaved but seems to have been purposely strewn with lava chunks by some volcanic witch intent on foiling tourism. Rocks pop against the underside of the car like small bombs and the typical Icelandic driver—always approaching from the opposite direction around a curve and over a hill—aims straight for you at breakneck speeds. But the trip is a glorious one and certainly anyone traveling in Reykjavik for more than one day should take this opportunity.

Thingvellir

> The first stop on the Golden Circle tour is the national shrine. It is the site of the country's ancient Parliament, the original Althing, which met on this plain for 868 years beginning in A.D. 930, just after the settlement of Iceland. A path has been laid from the parking lot to the Icelandic flag which flies at the spot where the Law Speaker used to stand to read the laws, reading through one third of the laws in each of the three years of his term. This was also the occasion when disputes were settled. Thingvellir is significant from a geological as well as a historical viewpoint for it sits on the fault that

runs beneath all of Iceland from the southwest to the northwest which is in turn part of the Mid-Atlantic Ridge. The North American and Eurasian continental plates are considered to meet here, as they do on the Reykanes Peninsula. Thingvellir is a vast plain and there is ample opportunity for wandering, but you should stay on the paths as the moss covered lava fields hold literal pitfalls for the unwary walker. For information on various walks and on camping and fishing permits, stop at the Warden's Lodge at the Thingvellir Church. ☎ *98-22677.*

Note for hungry travelers: The **Hotel Valholl** houses one of Iceland's best restaurants so try to schedule your arrival for either lunch or dinner. The trout come from Lake Thingvellir, about as fresh as you will find anywhere, and the lamb, served with an Icelandic herb sauce, is superb. You can also plan your trip to include an overnight stay at the hotel in the simple but comfortable rooms. At the last visit, some of the rooms needed redecorating and the housekeeping could have been more careful, but the beauty of the setting, the ambience of the public rooms and the excellence of the restaurant make up for those shortcomings. And it is nice to be able to fall into bed after a sumptuous dinner rather than making the hour drive back to Reykjavik.

Geysir

As you might have guessed, the attraction here is the kind of underground fountain of which Old Faithful is our most famous example. But here you will find geysers beyond anything you might imagine. Wide, menacing grins in the earth's crust, little impish smiles, seething holes that appear absolutely malignant, burbling pots that cook up a colorful brew—the variety is remarkable and the visitor can stroll along the paths, safely out of the way of the hot and faintly sulfurous spume, and observe all of these windows in the earth's crust. Here, the independent driver will be rewarded for his roadway agonies for he can stay as long as he likes and the place does invite the lingerer. The bus trip does not allow quite enough time here, but if you skip the snack bar and souvenir stand, you will get a bit more of a chance to peer and meditate and make acquaintance with these natural wonders that in ways seem almost to be talking to you.

Gullfoss

Here is nature at its most spectacular and unspoiled. No Niagara Falls hype here, not even a souvenir stand or a safety fence. The Golden Falls, the largest in Europe, splash down from shelf to shelf of black rock to a deep and misty gorge. Though there could be a tour bus and plenty of visitors, the majesty of the falls is not marred by what might be, for Iceland, a crowd. Tourists are at their best here, reverent and silent in the face of this spectacle.

Skalholt

This stop is included on most of the scheduled Golden Circle tours. Skalholt, a historic cultural and religious center, is the site of the oldest bishopric in Iceland. The oldest school, which was later moved to Reykjavik was established here, and the spot attracted scholars and poets as well as religious leaders from all over Iceland. Several churches were built on the site, always over the foundations of the predecessors. In the 19th century, the church was destroyed by a volcanic eruption, but a new one was constructed again on the foundations of the old in the 1960s under a joint effort of all the Scandinavian countries. Services are held on Sunday, and the school has been reestablished. In addition, the Skalholt Church is the setting for many concerts, and a concert series is held on weekends in July and August. Of special note is the artwork, especially the stained-glass windows and the mosaics which are constructed of Italian stones using all the colors found in Iceland's landscape. In the cellar are catacombs from the 13th century, and the crypt holds the remains of Bishop Pall Jonsson, who died in 1211. There is a summer hostel and a guesthouse not far from the church.

SUMMER SKIING ON THE SNAEFELLSNES PENINSULA

From **Reykjavik** in summertime, you can get in a little downhill skiing on the **Snaellsness Glacier**. Call **Add-Ice**, *from the US,* ☎ *011-354-1 first then— 676755; from Reykjavik* ☎ *676755.* The same company also offers longer ski trips to the Vatnajokull, the largest glacier in Europe.

SNOW SAFARI

For the intrepid tourist who is willing to brave Iceland in wintertime, this is a reward. Actually, Iceland is warmer than one might expect in winter, usually about 32°F, but the weather is so changeable that travelers should be warned that planned excursions could be cancelled and that a one-day trip could extend into two days, if the weather turns and a little Iceland blizzard blows in. But if you are lucky, there will be enough snow and you can take this extraordinary adventure for one or two days. Transportation is by an all-terrain, tank-like vehicle which can take the rigors of road and stream. Most of the time is spent in the wilderness, climbing (and sliding) up the hills and fording rivers by safari jeep because there are no bridges. The cost is $150 for one day or $300 for two. Lunch and a hearty afternoon snack are included on the one-day trip. The two-day price includes lunch, dinner, breakfast and overnight accommodations in a wilderness hut with electricity and a shower (one for all). Be sure to bring extra socks and mittens in case you get wet. For arrangements contact: **Add-Ice**, ☎ *from the US,* ☎ *011-354-1 first then—676755; from Reykjavik* ☎ *676755. The mobile telephone is* ☎ *011-354-1-25500.*

THORSMORK

This complex of valleys at the feet of the glaciers has an abundance of hiking trails through Iceland style "forests," up flower-blanketed hills and beside glacial river deltas. The bus trip from Reykjavik allows three to four hours here, ample time to sample the natural beauty and get some healthy exercise, and it is highly advisable to take the bus rather than to take on the rather formidable task of driving yourself as there are at least a dozen rivers to ford, no bridges and enough quicksand to make an Oldsmobile quiver. The trip which leaves the BSI bus terminal in Reykjavik at 8:30 a.m. (check for exact time as it could change) will take you southeast through Selfoss and Hella to the interior valley of Thorsmork. A guide meets the bus on arrival, not for leading hikers, but rather for answering

questions and recommending suitable hiking trails. This is a favorite spot of Icelanders so if you wish to overnight here in the huts which have electricity and a
shower, you must reserve far ahead of time.

ONE- AND TWO-DAY EXCURSIONS BY AIR

Icelandair has several one day trips from Reykjavik to farther flung destinations. Book through **Travel City**, *Hafnarstraeti 2, 101 Reykjavik,* ☎ *623020.*
Reykjavik Excursions also can book some of these tours. Or you can contact
Icelandair, any travel bureau in Reykjavik or your hotel. Meals and optional
guided tours are not included in fare. Pick-up service at no additional charge is
available at all hotels and guesthouses in Reykjavik. Contact the reception at
your hotel and be in lobby 15 minutes ahead of scheduled departure.

Isafjordur Tour

A 45-minute flight from Reykjavik will bring you to the capital of the Westfjords where, for an additional fee, you can choose either aerial sightseeing
or a boat trip to the fjords north of Isafjordur. There is also a tour of Isafjordur which begins at 2:00 p.m. and is included in the price.

Westman Islands

The tour lasts from four hours to all day, depending on whether or not you
choose to take an optional two to three hour boat trip to see the caves and
bird cliffs. A guided tour of Heymaey is included in the fare.

Special Flight to Heymaey

A three-hour trip which includes a guided tour of the island can be arranged
any day throughout the year for a minimum of three passengers.

Akureyri and Lake Myvatn

A guide will meet you in Akureyri and will take you by bus to Lake Myvatn
where you will visit, among other spots, the eerie mud pots and the lava formations of Dimmuborgir. An optional lunch at the nearby hotel is a possibility and you can either return for the evening flight to Reykjavik or stay
overnight at your own expense, picking up the second half of the tour the
following afternoon. Departs June–September at 7:30 a.m. from Reykjavik
City Airport.

Greenland

A two-hour flight from Reykjavik will take you to the other-worldly won-
derland of Greenland. The flight lands at Kulusuk, an island in the
Angmagssalik fjord. From the airport, a guide will lead you on the half-hour
walk across the tundra to the village of Kulusuk. This village has only been
resurrected from the Stone Age in this century when a Danish sailor discovered the natives living in dire poverty and convinced the Danish state to
help. The villagers endure a meager subsistence, even with the government's help, and though the scenery is beautiful and it is fascinating to
enter into this other world, you should be aware that you might not feel
entirely comfortable here. The village is littered with soda cans and paper;
the adults watch the tourists, who are important to their subsistence, warily.
They need us, but though they are perfectly polite, one senses that they
would rather not have to rely on this tiny bit of tourism. If you are lucky

and the ice has melted enough, you might get a fisherman to take you back to the airport by boat through the iceberg-maze of the fjord. The trip takes eight hours in all and includes lunch and dinner on the plane. Departs from Reykjavik Airport at 11:30 a.m. on Monday, Wednesday, Thursday and Friday from mid-June until the beginning of September. You must check in 45 minutes ahead of departure.

THE SOUTH COAST

The south coast of Iceland is extraordinarily beautiful with its black sand beaches against green swaths of moss-covered slopes. Over much of it, the snow-draped Hekla, Iceland's most active volcano once considered the Gate to Hell, hovers, an awe-inspiring reminder of the fact that this country is still seething with geological threats and possibilities. The other geological giant presence in the area is the Vatnajokull, Europe's largest glacier. You can explore the glacier by boat or four-wheel drive on organized tours from Hofn. The region of the south coast near Hofn is also the main nesting place in the northern hemisphere for the great Skua. The towns here, including Hofn, the largest, with a population of 1600, are minuscule with little to offer beyond acting as good bases for exploring the natural beauty of the region.

GETTING THERE

If you are interested primarily in getting to Hofn and using that as your base, there are year-round flights between Reykjavik and Hofn and between Egilsstadir and Hofn. Bus service is also available. The ride from Reykjavik is about seven hours, but in summer a bus service is in operation between Hofn, Egilsstadir and Seydisfjordur and the trip takes approximately six hours. You can also drive though the road from Hveragerthi on is rather narrow. The drive is beautiful, especially after you leave Hvolsvollur. You will pass farm lands with green meadows sweeping up to the mountains, waterfalls, cliffs, the sea, even two smaller glaciers in addition to the vast Vatnajokull which lies across the southeast corner of Iceland. If you are driving, stop at **Vik**, a minute town with a cafeteria, a gas station and snack shop. Set at the bottom of astonishingly green mountains and at the edge of a black sand beach, this is a good spot to stop for a breather, pick up some snacks and get a bit of exercise walking along the beach or running up the inviting green slopes. I do not recommend spending the night here as the hotel accommodations are less than adequate, though you might be able to arrange to stay in one of the small chalets which belong to the hotel.

As you drive farther east, you will be entering the fjord region of Hornafjordur. Except for the obvious violence of the geologic activity, the history of this region is very peaceful, starting with one of its earliest settlers, the Norwegian Earl Hrollaugur Rognvaldsson, who was banished to Iceland because he did not measure up as a warrior in his father's eyes. Aside from the natural beauty, the region's claim to fame is its local son. Thorbergur Thordarson, one of Iceland's 20th-century literary lights.

HVERAGERDI

Though less than an hour's drive from Reykjavik, this is a good place to spend the night on your drive south as it has one of Iceland's nicest hotels, the Hotel Ork. So you could leave Reykjavik late in the day and arrive at the Ork in time for dinner. Most of the produce of Iceland is grown in greenhouses here, and this is also a good spot to buy woolens.

WHERE TO STAY

Hotel Ork
Modern and attractive, this is Iceland's only spa hotel. The 76 rooms all have baths, and there is the added attraction of a huge geothermal swimming pool with a giant water slide. The very up-to-date spa offers plenty of exercise equipment as well as tanning beds and clay mud-pot baths. The sauna is coed, so you do need a bathing suit. There are also tennis courts and a golf course. The restaurants in the hotel are all good.

WHAT TO DO

Investigate the greenhouses which supply much of Iceland's produce as well as flowers. **Kaldidalur**, outside Hveragerdi, is one of the oldest farms in Iceland. It was settled around A.D. 1100 and was inhabited until 1910, but even now, with just a tiny deserted sod house, it is a beautiful and haunting place. Hveragerthi has a small amusement park, the only one in Iceland. The Hotel Ork will also arrange pony treks for you.

SHOPPING

The Eden Shop is located in the midst of the greenhouses and has an extensive inventory of woolen goods, with everything from mittens to one of the best selections of rugs in the country. There is a greenhouse attached to the shop so you can pick up fresh fruit for your car trip. There is a restaurant here, but for dining, I'd recommend the Ork. However, the Eden sells snacks and soft drinks so you could stock up on those.

HVOLSVOLLUR

This is another good stopping-over point on your trip south simply because its hotel is more pleasant than anything you'll find farther along the coast.

WHERE TO STAY

The Hotel Hvolsvollur
Not all 28 rooms have baths but the hotel is comfortable, light and airy. There is an excellent dining room, small but friendly and expensive, as are all Icelandic restaurants.

WHAT TO DO

Horseback riding, ☎ *78138* or *78133*. **Glacial exploration tours**, ☎ *78187* or *78243*.

HOFN AND SKAFTAFELL NATIONAL PARK

Hofn, one of Iceland's youngest towns, is the biggest town in this region and even at that it is small. A fishing and fish-processing center, it boasts a population of 1600. The completion of the Ring Road in 1974 added significantly to the development of Hofn and to its communication with other parts of the country, but there is not much here to hold the traveler captive. It serves, however, as a good place from which to explore the glacier.

WHAT TO DO

Skaftafell National Park

One of the most beautiful spots in Iceland, it offers accessible natural spectacles for there are many well-marked and easy trails.

Adventure Outings

Boat trips on the glacial lake at Breidamerkusandur can be booked either through the **Hotel Hofn** or through **Fjolnir Torfason**, *Hali, Sudursveit, 781 Hofn,* ☎ *97-81065.* Or you can usually just stop on your way and take the trip without advance booking. Snowmobile rides on the glacier are offered daily from June 15 to August 30. Snowcats, either with or without a guide, are also available for rental. The *Snowcat Adventure Trip* to Brokarjokull is a guided trip which runs about $125 per day per person. The price includes insurance, helmets and fuel. Pony treks can also be booked through the Hotel Hofn. You must arrange for all these trips at least one day in advance. *Contact Hotel Hofn, c/o Arni Stefansson, 780 Hofn,* ☎ *97-81240.*

Skiing on the Vatnajokull

Skiers can enjoy the sport both winter and summer. The slopes, ranging from two to five kilometers are served by a 1600-meter rope tow. Visitors can rent skis and boots, and there is a hut at the top which sleeps up to 10 people but must be booked ahead.

Folk Museum

Located in Hofn, the museum houses exhibits of domestic tools and utensils as well as a natural science exhibit and a small art collection. *Open 2:00 a.m.–6:00 p.m. daily, June 15–August 30.*

WHERE TO STAY

The Hotel Hofn

Though an improvement on any other place between Hvolsvollur and Hofn, the Hotel Hofn is not luxurious, and your chances of getting a room with a bath are remote unless you book well in advance. The hotel also has a few rooms in their annex, part of the dormitory of the local fish factory, and these, while very basic, do have private baths. You have to ask for a room there, and will only get one if the hotel itself is fully booked. Whichever you choose, request a room with a view of the glacier. There is a restaurant in the hotel which offers a good selection of both international and Icelandic dishes. If you do not feel like a big dinner, you can eat lightly but not cheaply at the self-serve buffet.

Not far from Skaftafell National Park is **Bolti**, a farm with beds and sleeping-bag accommodations in three double or two single rooms. The farm will serve breakfast and dinner if you arrange it. *Book through Bolti, c/o Gudveig Bjarnadottir, 785 Fagurholsmyri,* ☎ *97-81717.* Also in the area is the **Hrollaugsstadir** district school, which like so many schools in Iceland, operates as a simple hotel during the summer. There are beds or accommodations for sleeping bags, and breakfast is served. You can arrange for other meals as well. *Hrollaugsstadir c/o Thorunn Petursdottir, 781 Hofn,* ☎ *97-81057 or 97-81318.* At Stafafell, the bus will drop you right in front of the guesthouse which offers beds and sleeping-bag accommodations for as many as 30 guests in eight rooms. Breakfast is available and other meals can be arranged. You can arrange sightseeing and glacier tours as well as boat trips, pony treks and car rental.

Edda Hotel

Though I have not seen this, it should be clean with basic comforts, as are all the Edda hotels, which are school dormitories converted to hotels in summertime. This one is located about 10 kilometers west of Hofn. There is also a campgrounds in Skaftafell.

VESTMANNAEYJAR (THE WESTMANN ISLANDS)

Though archeological findings indicate that the Westmann Islands were inhabited before the settlement of the mainland, one might think that life here didn't begin until it almost ended, on January 23, 1973. For it is the volcanic eruption on Heymaey that is still the foremost topic of conversation in the town, and it is that eruption that has brought Heymaey its primary claim to fame. Most residents older than 25 years of age will be happy to tell you just where they were when the lava started flowing. The eruptions continued until July 3 of the same year, but the most remarkable accomplishment of the January day was that all 5000 inhabitants of Heymaey were safely evacuated to the mainland within a matter of hours. The town has now been completely rebuilt, but one half-buried house remains to give tourists a sense of what a mammoth undertaking the digging out must have been. The town of Heymaey is small and friendly. Many of its buildings are bright with the murals which school children paint each year in the annual contest. But the main attractions are the natural surroundings.

GETTING THERE

Daily flights to Heymaey are available from Reykjavik city airport, but if you are driving, you could head from Hveragerthi south towards Thorlakshofn, which is the port for the Westmann Islands car ferry. A word of warning: The ferry can be very rough, so if at all possible, take the quick flight from Reykjavik.

WHAT TO SEE AND DO

Hike up the volcano; walk down to the harbor; stroll the black sand beaches; and watch for the ubiquitous puffins and the occasional seal. You can even try your hand at the rope-swinging method of puffin-hunting, or if you're not brave enough for that, just observe the children of Heymaey as they swing on the cliff rope.

Sightseeing Tours

Tours are available by bus and boat or by a combination of both. This is the place where you really must get out onto the water, and onto this sweep of ocean punctuated with the skerries that testify to ancient undersea unrest. Your tour will probably take you into the sea caverns with their high sheer lava walls which are populated more densely than city tenements by the varied and multitudinous birds of the region. You will also have an extraordinary view of the mainland and the snow-clad volcano of Hekla. And a boat trip is the only way to get a glimpse of **Surtsey**, the newest island on earth, formed 25 years ago by an undersea volcanic eruption. In an effort to allow the animal and plant life to develop undisturbed, visitors (other than a few scientists and environmentalists) are not allowed on the island. For boat trips, contact either *Bravo Boat Tours,* in Hjalmar ☎ *(98)11616,* in Olafur ☎ *(98)11195,* or through the Hotel Thorshamar ☎ *(98)12900* or *Pall Helgason Travel Service,* ☎ *(98)11515.*

Volcano Show

The show consists of two films, one on the eruption of 1973 and the other a locally produced documentary about the shipwreck survival of a Heymaey resident. The show is presented in English at 3:00 p.m. and 5:00 p.m. and during July and August at 9:00 p.m. It lasts 55 minutes. Extra showings can be scheduled. For arrangements and to check on the times, ☎ *11045.*

Aquarium and Natural History Museum

This is one of Iceland's typically small museums, crammed with specimens of rock, stuffed birds and live fish. A naturalist on duty will offer plenty of valuable information in English. *Open every day 11:00 a.m.–5:00 p.m., May 1–September 1.*

WHERE TO STAY

Hotel Thorshamar

Located near the harbor and the center of town, this modern, small hotel has a truly Scandinavian flavor to it. The rooms are simple, but clean and comfortable. The rooms on the street side and those on the first floor near the breakfast room could be noisy, so request a second-floor room at the back of the hotel. All rooms have private baths, TV and minibar. Breakfast in the first floor breakfast room is included in the rate. The restaurant, Munnin, is first-rate. The hotel also owns and runs a guesthouse which offers accommodations for travelers with sleeping bags.

The Hotel Braedraborg

I mention this more to warn you away than to recommend staying here, at last check its standards were not up to par. If it's the only bed in town you could sleep here, but do not eat in the restaurant. The hotel occupies two separate buildings, one with 14 rooms, the other with 15. Only five of the rooms have private baths.

WHERE TO EAT

Munnin

In the Hotel Thorshamar • This is the place if you want something a bit up-scale, though not formal or fancy. The food is excellent, and the menu is filled with Icelandic specialties like lamb, steak, puffin and guillemot. A note to the softhearted: puffin are not an endangered species in Iceland. In fact, in summertime the puffin population swells to about 8 million. So ecological reasons need not deter you from enjoying this dish, though you may feel some reservations about consuming one of those adorable birds. The food here is excellent, whatever you order.

Besta Fisk

A cute little fish restaurant near the lava-crushed house. I have not eaten here, but it looks attractive and clean.

Bjossabar

A simple restaurant serving pizza and fried chicken. There are a few tables outside and a walk-up window where you can order soft drinks; hamburgers made from mutton rather than beef.

NORTHEAST ICELAND

The road between Egilsstadir and Husavik will take you farther inland, through a wide green valley ribboned with glacial rivers. The lava fields with their mossy covering are testimony to the relatively old age of the area. The volcano responsible for much of this terrain is Krafla, which is still active; in fact, it could erupt at any time in streams of slow-moving basalt.

GETTING THERE

The driving here is difficult to say the least, but not impossible. There are daily scheduled flights to Egilsstadir from Reykjavik and in summer between Hofn and Egilsstadir. There are also buses to Egilsstadir, Husavik and Akureyri which will give you a chance to see the scenery. If you do drive, the worst of the road is between Hofn and Egilsstadir and then again as you near Lake Myvatn, an area full of the relics of Krafla's rambuctiousness. But the ever-changing landscape makes the effort worthwhile, and you can get out of your car near the main crater of Krafla in the high-temperature area, and hike up the volcano to see the beautiful crater lake.

EGILSSTADIR

Egilsstadir is the administrative center of the region and, as Icelandic towns go, fairly sizable, with a lake where you can rent jet skis, a river and cows grazing in the middle of town. There is also a tourist information center here. But aside from tanking up, both the car and your stomach, there is not a lot of reason for staying here overnight, although the Hotel Valaskjalf is comfortable and modern and the small restaurant inviting. If you are planning to stay overnight, request Room No. 259, but all the rooms are pleasant and comfortable.

LAKE MYVATN

The lake is the fourth largest lake in Iceland and lies on the western edge of the volcanic belt running from north to south. Because the earth's crust here is very thin and the heat of the inner earth very close, the geological formations are relatively young and the variety of the volcanically formed landscape is extensive. The lake, whose name means midge lake, harbors an extraordinary variety of waterfowl. As you might expect, the namesake insect is also in abundance here, but these do not bite and seem to have a natural flair for public relations and tourism as they are present in June and August and not in July, the height of the tourist season. The lake is one of Iceland's best fishing spots, along with the nearby Laxa River. The town beside the lake is Reykjahlid. Though very small, the town does have two hotels and a bank, which is open Monday, Wednesday and Friday from 10:15 a.m. to 2:00 p.m. There are also gas pumps at the hotel.

GETTING THERE

Icelandair has flights from Reykjavik to Husavik every day during the summer and six days a week in winter. From the airport you can take a shuttle bus to Myvatn. The bus runs every day in summer and four days a week in winter. You can also fly from Reykjavik to Akureyri. In summer a bus to Myvatn meets the morning flight. In July and August a bus runs to Myvatn twice a week from Reykjavik. The bus takes the route over the highlands by way of Sprengisandur. From Akureyri there are also daily trips in summer and twice a week in winter. From June 22 through August 31, a bus runs everyday between Myvatn and Egilsstadir. In spring and fall the Egilsstadir bus runs three times a week.

SIGHTSEEING TOURS

For a one-day trip, take Icelandair's scheduled morning flight at 7:20 a.m. which connects with the local sightseeing tours or with its own air tour. Departure time to Reykjavik is 8:00 p.m. Guided tours through the Myvatn area and to other points of interest are available in summer, and a few begin as early as late May and run to September. A three-day guided tour from Myvatn to Kverkfjoll is offered on Monday and Friday. The Grand Tour of Myvatn is an eight-hour trip on Tuesday, Thursday and Sunday from May 26–September 15. You can also split up the Grand Tour and take one-half of it, or take it on two different days. A two-hour tour of Myvatn is given daily in summertime. There are also sightseeing flights by air over the area. For information and booking, contact: **Elda Travel Service**, ☎ *(96)44220;* **Jon Arni Sigfusson Bus Services**, ☎ *(96)44196;* or **Myflug Air**, ☎ *(96)44107.* For the Icelandair day trip, ☎ *(96)44107* or inquire at any Icelandair office.

WHAT TO DO

Nature is the star attraction in the area and hiking, fishing and in winter, cross-country skiing are the ways to enjoy it. You can also rent Icelandic ponies and bicycles at the Reynihlid Hotel. Among the attractions worth visiting are **Askja**, a caldera formed during the eruption of 1875. It holds the deepest lake in Iceland. You should be aware, however, that Askja, though often listed as one of the sights of the Myvatn area, is quite far from Myvatn and, since it is reachable along the trail into the interior you do need a four-wheel drive. **Dettifoss** is the spectacular waterfall site located about 30 kilometers northeast of Myvatn in the Jokulsa Canyoun National Park. Drive to **Dimmuborgir** and walk through and around the naturally formed lava sculptures. There is a path through this "lava garden," but the way is confusing and people do get lost. If you lose your bearings, stay within the fenced area and eventually you will come to the only gate. The perfect volcanic cone of **Hverfjall**, which is 150 meters high, was formed during an eruption 2500 years ago. **The Krafla** volcanic ridge extends for miles, but it holds at its core a still active volcano and a huge and most beautiful caldera to which you can drive. If you are a fisherman, by all means try your hand at the Laxa River, one of Iceland's most prized fishing rivers. *For fishing permits for*

the Laxa River, contact **Arnarvatn,** ☎ *(96)44255. For Lake Myvatn,* **Elda,**
☎ *(96)44220.*

WHERE TO STAY

The Hotel Reynihlid

This is the main hotel in town. Twenty-six of the 44 rooms have baths. For
an interesting view, request a room on the side facing the church where, in
what some people might call divine intervention, the lava stopped just
before reaching the entrance. The hotel has a restaurant. Visitors can rent
horses and bicycles, and car rental can be arranged.

Hotel Reykjahlid

This is a summer hotel situated by the lake, with just 12 rooms, none with
bath.

Farm Guesthouses

The Laxarbakki, ☎ *(96)44242,* and *Stong,* ☎ *(96)44252,* are both situated out of town. Breakfast is available, and the Stong has kitchen facilities.

HUSAVIK

This town of 2500 situated on Skjalfanda Bay, was first mentioned
in the *Book of Settlement.* According to the record, it was settled by
the second Scandinavian to reach Iceland, Gardar Svavarsson of Sweden, who landed at Skjalfandi and made a winter camp there. He
built houses by the bay which gave the town (Husavik means house
cove) its name.

GETTING THERE

There are daily flights in summer from Reykjavik and six times a week in winter. Buses also run from Egilsstadir but check the schedule.

WHAT TO DO

Husavik is the jumping-off spot for tours of the area's natural wonders. (See
"Lake Myvatn.")

Harbor

The picturesque harbor on Skjalfanda Bay is the heart of the town, and a
good place to strike up your acquaintance with Husavik.

Husavik Church

The major attraction of the town for tourists is the Husavik Church which
was built in 1907.

Budara River

Lake Botnsvatn is the source for the Budara river which runs through town.
Nearby, the park is filled with an extensive sampling of wildlife and plants.

The Town Museum

Artifacts, photographs, paintings and a copy of the Gudbrands Bible
printed in 1584 are on display.

The Natural History Museum

You will find an extensive collection of Icelandic birds, rocks and minerals as well as dried plants and a stuffed polar bear.

WHERE TO STAY

Hotel Husavik

The rooms are basic and very few have private baths. My suggestion would be to stay in Myvatn.

AKUREYRI

Tourist Office: *82 Hafnarstraeti. Open June, July and August, Monday–Friday from 8:00 a.m.–7:00 p.m.; Saturday and Sunday, 7:30 a.m.–11:30 a.m. Winter weekdays, 9:00 a.m.–5:00 p.m.*

Iceland's second largest town is a real surprise, beautifully situated on a fjord with much more vegetation than any other spot in the country. You will even find full-sized trees—poplars and mountain ash—and the climate here is more agreeable than most of the country with enough snow for skiing in the winter and warm weather in summer. This is also one of the oldest towns in Iceland. Iceland's northern commercial hub, Akureyri has been a trading center for 300 years, developing under the Danes during the time when Denmark, by royal decree, held the monopoly over all trade with Iceland. Though it grew slowly—the records of 1785 indicate the population at 10, and by 1862, when it was given its town charter, the population had only reached 286. Akureyri has grown rapidly in this century and now has a population of about 14,000. There is a new, very small university with schools of nursing, management and marketing, and a fishery school.

GETTING THERE

Icelandair runs several flights a day from Reykjavik in both winter and summer. There are also flights between Isafjordur and Akureyri. Buses connect with Akureyri from Egilsstadir and Husavik in summer time. Flights also are available to Grimsey Island, above the Arctic Circle. Bus service between Akureyri and Reykjavik is available throughout the year. There is a ferry to Grimsey and to Hrisey island, which sits in the middle of the Akureyri fjord as well.

DIRECTORY

Auto Repair • For Nissan and Subaru: *Bilaverkst. Sigurdar Valdimarssonar,* ☎ *22520.* For Ford, Mazda, Suzuki, Lancia: Bilasalan, Laufasgotu, ☎ *26300.* For Volvo, Honda, Chevrolet, Isuzu, Opel, Man: *Porshamar, Tryggvabraut,* ☎ *22700.* For lubrication and tire service: Smurstod Shell Olis, *4a Fjolnisgata,* ☎ *21325.*

Banks • Open Monday–Friday from 9:15 a.m. to 4:00 p.m. and Thursday nights, 5:00 p.m.–6:00 p.m.

Car Rental • Interrent, *14 Tryggvabraut,* ☎ *21715* or *26476.* **Orn Car Rental**, ☎ *24838.* **Icelandair Car Rental**, *Akureyri Airport,* ☎ *(96)11005.*

Emergency • Police. ☎ *23222.* Fire and ambulance, ☎ *22222.* Doctors on duty evening and weekends, ☎ *985-23221.*

Ferry service • Hrisey Ferry, Hrisey, ☎ *(96)61797.* Saefari, Hrisey-Grimsey Ferry, ☎ *985-32211.*

Pharmacy • Stjornu Apotek, *97 Hafnarstraeti,* ☎ *(96)23718.*

Post Office • *102 Hafnarstraeti.* Open weekdays 9:00 a.m.–4:30 p.m. Telegraph Office open for long distance calls and stamps 9:00 a.m.–6:00 p.m., Monday–Friday; 10:00 a.m.–3:00 p.m., Saturday.

Taxi. • B.S.O. Strandgata, ☎ *111010.* 24-hour service.

SIGHTSEEING TOURS

Tours to the Lake Myvatn area leave daily June 1–September 15 at 8:15 a.m. from the bus terminal.

Places of Historical Interest

A five-hour tour includes the Akureyri museums, Modruvellir and Hrisey Island. It leaves from the square on Monday and Thursday at 2:00 p.m.

Eyjafjordur Pastoral

This 3-1/2 hour tour includes Akureyri sightseeing and the country churches of Grund and Saurbaer. Wednesday.

Laufas Farm and Museum, Icelandic Ponies, Grenivik Village

A four-hour trip given on Thursday and Friday. For all the above except the Lake Myvatn tour, *contact Akureyri Travel Bureau, 3 Radhustorg,* ☎ *(96)25000.* All the tours are given from June 18–August 15. For *arrangements contact Nonni Travel, 3 Brekkugata,* ☎ *(96)60227922.* Farmhouse accommodations, hiking tours, horseback riding. Mailing address: *Nonni Travel. P.O. Box 726 Akureyri, Iceland.*

WHAT TO DO

Botanical Gardens

This would be an extraordinary collection of plants anywhere, but it is all the more remarkable in this northern climate. Established in 1912, it offers a sample of almost all the native plants of Iceland. Open in summer from 9:00 a.m.–10:00 p.m.

Akureyri Municipal Museum

This regional museum houses displays illustrating the everyday life and the cultural history of the area in the 19th and 20th centuries. Of particular interest are the needlework and national costume displays. Open June 1–September 15 every day from 1:30 to 5:00 p.m. Rest of the year, Sunday, 2:00 p.m.–4:00 p.m.

Davidshus

David Stefansson Memorial Museum • The writer lived here from 1944 until his death in 1964.

Museum of Natural History

Here you will find a large collection of plant specimens from Europe and Iceland and a display of Icelandic animal life. The exhibit of native birds and eggs contains a specimen of every nesting bird in Iceland. There are also displays of fish, shells and sea life. Open from June 1–Sept. 10 every day but Saturday from 1:00 p.m.–4:00 p.m. In winter, Sunday from 1:00 p.m.–3:00 p.m.

Nonnahus

Jon Sveinsson Memorial Museum • This was the childhood home of Jon Sveinsson, a Jesuit priest known for his children's books. The house is one of the oldest in Akureyri. Open June 15–August 31 daily from 2:00 p.m.–4:30 p.m.

Sigurhaediar

Matthias Jochumsson Memorial Museum • Matthias Jochumsson was the national poet of Iceland who translated Shakespeare into Icelandic. Open June 15–Sept. 15 from 2:00 p.m.–4:00 p.m. daily.

SPORTS AND RECREATION

GOLF

Akureyri has an 18-hole golf course, the world's northernmost 18–hole course, in fact, and in summer, during the light nights, you can play all night. The clubhouse serves light meals. The Arctic Open International Tournament is played through the night in late June. ☎ *(96)22974* or *24459.*

HORSEBACK RIDING

For trips of one hour to six days, call any of the following. **Alda, Melgerdi, Eyjafirdi.** ☎ *(96)31267.* **Jorunn, Hamraborgir, Aklureyri.** ☎ *(96)23863,* from 9 a.m.–1p.m. **Petursborg, Glaesibaejarhreppi.** ☎ *(96)25925.* **Polar Horses,** *Grytubakka.* ☎ *(96)33179.* All the above will pick you up.

KJARNASKOGUR WOOD

For walking or jogging, this area south of the airport is the spot. There is a walking route through the woods with exercise stations, tables and benches.

SKIING

Hlidarfjall mountain has five chair lifts and tows that service slopes running down from an altitude of 900 meters. There are also tracks for cross-country skiing.

SWIMMING POOL

There is an outdoor pool, hot pots, a sauna and solarium here as well as tennis courts and miniature golf. Call for hours as the sauna times vary for men and women. ☎ *(96)523260.*

SHOPPING

The pedestrian street, Hafnarstraeti, is the main shopping area. Here you will find several jewelry stores and art galleries selling Icelandic-made wares as well as bookstores, restaurants and snack shops. Shops open at 9:00 a.m. or 10:00 a.m. and remain open until 6:00 p.m. On Saturday, regular hours but most shops close at 2:00 p.m.

Alafoss Wool Factory • Though a bit out of the way, it is worth the trip to come here, even to pay the taxi fare, for the prices are excellent and the selection extensive. The shop takes credit cards but it will not ship merchandise. It is open Monday–Friday from 9:00 a.m. to 6:00 p.m. and Saturday from 10:00a.m. to noon. For special hours, ☎ *985-3 11 65*.

WHERE TO STAY

Hotel KEA
89 Hafnarstraeti • Request an inside room above the third floor in this attractive, modern hotel, which with 73 rooms is Akureyri's largest and most deluxe. All the rooms here have been renovated in the last three years and are very pretty and comfortable. They vary in size but not in decor, and all have private bathrooms, TV and minibar. The dining room is large but it is divided in a way that makes it intimate. The ambitious and imaginative menu, which offers fish, meat and game, changes frequently. Saturday nights there is dancing which is one of the reasons for having a room above the third floor. A lovely cafeteria is open from 8:00 a.m.–8:00 p.m., later in summer. A double room will run about $150. Breakfast is $12.

Hotel Stefania
85 Hafnarstraeti • A small, simple, but very pleasant hotel, the Stefania has just 25 rooms, most with private baths. The dining room has a fireplace and an inviting bar. One warning, there are four floors in the hotel and no elevator. A double room with bath will cost you about $125.

Hotel Nordurland
7 Geislagotu • Most of the 28 rooms here have private baths and all have TV and minibar. The hotel was renovated in 1989 and the rooms are lovely. Because it is right on a busy street, the hotel could be noisy on weekends, so request a quiet room. A double with bath will be about $125.

Hotel Edda
Hrafnagilsstraeti • Located outside town, this is a summer hotel, as are all the Eddas, open from mid-June to September 1. There are 79 rooms, only seven with private baths. The hotel has a restaurant.

There are several **guesthouses** in Akureyri which I have not seen. For information, contact the tourist office, ☎ *(96)27733*.

Camping
The camp grounds, located south of the swimming pool, are open from June 10–September 1. There are restrooms, hot and cold water, a telephone and a washer and dryer. ☎ *(96)23379*.

WHERE TO EAT

The Hotel KEA
This is the most upscale spot in town with a very interesting and well-prepared selection of Icelandic as well as international dishes. Try the Icelandic Lobster as an appetizer if you don't mind the price of about 1530kr.

Among the offerings that are unusual in Iceland are pork and a beef Wellington-style creation with truffle sauce.　　　　　*Expensive.*

Fidlarinn

Located on the fifth floor of the building at 14 Skipagata, the restaurant has an international menu, but it is most known for its fish.

Smidjan

92 Hafnarstraeti • An interesting, international menu. The restaurant is open for lunch from noon to 2:00 p.m. as well as for dinner from 6:00 p.m. to midnight.　　　　　*Moderate.*

Hotel Stefania

The cozy, pleasant restaurant is open for lunch in summer and for dinner from 6:00 p.m.–10:00 p.m. The menu is varied, with pork and T-bone steaks, the non-Icelandic surprises, as well as plenty of fish. There is also a children's menu. *Expensive*, though perhaps not quite so high as the KEA.

Sjallinn

14 Geislagata • In addition to a full dinner menu, there is a pub and on weekends both live music and a disco.

The Hotel Nordurland

The dining room here serves Icelandic dishes and Monday, Wednesday and Friday at 7:30 p.m., there is an evening of folklore which includes traditional Icelandic food, music and films.

Uppinn

Raedhustorg • This spot serves dinners as well a pizza and has live music most evenings.

EXCURSIONS FROM AKUREYRI

GRIMSEY

This is your one chance to get above the Arctic Circle in Iceland, and you can do it quickly by plane or more leisurely by ferry. Generally there is just one flight a day, leaving about 11:20 a.m. and it is spectacular, ranging over the mountain-ringed fjord and then through the mountains. This is a tiny island and unless you are camping and hiking, there is not a lot to attract you besides the adventure of being this far north. The arctic terns are a nuisance here, to say the least. They will dive-bomb you as soon as you set foot beyond the confines of the minuscule airport; so if you want to wander a bit and don't mind looking like an arctic Mary Poppins, bring an umbrella for protection. For those who go in for that sort of thing, you can leave your postcards at the airport, and they will be postmarked Arctic Circle.

HRISEY ISLAND

An hour's drive north along the side of the bright blue Akureyri fjord will bring you to the tiny, white-washed town of Olafsfjordur. Stop at one of the bakeries or the grocery for a picnic lunch and find a spot to look straight north towards Grimsey and the Arctic Circle. Leave Olafsfjordur in time to catch the 3:30 p.m. ferry from Arsksogsandur to Hrisey, a flat green slap of land in the middle of the fjord. The boat trip is a short one, just 10–15 minutes, and a beautiful one. Once you arrive at Hrisey, allow yourself time to hike on the island's very pleasant hiking trail and to take in the thriving little town and its dazzling view of the fjord. There is a full restaurant on Hrisey, near the boat pier.

THE SNAEFELLSNES PENINSULA

Hugged by the fjords of Faxafloi and Breidafjordur and sliced by a mountain range, the Snaefellsnes Peninsula is the site of the Snaefellsjokull Glacier, the spot from which Jules Verne sent his heroes towards the center of the earth. For tamer journeys, a drive around the peninsula will reward the traveler with lovely and haunting panoramas of a lava-formed landscape. Here you will find a variety of lava fields and great sweeps of black terrain. For the adventurous, this is an excellent area for hiking, horseback riding, fishing and snow mobiling.

GETTING THERE

If you are driving you can either take the ferry from Reykjavik to Akranes or go the longer way around the beautiful Hvalfjord. Whichever route you choose, head for Stykkisholmur where the hotel makes a pleasant stopping over spot. The roads, as expected, are difficult in places, but they are always passable and the scenery interesting enough to make the struggle worth it. There are flights to Stykkisholmur by way of Isflug Airlines. Day-long sightseeing tours by bus are available from Reykjavik. Information at the BSI bus terminal in Reykjavik. ☎ *(91) 22300.*

AKRANES TO BOGARNES

If you are driving, head out towards the west end of the peninsula. Your destination for the night will be Stykkisholmur as the best hotel is there, but you can also find farmhouses and simpler lodgings along the way if you prefer. The attraction of the peninsula is its scenery. The small towns are very small indeed and some more attractive than others. But don't expect to find any burgeoning metropolis here. Borgarnes is the first town of any note, prettily set between a river and a bay. Borgarnes was primarily the trading center for the nearby farms, but the construction of the bridge in 1980 opened it up to traffic and tourism. Egil Skallagrimsson, the hero of *Egil's Saga* is connected with the area through his father who is reputedly buried here. There is a district museum here as well as an art gallery.

PRACTICAL CONSIDERATIONS

There are service stations, a bank and a pharmacy in town, also a nice Verslun (convenience store) where you can stock up for the drive onto the peninsula. Tours of the town can be arranged at the Hotel Borgarnes, but it is easy enough just to walk around town on your own.

WHERE TO STAY AND EAT

The Hotel Bogarnes

The only game in town. The rooms are comfortable but undistinguished, and you will probably want to get on your way. But this is a good stopping place for lunch, as the hotel cafeteria serves a light menu of sandwiches as well as a good selection of fish and lamb at, what are for Iceland, reasonable prices.

DRIVING FROM BOGARNES TO STYKKISHOLMUR

Leaving Borgarnes, you will wind through a variety of lava fields, from the relatively young black heaps of newly laid rock to the soft, mossy carpets which are deceptively inviting. Watch out for these as the moss disguises deep crevices. The next stop on the northwest shore of the peninsula is **Hellissandur**, an old fishing village. A small open-air museum has a turf house on exhibit. **Grundarfjordur**, a tiny fishing village sits in a crescent of mountains, crowned by **Helgrindur**, a name which means Ridges of Hell. **Kirkjufell**, a smaller mountain by the water, is a favorite with very experienced mountain climbers. There is a farm guesthouse, Kverna, in the area. In most of these diminutive towns, you will find a Verslun, the kind of grocery/snack shop that seems to pop up in even the most remote villages. There is also auto service at Hellissandur. **Olafsvik** is the best center for hiking on the Snaefellsjokull. Beyond that and the existence of a service station and snack bar, there is not much reason for lingering. There is a hotel, but I do not recommend it.

Farmhouse Stay: Snorrastadir Snaefellsnes, ☎ *93-56627.* The farm, which has four modern, comfortable, well-equipped cabins, is located 39 km from Borgarnes. Riding and fishing available.

STYKKISHOLMUR

Because of its excellent natural harbor, Stykkisholmur was a busy trading spot as long ago as the 16th century. By the mid-19th century, the town was a major administrative center, and you will still find several buildings from this time standing. Stykkisholmur's fishing economy is based on scallops and other shellfish. Shipbuilding is another active industry. However, the principal employer is the Catholic convent which runs a hospital, a kindergarten and a printing operation. Stykkisholmur's location at a point of land jutting north into the Breidafjordur affords it a splendid view of the water and the mountains. The **Draphulidarfjall** mountain is known for the unusual colors of its rocks, and the mountain **Helgafell** is a landmark of the *Laxdaela Saga.* Gudrun, one of the main characters of that saga, is said to be buried nearby.

WHAT TO DO

Sightseeing tours: You can go by boat on a tour of the Southern Islands of Breidafjordur. The trip will take you out to the bird colonies of the islands as well as to **Dimonarklakkar**, the setting for one of the sagas of Eric the Red, and onto **Hvammsfjardarrost** where you will find one of Iceland's most powerful currents. The island of **Hvitabjarnarey**, also linked to many of the sagas, is densely populated with birds. The trip lasts about two hours.

Another boat trip will take you to **Flatey**, the largest of the Breidafjordur islands. As long ago as A.D. 1100 a monastery was established on the island. In the 18th century, Flatey was a major trading post for both the West and Europe. A center for Icelandic literature, it possesses the oldest library in Iceland. The library and the old village have both been restored. The boat stops for two hours to allow for a tour of the island with a local guide. The trip also takes you past several other islands: **Ellidaey** which boasts the largest colony of Kittiwakes in the Breidafjordur islands; **Stagley,** to the south, an old fishing station; and **Bjarneyjar**, which was, until the mid-1950s, the main fishing station of the Breidafjordur islands. If you have the time, you can take a combination of the southern islands tour and the Flatey tour. Arrangements can be made through the Hotel Stykkisholmur.

Adventures on the Glacier: You can arrange for snowmobile trips of from one-to-three hours on the glacier. Contact Tryggvi Konradsson, at *Ferdapjonustan Snjofell., 355 Arnarstapa, Snaefellsnes.* ☎ *93-56783.* This company will provide everything you need, including insulated outerwear and even boots. Located at Arnarstapi, the company also has a restaurant and sleeping bag accommodations, with cooking facilities and showers. There is also a guest house with nine rooms, just one with private bath.

The Norwegian House Museum

Lodged in one of Stykkisholmur's oldest houses, dating from 1829, is a small museum worth a look. The house gets its name from the fact that the wood used to build it was brought from Norway by its owner, Arni Thorlacius, who was the first man in Iceland to make weather forecasts.

WHERE TO STAY AND EAT

The Stykkisholmur Hotel

The 33 rooms of this hotel are simple and utilitarian, but very comfortable and all have private baths. The location on the water affords lovely views and the hotel is quiet, even on Saturday nights when there is live music in the restaurant. The large, airy dining room is pleasant with a surprisingly varied and sophisticated menu of well-prepared items.The hotel participates in a "stopover" program with Icelandair for a three-day visit to Iceland, including two nights at the Hotel Stykkisholmur with pick-up and return to the airport where you spend the last night. The service is available for a minimum of four people.

At some point during your visit to Stykkisholmur, you should try Stykkisholmur scallops, a staple of the fishing industry here. It you're lucky, on one of the boat tours, the captain might sling a net overboard and pull up a haul of the delicate sea creatures which are delicious even raw. And this is a place where you need not worry about pollution.

Egilshus Guesthouse

If you are looking for something simpler and less expensive, this is a possibility. I have not seen the rooms here but most of these guesthouses in Iceland are more than adequate. This one has a restaurant. ☎ *(93)81450*.

The **youth hostel** on Flatey is highly recommended.

ISAFJORDUR: THE WESTFJORDS

Tourist Information and Travel Bureau • *Adalstraeti 11* • Open Monday–Friday 9:00 a.m.–noon and 1:00 p.m.–5:00 p.m.

Isafjordur is the capital of the Westfjords and the best place at which to base yourself for exploration of the area. The Westfjords offers some of the most rugged scenery in Iceland, snow-laced black mountains seemingly tortured from the earth, glacier-raked morains, deep fjords. Snow dots the landscape much of the year, though in summer, the warming effects of the Gulf Stream can make for pleasant, balmy days. The bird life is rich here, especially the sea birds which populate the spectacular bird cliffs and islands. The region is one of the oldest, both geologically and historically, in the country. The earliest settlers arrived from Norway and also from Iceland almost 1100 years ago and many of the sagas are set in this area. Fishing and fish processing are the major industries. There is some farming, but most of the land is not arable and farmers depend to some extent on fishing as well as farming. The mail plane or a boat are the only ways in many of these spots to get from fjord to fjord. Except for Isafjordur, the administrative and commercial center of the area, the towns are minute, mostly fishing villages or farming towns which developed in the late 19th century.

GETTING THERE AND GETTING AROUND

The drive from Stykkisholmur to Isafjordur will take about five or six hours without stops, as there are several long fjords which you must drive around. Flights leave daily from Reykjavik and Akureyri for Isafjordur. Once there, you will have to rent a car, though if you really want a view from the top, you can make arrangements to fly on the mail plane which hops across the fjords and mountains, landing at various towns along the way. There is regular bus service in the summer to Reykjavik. A bus from the airport runs to the Hotel Isafjordur and the Summer Hotel. Several car rental agencies operate in town. The Fagranes boat sails four days a week in summertime to Hornstrandir and Jokulfirdir. Call ☎ *3155* to arrange booking.

DIRECTORY

Banks • Banks are open Monday–Friday from 9:15 a.m.–4:00 p.m.

Car Rental • Ernir, at the airport. ☎ *4200*. Only stick shift cars are available.

Emergency • Police, ☎ *4222*, 24-hour. Hospital, ☎ *4500*, 24-hour. Ambulance and Fire Station, ☎ *3333*.

Gas Station • Open Monday–Saturday, 7:30 a.m.–8:00 p.m.; Sunday, 9:00 a.m.–8:00 p.m. There is self-service available after closing.

Laundry and Dry Cleaning • Efnalaugin Albert, at Fjardarstraeti 16. Open Monday–Friday, 7:00 a.m.–6:00 p.m.

News in English • Weather and news are broadcast in English on radio station 1 every morning at 7:30 a.m. You can also ☎ (91)693690 for a recorded report of the news in English.

Road Conditions • ☎ 3911.

Shopping Hours • Monday–Friday from 9:00 a.m.–noon and 1:00 p.m.–6:00 p.m.

Swimming Pool and Sauna • Located at Austurvegur 9, the facilities are open weekdays 7:00 a.m.–5:30p.m. and 8:00 p.m.–9:30 p.m.; Saturday 10:00 a.m.–noon and 1:00 p.m.–4:00 p.m.; Sunday, 10:00 a.m.–noon.

Taxi • You need to call ahead. ☎ 3418.

WHAT TO DO

Sightseeing Tours

Sightseeing tours around Isafjordur and Bolungarvik are offered daily in summer and boat trips leave at 2:00 p.m. every day as well. Contact the Isafjordur Tourist Office. Also available are guided hiking tours through the Hornstrandir nature preserve. ☎ (94)4767. The **Fagranes Ferry** goes to Hornstrandir as well as to Adalvik and Hornvik. The trip to Adalvik is about 2-1/2-hours and another 2-1/2 to Hornvik. If you choose to go by boat to Hornstrandir, you will have to wait until the next day to catch the return boat. The **Eyjalin** is a 21 passenger speed boat which offers sightseeing trips to Jokulfirdir as well as an extraordinary tour around the Isafjardardjup, stopping at Adaey and Vigur to visit one of the region's largest eider duck farms. This is an especially interesting trip as it gives you a chance to visit a sparsely populated island that you would not otherwise see. In winter, sometimes as few as seven people live there. In summer, the population rises to between 20 and 30 with the addition of summer help. ☎ (94)3155. It is also possible to fly on the six passenger mail plane which makes stops at, among other places, Thingeyri and Patreksfjord. You must book ahead. Contact the Isafjordur Tourist Office. The trip lasts about 2-1/2 hours and is a spectacular way to see the landscape. The cost per person is about 5000kr.

Nedstikaupstadur

A cluster of five trading buildings which were constructed in the 18th century by merchants from Bergen, Norway. These are among the oldest buildings still standing in Iceland.

Westfjords Folk Museum and Maritime Exhibit

These exhibits are housed in the old buildings mentioned above. Open in summer, Tuesday–Sunday in from 1:00 a.m. to 5:00 p.m.

WHERE TO STAY

Hotel Isafjordur

Situated in the center of town, beside the fjord. The rooms are modern, bright and comfortable. All the rooms have private bathrooms and mini-bars. Request a room with a view of the fjord. The staff is very accommodating and will help you with sightseeing information and arrangements.

Isafjorduar Summer Hotel

Located at the dormitory of the Isafjordur College, the hotels have single and double rooms with bathrooms on each floor. There are also sleeping-bag facilities.

WHERE TO EAT

The Hotel Isafjordur

This pleasant hotel has an airy, lovely dining room with a view of the fjord and ample menu offerings to choose from. There is always a summer tourist menu item, marked by a smiling chef face. The summer tourist dinner includes coffee and soup with the main course. The dining room serves lunch and tea as well as dinner. Breakfast is included in the room rate.

Frabaer Snack Bar

A little restaurant serves pizza, hamburgers and fish and occasionally will have something more substantial, like lamb chops, on the menu. There is also a children's menu.

Sjomannastofan

A family restaurant at the harbor, this is a lively place. It does not serve alcohol, but the food is hearty and reasonably priced. **Upsalir** and **Krusin** are the two dance spots in town.

INDEX

Introducing first hand, "fresh off the boat" reviews for cruise fanatics.

Order Fielding's new quarterly newsletter to get in-depth reviews and information on cruises and ship holidays. The only newsletter with candid opinions and expert ratings of: concept, ship, cruise, experience, service, cabins, food, staff, who sails, itineraries and more. Only $24 per year.

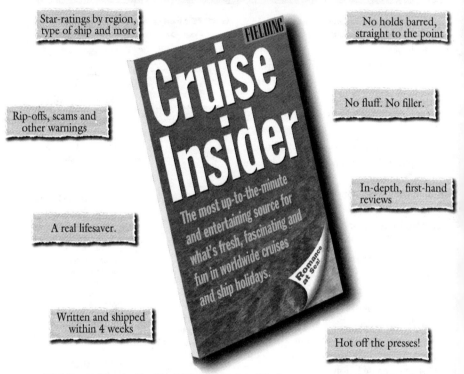

Star-ratings by region, type of ship and more

No holds barred, straight to the point

Rip-offs, scams and other warnings

No fluff. No filler.

In-depth, first-hand reviews

A real lifesaver.

Written and shipped within 4 weeks

Hot off the presses!

Fielding's "Cruise Insider" Newsletter is a 50-plus page quarterly publication, available at an annual subscription rate of only $24.00, limited to the first 12,000 subscribers.

Call 1-800-FW2-GUIDE to reserve your subscription today.
(VISA, MasterCard and American Express accepted.)

Order Your Fielding Travel Guides Today

BOOKS	$ EA.
Amazon	$16.95
Australia	$12.95
Bahamas	$12.95
Belgium	$16.95
Bermuda	$12.95
Borneo	$16.95
Brazil	$16.95
Britain	$16.95
Budget Europe	$16.95
Caribbean	$18.95
Europe	$16.95
Far East	$19.95
France	$16.95
Hawaii	$15.95
Holland	$15.95
Italy	$16.95
Kenya's Best Hotels, Lodges & Homestays	$16.95
London Agenda	$12.95
Los Angeles Agenda	$12.95
Malaysia and Singapore	$16.95
Mexico	$16.95
New York Agenda	$12.95
New Zealand	$12.95
Paris Agenda	$12.95
Portugal	$16.95
Scandinavia	$16.95
Seychelles	$12.95
Southeast Asia	$16.95
Spain	$16.95
The World's Great Voyages	$16.95
The World's Most Dangerous Places	$19.95
The World's Most Romantic Places	$16.95
Vacation Places Rated	$19.95
Vietnam	$16.95
Worldwide Cruises	$17.95

To order by phone call toll-free 1-800-FW-2-GUIDE
(VISA, MasterCard and American Express accepted.)

*To order by mail send your check or money order,
including $2.00 per book for shipping and handling (sorry, no COD's) to:
Fielding Worldwide, Inc. 308 S. Catalina Avenue, Redondo Beach, CA 90277 U.S.A.*

Get 10% off your order by saying "Fielding Discount" or send in this page with your order

Favorite People, Places & Experiences

ADDRESS:	NOTES:

Name

Address

Telephone

Name

Address

Telephone

Name

Address

Telephone

Name

Address

Telephone

Name

Address

Telephone

Name

Address

Telephone

Name

Address

Telephone

Favorite People, Places & Experiences

ADDRESS:	NOTES:

Name

Address

Telephone

Name

Address

Telephone

Name

Address

Telephone

Name

Address

Telephone

Name

Address

Telephone

Name

Address

Telephone

Name

Address

Telephone

Favorite People, Places & Experiences

ADDRESS:	NOTES:

Name

Address

Telephone

Name

Address

Telephone

Name

Address

Telephone

Name

Address

Telephone

Name

Address

Telephone

Name

Address

Telephone

Name

Address

Telephone

Favorite People, Places & Experiences

ADDRESS:	NOTES:

Name

Address

Telephone

Name

Address

Telephone

Name

Address

Telephone

Name

Address

Telephone

Name

Address

Telephone

Name

Address

Telephone

Name

Address

Telephone

Favorite People, Places & Experiences

ADDRESS:	NOTES:

Name

Address

Telephone

Name

Address

Telephone

Name

Address

Telephone

Name

Address

Telephone

Name

Address

Telephone

Name

Address

Telephone

Name

Address

Telephone

Favorite People, Places & Experiences

ADDRESS:	NOTES:

Name

Address

Telephone

Name

Address

Telephone

Name

Address

Telephone

Name

Address

Telephone

Name

Address

Telephone

Name

Address

Telephone

Name

Address

Telephone

Favorite People, Places & Experiences

ADDRESS:	NOTES:

Name

Address

Telephone

Name

Address

Telephone

Name

Address

Telephone

Name

Address

Telephone

Name

Address

Telephone

Name

Address

Telephone

Name

Address

Telephone

Favorite People, Places & Experiences

ADDRESS:	NOTES:

Name

Address

Telephone

Name

Address

Telephone

Name

Address

Telephone

Name

Address

Telephone

Name

Address

Telephone

Name

Address

Telephone

Name

Address

Telephone

Favorite People, Places & Experiences

ADDRESS: **NOTES:**

Name

Address

Telephone

Name

Address

Telephone

Name

Address

Telephone

Name

Address

Telephone

Name

Address

Telephone

Name

Address

Telephone

Name

Address

Telephone